Language and Linguistics in Context

Readings and Applications for Teachers

Language and Linguistics in Context

Readings and Applications for Teachers

Edited by

Harriet Luria
Hunter College, CUNY

Deborah M. Seymour
Laureate Education, Inc.

Trudy Smoke
Hunter College, CUNY

2006

LAWRENCE ERLBAUM ASSOCIATES, PUBLISHERS

Mahwah, New Jersey   London

Senior Acquisitions Editor:	Naomi Silverman
Assistant Editor:	Erica Kica
Cover Layout:	Tomai Maridou
Textbook Production Manager:	Paul Smolenski
Full-Service Compositor:	TechBooks
Text and Cover Printer:	Hamilton Printing Company
Book Cover Design:	Alan Robbins
Cover Illustration:	Abstract by Alan Robbins

This book was typeset in 10/12 pt. ITC New Baskerville, Bold, Italics.
The heads were typeset in ITC New Baskerville Bold.

Lawrence Erlbaum Associates, Inc., Publishers
10 Industrial Avenue
Mahwah, New Jersey 07430
www.erlbaum.com

Library of Congress Cataloging-in-Publication Data

Language and linguistics in context : readings and applications for teachers/edited
by Harriet Luria, Deborah M. Seymour, Trudy Smoke.
        p. cm.
  Includes bibliographical references and indexes.
  ISBN 0-8058-5500-9 (pbk. : alk. paper)
  1. Language and languages.   I. Luria, Harriet.   II. Seymour, Deborah M.   III. Smoke, Trudy.
  P107.L3594   2006
  400–dc22

                                                     2005021677

Printed in the United States of America
10 9 8 7 6 5 4 3 2 1

To our students and colleagues

Contents

Preface

Language and Linguistics in Context: Readings and Applications for Teachers came about as we tried to remake our introductory linguistics courses—"The Structure of Modern English" and "The History of the English Language"—by presenting readings from a variety of language fields that both introduce and clarify linguistic concepts. Because the cultural and political contexts of linguistic study have shifted and broadened, we felt the need to acknowledge the role of linguists in current policies involving language. In addition, we conceived of the readings as providing valuable insights into the relationship between the structure of language systems and first and second language acquisition, the study of language across culture, race, gender, and ethnicity, and between language study and literacy and education. To achieve this breadth and depth—that is, to provide "a big picture" view of basic linguistics and at the same time make it specific enough for the beginner—we chose selections by well-known theoretical linguists and by researchers from various disciplines.

We believe the selections we have chosen will be important for students in a variety of disciplines. In the preparation of *Language and Linguistics in Context: Readings and Applications for Teachers*, we class tested the readings in our courses. Students' comments about the articles have persuaded us that for the education major, the text provides the basis for discussion of current educational debates swirling around bilingual education, nonstandard dialects, English-Only movements, literacy methodologies, and, more generally, the importance of the study of language to teaching. And, for the anthropology or sociology major, these readings provide a context for language study and variation within different speech communities.

One of the main ways in which we have conceived the text is to reconstruct questions students have asked during our courses. Thus, three broad questions form the organizing principles of *Language and Linguistics in Context*: What is language and how is it acquired?; How does language change?; and What is literacy? In response to these questions, we have developed three units addressing the areas these questions raise.

In response to the query What is language and how is it acquired?, in Unit I we look at the nature versus nurture debate, predominant theories of second language acquisition, controversies and perspectives on bilingualism and bilingual education, and at linguistic research itself. In Unit II, in response to the question How does language change?, we look at influential trends in the history of English and at factors related to culture, geography, ethnicity, gender, race, and class and their connection to language and dialect use and variation. In Unit III, we explore our final question, What is literacy?, through a discussion of the ongoing political and educational issues that influence literacy practices.

In responding to these questions, we tried to select readings that focus on linguistic variation, applications, and literacy along with readings concerning traditional, formal linguistic notions. As a key feature of the text, we included selections combining theoretical and ethnographic analysis that demonstrate varieties of global discourse through linguistic data. We have also incorporated several personal narratives relating the language experiences of writers with a wide range of linguistic backgrounds. These perspectives map current language controversies onto the lives and experiences of real people, making it easier for readers to identify with the issues.

NOTES ON USING THIS BOOK

Because the readings in the book are diverse in level and range of topics and vary in level of linguistic formalism, its use in a half-year or one-year course would be appropriate. Choices could be made from among the introductory-level selections for a one-semester course, whereas a one-year course might make use of a larger number of the selections for in-depth analyses and more classroom discussion. Each unit begins with an introductory essay on the topic of the unit, followed by readings at various levels on that topic. Each reading is followed by *Questions to Think About,* including one *Extending Your Understanding* question, and a short list of *Terms to Define.* Each unit concludes with additional *Extending Your Understanding and Making Connections* questions, *Applications for Teaching* activities, and *Print and Web Resources.*

One way to use *Language and Linguistics in Context* would be to assign the readings in the order in which they appear in the book. However, we also include a set of matrixes with lists of suggested readings for different types of linguistics and education classes. In organizing the readings and apparatus in this volume, therefore, we arrange the material in such a way that it can be modified to fit many course plans and schemes of presentation.

Matrixes

Second Language Acquisition Pedagogy

Gleitman, Lila R.	A Human Universal: The Capacity to Learn a Language
Kuhl, Patricia K.	A New View of Language Acquisition
Gass, Susan	Fundamentals of Second Language Acquisition
Novakovich, Josip	This Is No Language (Intimate Exile)
Lvovich, Natasha	Russian as a Second language
Zentella, Ana Celia	Hablamos Spanish and English
Martin, David S.	The English-Only Movement and Sign Language for Deaf Learners
Gilyard, Keith	From "*Let's Flip the Script: An African American Discourse on Language, Literature, and Learning*"
Parry, Kate	People and Language
Edwards, John	Language and Language Learning in the Face of World English
Kubota, Ryuko	Unfinished Knowledge: The Story of Barbara
Canagarajah, A. Suresh	Understanding Critical Writing
Nieto, Sonia	Linguistic Diversity in Multicultural Classrooms
Ku, Robert Ji-Song	Confessions of an English Professor: Globalization and the Anxiety of the (Standard) English Practice
Pennycook, Alastair	Sociolinguistics and Power
Pita, M. & Utakis, S.	Educational Policy for the Transnational Dominican Community

The Structure of Language

Gleitman, Lila R.	A Human Universal: The Capacity to Learn a Language
Kuhl, Patricia K.	A New View of Language Acquisition
Gass, Susan	Fundamentals of Second Language Acquisition
Martin, David S.	The English-Only Movement and Sign Language for Deaf Learners
Trask, R. L.	Where Did English Come From?
Green, Tamara M.	Language Families
Barber, Charles	The Norman Conquest
Parry, Kate	People and Language
Bhaba, Homi K.	Queen's English
Fishman, Joshua A.	The New Linguistic Order
Newman, Michael	Definitions of Literacy and Their Consequences
Gee, James Paul	What Is Literacy?
Delpit, Lisa D.	The Politics of Teaching Literate Discourse
Gilyard, Keith	From "*Let's Flip the Script: An African American Discourse on Language, Literature, and Learning*"
Canagarajah, A. Suresh	Understanding Critical Writing
Pita, M. & Utakis, S.	Educational Policy for the Transnational Dominican Community

Literacy

Gleitman, Lila R.	A Human Universal: The Capacity to Learn a Language
Gass, Susan	Fundamentals of Second Language Acquisition
Alexander, Meena	Language and Shame
Parry, Kate	People and Language
Achebe, Chinua	The African Writer and the English Language
Edwards, John	Language and Language Learning in the Face of World English
Fasold, Ralph W.	Ebonic Need Not Be English
Zentella, Ana Celia	Hablamos Spanish and English
Newman, Michael	Definitions of Literacy and Their Consequences
Hull, Glynda & Schultz, Katherine	Literacy and Learning Out of School: A Review of Theory and Research
Gee, James Paul	What Is Literacy?
Delpit, Lisa D.	The Politics of Teaching Literate Discourse
Gilyard, Keith	From *"Let's Flip the Script: An African American Discourse on Language, Literature, and Learning"*
Canagarajah, A. Suresh	Understanding Critical Writing
Nieto, Sonia	Linguistic Diversity in Multicultural Classrooms
Ku, Robert Ji-Song	Confessions of an English Professor: Globalization and the Anxiety of the (Standard) English Practice
Nardini, G.	Italian Patterns in the American Collandia Ladies' Club: How Do Women Make *Bella Figura*?
Ghose, Malini	Women and Empowerment Through Literacy
Tate, G., McMillan J., & Woodworth, E.	Class Talk
Pita, M. & Utakis, S.	Educational Policy for the Transnational Dominican Community

We hope that instructors, students, and anyone whose interest is generally captured by language, its structure, and its functions will find this book creative, engaging, and informative—and will learn from its readings as much as we and our students have.

Harriet Luria
Hunter College, CUNY

Deborah M. Seymour
Laureate Education

Trudy Smoke
Hunter College, CUNY

Acknowledgments

We want to acknowledge the many people—family, friends, and colleagues—who helped to make this book possible. We would like to thank our colleagues and our students at Hunter College, Orange Coast College, and the University of California, Irvine, for their careful readings and enthusiastic responses to the selections in this text. We also want to express our gratitude to the Presidential Incentive and Teaching Grants Awards at Hunter College for the support given to this project. In addition, we thank the publishers and authors who allowed us to reprint articles, as well as the authors who contributed original work to our text. The reader should note that because this volume is a compilation of mostly previously published journal articles and book chapters, there may be inconsistencies of style in some reference citations.

We are particularly grateful to our editor, Naomi Silverman, for her recognition of the importance of this book, her knowledge of the field, and the insightful direction she gave our project. We are also grateful to her assistant, Erica Kica of Lawrence Erlbaum Associates, for her attention to detail and general helpfulness.

Finally, we wish to thank our family members. Harriet Luria is grateful to Jeremiah Luria Johnson and Ines Vigil for their encouragement and ideas. Trudy Smoke expresses her gratitude to Alan Robbins for his intelligent support and contribution. We all want to thank Dan Seymour for his valuable insights and technical help in preparing the manuscript for submission. We are indebted to them all.

About the Authors

Chinua Achebe, who was born in Nigeria, has been a professor of English at the University of Massachusetts, Amherst; at the University of Connecticut, Storrs; at UCLA; and is presently at Bard College. Achebe has written numerous novels, short stories, essays, and children's books, including *Things Fall Apart* and *Anthills of the Savannah.* He has published widely on African social issues and political ideas.

Meena Alexander is Distinguished Professor of English at Hunter College and the Graduate Center of the City University of New York. She has written seven volumes of poetry, including *River and Bridge* and two novels, including *Manhattan Music.* Her autobiography is titled *Fault Lines.*

James D. Armstrong is Professor of Anthropology at the State University of New York at Plattsburgh where he teaches courses on culture, sexuality, and global issues. He has conducted research into issues of identity and social structure on both an American and an international scale and co-authored *Distant Mirrors: America as a Foreign Culture.*

Charles Barber is the author of *The English Language: A Historical Introduction.* He is former Reader in English Language and Literature, School of English, University of Leeds.

Homi K. Bhabha was born into the Parsi community of Bombay. He received a B.A. from Bombay University and his D.Phil. from Oxford University. He is currently Chester D. Tripp Professor of Humanities at the University of Chicago, and has become recognized for his work in the critical theory of post-Colonialism. Among his many influential publications are *The Location of Culture* and *Nation and Narration.*

Deborah Cameron is Professor of Languages and Education at the University of London, and has been appointed to the Rupert Murdoch Professorship. Educated at Newcastle and Oxford, Professor Cameron held academic positions at the Roehampton Institute, the College of William and Mary, Virginia, and Strathclyde University. She specializes in spoken discourse, as well as gender and language. Among her many publications are *The Feminist Critique of Language*, *Working with Spoken Discourse*, and *Language and Sexuality*.

A. Suresh Canagarajah is Associate Professor in the Department of English, Baruch College, City University of New York. Previously, he taught for 10 years at the University of Jaffna in Sri Lanka. Reflecting his research interests in bilingualism, discourse analysis, academic writing, and critical pedagogy, his most recent writing includes *Resisting Linguistic Imperialism in English Teaching*, *Geopolitics of Academic Literacy and Knowledge Construction*, and *Critical Academic Writing and Multilingual Students*, and *Reclaiming the Local in Language Policy and Practice*.

Lisa D. Delpit received her doctorate from Harvard University. She holds the Benjamin E. Mays Chair of Urban Educational Leadership at Georgia State University and directs its Center for Urban Educational Excellence. Recipient of a MacArthur Foundation award, Dr. Delpit has written and presented widely on language, literacy, and educational practice. Her most recent books include *Other People's Children*, and she is coeditor of *The Real Ebonics Debate*, and coeditor of *The Skin That We Speak: Thoughts on Language and Culture in the Classroom*.

John Edwards teaches at St. Francis Xavier University in Nova Scotia. He is a specialist in the psychology of personality, dealing mainly with the major theorists—Freud, Jung, Rogers, and others. He also conducts a senior seminar course on the social psychology of language. His own research interests center on the relationship between language and group identity (with its important social ramifications, such as ethnicity, nationalism, multiculturalism, and social pluralism). His publications include *Language in Canada*.

Ralph Fasold is Professor of Linguistics at Georgetown University, Washington, D.C. He is a renowned sociolinguist who has published numerous books and articles and delivered presentations worldwide. Among his many publications are *The Sociolinguistics of Language* and *Language Change and Variation*.

Joshua A. Fishman earned his doctorate in social psychology from Columbia University. He is Professor Emeritus of Social Sciences at Yeshiva University and has been a visiting fellow at many respected academic centers throughout the world. He is the author of more than 800 scholarly articles and books in Yiddish and in English. Among his distinguished publications are *The Handbook of Language and Ethnic Identity* and *Can Threatened Languages Be Saved?*

Susan Gass is University Distinguished Professor of English, Director of the English Language Center, and Adjunct Professor of Linguistics at Michigan State University. Her research and teaching focus on second language acquisition (SLA). Her most recent book is *Input, Interaction and the Second Language Learner*. Dr. Gass, who served as President of the American Association for Applied Linguistics, is on a number of editorial boards and is currently Associate Editor of Studies in Second Language Acquisition.

James Paul Gee received his Ph.D. from Stanford University, taught at the University of Southern California and Clark University, and is presently the Tashia Morgride Professor of Reading in the Department of Curriculum and Instruction at the University of Wisconsin at Madison. Part of the "New Literacies Group," Gee is concerned with the applications of linguistics to literacy and education. His most recent works include coauthorship of *The New Work Order: Behind the Language of the New Capitalism, An Introduction to Discourse Analysis: Theory and Method,* and *Situated Language and Learning: A Critique of Traditional Schooling.*

Malini Ghose is a founding member of Nirantar, a Centre for Women and Education in New Delhi, India. She reports on violence against women and advocates for justice and empowerment of women in India.

Keith Gilyard is Professor of English at Pennsylvania State University. He received his Ph.D. from New York University. He has written and lectured extensively on language and literacy and is former Chair of the Conference on College Composition and Communication. He is author or editor of 12 books, including *Race, Rhetoric, and Composition* and *Voices of the Self,* for which he received an American Book Award.

Lila R. Gleitman is Professor Emerita of Linguistics at the University of Pennsylvania. Her most recent books are *An Invitation to Cognitive Science* and *Language Acquisition: The State of the Art.* Her research is in language and communication, as well as developmental psychology.

Tamara M. Green is Professor in and Chair of the Department of Classical and Oriental Studies at Hunter College in New York City. She received her Ph.D. from New York University. Among her specializations is the study of Greek and Latin roots in English. Her most recent publications include *The Greek and Latin Roots of English* and *The City of the Moon God: Religious Traditions of Harran.*

Glynda Hull received her Ph.D. from the University of Pittsburgh. She is Professor and Cochair of Language, Literacy, Society, and Culture at the Graduate School of Education at the University of California, Berkeley. In addition to her teaching and research in literacy, adult learning, and community-based education, Dr. Hull's most recent writing includes coauthorship of *The New York Order: Behind the Language of the New Capitalism; Changing Work, Changing Workers: Critical Perspectives on Language, Literacy, and Skills* and *School's Out: Bridging Out-of-School Literacies with Classroom Practice.*

Robert Ji-Song Ku received his Ph.D. from the Graduate Center of the City University of New York. He is Associate Professor and Chair of the Ethnic Studies Department at California Polytechnic State University, San Luis Obispo. His scholarly interests encompass 20th century American literature, Asian-American literature, and Anglophone creole and pidgin literatures. Dr. Ku's essays, reviews, and other writings appear in numerous journals, including *Amerasia Journal, The Journal of Asian American Studies,* and *The Journal of American Drama and Theatre* and in several anthologies, including *Asian American Literature* and *Crossing Into America.*

Ryuko Kubota is Associate Professor in the School of Education and Curriculum in Asian Studies at the University of North Carolina at Chapel Hill. Her most recent publication is "Critical Multiculturalism and Second Language Education" in *Critical Pedagogies and Language Learning,* edited by B. Norton and K. Toohey.

Patricia K. Kuhl is the William P. and Ruth Gerberding University Professor in the Department of Speech and Hearing Sciences and the Co-Director of the Center for Mind, Brain, and Learning at the University of Washington, Seattle. Her research focuses on language acquisition and language processing. She has played a major role in demonstrating how early language exposure alters the mechanisms of perception. Dr. Kuhl is a coauthor of *The Scientist in the Crib: Minds, Brains, and How Children Learn.*

Harriet Luria received her doctorate from Teachers College, Columbia University, and is Associate Professor in the Department of English, Hunter College, City University of New York, where she developed the College Reading Program. Her research and teaching interests are in the areas of the application of linguistics to teaching, and women and literacy. She is the author of *Ideas in Context: Strategies for College Reading* as well as workplace literacy studies through the Center for Advanced Studies in Education.

Natasha Lvovich is Associate Professor of English at Kingsborough Community College in Brooklyn, New York. Her research interests include second language acquisition: psycho- and sociolinguistic perspectives, intercultural and affective dimensions of bilingualism, acculturation and language learning, whole language and content-based language instruction, synesthesia, and multilingualism. She wrote a linguistic autobiography, *The Multilingual Self.* Her article "Socio-Cultural Identity and Academic Writing: A Second Language Learner Profile" was recently published.

David S. Martin is Professor in the Department of Education at Gallaudet University. He is the editor of *Cognition, Education, and Deafness,* a book that resulted from the 1989 International Symposium on Cognition, Education, and Deafness hosted by Gallaudet University.

John McMillan teaches at Texas Christian University. He is a rhetoric and composition specialist and coeditor of *Coming to Class: Pedagogy and the Social Class of Teachers.*

Gloria Nardini received her doctorate from the University of Illinois at Chicago where she currently teaches in the Department of Managerial Studies. Bilingual and bicultural, Nardini's recent research is a study of the Carnival in Viareggio, Italy. Her many presentations and publications include *Che Bella Figura! The Power of Performance in an Italian Ladies' Club in Chicago* and studies in *Ethnolinguistic Chicago, Vol. I and Vol. 2.*

Michael Newman received his doctorate from Teachers College, Columbia University, and is Associate Professor in the Department of Linguistics and Communication Disorders at Queens College, City University of New York. Dr. Newman has been involved in teacher education in a number of universities, and is the author of literacy-related articles, as well as *Designs of Academic Literacy: A Multiliteracies Approach to Post-Secondary Achievement.* His current work is on rap music as literacy.

Sonia Nieto received her doctorate from the University of Massachusetts and is presently Professor of Language, Literacy, and Culture in the Department of Teacher Education and Curriculum Studies at the University of Massachusetts, Amherst. Widely published in the fields of multicultural and bilingual education, Nieto's most recent books include *Language, Culture, and Teaching; What Keeps Teachers* Going?; and *Affirming Diversity: The Sociopolitical Context of Multicultural Education.*

Josip Novakovich is Associate Professor of English in the MFA program at Pennsylvania State University. Novakovich, who was born in Croatia and moved to the United States at the age of 20, has published two story collections (*Yolk and Salvation* and *Other Disasters*), two collections of essays (*Plum Brandy: Croatian Journeys* and *Apricots from Chernobyl*), and a novel, *April Fool's Day.* In 2002, he was a recipient of the National Endowment of the Arts Fellowship—one of many awards Professor Novakovich has received.

Kate Parry, who received her doctorate at Teachers College, Columbia University, is Professor of English at Hunter College in New York City. She also teaches at Makerere University in Uganda. A specialist in the history of the English language and its dialects, her recent publications include *Culture, Literacy and Learning English* and *Language and Literacy in Uganda.*

Alastair Pennycook is Professor of Language in Education at the University of Technology, Sydney, Australia. He has also taught at the University of Melbourne, Sydney, as well as in Germany, Japan, China, and Canada. He has published widely in areas of language; in particular, on critical theory and linguistics and the global spread of English. Among his many publications are *The Cultural Politics of English as an International Language, English and the Discourses of Colonialism,* and *Critical Applied Linguistics: A Critical Introduction.*

Marianne D. Pita, who received her Ph.D. from New York University, is Assistant Professor in the Department of English at Bronx Community College, City University of New York. She has recently published (cowritten with Sharon Utakis) "Educational Policy for the Transnational Dominican Community" in the *Journal of Language, Identity and Education,* and "Placing our Students at the Center of the Curriculum: Literature for Dominican-Americans" in the *Community College Humanities Review.*

Katherine Schultz received her Ph.D. from the University of Pennsylvania and is Associate Professor and Chair of the Educational Leadership Division in the Graduate School of Education at the University of Pennsylvania. Concerned with urban teacher education and urban literacy, Schultz has published several related works, including *Listening: A Framework for Teaching Across Differences* and coauthored *School's Out: Bridging Out-of-School Literacies With Classroom Practice.*

Deborah M. Seymour received her Ph.D. in theoretical linguistics from the CUNY Graduate Center. She has taught at CUNY's Queens College, Hunter College, and City College; the 92nd Street Y in New York City; and Orange Coast College and the University of California-Irvine in California. She currently works on curriculum design and course development at Laureate Education, Inc. Dr. Seymour's publications include *Building Academic Vocabulary* and *Strategies for English Language Learners.*

Trudy Smoke, who received her Ph.D. from New York University, is Professor of English at Hunter College, City University of New York. She has published widely in the areas of second language acquisition, ESL, and Writing Across the Curriculum. Her most recent publication is *A Writer's Workbook*, 4th edition. Her work has also recently appeared in *Crossing the Curriculum: Multilingual Learners in College Classrooms*, edited by Vivian Zamel and Ruth Spack, and in *Mainstreaming Basic Writers: Politics and Pedagogies of Access*, edited by Gerri McNenny and Sallyanne H. Fitzgerald.

Gary Tate was the Addie Levy Professor of Literature at Texas Christian University. He is coeditor of *Teaching High School Composition* and coeditor of *Coming to Class: Pedagogy and the Social Class of Teachers*.

Robert L. Trask (1944–2004) obtained his Ph.D. in Linguistics from the University of London in 1983. From 1988 until his death in 2004, he taught in the School of Cognitive and Computing Sciences at the University of Sussex. His special interests were historical linguistics, grammar, and the Basque language. His most recent publications were *The Dictionary of Historical and Comparative Linguistics* and *Language: The Basics*.

Sharon L. Utakis received her Ph.D. in Linguistics from the Graduate Center of the City University of New York. She is Assistant Professor in the Department of English at Bronx Community College, City University of New York, where she serves as ESL Coordinator. Her most recent publications (cowritten with Marianne Pita) include "Educational Policy for the Transnational Dominican Community" in the *Journal of Language, Identity and Education* and "Placing Our Students at the Center of the Curriculum: Literature for Dominican-Americans" in the *Community College Humanities Review*.

Elizabeth Woodworth teaches at Texas Christian University where she directed the University's composition and writing-across-the-curriculum programs. Her area of specialization is Victorian women writers.

Ana Celia Zentella, Professor of Ethnic Studies at the University of California at San Diego, identifies herself as an anthropolitical linguist. Professor Zentella is a central figure in the study of U.S. Latino varieties of Spanish and English, bilingualism, Spanglish, and English-only laws. Her book, *Growing Up Bilingual: Puerto Rican Children in New York*, won the 1998 Book Prize of the British Association of Applied Linguistics and the 1999 Book Award of the Association of Latina and Latino Anthropologists of the American Anthropology Association. Her most recent publications are "José Can You See?: Latino Responses to Racist Discourse" in *Bilingual Aesthetics* and "Spanish in the Northeast" in *Language in the USA: Themes for the 21st Century*.

Language and Linguistics in Context

Readings and Applications for Teachers

WHAT IS LANGUAGE AND HOW IS IT ACQUIRED?

Introduction to Unit I:
Language and Its Acquisition

Trudy Smoke
Hunter College, CUNY

WHAT IS LANGUAGE?

The word "language" is one of the most commonly used words in English; in fact, typing the word "language" into Google nets 85,800,000 hits. Thousands of languages exist on our planet. We all use language as speakers, signers, thinkers, readers, and writers. Language fascinates us with its enormous power: It brings us together and it divides us; it is used to assess our intelligence, our sociability, our class, our potential. Linguistics, or the study of language, includes a variety of perspectives: theoretical, applied, historical, psychological, cognitive, and social among others. Linguists research the relationship between humans and language as well as investigate animal and machine language.

To be able to describe and analyze language better, linguists examine language through its sounds, words, sentences, and meaning. *Phonology* is the study of sounds and the rules for the combination and pronunciation of sounds. *Morphology* is the study of words—the structure of words, the ways words are created, and the ways new words enter a language. One aspect of this is *etymology* or the historical derivation of words. *Syntax* is the study of the rules for combining words into sentences. *Semantics* is the study of linguistic meaning—the meaning of words, phrases, and sentences. *Discourse analysis* is the tool for analyzing texts of more than one sentence. The study of how people use language to interact with one another and convey meaning in a variety of contexts is *pragmatics*.

Along with the particular areas of study that make up linguistics mentioned above, there is also the philosophy of linguistics, which asks such intriguing questions about language as these: Is language only possible among humans? Is language innate in humans or did language ability evolve? What is the role of language in consciousness and sentience? Are there universal aspects to language? Does language construct our world or simply describe what is already in the world? There are many perspectives with which to approach these questions.

3

The philosophy of linguistics has a long history going all the way back to Plato, whose *Cratylus* dialogue is about the origins of language and the nature of meaning. In the 19th century, the Swiss linguist Ferdinand de Saussure made the distinction between *langue,* the abstract system of language, and *parole,* the physical, concrete manifestation of language. More recently in the 20th century, linguistics and the philosophy of language came into the forefront again in part because of an American theoretical linguist, Noam Chomsky. Chomsky is termed a *Nativist,* one who views language as innate and in some way hardwired in the human brain. (For more discussion of this, see the Gleitman article in this unit.) Chomsky wrote: "When we study language, we are approaching what some might call the 'human essence,' the distinctive qualities of mind that are so far as we know, unique to man" (1968, 1972, p. 100). He sees the aim of linguistics as going beyond individual languages toward the universal or general principles of a "universal grammar." Critics of Chomsky, for example, those in the Prague School of linguistics begun by Vilém Mathesius, view language through a *functional* approach that involves social interactions and sees language as a product of cultural evolution that evolved to satisfy human needs. As linguist Robert de Beaugrande writes: "Some of the [language] learning is biologically prepared and genetically transmitted as innate capacities; some of it is derived from experience in real-life situations; and some of it is explicitly and consciously learned from parents, siblings, friends, teachers, and so on. So humans come by their 'language competence' partly by subconscious, automatic processes, partly by conscious learning, and partly by making canny guesses about what words or people mean in the contexts where you hear or read them" (1997, p. 294).

Even though the linguists mentioned so far have focused on language as a human system, many linguists are fascinated by the question of whether animals or machines are capable of making and communicating meaning through language. They are concerned with consciousness and sentience—how we understand and are aware of ourselves and the world. At present, it is thought that humans alone are sentient, or have a conscious understanding of the world. On the other hand, animals have some level of understanding of their world and use gestures and sounds to communicate danger, food, and intimacy about their immediate environment. In the summer of 2004, Koko, a gorilla who had been trained in American Sign Language, signed to her trainers that she had pain in her mouth. A visit to the dentist revealed a diseased tooth. This was a news-making event because it was so unusual for a nonhuman animal to use a human language to communicate to a human. However, in keeping with what we know about animals: Koko was communicating, albeit in an unusual way, awareness of her immediate stimuli. As far as we know, nonhuman animals do not have cognizance of their past, their future, or their own future death.

Machines are programmed by humans and, despite having vast storage and memory capacity as well as extraordinary speed in performing calculations, do not have self-awareness or sentience. There is much discussion in the computer world about "when," "if," and "how" machines will become sentient. Many science fiction novels and movies have dealt with this possibility and, generally, humans anticipate the possibility of brilliant conscious machines with great anxiety. But, this is a thought for the future.

So, although there is much to be said about animal and machine communication, in this book, we will restrict ourselves to examining human languages that occur through the use of sounds, signs, gestures, and symbols.

We humans utilize all our senses to communicate, and when we have limited use of any of those senses—because of deafness, blindness, paralysis, or an inability to make sounds—we find other ways to communicate our feelings, needs, and ideas. A typically developing infant almost immediately begins to make sounds to communicate hunger, discomfort, or need for affection. These sounds are reinforced by those who respond to the infant's needs. Soon after birth, at around six months of age, babies begin to babble and create a wide variety of sounds and gestures. This exploratory babbling and gesturing suggest an innate sensitivity to linguistic or language cues and an inborn need to communicate in some way. As babies develop, their babbling and gesturing moves from generalized sounds and signs to those of the language community in which they live.

We know there are thousands of languages in the world, and linguists tell us that no language is better than any other, no language is harder or easier to acquire as a first language, and no living language remains totally static. However, just as babies begin to restrict their babbling and gestures to the language heard or signed in their environment, we will restrict our study in this book to primarily one language—in this case, English. In this unit, we will look at language—first language acquisition both spoken and signed, bilingualism, and second language acquisition.

FIRST LANGUAGE ACQUISITION

Spoken Language

Most researchers agree that typically developing healthy babies go through the same language acquisition stages no matter what their first language is. Newborn infants cry, but they do not make speechlike sounds until they are about three months, when they begin to make what are called *ooing* vowel sounds. Then, at about six months of age, babies begin to babble and make consonant–vowel combination sounds like *ba-ba-ba* and *da-da-da*. They practice these sounds, developing intonation patterns similar to whatever language is spoken in their environment. They keep trying out varieties of consonant–vowel combinations until the next stage in their development, which is the first word.

Usually, the first word is the name of a family member, a favorite food or toy, or an action word, such as for future English speakers *bye-bye, up, down,* or *no*. New words are gradually added, and babies usually overgeneralize words such as *mommy* to mean all women, or *doggy* to mean all four-legged, furry creatures. Very soon, the one-word utterance is extended to have sentence meaning: the holophrastic stage. In the holophrastic stage, the one-word such as *more* means *I want more*, or *up* means *Pick me up*. Most linguists think that children at this stage understand more language than they can produce.

Between one and one-half and two years of age, children begin to put two words together and form two-word sentences. We know that children already can recognize and even produce many words, but it is here that we witness the beginnings of syntactical and semantic relations: *Give me. All gone. Daddy home. Bye Mommy.* Children do not mark the words with inflections for tense, number, or person. At this stage, they do not usually use pronouns, except for *me* to refer to themselves. The next stage is the telegraphic stage, when children start to form sentences that sound like telegrams because these three-, four-, and several-word sentences are made up of nouns, verbs, adjectives, and some pronouns sequenced in the correct word order, but without inflectional endings or function words such as *the, a,* or prepositions. We hear sentences like: *Doggy play ball. Chair fall down. What her name? Me want that.*

Roger Brown (1973) and his colleagues at Harvard observed several children as they learned to talk in English and discovered that the sequence of acquisition of morphemes was similar for all the children they observed. Subsequently, other researchers have replicated his work and had similar findings.

After the telegraphic stage, language development proceeds rapidly. By the age of five when most children enter school, although their vocabulary may be limited and they may still have problems with irregular past and participle verb forms, some pronouns, and some types of subordinate clauses, they have a command of English that is almost indistinguishable from that of the adults surrounding them.

Dialects and the Standard. A dialect is a variety of a language with a grammar and *lexicon* (inventory of words) that is different from another form of the language. There are regional, social, and prestige dialects. Moreover, within a language, each person has his or her own lexicon and *idiolect* or individual way of speaking. People in particular communities often share a dialect. If you visit Boston, New York, Los Angeles, Dallas, or Atlanta, you will hear different dialects of English, dialects that are mutually understood as English but that sound different from one another in accent or idiom. A language may be termed "a collection of dialects" (Fromkin, Rodman, & Hyams, 2003, p. 445). Nevertheless, all dialects are not alike. Some are accepted as part of the standard and some are not. Children tend to grow up speaking the dialect of the family and community in which they are raised. The branding of some dialects as nonstandard or unacceptable has a powerful effect on the speakers of those dialects. How language patterns and dialects are developed, acquired by speakers, and judged by others are issues that are discussed by Gilyard and Zentella in this unit.

Two approaches to language study include the *descriptive* and *prescriptive*. The descriptive approach tells how language is actually used by a person or group of people at a particular time and place. As one introductory linguistics textbook explains the descriptive approach: "It does not tell you how you should speak; it describes your basic linguistic knowledge. It explains how it is possible for you to speak and understand, and it tells you what you know about the sounds, words, phrases, and sentences of your language" (Fromkin et al., 2003, p. 14). On the other hand, the prescriptive approach tells what "should" be and what is correct in the standard or prestige form of a language. This language standard for pronunciation and for grammatical use is usually based on the language of the people in power, the people in the media, and the people who control how language is disseminated to the public. However, no matter how we look at language, it is important to understand that no language is static. Language changes; new words come into the system; and rules are revised over time. (See Novakovich in this unit.)

Although many linguists think of the descriptive approach as unbiased, critical linguists question whether description can ever be neutral or unbiased. Description, by its very nature, focuses on a particular form of language spoken by a particular people at a particular time and in a particular place. Thus, a third perspective from which to examine language emerges: the critical perspective that questions the conduct of language research itself and raises questions about social class, hierarchy, privilege, and gender, among other issues. (For more on this, see Pennycook in this unit.)

Signed Language

All babies use gestures to indicate a range of emotions including affection, discomfort, and joy. Research suggests that when deaf infants are signed to at an early age, they learn to refine their gestures into recognizable signs and, thereby, communicate more easily. (See Gleitman in this unit.) Deaf babies who are signed to early on may even be more successful later in life both in the ability to communicate through signing and understanding spoken language.

Performing much the same functions as spoken and written languages, sign languages have a comparable structure and complexity of their own. Throughout the world, there are different sign languages, which are not mutually intelligible to one another. The various sign languages have their own signs and sentence structure regardless of the spoken language in their country; for example, British and American Sign Language are not mutually comprehensible. American Sign Language (ASL) is used by more than a half million people and for many of these, it is the native or first language. ASL users may study English as a second language. (See Martin in this unit.)

Finger spelling is not the same as sign language, although it may be used as an auxiliary system, a bridge between signed and written language. Finger spelling is used for proper names, for example. But, the system is slow as compared to a true sign language, which may be signed at much the same rate as a spoken language. However, for a person who is blind and deaf, such as Helen Keller, finger spelling on the hand, a type of touch language, can provide an effective mode of communication and, in her case, helped her to construct a world devoid of visual and auditory sensations. In James Berger's preface to the 100th year anniversary edition of Helen Keller's *The Story of My Life,* he describes language and how it relates to Keller's situation in the following way: "Language . . . is not primarily a way of describing or referring to the world. It is rather our means of creating, of shaping, of populating the world; it is what makes the world *our* world" (2003, p. xvii).

BILINGUALISM

"Multilingualism is the natural way of life for hundreds of millions all over the world" (Crystal, 1995, p. 362). On an individual level, multilingualism is usually "bilingualism," a term that can refer to either the acquisition of two primary or first languages at the same time or in very close proximity or simply to fluency in two or more languages. A child growing up in a household where two languages are interchangeably spoken by different members of the household usually is bilingual. A child who grows up in a home where one language is spoken and then at an early age, attends school, where a second language is spoken often becomes bilingual. Bilingualism often occurs spontaneously when an infant is in the care of individuals who speak more than one language (see Kuhl in this unit). Hearing children of deaf parents may acquire both sign and spoken language. A recent study showed that children in this circumstance develop the spoken and sign language in the same way that bilingual children acquire two spoken languages (Petitto, Katerelos, Levy, Guana, Tetreault, & Ferraro, 2001). Whereas most studies of bilingualism look at languages acquired by children, we also need to think about the possibility of bilingualism for adults who are learning to live in a new language while maintaining a first language. (See Lvovich in this unit.)

In reality, the actual determination of bilingualism is complicated: Does someone have to have equal fluency in both languages to be bilingual? Is a bilingual someone who is fluent only in speaking both languages? In writing two languages? In reading two languages? Is someone who can read a second language with proficiency but is unable to speak it bilingual? Is someone who can speak but not read a second language bilingual? The question of proficiency is a difficult one. Most researchers have found that the majority of bilinguals are not equally fluent in both languages. There is often a dominant language and a continuum of fluency in each language. Not only is a person usually more fluent in one language than the other, but the person may prefer one language over the other and may feel more comfortable with one language than the other. A person may communicate in one language only in specific situations. The linguist David Crystal tells of a child of French/English parents who went to school and university in France. "She became a geography teacher, married a British doctor, and came to live in England, where she had her first child. In general conversation, she could cope with ease in either language; but she found herself unable to teach geography in English, and she was extremely reluctant to discuss baby care in French" (1995, p. 364).

Code Switching.   Code switching is a phenomenon of bilingualism. Often when bilingual persons who speak the same languages communicate with one another, they engage in code switching: they speak some words or phrases in one language and some in the other. There is much speculation about the reasons for code switching: the need for a specific word or phrase that the speaker only knows or prefers in one language, the desire to express solidarity with a person or a group, or the desire to set a mood or attitude in relation to a subject or person. (For more on this, see Zentella in this unit.)

SECOND LANGUAGE ACQUISITION

People acquiring a second or additional language already know another language. They usually are acquiring the new language outside of the home environment—in a school or in a social situation. The learning may be decontexualized, where a learner may have to discuss events and ideas that are not current or real. Second language learners usually have meta-knowledge about their first language as well as language in general, and often have a conscious knowledge of grammar and how it works.

Much research has been conducted on people learning a second language at various points in their lives. The theory of second language acquisition is described more thoroughly in Susan Gass's article in this unit. However, to provide some background in the theory of second language acquisition, we need to have a general sense of American linguist Stephen Krashen's ideas, which he based on the teaching of English as a Second Language. Although Krashen terms his ideas hypotheses, many researchers in second language acquisition reference them and then contrast their own findings using these terms from Krashen's work. It is, therefore, important to know about them. Krashen's theory includes five basic tenets: acquisition versus learning, natural order hypothesis, monitor hypothesis, comprehensible input hypothesis, and affective filter hypothesis.

Acquisition versus learning refers to two different ways of gaining ability in a language: Acquisition is informal, natural, and subconscious, such as primary language learning in the home. Learning is formal, rule-conscious, and often gained in an artificial setting, such as a school. The contrast between acquisition and learning is applied to first and additional language learning as well as to many other instances of learning new abilities, such as how to drive or how to play a sport. The *natural order hypothesis* suggests that adults learning a new language follow a sequence similar to that of a child acquiring a first language, as described above in relation to Roger Brown's research with children learning English. According to this hypothesis, the *–ing* ending is acquired first and, then, the regular plural, and so on. With the *monitor hypothesis,* Krashen alleges that acquisition initiates one's utterances in a second language and is responsible for fluency, whereas learning functions to edit or monitor. Someone uses learning to make changes or edit an utterance after producing it; and in order for this monitoring to be effective, the learner needs to know the rule, have enough time to think about it, and must be thinking about correctness or the rule. The *comprehensible input hypothesis* means that people acquire a new language by receiving input that contains structures that are slightly beyond one's present level of competence although not too far beyond that. The job of the language teacher is to create an atmosphere where the learner receives extralinguistic and contextual cues to facilitate understanding. The *affective filter hypothesis* refers to what Krashen has identified as the three categories of affect that are important for language learning: motivation, self confidence, and low anxiety. Students who have a high affective filter—low motivation, little self confidence, and high anxiety—will have more difficulty with language learning than those with a low affective filter—high motivation, self confidence, and low anxiety.

In addition to Krashen's influential work, other second language acquisition researchers have focused on a variety of variables in understanding how people acquire new languages.

Motivation.   Motivation is divided into two general categories: instrumental and integrative. *Instrumental motivation* occurs when a learner believes that the language being studied will help achieve a specific goal: making friends, getting a job or a promotion, finding a partner, understanding scientific terminology. *Integrative motivation* occurs when a learner is immersed in a new language environment as a result of moving to a new country or community. Integrative motivation often leads to the successful acquisition of native-like pronunciation and the ability to communicate effectively in social interactions.

Critical Age hypothesis.   Most of us recognize that the younger we are, the easier it is for us to learn a language. Children born in families where two or more languages are spoken become bi- or trilingual with ease. Young children who have spoken one primary language at home and then start school where a different language is spoken also learn the new language quickly. The critical age hypothesis tells us that up until puberty, most people are able to easily learn a second or additional language and speak it without an accent. However, after puberty it becomes increasingly difficult as many adult language learners will attest. The problems have been ascribed to social and psychological factors such as embarrassment about mispronouncing words or using the wrong word, and self-consciousness about making mistakes. In her article in this unit, Patricia K. Kuhl presents evidence that physiological changes might also be involved in the difficulty that people beyond puberty have in learning a language, and especially in learning to speak a new language without an accent.

However, we have to be careful not to overgeneralize about the critical age hypothesis. It must be kept in mind that adults have knowledge about language in general and vocabulary and grammar in particular that gives them a metaknowledge of language, a knowledge that aids their acquisition, particularly in reading, writing, and understanding a new language. They may also have the motivation, specifically integrative motivation, which compels them to learn. We can think of many political situations in which adults have been forced from their homelands into new countries where they had to learn new languages, and they were quite successful. (In their articles, Josip Novakovich and Natasha Lvovich describe their experiences learning a new language as young adults.)

Contrastive Rhetoric.   This area of study examines the writing done by students (usually English as a Second Language students) from a variety of backgrounds and compares it to what is typically considered the "standard" American English writing pattern. Researchers in this field posit that writers from particular language and cultural backgrounds are more likely to exhibit particular patterns: longer or shorter sentences, more embedded sentences, a direct or indirect style, inductive or deductive reasoning, use of passive voice, or subordination over coordination among others. Although several decades of research have been compiled on this complex topic, many view the overall findings as overly determined, simplistic, and reductive. They also question the use of the American English writing pattern as the standard against which all other patterns are compared—"othering" other writers in a sense. Ryuko Kubota discusses this in her article in Unit I.

Generation 1.5.   In recent scholarship on English as a Second Language students in U.S. colleges, researchers have used the term "generation 1.5," a term coined by sociologists, to describe students who evidence writing problems and fit in one or more of the following three categories: a person who arrived in the United States as a child or young adolescent who speaks a first language other than English and obtained part of his or her education in the U.S.; a person born in the United States who speaks a language other than English at home, with friends, and in the neighborhood; a person living at home with a family that is in the process of acquiring English. More research needs to be done to determine how the use of this term will influence scholarship and teaching in the area of second language acquisition. (This issue is alluded to in Ana Celia Zentella article in Unit I.)

As you can see, language is a rich and complex topic and the study of it is both challenging and fascinating. Although the word "language" itself is one of the most commonly used words in English, it holds within it enormous power—the power to understand ourselves, to think and reason, to communicate with others, to know the past, and to live together in societies. In fact, language may, as Chomsky suggests, represent our true "human essence."

REFERENCES

Beaugrande, R. de. (1997). Theory and practice in applied linguistics: Disconnection, conflict, or dialectic? *Applied Linguistics, 18*(3), 279–313.

Berger, J. (2003). Editor's preface. In *The story of my life: Helen Keller* (Restored ed.). New York: Modern Library.

Brown, R. (1973). *A first language.* Cambridge, MA: Harvard University Press.

Chomsky, N. (1968, 1972). *Language and mind* (Enlarged ed.). New York: Harcourt, Brace, Jovanovich.

Crystal, D. (1995). *The Cambridge encyclopedia of the English language.* Cambridge, UK: Cambridge University Press.

Fromkin, V., Rodman, R., & Hyams, N. (2003). *An Introduction to language* (7th ed.) Boston: Heinle/Thomson.

Krashen, S. (1982). *Principles and practice in second language acquisition.* Oxford: Pergamon Press.

Petitto, L. A., Katerelos, M., Levy, B. G., Guana, K., Tetreault, K., & Ferraro, V. (2001). Bilingual signed and spoken language acquisition from birth: Implications for the mechanisms underlying early bilingual language acquisition. *Journal of Child Language, 28,* 453–496.

A BRIEF OVERVIEW OF UNIT I SELECTIONS

The focus of Unit I is language acquisition and language study itself. Beginning with first language acquisition, in "A Human Universal: The Capacity to Learn a Language,"

Lila R. Gleitman portrays language learning as universal and innate, supporting the nativist contention that "language capacity...is preprogrammed in the human brain." She sees language learning as following similar stages and time frames across linguistic communities, whether for spoken or signed language. Patricia K. Kuhl in "A New View of Language Acquisition," stresses the interrelationship of nature and nurture. Kuhl views caretaker language as vital to language acquisition and provides evidence from her research to show that infants "map" critical aspects of ambient language in the first year of life before they can speak.

Of course, studies about first language acquisition present only part of the picture. In "Fundamentals of Second Language Acquisition," Susan Gass considers practical and theoretical issues related to second language learning: where it takes place, how learners create a language system, the nature and consequences of speech interaction between native and non-native speakers, and how the "negotiation of meaning" affects language learning. She also discusses language interference and transfer, as well as the importance of context in language learning.

Related to second language acquisition is bilingualism, a subject which David S. Martin examines in "The English-Only Movement and Sign Language." To make his case, Martin makes connections among three, at first seemingly unrelated, language issues: the passage of the English Only law in California, the debates surrounding the use of sign language in the education of deaf and hard-of-hearing students, and the prohibition against the use of Hungarian by Hungarians in the province of Slovakia. In the next chapter, Keith Gilyard looks at another aspect of bilingualism in "Let's Flip the Script: An African American Discourse on Language, Literature, and Learning." He opens with an overview of the history of English, connects this to the development of language varieties spoken by African Americans and Afro-Caribbeans, and then presents some of the systematic linguistic features of these varieties. In his second part, Gilyard considers the politics of teaching and language. Continuing the discussion of bilingualism, Ana Celia Zentella in "Hablamos Spanish and English," describes the experiences of Puerto Rican immigrants to the U.S. who speak variations of both Spanish and English. As part of this, she theorizes about the purposes and meaning of "code switching," the rapid alternation of two languages within a single discourse by speakers who have command of both languages.

The next three chapters consist of language narratives: essays by people who have acquired a new language and to some degree feel a sense of divided identity. In his "This is No Language," Josip Novakovich recounts how he learned English more through the Voice of America, the BBC, and Christian radio programs, and by reading books in English from the library in Daruvar than from his school in Croatia. In explaining his decision now to write in English, Novakovich considers the language and politics of his first language, of English, and of his bilingualism. In "Russian as a Second Language," Natasha Lvovich discusses her ambivalence about the maintenance of one's first language as a tie to one's history and culture. She discusses not only her own language and cultural experiences but also those of her two daughters—one who moved to the U.S. when she was five and the other who was born here. Meena Alexander also takes a personal view of multilingualism in "Language and Shame." Alexander describes herself as divided, divided linguistically between Hindi and Malayalam, Alexander's true mother tongue, a language in which she is orally fluent but unable to read or write. She sees herself as a "truly postcolonial creature, who [has] had to live in English." Despite her internal conflicts, she warns readers about the price of fluency in only one language.

Having focused on the experience of being a learner, we move to that of being a teacher. Ryuko Kubota's essay takes the form of a fictional narrative. Kubota's

"Unfinished knowledge: The Story of Barbara," describes the conflicts faced by Barbara, a novice writing teacher who through a process of stages transforms her teaching and concepts of cultural difference. Kubota tells Barbara's story through the lens of critical pedagogy enabling her to critique taken-for-granted knowledge on cultural difference.

Finally, Alastair Pennycook takes linguistics and language study to task for not fully acknowledging the relationship between language and power. In "Sociolinguistics and Power," Pennycook makes a case against both prescriptive and descriptive approaches to language study. Instead Pennycook advocates using a critical approach to language study, one that considers language not apart from but as part of and, in fact, as an active element in constructing society.

As the writers in this unit illustrate, language is more than words. It helps create our identity and place in the world. So whether we focus on acquiring a first language, an additional language, or on being bi- or multilingual, on language as spoken or signed, or look at it from the perspective of learners or teachers, it is important to realize that the way we examine and present our ideas about the acquisition, use, and value of language in our classrooms, neighborhoods, and society tells something about who we are and how we see the world.

A Human Universal: The Capacity to Learn a Language

Lila R. Gleitman
University of Pennsylvania

Human skills, activities, emotions, and beliefs present a picture of bewildering variety, attributable to the cultural settings in which individuals learn and mature and to preexisting differences among individual species members. Is there anything about mental life that is universal across our species, and that typifies what it means "to be human"? The candidate universal function I discuss here is language—more specifically, the capacity of the young human brain to acquire a human linguistic system. Under widely varying environmental circumstances, while learning different languages under different conditions of culture and child rearing and with different motivations and talents, all nonpathological children acquire their native tongue at a high level of proficiency within a narrow developmental time frame. Evidence from the learning process for language suggests that this sameness of outcome despite variation in environment has its explanation in biology. Language is universal in the species just because the capacity to learn it is innately given. In Descartes's words, "It is a very remarkable fact that there are none . . . , without even excepting idiots, that they cannot arrange different words together, forming of them a statement by which they make known their thoughts; while on the other hand, there is no other animal, however perfect and fortunately circumstanced it may be, which can do the same."[1]

I will not try to sustain the claim that human language is innate in exactly the same sense that bee-language or horse-language may be innate or in the sense that the functioning of the visual system may be innate—that is, utterly unlearned and virtually impervious to environmental influence. Any such claim is immediately falsified by a glance at language in different human societies. There are about four thousand different languages now in use on the earth, and the speakers of one cannot understand the speakers of the next. Moreover, specific exposure conditions strikingly influence how each of these is acquired: there is a massive correlation between being born in England and coming to speak English and being born in France and speaking French. This immediately shows that the language function is heavily affected by specific environmental stimulation.

Reprinted with permission of the University of Chicago Press, from *Modern Philology* 90:4 (1993): 513–33.

Clearly, then, no specific language is universal to humankind. However, the commonalities among human languages are, upon careful study, far more striking than the differences among them. Every human language is organized in terms of a hierarchy of structures, composed of speech sounds that lawfully combine into morphemes and words, which in turn combine into phrases and sentences. Every human language has the wherewithal to express approximately the same meanings (i.e., they are intertranslatable). By innateness of the human language-learning machinery I mean that learners are prepared by nature to expect the language they hear to partake of just these formal and substantive properties and are able to acquire languages of this well-defined sort effortlessly during the natural course of maturation. To use Derek Bickerton's term, the learner is equipped with a "bio-program" that guides the acquisition process and makes the learning of specific languages possible.[2] Two kinds of argument favor this position: (1) language learning proceeds uniformly within and across linguistic communities despite extensive variability of the input provided to individuals; and (2) the child acquires many linguistic generalizations that experience could not have made available.

UNIFORMITY OF LEARNING

Language learning follows the same course in all of the many languages where this has been investigated. Isolated words appear at about one year of age. These are mainly nouns that describe simple objects and a few social words (e.g., "bye-bye"). Sometime during the third year of life, there is a sudden spurt of vocabulary growth accompanied by the appearance of rudimentary sentences: At first these are limited to two or three words, for example, "Throw ball," "Kiss teddy," and the like. These early sentences display considerable structure despite their brevity. Roughly speaking, there is a place for the noun and a place for the verb; moreover, the subject and object noun are positioned differently within the sentence. Thus, though the young learner never says long sentences like "Mommy should promptly throw that ball," the subject/object distinction will show up in such foreshortened attempts as "Mommy throw" (the subject precedes the verb) versus "Throw ball" (the direct object follows the verb). As soon as children begin to combine words at all, they reserve structurally determined positions for subjects and direct objects. It is the level of knowledge of language that makes such sentences possible to utter (however this stage of learning may ultimately be characterized) that I will refer to as representing the "skeletal base" of language learning, a sophistication that shows up early and in much the same way in all mentally intact two-year-olds, all over the world.

Between the ages of three and five years, language use by the child in normal learning settings undergoes considerable elaboration. Complex (multiclausal) sentences appear, and the function words (prepositions, articles, and so forth) make their appearance. Thus by age five or before, youngsters sound essentially adult. In his *Biological Foundations of Language* (New York, 1967) Eric Lenneberg argued that these uniformities in the course of learning for children exposed to different languages are first indicators that language learning has a significant biological basis. He provided some normative evidence that the achievement of basic milestones in language learning can be predicted from the child's age and seem to be intercalated tightly with developments that are known on other grounds to be maturationally dependent. For instance, youngsters utter first words just when they stand, two-word sentences just when they walk, and elaborate sentence structures just when they jump.

However, these findings are consistent with quite distinct conjectures about the processes that underlie language learning. Possibly children talk childishly because of limitations in their mental status, but on the other hand they may talk childishly because they have had insufficient time and exposure to learn all the detailed facts about the language that they are hearing from adults around them. (After all, foreign adults first arriving in a new linguistic community will also say things like "Throw ball," but surely not because they are unaccountably returning to a primitive maturational state.) These quite different conjectures about the roots of language learning have been investigated by considering how language learning proceeds, first, when the learning environment is changed and, second, when the maturational status of the learners themselves is changed.

I. Altering the Learning Environment

It is obvious that mothers talk differently to their young children than they do to learned professors of literature. This natural simplification is clearly an adaptation both to the fact that children are cognitively immature and to the fact that their understanding of the language is primitive. But it has sometimes been asserted that this simple kind of speech does more than serve the immediate communicative needs of caretakers and infants. Simplified speech (often fondly called "Motherese") may play a causal role in the language-learning process itself. The idea would be that the caretaker first teaches the child some easy structures and contents, and then moves on to more advanced lessons—essentially, provides smallest sentences to littlest ears. For instance, perhaps the fact that the child learns nouns before verbs and declarative sentences before interrogative sentences is a straightforward consequence of caretakers' natural behavior toward infants. This hypothesis, though plausible, turns out to be false. By and large, mothers speak in whole sentences even to youngest learners. Nouns, verbs, prepositions, and so forth occur in speech even to the youngest learners, and yet the children all select the nouns as the first items to utter. Worse, contrary to intuition, maternal speech is not characterized by simple declarative sentences of the kind that children utter first, such as "Mommy throw ball." In fact, these apparently simplest declarative formats occur in speech to youngest learners only about 10 percent of the time. Instead, the mother's speech is replete with questions ("Where is your nose?") and commands ("Get your foot out of the laundry!"), while the child's own first sentences are declaratives.

Most interestingly, variations in maternal speech forms have been investigated to see if they are predictive of the child's learning: perhaps some mothers know just how to talk to help their children learn; other mothers may not be inclined to speak in ways that facilitate the learning process, in which case their children should progress more slowly in language knowledge. One method for studying this is to select a group of young children who are at the same stage of language knowledge (e.g., fifteen-month-olds who speak only in single isolated words) and to collect samples of their caretakers' speech.[3] If learning is a function of the caretaker's speech style, then variation among the mothers at this time should predict the further progress of these children. To study this, the children's speech was sampled again six months later. Analyzing the children's speech at these two times (fifteen months, then twenty-one months), one can compute growth scores for each child on various linguistic dimensions (e.g., the length and structure of the sentences, the size of the vocabulary, and so forth). The question is whether properties of the mother's speech (in the first measurement, at fifteen months) predict the child's rate of growth on each measured dimension and explain his or her language status at the second measurement six months later.

The outcome of these studies was that the children's learning rate was largely unaffected by differences in their mothers' speech. Each child seemed to develop according to a maturational schedule that was essentially indifferent to maternal variation.

While such studies preclude certain strong versions of the view that language is learned just because it is taught, they also unfortunately leave almost all details unresolved. This is because the absence of measurable environmental effects may be attributable to threshold effects of various sorts. After all, though the mothers differed in their speech styles to some degree, presumably they all uttered speech that fell into some "normal range" for talking to children. This complaint is quite fair. To find out how the environment causes (or does not cause) a child to learn its native tongue, we would need to look at cases in which the environment is much more radically altered. The most straightforward technique would be to maroon some infants on a desert island, rearing them totally apart from adult language users. If they could and would invent a human language on their own hook, and if this invented language developed just as it developed in infants acquiring English or Urdu, this would constitute a stronger argument for a biological basis for language learning.

Classical cognoscenti will recall that, according to Herodotus, this ultimate language-learning experiment has been performed. A certain Egyptian king, Psammetichus, placed two infants ("of the ordinary sort") in an isolated cabin. Herdsmen were assigned to feed them but were not to speak to them, on pain of death. Psammetichus's experimental intent was to resolve the question of which (Egyptian or Phrygian!) was the first of all languages on earth. Appropriately enough for a king, he appears to have been a radical innatist, for he never considered the possibility that untutored children would fail to speak at all. In the event, Herodotus tells us, two years later ("after the indistinct babblings of infancy were over"), these children began to speak Phrygian, whereupon "the Egyptians yielded their claims, and admitted the greater antiquity of the Phrygians."[4]

In effect, if Herodotus is to be believed, these children invented Phrygian rather than merely learning it. No matter that this language had been in use long before they were born, these children did not learn Phrygian from their predecessors. For the isolates, Phrygian emerged as the pure reflection of the language of the soul, the original innate language.

Surprisingly enough, it has been possible to reproduce some of the essentials of Psammetichus's experiment in modern times. I discuss below three extreme examples of language learning in environmentally deprived circumstances. As we shall see, the outcome is not Phrygian. All the same, I will apply the same reasoning to the findings as did Psammetichus: those aspects of language that appear in children without environmental stimulation or support must be reflections of the language capacity as preprogrammed in the human brain.

Example 1. Language Invention by the Isolated Deaf Child.   Extensive study over the past thirty years has shown that the sign languages used among the deaf differ but little from the spoken languages of the world.[5] Their vocabularies are the same, and their organizational principles are the same; that is, they are composed of a small set of primitive gestures (analogous to speech sounds), organized into morphemes and words, which in turn are organized into meaningful phrases and sentences. Moreover, deaf or hearing children acquiring a sign language from their deaf parents follow the learning course typical of spoken-language learning.

But most deaf infants are born into hearing families in which the parents know no sign language. In many cases, the parents make the decision not to allow the children access to sign language at all. This is because they believe the children can come to know a spoken language by later formal "oralist" training in which the children are taught to lip-read and utter English. (This method has at best mixed results; few totally deaf children ever come to control spoken English adequately.) These children are thus deprived of linguistic stimulation until they are about three to five years of age. They cannot learn the language around them just because they cannot hear it. And they cannot learn the alternative, one of the sign languages of the deaf, because they have not been exposed to it. The question is whether, like the Psammetichus children, these youngsters will invent a language in circumstances where they have no opportunity to learn one.

Heidi Feldman, Susan Goldin-Meadow, and I studied the development of language in six of these language-isolated, congenitally deaf children, in the time period preceding their oralist training in English.[6] The findings were quite startling. As mentioned earlier, normally circumstanced learners acquiring English or Urdu from their caretakers produce isolated words starting around their first birthday. The deaf isolates in this same time period began to produce single manual gestures, much like the single words of the youngsters next door who were learning English "from" their caretakers. These gestures were understandable because of their iconicity, for example, the deaf children would flutter their fingers for "snow" and cup their hands behind their ears to render "Mickey Mouse." The hearing parents rarely attempted such gesturing. Insofar as they did, it could be shown that they learned the specific gestures from the deaf children.[7] The size and content of the children's gestural vocabulary approximated that of their hearing peers even though they had to invent their own "words."

At age two, again in common with their hearing peers, the deaf children began to put the gestures together into rudimentary two- and three-sign sentences, with occasional examples of yet further complexity. For example, a child would extend his open palm ("give"), point to some grapes on the table, and finally close the hand and move it to his mouth ("to eat"), thus approximating a request that he be given some grapes to eat. Most surprising of all, these signed sentences were structurally organized, with distinct structural positions assigned to the verb and nouns in each utterance. For instance, just like the youngest English speakers, they had structurally distinctive ways of expressing "Chicken eats" and "Eat chicken." This syntactic structuring of signed sentences was never observed in their hearing caretakers. Evidently, where the environment provides no language samples, children have the internal wherewithal to invent their own forms to render the same meanings. What is more, the timing of language development—at least at the early stages investigated here—is the same whether one is exposed to a fully elaborated natural language or not: first words at age one, rudimentary sentences at age two, with elaborations beginning to appear at age three. The skeletal base of a language appears to be given in the biology of normally developing children. At the same time, it is important to point out that the development of this homemade system does not appear to advance to anywhere near the level of the elaborated natural languages, whether signed or spoken. The "little words," such as articles, prepositions, verbal auxiliaries, did not occur in these youngsters' spontaneous signing, nor did multiclause sentences. We will return to discuss some possible explanations of this apparently stunted development later. Here, we have emphasized what isolated learners can do without environmental stimulation, reserving for later the question of what they perhaps cannot do.

Example 2. Language Development in the Blind Child. The case just considered involved children who were cut off from opportunities to observe the language sounds (or equivalent manual gestures). Evidently, they could invent something like a skeletal human language all the same, demonstrating that there is something within the human child that makes it "natural" to develop a language of a certain type—one that has words, phrases, and so forth. But a little reflection reveals that, in some ways, language invention seems an easier task than ordinary language learning. After all, the inventor of a new language is free to choose instantiations of each item that is specified by the hypothesized "bioprogram" for language. If he or she wants a word for Mickey Mouse, she can just make one up, say, by mimicking Mickey's big ears through an iconic gesture. The learners of English or Greek have no such freedom. They must learn just which sound (e.g., the sound "snow") is used to express the concept "snow" in the linguistic community around them.

How is this to be done? Clearly learners observe the real world contexts in which words are uttered. Thus presumably they will notice that "cup" is uttered in the presence of cups, "jump" is uttered in the presence of jumping, and so forth. But if this is the whole story of vocabulary learning, then we should expect delays and perhaps distortions in the language learning of the blind. After all, some words refer to things that are too large, distant, or gossamer for the blind child to apprehend through manual exploration—such as mountains, birds, and clouds. Overall, the restrictions on blind children's access to contextual information ought to pose acquisitional problems. Yet study of their progress demonstrates that there is neither delay nor distortion in their language growth.[8] They acquire approximately the same words at the same maturational moments as do sighted children, and their syntactic development is unexceptional, with phrases and sentences occurring at the ordinary time. A particularly surprising aspect of blind children's learning has to do with their acquisition of terms that (seem to) describe the visual experience in particular—words like "look" and "see." Because blind children cannot experience visual looking and seeing, one would think that these terms would be absent from their early spoken vocabularies. Yet, in fact, these are among the very first verbs to appear in blind (as well as sighted) children's spontaneous speech. And these words are meaningful to their blind users. For instance, sighted three-year-olds (even if blindfolded) will tilt their faces upward in response to the command, "Look up!" presumably because they understand that "look" has to do with visual-perceptual inspection. Blind children raise their hands instead, keeping the head immobile, as though they too realize that "look" has to do with perceptual inspection—but in the absence of a working visual system, this perceptual inspection must necessarily be by hand. This interpretation is reinforced by the finding that blind youngsters distinguish between the perceptual term "look" and the contact term "touch". Thus, if told "You can touch that table but don't look at it!", the blind three-year old responds by gingerly tapping the table. And then if told, "Now you can look at it," the child systematically explores all the surfaces of the table with her hands. Thus despite radical differences in the observational opportunities offered to blind and sighted babies, both populations come up with interpretations of quite abstract words in a way that is fitting to their own perceptual lives.

Let me now try to organize these facts. Clearly, learning a language is a matter of discovering the relations between the sounds (or gestures) and the meanings that language can express. Thus the novice English speaker must learn that there is a relation between the sound "see" and the meaning "inspect by eye" (or by hand, if the learner is blind), while the Spanish novice must discover that the sound "see" (*Si*) means "yes". The deaf isolates were deprived of the sound side of this equation. They neither heard sounds nor saw gestures, and thus they could not learn the language of the community around them. All the same, they were capable of inventing the rudiments of such a system, assigning distinct, spontaneously invented gestures to particular objects and events that they could observe in the world around them. In contrast, the blind children had access to all the sounds and structures of English, for they could hear. Their deprivation had to do with simultaneous observation of some of the things in the world to which their parents' speech referred, and which could provide the clues to the meanings of the various words. For instance, when the blind child's mother asks her to "Look at the pumpkin," the child decidedly cannot look, in the visual sense of this term. All the same, blind learners come up with a perceptual interpretation of the word—a haptic-perceptual interpretation, to be sure—that is relevant to their perceptual functioning. In content as well as in form, properties of mind appear to legislate the development and character of human language.

II. Changing the Learner's Mental Endowment

I have argued thus far that language learning is the natural product of the developing human brain, that linguistic-learning events in the child's life are the natural consequences of maturation rather than rote outcomes of what children hear and see in the world around them. After all, various children hear different sentences in different contexts, but they all learn the language of their communities in just the same way. But if maturation is a serious limiting factor in acquisition, learning should look different if it takes place later in life than in the usual case. One such case would pertain to the occasional situations in which children have been reared, like Romulus and Remus, by wolves or bears, and then attempts are made to rehabilitate them into human society. Unfortunately such "pure" cases of isolation defy interpretation owing to the collateral physical, nutritional, and other deprivations that accompany such individuals' language deprivations.[9]

More interpretable cases involve children raised by humans under conditions that are almost unimaginably inhumane. "Isabelle" (a code name, not the child's real name) was hidden away in an attic by a deranged mother, apparently never spoken to at all, and provided with only the minimal attention necessary to sustain her life. She was discovered at age six. Unsurprisingly, she had learned no language, and her cognitive development was below that of a normal two-year-old. But within a year, Isabelle learned to speak at the level of her seven-year-old peers. Her tested intelligence was normal, and she took her place in an ordinary school.[10]

The first lesson from this case is that a child at seven years, with one year of language practice, can speak about as well as her second-grade peers, all of whom had seven years of practice. Relatedly, bilingual children (who presumably hear only half as much of each language they are learning as do monolingual children, unless they sleep less) acquire both languages in about the same time that it takes the monolingual child to learn one language. That is, bilinguals speak at the level appropriate to their age, not the level appropriate to their exposure time. Such findings argue that maturational level, not extent of opportunities for practice, is the chief limiting factor in language growth. But the second inference from Isabelle's case seems to be that learning can begin late in maturational time and yet have the normal outcome: native-level fluency.

However, any such conclusion would be premature. Rehabilitation from isolation does seem to depend on maturational state. A child, "Genie," discovered in California about twenty years ago, was fourteen years old when she was removed from the hideous circumstances of her early life. From the age of about twenty months, she had lived tied to a chair in a darkened attic room, was frequently beaten, and never was spoken to—in fact, she was barked at because her deranged father said she was no more than a dog. But despite intensive, long-term rehabilitation attempts by a team of sophisticated psychologists and linguists, Genie's language learning never approached normality.[11] She did rapidly pass through the stages we have discussed thus far and identified as the skeletal base of the language-learning capacity: she acquired vocabulary items and put them together in meaningful propositions much as two-year-olds do—for example, "Another house have dog," "No more take wax." But she never progressed beyond this stage to complex sentences or acquisition of the function words that characterize normal three- and four-year-olds' speech.

Why did Genie not progress to full language knowledge while Isabelle did? The best guess is that the crucial factor is the age at which exposure to linguistic stimulation began. Six years old (as in Isabelle's case) is late, but evidently not too late. Fourteen years old is too late by far. There appears to be a critical or sensitive period for language acquisition, a consequence of maturational changes in the developing human brain.

The notion of a critical period for learning has been studied primarily in animals. Acquisition of a number of important animal behavior patterns seems to be governed by the timing of environmental stimulation. One example is the attachment of the young of various species to their mothers, which generally can be formed only in early childhood.[12] Another is bird song. Male birds of many species have a song that is characteristic of their own kind. They learn this song by listening to adult males of their own species. But this exposure will be effective only if it occurs at a certain period in the fledgling's life. This has been documented for the white-crowned sparrow. To learn the white-crowned sparrow song in all its glory (complete with special trills and grace notes), the baby birds must hear an adult song sometime between the seventh and sixtieth days of life. The next forty days are a marginal period. If the fledgling is exposed to an adult male's song during that period but not before, he will acquire only some skeletal basics of the sparrow song, without the full elaborations heard in normal adults. If the exposure comes still later, it has no effect at all: the bird will never sing normally.[13]

It is tempting to extend such findings to the cases of Isabelle and Genie. Though Isabelle's exposure to language was relatively late, it might have fallen full square within the critical period. Genie's later exposure might have been at the "marginal" time, allowing her to achieve only the skeletal base of a human language. But in order to draw any such grand conclusions, it is necessary to look beyond such tragic individual cases at a more organized body of evidence to examine the effects of brain state on the capacity to learn a language.

Second-Language Learning.   Much of the literature on this topic has traditionally come from studies of second-language learning, for the obvious reason that it is hard to find adults who have not been exposed to a first language early in life. But individuals acquire second—and third, and fifth—languages throughout their life spans. Do they acquire these differently as a consequence of differences in their degree of brain maturation?

The facts are these. In the first stages of learning a second language, adults appear to be more efficient than children.[14] The adult second-language learners produce primitive sentences almost immediately while the young child displaced into a new language community is often shocked into total silence and emotional distress. But the long-range outcome is just the reverse. After one to two years, very young children speak the new language fluently and sound just like natives. This is highly uncommon in adults.

This point has been made by investigators who studied the long-run outcome of second-language learning as a function of the age of first exposure to it.[15] The subjects were native Chinese and Korean speakers who came to the United States at varying ages. The East Asian languages were chosen because they are maximally dissimilar to English. The subjects were tested for English-language knowledge after they had been in the United States for at least five years, so they had ample exposure and practice time. Finally, all of them were students and faculty members at a large midwestern university, so they shared some social background (and presumably were about equally motivated to learn the new language to succeed in their jobs and social roles). These subjects listened to English sentences, half of which were grossly ungrammatical (e.g., *The farmer bought two pig at the market, The little boy is speak to a policeman*); the other half were the grammatical counterparts of the ungrammatical sentences. The task was to identify the grammatical and ungrammatical sentences. The results were clear-cut. Those learners who (like Isabelle) had been exposed to English before age seven performed just like native speakers. Thereafter, there was an increasing decrement in performance as a function of age at first exposure. The later they were exposed to English, the worse they performed.

Late Exposure to a First Language.   Immediate objections can be raised to the outcomes just described as bearing on the critical period hypothesis. The first is anecdotal. All of us know or know of individuals (e.g., Joseph Conrad or Vladimir Nabokov) who learned English late in life and controlled it extraordinarily well. But the point of the studies just mentioned has to do with population characteristics, not extraordinary individuals. Every child of normal mentality exposed to a (first or second) language before age six or seven learns it at native level. It is a rarity, the subject of considerable admiration and awe, if anyone does as well when exposure begins in adulthood.

The second objection is more substantive. Perhaps the difficulties of the learners just discussed had to do specifically with second language learning. Maybe older individuals are not worse at learning language but rather are troubled by their sophisticated knowledge of the first language. One body of language knowledge may "interfere" with the other.

For this reason, it is of interest to look at acquisition of a first language late in life. The best available line of evidence comes from work on the acquisition of sign language. As we saw earlier, most deaf children are born into hearing families and are therefore not exposed to a gestural language from birth. These individuals invent a skeletal communication system that compares quite well with language in the normally circumstanced two-year-old. Yet, they do not advance to an elaborate language system containing complex sentences, function words such as "the" and "to", and so forth. In some ways, their spontaneous development seems akin to Genie's. Thus early in life these isolates control no elaborate linguistic system.

At varying points in life, as accidents of personal history, most of these individuals do come in contact with a formal language of the deaf, such as American Sign Language (ASL), which they then learn and use for all their everyday communicative needs. Sometimes contact with a formal sign language comes relatively early in life but sometimes as late as forty or fifty years of age. These individuals are essentially learning a first language at an unusually late point in maturational time.

Does this late start matter? Elissa Newport studied the production and comprehension of ASL in three groups of congenitally deaf people.[16] All of them had been using ASL as their sole means of communication for at least thirty years, a virtual guarantee that they were as expert in this language as they would ever be. The only difference among them was the age at which they had first been exposed to ASL. The first group consisted of deaf children of deaf parents who had been exposed to ASL from birth. The second consisted of early learners, those who had been exposed to ASL between ages four and six. The third group had come into contact with ASL after the age of twelve. All subjects were at least fifty years of age when tested. The findings were dramatic. After thirty years or more of exposure and constant use, only those who had been exposed to ASL before age six showed native-level fluency. There were subtle defects in the middle group, and those whose exposure occurred after the age of twelve evinced significant deficits. Their particular problems (as usual) were with the ASL equivalents of the function words and with complex sentences.

Pidgins and Creoles.   A fascinating line of research concerns the process of language formation among linguistically heterogeneous adults who are thrown together for limited times or purposes.[17] They may be occasional trading partners of different language backgrounds who have to communicate solely about the costs of fish and vegetables, or foreign co-workers who come to a new country to earn money and then return to their native land. These individuals often develop a rough-and-ready contact language, a lingua franca, or pidgin. Not surprisingly from what we have discussed so far, these pidgin languages are rudimentary in form, perhaps because all their speakers are late learners. Thus there are interesting overlaps between the pidgins and the first attempts of young children learning an elaborated natural language. For example, at the first stages of both, the sentences are one clause long and have a rigid canonical structure and few if any function words.[18]

Very often, a pidgin will develop into a full language. An example is Tok Pisin ("Talk Pidgin"), a language of Papua New Guinea that had pidgin origins. However, the foreign visitors began to settle down, using the pidgin as the only means of linguistic communication, and—most important—had babies. The only language stimulation these babies heard was the pidgin itself. Now, once a pidgin language has native speakers (and thus by definition is called a "creole"), it undergoes rapid change and expansion of just the sort one might expect based on the learning data I have presented so far: multiclausal sentences and a variety of function words appeared in the users who heard the pidgin from birth rather than acquiring it during adulthood. Gillian Sankoff showed that this elaboration of structure was carried out by the child learners who, between the ages of about four and eight years, refined and expanded upon the formal resources available in the pidgin.[19]

Elissa Newport and Ted Supalla showed a related effect for the children of late learners of ASL.[20] We recall that these late learners, even after thirty years of exposure and practice, controlled only a rudimentary—"pidginized"—form of ASL. Perforce, it is this pidgin to which their own children are exposed. Again, at the appropriate maturational moments (ages four to eight), these learners refine, expand, and grammaticize the pidgin resources, creating an elaborated language complete with complex sentences and function words.

In a nutshell, both for the spoken pidgin of Sankoff and the gestural pidgin of Newport and Supalla, the first language-learning situation, carried out at the correct maturational moment, creates new resources out of the air—resources that are not properties of the input pidgin, are highly abstract, and are the very hallmarks of full natural languages.

EVERY LEARNER IS AN ISOLATE

The bulk of this article has focused on language learning in unusual and apparently especially difficult conditions—when the learner was blocked from getting information of various kinds by accidents of nature or circumstance, or even when there was no full language out there in the world for the learner to observe. Rising above these inadequacies in the data provided, children learned language even so. I have argued that this points to a human "linguistic nature" that rescues learners from inadequacies in relevant nurture.

But in an important sense, it was not really necessary to look at special populations to conclude that language learning must be largely "from the inside out" rather than being "outside in," a behavioral response to external stimulation. The special cases serve only to dramatize the ordinary conditions for language acquisition, rather than being different in kind from these. For every learner of a human language, no matter how fortunately circumstanced, is really in the same boat as, say, the blind child or the learner exposed to a rudimentary contact language: isolated from the information required to (literally) learn a language. At best, the child's environment offers some fragmentary and inconclusive clues, with human nature left to fill in the rest. In short, children are able to acquire English or German or Tlingit just because they know the essence of language in advance of exposure and without learning, by biological fiat.

Let me document this point with a few examples. Consider the information children are given such that they come to know that the sound "dog" means "dog" and that, therefore, this sound is appropriate to utter when referring to dogs. No one tells the child the meaning of the word (perhaps, "cute, furry, tame, four-legged, midsized mammal of the canine variety"). Instead, the child will see a few dogs—say, a chihuahua and a Great Dane—and in their presence the caretaker will utter, "That's a dog," "Be careful; that dog bites!" "I'm glad we don't have a dirty dog like that at home," or something of the sort. From such adventitious encounters with dogs and sentences about dogs rather than from any direct encounters at all with the "meaning of 'dog'," novices must deduce that there is a category 'dog', labeled "dog" in English, that can be applied to creatures of a certain kind. Though their observations may include only the chihuahua and the Great Dane, they must be able to apply the word to terriers and poodles as well, yet not to cats or elephants. In sum, the use of even the homeliest words is creative. Once learned, they are applicable to instances never previously observed, so long as they fit the category. But just what the appropriate extensions are from the introducing examples to new things in the world is left to the children to figure out on their own.

Such are the real conditions for vocabulary acquisition. The category (or "concept") is never directly encountered, for there are no categories "in the world" to encounter, only things, events, and so forth. The learner is thrown upon his or her own internal resources to discover the category itself. Yet the most ordinary child by age six has acquired about ten thousand such items, hardly any of them ever "defined" by the adult community.

To see the real dimensions of this vocabulary acquisition task, consider now the acquisition of "know," a vocabulary item within the range of every self-respecting four-year-old. In certain conversational contexts the novice will hear, "Do you know where your blocks are?" "I don't know what you're crying about," "You know Aunt Mary, don't you? You met her at Bobby's house last week." In consequence of such sometime contacts with the world and the word, children come to understand the meaning of "know." How do they manage to do so? What is the meaning of "know," such that it refers truly and relevantly to the (infinitely many) new "knowing situations" but not to the infinitely many other new situations that involve no knowing? Just what are the situations that license uttering "know"?

All in all, it seems that the word learner even under optimal environmental conditions is "isolated" from direct information about word meanings, even though his or her job is, inter alia, to acquire these. The instances offered by experience are insufficient to warrant discovery of these meanings, but the child does so anyway, and for a formidably large set of words.

Lay observers are often impressed with the fact that very young children may sometimes overextend some term—for example, calling the dog in the street "Fido" if that is the name of the child's own dog, or calling the man in the street "Daddy." But these errors are quite rare, even in the toddler (perhaps that is why they are so treasured) and have largely disappeared by age two. More important, the rare errors in applying a word are highly constrained: no child calls an onion or jumping or redness, "dog." Even when toddlers are slightly off the mark in using first words, they are admirably close to correct, despite the fact that the information presented in the environment is ludicrously impoverished. It must be that the categories in which language traffics are lavishly prefigured in the human mind.

Similar arguments for the poverty of the stimulus information (and thus the need to look to nature to understand the emergence of language in children) can be made by look-ing at almost any property of syntactic structure. No mother explains English grammar to her child. One reason is that no one "knows" the grammar in any conscious way. Another is that the babies would not understand the explanations. Just as in the case of vocabulary, acquisition of syntactic structure proceeds on the sole basis of examples rather than ex-planations. Regarding the instances now discussed, I will ask—following Noam Chomsky, in *Reflections on Language*—whether the example utterances that children hear are really sufficient to account for what they come to know about the structure of their language.[21]

English declarative sentences of the simplest sort position the verb after the subject noun phrase: for example, *The man is a fool.* To form the interrogative, the *is* "moves" into initial position preceding the subject (*Is the man a fool?*). But can any *is* in a declarative sentence be moved to form an interrogative? It is impossible to judge from one-clause sentences alone. The issue is resolved by looking at more complex sentences, which can contain more than one instance of *is*, for example:

(1) *The man who is a fool is amusing.*
(2) *The man is a fool who is amusing.*

Which of the two *is*'s in each of these sentences can move to initial position to form an interrogative? Suppose we say that it is the first of the two *is*'s that can move. This will yield:

(1′) *Is the man who a fool is amusing?*
(2′) *Is the man a fool who is amusing?*

Sentence 2′ is fine, but 1′ is clearly ungrammatical. No one talks that way. Therefore, the "rule" for forming an interrogative cannot be anything like "move the first *is*." But a new trouble results if we try to move the second *is* instead. This would yield:

(1″) *Is the man who is a fool amusing?*
(2″) *Is the man is a fool who amusing?*

Now sentence 2″ has come out wrong. Thus no rule that alludes to the serial order of the two *is*'s will do to account for what is and what is not a grammatical interrogative. The only generalization that will work is that the *is* in the main clause (rather than the subordinate clause, the one introduced by *who*) moves. The problem with 1′ and with 2′ is that we tried to move the *is* in the subordinate clause, a violation of English syntactic structure.

English speakers by age four are capable of uttering complex interrogatives like those we have just looked at. No one has ever observed a youngster to err along the way, producing sentences like 1′ or 2′. But how could they have learned the appropriate generalization?

No one whispers in a child's ear, "It's the *is* in the main clause that moves." And even such a whispered hint would be insufficient, for the task would still be to identify these clauses. Sentences uttered to children are not marked off into clauses such as:

(3) *The man [who is a fool] is amusing.*

nor are clauses marked "main" and "subordinate" anywhere in the speech stream. No one hears sentences like:

(4) *beginning-of-main clause "The man" subordinate clause "who is a fool" end-of-main clause "is amusing."*

In short, the analysis of heard utterances that is required for forming the correct generalization is not offered in the language stimulation that the child receives. Even so, every child forms this generalization, which operates in terms of structures (such as main clause) rather than according to the serial order of items (such as "the first *is*").

The distinction between main and subordinate clauses—or, in modern linguistic parlance, "higher" and "lower" clauses—is no arcane byway of English grammar. Consider as one more instance the interpretation of pronouns. Very often, pronouns follow their antecedents, as in:

(5) *When John arrived home, he ate dinner.*

But we cannot account for the antecedent/pronoun relation simply by alluding to their serial order in the sentence (just as we could not account for the movement of *is* by alluding to its serial position in a sentence). This is because a pronoun can sometimes precede its antecedent noun as in:

(6) *When he arrived home, John ate dinner.*

But this is not always possible, as shown by:

(7) *He arrived home when John ate dinner.*

Sentence 7 is perfectly grammatical but its *he* cannot be John, while the *he* in sentence 6 can be John.

What is the generalization that accounts for the distinction in the interpretation of 6 and 7? It is (very roughly) that the pronoun in the main (higher) clause cannot co-refer with a noun in the subordinate (lower) clause. Again, it was necessary to invoke structures within sentences rather than the serial order of words (here, nouns and pronouns) to understand how to interpret the sentences.

How could a child learn that the principles of English syntax are—always, as it turns out—structure-dependent rather than serial-order-dependent? Why are errors not made on the way to this generalization? The problem is that sentences spoken and heard by children in no way transparently provide the structural information. The "stimulus information" (the utterances) is too impoverished—just a bunch of words strung in a row—to sustain the correct generalizations. And yet these generalizations are formed anyway.

The solution seems to be that learners are innately biased to assume that natural-language generalizations will inevitably be structure-dependent rather than serial-order-dependent. Indeed, extensive linguistic investigation shows this to be true of all languages, not just English. With this principle in hand, a child has a crucial leg up in acquiring any natural language to which he or she is exposed.

To summarize this discussion, every real learner is isolated from the kinds of elaborate information that would be necessary for discovering the word meanings and grammatical forms of a human language. Children use neither dictionaries nor grammar texts to redress this paucity of the information base. It follows that innate principles are guiding their linguistic development. Children can learn language because they are disposed by nature to represent and manipulate linguistic data in highly circumscribed ways.

CONCLUSIONS

I have tried to describe some of the complex facts about language and language learning that I consider to be at least within calling distance of an explanation, just in case there are biologically given dispositions in humans to support them. Primarily, I have given evidence that language is the product of the young human brain, such that virtually any exposure conditions short of total isolation and vicious mistreatment will suffice to bring it forth in every child. In retrospect, this is scarcely surprising. It would be just as foolish for evolution to have created human bodies without human "programs" to run these bodies as to have created giraffe bodies without giraffe programs or white-crowned-sparrow bodies without white-crowned-sparrow programs. It is owing to such biological programming that language is universal in our species and utterly closed to other species—including even college-educated chimpanzees.

The universality of language is, moreover, no quirk or back corner of human mentality but rather one of the central cognitive properties whose possession makes us truly human. If we humans ever get to another planet and find organisms who speak like us, I predict that we will feel some strong impetus to get to know them and understand them—rather than trying to herd them or milk them—even if they look like cows.

Returning now to an issue that I may well have underemphasized throughout this discussion, it remains the fact that specific languages must be acquired by human babies even though the capacity to accomplish this is based on a specialized and highly evolved biological endowment. This is because the surface manifestations of human language capacity are marvelously variable. To repeat an obvious point, English children learn English, not Greek or Urdu. For this reason it is realistic to regard the language-acquisition task as a complex interaction between the child's innate capacities and the social, cognitive, and specifically linguistic supports provided in the environment. What I have tried to emphasize, however, is that acknowledgment of significant environmentally caused variation should not blind us to the pervasive commonalities among all languages and among all their learners.

Perhaps it would repay serious inquiry to investigate other complex human functions in ways related to those that have been exploited in the study of language learning. Palpably, there are vast differences in human artifacts and social functions in different times and places, with some humans riding on camels while others rocket to the moon. All the same, it may well be that—as is the case for language—human individuals and cultures cannot differ from each other without limit. There may be more human universals than are visible to the naked eye. Beneath the kaleidoscopic variation in human behavior that we easily observe, there may be universal organizing principles that constrain us and contribute to the definition of what it is to be a human.

NOTES

[1] Rene Descartes, *Discours de la méthode*, pt. 5, in *Philosophical Works*, trans. E. Haldane and G. Ross (Cambridge, 1911), 1:116–17.

[2] Derek Bickerton, *Dynamics of a Creole System* (New York, 1975), pp. 167–70.

[3] Elissa Newport, Henry Gleitman, and Lila R. Gleitman, "Mother, I'd Rather Do It Myself: Some Effects and Noneffects of Maternal Speech Style," in *Talking to Children: Language Input and Acquisition*, ed. C. Snow and C. Ferguson (New York, 1977), pp. 109–49.

[4] Herodotus, *The Persian Wars*, bk. 2, chap. 2, trans. G. Rawlinson (New York, 1942), p. 117.

[5] Ursula Bellugi and Edward S. Klima, "Aspects of Sign Language and Its Structure", in *The Role of Speech in Language*, ed. J. Kavanagh and J. Cutting (Cambridge, Mass., 1975), pp. 171–203.

[6] Heidi Feldman, Susan Goldin-Meadow, and Lila R. Gleitman, "Beyond Herodotus: The Creation of Language by Linguistically Deprived Deaf Children," in *Action, Symbol. And Gesture: The Emergence of Language*, ed. A. Lock (New York, 1978), pp. 352–415.

[7] Susan Goldin-Meadow and C. Mylander, "Gestural Communication in Deaf Children: The Non-Effects of Parental Input," *Science* 221 (1983): 372–74.

[8] Barbara Landau and Lila R. Gleitman, *Language and Experience: Evidence from the Blind Child* (Cambridge, Mass., 1985), pp. 22–50.

[9] See Roger Brown, *Words and Things* (New York, 1958), pp. 186–93.

[10] K. Davis, "Final Note on a Case of Extreme Social Isolation," *American Journal of Sociology* 52 (1947): 432–37.

[11] Victoria Fromkin, Steven Krashen, Susan Curtiss, D. Rigler, and M. Rigler, "The Development of Language in Genie: A Case of Language Acquisition beyond the 'Critical Period,'" *Brain and Language* 1 (1974): 81–107.

[12] S. Suomi and Harry Harlow, "Abnormal Social Behavior in Young Monkeys," in *Exceptional Infant: Studies in Abnormalities*, ed. J. Helmuth (New York, 1971), 2:483–529.

[13] Peter Marler, "A Comparative Approach to Vocal Learning: Song Development in White Crowned Sparrows," *Journal of Comparative and Physiological Psychology*, monograph 7 (1970), pp. 1–25.

[14] Catherine Snow and Marilyn Hoefnagel-Hohle, "The Critical Period for Language Acquisition: Evidence from Second Language Learning," *Child Development* 49 (1978): 1114–28.

[15] Jenny Johnson and Elissa Newport, "Critical Period Effects in Second-Language Learning: The Influence of Maturational State on the Acquisition of English as a Second Language," *Cognitive Psychology* 21 (1989): 60–90.

[16] Elissa Newport, "Maturational Constraints on Language Learning," *Cognitive Science* 14 (1990): 11–28.

[17] Gillian Sankoff and S. LaBerge, "On the Acquisition of Native Speakers by a Language," *Kivung* 6 (1973): 32–47; Bickerton (no 2 above), pp. 175–77.

[18] For the connection between pidgin and child language, see Daniel I. Slobin, "Language Change in Childhood and in History," in *Language Learning and Thought*, ed. John Macnamara (New York, 1977).

[19] Sankoff and LaBerge, pp. 35, 45.

[20] Elissa Newport and Ted Supalla, "The Structuring of Language: Clues from the Acquisition of Signed and Spoken Language," in their *Signed and Spoken Language: Biological Constraints on Linguistic Form* (Weinheim, Berlin, and Deerfield Beach, Fla., 1980), pp. 187–212.

[21] For a discussion along these lines, see Noam Chomsky, *Reflections on Language* (New York, 1975), pp. 30–33.

QUESTIONS TO THINK ABOUT

1. According to Gleitman, all languages have certain commonalities. Which specific commonalities does she mention? Choose one of these commonalities and explain it, referring to and giving specific examples from a language with which you are familiar.

2. What is the "skeletal base" of language learning? What are the next two steps in language learning? Do the notions of these basic learning steps hold up for the deaf, blind, second language learners, and late language learners described by Gleitman? What differences does she notice? What is the importance of the "correct maturational moment" for language learning?

3. How does Gleitman explain the fact that children are able to categorize both a Great Dane and a Chihuahua as a dog, despite the differences between them? How are they able to understand the various meanings for common words such as "know"? How do these and other examples support the idea that "children can learn language because they are disposed by nature to represent and manipulate linguistic data in highly circumscribed ways"? How else might you interpret these examples?

4. *Extending your understanding*: What linguistic principles should teachers keep in mind when working with children learning a second language? Should the principles be different for adults learning a second language? Should the expectations be the same?

TERMS TO DEFINE

Define the following words and phrases as they are presented within the context of the article. Comment on your understanding of the significance of each one.

Complex (multiclausal) sentences
Function Words
Haptic-perceptual
Lingua Franca
Morpheme
Pidgin and Creoles

A New View of Language Acquisition

Patricia K. Kuhl
University of Washington, Seattle

The last half of the 20th century has produced a revolution in our understanding of language and its acquisition. Studies of infants across languages and cultures have provided valuable information about the initial state of the mechanisms underlying language, and more recently, have revealed infants' unexpected learning strategies. The learning strategies—demonstrating pattern perception, as well as statistical (probabilistic and distributional) computational skills—are not predicted by historical theories. The results lead to a new view of language acquisition, one that accounts for both the initial state of linguistic knowledge in infants and infants' extraordinary ability to learn simply by listening to ambient language. The new view reinterprets the critical period for language and helps explain certain paradoxes—why infants, for example, with their immature cognitive systems, far surpass adults in acquiring a new language. The goal of this paper is to illustrate the recent work and offer six principles that shape the new perspective.

HISTORICAL THEORETICAL POSITIONS

In the last half of the 20th century, debate on the origins of language was ignited by a highly publicized exchange between a strong nativist and a strong learning theorist. In 1957, the behavioral psychologist B. F. Skinner proposed a learning view in his book *Verbal Behavior*, arguing that language, like all animal behavior, was an "operant" that developed in children as a function of external reinforcement and shaping (1). By Skinner's account, infants learn language as a rat learns to press a bar—through the monitoring and management of reward contingencies.

Noam Chomsky, in a review of *Verbal Behavior*, took a very different theoretical position (2, 3). Chomsky argued that traditional reinforcement learning had little to do with humans' abilities to acquire language. He posited a "language faculty" that included innately specified constraints on the possible forms human language could take. Chomsky argued

Reprinted with permission of P. K. Kuhn and PNS, www.pnas.org. © 2000 by P. K. Kuhn.

that infants' innate constraints for language included specification of a universal grammar and universal phonetics. Language was one of the primary examples of what Fodor called a module—domain-specific, informationally encapsulated, and innate (4).

The two approaches took strikingly different positions on all of the critical components of a theory of language acquisition:(*i*) the initial state of knowledge, (*ii*) the mechanisms responsible for developmental change, and (*iii*) the role played by ambient language input. On Skinner's view, no innate information was necessary, developmental change was brought about through reward contingencies, and language input did not cause language to emerge. On Chomsky's view, infants' innate knowledge of language was a core tenet, development constituted "growth" or maturation of the language module, and language input triggered (or set the parameters for) a particular pattern from among those innately provided.

A great deal has been learned since the debate ensued, caused largely by experiments conducted on infants. Infants' perception of the phonetic units of speech, which requires tracking the formant frequencies (5), and their detection of words from cues in running speech (6) support a different view. The emerging view argues that the kind of learning taking place in early language acquisition cannot be accounted for by Skinnerian reinforcement. On the other hand, the idea that language acquisition involves a selectionist process wherein language input operates on innately specified options also is not supported. The emerging view suggests that infants engage in a new kind of learning in which language input is mapped in detail by the infant brain. Six principles reflecting this view are offered.

INITIAL PERCEPTION PARSES SPEECH CORRECTLY AND IS UNIVERSAL, BUT NOT DOMAIN SPECIFIC OR SPECIES SPECIFIC

Any theory of language acquisition has to specify how infants parse the auditory world to make the critical units of language available. This is a formidable problem as indicated by the difficulty computers have in segmenting speech (7–9). Early experiments on infants confirmed their abilities to parse speech correctly at the phonetic level and revealed that their abilities are universal across languages. Interestingly, however, the data also demonstrated that the kind of partitioning seen for speech is not limited to humans or limited to speech.

The evidence derived from tests of categorical perception (10). When adult listeners were tested on a continuum that ranges from one syllable (such as "bat") to another ("pat"), perception appeared absolute. Adults discriminated phonetic units that crossed the "phonetic boundary" between categories but not stimuli that fell within a category. The phenomenon was language-specific; Japanese adults, for example, failed to show a peak in discrimination at the phonetic boundary of an American English ra-la series (as in "rake" vs. "lake") (11).

Categorical perception provided an opportunity to test whether infants could parse the basic units of language, and discrimination tests confirmed that they did. Infants discriminated only between stimuli from different phonetic categories (12–14). Moreover, unlike adults, infants demonstrated the effect for the phonetic units of all languages (15, 16). Eimas hypothesized that infants' abilities reflected innate "phonetic feature detectors" that evolved for speech and theorized that infants are biologically endowed with neural mechanisms that respond to the phonetic contrasts used by the world's languages (17).

Experimental tests on nonhuman animals altered this conclusion (18, 19). Animals also exhibited categorical perception; they demonstrated perceptual "boundaries" at locations where humans perceive a shift from one phonetic category to another (18, 19). In tests of discrimination, monkeys showed peaks in sensitivity that coincided with the phonetic boundaries used by languages (20–22). The results were subsequently replicated in a number of species(23, 24). Recently, additional tests on infants and monkeys revealed similarities in their perception of the prosodic cues of speech as well (25).

Two conclusions were drawn from the initial comparative work (26). First, infants' parsing of the phonetic units at birth was a discriminative capacity that could be accounted for by a general auditory processing mechanism, rather than one that evolved specifically for speech. Differentiating the units of speech did not imply *a priori* knowledge of the phonetic units themselves, merely the capacity to detect differences between them, which was constrained in an interesting way (18, 19, 25, 27). Second, in the evolution of language, acoustic differences detected by the auditory perceptual processing mechanism strongly influenced the selection of phonetic units used in language. On this view, particular auditory features were exploited in the evolution of the sound system used in language (19, 26, 27). This ran counter to two prevailing principles at the time: (*i*) the view that phonetic units were prespecified in infants, and (*ii*) the view that language evolved in humans without continuity with lower species.

Categorical perception also was demonstrated with nonspeech stimuli that mimicked speech features without being perceived as speech, in both adults (28, 29) and infants (30). This finding supported the view that domain-general mechanisms were responsible for infants' initial partitioning of the phonetic units of language.

DEVELOPMENT IS NOT BASED ON SELECTION

Eimas' early model of speech perception was selectionist in nature. An innate neural specification of all possible phonetic units allowed selection of a subset of those units to be triggered by language input (17). The notion was that linguistic experience produced either maintenance or loss. Detectors stimulated by ambient language were maintained, whereas those not stimulated by language input atrophied.

Developmental studies were initially seen as providing support for the selectionist view. Werker and her colleagues demonstrated that, by 12 months of age, infants no longer discriminate nonnative phonetic contrasts, even though they did so at 6 months of age (31). The finding was interpreted as support for a selectionist theory; there was a "loss" of a subset of phonetic units initially specified.

Modifications regarding the extent to which listeners "lost" the ability to discriminate nonnative phonetic units were quick to follow (32). Adult performance on nonnative contrasts could be increased by a number of factors: (*i*) the use of techniques that minimize the effects of memory (33, 34), (*ii*) extensive training (35, 36), and (*iii*) the use of contrasts, such as Zulu clicks, that are not related to native-language categories (37, 38). These data, indicating that there is not an immutable loss of phonetic abilities for non-native units (32), did not refute the selectionist position. The fact that listeners do not completely lose the ability to discriminate nonnative contrasts does not alter the basic tenet of the selectionist view, which is that the role of language experience is to maintain or decrease the activity of innately specified neural detectors. To refute the selectionist position, studies must demonstrate that infants listening to ambient language are engaged in some other kind of learning process, a process that is not fundamentally subtractive in nature. New studies on learning provide that demonstration.

INFANTS' LEARNING STRATEGIES "MAP" LANGUAGE INPUT

Learning theory as a mechanism for language acquisition had been dismissed by early theorists because of the failure of existing learning models, such as Skinner's, to explain the facts of language development (2). At present, however, learning models figure prominently in debates on language (39–42). What has changed? The discoveries of the last two decades, demonstrating that by simply listening to language infants acquire sophisticated information about its properties, have created new views of learning.

Three important examples of a new kind of learning have emerged. First, infants detect patterns in language input. Second, infants exploit the statistical properties of the input, enabling them to detect and use distributional and probabilistic information contained in ambient language to identify higher-order units. Third, infant perception is altered—literally warped—by experience to enhance language perception. No speaker of any language perceives acoustic reality; in each case, perception is altered in the service of language.

Infants' Abstract Patterns.   A major requirement of language processing is the detection of similarities, or patterns, in language input, a stumbling block for computer speech recognition (7). Infants demonstrate excellent skills at pattern recognition for speech. A number of studies have shown that 6-month-old infants, trained to produce a head-turn response when a sound from one category is presented (such as the vowel /a/ in "pop"), and to inhibit that response when an instance from another vowel category is presented (/i/ in "peep"), demonstrate the ability to perceptually sort novel instances into categories (43). For example, infants perceptually sort vowels that vary across talkers and intonation contours (44, 45), as well as syllables that vary in their initial consonant (those beginning with /m/ as opposed to /n/, or those beginning with /s/ versus /ʃ/) across variations in talkers and vowel contexts (46, 47). Moreover, infants perceptually sort syllables based on a phonetic feature shared by their initial consonants, such as a set of nasal consonants, /m/, /n/, and η as opposed to a set of stop consonants, /b/, /d/, and /g/ (46). Recent tests show that 9-month-old infants are particularly attentive to the initial portions of syllables (48).

Infants' detection of patterns is not limited to phonetic units. More global prosodic patterns contained in language also are detected. At birth, infants have been shown to prefer the language spoken by their mothers during pregnancy, as opposed to another language (49–51). This skill requires infant learning of the stress and intonation pattern characteristic of the language information that is reliably transmitted through bone conduction to the womb (52). Additional evidence that the learning of speech patterns commences *in utero* stems from studies showing infant preference for their mother's voice over another female at birth (53) and their preference for stories read by the mother during the last 10 weeks of pregnancy (54).

Between 6 and 9 months, infants exploit prosodic patterns related to the stress or emphasis typical of words in their native language. In English, a strong/weak pattern of stress, with emphasis on the initial syllable ("*ba*by," "*mom*my," "*ta*ble") is typical, whereas a weak/strong pattern predominates in other languages. American infants tested at 6 months show no listening preference for words with the strong/weak as opposed to the weak/strong pattern, but by 9 months they exhibit a strong preference for the pattern typical of their native language (55). Infants also use prosodic cues to detect major constituent boundaries, such as clauses. At 4 months of age, infants listen equally long to Polish and English speech samples that have pauses inserted at clause boundaries as opposed to within clauses, but by 6 months, infants listen preferentially to pauses inserted at the clause boundaries appropriate only to their native language (41, 56).

By 9 months of age, infants detect patterns related to the orderings of phonemes that are legal for their language. In English, for example, the combination *zw or vl* is not legal; in Dutch, they are permissible. By 9 months of age, but not at 6 months of age, American infants listen longer to English words, whereas Dutch infants show a listening preference for Dutch words (57). At this age, infants do not recognize the words themselves, but recognize the perceptual patterns typical of words in their language. They develop a "perceptual sleeve" in which words fit; a description of word candidates assists them in identifying potential words in running speech.

Infants Exploit Statistical Properties of Language Input.   Running speech presents a problem for infants because, unlike written speech, there are no breaks between words. New research shows that infants detect and exploit the statistical properties of the language they hear to find word candidates in running speech before they know the meanings of words. Goodsitt, Morgan, and Kuhl (58) demonstrated this in 7-month-old infants by using artificial words.

Goodsitt *et al.* examined infants' abilities to maintain the discrimination of two isolated syllables, /de/ and /ti/, when these target syllables were later embedded in three-syllable strings. The three-syllable strings contained the target syllable and a bisyllable composed of the syllables /ko/ and/ga/. The arrangement of /ko/ and /ga/ was manipulated to change the degree to which they could be perceived as a likely word candidate. Three conditions were tested. In *a*, /koga/ was an invariantly ordered "word," appearing either after the target syllables, /dekoga/ and /tikoga/, or before it, /kogade/ and /kogati/. In this condition, the transitional probability between the /ko/ and /ga/ was always 1.0. If infants detect /koga/ as a unit, it should assist infants in detecting and discriminating /de/ from /ti/. In *b*, the two syllables could either appear in variable order, either /koga/ or /gako/, reducing the transitional probabilities to 0.3 and preventing infants from perceiving /koga/ as a word. In *c*, one of the context syllables was repeated (e.g., /koko/). In this case, /koko/ could be perceived as a unit, but the basis of the perception would not be high transitional probabilities; the transitional probabilities between syllables in *c* remain low (0.3).

The results confirmed the hypothesis that 7-month-old infants exploit transitional probabilities. Infants discriminated the target syllables in condition *a* significantly more accurately than in either *b* or *c*, the latter of which showed equally poor discrimination. These strategies also have been shown to be effective for adults presented with artificial nonspeech analogs created by computer (42, 59).

In further work, Saffran, Aslin, and Newport (42) directly assessed 8-month-old infants' abilities to learn pseudowords based on transitional probabilities. Infants were exposed to 2-min strings of synthetic speech composed of four different pseudowords that followed one another equally often. There were no breaks, pauses, stress differences, or intonation contours to aid infants in recovering these "words" from the strings of syllables. During the test phase, infants listened to two of the original pseudowords and two new words formed by combining parts of two of the original words. The results demonstrated that infants listened longer to the new words, demonstrating that they are capable of using statistical regularities to detect words (60).

Additional examples of the computation and use of probability statistics have been uncovered. Nine-month-old infants detect the probability of occurrence of legal sequences that occur in English (61). Certain combinations of two consonants are more likely to occur within words whereas others occur at the juncture between words. The combination "ft" is more common within words whereas the combination "vt" is more common between words. Nine-month-olds were tested with consonant (C) and vowel (V) strings of the form CVCCVC. These items contained embedded CCs that were either frequent or infrequent in English. Infants listened significantly longer to the lists containing frequent within-word CCs.

The results reveal that an old principle of Gestalt psychology, referred to as "common fate" (58), plays a role in speech perception. Phonemes that are typically linked, and thus share a common fate, are perceived as units by infants. It is interesting to note that early object perception also may rely on this principle. Physical entities whose properties cohere in space, and move together, are perceived as individuated objects (62). Whether the constraints underlying infants' detection of common fate information for physical objects and speech are identical or different is important to theory and remains to be examined.

Language Experience Warps Perception.   Language experience not only produces a change in infants' discriminative abilities and listening preferences, it results in a "mapping" that alters perception. A research finding that helps explain this is called the perceptual magnet effect. The magnet effect is observed when tokens perceived as exceptionally good representatives of a phonetic category ("prototypes") are used in tests of speech perception (63–66). Many behavioral (63–69) and brain (70–73) studies indicate that native-language phonetic prototypes evoke special responses when compared with nonprototypes.

When tested with a phonetic prototype as opposed to a nonprototype from the same category, infants show greater ability to generalize to other category members (63, 64). The prototype appears to function as a "magnet" for other stimuli in the category, in a way similar to that shown for prototypes of other cognitive categories (74, 75). Moreover, the perceptual magnet effect depends on exposure to a specific language (65). Six-month-old infants being raised in the United States and Sweden were tested with two vowel prototypes, an American English /i/ vowel prototype and a Swedish /y/ vowel prototype, using the exact same stimuli , techniques, and testers in the two countries. American infants demonstrated the magnet effect only for the American English /i/, treating the Swedish /y/ like a nonprototype. Swedish infants showed the opposite pattern, demonstrating the magnet effect for the Swedish /y/ and treating the American English /i/ as a nonprototype. The results show that by 6 months of age, perception is altered by language experience.

Categorical perception and the perceptual magnet effect make different predictions about the perception and organization underlying speech categories and appear to arise from different mechanisms (76). Interestingly, comparative tests show that, unlike categorical perception, animals do not exhibit the perceptual magnet effect (64).

In adults, the distortion of perception caused by language experience is well illustrated by a study on the perception of American English /r/ and /l/ in American and Japanese listeners. The /r-l/ distinction is difficult for Japanese speakers to perceive and produce; it is not used in the Japanese language (77, 78). In the study, Iverson and Kuhl (79) used computer-synthesized syllables beginning with /r/ and /l/, spacing them at equal physical intervals in a two-dimensional acoustic grid. American listeners identified each syllable as /ra/ or /la/, rated its category goodness, and estimated the perceived similarity for all possible pairs of syllables. Similarity ratings were scaled by using multidimensional scaling techniques. The results provide a map of the perceived distances between stimuli—short distances for strong similarity and long distances for weak similarity. In the American map, magnet effects (seen as a shrinking of perceptual space) occur in the region of each category's best instances. Boundary effects (seen as a stretching of perceptual space) occur at the division between the two categories.

The experiment has recently been completed with Japanese monolingual listeners, and the results show a striking contrast in the way the /r-l/ stimuli are perceived by American and Japanese speakers. The map revealed by multidimensional scaling analysis is totally different—no magnet effects or boundary effects appear. Japanese listeners hear one category of sounds, not two, and attend to different dimensions of the same stimuli. The results suggest that linguistic experience produces mental maps for speech that differ substantially for speakers of different languages (40, 69, 79).

The important point regarding development is that the initial perceptual biases shown by infants in tests of categorical perception (12–16), as well as asymmetries in perception seen in infancy (80, 81), produce a contouring of the perceptual space that is universal. This universal contouring soon gives way to a language-specific mapping that distorts perception, completely revising the perceptual space underlying speech processing (65).

A model reflecting this developmental sequence from universal perception to language-specific perception, called the Native Language Magnet model, proposes that infants' mapping of ambient language warps the acoustic dimensions underlying speech, producing a complex network, or filter, through which language is perceived (39, 40, 82). The language-specific filter alters the dimensions of speech we attend to, stretching and shrinking acoustic space to highlight the differences between language categories. Once formed, language-specific filters make learning a second language much more difficult because the mapping appropriate for one's primary language is completely different from that required by other languages. Studies of adult bilinguals, who were exposed to their second language after the age of 6, demonstrate magnet effects only for the first language, illustrating the potent effects of early linguistic experience (66). According to the Native Language Magnet theory, infants' transition in speech perception between 6 and 12 months reflects the formation of a language-specific filter.

In summary, the studies on speech learning, demonstrating that infants detect patterns, extract statistical information, and have perceptual systems that can be altered by experience, cannot be explained by recourse to Skinnerian reinforcement learning. This is a different kind of learning, one ubiquitous during early development. Its study will be valuable beyond what it tells us about language learning.

Are the new learning strategies observed for speech domain-specific and/or species-specific? Research on cognitive development confirms the fact that categorization (83), statistical learning (84), and prototype effects (85) are not unique to speech. Further tests need to be done to determine the constraints operating on these abilities in infants by using linguistic and nonlinguistic events. What about animal tests? Thus far, the data suggest differences between animals and humans on these kinds of learning. For instance, monkeys do not exhibit the perceptual magnet effect (64). Animals do show some degree of internal structure for speech categories after extensive training (24), but it is unlikely the perceptual magnet effect would be spontaneously produced in an animal after 6 months' experience listening to language, as seen in human infants. Similarly, animals are sensitive to transitional probabilities (86), but it is unlikely that an animal would spontaneously exhibit statistical learning after simply listening to language, as human infants have been shown to do. These issues can be resolved with empirical tests.

VOCAL LEARNING UNIFIES PERCEPTION AND PRODUCTION

Infants not only learn the perceptual characteristics of their language, they become native speakers, which requires imitation of the patterns of speech they hear others produce. Vocal learning critically depends on hearing the vocalizations of others and hearing oneself produce sound. This is true both for humans, who do not learn spoken language (or even babble normally) if they are deaf (87), and also for song birds (88). Production plays a role in normal language development; infants tracheostomized at the time at which they normally would babble show abnormal patterns of development that persist (89). These cases illustrate the strong dependency between perception and production and suggest why speech motor patterns learned early in life become difficult to alter later. Speakers who learn a second language after puberty produce it with an "accent" typical of their primary language, even after long-term instruction (90).

Imitation forges this early link between perception and production. By 1 year of age infants' spontaneous utterances reflect their imitation of ambient language patterns (91, 92). Laboratory studies indicate that the fundamental capacity to imitate sound patterns is in place even earlier. In a recent study, Kuhl and Meltzoff (93) recorded infant utterances at 12, 16, and 20 weeks of age while the infants watched and listened to a video recording of a woman producing a vowel, either /a/, /i/, or /u/ for 5 min on each of 3 successive days. The results demonstrate developmental change between 12 and 20 weeks—by 20 weeks, there is clear separation between the three vowel categories for infants. At this age, infants clearly imitate the model, and their vowels have appropriate formant frequency values in relation to one another, even though infants' vowels occur in a much higher frequency range (93).

Early theories of speech perception held that speech was perceived with reference to production (10). The developmental data suggest a different conclusion—early in life, perceptual representations of speech are stored in memory. Subsequently, these representations guide the development of motor speech. The two systems are thus tightly coupled early on, but the coupling is seen as a coregistration of auditory and motor information, a polymodal mapping, rather than one in which the representation is specified in motor terms. Perceptual experience that guides sensory-motor learning also is seen in infants' imitation of nonspeech oral movements (94, 95) and in sign language (96). The perception-action links observed for speech thus may rely on domain-general capabilities.

In related studies, infants also show an ability to link mouth movements they see to auditory signals they hear. Studies on 18- to 20-week-old infants show that they look longer at a face pronouncing a vowel that matches one they hear as opposed to a mismatched face (97). Infants' polymodal speech representations are thus likely to contain information regarding visual, as well as auditory instantiations of speech (ref. 98, see also refs. 99–101).

"MOTHERESE" IS INSTRUCTIVE

Historically, language input was seen as a trigger for selecting among innately specified options. New data suggest that language addressed to infants plays a much more important role. The universal speaking style used by caretakers around the world when they address infants, often called "motherese" or "parentese" (102), has been shown to be preferred over adult-directed speech by infants given a choice (103, 104). Moreover, the exaggerated stress and increased pitch typical of infant-directed speech assists infants in discriminating phonetic units (105).

Infant-directed speech also is altered at the phonetic level and these alterations are argued to help infants learn. In a recent study, women were recorded while speaking to their 2-month-old infants and to another adult in the United States, Russia, and Sweden (106). Mothers used the vowels /i/, /a/, and /u/, in both settings, and their speech was analyzed spectrographically. The results demonstrated that the phonetic units of infant-directed speech are acoustically exaggerated. The results show a stretching of the acoustic space encompassing speech. Exaggerating speech not only makes it more discriminable for infants, it highlights critical parameters used in the native language. This may aid infants' discovery of the dimensions of sound used in their native language. Mothers addressing infants also increase the variety of exemplars they use, behaving in a way that makes mothers resemble many different talkers, a feature shown to assist category learning in second-language learners (107). In recent studies, language-delayed children show substantial improvements in measures of speech and language after listening to speech altered by computer to exaggerate phonetic differences (108, 109).

Mothers addressing infants make other adjustments that appear to aid learning. When introducing new words, parents repeat the word often in stereotyped frames ("Where's the____," "See the____," "That's a____;" 110), which would highlight the items in sentence-final position. They also present new words in a great variety of contexts, which would highlight the internal transitional probabilities of the new words against the backdrop of a variety of contexts (58). These new data suggest that the modifications made by adults unconsciously when they speak to infants plays a role in helping infants map native-language input. This represents a change in theoretical perspective with regard to the role of motherese in language acquisition.

THE CRITICAL PERIOD FOR LANGUAGE LEARNING DEPENDS ON EXPERIENCE, NOT JUST TIME

There is no doubt that children learn language more naturally and efficiently than adults, a paradox given adults' superior cognitive skills. The question is: Why?

Language acquisition often is cited as an example of a "critical period" in development, a learning process that is constrained by time, or factors such as hormones, that are outside the learning process itself. The studies on speech suggest an alternative (40, 82). The work on speech suggests that later learning may be constrained by the initial mapping that has taken place. For instance, if learning involves the creation of mental maps for speech, as suggested by the Native Language Magnet model (65, 82), it likely "commits" neural structure in some way. Measurements of brain activity, for example, confirm left-hemisphere effects for native-language sounds in the mismatched negativity (MMN), an event-related potential elicited by a change in a repetitive sound pattern (72). In infants, the MMN is observed to changes in both native and nonnative contrasts at 6 months of age. At 12 months of age, the MMN exists only for native language contrasts (73). Neural commitment to a learned structure may interfere with the processing of information that does not conform to the learned pattern. On this account, initial learning can alter future learning independent of a strictly timed period.

Support for the neural commitment view comes from two sources, second language learning, and training studies. When acquiring a second language, certain phonetic distinctions are notoriously difficult to master both in speech perception and production, as shown, for example, by the difficulty of the /r-l/ distinction for native speakers of Japanese, even after training (11, 78, 111, 112). The hypothesis is that, for Japanese people, learning to process English requires the development of a new map, one more appropriate for English. New training studies suggest that exaggerating the dimensions of foreign language contrasts (36), as well as providing listeners with multiple instances spoken by many talkers (113), are effective training methods. These studies show that feedback and reinforcement are not necessary in this process; listeners simply need the right kind of listening experience (36, 113). Interestingly, the features shown to assist second-language learners—exaggerated acoustic cues, multiple instances by many talkers, and mass listening experience—are features that motherese provides infants.

Early in life, interference effects are minimal and two different mappings can be acquired, as is the case for infants learning two languages. Anecdotal evidence suggests that infants exposed to two languages do much better if each parent speaks one of the two languages, rather than both parents speaking both languages. This may be the case because it is easier to map two different sets of phonetic categories (one for each of the two languages) if they can be perceptually separated. A second language learned later in life (after puberty) may require another form of separation between the two systems to avoid interference. Data gathered by using functional MRI techniques indicate that adult bilinguals who acquire both languages early in life activate overlapping regions of the brain when processing the two languages, whereas those who learn the second language later in life activate two distinct regions of the brain for the two languages (114). This is consistent with the idea that the brain's processing of a primary language can interfere with the second language. The problem is avoided if both are learned early in development.

CONCLUSIONS

The framework that emerges from this research is very different from that held historically. Infants are neither the *tabula rasas* that Skinner described nor the innate grammarians that Chomsky envisioned. Infants have inherent perceptual biases that segment phonetic units without providing innate descriptions of them. They use inherent learning strategies that were not expected, ones thought to be too complex and difficult for infants to use. Adults addressing infants unconsciously modify speech in ways that assist the brain mapping of language. In combination, these factors provide a powerful discovery procedure for language. Six tenets of a new view of language acquisition are offered:

(*i*) infants initially parse the basic units of speech allowing them to acquire higher-order units created by their combinations;

(*ii*) the developmental process is not a selectionist one in which innately specified options are selected on the basis of experience;

(*iii*) rather, a perceptual learning process, unrelated to Skinnerian learning, commences with exposure to language, during which infants detect patterns, exploit statistical properties, and are perceptually altered by that experience;

(*iv*) vocal imitation links speech perception and production early, and auditory, visual, and motor information are coregistered for speech categories;

(*v*) adults addressing infants unconsciously alter their speech to match infants' learning strategies, and this is instrumental in supporting infants' initial mapping of speech; and

(*vi*) the critical period for language is influenced not only by time, but by the neural commitment that results from experience.

Taken together, these principles suggest that what is innate regarding language is not a universal grammar and phonetics, but innate biases and strategies that place constraints on perception and learning. They allow infants to recover from language input the rules by which people in their community communicate. Language is thus innately discoverable, but not innate in the way that selectionist models suggested. The learning strategies used by infants may themselves have influenced the nature of language, in much the same way that general auditory processing influenced the selection of phonetic units for language during its evolution. The continued study of language development by infants promises to reveal the precise nature of the relationship between language and mind.

ACKNOWLEDGMENTS

I thank Erica Stevens and Feng-Ming Tsao for assistance on preparation of the manuscript and Andy Meltzoff for comments on the issues discussed. The preparation of this manuscript and my research are supported by grants from the National Institutes of Health (HD37954) and the Human Frontiers Science Program (RG0159).
E-mail: pkkuhl@u.washington.edu .
This paper was presented at the National Academy of Sciences colloquium "Auditory Neuroscience: Development, Transduction, and Integration," held May 19–21, 2000, at the Arnold and Mabel Beckman Center in Irvine, CA.

REFERENCES

1. Skinner, B. F. (1957). *Verbal Behavior* (Appleton-Century-Crofts, New York).
2. Chomsky, N., (1957). *Language 35*, 26–58.
3. Wexler, K. & Culicover, P. W. (1980). *Formal Principles of Language Acquisition* (MIT Press, Cambridge, MA).
4. Fodor, J. A. (1983). *The Modularity of Mind: An Essay on Faculty Psychology* (MIT Press, Cambridge, MA).
5. Stevens, K. N. (1998). *Acoustic Phonetics* (MIT Press, Cambridge, MA).
6. Pickett, J. M. (1999). *The Acoustics of Speech Communication* (Allyn and Bacon, Boston).
7. Gross, N., Judge, P. C., Port, O., & Wildstrom, S. H. (1998). *BusinessWeek* February 23, 60–72.
8. Waibel, A. (1986). in *Pattern Recognition by Humans and Machines*, eds. Schwab, E. C. & Nusbaum, H. C. (Academic, New York), pp. 159–186.
9. Bernstein, J., & Franco, H. (1996). in *Principles of Experimental Phonetics*, ed. Lass, N. J. (Mosby, St. Louis), pp. 408–434.
10. Liberman, A. M., Cooper, F. S., Shankweiler, D. P., & Studdert-Kennedy, M. (1967). *Psychology Review 74*, 431–461.

11. Miyawaki, K., Strange, W., Verbrugge, R., Liberman, A. M., Jenkins, J. J., & Fujimura, O. (1975). *Percept. Psychophys. 18*, 331–340.
12. Eimas, P. D., Siqueland, E. R., Jusczyk, P., & Vigorito, J. (1971). *Science 171*, 303–306.
13. Eimas, P. D. (1974). *Percept. Psychophys. 16*, 513–521.
14. Eimas, P. D. (1975). *Percept. Psychophys. 18*, 341–347.
15. Lasky, R. E., Syrdal-Lasky, A., & Klein, R. E. (1975). *J. Exp. Child Psych. 20*, 215–225.
16. Streeter, L. A. (1976). *Nature* (London) *259*, 39–41.
17. Eimas, P. D. (1975). in *Infant Perception: Vol. 2. From Sensation to Cognition*, eds. Cohen, L. B., & Salapatek, P. (Academic, New York), pp. 193–231.
18. Kuhl, P. K., & Miller, J. D. (1975). *Science 190*, 69–72.
19. Kuhl, P. K., & Miller, J. D. (1978). *J. Acoust. Soc. Am. 63*, 905–917.
20. Kuhl, P. K., (1981). *J. Acoust. Soc. Am. 70*, 340–349.
21. Kuhl, P. K., & Padden, D. M. (1982). *Percept. Psychophys. 32*, 542–550.
22. Kuhl, P. K., & Padden, D. M. (1983). *J. Acoust. Soc. Am. 73*, 1003–1010.
23. Dooling, R. J., Best, C. T., & Brown, S. D. (1995). *J. Acoust. Soc. Am. 97*, 1839–1846.
24. Kluender, K. R., Diehl, R. L., & Killeen, P. R. (1987). *Science 237*, 1195–1197.
25. Ramus, F., Hauser, M. D., Miller, C., Morris, D., & Mehler, J. (2000). *Science 288*, 349–351.
26. Kuhl, P. K. (1991). in *Plasticity of Development*, eds. Brauth, S. E., Hall, W. S., & Dooling, R. J. (MIT Press, Cambridge, MA), pp. 73–106.
27. Kuhl, P. K. (1988). *Hum. Evol. 3*, 19–43.
28. Miller, J. D., Wier, C. C., Pastore, R. E., Kelly, W. J., & Dooling, R. J. (1976). *J. Acoust. Soc. Am. 60*, 410–417.
29. Pisoni, D. B. (1977). *J. Acoust. Soc. Am. 61*, 1352–1361.
30. Jusczyk, P. W., Rosner, B. S., Cutting, J. E., Foard, C. F., & Smith, L. B. (1977). *Percept. Psychophys. 21*, 50–54.
31. Werker, J. F., & Tees, R. C. (1984). *Inf. Behav. Dev. 7*, 49–63.
32. Werker, J. F. (1995). in *An Invitation to Cognitive Science: Language*, eds. Gleitman, L. R., & Liberman, M. (MIT Press, Cambridge, MA), pp. 87–107.
33. Werker, J. F., & Logan, J. S. (1985). *Percept. Psychophys. 37*, 35–44.
34. Carney, A. E., Widin, G. P., & Viemeister, N. F. (1977). *J. Acoust. Soc. Am. 62*, 961–970.
35. Logan, J. S., Lively, S. E., & Pisoni, D. B. (1991). *J. Acoust. Soc. Am. 89*, 874–886.
36. McClelland, J. L., Thomas, A., McCandliss, B. D., & Fiez, J. A. (1999). in *Brain, Behavioral, and Cognitive Disorders: The Neurocomputational Perspective*, eds. Reggia, J., Ruppin, E., & Glanzman, D. (Elsevier, Oxford), pp. 75–80.
37. Best, C. T., McRoberts, G. W., & Sithole, N. M. (1988). *J. Exp. Psych. Hum. Percept. Perform. 14*, 345–360.
38. Best, C. T. (1995). in *Advances in Infancy Research*, eds. Rovee-Collier, C., & Lipsitt, L. P. (Ablex, Norwood, NJ), pp. 217–304.
39. Kuhl, P. K. (1994). *Curr. Opin. Neurobiol. 4*, 812–822.
40. Kuhl, P. K. (2000). in *The New Cognitive Neurosciences*, ed. Gazzaniga, M. S. (MIT Press, Cambridge, MA), pp. 99–115.
41. Jusczyk, P. W. (1997). *The Discovery of Spoken Language* (MIT Press, Cambridge, MA).
42. Saffran, J. R., Aslin, R. N., & Newport, E. L. (1996). *Science 274*, 1926–1928.
43. Kuhl, P. K. (1985). in *Neonate Cognition: Beyond the Blooming Buzzing Confusion*, eds. Mehler, J., & Fox, R. (Erlbaum, Hillsdale, NJ), pp. 231–262.
44. Kuhl, P. K. (1979). *J. Acoust. Soc. Am. 66*, 1668–1679.
45. Kuhl, P. K. (1983). *Inf. Behav. Dev. 6*, 263–285.
46. Hillenbrand, J. (1983). *J. Speech Hear. Res. 26*, 268–282.
47. Kuhl, P. K. (1980). in *Child Phonology: Vol. 2. Perception*, eds. Yeni-Komshian, G. H., Kavanagh, J. F., & Ferguson, C. A. (Academic, New York), pp. 41–66.
48. Jusczyk, P. W. (1999). *Trends Cognit. Sci. 3*, 323–328.
49. Mehler, J., Jusczyk, P., Lambertz, G., Halsted, N., Bertoncini, J., & Amiel-Tison, C. (1988). *Cognition 29*, 143–178.
50. Moon, C., Cooper, R. P., & Fifer, W. P. (1993). *Inf. Behav. Dev. 16*, 495–500.
51. Nazzi, T., Bertoncini, J., & Mehler, J. (1998). *J. Exp. Psychol. Hum. Percept. Perform. 24*, 756–766.
52. Lecanuet, J. P., & Granier-Deferre, C. (1993). in *Developmental Neurocognition: Speech and Face Processing in the First Year of Life*, eds. de Boysson-Bardies, B., de Schonen, S., Jusczyk, P., McNeilage, P., & Morton, J. (Kluwer, Dordrecht, The Netherlands).

53. DeCasper, A. J., & Fifer, W. P. (1980). *Science 208.*
54. DeCasper, A. J., & Spence, M. J. (1986). *Inf. Behav. Dev. 9,* 133–150.
55. Jusczyk, P. W., Cutler, A., & Redanz, N. J. (1993). *Child Dev. 64,* 675–687.
56. Hirsh-Pasek, K., Kemler Nelson, D. G., Jusczyk, P. W., Cassidy, K. W., Druss, B., & Kennedy, L. (1987). *Cognition 26,* 269–286.
57. Jusczyk, P. W., Friederici, A. D., Wessels, J. M. I., Svenkerud, V. Y., & Jusczyk, A. M. (1993). *J. Mem. Lang. 32,* 402–420.
58. Goodsitt, J. V., Morgan, J. L., & Kuhl, P. K. (1993). *J. Child Lang. 20,* 229–252.
59. Wolff, J. G. (1977). *Br. J. Psych. 68,* 97–106.
60. Aslin, R. N., Saffran, J. R., & Newport, E. L. (1998). *Psychol. Sci. 9,* 321–324.
61. Mattys, S. L., Jusczyk, P. W., Luce, P. A., & Morgan, J. L. (1999). *Cog. Psych. 38,* 465–494.
62. Spelke, E. (1994). *Cognition 50,* 431–445.
63. Grieser, D., & Kuhl, P. K. (1989). *Dev. Psych. 25,* 577–588.
64. Kuhl, P. K. (1991). *Percept. Psychophys. 50,* 93–107.
65. Kuhl, P. K., Williams, K. A., Lacerda, F., Stevens, K. N., & Lindblom, B. (1992). *Science 255.*
66. Bosch, L., Costa, A. & Sebastian-Galles, N. (2000). *Eur. J. Cognit. Psychol. 12,* 189–221.
67. Samuel, A. G. (1982). *Percept. Psychophys. 31,* 307–314.
68. Miller, J. L. (1994). *Cognition 50,* 271–285.
69. Iverson, P., & Kuhl, P. K. (1995). *J. Acoust. Soc. Am. 97,* 553–562.
70. Aaltonen, O., Eerola, O., Hellström, A., Uusipaikka, E., & Lang, A. H. (1997). *J. Acoust. Soc. Am. 101,* 1090–1105.
71. Sharma, A., & Dorman, M. F. (1998). *J. Acoust. Soc. Am. 104,* 511–517.
72. Näätänen, R., Lehtokoski, A., Lennes, M., Cheour, M., Huotilainen, M., Iivonen, A., Vainio, M., Alku, P., Ilmoniemi, R. J., Luuk, A., et al. (1997). *Nature* (London) *385,* 432–434.
73. Cheour-Luhtanen, M., Alho, K., Kujala, T., Sainio, K., Reinikainen, K., Renlund, M., Aaltonen, O., Eerola, O., & Näätänen, R. (1995). *Hear. Res. 82,* 53–58.
74. Medin, D. L. & Barsalou, L. W. (1987). in *Categorical Perception: The Groundwork of Cognition,* ed. Harnad, S. (Cambridge Univ. Press, New York), pp. 455–490.
75. Mervis, C. B., & Rosch, E. (1981). *Annu. Rev. Psychol. 32,* 89–115.
76. Iverson, P., & Kuhl, P. K. (2000). *Percept. Psychophys. 62,* 874–886.
77. Strange, W., & Dittmann, S. (1984). *Percept. Psychophys. 36,* 131–145.
78. Goto, H. (1971). *Neuropsychologia 9,* 317–323.
79. Iverson, P., & Kuhl, P. K. (1996). *J. Acoust. Soc. Am. 99,* 1130–1140.
80. Polka, L., & Bohn, O. S. (1996). *J. Acoust. Soc. Am. 100,* 577–592.
81. Miller, J. L., & Eimas, P. D. (1996). *Percept. Psychophys. 58,* 1157–1167.
82. Kuhl, P. K. (1998). in *Mechanistic Relationships Between Development and Learning,* eds. Carew, T. J., Menzel, R. & Shatz, C. J. (Wiley, New York), pp. 53–73.
83. Younger, B. A., & Cohen, L. B. (1985). in *The Psychology of Learning and Motivation,* ed. Bower, G. H. (Academic, San Diego), Vol. 19, pp. 211–247.
84. Saffran, J. R., Johnson, E. K., Aslin, R. N., & Newport, E. L. (1999). *Cognition 70,* 27–52.
85. Quinn, P. C., & Eimas, P. D. (1998). *J. Exp. Child Psychol. 69,* 151–174.
86. Gallistel, C. R. (1990). *The Organization of Learning* (MIT Press, Cambridge, MA).
87. Oller, D. K., & MacNeilage, P. F. (1983). in *The Production of Speech,* ed. MacNeilage, P. F. (Springer, New York), pp. 91–108.
88. Doupe, A., & Kuhl, P. K. (1999). *Annu. Rev. Neurosci. 22,* 567–631.
89. Locke, J. L., & Pearson, D. M. (1990). *J. Child Lang. 17,* 1–16.
90. *Flege, J. E. (1993). J. Acoust. Soc. Am. 93,* 1589–1608.
91. de Boysson-Bardies, B. (1993). in *Developmental Neurocognition: Speech and Face Processing in the First Year of Life,* eds. de Boysson-Bardies, B., de Schonen, S., Jusczyk, P., McNeilage, P., & Morton, J. (Kluwer, Dordrecht, The Netherlands), pp. 353–363.
92. Vihman, M. M., & de Boysson-Bardies, B. (1994). *Phonetica 51,* 159–169.
93. Kuhl, P. K., & Meltzoff, A. N. (1996). *J. Acoust. Soc. Am. 100,* 2425–2438.
94. Meltzoff, A. N., & Moore, M. K. (1977). *Early Dev. Parent. 6,* 179–192.
95. Meltzoff, A. N., & Moore, M. K. (1994). *Inf. Behav. Dev. 17,* 83–99.
96. Petitto, L. A., & Marentette, P. F. (1991). *Science 251,* 1493–1496.
97. Kuhl, P. K. & Meltzoff, A. N. (1982). *Science 218,* 1138–1141.
98. Kuhl, P. K., & Meltzoff, A. N. (1997). in *The Inheritance and Innateness of Grammars,* ed. Gopnik, M. (Oxford Univ. Press, New York), pp. 7–44.

99. MacKain, K., Studdert-Kennedy, M., Spieker, S., & Stern, D. (1983). *Science 219*, 1347–1349.
100. Rosenblum, L. D., Schmuckler, M. A., & Johnson, J. A. (1997). *Percept. Psychophys. 59*, 347–357.
101. Walton, G. E., & Bower, T. G. R. (1993). *Inf. Behav. Dev. 16*, 233–243.
102. Ferguson, C. A. (1964). *Am. Anthropol. 66*, 103–114.
103. Fernald, A. (1985). *Inf. Behav. Dev. 8*, 181–195.
104. Fernald, A., & Kuhl, P. (1987). *Inf. Behav. Dev. 10*, 279–293.
105. Karzon, R. G. (1985). *J. Exp. Child. Psych. 39*, 326–342.
106. Kuhl, P. K., Andruski, J. E., Chistovich, I. A., Chistovich, L. A., Kozhevnikova, E. V., Ryskina, V. L., Stolyarova, E. I., Sundberg, U., & Lacerda, F. (1997). *Science 277*, 684–686.
107. Lively, S. E., Logan, J. S., & Pisoni, D. B. (1993). *J. Acoust. Soc. Am. 94*, 1242–1255.
108. Merzenich, M. M., Jenkins, W. M., Johnston, P., Schreiner, C., Miller, S. L., & Tallal, P. (1996). *Science 271*, 77–81.
109. Tallal, P., Miller, S. L., Bedi, G., Byma, G., Wang, X., Nagarajan, S. S., Schreiner, C., Jenkins, W. M., & Merzenich, M. M. (1996). *Science 271*, 81–84.
110. Peters, A. M. (1983). *The Units of Language Acquisition* (Cambridge Univ. Press, Cambridge).
111. Flege, J. E., Takagi, N., & Mann, V. (1995). *Lang. Speech 38*, 25–55.
112. Yamada, R. A., & Tohkura, Y. (1992). *Percept. Psychophys. 52*, 376–392.
113. Pisoni, D. B. (1992). in *Speech Perception, Production and Linguistic Structure*, eds. Tohkura, Y., Vatikiotis-Bateson, E., & Sagisaka, Y. (Ohmsha, Tokyo), pp. 143–151.
114. Kim, K. H. S., Relkin, N. R., Lee, K. M., & Hirsch, J. (1997). *Nature* (London) *388*, 172–174.

QUESTIONS TO THINK ABOUT

1. Why does Kuhl begin by describing the Skinner and Chomsky theories of language acquisition—the two leading recent theories that preceded hers? Why might a researcher do this? What is Skinner's theory? What is Chomsky's theory? How does Kuhl's research counter Skinner's theory? How does her research counter Chomsky's? What aspects of her research support both or either of these theories?

2. What evidence has been found to suggest that the learning of speech begins *in utero*. What evidence does Kuhl present that supports the idea of a critical period in language acquisition? What does her research suggest about children growing up in a home where two (or more) different languages are spoken?

3. What are the characteristics that mark "motherse" or "parentese"? What seems to be the function of this exaggerated type of speech used by caretakers when talking to young children? What aspects of language development seem to be affected by this style of talking? Based on Kuhl's findings, would you advise parents or caretakers to adopt certain behaviors with their babies to facilitate language development? Why or why not?

4. *Extending your understanding:* How does Kuhl's research in first language acquisition inform you about problems children may have with language development? What does the research about first language acquisition suggest about issues that may emerge with second language acquisition? What insights might be helpful for second language teachers to be more effective?

TERMS TO DEFINE

Define the following words and phrases as they are presented within the context of the reading. Comment on your understanding of the significance of each one.

Critical Period
Universal Grammar
Innate Knowledge
Skinnerian Reinforcement
Native Language Magnet Model
Domain Specific/Species Specific

Fundamentals of Second Language Acquisition

Susan Gass
Michigan State University

WHAT IS THE FIELD OF SECOND LANGUAGE ACQUISITION?

Second language acquisition (SLA) is a relatively young field, having its systematic origins in the 1950s and 1960s (see the exchange by Thomas, 1998, and Gass, Fleck, Leder, & Svetics, 1998). Briefly put, the study of SLA is the study of how nonprimary language learning takes place. The International Commission of Second Language Acquisition (ICoSLA) defined SLA, in part, as follows (http://www.let.ruu.nl/~icsla/):

> SLA is a theoretical and experimental field of study which, like *first language acquisition studies,* looks at the phenomenon of language development.... SLA researchers... *describe and explain nonnative language behavior.* SLA... research includes, for instance, studying the complex pragmatic interactions between learners, and between learners [and] native speakers, examining how non-native language ability develops, stabilizes and undergoes attrition, and carrying out a highly technical analysis and interpretation of all aspects of learner language with the help of, amongst other things, current linguistic theory.

It is commonly believed that SLA refers to language teaching, but as the ICoSLA clearly stated,

> SLA is not about language teaching. Although it is focused on examining acquisition as a phenomenon in its own right and not on how acquisition is facilitated, the hope is often voiced that SLA research, will, together with other relevant disciplines, provide a firmer scientific basis for language instruction.

The purpose of this chapter is to lay out some of the accumulated knowledge of the field of SLA and, hopefully, to put to rest some of the naive assumptions that exist about language learning. It is further hoped that through this chapter I succeed in convincing the reader that the study of SLA represents a vibrant field with a sophisticated knowledge

Reprinted, with changes, from *Handbook of undergraduate second language education,* edited by J. W. Rosenthal. © 2000 by Lawrence Erlbaum Associates, Inc.

base. Finally, it is my goal that the reader will come to understand some of the complexities involved in L2 learning and by extension in the related field of L2 and foreign language teaching.

TERMINOLOGY

Because I deal with basic issues of nonprimary language learning, as a way of introduction, I explain my use of key terminology. First, *nonprimary*. I use this term to refer to language learning after the first language (L1) has been learned. I do not differentiate in this chapter between second and foreign language learning, where the former refers to language learning in the environment where that language is spoken (Italian in Italy, English in Australia, Japanese in Japan, etc.) and the latter refers to language learning in one's "home" environment (French in the United States, English in China, etc.). The reason for this lack of differentiation is that there is little evidence that the mental processes involved in learning a language beyond the native language (NL) differ as a function of whether the learning is in a second versus a foreign language environment. This is not to say that there are not significant differences in terms of the context itself, and hence the language material (both quantitative and qualitative) available to learners. The claim that is made is that the processes involved in learning a nonnative language are not dependent on the location of learning. I use the broad term *second language (L2) learning*, also not differentiating between second, third, or fourth languages.

The second set of key words is *acquisition* and *learning*. In the early 1980s, based on work by Krashen (1980, 1982, 1985), a distinction was proposed between acquisition and learning. Basic to Krashen's approach is the assumption that in learning an L2, learners develop two independent L2 knowledge systems, one referred to as acquisition and the other as learning. In nontechnical language, acquisition is the unconscious "picking-up" of a language whereas learning refers to conscious knowledge of an L2 (i.e., knowing the rules, being aware of them, and being able to talk about them). (See criticisms of Krashen's work by Gregg, 1984, 1986, and articles in Barasch & James, 1994.)

With regard to the function of these systems, Krashen argued that the acquired system is used to produce language. The acquisition system generates utterances. The learned system serves as an "inspector" of the acquired system; it checks to ensure the correctness of the utterance against the knowledge in the learned system.

The distinction between acquisition and learning has had a much greater impact on the "lay" community than on the SLA research community (mainly due to the proposed independence of the two systems). In fact, many researchers use the two terms (acquisition and learning) interchangeably and without the theoretical connotations associated with Krashen's theory. Although Krashen's ideas regarding L2 learning are appealing, when examined in depth, they lack theoretical rigor and, hence, are of limited value.

SECOND LANGUAGE ACQUISITION FINDINGS

This section is intended to address some of the major issues and findings that SLA research has uncovered over the past few decades. Because of the scope of this article, the topics are selective and designed to give only an overview. Most SLA research has been conducted with adult L2 learners. There are studies, however, that are selected for discussion in this section that deal primarily or exclusively with child L2 learning. In such instances, the principles that they illustrate are general principles of L2 learning and therefore cross age boundaries.

The Development of L2 Knowledge

A basic concept in SLA is that of "interlanguage" (Selinker, 1972). The assumption under-lying this concept is that learners *create a language system*, known as an *interlanguage*. This system is composed of numerous elements, not the least of which are elements from the NL and the language being learned, known as the target language (TL). There are also el-ements in the interlanguage that do not have their origin in either the NL or the TL. What is important is that the learners themselves impose structure on the available linguistic data and formulate and internalize a linguistic system. Consider the following utterances from an adult native speaker of Arabic who is in the early stages of her acquisition of English:

> Example 1. Data from Hanania (1974)
>   a. He's sleeping
>   b. She's sleeping
>   c. It's raining
>   d. He's eating
>   e. Hani watch TV (Hani is watching TV)
>   f. Read the paper (He is reading the paper)
>   g. Drink the coffee (He is drinking the coffee)

It appears that this learner has created a system (unlike the system of either Arabic or English) where the progressive is used only when there is no overt direct object (Examples a–d). When the direct object is present, the present tense form is used (Examples e–g). Implied in the concept of interlanguage is the centrality of the learner (as opposed to the teacher, textbook, materials, etc.) in the learning process. It therefore follows that there is not a one-to-one relationship between learning and teaching.

Input

How do learners "create" interlanguages? One of the most important contributing factors is *input*. This refers to the TL that is "available" to learners. It comes from a variety of sources including the language that the learner hears (e.g., in the classroom by the teacher, outside of the classroom by speakers of the second language), reads (in textbooks, in other reading materials), or sees, in the case of a signed language. Input is to be distinguished from intake, which is the language that is not just available to a learner, but is the language comprehended and utilized in some way by the learner (for further elaboration, see Gass, 1997).

In other words, the mere presence of input is not a sufficient condition for language learning. The fact of its presence must be noticed in some way. As a prerequisite to noticing some feature of the input, learners must focus their attention on and isolate some portion of the input. Once the input is noticed, learners have to determine what patterns are present. And, to do this, they first have to segment a stream of speech (if it is a written text, the task is easier because spaces usually exist between words) into meaningful units (probably words). Then they have to organize the words into syntactic units and come up with hypotheses about what the grammar *might* be like.

In the 1960s and 1970s, SLA researchers believed that L2 learning was based on a behav-iorist view of language. Within this framework the *major* driving force of language learning was the language to which learners were exposed (the input). Input had major importance because it was believed that learning a language involved imitation as its primary mech-anism. Subsequent research made it clear that L2 speakers do not merely imitate; they create a system that allows them to produce novel utterances.

Since the early years of SLA research in the 1960s and 1970s, many studies have been conducted and numerous observations have been made of the speech used by native speakers (NSs) (teachers and nonteachers) when addressing nonnative speakers (NNSs). Language addressed to NNSs has been referred to as *foreigner talk*. In contrast to speech directed toward proficient speakers, foreigner talk has some of the following characteristics: louder speech, speech that is slower and more carefully articulated, simpler vocabulary, less frequent use of idioms, less complex syntax, and fewer contractions (see Hatch, 1983, for a fuller description).

Interaction

Long (1980) was the first to point out that conversations involving NNSs exhibit forms that do not appear to any significant degree when only NSs are involved (see also Scarcella & Higa, 1981, for similar research on children, and Gass, 1997). For example, confirmation checks, comprehension checks, and clarification requests are peppered throughout conversations in which there is a nonproficient NNS participant, in either NS–NNS or NNS–NNS conversation. Following are examples of each taken from Varonis and Gass (1985):

    Example 2. Confirmation check
       NNS1: When can you go to visit me?
→   NNS2: visit?

    Example 3. Comprehension check
       NNS1: and your family have some ingress
       NNS2: yes ah, OK OK
→   NNS1: more or less OK?

    Example 4. Clarification request
       NNS1: . . . research
→   NNS2: research, I don't know the meaning.

In addition to these features, different kinds of questions are asked, often with the answer being suggested by the speaker immediately after the question is asked. The "or-choice" question in Example 5 exemplifies this phenomenon:

    Example 5. From Long (1983)
→   NS: Well, what are you doing in the United States? Are you just studying or do you have a job? Or . . .
       NNS: No. I have job

A similar example of modification is given in Example 6 where the NS gives a suggested answer to the question he just posed.

    Example 6. Long (1980)
       NS: When do you take the break? At ten-thirty?

The effect of such modifications (whether intentional or not) is to aid the NNS in understanding what is being said. This reduces the linguistic burden for NNSs in that they are assisted by others in understanding and in producing language appropriate to the situation.

Teachers, too, often adjust their speech according to the perceived proficiency level of the addressee. Example 7 illustrates the adjustment that a kindergarten teacher made in her mixed class (for similar adjustments to adult university-level learners, see Gaies, 1979):

Example 7. Data from Kleifgen (1985)
Speech to:

A single NS
Now, Johnny, you have to make a great big pointed hat.

NS of Urdu; intermediate-level English
Now her hat is big. Pointed.

NS of Arabic; low intermediate-level English
See hat? Hat is big. Big and tall.

NS of Japanese; beginning-level English
Big, big, big hat.

NS of Korean; beginning level-English
Baby sitter. baby.

In looking at Kleifgen's data, one finds another interesting phenomenon. For those students whose English proficiency showed improvement over time, the teacher's talk changed; for those students who did not improve, the dynamic and changing nature of the teacher's talk was not apparent. Thus, foreigner talk changes according to individual and contextual factors. The use of foreigner talk appears to result from prior experience as well as from a basic human desire to maintain the smooth flow of a conversation.

In sum, we have seen that it is frequently the case that the language addressed to NNSs is modified and that one of the main purposes of modification is to aid comprehensibility. However, although comprehensibility is a necessary condition, it is clearly not a sufficient condition for learning the TL.

As mentioned earlier, conversations with L2 learners have characteristics that differ from those between or among native speakers. Beginning more than two decades ago with work by Wagner-Gough and Hatch (1975) and developed in the following years by many researchers (see the summary in Gass, 1997), L2 research has emphasized the role that conversations play in the development of an L2. *Conversational interaction* in an L2 forms the *basis* for the development of syntax rather than being only a forum for practice of grammatical structures.

One way that a lack of understanding in conversation can be handled is through an interruption in the conversation itself through confirmation checks and other ways of seeking clarification and of thereby coming to a mutual understanding of what is intended. This is referred to as *negotiation of meaning*, and it is negotiation that is claimed to have significance for SLA (see Gass, 1997; Long, 1996).

How does negotiation itself aid learning? Negotiation routines do more than just straighten out language difficulties. Negotiation forces a learner's attention on parts of the language that need modification in order to be comprehensible. Language per se therefore becomes the focus of attention. Example 8, from adult language learning, shows how the focus on form results in later incorporation into the learner's speech. The arrows indicate where negotiation is occurring:

Example 8. (Data from Gass & Varonis, 1989)
  NNS1: A man is uh drinking c-coffee or tea uh with uh the saucer of the uh uh coffee set is uh in his uh knee
→ NNS2: in him knee
→ NNS1: uh on his knee

NNS2: yeah
→   NNS1: on his knee
→   NNS2: so sorry on his knee

The two NNSs in this example have used the conversation as a learning device. The negotiation per se provided NNS2 with usable information (about the correct preposition and the correct form of the possessive), which was then used to make appropriate modifications.

The claim is not that negotiation causes learning nor that there is a "theory" of learning based on interaction. What is claimed is that negotiation is a facilitator of learning; it is one means, but not the only means of drawing attention to areas of needed change.

U-Shaped Learning

A naive view of language learning is that it proceeds in a linear fashion. That is, one learns one grammatical structure and then another, and presumably, previously "learned" structures are retained as new ones are acquired. In fact, many language textbooks are based on this assumption with each chapter focusing on a different structure. Although it is true that there are predictable stages for learning (see the following section), it is also the case that in other ways language learning cannot be described in a step-by-step fashion.

U-shaped behavior (see Kellerman, 1985, for use of this term in SLA) refers to stages of linguistic use. In the earliest stage, a learner produces some linguistic form that appears to conform to TL norms (i.e., error-free). Then, at a subsequent stage the learner appears to lose what she or he knew at Stage 1; the linguistic behavior at Stage 2 now deviates from TL norms. Stage 3 looks just like Stage 1 in that there is again correct TL usage.

Lightbown (1983) presented data from French learners of English in a classroom context, examining the use of the *-ing* form in English among sixth-, seventh-, and eighth-grade learners. A typical Grade 6 utterance was:

Example 9.   He is taking a cake.

By Grade 7, the response was:

Example 10.   He take a cake.

This is a common phenomenon of language learning and one that causes great consternation and confusion for language teachers. How can we account for an apparent decrease in knowledge? Lightbown hypothesized that initially these students were only presented with the progressive form. With nothing else in English to compare it to, they equated it with the simple present of French. That is, in the absence of any other verb forms, there was no way of determining what the limits were of the present progressive. In fact, with no other comparable verb form in their L2 system, learners overextended the use of the progressive into contexts in which the English present would have been appropriate. When the simple present was introduced at a later point in time, learners not only had to learn this new form, but they also had to readjust their information about the present progressive, in essence, redefining its limits. Evidence of the confusion and subsequent readjustment of the use of the progressive was seen in the decline in both use and accuracy. It takes time before learners restructure and reorganize their L2 knowledge appropriately and are able to use both the progressive and the present in targetlike ways. Thus, given these data, a U-shaped curve results, as can be seen in Fig. 3.1.

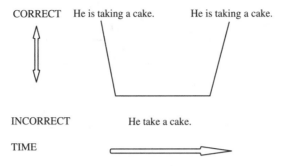

Fig 3.1.   U-shaped curve.

Stages

The preceding discussion focused on the nonlinear nature of L2 learning. However, this is not to say that there are not predictable sequences in L2 learning. This section deals with such stages in grammatical development.

Corder (1967) noted that learners have a "built-in" syllabus. Regardless of what they are presented with, certain parts of the language develop in a regular, predictable fashion. An example from syntax illustrates this. Pienemann and Johnston (1987) presented the stages shown in Table 3.1 in the acquisition of question forms in English. These stages are independent of any pedagogical syllabus and are a result of learners creating their own systems, perhaps limited in this case by processing constraints. Mackey (1995), in her study of the acquisition of English questions, showed that with regard to questions, stages are not skipped, even though the path through them can be accelerated.

A similar example of stages in learning can be seen in the following sequence reflecting the acquisition of negation in English. Schumann (1979), in data from an adult NS of Spanish learning English, noted that initially negative utterances are formed by using the word *no*, which is placed before the verb as in the following examples:

Example 11.   no understand
              no you told me
              no swim
              no correct

A second stage of development is seen with the occurrence of *don't*, even though this element is placed preverbally, as in Example 12:

Example 12.   don't like
              I don't saw him

Next, learners show an increased use of *not* as opposed to *no* as a negator in Example 13:

Example 13.   not today

They also use *not* following the verb "to be" and the auxiliary as in Example 14:

Example 14.   I'm not old enough
              I will don't see you tomorrow

TABLE 3.1
Example Table for Question Forms and Developmental Stages

Developmental Stage	Example
Stage 1	
Single units	
Single words	What?
Single units	What is your name?
Stage 2	
SVO	
	It's a monster?
Canonical word order with question intonation.	Your cat is black?
	You have a cat?
	I draw a house here?
Stage 3	
Fronting: Wh-word/Do	
	Where the cats are?
Direct questions with main verbs and some form	What the cat doing in your picture?
of fronting.	Do you have an animal?
	Does in this picture there is a cat?
Stage 4	
Pseudo Inversion: Y/N, verb "to be"	
In y/n questions an auxiliary or modal	(Y/N) Have you got a dog?
(e.g., can/could) is in sentence-initial position.	(Y/N) Have you drawn the cat?
In wh-questions the verb "to be" and	("to be") Where is the cat in your picture?
the subject change positions.	
Stage 5	
Do/Auxiliary 2nd	
Q-word → Auxiliary/modal → subj	Why (Q) have (Aux) you (subject)
(main verb, etc.)	left home?
Auxiliary verbs and modals are placed in second	What do you have?
position after Wh-question words and before	Where does your cat sit?
subject (applies only in main clauses/direct	What have you got in your picture?
questions).	
Stage 6	
"Can" Inversion, Negative Q, Tag Question	
Cancel Inversion: Wh-question inversions are not	(Can Inv) Can you see what the time is?
present in relative clauses	(Can Inv) Can you tell me where the cat is?
Neg Q: A negated form of do/auxiliary is placed	(Neg Q) Doesn't your cat look black?
before the subject	(Neg Q) Haven't you seen a dog?
Tag Q: An auxiliary verb & pronoun are attached	(Tag Q) It's on the wall, isn't it?
to end of main clause.	

Note. From Mackey (1995). Copyright 1995 by Mackey. Reprinted with permission.

Still later, learners begin to use variants of don't (i.e., *doesn't, didn't*), as can be seen in Example 15:

Example 15. I didn't went to Costa Rica

And finally, most learners sort out the facts of negation and learn that in negation, *do* is the element that bears tense and person distinctions.

In this section we have seen examples in which learners appear to follow predictable stages, immutable by instruction. This contrasts with the U-shaped learning curve that was discussed previously. That there is evidence for both predictable stages as well as nonlinear learning highlights the complexities of the process of SLA.

WHAT DO LEARNERS START WITH?

Thus far, I have presented some of the characteristics of the linguistic system that L2 learners create. I have dealt with the input that learners have available to them and how they might manipulate the input through conversation to create new knowledge. In the sections that follow, I consider various perspectives on the starting point of learning. In other words, I look at what linguistic information learners start with as they enter the new language-learning process.

Innateness

A current question in L2 research is the starting point of language learning. To deal with this topic, I refer to some of the assumptions from the literature on child language learning. One theory of child language learning holds that children are born with a language faculty known as Universal Grammar (UG; for a discussion of UG as it relates to SLA, see Cook 1988, 1993; White, 1989). The theory underlying UG assumes that language consists of a set of abstract principles that characterize core grammars of all natural languages. The necessity of positing UG comes from the fact that all children have to learn a complex set of abstractions as they acquire their NL. There must be something *in addition to* the language input (which is "impoverished" in that it does not contain direct evidence of abstract knowledge) to which children are exposed in order for them to learn the TL with relative ease and speed. UG is postulated as an innate language faculty that specifies the limits of a possible language. The task for learning is greatly reduced if one is equipped with an innate mechanism that constrains possible grammar formation. In other words, certain kinds of linguistic systems are ruled out a priori. A similar situation applies in the case of L2 learning, and an even more complex problem exists because not only is the input impoverished, but also learners are influenced by their L1 or other languages known (White, 1992).

But the UG position is not a uniform one. White (1996) pointed out that there are four current positions with regard to UG:

One position maintains that the initial state of L2 is actually the final state of L1; that is, UG has atrophied and is, therefore, no longer available for building L2 knowledge. White argued that the input feeds directly into the L2 system, which initially is essentially the L1 system.

A second position also assumes that the starting point for L2 acquisition is the final state of L1, but unlike the previous position, assumes the availability of UG. Here the learner is assumed to use the L1 grammar as a basis, but to have full access to UG when the L1 is deemed insufficient for the learning task at hand. This differs from the first position in that the L2 input feeds into both the initial state system (= L1) and UG.

A third position maintains that the initial state of L2 is the same as the initial state for L1, that is, UG. Here, the input is mediated through UG and not through the L1, as in the previous two positions. Thus, UG serves as a filter through which the L2 input passes.

There is yet a fourth position, the compromise position. The L2 initial state is affected by both UG *and* the L1. Certain aspects of the initial state are based on UG and other aspects from the L1.

This section has described the position that states that there is an innate mechanism that is responsible for language learning. In other words, this theoretical position argues for an innate language-learning mechanism as the starting point for learning.

General Nativism

There are other theoretical positions with regard to the starting point of L2 learning. The best articulated position of these is the general nativist approach of O'Grady (1996, 1997). In essence, in general nativist approaches it is argued that one does not have to invoke UG—or any other innate language module—to explain SLA. According to general nativist positions, whatever learning mechanisms are available for general (non-language) learning (e.g., issues relating to memory, chunking of units, processing constraints) are also available for SLA (Eckman, 1996; Hamilton, 1996; O'Grady, 1996; Wolfe-Quintero, 1996).

What is common to both innate and general nativist positions is that they consider language devoid of the context in which it occurs. The criticism leveled against both of these approaches is that because language is used in context, one cannot understand SLA without a theoretical recognition of this fact. (I return to this briefly in the section on variation.)

First Language

Research on the importance of the NL in the learning of an L2 has had a rocky history over the past few decades. Early work in L2 learning, stemming primarily from an interest in language teaching, made the assumption that learners transferred forms and meanings from the NL to the TL (Lado, 1957). The terminology used in a language-learning setting and the associated concepts (e.g., interference/facilitation) come from the literature on the psychology of learning, and more specifically from work done within a behaviorist framework (see Gass & Selinker, 1994 for a more complete discussion of these issues). Central to this school of thought were the notions of *transfer* and *interference*. Transfer refers to the psychological process whereby prior learning is carried over into a new learning situation; interference refers to incorrect (L2) learning based on NL forms. I use only the term transfer or NL influences because there is little evidence that interference (as a process) impedes L2 learning. It only describes incorrect forms of language use.

During the 1960s there were challenges to the behaviorist theory of language and language learning. According to behaviorist theory, language was believed to be acquired by imitation, and language itself was conceived as a set of habits. However, it became clear that language could not be conceptualized as a set of automatic habits, but as a set of structured rules. These rules are learned by actively formulating them on the basis of innate principles coupled with exposure to the language being learned. An example from the child language literature is often cited as evidence *against* the imitation view of language acquisition:

> Example 16. From Cazden (1972, p. 92)
> Child: My teacher holded the baby rabbits and we patted them.
> Adult: Did you say your teacher held the baby rabbits?
> Child: Yes.
> Adult: What did you say she did?
> Child: She holded the baby rabbits and we patted them.
> Adult: Did you say she held them tightly?
> Child: No, she holded them loosely.

Despite the modeling of the correct past tense form, the child continues to "regularize" the past tense by adding "ed" rather than changing the vowel. Imitation clearly played no role at this point in this child's speech.

As Example 16 showed for child language learning, L2 learners also produce errors that could not have been heard in the surrounding speech. For example, common errors such as "She goed yesterday" demonstrate that learners attempt to impose regularity on an irregular verb (not dissimilar to what the child was doing in trying to regularize the verb *hold* in Example 16 discussed earlier). There is no way to account for this fact within a theory that was based primarily on a learner transferring forms from the NL to the TL.

One way that researchers in SLA approached the study of transfer was to compare different groups of learners with different NLs, to determine the similarity of patterns of acquisition. Dulay and Burt (1974) found similar patterns of acquisition of English between two groups of children with different NL backgrounds (Spanish and Chinese) They concluded, contrary to the behaviorist view of automatic transfer of NL forms, that developmental factors rather than NL factors were at play and that universal mechanisms for SLA had to be considered primary. Similar results were noted in a study by Bailey, Madden, and Krashen (1974), who dealt with adult learners.

Work in the 1970s on the role of the NL tended to take one side or the other of the dichotomous question: Is the NL important in L2 learning? In research over the past two decades, a more measured view of the role of the NL has been noted, with researchers observing different rates of learning, different paths of learning, and overproduction of use. Indirect influences such as these clearly depart from the earlier approach of automatic transfer of forms.

Ard and Homburg (1992) viewed transfer as a facilitation of learning. They compared the responses of two groups of learners whose NLs were Spanish and Arabic on the vocabulary section of a standard test of English. Of major interest were the response patterns to noncognate items (in general, words of Germanic origin in English) on which the Spanish learners outperformed the Arabic learners. Ard and Homburg hypothesized that this suggests accelerated learning rates. The Spanish speakers, because so many cognates exist between their NL and the TL, can focus more of their "learning time" on other aspects of language (in this case other vocabulary items). Thus, knowing a language that is related in some way to the TL can help in many ways, only some of which can be accounted for by the mechanical carry-over of items and structures.

Zobl (1982) pointed out the importance of developmental pace. He reanalyzed data from Henkes (1974) in which three children (French, Arabic, Spanish) were observed in their acquisition of the English copula (the verb "to be"), a form that is present in French (*sa maison est vielle* "her or his house is old") and Spanish (*su casa es vieja* "her or his house is old"), but absent in Arabic (*baytuhu* [house] *qadimun* [old]). Copula use was not consistent for any of the three children. However, whereas the Arabic child continued to use the copula variably, even at a fairly advanced state of syntactic acquisition, the other two children regularly employed the copula. Thus, although the same phenomenon of copula use was observed in all three children, it took the Arabic child longer to use the English verb "to be" appropriately due to the absence of the category in his NL.

Although we have seen that there are stages in acquisition, there are instances in which these stages of acquisition are not identical for speakers of all languages. Zobl (1982) compared the acquisition of the English definite article by a native Chinese-speaking child and a native Spanish-speaking child. The Chinese speaking child, whose language does not have a definite article, used the English word *this* for the same function that *the* serves in English. The data also show that the definitizer *this* developmentally precedes the true English definitizer, the article *the*. On the other hand, the Spanish-speaking child, whose language does have definite articles, showed frequent use of both *this* and *the*. The differences between these two children suggest that their NLs led them down different paths— the Chinese child through a stage in which *this* occurs before the definite article and the Spanish child to a starting point in which the definite article *the* and the demonstrative *this* co-occur.

Not only are there different paths of development, but we also find quantitatively different uses of forms depending on the NL. Schachter and Rutherford (1979) examined compositions written by university students who were NSs of Chinese and Japanese learning English. Both Chinese and Japanese rely heavily on the concept of topic with sentences organized around a "topic comment" structure (As for meat [topic], we don't eat it anymore [comment]). What Schachter and Rutherford found was an overproduction of sentences such as "It is very unfortunate that..." and sentences with *there is* or *there are* ("There is a small restaurant near my house in my country. Many things of the restaurant are like those...."). They claimed that these structures were being used to carry the weight of a particular discourse function, even though the TL makes use of other forms for that same function. They hypothesized that the NL is at play here: There is an influence of NL function (the need to express topic–comment type structures) to L2 form.

All of these examples show indirect influence of the NL on the SLA process. An interesting proposal in the area of transfer is that made by Kellerman (1979). Basic to his view of the role of the NL is the learner's perception of the distance between the L1 and the L2. For example, a Spanish speaker learning Italian may consider a good portion of the NL grammar as being "the same" as that of the TL syntax. Hence, in this particular situation, we would expect to find a greater amount of reliance on the NL than we would if the same learner were learning Japanese. Kellerman's work and that of Gass (1979) is significant in that they attempt to place the study of transfer within a cognitive framework, thereby discrediting the implicit assumption of the necessary relationship between transfer and behaviorism. In this view, the learner is seen as "making decisions" about which forms and functions of the NL are appropriate candidates for use in the L2. The constraints on language transfer transcend the linguistic boundaries of similarity/ dissimilarity of the NL and TLs and encompass as a major variable the learner's decision-making processes relating to the potential transferability of linguistic elements.

If learners use the NL to make predictions about the TL, what is the basis on which these decisions are made? Linguistic information can be categorized along a continuum that ranges from those parts of language that a learner believes to be common to both the NL and the TL (e.g., writing conventions, certain aspects of semantics, stylistics, certain grammatical structures) to those parts of language where a learner anticipates differences between the NL and the TL (e.g., most of the syntax, pronunciation, idioms, inflections). Those parts of language that the learner perceives as similar will more likely be used in an L2 situation.

Variation

There is much variation in the language that learners produce. Some of the variation is a reflection of learning. As learners are testing out various hypotheses about the L2, they inevitably do not produce correct forms at all times. Some of the variation is *systematic* (i.e., it reflects a [faulty] hypothesis that learners have—see Example 1) and some of it is *free* (i.e., learners use one form one time and another form another time—all with apparent randomness). However, there are times when variation is important as far as actual learning is concerned, in particular variation due to factors of context.

Tarone and Liu (1995) argued, on the basis of interactional data in three settings, that a learner's involvement "in different kinds of interaction can differentially affect the rate and route of the acquisition process" (p.108). They examined data from a Chinese NS learning English in Australia (from age 5 to age 7). Data were collected in three situations: (a) in interactions with teachers, (b) in interactions with peers, and (c) in interactions with the researcher (in English, although the researcher was a native speaker of Chinese). With regard to rate of acquisition, Tarone and Liu argued that new forms nearly always emerge in one context (in this case, interaction with the researcher) and then spread to the context with peers and then to interactions with teachers. What is important, however, is the fact that new forms emerge from interactions themselves, and it is the unique demands of each interaction that differentially allow for the emergence of new forms. In other words, different contexts push the learner to produce new forms to a greater extent than other contexts.

ULTIMATE ATTAINMENT

Age Effects

One recognized fact about L2 learning is that it is rare to become completely proficient in more than one language when the learning of the L2 begins as an adult. There have been a number of proposals over the years as to why a nonnative-like end state for acquisition is common. Among the arguments that have been put forth are (a) loss of neural plasticity. (b) lack of access to the innate module proposed for first language learning, and (c) cognitive maturity.

Lenneberg (1967) made the strongest argument relating to the so-called "critical period hypothesis" (although it should be noted that his main claims were with regard to L1 rather than L2 learning). The critical period hypothesis holds that there is a critical period for language learning. Although the age at which this occurs is in debate, some parts of language, for example pronunciation, might have a critical age as early as 6. If learning does not occur prior to that point, the ultimate attainment for L2 learning will be something less than nativelike ability. His argument rested on the assumption that there was a "termination of a state of organizational plasticity linked with lateralization of function" (p. 167). In other words, lack of language learning was directly related to brain functions due to the normal process of aging.

A second explanation that has been posited is that there is a loss of access to UG, the innate mental faculty responsible for learning one's L1 (see discussion in Birdsong, 1999). One means by which this can happen is the "use it and lose it" phenomenon; that is, once it is used it disappears. A second way is that UG is still present, but for some reason not available for language learning.

A third possible explanation for lack of completeness of adult language learning has been put forth by Newport (1990, 1991) and has to do with the greater cognitive maturity of adults. Children, with small memory capacity, are able to process the input more efficiently. That is, they take in smaller bits of input and can more readily analyze those small chunks. Adults, on the other hand, take in greater bits of information and have the concomitant problem of being confronted with the need to analyze large amounts of language, a process that is not successful given the onerous task involved.

There is research addressing both sides of the critical period issue (i.e., that a critical period exists and that a critical period does not exist). There are those who make the argument that adult L2 learning is indeed constrained by age. Johnson and Newport (1989) in a study of Korean and Chinese learners of English (all with greater than 5 years of residence in the United States) in which age of arrival was varied, found that up until age 17, there was an age-of-arrival effect (knowledge of English decreased as a function of age of arrival), but after age 17, results on a test of linguistic knowledge were more or less random. These results have been challenged by a number of other researchers who have found age-of-arrival effects for learners who arrived in an L2 environment after age 17 (Bialystok & Hakuta, 1999; Birdsong, 1992); for further discussion, see Birdsong, 1999).

Birdsong (1999) reported a number of studies that show nativelike attainment for learners who began learning an L2 after childhood (e.g., Cranshaw, 1997; White & Genesee, 1996). It should be noted that many of these studies deal with specific features of language and do not look at the entire picture of the learner's language. In a study that looked at a number of linguistic features, Coppetiers (1987) found that although many late learners could "pass" as NSs, they often had intuitions about the L2 that were dissimilar from those of NSs (however, see Birdsong, 1992, whose results differed).

The jury is still out on the question as to the validity of the critical period hypothesis. What does seem to be relatively clear is that there are various "windows of opportunity" for L2 learning. For example, Long (1990) proposed that the window for pronunciation may be as young as age 6, but the window for other parts of language considerably later, perhaps as late as age 15.

Aptitude and Motivation

In addition to age-related explanations for lack of L2 learning are individual features such as motivation (i.e., attitude and other affective factors) and aptitude (relating to cognitive capacities). With regard to motivation, like all types of learning, motivation to learn a language is undoubtedly at play in the success or lack of success in learning. Although IQ does not seem to relate to ultimate success, there do seem to be individual propensities toward language learning (language aptitude) (see Ellis, 1994; Gass & Selinker, 1994; Larsen-Freeman & Long, 1991).

In sum, the preceding sections have discussed issues of ultimate attainment and some of the possible reasons why L2 learning in adults almost inevitably falls short of native-like abilities. Clearly, SLA in adults differs from the seemingly effortless acquisition of one's NL by all normal children.

PEDAGOGICAL IMPLICATIONS

This brief summary of SLA has not dealt with teaching, partly out of a belief held by most researchers that we can only apply our findings with caution (see Hatch, 1978). However, there are some general lessons that we can learn. First, given that L2 systems are created by individual learners, it is inevitable that not all learners will organize their L2 grammars in exactly the same way. Therefore, it is reasonable to assume that although teachers can teach (i.e., organize the language for students), learners may or may not learn precisely what teachers believe they are teaching. Second, language learning is a long process; results are not instantaneous. Learners must take the input and have the opportunity to "work" with it by using it (see Swain, 1985, 1995) in an interactive setting. Presenting bits of language and expecting that language to be assimilated by learners is a basic misunderstanding of how the process of language learning takes place. Third, as we have seen, language learning is arduous; it does not come easily. As Lightbown (1985) pointed out, we as teachers need to have realistic expectations of our students' successes as well as their lack of success. It is through an understanding of the processes involved in learning an L2 or a foreign language that we can ultimately come to appreciate the task that confronts students in language classrooms.

A POSSIBLE SCENARIO

Early in this chapter, I mentioned that I would not differentiate between L2 and foreign language learning because there is little evidence that the mental processes involved differ. Nonetheless, in spite of all they do have in common in terms of both theory and peda-gogical issues, language professionals (whether in foreign languages, English as a second language [ESL] or a bilingual/dual language program) are often isolated from each other. For example, in a foreign language department, there may be only one person who has expertise in German language learning and/or teaching, one person with expertise in French language learning and/or teaching, and so forth. Further, on a given campus, the ESL and foreign language faculty may be housed in different departments and, as a result, rarely interact with each other. What is particularly unfortunate is that the discrete entities represented by departmental boundaries perpetuate the isolationism (noted also in high schools): The French language coordinator does not regularly talk with the German language coordinator. This same isolation is also seen in professional organizations, such as the AATs (American Association of Teachers of [your language here]), which are divided up by language, TESOL (Teachers of English to Speakers of Other Languages), which deals with English, LCTL (less commonly taught languages) organizations, and so forth. A greater sense of language community is needed as a way of exploiting what we know of the commonalities of research in the learning and teaching of diverse languages.

At Michigan State University we recently established, with federal funds, the Center for Language Education and Research (CLEAR) (http://clear.msu.edu/). The Center has as its major goal the improvement of language teaching and language learning throughout the United States; it is doing this through greater coordination of L2 and foreign language-related activities. For example, individuals from Spanish and ESL are working together on joint research projects. Individuals with expertise in African languages are developing, together with those with expertise in ESL, a tutor's manual. What is being created on campus through a research center (other campuses [e.g., University of Arizona, University of Illinois] have accomplished similar goals through joint graduate programs) is a framework for cooperation and sharing of information. We firmly believe that there is no such thing as a theory of learning or teaching French that is separate from a theory of learning or teaching Spanish or English. As stated earlier, this is not to say that there are not contextual differences, but that as a profession, we all have the same objectives. To meet our common goals, greater efforts must be made to exploit our areas of common concern and to feed our areas of similarity while, at the same time, being mindful of where different languages force divergence.

REFERENCES

Ard, J. & Homburg, T. (1992). Verification of language transfer. In S. Gass & L. Selinker (Eds.), *Language transfer in language learning* (pp. 47–70). Amsterdam: John Benjamins.

Bailey, N., Madden, C., & Krashen, S. (1974). Is there a "natural sequence" in adult second language learning? *Language Learning, 24,* 235–243.

Barasch, R., & James, C. (Eds.), (1994). *Beyond the monitor model: Current theory and practice in second language acquisition.* Boston: Heinle & Heinle.

Bialystok, E., & Hakuta, K. (1999). Confounded age: Linguistic and cognitive factors in age differences for second language acquisition. In D. Birdsong (Ed.), *Critical period hypothesis* (pp. 161–181). Mahwah, NJ: Lawrence Erlbaum Associates.

Birdsong, D. (1992). Ultimate attainment in second language acquisition. *Language, 68,* 706–755.

Birdsong, D. (1999). Introduction: Whys and why nots of the critical period hypothesis for second language acquisition. In D. Birdsong (Ed.), *Critical period hypothesis* (pp. 1–22). Mahwah, NJ: Lawrence Erlbaum Associates.

Cazden, C. (1972). *Child language and education.* New York: Holt, Rinehart & Winston.

Cook, V. (1988). *Chomsky's universal grammar.* Oxford, England: Basil Blackwell.

Cook, V. (1993). *Linguistics and second Language acquisition.* London: Macmillan.

Coppetiers, R. (1987). Competence differences between native and non-native speakers. *Language, 63,* 544–573.

Corder, S. P. (1967). The significance of learner's errors. *International Review of Applied Linguistics, 5,* 161–170.

Cranshaw, A. (1997). *A study of Anglophone native and near-native linguistic and metalinguistic performance.* Unpublished doctoral dissertation, University of Montreal, Quebec.

Dulay, H., & Burt, M. (1974). Natural sequences in child second language acquisition. *Language Learning, 24,* 37–53.

Eckman, F. (1996). On evaluating arguments for special nativism in second language acquisition theory. *Second Language Research, 12,* 398–419.

Ellis, R. (1994). *The study of second language acquisition.* Oxford, England: Oxford University Press.

Gaies, S. (1979). Linguistic input in first and second language learning. In F. Eckman & A. Hastings (Eds.), *Studies in first and second language acquisition* (pp. 185–193). Rowley, MA: Newbury House.

Gass, S. (1979). Language transfer and universal grammatical relations. *Language Learning, 29,* 327–344.

Gass, S. (1997). *Input, interaction, and the second language learner.* Mahwah, NJ: Lawrence Erlbaum Associates.

Gass, S., Fleck, C., Leder, N., & Svetics, I. (1998). Ahistoricity revisited: Does SLA have a history? *Studies in Second Language Acquisition, 20,* 407–421.

Gass, S., & Selinker, L. (1994). *Second language acquisition: An introductory course.* Hillsdale, NJ: Lawrence Erlbaum Associates.

Gass, S., & Varonis, E. (1989). Incorporated repairs in NNS discourse. In M. Eisenstein (Ed.), *The dynamic interlanguage* (pp. 71–86). New York: Plenum.

Gregg, K. (1984). Krashen's monitor and Occam's razor. *Applied Linguistics, 5,* 79–100.

Gregg, K. (1986). Review of Krashen (1985). *TESOL Quarterly, 20,* 116–122.

Hamilton, R. (1996). Against underdetermined reflexive binding. *Second Language Research, 4,* 420–446.

Hanania, E. (1974). *Acquisition of English structures: A case study of an adult native speaker of Arabic in an English-speaking environment.* Unpublished doctoral dissertation, Indiana University, Bloomington.

Hatch, E. (1978). Apply with caution. *Studies in Second Language Acquisition, 2,* 123–143.

Hatch, E. (1983). *Psycholinguistics: A second Language perspective.* Rowley, MA: Newbury House.

Henkes, T. (1974). *Early stages in the non-native acquisition of English syntax: A study of three children from Zaire, Venezuela, and Saudi Arabia.* Unpublished doctoral dissertation, Indiana University, Bloomington.

Johnson, J., & Newport, E. (1989). Critical period effects in second language learning: The influence of maturational state on the acquisition of ESL. *Cognitive Psychology, 21,* 60–99.

Kellerman, E. (1979). Transfer and non-transfer: Where we are now. *Studies in Second Language Acquisition, 2,* 37–57.

Kellerman, E. (1985). If at first you do succeed.... In S. Gass & C. Madden (Eds.), *Input in second Language acquisition* (pp. 345–354). Rowley, MA: Newbury House.

Kleifgen, J. (1985). Skilled variation in a kindergarten teacher's use of foreigner talk. In S. Gass & C. Madden (Eds.), *Input in second language acquisition* (pp. 59–68). Rowley, MA: Newbury House.

Krashen, S. (1980). The input hypothesis. In J. Alatis (Ed.), *Current issues in bilingual education* (pp. 168–180). Washington DC: Georgetown University Press.

Krashen, S. (1982). *Principles and practice in second language acquisition.* London: Pergamon.

Krashen, S. (1985). *The input hypothesis: Issues and implications.* New York: Longman.

Lado, R. (1957). *Linguistics across cultures.* Ann Arbor: University of Michigan Press.

Larsen-Freeman, D., & Long, M. (1991). *An introduction to second language acquisition research.* London: Longman.

Lenneberg, E. (1967). *Biological foundations of language.* New York: Wiley.

Lightbown, P. (1983). Exploring relationships between developmental and instructional sequences in L2 acquisition. In H. Seliger & M. Long (Eds.), *Classroom oriented research in second language acquisition* (pp. 217–243). Rowley, MA: Newbury House.

Lightbown, P. (1985). Great expectations: Second-language acquisition research and classroom teaching. *Applied Linguistics, 6,* 173–189.

Long, M. (1980). *Input, interaction, and second language acquisition.* Unpublished doctoral dissertation, University of California, Los Angeles.

Long, M. (1983). Linguistic and conversational adjustments to nonnative speakers. *Studies in Second Language Acquisition, 5,* 177–193.

Long, M. (1990). Maturational constraints on language development. *Studies in Second Language Acquisition, 12,* 251–285.

Long, M. (1996). The role of the linguistic environment in second language acquisition. In W. Ritchie & T. Bhatia (Eds.), *Handbook of second language acquisition* (pp. 413–468). San Diego: Academic Press.

Mackey, A. (1995). *Stepping up the pace: Input, interaction and interlangauge development, an empirical study of questions in ESL.* Unpublished doctoral dissertation, University of Sydney, Australia.

Newport, E. (1990). Maturational constraints on language learning. *Cognitive Science, 14*, 11–28.

Newport, E. (1991). Contrasting conceptions of the critical period for language. In S. Carey & R. Gelman (Eds.), *The epigenesis of mind* (pp. 111–130). Hillsdale, NJ: Lawrence Erlbaum Associates.

O'Grady, W. (1996). Language acquisition without universal grammar: A general nativist proposal for learning. *Second Language Research, 4*, 374–397.

O'Grady, W. (1997, October). *Plenoquium: SLA and theories of mind.* Paper presented at the Second Language Research Forum, East Lansing, MI.

Pienemann, M., & Johnston, M. (1987). Factors influencing the development of language proficiency. In D. Nunan (Ed.), *Applying second language acquisition research* (pp. 45–141). Adelaide, Australia: National Curriculum Resource Centre, AMEP.

Scarcella, R., & Higa, C. (1981). Input, negotiation and age differences in second language acquisition. *Language Learning, 31*, 409–438.

Schachter, J., & Rutherford, W. (1979). Discourse function and language transfer. *Working Papers in Bilingualism, 19*, 3–12.

Schumann, J. (1979). The acquisition of English negation by speakers of Spanish: A review of the literature. In R. Andersen (Ed.), *The acquisition and use of Spanish and English as first and second languages* (pp. 3–32). Washington, DC: TESOL.

Selinker, L (1972). Interlanguage. *International Review of Applied Linguistics, 10*, 209–231.

Swain, M. (1985). Communicative competence: Some roles of comprehensible input and comprehensive output in its development. In S. Gass & C. Madden (Eds.), *Input in second language acquisition* (pp. 235–253). Rowley, MA: Newbury House.

Swain, M. (1995). Three functions of output in second language learning. In G. Cook & B. Seidlhofer (Eds.), *Principle and practice in applied linguistics: Studies in honour of H. G. Widdowson* (pp. 125–144). Oxford, England: Oxford University Press.

Tarone, E., & Liu, G. (1995). Situational context, variation, and second language acquisition theory. In G. Cook & B. Seidlhofer (Eds.), *Principle and practice in applied linguistics: Studies in honour of H. G. Widdowson* (pp. 107–124). Oxford, England: Oxford University Press.

Thomas, M. (1998). Ahistoricity. *Studies in Second Language Acquisition, 20*, 387–405.

Varonis, E., & Gass, S. (1985). Non-native/non-native conversations: A model for negotiation of meaning. *Applied Linguistics, 6*, 71–90.

Wagner-Gough, J., & Hatch, E. (1975). The importance of input data in second language acquisition studies. *Language Learning, 25*, 297–307.

White, L. (1989). *Universal grammar and second language acquisition.* Amsterdam: John Benjamins.

White, L. (1992). Universal grammar: Is it just a new name for old problems? In S. Gass & L. Selinker (Eds.), *Language transfer in language learning* (pp. 217–232). Amsterdam: John Benjamins.

White, L. (1996, November). *The tale of the ugly duckling (or the coming of age of second language acquisition research).* Paper presented at the Boston University Conference on Language Development, Boston.

White, L., & Genesee, F. (1996). How native is near-native? The issue of ultimate attainment in adult second language acquisition. *Second Language Research, 12*, 238–265.

Wolfe-Quintero, K. (1996). Nativism does not equal Universal Grammar. *Second Language Research, 12*, 335–373.

Zobl, H. (1982). A direction for contrastive analysis: The comparative study of developmental sequences. *TESOL Quarterly, 16*, 169–183.

QUESTIONS TO THINK ABOUT

1. Gass cites Stephen Krashen's concept that language learners develop their abilities through two processes: "acquisition" and "learning." Define acquisition according to Krashen's theory. What particular aspects of language learning exemplify acquisition? Define learning according to Krashen's theory. What aspects of language learning exemplify learning? What aspects of language learning involve both processes? Give a specific classroom example of each aspect of language learning.

2. According to Gass, what evidence is there to support the idea that language learning is not simply imitation? How might participants in a conversation help an NNS (nonnative speaker) to understand what is being said? How does the idea of UG (universal grammar) influence SLA (second language acquisition)? How does someone's NL (native language) influence the learning of an additional language?

3. Although our intuition tells us that language learning proceeds in a linear fashion, SLA research tells us otherwise. What stages do researchers observe in SLA learners? Why might there be ups and downs in the process—times when a learner seems to have decreased in knowledge of the TL (target language)?

4. *Extending your understanding*: Citing SLA research, Gass explains that "foreigner talk" serves the human need "to maintain the smooth flow of a conversation." What does she describe as the characteristics of "foreigner talk"? Observe an NS (native speaker) of a language speaking to an NNS (or even observe your own patterns in such a situation). Notice what goes on in the interaction. In what ways does each person change his/her vocabulary or way of speaking to accommodate the NNS? Write out your observations thinking about whether or not they correspond to the Gass description.

TERMS TO DEFINE

Define the following words and phrases as they are presented within the context of the reading. Comment on your understanding of the significance of each one.

Behaviorist Theory
English Copula
Nonprimary
Progressive Tenses
Simple Present Tense
Transfer

The English-Only Movement and Sign Language for Deaf Learners: An Instructive Parallel

David S. Martin
Gallaudet University

The passage and implementation of a law requiring that English be the primary language of instruction in California marked 1998 as a historic year in the teaching of English in the United States. However, not only did this movement not happen suddenly (it actually began more than twenty years earlier), it also is not isolated as an example of excluding learners' first languages in schools. In the education of deaf and hard of hearing learners, to take another prime example, whether to use sign language or English as the primary language of instruction is a long-standing issue in countries in which English is the first language of hearing people. Examples can also be found outside the English-speaking world; for example, in Slovakia, a prohibition is in effect against the use of Hungarian by resident Hungarians, and the government has required the removal of Hungarian expressions on public signage that had previously been bilingual in those parts of the country with a large Hungarian population.

To what extent are these movements and issues parallel, and how may they inform each other? Let us address these issues in relation to both differences and, especially, similarities in terms of what we may learn from them in order that educators and others may develop a balanced perspective on the issue of the language of instruction.

THE HUNGARIAN EXAMPLE

Ethnic and linguistic minorities exist in many different countries of the world for a variety of reasons—some because of immigration, others because of an influx of resident foreign workers, and still others because of the sometimes arbitrary redrawing of national boundaries that then "entrap" native speakers of one language within an entirely different linguistic context—against their choice or will.

Such an example among many is that of the ethnic Hungarians who currently live inside the borders of the relatively new country of Slovakia. Historically, these people have

---

lived in that same region for many years, going back to the time of the Austro-Hungarian Empire, which was much larger than the current boundaries of Hungary today. The treaty ending World War I, which dissolved the Austro-Hungarian Empire, left these people inside a different country (Czechoslovakia), but they had not changed their actual residence. Since the nation known as Czechoslovakia has separated into two countries, the Hungarian ethnic and linguistic minority has been the target of increasing discrimination at the official level in the country now known as Slovakia. At the time of this writing, the Slovakian government—in an attempt to give primacy to the Slovakian majority—had recently passed a regulation forbidding the use of the Hungarian language in public places and in instruction in schools. Of course, various other examples can be found, particularly in Eastern Europe with its many boundaries that have been redrawn numerous times during past centuries.

This Slovakian regulation has, not unexpectedly, outraged Hungarians living in nearby Hungary as well as Hungarians within Slovakia. Kontra (1995, 1996), in a penetrating analysis of this situation, refers helpfully to the pronouncements of the Linguistic Society of America (LSA), which proclaim that any linguistic minority has a *human right* to use the language of its preference in all areas of life (1996). This statement by the LSA is most helpful in analyzing the various dimensions of such situations but of course is not universally accepted, especially at governmental and policy levels, in many countries.

The outcome of the Slovakian situation is uncertain, due to the question of whether this disenfranchised minority will resist this governmental ruling in some strident manner that will bring increased public attention to the situation. Regardless of the outcome, this example illustrates the international dimension of this interaction among the triad of nationalism, language, and political power.

THE ENGLISH-ONLY MOVEMENT IN THE UNITED STATES

During the 1970s, several individuals, notable among them S. I. Hayakawa (then a linguist at San Francisco State University and later a U.S. senator from California), began to call for an end to bilingual education in the state of California and elsewhere for children whose first language was other than English. As early as 1985 and before, Hayakawa— through a group called "U.S. English"—lobbied Congress to pass a law declaring English to be the official language of the United States, in the belief that a common language is essential to ensuring the nation's survival and to providing access to wealth and power for its citizens. His reference to the success of millions of immigrants in the past demonstrates that concept (Armstrong 1985). The call among certain political leaders, scholars, and laypersons (including some parents and educators) was to question the merits of providing bilingual instruction for children who had recently arrived in the United States from other language regions and to instead require instruction only in English in an immersion manner, prohibiting the maintenance of the child's first language within the school setting.

The interests and motivations among what became a growing coalition of individuals from several domains was varied; for some, it was and is an expression of political conservatism, returning the United States to its supposed first roots of English (ignoring the fact that the true native languages of America were those used by its indigenous peoples, who arrived in America thousands of years before the first English-speaking settlers). In other cases, the motivation was linked to the conviction that an early mastery of English and a setting aside of the child's original ethnic identity and language would be in the best interests of the child's future economic well-being and ultimate integration into American society. Still others maintain this position from a thinly disguised intolerance of anyone who is different from the traditional white middle-class American stereotype.

Numerous attempts were made through the 1980s and the 1990s to the present to establish an English-only policy not only in California, but also at the national level—on each occasion until 1998 without sufficient political support for passage.

To analyze the events of 1998, it is important to understand the varied meanings of bilingual education as it is practiced in American schools, including California, until now. It would be fair to say that there is a range of options on a continuum, which includes such varieties as

1. immersion programs in which the children are exposed daily to English and very little, if at all, to their own original language in schools;
2. instruction in English for some of the school day and instruction in the child's first language for other parts of the school day by a bilingual specialist;
3. instruction in the child's first language for some or all of the school subjects, with separate instruction in English as a second language and as a school subject; and
4. instruction by a bilingual teacher who may teach some of the time in English and some of the time in the child's first language, but who is adept at codeswitching in order to provide full access to the subject content for the child whose first language is other than English.

The California law, enacted through a public referendum in the spring of 1998, sought to eliminate this variety of practices.

It is interesting to note the identity of some of the supporters of that 1998 referendum. Parents appear to have been quite divided on the topic, with some parent groups of Spanish-speaking children actually in favor of the new law, while teachers as a group demonstrated a solid opposition to the referendum, even continuing their protest at the public hearings in front of school boards when implementation of the new law was being discussed throughout the state during the summer of 1998. An analysis of the political dimensions of the entire issue is also illuminating since languages are embedded in social systems. Candidates who run for state or federal office from heavily Hispanic communities in state and federal legislatures encounter these opposing viewpoints in their districts. Some voting parents see English as the key to their children's future success. Immigration to the United States (legally or illegally) is based on a mixture of adult economic motives and aspirations for their children.

On the other hand, other Hispanic adults feel victimized by an environment in which many of those in authority, as well as in the public media, do not provide them with linguistic access to English as the official language. Teachers' unions constitute still another political force and represent highly organized influences to which American politicians must listen; teachers are frequently strong advocates for the rights of their students to have access to information. By publicly taking a stand in favor of the right of Hispanic children to be educated in Spanish or to use Spanish for part of the school day, teacher groups add to the strident political overtones of this dilemma.

The terms of the law are important to understand before any discussion of the possible responses to it. The new law states that students with limited English skills must be taught in "structured immersion" English classrooms in which "nearly all" instruction is in English but in which the curriculum is designed for learning English as a second language; students are expected to be in such programs not more than one year before moving to a mainstream classroom (Schnaiburg 1998).

The response to the law is indeed fascinating because of the variety of ways in which school districts are wrestling with implementation. The Los Angeles school district, for example, developed a set of options for implementation, from which schools and teachers must choose; parents may choose to place their children in: (1) an all-English mainstream class, (2) a bilingual class requiring some kind of waiver, or (3) in one of two different versions of immersion in English that provide a varying amount of native-language assistance (ibid.). On the other hand, the San Francisco school district superintendent announced that he would *not* be following the mandate of the new law because of a federal court decision some years before (the *Lau v. Nichols* decision), which mandated provision of bilingual education for students who need and prefer that option; the superintendent argued that this federal mandate overrides any state law. This rationalized defiance adds a particularly poignant dimension to implementation.

American educators have often remarked that events in California are frequently bell-wethers of trends to come elsewhere in the country. For this reason, great interest is and should be focused on this implementation and also on efforts by either individuals or schools to resist the law in what they regard as the better interests of the child in continuing instruction in more than English.

In a recent study, Chey and Gittelsohn (1999) reported that in Orange County, California, students in bilingual and English-immersion classes had shown equal levels of improvement, but that parents had exercised their legal option to have Spanish bilingual programs continue in some schools; thus, native-language teaching has turned out not to have been totally forbidden under the new California law.

A far larger question looms beneath all of these arguments: Does the placement of one's first language in a position that is subordinate to the majority-culture language constitute a form of cultural subordination? The next logical question then is, Does cultural subordination affect academic achievement (Porter 1999)? The possible implications of the answers to this question are enormous and would apply to many linguistic minorities. An alternative to this possible threat is the approach favored by Glenn (1990), and used in Canada and Europe, where students have heritage-language education if they are minority group members, in addition to learning the majority language.

The issue, clearly, is about much more than the language of instruction; it is also about an individual's human right to maintain an identity with an original language while at the same time moving toward integration within a new society. The policy statement of the Linguistic Society of America, referred to earlier, fits this situation very well.

SIGN LANGUAGE FOR DEAF LEARNERS

A growing body of evidence and opinion now is beginning to indicate that sign language is a most appropriate first language for learners who are severely or profoundly deaf in any country. Implementation of this idea has been underway in several countries for some time, notably in Sweden. Increasing interest in sign language as a first language for deaf students and bridging to English as a second language is seen currently in the United States but by no means universally throughout the country.

Some established linguistic points may clarify this movement. Since the 1960s, linguists (e.g., Stokoe 1970) have established that sign languages (different in each country) are identifiably full languages—each having a grammar, a syntax, and a lexicon capable of expressing any idea or thought, no matter how abstract. The fact that sign languages are not written does not eliminate them from consideration as full languages—a number of the world's languages do not have a written form. Reports of numerous studies and influential publications on sign languages have been written in various settings within and outside the United States. Lane (1984) describes the history of sign language in deaf education in France, which influenced early deaf education in the United States. Others have asserted the right of deaf learners to grow up bilingually (e.g., Grosjean 1982, 1992, 1996). Thus, we see parallels to the earlier discussion of the California situation.

Sign languages are not isolated but rather are usually part of the subculture of the Deaf community in many countries—growing, evolving, and transmitted as a dynamic part of a tradition in that subculture. Thus, just as Spanish is a part of the life of groups in the United States who share a version of Hispanic culture, so sign languages are also important components of deaf subcultures.

However, for centuries, the prevailing philosophy in the instruction of children who are deaf has been to teach them exclusively how to try to imitate the sounds of the local spoken language (with very mixed success in a number of cases) and to read that language on the lips of speakers, to the exclusion of the use of sign language as a full visual language system for those learners in the classroom. At this time in many countries and in numerous settings, sign language is still forbidden by educational policy in the deaf education classroom, in spite of the concept that access to information through a visual language is essential to the full education of individuals who cannot hear. Some countries have developed an educational policy that, apparently begrudgingly, permits sign language in the classroom for deaf students *after* and only after the students seem not to have succeeded with the use of oral-aural methods. In China, for example, the policy is to try oral-aural methods first and sign language only later in the intermediate and secondary school years, with the result that for a number of deaf children, valuable years of access to information have been lost. Although the era of requiring deaf children to sit on their hands or sit with hands tied behind their backs is largely gone, these current policies have the same effect because they are strictly enforced by teachers in the early years.

For deaf persons, as with Hungarians living in Slovakia and Hispanic individuals living in California, the issue is fundamentally related to access—to an education and to a successful life as an adult. However, for deaf persons, the concept of access is special; it means not simply providing oral/aural/written access to another auditory language (as it does with the Slovak/Hungarian and the Spanish/English examples) but involves the use of a different *modality*—the visual. It also involves the concomitant complexities of codeswitching between a visually based language represented primarily on the hands and with gestures and an auditory language (in this case, English) represented publicly in written form, such as through captions. Thus, with deafness the matter of access has multiple dimensions. The parallels between examples such as the Hungarian/ Slovakian situation, the English-only movement for non-English-speaking children in California, and deaf children being prevented from using sign language are striking. The policy of the Linguistic Society of America would clearly benefit the struggling movement in deaf education and should be brought to the attention of policymakers as well as parents, inasmuch as it is appropriate to view the Deaf community not as a community of "disabled" individuals but rather as a linguistic minority. This sense of identity is strongly endorsed by the Deaf community itself. Unfortunately, deaf persons numerically compose a very small proportion of individuals in any society because of the low incidence of deafness; thus, it is far less likely that the strong public attention and awareness that is found in the English-only movement or in the Hungarian/Slovakian situation can ever be focused on the needs of a rather small group of deaf sign language users.

Thus, it is now essential that linguists, anthropologists, parents, and educators unite to bring the human rights dimension of this linguistic situation to far more public attention by drawing inferences about such parallels. Only then will it be possible for deaf learners to develop a strong linguistic base from which they will move forward into the learning of other languages that are important for their economic and social well-being.

RECOMMENDATIONS

The parallels among these three examples are apparent, although, of course, they are limited in other ways because of either the different nature of their respective languages or the cultural context. However, a unifying theme appears to be the threat of loss of the opportunity to use a language that is traditionally appropriate, natural, and at least partially within the context of an individual's own culture. Thus, the following action is needed on two fronts in all three types of instances:

1. Conduct relevant and consistent linguistic research in educational settings to determine the manner in which these first languages are not only important but also how they may be used most effectively for instruction; and

2. Provide parallel teacher development for teachers who can become skilled codeswitchers in the classroom, able to move easily between the child's first and second languages while attending to both the child's first language and building on it toward a second.

The case for initiating and maintaining a policy of bilingual education in all three of these cases is also supported by research and practice indicating that, worldwide, students in well-implemented bilingual programs do not lose out in the development of their academic skills in the majority language, despite spending considerable instructional time in learning through the minority language (Rossell & Baker 1996).

In order to implement such a two-part recommendation, however, coalitions of educators, informed parents, anthropologists, and linguists must come together to oppose policies that in various ways forbid the very practices being discussed here. Such coalitions are indeed historically unnatural among those particular constituencies, but the time for action is now in order to enable a whole generation of young learners to achieve their full potential. A positive trend can be found in some countries where sign language, the child's first language, is the medium of instruction, and English or the other spoken language of the community is taught as the second language for purposes of reading and writing. This trend must be encouraged and spread to other countries. Based on what is known today about language development and education, to do less is indeed a denial of universal individual human rights.

REFERENCES

Armstrong, D. F. (1985). Will it ever: A review of *When the mind hears. Sign Language Studies 48* (Fall): 223–48.

Chey, E., & Gittelsohn, J. (1999). Educators review lessons of Prop. 227. Orange County, Calif.: *Orange County Register* 1. Prop. 227 (August 8).

Glenn, C. L. (1990). Introduction. In *Two-way integrated bilingual education.* Boston: Massachusetts Department of Education, Department of Educational Equity.

Grosjean, F. (1982). *Life with two languages: An introduction to bilingualism.* Cambridge, Mass.: Harvard University Press.

Grosjean, F. (1992). The bilingual and the bicultural person in the hearing and in the deaf world. *Sign Language Studies* 77:307–20.

Grosjean, F. (1996). Living with two languages and two cultures. In I. Parasnis, (Ed.), *Cultural and language diversity: Reflections on the deaf experience* (20–37). Cambridge: Cambridge University Press.

Kontra, M. (1995). English Only's cousin: Slovak Only. *Acta Linguistica Hungarica* 43:345–72.

Kontra, M. (1996). The wars over names in Slovakia. *Language Problems and Language Planning* 20(2):260–67.

Lane, H. (1984). *When the mind hears.* New York: Vintage Books.

Linguistic Society of America. (1996). Statement on language rights. *LSA Bulletin* 151 (March).

Porter, R. P. (1999). The benefits of English immersion. *Educational Leadership 57, 4* (December):53–61.

Rossell, C. H., & Baker, K. (1996). Effectiveness of bilingual education. *Research in the Teaching of English* 30:7–74.

Schnaiburg, L. (1998). Schools gear up as bilingual education law takes effect. *Education Week 1* (August 5):29.

Stokoe, W. C. (1970). *The study of sign language.* Washington, D.C.: Center for Applied Linguistics.

QUESTIONS TO THINK ABOUT

1. Martin quotes from the pronouncement of the Linguistic Society of America that "any linguistic minority has a *human right* to use the language of its preference in all areas of life." How does he apply the tenets of this pronouncement to the linguistic situations he describes in this article? How does he connect the needs of the deaf community with those of the hearing community?

2. What evidence does Martin provide to support the idea that language is political? What do supporters of the Official English (or English-Only) movement think would be the benefit to the United States to have English designated as the official language of this country? What do opponents to this plan see as its detriment? How might people be affected on a day-to-day basis if English became the official language?

3. Martin writes: "However, for centuries, the prevailing philosophy in the instruction of children who are deaf has been to teach them exclusively how to try to imitate the sounds of the local spoken language (with very mixed success in a number of cases) and to read that language on the lips of speakers, to the exclusion of the use of sign language as a full visual language system for those learners in the classroom." What is Martin's position on this? How does he support his position? Looking at the various models Martin provides for bilingual education, how might you apply these to the education of the deaf? Which do you prefer and why?

4. *Extending your understanding*: Many visitors from countries around the world have criticized what they view as the United States' monolingualism. They believe that the country would be enriched if all students were required to learn a second language to the point where they could speak or sign with ease, read, and write in that second language. What do you think would provide the best approach to ensuring that the next generation of young people in the U.S. will be bilingual? What steps might you take in your classroom to promote the concept that knowing a second language is an asset and not a detriment?

TERMS TO DEFINE

Define the following words and phrases as they are presented within the context of the reading. Comment on your understanding of the significance of each one.

Political conservatism
Immersion programs
Lau v. Nichols decision
Heritage language education
Oral-aural method
Sign language

From "Let's Flip the Script: An African American Discourse on Language, Literature, and Learning"

Keith Gilyard
Pennsylvania State University

ONE MORE TIME FOR PROFESSOR NURUDDIN

Yusuf Nuruddin, MY BROTHER. Surely the best arrangement is for me to be there at Medgar Evers College to visit your Black Studies courses. But now that I live two hundred fifty miles from Brooklyn, that option is no longer convenient. So, as per your request, I have sent what you need to do justice to the language unit in your classes. I hope you'll appreciate that I treat African American and Caribbean varieties of English together. You may catch some flak for this. As you know, you teach at the college with the largest concentration in the country of Caribbean students with African bloodlines, many of whom insist upon a cultural distinction in every detail between themselves and African Americans. On the other hand, as you are also well aware, African American students on campus haven't always welcomed their Caribbean schoolmates warmly. So expect some tension. But hold your ground, for this is the way to go. And perhaps this current crop is much hipper anyway, past all that jingoism.

My examples of linguistic features are purposely restricted to the sentence level. I feel you can talk well enough about discourse features such as call-response, talking sweet, toastin', and so on. If not, we can consult some more sources. That analysis is never as complicated as the syntactic stuff, and I imagine it would be more interesting for you to read.

You may get to repay this favor, as I may need a good sociological and historical analysis for an English class soon, you know, with new historicism and all. I'll call.

Overview

Certain language varieties spoken by African Americans and Afro-Caribbeans have often been termed "Broken English" by teachers, students, and the general public. The underlying assumptions are that the language varieties in question are unsystematic, inferior, and

---

the direct cause of poor reading and writing. Nothing could be more inaccurate. These language varieties are rule-governed systems that have developed as a result of conflict, conquest, and cultural mixing. They are equal in a linguistic sense to any other varieties of English and are not a major obstacle to literacy.

Origin and Development

Just as English grew and changed because of the Anglo-Saxon invasions, the Danish raids, the Norman conquest, and class divisions within Great Britain, the language changed again when it was exported overseas. Because of British colonizing activity in the New World accompanied by the mass importation of African slaves, the dialects, to use the most familiar label, spoken by most African Americans and Anglophone Caribbeans represent a merging of some aspects and practices of English and several languages of Africa. Although it was standard procedure to mix slaves from different groups together in an attempt to stifle their verbal interaction, some degree of verbal communication among them was necessary for plantations to operate effectively. In addition, masters and overseers needed to be able to address and receive reports from their workers. To accomplish these ends, new language varieties were created by combining what appeared to be the simplest (which usually meant least redundant) elements of two or more existing languages. Such newly created language systems are called *pidgins*.

In time, children are born who acquire a pidgin as their first language. The language combination is then said to have *creolized* and is referred to as a *creole*. People from the Caribbean sometimes say they speak Creole, which is true, but they are really talking about a particular creole, as *creole* also functions as a generic term. Jamaican Creole, for instance, also known as *patois*, is indeed a creole. But so are the range of dialects we generally call Black English.

The language varieties being considered can all be classified, following the lead of John Holm, under the heading *Atlantic Creole, AC* for short.[1] Creoles basically contain the syntax of the language of less or least prestige and the lexicon of the privileged tongue. AC, then, is an amalgam of English and structures from several African languages. But proportions are not absolute. Some brands of AC are closer to Standard English syntax than others, and African lexical items have been incorporated into Standard English. Words borrowed from Africa include *yam, tote, gumbo, gorilla, elephant, okra, jazz, oasis, sorcery, cola, banana,* and *banjo.*

The above view of language formation is known as the *creole hypothesis* and is the explanation for AC given the most credence by contemporary linguists. Competing claims that AC symbolizes cognitive deficiency, or attests to physiological differences, or derives from white regional speech, or mostly signifies an evolution of Portuguese trade pidgin lack compulsion.

Creoles change over time, as all varieties do, usually moving closer to the dominant language. This is *decreolization*. Language varieties can also *recreolize*, that is, move in the opposite direction. It all depends upon social activities at large. That African Americans have been a numerical minority in the United States accounts for the great degree of decreolization in this country. Differences between AC in Jamaica and Barbados result largely from different histories of colonization and economic organization. Jamaica, for example, was ruled by Spain, then Britain, and housed large sugar plantations with relatively high slave-to-master ratios, while Barbados, "Little England," was never colonized by anyone but Big England and featured mainly small farms and low slave-to-master ratios.

Geography also accounts for differences. Jamaica, after all, is one thousand miles from Barbados, roughly the distance from New York to St. Louis. Usage is also influenced by gender, class, education, attitude, age, degrees of assimilation, contact with languages other than English, and so on. AC will vary slightly, therefore, from nation to nation and within nations, similar to how Standard English varies from Australia to New Zealand and from New England to Texas. What must be stressed, however, is AC's essential character. Despite differences among varieties, their similarities are far greater. They don't vary as much from one another as they do from Standard English. As J. L. Dillard points out, "the English of most American Blacks retains some features which are common to both Caribbean and West African varieties of English" (1972, 1973, 6).

Language Features

The following examples come from speech samples or student essays. The country where each subject spent his or her formative years is noted in parentheses. Although I approach them from the angle of inflections and spelling, there are other classification schemes for discussing syntax and phonology issues. I am not attempting an exhaustive or theoretically sophisticated review. I wish to keep this both condensed and useful.

Inflections

Inflections are changes in word form that indicate how a particular word is being used. For example, in the statement "We are interested in Malcolm's ideas," the 's is a suffix that completes the possessive construction. Generally, inflections proliferate when word order is relatively unimportant. That is why English, centuries ago, deriving mainly from German, had many noun and verb inflections. Word order wasn't an overriding feature of the language then. It since has become so. Subject, object, and possession can all be demonstrated by word order, and inflections are not needed to convey meaning—the reason, in fact, many have become obsolete. Even the distinction between *who* and *whom* is weakening and perhaps disappearing.

Inflections were not a feature of West African languages, and in the merger of those languages with English, inflections, being unnecessary to making meaning, did not become a significant feature of the creoles. Speakers of AC systematically eliminate certain redundancies relative to nouns, pronouns, and verbs. Instances commonly described as subject-verb (dis)agreement, tense, pronoun, or possessive errors are directly tied, as illustrated below, to this practice.

1. *She have* a Benz that she and Carl call the Status Symbol. (Guyana)
2. When *a young child have* a baby she is not ready for, problems come. (Guyana)
3. *A student do* have some say in the matter. (Jamaica)
4. *He need* to get with the program. (U.S.A.)
5. *Blacks* in South Africa *is refused* decent health care. (Barbados)
6. *He play* four instruments. (Trinidad).

No doubt, these types of constructions irk more than a few speech and English teachers, many of whom would be quick to assert that the speakers or writers don't know grammar or, even worse, that the sentences make no sense. But these configurations result from the application of a specifiable rule, in this case that only one form of a verb be used with all subjects. In an absolute sense, these constructions are no less meaningful or more ambiguous than their Standard English translations:

7. *She has* a Benz that she and Carl call the Status Symbol.
8. When *a young child has* a baby she is not ready for, problems come.
9. *A student does* have some say in the matter.
10. *He needs* to get with the program.
11. *Blacks* in South Africa *are refused* decent health care.
12. *He plays* four instruments.

The substitutions of *has* for *have*, *does* for *do*, *needs* for *need*, and *plays* for *play* don't clarify the statements. That the latter forms indicate singularity is true, but they don't create it.

A student and a young child would not be confused with plural forms by any native speaker of English. To inflect a verb to show singularity, plurality, or person is redundant because the subject alone denotes these attributes.

AC speakers will sometimes produce forms like *they does* because they are struggling with conflicting rule systems. This is called *hypercorrection*. Hypercorrect forms are actually incorrect in all varieties of English. It is the same type of overgeneralization committed when a speaker learns how to indicate past tense but says *he goed* instead of *he went*. An additional example:

13. Sometimes in life we experience certain things that tells us we have to make a decision. (Guyana)

As stated previously, speakers of AC often do not mark for tense:

14. I was on my own.
15. It was very hard because I *have* to work day and night. (Jamaica)
16. Back when I was fourteen, I *drop* out of school. (Antigua)
17. Most of the factors *mention* about teenagers in my paragraphs are trends followed by most teenagers today. (Grenada)
18. I finally got away from my family.
19. Then I *start* having children right after I got married. (U.S.A.)

One would be justified in saying, to the horror of many language guardians, that AC represents an advanced variety of English, historically speaking, particularly with respect to verb usage. As Frederic Cassidy explains:

> Those of us who were brought up on Latin Grammar sometimes do not realize that the Standard English verb today has only three living inflectional suffixes: (*e*)*s* of the third person singular (go*es*, sing*s*), (*e*)*d* (or *t*) of the weak past (tast*ed*, swep*t*) and *ing* of the present participle (com*ing*). One cannot even include the (*e*)*n* of such verbs as brok*en*, since it is never added to new verbs, and survives in a decreasing number of old ones. In the course of its history the English verb has been discarding inflection more and more. (1982, 57–58)

AC varieties of English assign a fixed form to nouns, usually the Standard English singular. Thus, we obtain the following:

20. Teenagers especially in America have the attitude of separating most *adult* from them. (Grenada)
21. Especially in those high technology *continent* such as America and Europe. (Grenada)
22. The hard facts hit us about a few *week* later when we had to start finding jobs to support ourselves. (Jamaica)

Hypercorrect utterances include:

23. I did not think *an adults* could say much.

One form of a pronoun is generally chosen or repeated. The subject pronoun may serve as the possessive pronoun also:

24. They still don't think that we are *they* equal. (Barbados)
25. They better bring *they* best! (U.S.A.)

Sometimes the Standard English subject pronoun becomes the object pronoun. Instead of *her* and *they*, we get:

26. Look at *she*! (Trinidad)
27. There are too many young people having babies and *them* themselves are still babies. (Guyana)

Along with possessive pronouns and "apostrophe *s*" (*town's people*), possession is indicated in Standard English by preposition (*people of the town*) or by juxtaposition (*townspeople*). Speakers of AC rely almost exclusively on juxtaposition:

28. *My parents business* was about to collapse. (Jamaica)

The convergence of AC pronunciation and the redundant aspect of all inflections determine the nature of auxiliary constructions:

29. This *has strengthen* me to be an example for my peers. (Trinidad)
30. But where his kids *were concern*, nothing was too strenuous for my dad. (Trinidad)

Hypercorrect forms produced include:

31. But he *did not succeeded* in doing so. (Jamaica)
32. This *could indicated* that this area was new to her. (Guyana)

Spelling

Anyone can have trouble with words that sound alike. Speakers of various English varieties confuse your/you're, no/know, to/too (and even two), and there/their. One can, of course, add other examples. Speakers of AC share the potential for these problems, and, because of pronunciation rules of AC, they have additional sets of homophones. Influenced heavily by the phonology of West African languages, speakers of AC soften consonant clusters at the beginning and end of many words. The initial *th* sound, for example, becomes *d* or *t*. So, where *taught* and *thought* are not homophones to speakers of Standard English (in this case, not for speakers of the U.S. creole either), they are to many speakers of AC. Sentences like these are written frequently:

33. Fred wrote an essay he *taught* was excellent. (Grenada)
34. One must be *thought* responsibility. (Trinidad)
35. The kids who were being *thought* by Miss Moore didn't have much pride because of their environment. (Trinidad)

Although the softening of the initial *th* is only one of many AC phonological rules, it receives a lot of attention because initial *th* is a feature of many of the most commonly used words in English.

The softening of final consonant clusters also creates homophones specific to AC. For example: *mine/mind, fine/find*:

36. I really wouldn't *mine* having an Acura Legend. (U.S.A.)
37. In the 1980s you will *fine* more people having sex than in the 1960s. (Guyana)

Among AC speakers, Jamaicans possess a distinct feature:

> ... *h* behaves in a non-Standard way. It is, as often as not, prefixed to stressed vowels or diphthongs, as in *heggs* and *hice*, and dropped irregularly from other words—*'ow*, *'igh*, *'ouse*. This is very much like Cockney usage—indeed, some historical connection is not at all impossible; yet the Jamaican and Cockney confusions with *h* may merely result from the same conditions: loss of the sound, followed by an attempt to replace it that goes awry and puts it in the un-Standard places. (Cassidy 1982, 36–37)

Educational Implications

I promise not to take you too far afield here, but I think it's important to indicate the major camps in terms of dialect and education issues. I term them *eradicationists, bidialectalists,* and *pluralists.*

The eradicationists would argue that schools should attempt to eradicate AC because it represents deficient speech and interferes with the acquisition of Standard English. But while linguistic variation can contribute to minor problems of reading and writing, it is not the major cause of reading and writing problems. (Remember, dialects of English are far more alike than they are unalike.) Grapholects (writing systems) bridge dialects, which is why people from various English-speaking regions can read common texts in Standard English, or even in dialects such as AC. People don't read solely the way they speak. Nor do they write the way they speak unless they draw only upon native oral resources. To develop a Standard English "writing voice" is the key, and that comes through continual and plentiful practice by motivated students, not through drills aimed at eliminating the vernacular. To spend time on eradicationist attempts, given the badge of identity that language is, invites cultural resistance that hampers, perhaps even dooms, instructional efforts. This is not to argue that teaching Standard English, the language of wider communication, is never a legitimate school goal, only that it is not likely to happen through a policy of eradicationism.

Pluralists would maintain that most of the educational problems encountered by speakers of AC stem from who they are, not which language variety they utter. They understand that AC and Standard English are linguistically equal and know that the fact that they are not equal in society is a matter of society, not linguistics. The crucial work for pluralists is expressly political: shake up school and society so language variation doesn't play out so negatively in classrooms. Get AC some real respect, some acceptance. Pluralists wouldn't ignore Standard English, but they do feel that in a more equitable societal arrangement and school situation, students generally would want to expand their use of Standard English and, in fact, do so very well.

Bidialectalists know what pluralists know, namely that AC is not inferior to Standard English in a linguistic sense. However, they would make the seemingly pragmatic argument that AC speakers will need Standard English to succeed in the mainstream. Theirs is an accommodationist strategy: they don't want to make much of a fuss.

I'm down with the pluralists. Educational initiatives that fail explicitly to consider or address social relations and student perceptions are impoverished in my view and are geared to fail students, like many of those of African descent, who feel reasons not to melt on into the program.

I'll stop for now. You easily have one whole class period covered. Maybe two. And you can assign field work.

REFERENCES

Cassidy, F. G. (1982). *Jamaica talk: Three hundred years of the English language in Jamaica.* London: McMillan Education.

Dillard, J. L. (1972, 1973). *Black English: Its history and usage in the United States.* New York: Vintage.

Holm, J. (1988). *Pidgins and creoles: Theory and structure.* Cambridge: Cambridge UP.

Holm, J. (1989). *Pidgins and creoles: Reference survey.* Cambridge: Cambridge UP.

Smitherman, G. (1977, 1986). *Talkin and testifyin: The language of black America.* Detroit: Wayne State UP.

LANGUAGE LEARNING AND DEMOCRATIC DEVELOPMENT[2]

I have sought to avoid hopping from one bandwagon to another, a behavior characteristic of American educators. My decisions to embrace or reject phonics or teaching grammar or back-to-basics or process writing instruction or critical thinking courses have not been based upon the shrillness or popularity of rhetoric but upon cautious consideration of practice and theory. As I have argued, often in a winding and inductive way, in favor of pluralistic educational initiatives, against monocultural ideals, in favor of emphasizing literature in basic writing courses, I have been approaching, sometimes unwittingly, a deductive vantage point from which I can efficiently analyze educational proposals. This viewpoint mainly entails a concern with democratic schooling and affords an extremely useful typology: either educational proposals promote democracy and thus are to be favored, or they do not. This is how I am viewing language arts learning proposals for all levels, including adult education programs.

Let me confess at this point, while I'm being purposely political, that a small part of me leans toward benevolent dictatorship as the superior form of government. I believe it was Sartre who asserted that when one chooses, one chooses for all, and I take those words too literally at times, as I'm sure Sartre would discourage. At any rate, since I would never trust any dictator to be totally beneficent other than myself, the greater part of me sees true democracy as our nation's best hope. If we're not struggling toward that as educators, we're not struggling toward anything worthwhile.

Our work as teachers is political—whether we construe it that way or not—and our obligation, which we sometimes shun, is to provide clarity of political vision regarding our teaching endeavors. My vision yields the following mission statement: literacy educators further the development of authentic democracy—enlightened citizenry and all that— by helping to create informed, critical, powerful, independent, and culturally sensitive student voices.

Of course, I'm not pretending to be original. Thomas Jefferson knew the value of heightened dialogue and asserted more than two hundred years ago that given a preference, he would choose newspapers without government rather than government without newspapers, although Jefferson may have softened that stance somewhat had he been around to discover how susceptible to propaganda, especially in the television age, many Americans have become. There can be no democracy in the full sense he envisioned without universal, critical literacy. This condition does not exist in our society and is why I have been qualifying the term *democracy* with descriptors like *true* and *authentic*. Because Jefferson was a slaveholder, he was more than a little bit hypocritical, but his better notions, like his understanding that governance by internal authority requires widespread informed debate, are yet worthwhile.

John Dewey took this conception a step further. In *Democracy and Education*, which appeared more than eighty years ago, he wrote:

> A democracy is more than a form of government; it is primarily a mode of associated living, of conjoint communicated experience. The extension in space of the number of individuals who participate in an interest so that each has to refer his own action to that of others, and to consider the action of others to give point and direction to his own, is equivalent to the breaking down of those barriers of class, race, and national territory which kept men from perceiving the full import of their activity. These more numerous and more varied points of contact denote a greater diversity of stimuli to which an individual has to respond; they

consequently put a premium on variation in his action. They secure a liberation of powers which remain suppressed as long as the incitations to action are partial, as they must be in a group which in its exclusiveness shuts out many interests. (87)

Paulo Freire also develops this idea of culturally diverse stimulation, while examining more directly the relative positions of students and teachers. In *Pedagogy of the Oppressed*, which appeared more than twenty-five years ago, he asserts:

A careful analysis of the teacher-student relationship at any level, inside or outside the school, reveals its fundamentally narrative character. This relationship involves a narrating subject (the teacher) and patient, listening objects (the students). The contents, whether values or empirical dimensions of reality, tend in the process of being narrated to become lifeless and petrified. Education is suffering from narration sickness. (57)

There was enough of a Jeffersonian-Deweyan-Freirean strain kept alive among language arts professionals to bring about the English Coalition Conference of 1987, convened in a nation probably more diverse and booming with more narration than could have been predicted by these intellectual antecedents of the conference participants. At the gathering, the theme of which was "Democracy through Language," old ideas were reworked and invigorated. An excerpt from the conference report reads:

The increased heterogeneity of our society also gives new urgency to enhancing students' ability to appreciate cultural diversity and multiple ways of reading and writing. The information explosion makes learning how to read and write absolutely vital for living, because without these abilities students will not be able to assimilate, evaluate, and control the immense amount of knowledge and the great number of messages which are produced every day. The development of new media similarly requires of citizens an enhanced ability to use different ways of reading and writing, and language arts instruction has an important role to play here. (86)

Perhaps no students have been more shut out, objectified, and bewildered than those who eventually enroll in adult education programs or those who enter so-called remedial programs in open-admissions colleges. These two groups can reasonably be viewed as one in some respects. I have, in fact, seen students proceed from adult education programs into colleges as discretionary admits, meaning without high school diplomas, and subsequently, be referred back to adult education programs. The important matter is that most of these students have not prospered in our system of public education.

Many adult education students are members of ethnic minority or immigrant groups, of a people whose numbers on these shores are tied directly either to bloodshed or to dreams. When we meet them, they have not given up hope of securing credentials that will, they feel, enable them to succeed. Unfortunately, however, a large percentage of these students (like too many students overall) will be subjected to instructional practices that will not help them toward their goal. They are eager yet passive, maybe the worst disposition, in the long run, any group of students can possess. They search for saviors, instead of guides, in teachers, many of whom all too willingly accept the role. These students search for magic in methods; they settle for getting taught at while they fail to see themselves as largely responsible for their own learning. And what is especially ironic and painful to realize, as a spectator to some of this educational parade, is that these students' lives in many instances are the very case studies that indicate the ineffectiveness, from the standpoint of their own benefit, of dictatorial teaching. They indeed suffer—they, not education—personally, not abstractly—from narration sickness. And we lose them again.

I always hope to get in my class students who have been rather rebellious in previous schools and who prove to be somewhat contentious in general. I want to work with these spunky souls, who often not only know where they want to go (which most students know at least vaguely) but may have some strong and sensible ideas about how they want to get there. But, alas, I don't start out with these nervy types very frequently. I see instead remedial students doing the good old remedial thing, waiting on the remedy. They are expecting isolated, prepackaged grammar lessons. They are waiting on presentation of written format divorced from ongoing reading. I have had basic writing students ask me why I put so many reading assignments on the syllabus. After all, they reason, ever mindful of their convoluted prose, they have taken the course to learn how to write. And they are almost hopelessly intimidated by literary texts. I'll stretch this last point out a bit further, for I think that attempting to resolve the problem indicated here is perhaps the most important work I have done in class.

Several years ago, when reading essays students had submitted after reading a William Faulkner short story, "Dry September," I encountered a startling beginning: "This story was written in 1931 on a hot dry day in the month of September."

I was taken aback because a hot dry September day is simply the backdrop in the tale, and 1931 is the publication date indicated on the opening page of the story as it appeared in the anthology. The student demonstrated no understanding of a writer's ability to use language to create a world. In her mind Faulkner was doing the work of a stringer, and she was content to summarize what she perceived to be his impartial recording of events.

When I shared my own reading of "Dry September," a story on one level about a rumor of rape, I started explaining how it spoke to me about a certain psychosexual sickness that lies just below the surface of Southern life easily exposed by even the slightest suggestion of black-on-white rape and how the description of aridity illustrates that sickness. This same student interrupted me. Peevishly she inquired, "Where did you get that from?" She wasn't challenging my originality; she didn't understand my symbol making. Prepared to scour the text for literal evidence, for some words she had missed, she failed to see that an examination of my belief system was more appropriate if she wished to know the total sources from which I derived meaning. Despite my subsequent request for interpretive papers, she penned one of the most detached efforts ever given to me in an English class. Indeed, she was far more concerned with her usage—which, no surprise to me, was poor— than with interpretation. This was a Freshman English class, not a basic writing course, mind you. She had passed one of those already.

Although the most memorable case of what I call low literary self-esteem, this student's plight is not uncommon. A number of students have, like her, staggered through watered-down basic skills or adult education courses only to be left with little or no conception about how to proceed successfully in, say, College English I. This episode helped to convince me that work in literary response should be a mainstay of all reading and writing courses I teach, basic and developmental classes as well as those designated Freshman English. But I still didn't have a broad view, not anything like a theory of democratic schooling. I saw myself as simply making a reasonable response to an immediate problem. As a practical matter, I figured, if students could write critical papers on literature, they could fulfill their English course requirements. The sooner they started working toward that goal, the better. Addressing the question of teaching literature, Peter Roberts writes:

> One answer to this argument is that in the teaching of Appropriate and Effective English, because people have always drawn on the techniques of persuasion inherent in the language of written literature, the study of written literature is the most fertile ground for understanding language use. In other words, the traditional categories of literature study—theme, structure/plot, style, content, purpose—are the very same factors that govern Effective English. Therefore, where once literature was an objective in itself, whose appreciation was aided by knowledge of its constituent factors, it can now be treated as general exemplification of factors which are used in specialized forms of persuasion (i.e. in advertising, labels, newspaper articles, etc.). (*West Indians and Their Language*, 201)

Influenced by the work of James Britton, through his book, *Language and Learning* and such essays as "The Role of Fantasy" and "English Teaching: Retrospect and Prospect," I became acutely aware of the possibilities of using literature as a way to expand students' conceptual powers and to foster expressive ability. Naturally, I held a vague notion that it had worked that way for me. Literature has always been a powerful way of reminding me that I am not just in the world but of it. Writing about literature or attempting to compose some myself makes up the bulk of the scribing I have managed. Through the realm of literature, it can be argued, runs the clearest path to proficiency in both reading and writing. In the wider world, stories engage people much more deeply than drills or restricted assignments, a relationship that should also hold in educational circles provided students are given a proper forum.

I came to recognize that the problem with students like the one who summarized the Faulkner story is not that they are totally devoid of critical ability. However, because they have learned to be intimidated, they usually don't bring what are at times substantial evaluative talents into the arena of formal education. They don't cope well with the surprising experience of being asked to pass judgment on texts already certified as great works, or so it appears, signified by their presence in an anthology or on a teacher's syllabus. Teachers themselves, sometimes merely by the sureness and forcefulness with which they speak about a piece of literature, frequently dominate class discussion and give the impression that their opinion is really the only important one, even as they push transactional or reader-response theory. I know I have quoted Louise Rosenblatt on the one hand, trying to persuade students that the primary subject matter of their papers had to be "the web of sensations and ideas that they spun between themselves and the text" (*The Reader, the Text, the Poem* 137), while on the other hand becoming too directive of their spinning. Such intrusion short-circuits the interpretive endeavor and fails to lend strength to student voices. Rather than look to deficit and skills models to explain student withdrawal from classroom literary encounters, teachers would do well to examine their own roles during such activities. There certainly are specific strategies that readers at every level can learn to employ to make better sense of texts, but these strategies are not the discrete "skills" about which many reading teachers are concerned. We could introduce teachers themselves to deconstruction, for example, as a critical tool without assuming a skills or decoding deficiency on their part. If we did assume deficiency of this sort, they would be right to feel insulted.

As my outlook broadened, with graduate study and the like, as well as finally and consciously linking political ideas I had held more explicitly to my work, I was able to articulate more substantial reasons for using literature in all language arts classes. I understood that along with passing courses and becoming more literate, it is fundamental that students begin practice in developing beliefs that are to be defended, amended, or discarded as they participate in the discourse of academic and wider formal settings, since informed and powerful voices existing in dialogic and critical relationships is the form of discourse this society supposedly privileges. Other voices, less informed, less powerful, generally are excluded from the dominant societal conversation. I wrote a few years back that surrounding a text in class, being united by it, being at odds with others because of it, approving and/or disapproving it, discussing it confidently, feeling passionate enough to write about it and want to share that writing (which then means attention to conventional usage), seeking new texts, and searching out new talk are some of the most important activities students can undertake—not because they are good ideas in and of themselves, I see now, but because they support democratic development and are on that basis to be favored.

By 1987, I was ready for the English Coalition Conference—if only I had been called. I'm not sure I would have gone anyway. It was held on an old plantation in Maryland, and that's a spooky kind of thing to me. Nonetheless, in my painstaking manner, I had moved very close in spirit to those who participated. To cite another section of their report:

> Teaching students how and why different ways of reading can find different meanings in the same text can provide important experience in understanding and appreciating opposing perspectives. Learning about the many different kinds of writing and ways of thinking which are the subject matter of the language arts curriculum can expand the capacity of students to imagine

and value worlds other than their own. The ability to communicate their views in oral and written form and to listen with comprehension to the views of others is also indispensable to citizens in a democracy, and enhancing this ability is a major aim of language arts education. (86)

So neither I nor the folks at the conference would support narrowly defined skills curriculums in adult literacy programs or in any other programs. Interpretive work should characterize the academic lives of students. Reader-response theory, though a step in the right direction, is no miracle cure for all that has gone wrong. And there were no miracles in the class I alluded to earlier. Some students showed marked improvement as critics, while others, including the woman who struggled with the Faulkner story, did not. And even the students who did progress significantly were not as ready for College English II as I would have liked. They were still too afraid of "literature" and not trusting enough of themselves. They didn't display enough of the arrogance that is part of the temperament of all good readers and writers—and viewers, too, I might add, having observed the critical activity surrounding the movie *Malcolm X*.

Some moviegoers pointed out the historical inaccuracies of the film, legitimately so, given that many less informed viewers were ready to accept the film as historically accurate in every detail. Director Spike Lee, equally correct, insisted the film was a dramatic representation of Malcolm's life, not a documentary. As a result, Lee felt justified in taking artistic license. I had no quarrel with any party on this score. In fact, I found this particular debate relatively boring. A more interesting activity for language arts classes is for students and instructors to question how valid the division is that Lee made between dramatic and documentary. Could any film, even a documentary, be completely objective? Or consider *The Autobiography of Malcolm X*, a text regarded as a virtually indisputable source of authority by Lee and many others. Does autobiography have an absolute claim on truth or just a particular one—a subject requesting that we believe the one story of his or her life that only he or she can narrate in first person? I'm not anywhere near commending Bruce Perry's misguided psycho-babble about Malcolm, and I'm certainly not disparaging autobiography as a genre. I wrote one myself. I raise these questions to suggest more ways of talking and getting students to talk about textual authority, maybe to change relations of power between students and texts, to get students to see that they can act powerfully on stories, that stories don't just act on them.

Oprah Winfrey, at least three times on her television talk show discussing Lee's film, implored people not to worry about *Malcolm X*'s length, 201 minutes, but to go see it anyway. I would have liked to hear students talk about why Winfrey felt such exhortation was necessary. To whom did they think Oprah was specifically addressing her remarks? Did they think that a comment was being made about their interests and abilities? If so, what was their response? And what I'd be most interested in regarding any venture involving Malcolm X is what do students, especially adult education students (of whom Malcolm was one), think is the crucial lesson to be learned from his life? Do they accept the weak, tepid line that the central import of his life is that he overcame obstacles and had a tremendous capacity for reinventing himself? I know I don't accept it. You can run to your nearest politician to find a master of hurdling and reinvention. Malcolm stood straight up and aimed a fiery verbal assault directly against white supremacy and economic exploitation. That is what thrilled me on the verge of adolescence. I didn't care that he liked jazz and danced the Jitterbug. I liked Motown and did the Brooklyn Hustle. I didn't care what hard times he had gone through to get to that stance. I had my own hard times to go through. No, what was essential was that he was on the scene by whatever circumstances, tall, majestic, being defiant, and mostly being right. While I am witness to the commodification of X, I'm looking for some X-ification, if you will, some basic decency and far less greed in our structures of commodity. I'm seeking some X-ification, some gentle equalities and student empowerment in our establishments of education. This is how I am reading X as text.

I may seem far afield from my basic argument, but actually I have merely stepped inside it for a moment, personifying critical reading ability, conceived broadly, though, of course, I don't imagine that everyone shares my views or endorses my explication.

Before I begin to wind down, and point out some specific contrasts between authoritarian and democratic practices, I want to be as clear as possible about some of my previous remarks concerning students. I don't mean to imply that all adult education students are so easily victimized or that all programs are set up in such a way as to achieve victimization. Neither do I mean to underplay psychological strategies that account for student behavior, a passive rejection of certain kinds of formal instruction, for example. Nor do I ignore external social factors that undermine success. I simply wish to emphasize what I feel most familiar with, a seemingly enabling eagerness and availability to learn rendered nearly useless in school by a learned passivity about how schooling should proceed.

A view of knowledge as lore, then, as accumulated information, is an authoritarian view. A teacher holding this view would consequently conduct classes in an authoritarian manner, assuming his or her rightful function to be that of distributing knowledge to his or her charges. This promotes the student passivity I have been describing. On the other hand, from a democratic view, knowledge is a process that is only successful in schools with active student participation, which is proper preparation for the active participatory lifestyles envisioned by some of the scholars mentioned earlier.

The construct that admirable progress is being made as teachers "cover the material" is an authoritarian construct. That more meaningful activity occurs when students "uncover material" is a democratic construct.

To focus exclusively on teachers' purposes is authoritarian. Cointentional education, as Freire puts it, is preferable—not because it has a nice ring to it, but because it is democratic.

A deficit model of language differences is also authoritarian. Deviations from standard or target usage are treated as deficiencies. Black English is "Broken English" and has to be repaired. Jamaican Creole is "Broken English" and has to be operated upon. There is a line on the back of the City University of New York Writing Assessment Test booklet on which students are to indicate their native language. Many students from the Caribbean indeed write "Broken English" on this line. The first few times I saw this, I thought the students were being facetious. But I soon changed my mind. The rate at which they were failing the exam was no joke. Students, not dialects, have been broken, and negative responses to language differences have been much of their problem. An equality model of language variation, the only one supported by modern sociolinguistic scholarship, does not support repair-model instruction. Understanding, as George Bernard Shaw did, that "a language is a dialect with an army behind it," democratic educators focus upon repertoire expansion. They accept the legitimacy of various types of English and study them so as to contribute to an enlightened discussion of learning and teaching with respect to the various speaking populations to be served.

I think the history of English, if only in a rudimentary way, is an important topic for language arts classrooms. We could all stand to know how closely the earlier evolution of English was tied to politics and warfare. We could start with the collapse of the Roman Empire in the fifth century, talk some about clashes among Jutes, Celts, Angles, and Saxons, and how this activity led to the development of certain Englishes, as did conflict with the Norse, from whom were borrowed such essential items as the pronouns *they, them,* and *their.* We could talk about Duke William and his posse of Normans, their (remember a word from the Norse) conquest causing a considerable "Frenchifying" of English. *Government,* a word central to this presentation, is a French word. Then we have to notice the Anglo-Saxons, back in charge and growing strong enough to export English around the world to become the tongue upon which the sun never set. During this period dictionaries and prescriptive grammar books were produced. Standards of usage were established.

Writing instruction in schools has much to do with standards set by powerful groups. Being able to produce texts that meet that standard may be a valuable ability. However, a focus on the standard to be reached, accompanied by disregard for different ways students may try to get there, is authoritarian and disabling. An approach in which the prevailing spirit is to take advantage of varying talents, strengths, and interests of students is more enabling, more democratic.

The final area I want to talk about is *multiculturalism*. I find it a term that obscures more than it illumines when forwarded as an educational concept; at least, that's what my conversations with people have led me to conclude. It is easy enough to argue against a monocultural ideal. To privilege one culture amid the wealth of diversity in this nation is certainly to be authoritarian. To celebrate cultural diversity is sensible. But of what is the celebration to consist? I often hear discourse on multiculturalism reduced to the level of cuisine, a chicken chow mein, chicken fettucini, Southern fried chicken, arroz con pollo kind of multiculturalism. I hear leaders say our nation's strength lies in its diversity, though I don't often hear them articulate why, that the real virtue of multiculturalism or ethnic diversity is that it supremely tests the nation's resolve to live up to the rhetoric contained in its most cherished documents. Will we comprehend the teasing oxymoron near the end of Ellison's *Invisible Man*? To quote:

> It's "winner take nothing" that is the great truth of our country or any country. Life is to be lived, not controlled; and humanity is won by continuing to play in the face of certain defeat. Our fate is to become one, and yet many—This is not prophecy, but description. (564)

Ira Shor, who is on the faculty at CUNY's Graduate Center, posed to me a question: what would college language arts classes look like if we took multiculturalism seriously? The obvious answer is that the content of curriculums would change. It would become more diversified. More and more literature by authors from so-called minority groups would be incorporated, and so on. Again, that's the easy answer. I contend, however, that three other results, usually overlooked, of taking multiculturalism seriously are ultimately more important than mere diversification of the canon.

The first result I'm thinking about is that whole departments would be more serious about multiculturalism. This may seem an odd point to make, since I have already mentioned a diversified canon. But such progressive activity is often confined to only a few members in a department. It becomes someone's specialty. We create a cadre of experts on multicultural-ism when, in fact, we should all be striving for expertise. Some usually well-intentioned colleagues are still asking me to, quote, "give them something on multiculturalism," like my name is Mr. Multicultural or something like that, like I'm not just one African American man. I see the term on numerous job announcements these days: "Candidate must have demonstrated commitment to multicultural education." I surmise that the insistence on this quality in applicants is because the employers possess so little of it themselves.

The second result I foresee is that the ethnic composition of classrooms would change, especially in upper-level literature courses. A higher concentration of students from so-called minorities might even become language arts professionals. I'm not sure what the exact effect would be on adult education programs, but it would ultimately be positive.

The third result, most important, of taking multiculturalism seriously is that it would disappear, that is, as a distinct educational concept, at least in the sense it now exists. At present, it is an *ism* that circumscribes the failure to take full advantage of the diversity that has always surrounded us. The United States has been a polylingual, multicultural nation since its inception, and if the educational system had reflected this reality all along, there would never have been a need to propose this particular *ism* as a panacea for educational ills. If a multicultural ideal were ever present, it would not have become a special move-ment. In fact, it may be time for another movement, one that stresses not just recognition of diversity but diverse interaction. This new movement, really an eve-of-the-twenty-first-century update of an intellectual tradition I sketched earlier, would emphasize not just multicultural existence but transcultural dialogue.

One evening in a restaurant, I remarked to my friend and colleague Nancy Lester that with all the new experts on multiculturalism running around, it was a clear signal to stop using the term to explain anything. It was time to light out, as Huck Finn might put it, for other rhetorical territory. I was amazed by the numbers. As I reexamined the program for the annual convention of the National Council of Teachers of English in 1981, the first year I attended, I hardly noticed any reference to multiculturalism, though by then I had heard the term used among literary artists for at least a decade. Of approximately two hundred panels and workshops at the six-day conference, only three were billed as multicultural or multiethnic in perspective, and one of those panels was composed entirely of presenters from Canada. The conference theme was "Sustaining the Essentials." For the 1989 NCTE annual convention, the theme was "Celebrating Diversity." Did I hear someone say bandwagon, that it won't last? We'll see.

Insofar as *multi* means diverse fluidity, it sounds good to me. But where *multi* means distinct, as the fixed tile in a mosaic, I think we have problems. This is one reason I enjoyed Toni Morrison's book *Playing in the Dark*. Her ideas about American Africanism— Morrison's phrase to describe how the African presence in the United States profoundly affected the work of writers such as Willa Cather, Ernest Hemingway, and Mark Twain— make for good cross-cultural conversation.

It is all before us now. There is a past to draw upon but not to duplicate. What about the golden age of American education when all was fine? Forget it. It never happened. Numerous scholars have argued convincingly that American education has generally focused on producing a highly literate elite and a minimally literate general populace. Never was it the most widely held view among administrators to provide high level literacy for everyone, what business leaders are calling for urgently. It is indeed a new literacy challenge we and our students face, a task we must be equal to if we are to have the most favorable participation in civic and business affairs, if our society is genuinely to become more inclusive and approach its full potential for humanism.

NOTES

[1] Atlantic Creoles also include those based on other dominant languages like Dutch, French, and Spanish. For convenience I limit the term's use to English-based creoles.

[2] Presented December 9, 1992 at the Graduate School and University Center of the City University of New York, as part of the Distinguished Speakers Series in Adult Learning sponsored by the CUNY Office of Academic Affairs.

REFERENCES

Britton, J. (1970, 1972). *Language and learning*. Harmondsworth: Penguin.

Britton, J. (1982a). English teaching: retrospect and prospect. In G. M. Pradl (Ed.), *Prospect and retrospect: Selected essays of James Britton* (pp. 210–215). Montclair, NJ: Boynton/Cook.

Britton, J. (1982b). The Role of fantasy. In G. M. Pradl (Ed.), *Prospect and retrospect: Selected essays of James Britton* (pp. 38–45). Montclair, NJ: Boynton/Cook.

Dewey, J. (1916, 1966). *Democracy and education*. New York: Free Press.

Ellison, R. (1952, 1972). *Invisible man*. New York: Vintage.

Freire, Paulo. (1970). *Pedagogy of the oppressed*. New York: Continuum.

Lloyd-Jones, R., & Lunsford, A. (Eds.). (1989). *The English Coalition Conference: Democracy through language*. Urbana, IL: NCTE.

Morrison, T. (1992). *Playing in the dark: Whiteness and the literary imagination*. Cambridge, MA: Harvard UP.

Perry, B. (1991). *Malcolm X: The life of a man who changed black America*. Barrytown, NY: Station Hill Press.

Roberts, P. (1988). *West Indians and their language*. Cambridge: Cambridge UP.

Rosenblatt, L. (1978). *The reader, the text, the poem: The transactional theory of the literary work*. Carbondale, IL: Southern Illinois UP.

QUESTIONS TO THINK ABOUT

1. What evidence does Gilyard provide to support the idea that language varieties spoken by some African Americans and Afro-Caribbeans "are rule-governed systems" that "are equal in a linguistic sense to other varieties of English and are not a major obstacle to literacy"? What features of AC does Kilyard suggest are evidence that "AC represents an advanced variety of English"? What changes have you noticed in standard English that support the idea that language changes, is dynamic, and is not a static system? How does knowing about the history of the English language give us a clearer understanding of the varieties of English spoken by many?

2. What does Gilyard mean by "eradicationists, bidailectalists, and pluralists"? How would each of these types of educators approach teaching students whose writing or speaking reflects AC features?

3. Gilyard gives three answers to the question of what would happen if schools took multiculturalism more seriously. What are they? Why does he think the disappearance of multiculturalism as a "distinct educational concept" would be a positive outcome? Is multiculturalism taken seriously in the school you attend? What evidence do you have to support your answer.

4. *Extending your understanding*: Kilyard sums up his ideas about democracy and education with his educational mission statement: "Literacy educators further the development of authentic democracy—enlightened citizenry and all that—by helping to create informed, critical, powerful, independent, and culturally sensitive student voices." What evidence have you seen of this in school systems in which you have participated? What changes, if any, would you like to see? Apply these concepts to your understanding of language and how it functions in our society today.

TERMS TO DEFINE

Define the following words and phrases as they are presented within the context of the reading. Comment on your understanding of the significance of each one.

Pidgin
Creole
Patois
Atlantic Creole (AC)
Decreolization/Recreolization
Hypercorrection

Hablamos Spanish and English

Ana Celia Zentella
University of California, San Diego

Near the elevators on the twelfth floor of Hunter College is a sign that reads "Monolingualism can be cured." It is not a malady from which many Hunter College students suffer. Our students converse in, among other languages, Haitian French or Creole, Italian, Chinese, Polish, Ukrainian, Greek, Yoruba, and Korean. But the language that is most frequently spoken in Hunter student homes and most frequently heard in the College halls and cafeteria is Spanish. Unlike the days in the late 1950s when I was a Hunter student and the few Spanish-speaking students all knew one another, today some 16 to 25 percent of Hunter's student body is of Hispanic background. Although the bulk are Puerto Ricans and Dominicans, others come from an increasing variety of countries in Latin America. This picture reflects the nationwide trend: Hispanics in the United States, presently numbering 15 million, are expected to become the largest minority in the country by 1990.

In the Northeast, Puerto Ricans represent the oldest and largest Spanish-speaking migration, and if our progress is to be taken as a yardstick for the newer Hispanic migrations, the prognosis is not good. The Puerto Rican Forum, Inc. has recently documented the fact that the Puerto Rican community is now the most disadvantaged ethnic group in America. In comparison with whites, Blacks, and people of other Spanish origin, Puerto Ricans as an urban group have the highest percentage of families living below poverty level, the highest percentage of families with children living in poverty, the lowest participation in the labor force, and the lowest median income. Sociologists, economists, political scientists, and educators cite various reasons for the deteriorating conditions in the Puerto Rican community, including the effects of colonialism, involuntary push-pull migration, non-European status, and non-white classification.

My own work and that of other linguists suggests that one of the severe identity conflicts suffered by Puerto Ricans concerns their Spanish and English, and that this conflict has negative repercussions for their social and educational development. The consistent attacks on how Puerto Ricans speak—the consequences of a linguistic posture which stresses the superiority of English in general and the inferiority of Puerto Rican Spanish in

Reprinted with permission of A. C. Zentella, from *Hunter Magazine* 9:1 (1982): 10–13.

particular—began as early as 1898, as the comments of a North American colonial administrator in the new colony of Puerto Rico indicates:

> Their language is a patois almost unintelligible to the native of Barcelona and Madrid. It
> possesses no literature and has little value as an intellectual medium. There is a bare possibility
> that it will be nearly as easy to educate these people out of their patois into English as it will be
> to educate them into the elegant tongue of Castile.[1]

In an attempt to make English the only language of Puerto Rico, Spanish was virtually
banished from the classrooms and the courts of Puerto Rico for fifty years. The immediate
repercussions of the imposition of English included the thwarted education of the 80 percent of the student population who failed and dropped out of school by 1930. The long-
term effects are still being felt by the offspring of those children, many of whom migrated
to the United States.

In this country, the low status of Spanish and of Spanish speakers was and is still reinforced by the schools. One of the most effective lessons that Puerto Rican children learn
in New York City classrooms is to be ashamed of the language variety spoken in their native
land and by their parents. This is achieved by various practices, including the constant
correction and denunciation of different aspects of Puerto Rican Spanish pronunciation,
vocabulary, and grammar. They are told to pronounce syllable final -s at all times (much*as*
gracias), never to omit intervocalic *d* (esta(d)o 'was'), to say *naranja* (orange) and *auto-
bus* instead of *china* and *guagua*. Words in their vocabulary such as *roofo* (roof) and *lonche*
(lunch) are called barbarisms. And, as if to clinch the argument, Puerto Ricans are told they
speak a dialect of Spanish that is not "real" Spanish, harkening back to the anti-linguistic
posture of the colonial administrator cited above.

Although there has been no consistent documentation of the psychological and emotional harm caused by these attitudes, case studies of disturbed Puerto Rican children
frequently mention language harassment as a significant source of friction and distress. It
is heartening to find, given the enormity of the pressures to the contrary, that many Puerto
Ricans have managed to survive with a positive sense of identity, and with both English and
Spanish separately and together as integral parts of that identity.

Those who design and implement policies that affect Puerto Ricans need to understand
the historical linguistic processes that characterize languages in close cultural contact and
the linguistic diversity that results from such contact. For example, the "barbarisms" that
cause such alarm are so few they pose no threat to the Spanish vocabulary. More important,
they constitute additions that reflect a new or different sociocultural reality: roofs and
lunches are not the same in Puerto Rico as they are on *el bloque* in New York City, and
roofo, lonche, and *bloque* capture the new connotations. The detractors of Puerto Rican
Spanish are unaware of word borrowing, loan translation, and other such processes, and
of basic notions of language variety and its social correlates. Speakers of every language
share certain features of pronunciation, grammar, and word formation with others in their
community, and these become important symbols of membership in a particular group.
This variety is what is meant by the word "dialect"; dialects distinguish each geographical
region, class, ethnic group, and race from the others. Just as people of Great Britain say
"lift" and "shedule" for what North Americans call "elevator" and pronounce "skedule,"
Puerto Ricans say *china* and *graciah* instead of *naranja* and *gracías*. Except in the minds of
some arch anglophiles, British English is not considered superior to American English.
Similarly, it is worth repeating that Puerto Rican Spanish, closer to all other varieties of
Spanish than American English is to world Englishes, should not be considered inferior
to any other dialect.

Perhaps the most misunderstood linguistic behavior in the Puerto Rican community
in the United States is the frequent and rapid alternation of English and Spanish that
is known in the literature as "code switching." Outside observers and even community
members are confused about how and why code switching occurs. Some instances are clear:
in a large community like *el Barrío* (East Harlem) or the South Bronx, for example, where

residents run the linguistic gamut from English monolinguals to Spanish monolinguals, bilinguals are frequently called upon to switch from one language to the other for different interlocutors. My own research with the children of *el Barrío* proves that youngsters learn the complex rules of code switching as they learn both languages. As the children develop the ability to switch between the phonological and grammatical systems of languages in their repertoire in order to address different people, they also learn to extend this ability to switch for stylistic purposes, and to accomplish it within the boundaries of a sentence.

It is precisely this alternation of languages within the same sentence that confuses outsiders. Code switchers themselves have only a partial understanding of the processes, and they learn to become ashamed of what is in reality a very creative verbal skill. It is frequently erroneously conceived of as limited to word borrowing, which it may include, and it is linked with language deterioration and/or the creation of a new language, now labeled Tex-Mex in the Chicano community and Spanglish in the Puerto Rican community. These terms often have pejorative connotations and reflect misconceptions about the linguistic or intellectual abilities of those who code switch; code switchers are judged sloppy, deficient, or even alingual. Such popular misconceptions have no basis in fact, but they contribute to the linguistic minority's feelings of inferiority.

We have discussed what code switching is not—it is not limited to word borrowing, it is not a new language, and it does not reflect sloppy thinking or speech. We can proceed to define code switching as an effective way of alternating two languages to capture new ways of meaning while it maintains the integrity of both languages. In the Puerto Rican community, far from creating a chaotic and haphazard Spanglish, code switching employs both English and Spanish to great advantage.

The multiple communicative purposes achieved by code switching can be grouped in three categories: switches that cover gaps in the speaker's knowledge (*crutching*), switches that realign the roles of speaker-hearer (*footing*), and switches that seek to emphasize and/or control (*appeal and control*). Crutching is the most frequently recalled reason for code switching, but switches for footing and appeal and control are four times as frequent. Bilinguals are liable to remember the lapses that occur whenever they do not know a word or construction in one language and turn to the other to fill in the gap, as in "Necesito un string para la kite" (I need a string for the kite). They tend to generalize that all code switching occurs for the same purpose. It is indeed employed to this advantage, and in this capacity it plays a useful role in resolving a potential lapse in communication, but it is far from being the only reason why bilinguals switch.

More frequently, code switching allows bilinguals to maneuver skillfully. By switching languages bilinguals can, for example, switch roles and go from narrator to actor or vice versa, or they can switch discourse modes and go from question to statement or vice versa. They can also switch topics, bracket appositions, check future references, and achieve many nuances of meaning that a monolingual does by intonation, style shifts, or dialect switching. The bilingual's shift to another language serves to highlight the change in footing, as in the following switch accompanying a topic shift: "Vamos a preguntarle. (Let's ask him.) It's raining!"

The third category of discourse strategies that code switching accomplishes for our community and others involves a special type of footing: attempts to convince or control the addressee via intensifying repetitions and aggravated, mitigated, or accounted-for requests. A most compelling example of an aggravated request occurs when a six-year-old admonishes a two-year-old with "Give me a kiss o te pego" (or I'll hit you). Despite the several dozen discourse strategies we have identified with code switching, many switches defy categorization because code switchers often switch as a sign of group solidarity, expressing a positive "we belong to both worlds" statement by the act of switching. Some of the most dramatic and creative word switching occurs in the works of our poets and writers: Tato La Viera, Pedro Pietri, and Sandra Esteves.

At present, young second generation Puerto Ricans and other Hispanics are not creating a new language, they are alternating between the languages in their repertoire in innovative ways for varied discourse purposes. Moreover, switchers display their control of the grammar of two languages by linking one language to the other at just the equivalent points: linguists have proved that the overwhelming majority of switches link constituents that are grammatical in one language with constituents that are grammatical in the other in a way that does justice to both grammars simultaneously. Instead of being ashamed of switching, bilinguals should be made aware of the complexity of their linguistic mastery, monolinguals should be made aware of their own ability to code switch between varieties of the one language they know, and both groups should be helped to develop these skills.

To date, the unfortunate experience of most Americans from homes where a language other than English is the mother tongue is that English is stressed to the exclusion of the native language. As a result, they go from being monolingual in their native language to being monolingual in English. In contrast to the Founding Fathers' openness to multilingualism, in today's America bilingualism is under siege. As a result, not only is monolingualism not cured for native English-speaking Americans, but the condition spreads to those groups which had the best chance of recovery, the children of the nation's immigrants. In this manner, the linguistic resources of the nation are sadly squandered: these resources could strengthen our appreciation of cultural diversity at home and internationally. The code switchers in our midst are a key to the opening of the linguistic frontiers of this nation, a key that must not be thrown away.

* * *

	may the sentiments
EXCOMMUNICATION GOSSIP	of the people rise
	and become espiritistas
	to take care of our religious
	necessities...
TATO LA VIERA	y echar brujos de fufú y
	espíritus malos a los que
	nos tratan como naborias
	y esclavos...
	and sentence them to hang
	desnudos tres días en orchard
	beach, pa que yemayá le saque
	sus maldades.*

*The last stanza of "excommunication gossip" by Tato La Viera, reprinted from *La Carreta Made a U-Turn* (Gary, Indiana: Arte Publico Press, 1979). As translated by Dr. Zentella, the Spanish reads: "and to cast black magic spells and bad spirits on those who treat us like Indians and slaves...naked three days in Orchard Beach so that Yemaya (one of the Yoruba gods in its spiritist religion) can rid them of their evil ways."

NOTE

[1] Juan Osuna. *A History of Education in Puerto Rico* (Rio Piedras: Editorial de la Universidad de Puerto Rico. 1949). p. 324.

QUESTIONS TO THINK ABOUT

1. The concept of "code switching" is a common and universal response to multi-language and dialect environments. Summarize Ana Celia Zentella's definitions both of what it is and what it is not, and then comment on why code switching is a significant language process. What purposes does it serve and what is its role in language change and variation?

2. Zentella says that "At present, young second generation Puerto Rican and other Hispanics are not creating a new language, they are alternating between the languages in their repertoire in innovative ways for varied discourse purposes." How does this represent a type of "linguistic mastery"? Can you think of other groups in American society, bound by age, culture, ethnicity, or something else, who create a similar language/discourse or style? What is gained by groups in doing this?

3. When Zentella writes, "The code switchers in our midst are a key to the opening of the linguistic frontiers of this nation," what does she mean? Do you agree with her perspective that monolingualism should be "cured"? In crafting your response, consider both the history of the United States as a home to peoples from all over the world as well as the present-day globalized world of culture and commerce.

4. *Extending your understanding*: Ana Celia Zentella writes: "In this country, the low status of Spanish and of Spanish speakers was and still is reinforced by the schools. One of the most effective lessons that Puerto Rican children learn in New York City classrooms is to be ashamed of the language variety spoken in their native land and by their parents." This is a very strong assessment, many would say indictment, of the school system in the United States. How does the classroom become a site for language denunciation? What are the implications of Zentella's article for teaching?

TERMS TO DEFINE

Define the following words and phrases as they are presented within the context of the reading. Comment on your understanding of the significance of each one.

Dialect
Bilingual
Code switching
Crutching
Footing
Appeal and control

This Is No Language. (Intimate Exile)

Josip Novakovich
Pennsylvania State University

Because I immigrated to the [United] States from Croatia at the age of twenty, people often ask me why I write in English rather than in Croatian. I give a silly answer that it's owing to my Achilles' heel that I do. The less silly—but not tragic—answer takes longer, even though it might start just as well with my injured foot.

When I was sixteen I sprained my left ankle, tearing its ligaments, and stayed in bed with a cast for a month. My brother, Ivo, to become a rock star and sing in English, bought a dozen of Langenscheidt's books in simplified English, with vocabularies of 450, 750, and 1,200 words. I grabbed the one with 450 words, *Greek Myths.* I used to read fairy tales—and to my mind myths were nothing but tales. Under the guise of learning English, I read the book in a couple of days, amazed that the meanings of the words came across, through a shroud of letters, from a long distance of memory and guessing; the chaotic letters ordering themselves through my leaps of faith spoke tales of men and women changing into animals, gods into lusty men. After that, that I should understand a language seemed modest and natural, no hubris. Then I read *Dr. Jekyll and Mr. Hyde.* Jovially, I wondered whether the new language would change me into a half-man, a half-goat, or a donkey, or, equally astounding, a foreigner. When I returned to school a week later and the teacher asked me to translate a text the class had studied in MY absence, I did it quickly. Till then I'd had a D in English—we had two hours a week of English (mostly in Croato-Serb) since the age of twelve—so my metamorphosis into an Anglophile amazed both the teacher and me.

After that, at night I listened to the Voice of America, the BBC, and Christian broadcasts on shortwave. In the dark, ominously sonorous Texan voices announced the Hour of Decision. I'd wake up early in the morning, when the stations went off the air, to a buzz sliding up and down the frequencies. One morning, I wrote to the radio station because the announcer had promised a free New Testament. (That was the second letter I had ever written in English. The first I had written when I was twelve with a dip-in steel pen, in calligraphy, to Roger Moore, who'd sent me his autograph, which I kept with autographs of my dead father.) Along with the New Testament came the station's monthly magazine

Reprinted with permission of J. Novakovich, from *Ploughshares* 20: 2-3 (Fall 1994): 40–47.

with my letter printed and highlighted—evidence that broadcasting the Good News into the communist bloc worked. Seeing that my words, not Croatian but English, were printed in Canada, indeed gave me a great confirmation in the faith—not in Christ, but in the word: the English word had become flesh, or at least lead on cellulose.

The library in our town, Daruvar, got a present of one hundred books in English from the U.S. Consulate in Zagreb. I read *The Old Man and the Sea* without a dictionary. Then I read the dictionary, marked the words I lusted after, wrote them down on lists, and walked in the park, memorizing fifty a day. During history lectures, I took notes in English. I remember where I learned some words: obtuse, obtrude, and obese I learned with my feet dangling in the town swimming pool, in water green from algae and brown from the spring rains. Mob, I learned at a cool water fountain in the park, as I let the water pour over my forearms to cool my blood. Bog, I learned while bathing in a large oval marble turkish bathtub in our hot springs—the letter sequence meant God in Croatian. (Now, years later, those tubs are no longer in service because a Yugoslav federal army jet rocketed the building, but vapors still have to do with both bog and god.)

I became so obsessed with English that I wanted to study in England or the States. I wrote to a hundred colleges, and after a year, Vassar, which did not charge any application fee, offered me admission and full financial aid.

The evening before my departure, I found my childhood friends sitting on a terrace in the park. I said, "Tomorrow I am going to the United States." They made no reply, but continued to slurp coffee and blow out cigarette smoke for a long time, not looking at me; then they raised their eyebrows and went on with their conversation about soccer. Offended and supercilious, I walked away: they did not believe me.

At Vassar, after reading "The Death of Ivan Ilyich," I wrote a death story, in Croatian. I mailed it off to a Serb friend of mine, editor of a literary journal in Zagreb. His reply astonished me. "What language are you writing in? This is no Croatian: too many Serb words, too much strange syntax, and not consistently enough to be mistaken for experimentation. First learn the language, then write." It turned out that my friend was half Croat, half Serb, and that he was openly and bravely critical of the Yugoslav police state because Serb police had tortured his father on the Naked island (our version of Siberia) for pro-Soviet sympathies. So he did not see any reason why Croatian should be filled with Yugoslavisms.

Croatian had been Serbanized for decades to fit the Yugoslav model, ever since the thirties and the dictatorship of King Alexander Karadjordjevic. I could understand why one would wish to distance oneself from Serb imperialism even in language. But whatever vocabulary I had grown up on was a living language, so why not use it and savor its nuances, all the more multiple because of a mix of cultures—and politics, too, is a form of culture. People in Daruvar did speak the way I wrote. The project to ethnically cleanse my native language depressed me since I did not want to deal with any kind of nationalism. Tito had made Yugoslavs terrified of the very word. But had I forgotten my love for English? I read in English, studied in English, wrote papers in English, talked in English for many hours in the dining halls. When it came to talk, students lived in an old-world rhythm. So I had a real friend to turn to, the English language.

I translated my story into English, brimming with conceit once again. Then my new American friends began to point out my awkward syntax—too many winding sentences and misplaced adverbs and wrong prepositions and lapses in diction: too much mixture of the high and the low style, and too many British words. This sounded familiar. In American culture a strong drive to purify the language by eliminating excessive Anglicanisms still lingered. I fell from the frying pan into the melting pot, in which not many ingredients were allowed to melt. In college, while I was invited to admire Joyce's word permutations, I was discouraged from experimenting, from deviating in any way from an imaginary standard English. I was invited to admire Faulkner's lengthy acrobatics but held fast to the rules of basic word order and exhorted to copy Hemingway's short sentences—which was all fine, but the accountability to write in the least common denominator of the language seemed to me deconstructive, inhibitory, humiliating. Soon, though, I realized that I needed the advice; in Croatia, under Austro-Hungarian and German influence, people strained the language, writing monstrously convoluted sentences. Under bureaucratic communism, where obfuscation was desirable, newspapers became unreadable. A comparative study of national newspapers showed that the Yugoslav press used more acronyms than any other press. I had not deviated from the Croatian style: the longer and the more confusing my sentences were, the prouder I was. My American teachers now taught me to make "precise" and "vivid" descriptions, to select "*Le mot juste.*"

These days after spending dozens of minutes making word choices, I am disconcerted when friendly writers tell me: "You know what? Your being a foreigner is an advantage. You accidentally pair up words in a strikingly fresh way. You probably don't even notice it. We native speakers have to work at it."

And when I don't get a shade of a word because I haven't grown up listening to American lullabies, my friends patronizingly smile; when I don't do dialects because I haven't grown up with them, my friends treat me as a comic alien, an aquamarine creature. Tell me about the advantage, then! My writer friends show me how superficial my project of writing in English must be. Where in me are those soulful contacts with words that can be made only with mother's nipple between your naked gums? Sometimes, for example in the movie *Crossing Delancy*, you find a stereotype of a foreigner who writes in English, and who for that reason is superficial.

But thousands of immigrants write in English as a second language—sometimes superficially, but more often deeply, because their immigrant experience does free them as well as hurt them. I can think of only one expatriated American adopting a foreign language and writing in it, Julien Green. How come? Isn't adventure the spirit of America? Or is the mythical adventure only the sort that comes to America, rather than adventuring from America? I marvel at American linguistic unexileability.

Yes, it's often troublesome writing in ESL. English, which at first came so quickly and easily, melodiously, in the long run proves highly evasive in its shadings. This is what David Godine, for example, said about a novel of mine several years ago: "Although I found your novel interesting, I cannot make an offer because it sounds like a bad translation of a good book."

And maybe I did sound like an English translation—maybe still do—because I read a lot of literature in translation, afraid to be "limited" to American outlooks. Still, do I have to put up with people constantly knocking down the language in which I write? Why don't I go home? Go back to Croatian?

All right, this is why. I don't know the new Croatian, nor the old Croatian. I remember how when I received a visitor from Hungary in my hometown, Daruvar, she conversed in Hungarian with the local Baptist minister at a dinner party, and she laughed at his Hungarian. He had grown up in a Hungarian family in Croatia, in isolation from Hungary. Hungarian had changed in several decades, but his belonged to the last century. My Croatian is an anachronism, or anatropism: it does not belong to another century but to another country—the Socialist Republic of Croatia in the Socialist Federative Republic of Yugoslavia, the country which has in the meanwhile vanished. The use for my language is gone. In the last three years, Croatian bureaucracy, to prove it is independent, has undertaken a revision of the language. Words I had never heard appear in daily newspapers. For example, *u pogledu toga* (in regard to this) has become *glede*. The linguo-ethnic purge affects not only Serb words and communist jargon but many words of foreign origin. *Avion* has become *zrakoplov* (airfloater, literally). Some Turkish words remain, such as *bubreg* (kidney); perhaps Croat bureaucrats like them because many Serbs hate these words as a reminder of the four-century long Turkish invasion of Serbia. Not only couldn't I keep up with all the changes, but I don't like most of them. Languages mix, interlink, and there's no such thing as a pure language. Language is used for mixing, not for refusing to communicate, though of course in many cases, yes, we do use language as a shield, a wall, psychologically, and obviously, politically. I prefer the mixing and the shades that come from various regions, like coffee aromas.

Another irksome thing about Croatian. Recently I bought a directory of Croatian writers, published in 1991 by Most (Bridge) magazine. (Ironically, it's Croats and Serbs who have demolished the bridge in Mostar.) Almost all the Croat writers come from and live in the major cities—Zagreb, Rijeka, Split, Osijek. I met some. They all sounded like the radio, stiffly correct, whatever that happened to be at the time. That, too, I would not want to adjust to. I would use the Daruvar—and Western Slavonian (different from Slovenian)— regional, provincial expressions. But that would not go over well in Zagreb, where I'd be immediately branded as a provincial unless I changed my speech into either standard Croatian (as though there were such a thing) or a Zagreb dialect.

If I meet a Croat, linguistically I'm walking barefoot on nails. Any word might be construed politically to show me to be a Yugoslav nostalgic, which I am not, but my not having purged my tongue of Serb words could create that impression. (For a year I studied in Serbia and that increased my spontaneous Serb vocabulary.) Some words peculiar to my region (many of them Czech, German, and Hungarian) could create a complex relation of Zagreb versus the provinces. I am not interested in proving that I am not a provincial. And if I become interested in that, I prefer to prove that I am not a Zagreber but an American, that is, a cosmopolitan—a different kind of provincial.

And this linguistic insecurity with Croatian is not unique to me. I exchanged several notes in English with a new writer from Croatia—Sanja Brizic-Llic, now residing in Venice, California—when I edited an anthology of stories in English as a second language, *Stepmother Tongue*. Recently when I talked on the phone with her, we spoke in English. She told me she did that because she was not sure what Croatian was anymore—just in case I was.

This politically induced linguistic confusion particularly affects small and weak countries such as Croatia, but though I sympathize with the confusion, I am not going to throw myself headlong into the muddy waters and write in Croatian again. I never liked jumping into the water headfirst. Stones may be too close to the surface. So I decide to stick with my English, such as it is. Here at least I have an excuse. No matter what awkwardness I commit, I can still say, What do you expect? I'm just a foreigner.

Do you miss Croatian? people ask me. No, I say, though I may, on some hearthy level. In Croatian I could do old dialects—I have a good ear for them—and I could play with old voices, with untranslatable shades of words, their histories and even their politics. But I'm not going to lament. I don't need to pull a Nabokov—the way he tried to show what he'd lost in translation by writing down the original Russian word and explaining its shadings as he did in *The Gift* and *Ada*. I don't mind losing some good stuff in translation because I have lost much more bad stuff.

The politics of Serbo-Croatian and Croato-Serbian and Croatian or Serbian (as for a while the language was called)—this was the only language in the world with a hyphen, and then later, even more absurdly and confusingly, with an or—these politics troubled me beyond words even when I lived in Croatia. I must admit I did not enjoy being forced to write compositions in the Cyrillic alphabet once a week at school. (In Croatia we wrote in the Latin alphabet.) Nor did I like getting conscription notices from the Yugoslav federal army in the Serbian variant of the language (*ekavski* rather than *ijekavski*). The army used only blatantly Serbian syntax, vocabulary, and it was a mostly Serb institution. Serb officers had ridiculed and abused several friends of mine in the army for their speaking the Croato-Serb rather than Serbo-Croat. Nor did I like Serb nationalists in our town artificially using Serbian vocabulary to make a statement. But I equally disliked the awkward purification of the Croatian language that followed.

So it's not that much of an accident—certainly not just an ankle injury, though more crippling—that I left the former Yugoslavia. Even while I was there physically, I tried to be away linguistically. After all, at the medical school in Novi Sad, I took down notes in human anatomy—in English.

Politics and words give me a headache, and a jaw-ache. (Switching between Croatian and English I did once hurt my jaw joint! I could barely open my mouth for days afterward. Perhaps it was a form of linguistic hysteria? Psychologically, I preferred no language at all rather than the choice between the two.) Feminists have rightly pointed to the patriarchal aspects of English, and I understand their purges even when they result in "or" expressions, such as *he or she*, no matter how awkward. I have been tempted to quit the business of words altogether, but I persevere, partly because I could not concentrate on anything else with sufficient enthusiasm, and partly because if it was enthusiasm I needed, I could not only wistfully recall but safely revert to one experience: grasping for tales through foreign words, as I used to do with those Greek myths. I have tried to learn other languages to recreate the revelatory sensation I once had with English, but after many bouts with German—and some with Greek, Hebrew, Russian, French—exhausted, forgetful, I come back to English, like a shaggy dog in heat, returning home and collapsing in his shanty on the familiar old rug that comfortingly smells of urine. Or better, it smells of goat turds. Having had chevre cheese in France, I can't help but think there's something ineluctably cosmopolitan—more than tragic—about that goat turd smell. English words to me are goat turds. With them, I don't feel like a linguistic exile. Despite the stink, I sniff in them the freedom to be away from Croatia and Yugoslavia.

QUESTIONS TO THINK ABOUT

1. Is the gain that Novakovich makes in English accompanied by a loss of his birth language and culture? Is he a true bilingual or multilingual? Does his experience support the idea of bilingual education? Explain why or why not.

2. For Novakovich, the language in which one writes is a political as well as a linguistic choice. His native language itself has become a new language because of political changes in his country. How does the history of his country influence his writing and his inability to publish in his first language? Novakovich writes, "Languages mix, interlink, and there's no such thing as a pure language." What examples in English reinforce this idea of language as a mix?

3. Novakovich mentions that although thousands of immigrants write in English as a second language, Americans rarely expatriate and write using a foreign language. Name any American writers who also write/wrote in a foreign tongue. Is what Novakovich terms "American linguistic unexileability" true? If so, how do you explain it?

4. *Extending your understanding*: What techniques does Novakovich use to teach himself English? As a teacher, how might you incorporate some of these strategies in the classroom? How is it possible to generate in a classroom the kind of enjoyment for language learning that Novakovich generates on his own? What resources would you want to have available for your students?

TERMS TO DEFINE

Define the following words and phrases as they are presented within the context of the reading. Comment on your understanding of the significance of each one.

Achille's Heel
Acronym
Anatropism
BBC
Syntax
Voice of America

Russian as a Second Language

Natasha Lvovich
Kingsborough Community College, CUNY

. . . the child may attempt to blend in and be like his or her peers; the child may assimilate and act as if the past never existed, denying his or her cultural self. If he or she can be helped by teachers to embrace both worlds, an integrated sense of self can develop and the child can make strides forward. If there is no intervention, either by teachers, other adults, or peers, the child may feel hopelessly shut off from his past and/or become stuck at that level. This stage is crucial; the child can either be guided to integrate his or her cultural self or be left alone to discard it, only to try to regain it in later life.
—Cristina Igoa, *The Inner World of the Immigrant Child*

This story, which describes the process of my writing it, also describes the transformational processes that occurred in me while I was writing. The discovery that I have made here goes beyond the topic of bilingualism, but includes it, and I hope it will make me a new person and a new mother. The underlying realities of this story are the accumulated effects of some valuable friendships and readings: in the process, there was "an impulse, an awareness, a goal and a will, a triggering event, and then—realignment" (Munaker, 1996). There was the GREAT AHA!—and the vicious circle of my mother's projection on me of what her mother had projected on her has been broken.

* * *

It was drizzling outside, and New York's dominant color was gray, except for the multicolored umbrellas people were opening and closing, uncertain about the almost invisible rain that seemed to be over and yet wasn't.

I was heading to a café in the Village where I had a rendezvous with my editor and one of the reviewers to talk about the final changes to the last draft of my book. I was ready to let it go; I had other projects in mind; I felt burnt out and tired. However, somewhere deep in my heart, I was opening and closing the umbrella. I was ready to put a fat black period at the last word of my stories, where the truth about the multilingual self refers to my past (close the umbrella!). However, I did not feel comfortable with the idea of the past perfect (open the umbrella!). My book is about discoveries. And discoveries are happening right now, invisible like this drizzle. There is something missing in that present perfect continuous

Reprinted with permission from *The Multilingual Self: An Inquiry into Language Learning.* © 1997 by Lawrence Erlbaum Associates, Inc.

mode of my existence, which is so beautifully grasped by English grammar, the tense that many second language learners have so much trouble with. Is that because they, like me, are trying to hide the truth from themselves?

The final reviews of my book, especially one of them, reached me right into the heart, asking the questions that I had been asking myself all along. The "painful topic" the reviewer alluded to is the issue of the present and of the future: the immigrant children, my bilingual children, what is their life in connection to ours? How can I see myself, in the consistency of my life continuum, not only as a multilingual and multicultural individual and language teacher and researcher, but simply as a parent, a mother of children growing up bilingual in a twofold world?

My little daughter, Julia (*Yulia* in Russian), is 14 months old now. She has just started walking and talking. Her baby language is a derivative of Russian: This is the only language she hears from her parents, her grandmother, and her babysitter. I am enjoying watching her form her first words: trying out the plural; not understanding the negation; expressing herself with nouns. As a linguist, I am fascinated by the way she is creating her language and experimenting with it. As a mother, I am filled with joy to know her first language is Russian. As a second language and culture researcher, I know that her first language will eventually shift giving its place to English. I am already wondering how she perceives Sesame Street every morning and how she differentiates the tone, the inflexions, and the whole different world of the American reality in her sister's English—not the meaning, not yet, oh please! I know, some day she will have to go to day care or to school; she will take in the language from her peers and from the street; she will enjoy television—and that will become her life and part of who she is. And that means, we will lose her the way we know her: What a terrible idea for any parent!

I am recalling a bitter complaint, almost a moan, of my older daughter's drama club teacher, a former Russian theater director, who thought of his work with American Russian children as the biggest failure in his life, "They are not our children!" Of course they are not. And that is the point.

My older daughter, Pauline, now is 12, and she is going through a difficult period of adjustment as a teenager growing into adulthood. Her bilingualism only adds to the confusion of the world perception, of wanting so badly to be like everybody else, her differentness being her a priori given. She was almost 5 when we came to this country. She did not know how to read and write in Russian. She learned English within 3 months, when she went to her first American school, where the kindness of her teacher was the only special help with her ESLness. Her Russian now is better than that of many of her Russian friends, even though she may occasionally make a grammar or a syntactical error. She is unwilling to read and to write in Russian, and her vocabulary is limited. But, most importantly, she does not want to learn more and she is resistant to be involved in any Russian culture-geared activities. When she is angry or upset, she throws her English at our faces as her only defense shield. Nevertheless, with all her American-like behavior, she is still my child. I desperately need her to be, to remain my child. And thus—this story.

Why are so many immigrant parents worried about their children Americanizing too fast, becoming deaf to the "home language" and culture? Besides the understandable pragmatic desire to raise our children enriched by the knowledge of two languages, there is some more dramatic meaning to our anxiety. Watching my daughter growing up American, whatever that term means, is somewhat disturbing, painful, and confusing.

I sat down and started writing. By the end of a few weeks I realized that I had numerous pieces that did not fit together and with which I was unhappy. I was writing about the beauty of bilingualism, my father teaching my daughter to read and write in Russian and her mysterious unwillingness to do it. There was no link between my ideas and my observations. There was no truth and no discovery. I also asked Pauline, my daughter, to write about her bilingual experiences, but her writing was equally confusing. After a great deal of struggling, I left a distress call message on my editor's answering machine and decided to "sleep on" the issue during the week of my summer vacation, the one I needed and could not afford for years.

The only vacation I had was my doctoral program that required some out-of-town seminars, which were fun and full of interesting people—but still, they were not real vacations. By the end of my doctoral program, there was the long sickness of my father, who died while I was heavily engulfed in the dissertation writing. There was teaching in two or even three jobs and the frustrating full-time substitute line at my college eliminated by the magic stick of the budget crunch. Then there was pregnancy, the baby, the job search, and my 12-year-old daughter becoming an American teenager. Preparing the book for publication under these circumstances was not an easy task. Vacation! I needed a real vacation!

I also wanted to take my older daughter away from her little sister and the noise of the house where the baby is always the center; to spend some quality time with her, to communicate in the silence of nature, and finally to be there for her, just for her. We booked a cottage in Cape Cod, with a friend of mine who took her 14-year-old son. We had planned that fun trip for years over the phone and it seemed such an important accomplishment to finally make it happen.

My friend's son, Andrei, is a quiet, intelligent boy, who loves clam chowder, pancakes, and poker. I am sure he is passionate about other things, too, but on that trip he seemed reserved, locked in his own world, and—unsafe. All children experience insecurity at a certain degree, but immigrant children are more insecure than others. In the desperate attempt to keep the native language alive, in my friend's house it is forbidden to say even one English word. Doesn't this seem like a plausible solution to the problem of language and culture attrition?

I remember how silly I felt in their house facing the dilemma of finding Russian words for certain nonexistent cultural realities and concepts. Let's say there is an equivalent in Russian to the word highway, but it is simply not at all what a highway really is—it is just a road. And even if one can find the exact equivalent, the word might be an archaism, no longer used in modern Russian; it might have taken on a different emotional connotation or need a long paraphrase because the equivalent does not exist. And how about the spontaneous stories, jokes, rhymes which create (or are created by) the whole different culture in school or at work or in the street? Not only did I feel silly and awkward, tormenting my mind to translate the untranslatable, but I also felt humiliated by the situation of someone's having control over my language, over me. Being a determined partisan of the importance of keeping the native language and of true bilingualism, I felt in contradiction with myself.

As a rule, we speak Russian at home. I know my daughter would sense the awkwardness and the wrongness if I spoke English to her. I only do it in the presence of her or my English-speaking friends, out of mere politeness. When she was in summer sleep-away camp, I faced the dilemma of printing to her some very simplistic messages in Russian or of writing to her in English. I did both, and she recognized both: These two voices are part of me and part of our relationship. Pauline (who adopted an American name, Paula, despite my attempts to explain that Pauline is a French, not a Russian name) is proud of my good English when I talk to people in front of her and especially when I talk to her teachers. I always try to suppress my discontent about her speaking English at home in certain situations, like passionate recollections of her experiences at school, or about code switching if there is no cultural equivalent in Russian. In all my good faith in bilingualism, I have to believe in my natural instincts. It is imperative for Pauline, a definite extrovert, to seek a place in the peer group. Part of the search is to see herself through the eyes of other girls and boys, who seem to be or are self-asserted Americans. Being or feeling American (like "everybody else"—her motto of the day) brings her security and stability.

Needless to say, my daughter did not get along with the introvert Russian-speaking Andrei, who insistently spoke Russian to his mother, me, and my daughter. He even spoke Russian to his mother in the presence of other Americans. It appeared a secret language in his secure world, where he could find a nest for their close relationship. Instead of being happy about our children's communication in Russian, the Russian world suddenly seemed like a prison to me. There was something artificial and dangerous about it.

Many Russian intellectuals fear their children's Americanization, their assimilation into the main-stream "anti-intellectual American culture." As opposed to them, who had come from the society of despotism, where Russian intelligentsia had to assume the passive role of learners and thinkers to escape servitude, their children are living in the free America, a world of mass culture, consumerism, and pragmatic scholarship. They don't read much and they don't read what their parents have read. With horror, we watch them drifting away, not only from our culture, but from our values. Here is the truth that makes this topic especially painful. "They are not *our* children!" But if we impose on them the artificial Russian world, imprinted in our powerful language, would that be the solution to the problem of raising them to be bilingual, intellectual, and inheritors of our idealism? Without any cultural and social context, the media, and the motivation to learn, would that make them "ours?"

Despite my painful longing for my children to be bilingual and bicultural, my heart twisted with pain for the boy locked in his punitive Russian mode. I suddenly wanted him to become an American kid, a healthy monolingual nonintellectual.

For the first year of our new life in New York, our daughter was endlessly sick with colds, infections, flus, and who knows what else. Her pediatrician, an attentive and caring Russian woman, told me, "They all go through this. Culture shock. They cannot cope with their internal struggle, so their body has to resist. Give her time; she will be okay."

And she was. She acquired English. She became American in her looks and her mannerisms. She does not read much. She does not seem to have any intellectual interests. But she is okay.

Most Russian kids speak English only. My daughter's friends from Leningrad, Kiev, Odessa hardly understand the limited Russian spoken at home and they answer their parents in English. They do not read or write in Russian, not only because they had never learned or forgot, but because they don't want to. They speak English to each other as a confirmation of their American belonging: They are "like everybody else!"

This is similar in some cultural groups but not in others. For example, as far as I know, the situation is quite different in most Chinese families, where, unlike Russian families, children grow up in America fully fluent in Chinese, but the same in Haitian families, where, my adult Haitian students report to me, Haitian children often cannot communicate with their grandmothers who don't speak any English. There must be something in the family structure and family traditions that creates such differences in bilingual development.

Regardless of the social, professional, or intellectual status of any particular family, there is a cultural pattern in families from the same cultural group. This pattern is about power and control in the parent-child relationship, heavily imposed by the ethnic culture. It is possible that in the Chinese family, the tradition of obedience and unquestionable respect to the parents' culture is so strong that the children have no choice but to subjugate themselves to their parents, which makes them keep their language and the surface attributes of the parents' culture. The question is how many of them would need psychological help?

When I returned from vacation, I got back to my writing. I reread the unfitting pieces for my story about a rosy picture of bilingualism, a celebration of harmony and of successful acculturation where the mother tongue and the mother culture are equally present. I also reread what my daughter had produced about her bilingual experiences and feelings. She did try hard, but only managed to write some strangely awkward unfinished pieces— exactly the same way I had done. I looked at my drafts and at hers. Her writing was mainly about how ugly, how abnormal she feels in Russian; about the horror of the first days in school, when the English spoken classroom felt as an animal roaring; about the crudeness of the kids who did not want to accept her; about how she had to prove herself (to be like everybody else!) to become part of the group. There was nothing positive about speaking or feeling Russian. There was just suffering, and nothing else. My writing and hers had one thing in common: Both of us did not want to talk about it!

The transformation that had occurred in me and made sense of my different selves, nourished and expressed by different languages, led me to the understanding of the multilingual personality as an enriched and harmonic social identity, the whole. If that ever happens to my daughter, it can only happen as a result of her own growth. I am tempted, as all parents are to substitute my daughter's world and its world-generated values for mine. My writing did not make sense because I wanted my daughter to be me. So, there was no truth and no discovery. The truth is that I want her to be healthy and at peace with herself. I want her to be secure. If I can make her feel comfortable with who she is, Russian or American, she will find strength to grow and, possibly, transform into a truly bilingual, self-asserted, and perhaps intellectual individual. I have to let it go. We can only motivate, but we can't force. Maybe one day she will enjoy being different.

It is crucial to know that our children carry on our ethnic and family culture, language, values, worldviews. That is what makes us feel immortal and helps to deal with the fear of disappearing forever. Transferring culture and language from generation to generation, we ensure life after life and our presence in the future. In his book, *Hunger of Memory*, Richard Rodriguez argued that the price he had to pay for his success in America is the loss of his own culture and language and the emotional distancing from his family. This is the price we, the parents, have to pay for our own and our children's acculturation, for the risk we took by immigrating in pursuit of the American dream. The responsibility of this act is both to the past generations, for cutting off the link with the old culture, and to the generations to come, who will test and value our contributions.

Most of my dear American friends, of Italian, Russian, or Eastern European Jewish origins, hardly know anything about their ancestors and their culture. Needless to say, neither their parents nor they speak their language of origin. They belong to this blend, the almost imperceptible chemistry that is called American culture, with a sparkle of something "Russian" or "Italian" in their eyes. There is an avid intellectual interest in their culture of origin and there is a manifest legacy of what is called national character in their sense of humor. Very often, there is some transferred cultural pattern of lifestyle: cuisine, hospitality, relationship styles. There are precious memories, even inherited political views, and the attraction to a certain type of people. My American friends' ancestors from Russia speak to me, recognizing my culture as theirs. All of them are liberal intellectuals, former Marxists, and hopeless idealists.

So, I have a chance to be immortal, too. If I can raise my daughter with love and kindness and respect her sense of identity, she might develop the Russian "sparkle." But right now I want her to be healthy and secure. This is the only guarantee that she will integrate in her being free development and at the same time the endurance of the great Russian culture and the powerful Russian language that my father taught her.

The monument on my father's grave represents two hands reaching for each other. One is a big masculine hand, and the other is the hand of a child. The engraving is in two languages: Russian and English.

REFERENCES

Igoa, C. (1995). *The inner world of the immigrant child*. Hillsdale, NJ: Erlbaum.

Munaker, S. (1996). *The great aha: A path for transformation*. Unpublished doctoral dissertation. Union Institute, Cincinnati, OH.

Rodriguez, R. (1982). *Hunger of memory: The education of Richard Rodriguez*. NY: Bantam Books.

QUESTIONS TO THINK ABOUT

1. In the second paragraph of her essay, Lvovich refers to the "past," the "past perfect," and "present perfect continuous" tenses. She uses these as metaphors for her life, but do you know to which grammatical tenses she is referring? How do you form them? When do you use these tenses? Do we need to understand the tenses to understand Lvovich's meaning?

2. Lvovich discusses the process by which her baby daughter is acquiring language. What aspects of language learning does she observe in the 14-month-old infant? What sounds make Lvovich think the child is speaking a derivative of Russian? What cultural influences will probably teach this child English? Do you think she will become bilingual—linguistically and/or culturally?

3. Lvovich quotes a Russian theater director who sees his work with American Russian children "as the biggest failure in his life." He says, "They are not our children!" Lvovich wonders why "so many immigrant parents worried about their children Americanizing too fast, becoming deaf to the 'home language' and culture." Have these children gained or lost more? Is assimilation a goal in the United States of the 21st century? Should it be?

4. *Extending your understanding*: Reread the Igoa quote that begins the Lvovich essay. How might you as a teacher help your students to develop an "integrated sense of self"? Should this goal be part of a teacher's responsibility? What might be included in a classroom that emphasizes multiculturalism and linguistic diversity? Should we be emphasizing multiculturalism and diversity in our schools today?

TERMS TO DEFINE

Define the following words and phrases as they are presented within the context of the reading. Comment on your understanding of the significance of each one.

Assimilation
Past Perfect Continuous Tense
Past Perfect Tense
Past Tense

Language and Shame

Meena Alexander
Hunter College and Graduate Center of CUNY

There is something molten in me. I do not know how else to begin, all over again as if in each attempt something needs to be recast, rekindled, some bond, some compact between flesh, clothing, words. There is something incendiary in me and it has to do with being female, here, now, in America. And those words, those markers, of gender, of time, of site, all have an extraordinary valency. When they brush up against each other, each of those markers—"female," "here," "now," "America"—I find that there is something quite unstable in the atmosphere they set up. I do not have a steady, taken for granted compact with my body. Nor indeed with my language. Yet it is only as my body enters into, coasts through, lives in language that I can make sense.

I need to go backwards, to begin: think of language and shame.

As a child, I used to hide out to write. This was in Khartoum, where I spent many months of each year—my life divided between that desert land and the tropical green of Kerala, where my mother returned with her children for the summer months. In Khartoum, I hid behind the house under a neem tree or by a cool wall. Sometimes I forced myself into the only room where I could close the door, the toilet. I gradually learnt that the toilet was safer, no one would thrust the door open on me. There I could mind my own business and compose. I also learnt to write in snatches. If someone knocked at the door, I stopped abruptly, hid my papers under my skirts, tucked my pen into the elastic band of my knickers, and got up anxiously. Gradually, this enforced privacy—for I absorbed and perhaps, in part, even identified with my mother's disapproval over my poetic efforts—added an aura of something illicit, shameful, to my early sense of my scribblings. Schoolwork was seen in a totally different light. It was good to excel there, interpreting works that were part of a great literary past. The other writing, in one's own present, was to be tucked away, hidden. No wonder then that my entry into the realm of letters was fraught.

The facts of multilingualism added complexity to this split sense of writing in English. Hindi washed over me in my earliest years. I chattered aloud in it to the children around. It was my first spoken language, though Malayalam, my mother tongue, has always been there

---

by its side, indeed alongside any other language I have used. What is my mother tongue now, if not a buried stream? At times, in America, I feel my mother tongue approaches the condition of dream. Its curving syllables blossom for me in so many scripts: gawky, dazzling letters spray painted in fluorescent shades onto the metal sides of subway cars or the dark walls of inner tunnels, shifting, metamorphic. Sometimes in chalk I read letters a man draws out laboriously on the sidewalks of Manhattan, spelling out the obvious, as necessity so often compels: I AM HOMELESS, I NEED FOOD, SHELTER. A smattering of dimes and quarters lie near his bent knees. Those letters I read in the only script I know make for a ferocious, almost consumptive edge to knowledge in me.

I have never learnt to read or write in Malayalam and turned into a truly postcolonial creature, who had to live in English, though a special sort of English, I must say, for the version of the language I am comfortable with bends and sways to the shores of other territories, other tongues.

Yet, the price of fluency in many places may well be loss of the sheer intimacy that one has with "one's own" culture, a speech that holds its own sway, untouched by any other. But perhaps there is a dangerous simplicity here. And, indeed, how might such an idealized state be maintained at the tail end of the century? And it is a dangerous idea that animates such simplicity, small and bloody wars have been fought for such ideals.

Of course, there are difficulties in the way of one who does not know how to read or write her mother tongue. For instance, I would love to read the prose of Lalithambika Antherjanam, the poetry of Nalapat Balamaniamma and Ayyappa Paniker rather than have them read to me. I would love to read Mahakavi K.V. Seemon's epic *Vedaviharam* rather than have it recited to me.

Or is there something in me that needs to draw on that old reliance, the voice of another reading, the sheer givenness of speech. After all, if it were just an issue of mother wit, I am sure I would be able to read and write Malayalam by now. So is there perhaps a deliberate dependency, revealing something of my childhood longings and fears, a community held in dream, a treasured orality? For the rhythms of the language first came to me not just in lullabies or in the chatter of women in the kitchen or by the wellside, but in the measured cadences of oratory and poetry, and nightly recitations from the Bible and the epics.

Perhaps there is a fear that learning the script would force me to face the tradition with its hierarchies, the exclusionary nature of canonical language. And how then would I be restored to simplicity, freed of the pressures of countermemory?

Sometimes all that has been forgotten wells up and I use my English to let it surface. At the end of "Night-Scene, the Garden," there is a vision of ancestors dancing free of the earth, permitting the "ferocious alphabets of flesh."

QUESTIONS TO THINK ABOUT

1. In "Language and Shame," Meena Alexander suggests complicated relationships between language and other markers: gender, geography, education, and hierarchy. What does she say about each of them? What is unique in her account and in her way of writing? How do her ideas connect to those of other writers in this text? For example, she says, "the price of fluency ... may well be loss of the sheer intimacy that one has with 'one's own' culture." Do other authors share her misgivings? What is lost, what is gained?

2. Alexander describes "hid[ing] out to write." Why might writing have been seen as a subversive or shameful act? In what language was she doing this private writing? In what sense is this act an example of the split that she seemed to feel within herself? Why might a child feel this way about her imaginative or personal writing?

3. Meena Alexander connects language and shame and language and memory; she also says she "has turned into a truly postcolonial creature." This term and concept are increasingly part of our lexicon today. What is there in the global English experience that Alexander both embodies and recounts, an experience recounted by many other authors in this text?

4. *Extending your understanding*: What does Alexander mean when she refers to the "orality" of her mother tongue and that to learn its script would interfere with her idealization of her initial language? How does her sentiment reflect the experience of those students in classrooms for whom the language of instruction and of texts differs from their "mother tongue"? What are the ramifications of this for teaching? What idealizations are interrupted when methodologies such as bilingual education are introduced with its insistence on literacy in both "mother tongue" (whether that is a first language or first dialect) and standard language, in this case standard English?

TERMS TO DEFINE

Define the following words and phrases as they are presented within the context of the reading. Comment on your understanding of the significance of each one.

Mother Tongue
Orality
Postcolonial
Shame

Unfinished Knowledge: The Story of Barbara

Ryuko Kubota
University of North Carolina at Chapel Hill

Issues of culture in teaching ESL, particularly academic writing, became a topic of debate in the 1990s, triggered by a series of articles highlighting cultural differences between ESL students' background and the expectations of the target English discourse community (e.g., Atkinson, 1997; Atkinson & Ramanathan, 1995; Carson, 1992; Carson & Nelson, 1994, 1996; Fox, 1994; Nelson & Carson, 1998; Ramanathan & Atkinson, 1999; Ramanathan & Kaplan, 1996). A common conception underlying these articles is that Western academic traditions emphasize such values as individualism, autonomy, creativity, voice, and critical thinking, whereas the cultural background of ESL students, particularly those from East Asia, reflects quite opposite characteristics, such as collectivism, memorization, and respect for authority. This view, however, met with criticisms from various scholars: It was criticized for manifesting a deterministic understanding of culture and a particular student population and for promoting "cultural essentialism" or the idea that certain objectively essential and stable properties exist in a culture (e.g., Kubota, 1999; Raimes & Zamel,1997; Spack, 1997; Zamel, 1997).

An article by Atkinson (1997), in particular, provoked controversy. In his article, Atkinson cautioned against an emphasis on critical thinking in ESL pedagogy, arguing that critical thinking is a social practice unique to Western cultural traditions and thus incompatible with the cultural assumptions that Asian students bring with them to U.S. classrooms. As a pedagogical approach, he proposed a cognitive apprenticeship model to teach thinking skills through modeling and coaching. Several critics took issue with the contentiousness of the definition of critical thinking, the notion that Asian students are not critical thinkers, and the proposed pedagogical approach (Benesch, 1993; Davidson, 1998; Gieve, 1998; Hawkins, 1998). Sarah Benesch recognized the controversial nature of this topic and organized a panel at the 2000 TESOL Convention, inviting Dwight Atkinson, Ruth Spack, Vivian Zamel, and me to debate issues of culture.

Reprinted with permission of *College ESL*, from *College ESL* 10: 1 & 2 (May 2003): 11–21.

The main points I wanted to make in my presentation were the following:

1. The prevalent view on culture in teaching ESL reflects teachers' good intentions to respect cultural difference rather than denying it altogether.

2. Nonetheless, this liberal view of cultural difference tends to fall into cultural relativism, essentializing cultures, and creating a dichotomy between "us" and "them."

3. This view also fails to examine how cultural differences are constructed by discourses and how power is exercised in perpetuating these differences (Kubota, 1999, 2001; Pennycook, 1998; Susser, 1998).

4. Thus, in order to understand cultural differences critically, issues of power and discourse need to be examined.

Although these issues could be discussed through a conventional academic discourse, I wanted to present them in a more accessible and light-hearted way for the audience. What follows is a fictional narrative about a writing teacher who experiences various understandings of cultural difference. In it, I use jargon from the field of cultural studies. Although this strategy may make the paper an unusual mix of fiction and academic writing, it reflects my experiment to make my points both academically valid and accessible. As the title suggests, there is no definite answer as to how we should understand cultural difference. I present this narrative in the hope that it inspires teachers and researchers to explore the issues further.

Barbara was a young writing teacher at a small, Midwestern university. She had grown up in a predominantly white community and was quite content with her life in a close-knit circle of friends and family. After obtaining her master's degree in English, she decided to teach at her alma mater so that she could be close to her friends and family. Unlike some of her friends who had participated in study abroad programs, Barbara was not particularly interested in learning about different languages and cultures. This was mainly because she had hated her French class in high school. It was so boring and the teacher was so mean. Consequently, she had a very limited experience of interacting with people from different countries.

One semester, Barbara looked at her class roll and noticed three foreign names. She assumed that they were second language learners. Because of her limited experience with second language learners, she felt nervous but decided to do her best. On the first day of class, Barbara found out that these three students were from China, Korea, and Japan. She felt relieved because they were quiet and polite. As a rather naive teacher, Barbara expected them to improve their writing just as native English speakers would. But their lexical and syntactic errors as well as incoherence and poor paragraph organization persisted. After a while, Barbara began to think there was something wrong with them—either low intelligence or some cognitive deficit that prevented them from thinking logically.

One day, Barbara talked to her colleague, Carol, about this problem. Compared to Barbara, Carol was much more worldly and interested in different cultures, particularly ethnic cuisine. Furthermore, Carol held a master's degree in TESOL. Listening to her, Carol thought that Barbara was in desperate need of cross cultural experience. So, Carol took Barbara out to a local Japanese restaurant.

At the restaurant, Barbara said, "I have no idea what to order. What do you recommend, Carol?" Carol thought that trying sushi would be too traumatic for her. So she said, "Why don't you try chicken teriyaki? It's pretty good." Barbara really liked the chicken teriyaki—it tasted much better than the so-called teriyaki she had once had on an airplane.

During dinner, Carol talked about the importance of recognizing and respecting cultural differences. She explained that different cultures have different social values, beliefs, and customs. When two people from different cultures meet, misunderstanding tends to occur, she said, because we tend to judge the other person with our own cultural frame of reference. However, neither culture is right or wrong or good or bad. They are just different. Carol explained that there are different thought patterns that influence written rhetorical structures. She drew a straight line representing the English thought pattern and a centripetal circle representing the Oriental counterpart and explained that these differences affect cross-cultural writing (Kaplan,1966). Carol mentioned the four-unit Japanese rhetorical style called *ki-shoo-ten-ketsu* (Hinds, 1983, 1987) and the Korean rhetorical style called *ki-sung-chon-kyal* (Eggington, 1987), representing *introduction, development, presentation of a different view or idea*, and *conclusion*. She further explained that the concept of writer-responsibility versus reader-responsibility represents, respectively, English versus Asian languages (Hinds, 1987). Carol explained to Barbara that Western cultures value individualism, whereas non-Western cultures value collectivism, and these differences are affecting the cultural adjustment of Barbara's Asian students (Atkinson, 1997; Fox, 1994; Ramanathan & Atkinson, 1999; Ramanathan & Kaplan, 1996). Carol told Barbara about a professor described in Fox (1994) as commenting, "If you can think clearly, you can write clearly. So those students who cannot write clearly cannot think at all" (p. xiv). Carol found this professor ethnocentric and unable to recognize cultural differences. Carol once again emphasized that none of the different values and customs are good or bad. Rather, they are all culturally specific and teachers need to recognize and respect them. That night, Barbara felt as though the relish of chicken teriyaki had led her to a completely new world.

After this awakening, Barbara became much more interested in different cultures. She started to read books and articles that Carol suggested.

Two years passed. Barbara now had a larger number of second language learners in her class and she felt more comfortable teaching them. In fact, she became so fascinated by cultural differences that she often had frank discussions about them with her students. In the discussions, she asked the students what kind of linguistic and rhetorical conventions existed in their native language and how they differed from those in English (Reid, 1989). She sometimes described characteristics of a language and asked for feedback from students who spoke that language. Barbara and her students often talked about the indirectness of Asian languages contrasted with the directness of English (Connor, 1996; Fox, 1994). They also discussed an emphasis on memorization in Asian education compared to an emphasis on self-expression and critical thinking in American education (Carson, 1992; Matalene, 1985). Barbara was fascinated by the fact that what her students told her often corresponded to what she read. For instance, Fox (1994) reported a Japanese student saying, "Japanese is more vague than English. You don't say what you mean right away. You don't criticize directly" (p. 8). Shen (1989), a Chinese writer of English, reported, "Rule number one in English composition is: Be yourself," whereas in China, "'I' is always subordinated to 'We'" and "presenting the 'self' too obviously would give people the impression of being . . . boastful in scholarly writing" (p. 460). At the end of the discussion, Barbara would emphasize that the students need not abandon their own culture—they simply need to acquire new cultural conventions in order to succeed in the academic community.

Barbara also learned from Carol that it is important to engage learners in topics that are relevant to their lives. She increasingly assigned compare/contrast composition tasks such as "Describe the ways children are raised in the United States and in *your country*" and "Compare attitudes toward the elderly in the United States and in *your country*" (Harklau, 1999, 2000). Barbara now felt that she had gained much knowledge of culture. Sometimes, she felt confident enough to point out cultural characteristics of a given country when a student from that country failed to notice them. Actually, she increasingly became like researchers such as Rubin, Goodrum, and Hall (1990). In reacting to a Japanese student's comment, "Japanese writing style has no conclusion. And the normal essay has only one paragraph. Japanese writing has no style except poem and polite letter," these researchers stated, "Of course this . . . student is quite mistaken in most of these assertions about Japanese writing. In fact, the paradigmatic macrostructure known as *ki-shoo-ten-ketsu* is well documented in Japanese exposition" (Hinds, 1987) (p. 69).

One day, Barbara met David at a local Korean restaurant. He was working there as a waiter while working on his Ph.D. in cultural studies. Barbara was attracted to him because by that time, she was quite fascinated by things *different*—she thought it was rare to see a white guy waiting tables in a Korean restaurant. Also, being interested in various cultures, she was curious to know what "cultural studies" was about. To David, Barbara was an attractive woman with a cheerful spirit.

The following weekend, Barbara and David had their first date at a local Chinese restaurant. David asked Barbara about her teaching. Barbara told him all about what she had experienced in the past two years with excitement and enthusiasm. David knew the next question coming up—"So, David, what topic are you working on?" David felt daunted by the huge chasm that they would need to bridge in order to have a decent conversation. When Barbara asked this question, he simply answered, "I'm exploring the 'politics of difference'." Barbara looked puzzled and said, " 'Politics of difference'? What is that?"

David thought that a feminist analogy would be a good start. So, he explained that there are two different views of womanhood: essentialist and constructionist (Fuss, 1989). Essentialists define womanhood by emphasizing pure sexual/biological femininity, whereas the constructionist view argues that womanhood is produced socially and historically. The difference lies, David said, between the idea that "woman is born" versus "woman is made." David then mentioned that the notion of culture could be seen in the same way. The essentialist position views culture as an objective, monolithic, and fixed category that can be discovered scientifically, whereas the constructionist position views culture as produced, as implicated in politics and ideology, and as employed in various convenient ways to exercise power. In constructionist thinking, cultural differences are constructed by discourses rather than existing a priori. There is no such thing as pure empirical cultural characteristics.

Listening to David, Barbara was getting uneasy. She interrupted David, "Wait a minute. Are you saying that there are no cultural characteristics? Of course, we shouldn't be deterministic, but anyone who has taught students from different cultures knows that there are certain predictable behaviors" (Sower, 1999). "How can you teach them effectively without knowing their cultural background? Also, you use too much jargon. Are you trying to intimidate me or are you playing a word game?" David told her that she misunderstood what he meant. At this point, he thought that a further discussion would ruin their dinner, so he suggested that Barbara talk to Eiko, a Japanese Ph.D. student in applied linguistics.

Barbara felt quite confused by what David had told her. A few days later, she met Eiko at a local Starbucks. Eiko familiarized Barbara with some criticisms of the popular descriptions of the rhetorical style of written Japanese. For instance, McCagg (1996) argued that the reason native English speakers find it difficult to understand texts written by Japanese writers is not so much that the texts are organized in a culturally specific way as that English readers lack cultural and linguistic knowledge. Kubota (1997) pointed out the multiplicity of the interpretation of *ki-shoo-ten-ketsu* as well as the influence of English on the development of contemporary Japanese written language, which makes it difficult to define this style as a paradigmatic macrostructure. Eiko also introduced some critical works in the field of teaching ESL and suggested some readings such as Kubota (1999, 2001) and Pennycook (1994, 1998) which discuss how images of culture are produced by discourses that reflect, legitimate, or contest unequal relations of power between the West and non-West. She recommended other works on critical approaches to TESOL such as Auerbach (1993), Benesch (1993), Canagarajah (1993), Morgan (1998), Norton (1997), Vandrick (1994), and so on. These studies examine how issues of politics, power, and resistance manifest themselves in teaching, learning, and identity construction; and they explore how teachers and students can work together toward counter-hegemonic uses of language, understanding of culture, and formation of identities. Eiko also introduced some concepts of critical pedagogy developed by Freire (1998) explaining that the goal of critical pedagogy is to seek social justice by raising critical consciousness as to how domination and oppression are legitimated and perpetuated in various social practices including language use. She mentioned that this could be achieved through problem-posing and genuine dialogue among the participants in the classroom rather than depositing knowledge into the empty heads of the students through "banking" education.

A few months later, Barbara was still in a state of confusion, but her inherent open-mindedness and mysterious love/hate feelings toward David helped her begin to reflect on her own teaching. She realized that asking students to compare the target language and culture with their native language and culture might have reinforced a fixed and polarized way of viewing these cultures (Harklau, 1999, 2000). She recognized that, by having a frank and uncritical discussion of cultural differences, she was also endorsing stereotypical cultural images. She also came to believe that the stereotypical view of American and Asian cultures reflects the colonial dichotomy between the colonizer and the colonized in cultural politics (Kubota, 1999, 2001; Pennycook, 1998; Willinsky, 1998). She realized that although she was reassuring her students that learning English should not lead to a rejection of their native language and culture, many of them ended up thinking that English and American culture were more sophisticated and developed than their own. Also, she noticed that some Asian students, in trying to adapt to the direct way of self-expression in English, sometimes sounded too blunt because they failed to use politeness strategies, just like the Japanese students in the study by Beebe and Takahashi (1989).

In her teaching, Barbara began to ask more critical questions about students' perceptions about cultures. For example, responding to a student's comment that English communication is more direct and assertive than communication in Asian languages, Barbara would ask whether this perceived characteristic of English applies to all social situations and all people. She would also ask who has more access to this communication mode, who is expected to use it, who benefits from it, and who is oppressed by it. She encouraged students to ask the same questions about their own language. Also, she began to look for materials from newspapers, magazines, books, and videos that questioned stereotypical assumptions about American culture, such as liberty and justice for all. Through dialogues with students, she tried raising their critical consciousness of how social injustice is concealed behind the commonly accepted glorious images of culture. She encouraged students to discuss what "acquiring English" meant to them. What linguistic and cultural standard did they want or have to acquire, and why? Did the acquisition of the language and culture automatically make them equal members of the dominant English-speaking society? Why or why not? How could they advocate for themselves in English and seek racial, ethnic, cultural, and linguistic equality?

Although Barbara began to understand the complexity of culture, she was still uneasy about the notion of culture as a discursive construct. She had many questions like "Does this mean that there are no cultural differences or unique cultural characteristics?" "Should teachers not take into account any cultural differences if they are to avoid stereotyping?" and so on. To get an expert's opinion, Barbara e-mailed David, who had left town a few weeks before to take up a dissertation fellowship in Washington DC. (Actually, the separation was quite traumatic for Barbara, even more than eating sushi.) Contrary to her expectation, David didn't respond to her e-mail. Barbara was disappointed. By that time, however, she had become well aware of the postmodern instability of human relationships, so she decided not to pursue this relationship. Feeling anxious to find answers to her questions by herself, Barbara made up her mind to pursue a doctoral degree in cultural studies.

One year passed. One day, she ran into David in the Korean restaurant where they first met. After an exchange of surprised feelings and affectionate hugging, David introduced the person standing beside him to Barbara, "This is my partner, Robin."

David and Robin excused themselves because they were rushing to a movie theater, but David promised Barbara to send e-mail to her. David vaguely remembered that he owed Barbara answers to her questions, but he didn't remember what the questions were. When he e-mailed Barbara, however, she already had tentative answers to her questions. In her response, she repeated the questions and wrote,

"Well, what I've learned is that not all cultural or ethnic essentialisms are negative. Sometimes, essentialism is used strategically by the oppressed in order to contest oppression and empower themselves, as seen in the Black movement and the Chicano movement. In essentializing their own culture, these groups try to attach positive attributes to their unique heritage and use this uniqueness for creating a new identity. In fact, there is a danger in essentializing essentialism as being always problematic (Fuss, 1989; Werbner, 1997). It is necessary to recognize not only how people with a culturally subordinate status get socially and culturally positioned through essentialism, as often in the case of Asian ESL students in U.S. classrooms, but also how essentialism is strategically used by these people who want to position themselves in an oppositional way to resist the existing power hierarchy. Cultural differences indeed exist in political spheres. It's important to recognize specific positionings from which people speak as well as the 'unfinished knowledge' (to use the term from Collins, 1990) that each such situated positioning can offer (Yuval-Davis, 1997).

In teaching, a thin line always exists between recognizing and essentializing cultural differences. A common consequence of neutral, superficial recognition of cultural differences is negative essentialism (or stereotyping). In order to avoid this, it's necessary to understand that much of our conception of cultural difference is politically implicated. Politicizing cultural difference allows us to examine the motivation or purpose of recognizing cultural differences—whether to assimilate, segregate, disempower, or empower the underprivileged students.

What do you think about these ideas? How are you tackling the politics of difference these days? Keep in touch. Barbara."

REFERENCES

Atkinson, D. (1997). A critical approach to critical thinking in TESOL. *TESOL Quarterly, 31*(1), 71–94.
Atkinson, D., & Ramanathan, V. (1995). Cultures of writing: An ethnographic comparison of Ll and L2 university writing/language programs. *TESOL Quarterly, 29*(3), 539–568.
Auerbach, E. R. (1993). Reexamining English Only in the ESL classroom. *TESOL Quarterly, 27*(1), 9–32.
Beebe, L. M., & Takahashi, T. (1989). Sociolinguistic variation in face-threatening speech acts: Chastisement and disagreement. In M. R. Eisenstein (Ed.), *The dynamic interlanguage: Empirical studies in second language variation* (pp. 199–218). New York: Plenum Press.
Benesch, S. (1993). ESL, ideology, and the politics of pragmatism. *TESOL Quarterly, 27*(4), 705–716.
Canagarajah, A. S. (1993). Critical ethnography of a Sri Lankan classroom: Ambiguities in student opposition to reproduction through ESOL. *TESOL Quarterly, 27*(4), 601–626.
Carson, J. G. (1992). Becoming biliterate: First language influences. *Journal of Second Language Writing, 1*(1), 37–60.
Carson, J. G., & Nelson, G. L. (1994). Writing groups: Cross-cultural issues. *Journal of Second Language Writing, 3*(1), 17–30.
Carson, J. G., & Nelson, G. L. (1996). Chinese students' perceptions of ESL peer response group interaction. *Journal of Second Language Writing, 5*(1), 1–19.
Collins, P. H. (1990). *Black feminist thought: Knowledge, consciousness and the politics of empowerment.* Boston, MA: Unwin Hyman.
Connor, U. (1996). *Contrastive rhetoric: Cross-cultural implications of second-language writing.* New York: Cambridge University Press.
Davidson, B. W. (1998). Comments on Dwight Atkinson's "A critical approach to critical thinking in TESOL": A Case for critical thinking in the English language classroom. *TESOL Quarterly, 32*(1), 119–123.
Eggington, W. G. (1987). Written academic discourse in Korean: Implications for effective communication. In U. Connor & R. B. Kaplan (Eds.), *Writing across languages. Analysis of L2 text* (pp. 153–168). Reading, MA: Addison-Wesley.
Fox, H. (1994). *Listening to the world.* Urbana, IL: National Council of Teachers of English.
Freire, P. (1998). *Pedagogy of the oppressed (New revised 20th-anniversary edition).* New York: Continuum Press.
Fuss, D. (1989). *Essentially speaking: Feminism, nature & difference.* New York/London: Routledge.
Gieve, S. (1998). Comments on Dwight Atkinson's "A critical approach to critical thinking in TESOL": A reader reacts.... *TESOL Quarterly, 32*(1), 123–129.
Harklau, L. (1999). Representing culture in the ESL writing classroom. In E. Hinkel (Ed.), *Culture in second language teaching and learning* (pp. 109–130). Cambridge: Cambridge.

Harklau, L. (2000). From the "Good kids" to the "Worst": Representations of English language learners across educational settings. *TESOL Quarterly 34*(1), 35–67.

Hawkins, M. R. (1998). Comments on Dwight Atkinson's "A critical approach to critical thinking in TESOL": Apprenticing nonnative speakers to new discourse communities. *TESOL Quarterly, 32*(1), 129–132.

Hinds, J. (1983). Contrastive rhetoric: Japanese and English. *Text, 3*, 183–195.

Hinds, J. (1987). Reader versus writer responsibility: A new typology. In U. Connor & R. B. Kaplan (Eds.), *Writing across languages: Analysis of L2 text* (pp. 141–152). Reading, MA: Addison-Wesley.

Kaplan, R. (1966). Cultural thought patterns in inter-cultural education. *Language Learning, 16*, 1–20.

Kubota, R. (1997). A reevaluation of the uniqueness of Japanese written discourse: Implications to contrastive rhetoric. *Written Communication, 14*(4), 460–480.

Kubota, R. (1999). Japanese culture constructed by discourses: Implications for applied linguistic research and English language teaching. *TESOL Quarterly, 33*(1), 9–35.

Kubota, R. (2001). Discursive construction of the images of U.S. classrooms. *TESOL Quarterly, 35*(1), 9–38.

Matalene, C. (1985). Contrastive rhetoric: An American writing teacher in China. *College English, 47*(8), 789–808.

McCagg, P. (1996). If you can lead a horse to water, you don't have to make it drink: Some comments on reader and writer responsibilities. *Multilingua, 15*(3), 239–256.

Morgan, B. (1998). *The ESL classroom. Teaching, critical practice, and community development.* Toronto: University of Toronto Press.

Nelson, G. L., & Carson, J. G. (1998). ESL students' perceptions of effectiveness in peer response groups. *Journal of Second Language Writing, 7*(2), 113–131.

Norton, B. (1997). Language, identity, and the ownership of English. *TESOL Quarterly, 31*(3), 409–429.

Pennycook, A. (1994). *The cultural politics of English as an international language.* New York: Longman.

Pennycook, A. (1998). *English and the discourses of colonialism.* New York/London: Routledge.

Raimes, A., & Zamel, V. (1997). Response to Ramanathan and Kaplan. *Journal of Second Language Writing, 6*(1), 79–81.

Ramanathan, V., & Atkinson, D. (1999). Individualism, academic writing, and ESL writers. *Journal of Second Language Writing, 8*(1), 45–75.

Ramanathan, V., & Kaplan, R. B. (1996). Audience and voice in current Ll composition texts: Some implications for ESL student writers. *Journal of Second Language Writing, 5*(1), 21–34.

Reid, J. (1989). English as second language composition in higher education: The expectations of the academic audience. In D. M. Johnson & D. H. Roen (Eds.), *Richness in writing: Empowering ESL students* (pp. 220–234). New York & London: Longman.

Rubin, D. L., Goodrum, R., & Hall, B. (1990). Orality, oral-based culture, and the academic writing of ESL learners. *Issues in Applied Linguistics, 1*(1), 56–76.

Shen, F. (1989). The classroom and the wider culture: Identity as a key to learning English composition. *College Composition and Communication, 40*(4), 459–466.

Sower, C. (1999). Comments on Ryuko Kubota's "Japanese culture constructed by discourses: Implications for applied linguistics research and ELT" Postmodern applied linguistics: Problems and contradictions. *TESOL Quarterly, 33*(4), 736–745.

Spack, R. (1997). The rhetorical construction of multilingual students. *TESOL Quarterly, 31*(4), 765–774.

Susser, B. (1998). EFL's othering of Japan: Orientalism in English language teaching. *JALT Journal, 20*(1), 49–82.

Vandrick, S. (1994). Feminist pedagogy and ESL. *College ESL, 4*(2), 69–92.

Werbner, P. (1997). Essentialising essentialism, essentialising silence: Ambivalence and multiplicity in the constructions of racism and ethnicity. In P. Werbner & T. Modood (Eds.), *Debating cultural hybridity. Multi-cultural identities and the politics of anti-racism* (pp. 226–254). London & New Jersey: Zed Books.

Willinsky, J. (1998). *Learning to divide the world: Education at empire's end.* Minneapolis, MN: University of Minnesota Press.

Yuval-Davis, N. (1997). Ethnicity, gender relations and multiculturalism. In R. Werbner & T. Modood (Eds.), *Debating cultural hybridity. Multi-cultural identities and the politics of anti-racism* (pp. 193–208). London & New Jersey: Zed Books.

Zamel, V. (1997). Toward a model of transculturation. *TESOL Quarterly, 31*(2), 341–352.

QUESTIONS TO THINK ABOUT

1. Using the cultural studies terminology that Kubota introduces in her article, explain the various stages that Barbara goes through in her teaching. Which of these stages seems closest to where you are in your thinking and/or teaching? What positive aspects do you find in each of the stages? What problems do you find in each of the stages?

2. Contrast essentialism and constructionism. Reread the way that Kubota applies these terms to "womanhood." Describe an issue that faces society today using essentialist and constructionist terms; think of, for example, genderism, racism, ethnocentrism, intolerance toward a religious belief, homophobia, or another issue about which you have some awareness. How does looking at the issue from these two perspectives affect your understanding of the issue you have chosen? What problems do you find in each looking at the issue using these terms?

3. What is the difference between cultural essentialism and stereotyping? What does Kubota mean when she writes that "the stereotypical view of American and Asian cultures reflects the colonial dichotomy between the colonizer and the colonized in cultural politics"? From another perspective, how may cultural essentialism be used as a strategic tool?

4. *Extending your understanding*: Imagine that you are the teacher in a situation such as the one Barbara faces in the beginning of the article. How would you work with the students in the class Barbara describes? What particular approaches might work best? What kinds of assignments might you require of your students?

TERMS TO DEFINE

Define the following words and phrases as they are presented within the context of the reading. Comment on your understanding of the significance of each one.

Constructionism
Cultural essentialism
Determinism
Paradigmatic macrostructure
Construction by discourse versus a priori existence

Sociolinguistics and Power

Alastair Pennycook
University of Technology, Sydney

Of course, some versions of language may disavow any connection to power: Language is language, and power is power, and ne'er the twain shall meet. But whatever view of language supports such a position, it is evidently not one that is concerned with language use, for even conservative views on language tend to draw connections between language and power. Indeed the main title of [John] Honey's (1997) conservative defense of standard English is *Language Is Power*. Such a title already points toward the arguments that underlie such a position: Particular forms of language (standard English) can convey social and economic power (language *is* power rather than [Norman] Fairclough's [1989] language *and* power). It is worth looking very briefly at this position not only because it has had wide coverage at least within Britain and enjoys fairly considerable support in popular media (Cameron, 1995) but also because it is a position against which much liberal academic work reacts.

Honey's (1983, 1997) arguments about standard English have been massively critiqued elsewhere (Bex & Watts, 1999): They are contradictory; they rest on the "astonishing proposition, which seems to be the basis of all Honey's thinking on the subject" that standard English is "the English he himself uses" (Harris, 1997, p. 19); they repeat old myths about "speaking only a preliterate language with a tiny vocabulary" (Honey, 1997, p. 21); and they slide all too easily into a view of intellectual deficit as a result of speaking in a certain way when he asks:

> whether some languages (or, to some extent, some varieties of one language) might be less well equipped as vehicles of certain kinds of intellectual activity than others, with consequent intellectual disadvantage to those people who can handle effectively that one language or dialect, and not any other, less limiting form. (Honey, 1983, p. 9)

Nevertheless, it is worth looking briefly at part of his argument, which can be summed up through the following example:

Reprinted with permission from *Critical linguistics: A critical introduction*, by A. Pennybrook. © 2001 by Lawrence Erlbaum Associates, Inc.

> I believe that one of the most powerful factors contributing to the disadvantage of America's underclass—Blacks and other ethnic groups, and lower-class whites—is in reality capable of being changed: I refer to their ability to handle standard English. A properly funded and effective programme designed to add standard English to their repertoire of speaking and writing skills has the potential to transform the educational and occupational opportunities of members [of] these groups. (Honey, 1997, p. 240)

Putting aside for a moment the many inaccuracies in Honey's position and his claims that speakers of nonstandard forms of English suffer both communicative and cognitive disadvantage, the main point worth considering here is whether access to standard English is indeed as "empowering" as is claimed. The problem here is that first Honey presents us with an undifferentiated Other—people of different class, regional, and ethnic backgrounds who speak in different ways—and an unexamined notion of an inherently powerful standard version of the language, the learning of which can act as a panacea for all sorts of other social ills—poverty, racism, class bigotry, and so on. And second, this is coupled with a sociological naiveté that learning a standard version of the language will bring about social and economic advantage. Honey's vision boils down to one in which difference will be effaced if everyone speaks like him. As Wiley and Lukes (1996) point out, following Wiggins (1976), "for all too many African Americans, the fact that mastery of the language does not ensure economic mobility or political access makes manifest the fallacy of standard English as the language of equal opportunity" (p. 530). The point here, of course, is not that learning standardized forms of English should be denied to students but rather that we need to understand in much greater depth how forms of language may be related to forms of power. On the one hand, the vision that access to standard forms will somehow be automatically empowering is inadequate; on the other hand, it is important not to fall into the trap of suggesting that power always lies outside language and that it is only with social change that different language forms may come to take on different roles.

LIBERAL SOCIOLINGUISTICS

One of Honey's main points of attack is against one of the central orthodoxies of (socio)linguistics, that all varieties of language are "equal." As he suggests:

> To deny children the opportunity to learn to handle standard English, because of pseudo-scientific judgements about all varieties of language being "equal," is to set limits *in advance* to their ability to express themselves effectively outside their immediate subculture, and to slam the door on any real opportunity for social mobility. (Honey, 1983, p. 24–25)

Honey's argument is problematic both because the pedagogical response to this stance has not been to deny access to standard English but to acknowledge alternatives and because once again he makes unwarranted claims about communication, subcultures, and social mobility. And yet, his critique resonates with more critical approaches to the question. As Giroux (1983) explains:

> Questions about the value of standard English as well as about the role of working-class culture in education become meaningful only if it is remembered that the skills, knowledge, and language practices that roughly characterize different classes and social formations are forged within social relations marked by the unequal distribution of power. Subordinate cultures are situated and recreated within relations of domination and resistance, and they bear the marks of both. To argue that working-class language practices are just as rule-governed as standard English usage and practice may be true, but to suggest at the same time that *all* cultures are equal is to forget that subordinate groups are often denied access to the power, knowledge, and resources that allow them to lead self-determined existences. (p. 229)

The problem here, then, is that while a conservative critique decries the liberal egalitarianism of (socio)linguistics, a more critical stance also finds fault with the liberal politics that wishes for equality where there is none. The liberal structuralism underlying the sociolinguistic argument—that we should deal with systems according to their own logics and eschew external evaluative positions—has been a highly significant one in promoting an antielitist stance on difference. It is worth looking in slightly greater depth at the problems with this liberal sociolinguistic vision of language and power.

It is important to acknowledge here that the work of sociolinguists such as William Labov was aimed directly to counter the sort of linguistic deficit arguments that Honey is still promoting (indeed, Labov is one of Honey's many antagonists). Labov took aim at what he called "verbal deprivation theorists," those who in the 1960s were arguing that nonstandard, particularly Black American, speech was illogical and malformed and that this showed an inability to think logically. For some (such as Arthur Jensen), this represented evidence of "the genetic inferiority of Negroes" (Labov, 1970, p. 181), while for others such verbal deprivation could be overcome through intervention programs such as Operation Head Start. Labov's (1970) argument was a crucial one in that he attempted to show how Black English vernacular (BEV) had its own rules and logic (and also that standard English has its own shortcomings). "Linguists," he suggested, "are in an excellent position to demonstrate the fallacies of the verbal deprivation theory. All linguists agree that nonstandard dialects are highly structured systems" (p. 184).

Although such arguments against the often blatant racism of theories that have connected nonstandard speech with cognitive difference—a position that reemerged all too quickly with the ebonics debates in the United States (Perry & Delpit, 1998)—have been extremely important, they have also led to shortcomings to the extent that they have been concerned principally with critiquing a conservative position and constructing a form of liberal structuralism in opposition. A key aspect, then, of the attempt to relate power to language lies in how we understand relations between language and society. The issue here is not only to relate language to broader social concerns but also to do so within a critical model of society. This is one of the major concerns that a domain of work such as (critical) applied linguistics faces: Any model of a relation between language and society will only be as good as one's understanding of society. Unfortunately, the model of society in sociolinguistics has tended to remain something of an unexamined given. Sociolinguists, as Cameron (1995) points out, "have been content to work with simple, commonsensical ideas about the social" (p. 15).

There are four principal concerns worth discussing in this context:

- The need for a critical social theory capable of dealing with the maintenance of inequality;
- The need for an approach to language that goes beyond description and moves toward critique;
- The need to understand the shortcomings of a model that emphasizes appropriacy;
- The need to view language as productive as well as reflective of social relations.

Williams (1992) critiques the sociolinguistic structural functionalist view of society in which rational actors follow social norms for the general good of society and their own social welfare. The understanding of society is therefore a consensual one in which we all agree to act together for a mutual good. Society is described in limited terms (e.g., unexamined notions of social class) with the focus ultimately being on the individual and her or his linguistic behavior, rather than the complex workings of language amid conflictual social contexts:

> Despite employing concepts such as social class, ethnicity or gender, which are explicitly related to domination and subordination, as independent variables within the empirical framework, the conflict which is implicit in such dimensions is missing as a consequence of the structural functionalist orientation. The emphasis on nonnative consensus as the guiding force of

individual speech results in the legitimisation of standard forms and the parallel marginalisa-
tion of non-standard forms. (p. 93)

Although as Giddens (1982) remarks, this consensual versus conflictual dichotomy in
sociology is not always helpful, it is nevertheless clear that a critical sociolinguistics needs
some model other than a bland consensual one in which all members of a society happily
work together for collective gain. The liberal structuralism of sociolinguistics may have
distanced itself from an elitist view of natural social hierarchies, but it still has little to say
about how inequality is created, sustained, or overturned.

From a critical standpoint, furthermore, the sociolinguistic tendency to engage merely
in description is problematic. As Cameron (1995) observes, the general tenet of linguistics
and sociolinguistics that it is involved in description rather than prescription is untenable
since "*both* prescriptivism *and* anti-prescriptivism invoke certain norms and circulate particular notions about how language ought to work." Thus, "'description' and 'prescription'
turn out to be aspects of a single (and normative) activity: a struggle to control language
by defining its nature" (p. 8). According to Harris (1981), the view of language sustained
by linguistics is in many ways "no less rigid than the authoritarian recommendations of
the old-fashioned grammarian pedagogue" (p. 46). Similarly, Parakrama (1995) points out
that so-called descriptive work always focuses on certain forms of language at the expense
of others. "This unequal emphasis," he goes on, "is not so much the fault of individual
descriptivists as a problematic of description itself, which can never be a neutral activity.
In other words, description is always a weak form of prescription" (p. 3). Thus, the claim
that linguistic or sociolinguistic descriptions of language somehow are objective or value
neutral goes against any more complex understanding of the politics of knowledge.

The insistence on description rather than a more sustained critique of the conditions
one is describing raises important questions about the politics of mainstream sociolinguistics. Jacob Mey (1985) has made this point forcefully in his argument that for "traditional
sociolinguistics, the present organization of society's material production is the only natural
one; so natural, in fact, that traditional sociolinguists, in their description of the language
people use, totally disregard the existence of social classes" (p. 342). The notion of class
that is employed in sociolinguistics (and against which linguistic phenomena are then correlated) tends "to refer to what might better be referred to as 'social strata'—groupings of
people who are similar to one another in occupation, education, or other standard sociological variables" (Fairclough, 1989, p. 8). A more critical view understands social class as
bound up with inequality, struggle, and opposition. Thus, Mey (1985) suggests, by avoiding
questions of social inequality in class terms and instead correlating language variation with
superficial measures of social stratification, traditional sociolinguistics fails to "establish a
connection between people's place in the societal hierarchy, and the linguistic and other
kinds of oppression that they are subjected to at different levels" (p. 342).

Third, the framing of debates between either the conservative emphasis on standards
or a more liberal model of diversity, in conjunction with a consensual view of society, leads
to a problematic emphasis on "appropriacy." This last argument is the liberal compromise
that suggests that we need to teach the appropriate forms at the appropriate times. But
as Ivanič (1990) suggests, there are problems with this notion: "'Appropriacy' sounds
more liberal and flexible than 'accuracy,' but I believe it is just as much of a straightjacket
for the bilingual trying to add English to her repertoire" (p. 124). The problem here,
according to Ivanič, is that "the dominant conventions of appropriacy are treated as natural
and necessary" (p. 125). Thus, although the unquestioned concept of accuracy according
to a "standard" version of the language can be criticized for its exclusionary linguistic
stance, an emphasis on appropriacy may be equally criticized for its discussion of social
appropriacy in normative terms. By contrast, "a critical view of language emphasizes the
fact that prestigious social groups have established these conventions: they are not 'natural'
or necessarily the way they are" (p. 126).

Fairclough (1992) develops this critique further, arguing first that "models of language variation based upon the concept of appropriateness project a misleading and unsustainable image of sociolinguistic practice and how sociolinguistic orders are structured" (p. 47). He suggests that the appropriateness version of language variation, with its presuppositions that the distinction between appropriate and inappropriate is clear-cut, that such appropriacy is the same for all members of a community, and that there is a clear match between language variants and contexts of use, simply does not hold up under critical scrutiny. In many contexts—Fairclough provides the example of a professional woman talking to a senior male colleague—it is far less obvious what forms will be seen by the participants as appropriate. Secondly, Fairclough argues that the notion of appropriacy needs to be understood ideologically, that is in terms of the claims made to represent a social reality. Thus, he suggests, appropriateness models "derive from a confusion between sociolinguistic realities and political projects in the domain of language" (p. 48). The view that there is a static social order, as we saw in Williams' critique of sociolinguistics, needs to be seen as a very particular political view of language and society, "the political objective of the dominant, 'hegemonic,' sections of a society in the domain of language as in other domains" rather than "sociolinguistic reality" (Fairclough, 1992, p. 48).

The sociolinguistic model of appropriacy underlies the widely promoted applied linguistic concept of sociolinguistic competence as an aspect of communicative competence (Canale & Swain, 1980). The resultant problem is that this view of communication has taken on board a notion of a static society with fixed social roles and hierarchies that are reflected linguistically, or as Fairclough (1992) puts it, "imaginary representations of sociolinguistic reality which correspond to the perspective and partisan interests of one section of society or one section of a particular social institution—its dominant section" (p. 48). Peirce (1989) has argued that instead of adopting such models of social appropriacy, we need to consider language use in terms of political desirability, and thus instead of working with a model of communicative competence based on a static and unquestioned version of social order, we need to consider how our notion of communicative competence might also have a more transformative social agenda.

Finally, for much of sociolinguistics, both society and language remain rather static entities. From this point of view, language merely *reflects* society. As Williams (1992) explains, this leads to the tendency to treat the social as some sort of "independent variable," a static, given series of social relations, while language is treated as the "dependent variable," a static reflection of social relations (p. 39). This positivistic and behaviourist view of society, in which a stimulus (independent variable) produces a response (dependent variable), is, to say the least, a very limited view of the dynamics of social relations. Cameron (1990, 1995) similarly criticizes sociolinguistic research for its static labeling and the belief that "people's use of linguistic variables can be correlated with their demographic characteristics: their belonging to particular classes, races, genders, generations, local communities" (Cameron, 1995, p. 15). Thus, whether the view is one in which language use simply reflects society or one that allows for slightly more agency in this relation (so that language users actively "mark" their social identity), "it is implicitly assumed that the relevant categories and identities exist prior to language, and are simply 'marked' or 'reflected' when people come to use it" (Cameron, 1995, p. 15).

An alternative view, as Cameron suggests, sees language itself as *part of* the social and indeed an active element in its construction. As Cameron explains, "any encounter with recent social and critical theory" will cast doubt on a view that language reflects society:

The categories sociolinguistics treats as fixed givens, such as "class," "gender" and even "identity," are treated in critical approaches as relatively unstable constructs which are therefore in need of explanation themselves. Furthermore, in critical theory language is treated as part of the explanation. Whereas sociolinguistics would say that the way I use language reflects or marks my identity as a particular kind of social subject . . . the critical account suggests language is one of the things that constitutes my identity as a particular kind of subject. Sociolinguistics says that how you act depends on who you are; critical theory says that who you are (and are taken to be) depends on how you act. (1995, pp. 15–16)

This moves us toward the crucial insight that using, speaking, learning, teaching language is a form of social and cultural action; it is about producing and not just reflecting realities.

The overriding problem here, then, is that in debates around language, social class, and variety, there has been little critical understanding of how such questions are linked to issues of power. Thus, in debates on standard language, grammar and so on, the conservative arguments for traditional grammar and standard English (which, as Cameron [1995] argues, serve as metaphors for greater social order, discipline, and authority) are countered only by a sociolinguistic liberalism. The same can be said of other domains of sociolinguistic interest such as language in the workplace and professional settings. Once again, while the principal goal of analyses of language in legal settings, doctor–patient in-teractions, or job interviews is usually to arrive at descriptive frameworks for generic forms of interaction, a second ostensible goal is to show how power may operate within such settings. Yet to the extent that such work operates with a model whereby personal and in-stitutional power rests in the hands of doctors, lawyers, and interviewers and is reflected in language, it fails to illuminate sociologically how language operates in more complex ways.

In their study of language, discrimination, and disadvantage in British workplaces, by contrast, Roberts, Davies, and Jupp (1992) argue for an understanding of language that includes not just the local context but also

an understanding of the wider context in which ethnic-minority workers live and work, an understanding of their experiences of racism and disadvantage and of the cultural knowledge which is part of their first language, and an understanding of how language in interaction creates a context which is particular to that interaction but which also reflects and helps to form social spheres and institutions. (p. 6)

Here we can see a more productive role for language, a more complex interweaving of social levels that goes beyond a simple micro/macro relation, and a diversity of forms of power operating through discrimination, social disadvantage, language, and cultural difference.

Similar interwoven layers of complexity emerge, for example, in Tara Goldstein's (1996) study of how social relations, language choice (Portuguese or English), and gender inter-act on the shop floor, or Crawford's (1999) study of communication in Cape Town (RSA) health services, where the relationship between patients, nurses, and doctors is interwo-ven with issues of power in language, culture, translation, race, and gender. But while some of this work on language in medical encounters, legal settings, and other workplaces attempts to relate the micro interactions of a conversation to complex institutional and social relations, far too much remains content with simplistic labels of power as simply reflected in the language of powerful individuals. Thus, although much of liberal struc-turalist sociolinguistics apparently has fairly emancipatory goals, it is frequently unable to do more than discuss differences and decry deficits, without being able to take on the re-lation between the two more critically. As Williams (1992) describes the problem, there is "evidence of an overriding desire to support the underdog, accompanied by a sociological perspective which reflects the power of the dominant" (p. 226).

REFERENCES

Bex, T., & Watts, R. J. (Eds.). (1999). *Standard English: The widening debate.* London: Routledge.
Cameron, D. (1990). Demythologizing sociolinguistics: Why language does not reflect society. In J. Joseph & T. Taylor (Eds.), *Ideologies of language* (pp. 79–96). London: Routledge.

Cameron, D. (1995). *Verbal hygiene.* London: Routledge.

Canale, M., & Swain, M. (1980). Theoretical bases of communicative approaches to second language teaching and testing. *Applied Linguistics, 1*(1), 1–47.

Crawford, A. (1999). "We can't all understand the whites' language": An analysis of monolingual health services in a multilingual society. *International Journal of the Sociology of Language, 136,* 27–45.

Fairclough, N. (1989). *Language and power.* London: Longman.

Fairclough, N. (1992). The appropriacy of "appropriateness." In N. Fairclough (Ed.), *Critical language awareness* (pp. 33–56). London: Longman.

Giddens, A. (1982). *Sociology: A brief but critical introduction.* London: Macmillan.

Giroux, H. (1983). *Theory and resistance in education: A pedagogy for the opposition.* South Hadley, MA: Bergin & Garvey.

Goldstein, T. (1996). *Two languages at work: Bilingual life on the production floor.* Berlin: Mouton de Gruyter.

Harris, R. (1981). *The language myth.* London: Duckworth.

Harris, R. (1997). Fighting the many enemies. A review of *Oxford English dictionary additions series volume three* and J. Honey *Language is power: The story of standard English and its enemies. The Times Higher 1296 September 5 1997,* 19.

Honey, J. (1983). *The language trap: Race, class and the "standard English" issue in British schools.* Kenton, UK: National Council for Educational Standards.

Honey, J. (1997). *Language is power: The story of standard English and its enemies.* London: Faber and Faber.

Ivanič, R. (1990). Critical language awareness in action. In R. Carter (Ed.), *Knowledge about language and the curriculum: The LINC Reader* (pp. 122–132). London: Hodder & Stroughton.

Labov, W. (1970). The logic of nonstandard English. In F. Williams (Ed.), *Language and poverty: Perspectives on a theme* (pp. 153–189). Chicago: Markham.

Mey, J. (1985). *Whose language? A study in linguistic pragmatics.* Amsterdam: John Benjamins.

Parakrama, A. (1995). *De-hegemonizing language standards.* New York: Macmillan.

Peirce, B. (1989). Toward a pedagogy of possibility in the teaching of English internationally. *TESOL Quarterly, 23,* 401–420.

Perry, T., & Delpit, L. (Eds.). (1998). *The real ebonics debate: Power, language, and the education of African-American children.* Boston, MA: Beacon Press.

Roberts, C., Davies, E., & Jupp, T. (1992). *Language and discrimination: A study of communication in multi-ethnic workplaces.* London: Longman.

Wiggins, M. E. (1976). The cognitive deficit difference controversy: A Black sociopolitical perspective. In D. Harrison & T. Trabasso (Eds.), *Black English: A seminar* (pp. 241–254). Hillsdale, NJ: Lawrence Erlbaum Associates.

Wiley, T., & Lukes, M. (1996). English-only and standard English ideologies in the U.S. *TESOL Quarterly, 30*(3), 511–536.

Williams, G. (1992). *Sociolinguistics: A sociological critique.* London: Routledge.

QUESTIONS TO THINK ABOUT

1. In linguistic terms, what is the difference between description and prescription? According to Pennycook, how is critique or a critical approach different from a descriptive or a prescriptive approach? What does Pennycook mean by the following statements: "'Description' and 'prescription' turn out to be aspects of a single (and normative) activity: a struggle to control language by defining its nature"; and "Description is always a weak form of prescription?" What differences does he make between these approaches and the critical approach toward language study?

2. What does Pennycook mean when he writes "the crucial insight [is] that using, speaking, learning, teaching language is a form of social and cultural action; it is about producing and not just reflecting realities." Contrast Pennycook's perspective to that of other writers quoted in the article.

3. Pennycook states: "Any model of a relation between language and society will only be as good as one's understanding of society." Do you agree with this idea? Why or why not? Why does Pennycook object to having "the focus ultimately [on] the individual and his or her linguistic behavior, rather than the complex workings of language amid conflictual social contexts"?

4. *Extending your understanding:* Pennycook questions "whether access to standard English is indeed as 'empowering' as is claimed." He continues, "On the one hand, the vision that access to standard forms will somehow be automatically empowering is inadequate; on the other hand, it is important not to fall into the trap of suggesting that power always lies outside language and that it is only with social change that different language forms may come to take on different roles." Think about your own response to this question. Is your opinion about this as a teacher different from your opinion about this as a general member of society? How do you think other writers in this unit would respond to the point of view Pennycook presents?

TERMS TO DEFINE

Define the following words and phrases as they are presented within the context of the reading. Comment on your understanding of the significance of each one.

Consensual versus conflictual dichotomy in sociology
Verbal deprivation theorists
Sociolinguistic structural functionalism
Appropriacy
Hegemonic

Unit I: Questions, Activities, and Resources

EXTENDING YOUR UNDERSTANDING AND MAKING CONNECTIONS

1a. Gleitman and Kuhl both examine acquisition of a first language. Describe each of their methodologies. Summarize each of their findings. In what ways are their methodologies and findings similar and in what ways are they different? What seems to be the most important concepts that unite their research?

1b. Kuhl and Gass each examine acquisition of a second language. In what ways are their findings similar and in what ways are they different? For example, think about the critical age hypothesis, bilingualism, and pronunciation.

2. Novakovich, Lvovich, and Alexander write personally about the experience of learning a second language—how it affects one's identity, one's children, one's ability to write, and one's relationship with the first language. What common threads do you find in the three essays? What connections can you make among these three essays and Zentella's discussion of bilingualism? What connections can you make between these essays and Gass's theory of second language acquisition? What benefit is to be gained from reading personal narratives along with theory?

3. Gilyard and Pennycook both write about the politics of language and more specifically about issues related to African American Vernacular English (AAVE). What ideas do they share in common? In relation to what issues might they disagree? Imagine a conversation between the two of them: What would they have to say to each other?

4. Kubota concludes her essay in the following way:

> In teaching, a thin line always exists between recognizing and essentializing cultural differences. A common consequence of neutral, superficial recognition of cultural differences is negative essentialism (or stereotyping). In order to avoid this, it's

123

necessary to understand that much of our conception of cultural difference is politically implicated. Politicizing cultural difference allows us to examine the motivation or purpose of recognizing cultural differences—whether to assimilate, segregate, disempower, or empower the underprivileged students.

How does one negotiate the "thin line" to which Kubota refers? Do any other writers in this unit address issues of essentializing and stereotyping? If so, how do they approach these issues?

APPLICATIONS FOR TEACHING

1. After reading Kuhl and Gleitman, you may find it interesting to do a small study of infant acquisition of language yourself. (It is easier to do this with a family member or friend.) Once they agree to do this, observe a baby under 2 years of age with an adult or older child in a natural environment. If possible, use a tape recorder or take careful notes of the interactions between the baby and adult. Try to observe for at least one or two 20-minute periods. Transcribe your tape or notes and analyze what happened in relation to language development. Did the baby make sounds? How did the adult respond? Who initiated the conversation? Analyze and describe how your findings correspond to what Kuhl and Gleitman describe in their essays?

2. Think about the ways in which one's knowledge of one's first language may be helpful in learning a second language. How might that knowledge hinder one's SLA? Discuss how a teacher in a class with students with different language backgrounds *might* use the students' abilities in their first languages to help them learn the TL.

3. Gass, Kubota, Gilyard, and Zentella all discuss aspects of teaching. Think about the situation that Kubota poses—a new teacher in a classroom of students with diverse linguistic and ethnic backgrounds. Which of these writers seems closest to your way of thinking about teaching? Why? Choose one specific aspect of each of their articles and apply it to your own pedagogy of teaching in relation to teaching one specific lesson.

4. *Lesson Plan:* Create a lesson plan for a second language class keeping in mind the second language acquisition (SLA) theories and practices you have read about in the articles, in this unit. Think about the different pedagogical approaches that promote learning and those that promote acquisition. Remember that the process of SLA is somewhat different for children and adults, so before you plan your lesson, decide on the age of your students—young children, teens, adults, etc. What aspect of language do you want to teach? What is the overall objective of your lesson? Here are some questions to think about as you conceive the lesson: What is the setting of your class— in a school or an out-of-school program? What is the language level of your students in the target language–beginning, intermediate, or advanced? Are they able to speak, read, and/or write in the new language? What other language/s do they know? What are their abilities in those languages? Why are they taking your class? Then decide on the teaching practices you will use to help this group to increase its understanding about a particular aspect of the target language. In your lesson plan, describe in detail your pedagogical plan including the basic steps of the lesson, the overall curriculum, and the specific methodology that you think would be effective in your imagined teaching and learning environment. Be prepared to present and discuss your lesson plan in class.

PRINT AND WEB RESOURCES

Print Resources

de Courtivron, I. (Ed.). (2003). *Lives in translation: Bilingual writers on identity and creativity.* NY: Palgrave.

Gass, S. M., & Selinker, L. (2001). *Second language acquisition.* Mahwah, NJ: Lawrence Erlbaum Associates.

Gilyard, K. (1991). *Voices of the self: A study of language competence.* Detroit: Wayne State University Press.

Kövecses, Z. (2000). *American English: An introduction.* Ontario, Canada: Broadview Press.

Lemberger, N. (1997). *Bilingual education: Teachers' narratives.* Mahwah, NJ: Lawrence Erlbaum Associates.

Li, X. M. (1996). *'Good writing' in cross-cultural context.* Albany: State University of New York Press.

Maurais, J., & Morris, A. M. (2003). *Languages in a globalizing world.* Cambridge: Cambridge University Press.

Pennycook, A. (1998). *English and the discourses of colonialism.* London: Routledge.

Rickford, J. R., & Rickford, R. J. (2000). *Spoken soul: The story of black English.* NY: John Wiley

Web Resources

http://www.aaal.org
(American Association for Applied Linguistics)

http://www.cal.org
(Center for Applied Linguistics)

http://www.carla.umn.edu
(Center for Advanced Research on Language Acquisition)

http://eric.ed.gov
(Educational Resource Information Center)

http://www.lsadc.org
(Linguistic Society of America)

http://www.tesol.org
(Teachers of English to Speakers of Other Languages)

HOW DOES LANGUAGE CHANGE?

Introduction to Unit II:
The History of English and Language Change

Deborah M. Seymour
Laureate Education, Inc.

HOW DO LANGUAGES CHANGE?

As C. M. Millward reminds us, to begin to respond to this question, we need to review some linguistic vocabulary as it pertains to language and linguistic change. Two critical things to remember about languages are that they are all both *conventional* and *arbitrary*. They are conventional in that communication fails if one violates the conventions of the language—one cannot just call a sock a "hanger" and expect people to know what they are talking about. Yet languages are arbitrary in that there is no inherent relationship between the word "sock" and its meaning—or, for that matter, the word "hanger" and its meaning. These words evolved over time to designate the items we put on our feet and the items on which we hang our clothes, respectively—but the things we call socks could just as easily have come to be called "hangers"; and the things we call hangers could just as easily have come to be called "socks."

Moreover, languages are *redundant*. The same information can be signaled in more than one way within a language. Take, for example, the sentence "He is a man" in Present Day English. Singular number is signaled in four ways in this sentence: "he" is singular, "is" is singular, "a" is singular, and "man" is singular. How is this notion of redundancy relevant to language change? Well, if over time one of these word forms changed so as to no longer signal singularity, singularity would still be clearly signaled by the other words in the sentence. The same would be true of the feature of plurality in the sentence "They are men," or the feature of being feminine in "She is a woman." In "They are men," all the words are plural in number; in "She is a woman" both "she" and "woman" are feminine in gender. (See Parry for similar cases, in this volume.)

Importantly, all languages change over time. Language is not *static*; it is *dynamic*. It doesn't "run in place;" it constantly changes as the years go by. There may be *language-external* pressures for change, such as sociological, economic, and political factors that cause a language to change; and there may be *language-internal* pressures for change, such as the misunderstandings caused by lexical ambiguity or the confusion caused by "exceptions to the rule." As the scope of this book is restricted to the study of the English language, however, what we are most interested in for the purposes of this unit are the issues of (1) the history of how the English language has evolved, (2) what has caused English to change, and (3) in what ways English has changed. Thus, we begin by looking briefly at the history of how English became the language it is today.

LANGUAGE FAMILIES AND THE ENGLISH LANGUAGE

If you have ever noticed distinct similarities between English and other languages, it might be because they are descended from the same mother language as English—and belong to the same *language family*, as *cognate* languages. The major language families of the world include the one to which English belongs, *Indo-European*. There are a number of other language families, such as the Finno-Ugric family, which includes Finnish, Hungarian, Lapp, and Estonian; the Hamito-Semitic family, which includes Hebrew, Arabic, and other Semitic and North African languages; as well as many other groupings, which include those that linguists have variously classified as the Niger-Congo, Khoisan, Sino-Tibetan, Tai, Mon-Khmer, and Austronesian families. The Indo-European grouping includes many of the languages spoken in Europe and parts of Asia and Africa over the years. These languages are thought to have descended from a common language, Proto-Indo-European, that might have been spoken as early as 5000 BC and, most likely, as late as 3000 BC. Sometime after 3000 BC, great migrations of the Indo-European speakers throughout Europe and Asia began.

Linguists today recognize ten major members of the Indo-European family, some of which are now moribund or even extinct. English descends from the Proto-Germanic branch of the Indo-European language family tree, which also gave rise to the German, Dutch, Swedish, Danish, Icelandic, Norwegian, Frisian, Swiss, Flemish, and Yiddish dialects of the present day. (See Green, in this volume.)

But how did English become the language it is in the present day? In the middle of the 5th century, several Germanic tribes began a series of invasions of the British Isles, which at the time were inhabited primarily by Celtic speakers—Celtic being a different branch than German of the Indo-European language tree. The invading tribes are historically believed to have been the Angles, Saxons, and Jutes. (There were probably Frisians among the invaders, as well.) The Celts called the invaders Saxons, but on the European continent they were always called the Angles, and their common language was English. After about a century of these invasions, the Germanic tribes had pretty well established themselves in Britain and, thus, the beginnings of the Old English language in Britain were introduced. (See Trask, in this volume.)

A BRIEF HISTORY OF ENGLISH

We may divide the history of English into four stages: Anglo-Saxon or Old English (446–1066), Middle English (1066–1500), Early Modern English (1500–1700), and Present Day English (1700–present). We also may view these stages through literary texts written during these times: *Beowulf* (8th century); the *Canterbury Tales* (Geoffrey Chaucer, 1387); Shakespeare's works (William Shakespeare, 1564–1616) and the *King James Bible* (1611); the Declaration of Independence of the United States (1776), the

Gettysburg Address (1863), *Things Fall Apart* (Chinua Achebe, 1959), and *Beloved* (Toni Morrison, 1987).

The changes that have taken place in English in these four stages are morphological, syntactic, semantic, lexical, and phonological. The grammar of Anglo-Saxon or Old English is so different from that of Present Day English that today, Old English is studied as a foreign language. One way in which it is different from Present Day English is in its many inflectional suffixes. Old English employed inflectional suffixes to indicate tense, person (first, second, third), gender, number, and case. Case endings indicated the subject, object of the verb, object of the preposition, possession, etc. Because of the system of inflections, word order was not important because the inflections indicated the grammatical function of each word in a sentence. The vocabulary was largely Germanic with some influence from Latin and Old Norse. Words, and particularly vowels, were pronounced differently from their pronunciations in Present Day English. In addition, because there was no system of standardization, words were not only pronounced but also spelled differently all throughout England. There are many stories of speakers of English who traveled from one district in England to another and were unable to be understood by the members of that community. Old English used several letters that we no longer use in English today; for example, þ, the *thorn*, which was the sound of "th" in "then," ð, *eth*, for "th" in "with," and æ, the *aesh*, which combined the "a" and "e" vowel sound in words such as "sat."

Middle English started to develop after the Norman Conquest in 1066, when England began to be ruled by the French, who brought their language with them and used it in the courts, the church, and the government. Thousands of Old French words were incorporated into what we now call Middle English. Many of the inflectional suffixes that existed in Old English were lost in Middle English, and therefore word order became the means of establishing relationships between, for example, subjects and objects in sentences. In many senses, Middle English was a tri-language—a combination of Anglo-Saxon, French, and Latin. We see this in the wedding vow "to cherish, honor, and obey"—words of Latin, French, and English derivation, which all had similar meanings but could be understood by family members who might know one of these languages better than English itself. (For a perspective on this, see Barber, in this volume.)

By 1500, Modern English was in its early developmental stage. When in 1475, William Caxton introduced the printing press to England and great numbers of books began to be produced, people felt the need to learn to read and write. Translations from Latin, Greek, and French were being produced so that the classics could be printed in English and read by many for the first time. As translations were made, additional words from Greek, Latin, and French entered the English language. Grammatical changes were taking place as language changed. One example is that the familiar form of the second person "thou" was in the process of being dropped in favor of the use of "you" for both the familiar and formal form of the second person. Starting at the end of the 15th century, a shift in the prestige pronunciation of words, especially of vowels, known as the Great Vowel Shift, was occurring. Historical linguists have posited a variety of reasons for the shift in the prestige pronunciation of English, but there is no definitive explanation (although we know that throughout history particular regional dialects have become more prestigious for political, economic, and social reasons).

Although most contemporary readers understand Shakespeare's English, we recognize differences in meanings of words, in some past tense forms, in pronoun usage, and in the vocabulary itself from the way that we use English today. Shakespeare used grammatical forms that are no longer in use today—"doth" and "hath" among others.

Later, in the 1800s, the need was felt to create dictionaries of English, which led to standardization of spelling and, to some degree, pronunciation. In some cases, this standardization solidified problematic Latinate spellings and grammatical rules. However, the overall result was that it became easier to produce books and pieces of writing that could be read by most literate users of English. Other aspects of English changed as well. English lost most of its inflections. Present Day English, with the exception of irregular verbs, has only eight bound inflectional suffixes: -s (for plural), 's or s' (for possession), -s (for third-person singular), -ed (for past tense), -ing (for progressive tenses), -en (for the past participle), -er (for comparative), and -est (for superlative). In addition, when new words are introduced into English, they are introduced as regular nouns and verbs, using the above inflectional suffixes to indicate plural and tenses. All the irregular plurals and verbs such as *dreamt, meant, written,* and *children* hark back to earlier stages of English.

SOCIOLINGUISTICS: LINGUISTIC VARIETIES

What has caused English to change over the years, and in what ways has it changed most recently? To consider this question, we need to define *sociolinguistics* and how it relates to language change. Sociolinguistics is a term referring to the connections between language and society, and the way we use language in different social situations. It ranges from the study of the wide variety of dialects across a given region to the analysis of the way men and women speak to one another. Sociolinguistics shows us how a dialect of a given language can often describe the age, sex, and social class of the speaker; it codes the social function of a language. (*Explore Linguistics,* 1997).

Included (among many other concepts) in the studies of sociolinguistics are the studies of *dialects, registers, diglossia,* and *slang.* Dialects are the individual varieties of a language spoken by different groups of speakers of that language. In general, they may be social dialects or geographical dialects. Social dialects include those spoken by particular ethnic groups and particular socioeconomic groups; examples would be AAVE (African American Vernacular English) and the Brahmin dialect of Massachusetts. Geographical dialects are spoken by groups of people in specific geographical areas, such as Australian English and Parisian French. Linguists distinguish the dialects of a single language from what are actually separate languages by their *mutual intelligibility,* or by whether speakers of one dialect can understand the speakers of another dialect of the language. This measure of distinction between languages and dialects can become a little slippery, however, in that some languages are more mutually intelligible than are some dialects of the same language. There are, for example, speakers of Flemish and Dutch who have an easier time understanding each other than do some speakers of American and Scottish English. What this represents is that not only does pure linguistics figure into what distinguishes a language from a dialect, but historical and political factors figure in, as well. Furthermore, all this having been said, one of the prime features of dialects to which politics and history contribute is that of what is the *standard* variety, or dialect, of the language—and which varieties, or dialects, are considered *nonstandard* by the majority of speakers. The standard dialect is generally the variety spoken by the educated, upper classes, whereas nonstandard varieties may be spoken by certain ethnic or socioeconomic groups, as well as in particular geographical areas.

The notion of a register is not the same as that of a dialect. Registers are the distinct varieties of a language spoken in distinct social situations. One would not address a judge in exactly the same style of language one uses with his or her friends. These two different styles of using language represent two different registers of the same language and, perhaps, even the same dialect—but they differ in level of formality, just the same. An instance of the difference in the use of a language can be seen in the following example from Janet Holmes' *An Introduction to Sociolinguistics* (2001). It is taken from the two main languages used in Paraguay—Spanish and Guarani:

Domain	**Addressee**	**Setting**	**Topic**	**Language**
Family	Parent	Home	Planning a party	Guarani
Friendship	Friend	Café	Humorous anecdote	Guarani
Religion	Priest	Church	Choosing the Sunday liturgy	Spanish
Education	Teacher	Primary	Telling a story	Guarani
Education	Lecturer	University	Solving a math problem	Spanish
Administration	Official	Office	Getting an important license	Spanish

Holmes' example demonstrates that in certain countries, not only are different registers appropriate for different social situations, but different social circumstances may actually suggest the use of different languages. These countries exhibit what linguists call diglossia or the use of different languages for different social situations. Janet Holmes defines diglossia as having three crucial features:

1. In the same language, used in the same community, there are two distinct varieties. One is regarded as high (H) and the other low (L).
2. Each is used for distinct functions.
3. No one uses the high (H) in everyday conversation.

In the following examples it is easy to tell which variety you will use given the social situations (*Explore Linguistics*, 1997):

- Telling a joke
- Interviewing for a job
- Giving a speech for a charity event
- Giving a speech for a friend for his/her birthday
- Church
- Cafeteria

The notion of slang is somewhat different from both the notion of a dialect and the notion of a register. Slang is more dynamic and, indeed, more volatile than either a dialect or a register. A particular dialect may contain some slang, as may the registers used in various situations. Slang is often the bit of a language that changes most frequently; what is "cool" or "hip" slang today may be outdated tomorrow. In American English, slang expressions from the 1960s like the word "groovy" lost their popularity by the 1970s. In the present day, slang from various dialects like "bling-bling" and "dude" may lose their popularity within 5 to 10 to 20 years as well. Slang can arise from many different aspects of life: social in-groups, various industries, political discourse, and, most notably, pop culture. The use of slang is, in general, most popular among the younger generations in society and may be frowned upon by older speakers. Thus, although the terms "slang" and "dialect" are often used interchangeably, linguists usually distinguish these by their staying power and, even more important, by their use across generations and their differences in critical mass of expressions.

In referring back to our brief outline of the history of English, we note that English has gone through many evolutions over the course of the past 1500 years. Prior to that, the Germanic languages that gave rise to English changed in multiple ways, similarly to the Proto-Indo-European language that gave rise to the earliest forms of Germanic. What causes all these changes, and how do they relate to the sociolinguistic ideas that we were just discussing?

Recall that there may be language-external reasons for change, as well as language-internal reasons. The latter reasons are generally complex linguistic phenomena that may cause one word form to split into two, or two word forms to merge into one, or a sound change that may propagate throughout the language or several of its dialects, or other similar changes. The former reasons, however, although they may be equally complex, may be simpler to describe and analyze without the use of complicated linguistic language and machinery. Language-external reasons for change include events, such as migrations, wars, inventions, political and legal decisions, social progress, religious changes, and so on. These events, which occur every day across the globe, affect the languages spoken by the people as a sort of "side effect" of their impacts. To cite just a few examples, the migrations of the Indo-European peoples are thought to have caused their language to split off into separate, unique, mutually unintelligible languages: the Norman Conquest gave rise to the incorporation of many French words into English; the invention of the printing press allowed for the spread of the written word, and thus more widespread literacy; and the desire for religious freedom brought many English people to the shores of the Americas, giving rise to the evolution of American English dialects.

More recent examples of language-external factors for change in English can be found in the selections in the latter part of this unit (Bhabha, Fishman, Achebe, Fasold, Edwards, Armstrong, Cameron). Some ideas to keep in mind while reading these selections are that geographical differences, including geographical isolation (being cut off geographically from other speakers), may bring about linguistic and, in particular, dialect, change; social differences among classes often bring about distinctions in dialect; ethnic differences may give rise to distinctions in dialect and slang; and, ultimately, the attitude of the speaker and those in his or her environment may play the largest role in determining his or her choice of dialect.

REFERENCES

Explore Linguistics: Sociolinguistics. (1997). Retrieved January 2004 from http://logos.uoregon.edu/explore/sociling

Holmes, J. (2001). *An introduction to sociolinguistics.* London: Longman. Retrieved January 2004 from http://logos.uoregon.edu/explore/sociling

Millward, C. M. (1996). *A biography of the English language* (2nd ed.). Fort Worth: Harcourt.

A BRIEF OVERVIEW OF UNIT II SELECTIONS

Tamara Green lists the different branches of the *Indo-European* language family tree in "Language Families," and then briefly summarizes the history of the English language. Examining in a bit more depth the issue of how the various Germanic dialects developed into different languages, R. L. Trask in "Where Did English Come From?" describes a Germanic language he calls *Ingvaeonic*, spoken more than 1500 years ago in Northern Europe. At the time English was merely a dialect of Ingvaeonic; yet geographical and social factors led it to become a distinct language. In "The Norman Conquest" Charles Barber talks about how the Norman Conquest of 1066 did not bring culture to the "backward and barbaric Anglo-Saxons," as is often assumed. According to Barber, "These people did not need William of Normandy and his adventurers to bring them civilization."

In "People and Language," Kate Parry gives us a clear overview of both how languages change over time and the particular changes that have taken place in English over the centuries, often as a result of language contact.

Quite relevant to what Parry explains, Homi Bhabha in "Queen's English" compares the status of teenage Ebonic speech in the United States with that of Bombay Bazaar English speech in India. Bhabha declares that

> . . . whether or not these hybrid speech genres are a species of African American Vernacular English (AAVE) or something like Bombay Bazaar Hindi-English (BBHE), whether the grammatical structure of 'Ain't nobody sing like Chaka Khan' comes from the Niger-Congo Basin, or the rhetorical peculiarity of 'Miss Pushpa is smiling and smiling/even for no reason' can be traced back to Hindi speech patterns common to Bombay's Bhindi Bazaar, the world of these utterances cannot be reduced to the description of speech as an 'object' of linguistic study without doing violence to the living tongue.

Bhabha makes us aware of the paradoxical quality of a dialect to act as a qualifier among its speakers for inclusiveness in the group, while at the very same time acting as a qualifier to exclude its speakers from the group associated with the standard variety.

Yet, what Joshua Fishman reports in "The New Linguistic Order" is that although English has become and remained a predominant language throughout the world over the past few centuries, there are reasons to believe that its influence may be waning. Despite the globalization of English in the technological age, for grassroots and traditional reasons many countries are returning to languages spoken in their past. Fishman also says that "the spread of English is closely linked to social class, age, gender, and profession," which leaves out millions around the globe who do not fit the profile of the typical international English speaker.

Chinua Achebe, in "The African Writer and the English Language," examines the decision that African writers whose first language is other than English must make: Should they write in English and reach a wide audience, or write in a local language to make the text accessible to those of their initial language and experience? Achebe reasons that it is necessary to write in English, even though it is the language of the colonizer; but writers must bend and change English to accommodate their varied experiences of the world.

"Since the 1996 Oakland School Board decision regarding the use of Ebonics as a tool of instruction, opinions have clashed over whether Ebonics is a separate language or merely a dialect of English," explains Ralph Fasold in "Ebonic Need Not be English." "Called Black Vernacular English (BVE) in the 1960s and 1970s and African American Vernacular English (AAVE) in the 1980s and 90s, Ebonics has traditionally been considered a dialect of English by educators and linguists," according to Fasold. Yet, Fasold looks at what it actually takes to make a language.

In a similar vein, John Edwards in "Languages and Language Learning in the Face of World English" poses the question, "How can you induce the learning of a language when its community of use is negligible, but how will that community ever grow unless more join it?" This is the question faced by many linguistic communities trying to preserve a native language that is, either more slowly or rather rapidly, falling into disuse because of the expansion throughout the world today of a more widely spoken language like English.

Deborah Cameron explains in "Gender Issues in Language Change" that although it has long been recognized by scholars that gender exerts an influence on language change, recent theories in sociolinguistics and linguistic anthropology have allowed for a reinterpretation of some of the empirical data from the 1970s and 1980s. Finally, James Armstrong's "Homophobic Slang as Coercive Discourse Among College Students" makes (among others) the points that heterosexual males, usually young, may use language that creates an atmosphere of intolerance toward gays; and that furthermore, in some contexts this language asserts male heterosexual dominance by confirming presumed masculine values, while degrading presumed feminine gender attributes.

Each of the selections helps to demonstrate that language, by any means, is not a static attribute of the community, but that it is a dynamic, ever-changing, living tool of expression for human beings. American awareness of the role that language varieties play in English education came into being in the latter half of the 20th century. As we continue to move forward in the 21st century, many of the same questions about how to integrate or distinguish standard and nonstandard varieties persist, not satisfactorily answered in the decades preceding us. With continued attention, however, perhaps our school systems can reinvent themselves into places that can educate all children equally well—whether some of the old debates must be resolved in order to do so, or whether they simply need to be put aside.

Language Families

Tamara M. Green
Hunter College, CUNY

LANGUAGE AND HISTORY

Language is a human activity and, like all human activities, it seems to have infinite variability. Nevertheless, within that variability, patterns and relationships can be discovered. The languages of the world (and the experts estimate that the number of languages ranges from 2,900 to nearly 10,000) are divided into various families, the members of which are considered by linguists to be related because of similarities in structure, grammar, and vocabulary. The major families, or trees, of human languages are the following:

1. Indo-European
2. Afro-Asiatic (formerly known as Semitic-Hamitic: Arabic, Hebrew, Amharic, Coptic)
3. Sino-Tibetan (Chinese, Tibetan, Thai, Burmese)
4. Japanese and Korean
5. Uralic-Altaic (Finnish, Estonian, Hungarian, Turkish, Mongol)
6. Caucasian (spoken in the Caucasus Mountains of Georgia, Armenia, and Azerbaijan)
7. Dravidian (spoken in Southern India)
8. Malayo-Polynesian (the languages of the South Pacific and Indian Ocean)
9. Austroasiatic (Cambodian, Vietnamese)
10. African[1]
11. North and South American Indian[1]
12. The orphans: single languages that seem to bear no connection with any other: e.g., Ainu, which is spoken by the aboriginal inhabitants of Japan, or Basque, the language of the inhabitants of the Pyrenees region of Spain and France.

Reprinted with permission from *The Greek and Latin Roots of English,* 3rd ed., by T. M. Green. © 2003 by T. M. Green.

THE BRANCHES OF THE INDO-EUROPEAN TREE

The largest and most widely diffused of these language families is Indo-European. Like everything else in the realm of human activity, language is subject to change, and many languages have disappeared or evolved into other languages over the centuries. For example, Latin is no longer spoken, but it survives through its direct descendants, Italian, French, and Spanish. Other ancient languages, however, have disappeared without a trace because they were not written down.

Linguists have classified the surviving branches of the Indo-European tree as follows:

1. *Indian*	2. *Iranian*	3. *Hellenic*	4. *Italic*
Sanskrit[2]	Avestan[2]	Ancient Greek[2]	Latin[2]
Hindi	Old Persian[2]	Byzantine Greek[2]	Italian
Bengali	Modern Persian	Modern Greek	French
Punjabi	Pashto	Macedonian[3]	Spanish
Mahrati	Kurdish	Yavanic	Portuguese
Urdu	Beluchi		Romanian
Sinhalese			
Romany			

5. *Germanic (Teutonic)*	6. *Celtic*	7. *Slavonic*
Gothic[2]	Galatians[2]	Great Russian
Middle High German[2]	Gaulish[2]	Belorussian
Modern German	Celtiberian[2]	Ukrainian
Yiddish	Brittonic[2]	Sorbian
Dutch	Cornish	Kashubian
Flemish	Welsh	Polish
Frisian	Breton	Slovene
Old English (Anglo-Saxon)[2]	Gaelic	Slovak
Middle English[2]	(a) Irish	Czech
Modern English	(b) Scottish	Serbo-Croatian
Afrikaans	(c) Manx	Bulgarian
Scandinavian		Macedonian[3]
(a) Norwegian		
(b) Icelandic		
(c) Swedish		
(d) Danish		
(e) Faroese		

8. *Baltic*	9. *Illyrian*	10. *Thraco-Phrygian*
Lithuanian	Albanian	Thracian[2]
Latvian		Phrygian[2]
		Armenian

AN OUTLINE OF THE HISTORY OF THE ENGLISH LANGUAGE

Although English is classified as belonging to the Germanic branch of the Indo-European tree because of its historical origins and development, its vocabulary has been strongly influenced, through the accidents of history and politics, by other Indo-European languages, most notably Latin and its offshoots and, to a lesser extent, Greek. What follows is a brief outline of the historical and cultural events that influenced the development of the English language.

The Roman Occupation of Britain: first century AD–AD 410

1. Celtic languages (also Indo-European)
2. Introduction of Latin, the language of Roman conquest and commerce
3. Withdrawal of the Roman army: 410

Old English: AD 450–AD 1150

1. Invasion of the Germanic tribes (Angles, Saxons, Jutes): 449
2. Conversion of the Anglo-Saxons to Christianity: 597: Reintroduction of Latin via the Church
3. Viking (Danish) raids on Britain: 8th–9th centuries
4. *Beowulf* (Anglo-Saxon): 8th–9th centuries
5. The Norman Conquest: 1066: Reintroduction of Latin-based vocabulary via French

Middle English: AD 1150–AD 1500

1. The Anglo-French connection
2. Changes in vocabulary: loss of many Old English (Germanic) words; addition of thousands of words from French and Latin
3. Changes in grammar: loss of inflection
4. The development of a vernacular literature: Chaucer: *Canterbury Tales*; Langland: *Piers Plowman*
5. First translation of Bible from Latin into English, perhaps by John Wycliffe
6. Introduction of the printing press into England by William Caxton (1476)

Modern English: AD 1500–present

1. Decline of Latin as a common European language of discourse and the rise of vernacular languages
2. Translations of classical Greek and Latin texts (Renaissance)
3. Shakespeare (1564–1616)
4. Standardization of spelling (orthography) and enrichment of vocabulary (16th–17th centuries)
5. Dr. Samuel Johnson: *A Dictionary of the English Language* (1755)
6. Grammarians and rhetoricians: the formation of rules (18th century)
7. The development of the scientific study of comparative, historical, and structural linguistics (18th century)
8. The influence of British and American colonialism and Empire (19th–20th centuries)

THE DEVELOPMENT OF AMERICAN ENGLISH

England and America are two countries separated by the same language.
George Bernard Shaw

From the settlement of Jamestown to the end of the colonial period: 1607–1790

1. The establishment of the forms and patterns of American English, as distinct from British English

The period of Westward expansion: 1790–1860

1. Immigration from Western Europe and Ireland
2. Noah Webster: *An American Dictionary of the English Language* (1828)
3. Mobility of the population; settlement of the Far West

The period since the Civil War: 1861 to the present

1. Emancipation of the slaves (1863)
2. Immigration from Eastern and Southern Europe (1880–1920)
3. Immigration from the Caribbean and South America (1945–present)
4. Immigration from Asia and the Pacific Rim (1975–present)
5. Uniformity of language vs. regionalism: the influence of radio, television, and the movies

SOME USEFUL TERMS

etymology: the study of the history of a particular word; the derivation or origin of a word
linguistics: the science of language, including the history, formation, and structures of languages

Note

Studying language can be glamorous. The words *grammar* and *glamour* have the same etymology. Grammar, a system that describes the structures of a particular language, is derived from the Greek word *gramma* (something written). In medieval Europe, few people could read, and those who could were thought to possess special magical power. The original meaning of *glamour*, which is a variant pronunciation of *grammar*, was magic or enchantment.

NOTES

[1] Strictly speaking, these are divisions that are based on geographic proximity, rather than on the usual rules of linguistic classification, because there is a great deal of disagreement about their relationship to one another. There are estimated to be over 700 African and 1200 American Indian languages.
[2] No longer spoken.
[3] Macedonian shows elements of both Slavic and Greek.

QUESTIONS TO THINK ABOUT

1. What are some of the language families listed by Green? Which relationships between languages surprised you? What evidence leads linguists to believe that these languages are related to each other?

2. What are "orphan languages," as described by Green? What are some examples of these languages? Where are they spoken?

3. In reading this selection, were you surprised to find out that English is a Germanic language? What other languages in the Germanic list were either unfamiliar to you or surprised you in being Germanic in origin? How does the historical summary that Green provides help to explain the many words of non-Germanic origin in English?

4. *Extending your understanding*: Choose a branch of the Indo-European language tree presented by Green. Research some of the characteristics that the languages in that branch possess. How are the languages similar? How are they different? Find some words that are similar within the languages of that branch. Would these *cognate words* lead you to suspect that the languages are related?

TERMS TO DEFINE

Define the following words and phrases as they are presented within the context of the reading. Comment on your understanding of the significance of each one.

Language family
Indo-European
Germanic
Vikings
Norman Conquest
Etymology

13

Where Did English Come From?

R. L. Trask
University of Sussex

When the Anglo-Saxons first settled in England around 1,500 years ago, there were already, of course, some regional differences in their speech, though these were not dramatic. With the passage of time, however, further differences began to accumulate. We have seen that an innovation that occurs in one area may spread to a larger area, but that it doesn't necessarily spread to the whole area occupied by the language. After some centuries, every area of England had undergone some changes in grammar, vocabulary, and pronunciation, but failed to undergo other changes that had affected different areas. Consequently, the English-speaking area gradually broke up into a number of regions all distinguished by an ever-greater number of differences. By about the year 1500, (a thousand years after the settlement), it was clear that speakers from different regions were often finding it very difficult to understand one another.

These regional differences are still with us, and they are very familiar. Not long ago, there was a striking example of the extent to which English has diverged: a television company put out a program filmed in the English city of Newcastle, where the local variety of English is famously divergent and difficult, and the televised version was accompanied by *English subtitles!* The producers were afraid that other speakers would be quite unable to understand the "Geordie" speech of the performers. This ruffled quite a few feathers in Newcastle, but the producers had a point: I recall that, the first time I met a Geordie speaker, it was some days before I could understand a single word he was saying.

As we shall see, the combination of language change with geographical separation is a powerful one and, in the case of English, the degree of separation was greatly increased by the settlement by English-speakers of North America in the seventeenth century and of Australia and New Zealand in the nineteenth. Already the speech of North America is noticeably different from anything heard in Britain, and the English of, say, Mississippi or North Carolina can be exceedingly difficult for a Briton to understand. Indeed, it is reported that, when American films with soundtracks were first shown in Britain in the

Reprinted with permission from *Language: The Basics.* © 2003 by Routledge Publishers.

1930s, British audiences, having had almost no previous exposure to American speech, often found them very difficult to understand.

If nothing were to intervene, what do you suppose the result of this growing divergence would be? Easy: Eventually the regional varieties of English would diverge so far as to become mutually incomprehensible and we would be forced to speak not of dialects, but of separate languages.

It is possible that this will not happen now, thanks to the dramatic advances in transport and communications we have seen in the twentieth century, but it would have happened otherwise. And, there is no doubt at all that such breaking up of a single language into several quite different languages has happened unaccountably many times before. Indeed, that's exactly how English came into existence in the first place.

More than 1,500 years ago, when most of Britain was still occupied by people who spoke the language that would eventually develop into Welsh and Cornish, the ancestor of English was spoken on the North Sea coast of the European continent, in areas that are now part of the Netherlands, Germany, and Denmark. If the speakers of that language had given it a name, it had not survived. For convenience, we call it Ingvaeonic. And, it was some of the Ingvaeonic-speaking tribes, including the Angles and the Saxons, who moved across the North Sea into Britain 1,500 years ago. But not *all* of them emigrated; many of them stayed behind in Europe. So what happened to *their* Ingvaeonic? It certainly didn't turn into English.

Of course not, but it did turn into something else, or rather several something elses. The Angles and Saxons took to Britain the same Ingvaeonic speech they were leaving behind, but the North Sea proved to be a formidable barrier to further contact. Ingvaeonic continued to change, but change occurring on one side of the sea almost never crossed over to the other side, and within a few centuries the insular varieties that we now call English were already sharply different from the continental varieties. And, whereas England gradually came to be united under a single political authority (a factor which to some extent helped to slow the fragmentation of English), the stay-at-homes on the Continent found their territory criss-crossed by political boundaries. Eventually, continental Ingvaeonic broke up into several regional varieties which were not even comprehensible to one another, let alone with English. Today, linguists recognize three continental languages derived from Ingvaeonic: Dutch, Frisian, and Low German (in fact, only some dialects of Dutch and of Low German derive from Ingvaeonic—the linguistic position was really somewhat complicated in this part of the world).

Dutch is spoken in the Netherlands, in half of Belgium, and in a small area of northern France around Dunkirk; like English, it has splintered into a number of regional dialects, and a speaker from Amsterdam cannot understand the local Dutch of western Belgium or France (these regional varieties of Dutch are sometimes called *Flemish*). Frisian was formerly spoken in much of the Netherlands and is still spoken on several islands off the coast of the Netherlands and Germany, and in one corner of the continent. Frisian too has broken up into at least two major dialect groups which are not very similar. Low German is spoken over a wide area of northern Germany, again in a number of quite different varieties. (There is one more modern descendant of Ingvaeonic, but it is not spoken in Europe: it is Afrikaans, a distinctive offshoot of the Dutch introduced into South Africa three centuries ago.)

English-speakers have not been able to understand these languages for many centuries, but we can still recognize tantalizing fragments of our common ancestry. What do you make of such Dutch phrases as *een goed boek* or *koud water* or *de open deur* or *een gouden ring*? Or how about a whole sentence: *Wat wilt u—een kopje koffie of een glas bier*?

We can represent the common ancestry of the Ingvaeonic group of languages by using a tree diagram, as in Fig. 13.1. The structure of this tree shows that Dutch and Afrikaans are much closer than the other languages, having diverged only about three centuries ago. These languages are still mutually comprehensible, although each sounds very strange to speakers of the other.

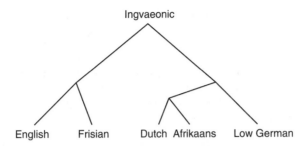

Fig 13.1. The Ingvaeonic family tree.

But the Ingvaeonic languages are far from being the only relatives that English has. A number of other European languages are also transparently related to English, if not quite so closely. German sentences like *Mein Haus ist alt* and *Dies Wein ist gut* are not so different from English, and even Swedish *Nils har en penna och en bok* you may be able to recognize as meaning "Nick has a pen and a book." Icelandic is far more difficult, but, if I tell you that *Folkid segir, ad hun se lik Anna* means "People say that she is like Anna," you will spot the resemblance. Also in this group are Danish, Norwegian, Faeroese (spoken in the Faeroe Islands), Norn (formerly spoken in the Shetland and Orkney Islands north of Scotland), Yiddish (a distinctive offshoot of German), and Gothic (an extinct language spoken by many of the barbarian invaders who overthrew the western Roman Empire).

These languages are called the Germanic languages, and they all started off millennia ago as nothing more than dialects of a single language, which we call *Proto-Germanic*. The Germanic family tree is shown in Fig. 13.2. Who spoke Proto-Germanic, and where and when? This is not a simple question, since the Proto-Germanic speakers were illiterate and left no written texts behind. But the consensus of scholars is that the language was probably spoken in southern Scandinavia around 500 BC, and that groups of Germanic speakers spread from there into northern, eastern, and southern Europe, and finally, a thousand years later, into Britain. The dialects spoken by these groups have diverged

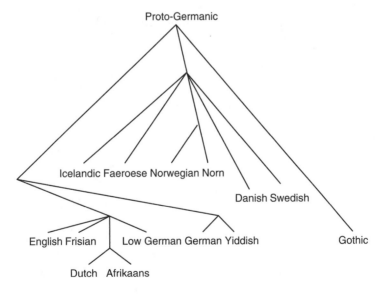

Fig 13.2. The Germanic family tree.

into a number of distinct languages, but the relatedness of these languages is still easy to see.

And Proto-Germanic is not the end of the story, or rather it is not the beginning. Two hundred years of careful research has demonstrated beyond any doubt that Proto-Germanic itself began life as a dialect of a still more ancient language, and that the Germanic languages are thus related to a vast family of languages spoken over most of Europe and much of Asia. This enormous family includes the Celtic languages like Irish and Welsh, the Romance languages like French, Spanish, and Italian, the Slavic languages like Russian, Polish, and Serbo-Croatian, the Baltic languages like Lithuanian, several rather isolated languages like Greek, Albanian, and Armenian, the Iranian languages like Persian and Kurdish, the north Indian languages like Hindi, Panjabi, Bengali, and Gujarati, and a number of now extinct languages formerly spoken in the Balkans, in modern Turkey, and in central Asia. We call it the Indo-European family, and the Indo-European languages are, of course, descended from a remote ancestor called Proto-Indo-European, or PIE. We think PIE was spoken around 6,000 years ago, probably somewhere in eastern Europe, possibly in southern Russia, by a group of people who rode horses and had wheeled vehicles, agriculture, and domesticated animals. We know this because such PIE words as those for "horse," "wheel," "axle," "grain," "cow," "sheep," and "dog" have survived in a number of daughter languages. For example, we're confident that the PIE word for "sheep" was *owis* (the asterisk marks an unattested form reconstructed by linguists) because of the existence of Sanskrit (an ancient language of India) *avis*, Latin *ovis*, Greek *ois*, Lithuanian *avis*, Old Irish *oi*, all meaning "sheep," and English *ewe*.

Naturally, PIE must itself have been descended from a still earlier ancestor, and so on, all the way back to the origins of human language perhaps 100,000 years or more ago, but it is exceedingly difficult to trace things back further into the past: eventually the weight of accumulated changes in languages becomes so great that we can no longer identify an ancient common origin with confidence—although a number of linguists are working very hard on this problem, and some of them are beginning to think that we might be able to derive the Indo-European and other families from a very remote ancestor which they call Proto-Nostratic and which they think was spoken perhaps 15,000 years ago. But this idea is still deeply controversial.

Nonetheless, we have succeeded in tracing the origins of English back to an unidentified, illiterate people living somewhere in eastern Europe around 6,000 years ago. These people gradually spread out over much of Asia and Europe, and one group moved first into Scandinavia, then south into much of Europe. Some of them eventually crossed the North Sea into Britain, where their Germanic language, eventually called English, became in turn the national language of England, the language of the British Empire and, finally, the most influential and widely used language in the world.

QUESTIONS TO THINK ABOUT

1. How does Trask demonstrate the relationship between language change and geographical separation? What are some of the examples he uses? What is the eventual outcome of the geographical separation of different dialects? What happens to the dialects?

2. How would you describe the language Trask calls *Ingvaeonic*? To what language might it refer? Into which languages did this ancestor language eventually evolve? Where are, or were, these languages spoken?

3. Who spoke Proto-Germanic and where and when, according to Trask? Into what linguistic branches did Proto-Germanic split off? Which languages look to be the closest relatives of English, according to the diagrams found in the reading?

4. *Extending your understanding*: Why do you think the history of the English language is important as a subject of study? How might it enlighten both your understanding of historical events and of language and how it develops? Form small groups in your class and discuss these questions. As you are having your discussion, compose a list of ways in which the subject of the history of English might aid in the learning and teaching of history, grammar, vocabulary, spelling, sociology, and geography.

TERMS TO DEFINE

Define the following words and phrases as they are presented within the context of the reading. Comment on your understanding of the significance of each one.

Regional dialect
Proto-Germanic
Frisian
Flemish
Dutch Afrikaans
Sanskrit

14

The Norman Conquest

Charles Barber
Formerly Reader in English language and literature, School of English,
University of Leeds

The Norman Conquest of 1066 was not such a violent break in English history as people sometimes imagine. There was already strong French influence in England before the Conquest, at any rate, in the higher levels of society: Edward the Confessor was half Norman, and his court had close relations with France. It is certainly true, however, that the Conquest had a profound influence on the English language. For some centuries, English ceased to be the language of the governing classes, and there was no such thing as standard literary English; and when English did once again become the language of the whole country it had changed a good deal under the influence of the conquerors.

The rulers of Normandy had originally been Scandinavian Vikings, who occupied parts of northern France and were eventually recognized by the French crown: in 912, Rollo became the first Duke of Normandy, and accepted the king of France as his overlord. By the middle of the eleventh century, however, the Normans had long lost their Scandinavian speech: they spoke French, and were essentially French in culture. People sometimes talk, therefore, as though the Norman Conquest were the coming of a higher civilization to the backward and barbaric Anglo-Saxons. This, however, is a misapprehension. Six hundred years had passed since the Anglo-Saxon invasion of Britain, and in that time the English had developed a sophisticated civilization. The Normans demonstrated their superiority in military techniques, for they had the new heavy cavalry that had been developed on the continent by the Franks, while the Anglo-Saxons still fought on foot behind a wall of round shields. The Normans also showed themselves superior at the construction of castles, and after the Conquest they built some fine churches and cathedrals. But it is difficult to see in what other ways they were culturally superior to the people they conquered.

The Anglo-Saxons had a fine literature, both in verse and in prose. They had traditions of scholarship which went back to the seventh century, and when Charlemagne, at the end of the eighth century, wanted to reform his educational system, he imported an Englishman to do it for him. This tradition had been badly disrupted by the Viking invasions, but there was a revival under West-Saxon leadership in the second half of the tenth century. The Anglo-Saxons were also fine artists and craftsmen: they produced beautiful carved crosses, and jeweler's work, and illuminated manuscripts to compare with any in the world. They were also famous for their needlework, and the celebrated Bayeux Tapestry was probably made in England.

These people did not need William of Normandy and his adventurers to bring them civilization. French became the language of the upper classes in England simply because it was the language of the conquerors, not because of any cultural superiority on their part. What happened was that the native aristocracy were largely destroyed, and their lands were distributed to William's Norman followers, who became the new ruling class. Many key ecclesiastical positions, such as bishoprics and abbacies, were also given to Normans in the years following the Conquest, so that the church and education were dominated by them. French, therefore, was the language of the aristocracy and the court, and it remained so for over two hundred years. So anybody whose native tongue was English, and who wanted to get on in the world, had to learn French. The following comment on the situation was made in the late thirteenth century in a long history of England written in verse, usually known as the Chronicle of Robert of Gloucester:

þus com, lo, Engelond in-to Normandies hond:
And þe Normans ne couþe speke þo bote hor owe speche,
And speke French as hii dude atom, and hor children dude also teche,
So þat helemen of þis lond, þat of hor blod come,
Holdeþ alle þulke speche þat hii of hom nom;
Vor bote a man conne Frenss me telþ of him lute.
Ac lowe men holdeþ to Engliss, and to hor owe speche ȝute.
Ich wene þer ne beþ in al þe world contreyes none
þat ne holdeþ to hor owe speche, bote Engelond one.
Ac wel me wote uor to conne boþe wel it is,
Vor þe more þat a mon can, þe more wurþe he is.

This can be translated as follows:

Thus came, lo, England into Normandy's hand: and the Normans then knew how to speak only their own language, and spoke French as they did at home, and also had their children taught (it), so that noblemen of this land, that come of their stock, all keep to the same speech that they received from them: for unless a man knows French, people make little account of him. But low men keep to English, and to their own language still, I think that in the whole world there are no countries that do not keep to their own language, except England alone. But people know well that it is good to master both because the more a man knows the more honored he is.

This bears witness to the prestige of French, and also to the fact that English was still spoken by the majority ("lowe men"). Now, however, that English was no longer the language of upper-class culture and administration, West Saxon lost its place as a standard literary language. For three centuries, no single form of English was recognized as a norm, and people wrote in the language of their own region. Early Middle English texts give the impression of a welter of dialects, without many common conventions in pronunciation or spelling, and with considerable divergences in grammar and phonology.

QUESTIONS TO THINK ABOUT

1. What was the "profound influence on the English language" of the Norman Conquest to which Barber refers? Why did the language change under Norman authority?

2. In what ways were the Normans superior to and more advanced than the Anglo-Saxons they conquered? In what ways, according to Barber, were they not superior? How do these assertions by Barber rest on his particular definition of what constitutes a superior civilization?

3. Barber says that after the Norman Conquest "anybody whose native tongue was English, and who wanted to get on in the world, had to learn French." Can you think of any more contemporary situations in which people who want to get ahead in society feel the need to learn another language or dialect? Explain.

4. *Extending your understanding*: Barber states that "the Anglo-Saxons had a fine literature, both in verse and in prose." Look up some of the Old English verse and prose to which Barber is referring, especially in translation to Present Day English. What can we learn about the speakers of Old English from the topics, style, and vocabulary of their writings? Describe your observations in writing.

TERMS TO DEFINE

Define the following words and phrases as they are presented within the context of the reading. Comment on your understanding of the significance of each one.

Edward the Confessor
Standard literary English
Cultural superiority
Rollo of Normandy
Charlemagne
The Franks

People and Language[1]

Kate Parry
Hunter College, CUNY

Mummy, Mummy; Mummy come ... Up, up. ... Cupboard. ... Up cupboard, up cupboard; up cupboard. ... Get up, get up. ... Cupboard, cupboard. ... Cupboard-up; Cupboard-up, cupboard-up. ... Telephone. ... Mummy. ... Mummy get out telephone.

—Bruner (1993, p. 65)

Richard is 2 years old, and he wants his mother to get a toy telephone out of a cupboard for him. She, we are told, is "very pregnant" and understandably reluctant to get up from her chair. So she does not immediately get up; she protests and holds out until Richard has achieved "something approaching a request in sentence form." In this way, she is leading him into acquiring language, always in the context of social interaction. It is a means of expressing his needs and desires and of influencing the world about him. It is also, of course, the means by which his mother attempts to control him. From any point of view, language—English, in this case—is playing a fundamental role in Richard's socialization, and as he grows aware of himself as a person, the language is an integral part of his identity.

Lem is another child who is learning English. On this occasion, he is in trouble because he has taken off his shoes, and his mother is angry with him. She asks him what he has done with the shoes and says, "You want me to tie you up, put you on de railroad track?" Lem, after a moment's hesitation, responds:

Railroad track
Train all big 'n black
On dat track, on dat track, on dat track
Ain't no way I can't get back
Back from dat track
Back from dat train
Big 'n black, I be back. (Heath 1983, p. 110)

153

Everyone laughs, and Lem's offence is forgotten. The incident is another example of a child acquiring language through social interaction. Lem, however, is growing up in a different community and is learning both different forms of English and different ways of using it. His mother does not ask him the same kinds of questions that Richard's mother asks, nor does she hold out in the same way for him to make his desires explicit, though she does reward him for using language imaginatively. The two children are also learning different pronunciations of the same words and, in some respects, a different grammar. These differences of language both indicate and help to perpetuate the cultural differences between the communities into which the children are born; and each child is learning to be part of his own community through the language that he is learning to speak.

Anthony is another English speaker, but, being Nigerian, he has learned the language in quite different circumstances. As a teenager, he tells the story of his first encounter with it:

> One day the thought of going to school came into my head, so I asked my father that I wanted to go to school too, so he enrolled my name.
>
> I bagan [*sic*] in class one, and was the tallest and clever b[o]y in class. We were taught A, B, C, D . . . in the usual way. I was appointed the monitor and every time the class remained silent, because I proved wicked to any one who disturbed.
>
> In the cause [*sic*] of the year, I was promoted to class two and remained monitor. Gradually we were taught how to read. . . .
>
> In class four, I was able to read. And those who could read like myself were appointed leaders in a group and I was appointed the leader of group "B." (Parry 1986, p. 133)

Anthony learned to read in English, but he did not speak it before going to school. In his family, he had learned the language of his own ethnic group, and with his friends he used Hausa, the lingua franca that the different peoples of Northern Nigeria use to communicate with one another. So English for Anthony is a language of the classroom, and, by his own account, it is a classroom in which social interaction is extremely limited. Yet, the language plays an important part in his life because he received most of his primary and all of his secondary education in it, and he needs to use it for any official business or large-scale commercial transaction. Thus, he has made strenuous efforts to learn it and, by the time he wrote this passage, he could speak it quite fluently. His English is not, however, the same as the English that either Richard or Lem is learning; it is more formal. Anthony uses words such as *wicked* and *disturbed* in distinctively Nigerian ways.

Sun Wenjing is another person who came to English relatively late in life:

> In 1973, when I was nine years old, there was a broadcast program that would teach English from ABC. My parents bought the teaching materials for that program—English written by Cheng Lin. . . . From that time, I had my first English teacher—the radio. I remember at the beginning they said, "Good morning, comrades. Long live Chairman Mao! Long live Marxism-Leninism and Mao Zedong thought!" After I learned the twenty-six letters, I realized that English words were all made up of combinations of these letters. How interesting English was! It only had twenty-six letters, but these twenty-six letters could express a person's feelings and thought. And people use English for international trade, international scholarship, and scientific research. . . . Now I still think English is a very interesting language. (Parry 1998, p. 125)

For Sun, English is no more the primary language for writing than it is for speech. It is an entirely foreign language, with characteristics notably different from her native Chinese (her surprise at what English can do with only twenty-six letters arises from the fact that the Chinese writing system uses thousands of characters). For her, the primary function of this language is communicating with foreigners, although she is learning it in a Chinese environment and through the expression of Chinese ideas and sensibilities. Her form of English is, thus, different again, and, although she listens to it on the radio and reads it in books, she speaks it only occasionally outside the English classes that she teaches.

These four people, so different from one another, represent only a small part of the immense diversity of people who now speak English. During the past half-century, the language has become a "global language" (Crystal 1998), used by different people for different purposes and expressing an extraordinary range of different cultures. Its speakers relate to it in a variety of different ways. For many, like Richard, it is their *mother tongue*, the language that they learned at the beginning of consciousness, in the context of their families. It is, thus, firmly associated with their own sense of identity. Moreover, many people, like Richard, grow up in educated families where the English spoken is the *standard* form of the language, one that is generally used by the people with authority and power in a centralized society. Its grammar and vocabulary vary relatively little (although its pronunciation does), and they correspond to the grammar and vocabulary of written texts. Indeed, mothers like Richard's ensure that their children's speech is similar to what they will encounter when they start to read by reading books aloud to them (Bruner 1993; Heath 1983). For such speakers then, English links them not only to their own families, but to people with power and authority at both national and international levels, and to a long historical tradition of writing. Their mother-tongue confers on them privileges, so they rarely feel constrained to learn any other.

English is no less a mother tongue for Lem than it is for Richard, but Lem, like the majority of native speakers of English (McArthur 1998, p. 7), is growing up speaking a *nonstandard* variety—in this case, an African American one. Such nonstandard varieties are usually spoken in working-class communities and are associated with particular localities. They often differ from the standard in grammar and vocabulary as well as pronunciation, and they are rarely used for writing, except in the representation of dialogue among working-class speakers. Because of their class associations and because they do not usually have written traditions, these varieties of English are commonly regarded as having less prestige than the standard; people often refer to them as *dialects*, using the word in a negative and disparaging sense. (Professional linguists, however, do not use the word in this way. When they refer to the dialects of a language, they usually mean that the language has a number of variants that, linguistically speaking, are all of equal status. See, e.g., Carver 1989, and the discussion in Leith 1997, pp. 9–10). Because of such public attitudes, speakers of nonstandard varieties of English often make great efforts to "correct" their speech, especially if they are ambitious. Yet, many nonstandard speakers cling to their variety: it is their mother tongue and to reject it would be to reject their most intimate relationships and their own family history. Some become *diglossic*, that is, they learn to use both varieties, switching from one to the other according to whom they are talking to and what they are talking about. Others keep firmly to their nonstandard speech, using it as an expression of rebellion against the powerful and the privileged and of solidarity with their own social group.

Whereas Lem may grow up diglossic, with control of two varieties of the same language, Anthony is not merely *bilingual* but *trilingual*, speaking three different languages.

His trilingualism, however, is like *triglossia* because he does not translate his experience from one language to another; rather, he uses each of his languages with different people and for different purposes. English is the language of the formal, educated part of his life, just as standard English is for many speakers of nonstandard varieties. This division of his life between languages undoubtedly creates complications: It makes it difficult, for example, to relate what he learns at school to what he learns at home; it is likely to prevent him from ever using English, especially in writing, with the ease and confidence of a native speaker; and it will inhibit the development of his own mother tongue because he will never use the latter for scholarly purposes. Yet large numbers of English speakers are in Anthony's position, and as they use the language among themselves they are changing it to express their own identities and to reflect the usages of their other languages.

Sun Wenjing is *bilingual*, but her use of her two languages is not the same as Anthony's use of his three. Although she was still a child when she began learning English, she could already read and write, as well as speak, Chinese well, and her acquisition of English has never been at the expense of developing her Chinese. Rather than leading a life in English that is distinct from her Chinese life, she is learning to translate her Chinese life into English. Nevertheless, learning English does to a degree change the kind of person she is; it opens up to her a world that is much wider than the world of Chinese—rich and varied though that world is—and it may make her, perhaps, more critical of her own background (Parry 1998, pp. 127–128). As for the form of English that she uses, Sun, even more than Anthony, models herself as closely as she can on the standard written language. Her usage is influenced by Chinese, of course, and as a teacher she may pass her usage on to others; but since English is not used in China for everyday purposes, a distinct Chinese variety is less likely to develop. On the other hand, her use of the Chinese language may well be influenced by her English, especially as she finds words relating to aspects of English-speaking culture untranslatable (Parry 1998, pp. 119–121).

English, then, as represented by these four speakers, is an extremely complicated phenomenon. Indeed, Tom McArthur argues that it is so diverse and is developing in so many different directions that we should not talk about the English language in the singular, but about the English languages in the plural (1998, pp. 57–67). The main purpose of this book is to explore this complex situation and examine how it came about. It will suggest that, despite their diversity, today's English speakers have *linguistic ancestors* in common, in that they have all learned the language from others who learned it from others who learned it from others, going back to a relatively small group of speakers. The book will begin with the first such ancestors that we can identify in historical records and will tell the story of how that society changed and developed, expanded and diversified, and of how its language changed and developed with it.

Such an historical approach will not lead all the way back to the origins of English, since the first speakers that we can identify obviously learned their language from others too. Scholars have taken the story further, into prehistory, by comparing different languages and showing, from their similarities, that they must have developed from a common source—in short that they were once varieties of the same language. A large group of European languages, for example, including English, Dutch, Low German, High German, Danish, Swedish, and Norwegian, can be thought of as divergent forms of a source language called *Proto-Germanic* or simply *Germanic* (the *Oxford English Dictionary* uses the term *Teutonic*). Another group, including French, Spanish, Portuguese, Italian, and Romanian, are known to have developed from *Latin*, the language of the *Romans*, and are accordingly described as *Romance* or sometimes *Italic* languages. A third group, which used to be dominant in Europe but is now represented only by Welsh, Breton, Irish, and Scots Gaelic, derives from a common *Celtic* language. In turn, the source languages, Germanic, Latin, and Celtic, together with classical Greek and Sanskrit (which is an ancient Indian language) have been shown to have a common origin in a language called by scholars *Indo-European*; and although no Indo-European records survive, inferences can be made about its sound system, grammar, and vocabulary by comparing the earliest records of its successor languages. (For discussion of the relationships among Indo-European languages, see Pyles & Algeo 1982, pp. 69–79; Millward 1989, pp. 46–53.) Some scholars go back even further than this, claiming that all human languages derive from a single source (Pinker 1995, pp. 255–259), and there has been much speculation about how that original language might have emerged from the calls, grunts, and lip-smackings of early hominids (Aitchison 1996, pp. 93–103). But, fascinating as these inferences and speculations are, they tell us nothing directly about speakers and about how their experiences and interactions led to changes in their speech. For this reason they lie outside the scope of the present chapter.

Nevertheless, to understand the history of English it is necessary to know about the major European groups of languages, especially Germanic, Romance, and Celtic. English speakers have never, in historical times, lived in isolation: They have interacted continually with speakers of other languages, especially of these three groups, and the resulting *language contact* has had important effects on the way English has developed. Language contact takes place in the minds of individuals who become bilingual, who, because they are bilingual, are able to participate in social networks of monolingual speakers of either language. (For a discussion of the role of social networks in language change, see J. Milroy 1993; L. Milroy 1987.) Bilingual speakers often incorporate elements of both languages in their speech: their first language almost invariably influences their second, and their second may also influence their first. As they interact with others, then, they may influence even monolinguals to adopt elements of the other language. Which elements these are and how widely they are adopted depends on the relative prestige of the two languages, the degree of similarity between them, and the proportion of bilingual speakers in the community.

Anthony, for example, has learned English, which is a language of prestige in Nigeria. So, even when he is speaking Hausa with other people who do not know English, he is quite likely to use English words, especially when referring to ideas or objects that were introduced to Nigeria by English speakers. The people he talks with may then adopt these words, even though they cannot speak English at all; and the words may become a regular part of their vocabulary if they hear other bilingual speakers, besides Anthony, use them. The words then will become, in effect, Hausa words, as has, indeed, happened many times: The words *sukuru dureba* in Hausa, for example, is the English word *screwdriver* adapted to Hausa pronunciation patterns; the word *peturur* is the English word *petrol.* The influence goes the other way too. Try as he will, Anthony does not produce English exactly like that of any native speaker; his English is inevitably affected by the fact that he is learning it as a foreign language. The influence shows especially in his grammar, as, for example, in "I asked my father that I wanted to go to school," and when he speaks English with other Northern Nigerians, they, coming from similar linguistic backgrounds, will probably use similar constructions. When the languages in question are more closely related to one another than Anthony's first two languages are to English, this kind of grammatical influence is particularly likely to happen, as is also the borrowing of common as well as specialized words. (For full discussion of different forms of language contact, see Weinreich 1966; Thomason & Kaufman 1988; and Thomason 2001.)

Although language contact may lead to *language mixing*, it can also lead, in extreme cases, to *language shifting*, that is, to speakers of one language abandoning it entirely in favor of another one. Speakers do this when they perceive the second language as being more prestigious than their own: The people who speak it are more powerful, more wealthy, and probably more numerous. The first stage in the process is for most speakers of the first language to become bilingual, whereas few if any speakers of the second do so. Speakers of the first group then begin to use their second language among themselves, and, most important, to pass it on to their children. The children may grow up with little knowledge of their parents' ancestral language, and the next generation will probably not speak it at all. Ultimately, the ancestral language is forgotten, although its influence may survive in the grammatical structures and vocabulary that its speakers introduced into their new language at the time when many of them were bilingual. English has been described as a "killer" language (Price 1984, p. 170; Fennel 2001, p. 264) because so many communities have felt constrained to adopt it; the result is that their ancestral languages, having no more speakers, are now dead.

Language contact is often the result of *migration*, the movement of communities of speakers from one region to another. English speakers have moved several times in recorded history and in so doing have encountered speakers of other languages, as well as new physical environments. They have adapted their language in response to the needs of these new environments, often drawing on the languages of the peoples that they have met there, while using the resources of their own language too. In this way, new linguistic communities have developed, with their own distinctive forms of speech. Meanwhile, the people left behind have continued in their old communities, still speaking the language and changing it according to their own needs. In such situations, the speakers of old and new communities can still understand one another for a time and as long as they continue to interact, their ways of speaking do not diverge so much as to become mutually incomprehensible. However, once the communities stop communicating—or if there is ill-feeling between them, so that their members want to establish distinct communal identities—the divergent varieties will eventually become so different as to be considered different languages. It was presumably through this process that Indo-European diverged and developed into so many different languages. In the case of English, however, we can document how this divergence and development happened and is still happening today.

Although language contact and migration are important factors in linguistic change, they are not the only ones. Another factor is *technological*, or, more broadly, *intellectual* change, which itself is often the result of contact between different peoples and different cultures. As a community acquires new technology and new knowledge—or, indeed, as its thinkers reconceptualize the knowledge that it has already—new vocabulary is needed to represent the new ideas. In a language contact situation, speakers will often take this vocabulary from the language of the people who introduced the ideas in question, but they may develop it from the resources of their own language. They may, for example, combine existing words to make new *compounds*, as, with the development of computer technology, people now talk of *booting up, system crash,* and *printout.* They may put new endings on existing root words, as they have in developing the word *emoticon.* They may use existing words in their entirety but with completely new meanings: An obvious example is *mouse* (the connection here is *metaphorical:* The computer mouse is like the animal). The resources of a language are endless, and if a community needs new words some of its members will come up with them; others in their social networks will then adopt them and absorb them into the language.

A particularly significant factor in language change, at least in the case of English, has been literacy. *Literacy*, like *dialect*, is a difficult term to use because it is associated with a great deal of prejudice: Modern English speakers who can read and write tend to despise those who cannot because they equate reading and writing with social integration and personal intelligence. But, as a number of studies show, reading and writing do not in themselves confer social, economic, or intellectual benefits (Graff 1979; Prinsloo & Breier 1996; Scribner & Cole 1981; Street 1984); their effects depend on how societies use written texts. That said, the ability to use language in a visual form does have certain practical consequences: A written message can be conveyed over distance and a written record can be preserved over time more effectively and efficiently than an oral message or record can. Thus, people who acquire a writing system acquire a means of organizing themselves over wider geographical areas and with more central direction. They also acquire a means of accumulating evidence of past events and, thus, of extending their collective memory. Both these factors are important in the building up of social institutions (Goody 1986), and they have played an essential role in the development of English-speaking societies.

More specifically, as far as language is concerned, literacy—especially *print literacy*—enables people to communicate directly not only over wider distances but also with more people than they can orally and, thus, the network through which they can influence one another's language is wider (Eisenstein 1979; Ong 1982). Through such a network of readers and writers, a standard variety or dialect can develop that transcends regional varieties, although it may be confined to a relatively small social group. Literacy also enables people to preserve examples of the language of the past so that even when words or structures are abandoned in the spoken form, they remain available in writing and may sometimes be revived and used again. The net effect is to expand the resources of the language, at least for those who read habitually. Finally, literacy creates the possibility of *translation*, which is a most intimate form of language contact. Translators who try to write in one language what they read in another are engaged in a constant struggle to find ways of expressing foreign meanings, and they are often led into borrowing foreign words and structures because those of their own language seem inadequate. When the texts they are working on have high status in the culture, their translations, with all the foreign forms that they include, can have considerable impact on the development of the language.

Literacy is especially important for the study of social and linguistic history. Written documents give a far fuller picture of past people and events than oral traditions or physical remains can do; and before the 20th century, writing was the only way of preserving records of language itself. Yet, it is important to recognize the limitations of written sources. Even now, not all English speakers can read and write, and in the past the literate proportion of the population was small indeed (Graff 1987). That proportion comprised distinct and privileged social groups: churchmen at first (and hardly any women), then royalty and aristocracy, and, later, the expanding and increasingly dominant middle classes. Those who wrote the records that we now have came from these social groups and naturally expressed their interests and perspectives; those of the common people, the majority of English speakers, were not, for the most part, represented, nor were the ways in which they spoke.

Another limitation of written sources is that even the most literate communities write only a fraction of what they say, and the kinds of interaction that are recorded in writing may be quite different from spoken ones. Writing takes longer than talking, and the materials used for it may be expensive, so it has at some periods and in some communities been used only for formal purposes. We must also remember that of all that was written in the past, much has been lost. What has survived has been determined partly by chance and partly by past people's decisions as to what was worth preserving—and what they considered important may well be different from what we would consider important now.

However much is written and preserved, it will in any case be an inadequate representation of speech because of the limitations of the writing system itself (Coulmas 1989, p. 268). The English writing system is based on the alphabet, which, in principle, uses a single symbol to represent each *phoneme*, or unit of sound in the language. The word *pin*, for example, includes three phonemes and so is represented by three letters; *spin* has four phonemes and is represented by four letters. The representation has never been exact, however, because the alphabet was not developed by speakers of English but by speakers of languages with different sound systems. The 26 letters of the alphabet, therefore, are not enough for the 40 or so English sounds–it is particularly short of symbols for vowels. In addition, people's pronunciation has changed over the centuries; writers have changed their spelling too, but not always consistently or systematically, and they have not kept pace with the sound change. In the past three to four hundred years, in particular, English spelling has become quite rigid, and because sound change has continued, the fit between the written and spoken language is now worse than ever. Besides these problems with the alphabet, there are many characteristics of speech that are not represented in writing at all. There are no symbols to represent speed, intonation, volume, or stress—readers have to supply those from their knowledge of speech, helped only minimally by punctuation. We can only guess, then, what texts written down in the past might have sounded like when read aloud, although, by careful comparisons with other texts and with modern pronunciations, we can make guesses that are probably quite accurate.

One final point needs to be made about literacy: Important and influential as it is, it is always secondary to *orality*. Children, like Richard and Lem, learn to speak before they learn to read and write; some, in fact, never learn to read and write at all, for whereas speaking is characteristic of all normal humans, reading and writing are not. Similarly, a natural language is always spoken before it is written, and although some innovations (new words, for example) may be introduced through writing, most appear in speech and become established in the language as speakers interact. And, because orality is primary, it follows that reference books on language, such as dictionaries and grammar books, can only be a record of how speakers have used words and structures up to a given point in time. Many books attempt to lay down rules as to what speakers should use, but these rules have little impact on the language; the rules that speakers have developed through interaction with one another are infinitely more powerful.

For as much as a language may vary and change, it is always rule-governed. Richard, for example, is, with his mother's help, constructing rules for expressing what he knows about the world. Lem is doing the same: "Ain't no way I can't get back" does not conform to the rules that Richard is learning, but it does conform to the rules of Lem's dialect. These rules operate at different levels, governing *pronunciation*, which includes *phonology*, *grammar*, which includes *morphology* and *syntax*, and *vocabulary*, which includes *lexis* and *semantics*. (For a fuller explanation of these levels, see Millward 1989, pp. 1–4.) The levels are interdependent, so that a change in one is likely to have a chain reaction in the others. For example, Ugandan speakers of English do not distinguish between the sounds represented by *i* as in *sit* and *ea* as in *seat*; their phonological rules allow for fewer vowels than other English varieties (Schmied 1991). Consequently, the words *sit* and *seat* sound identical. This has led to a change in both vocabulary and grammar: The verb *seat* (as in "to seat guests") is not used, and the use of *sit* is extended. A senior university administrator, for example, writes that one university library "can *sit* 40% of enrolled students" and that it is relatively well off for "*sitting* space"; thus, one vocabulary item is lost, and another is used with a new meaning and in new grammatical contexts.

This set of changes is tiny in relation to the language as a whole and is certainly not enough to make Ugandans' English incomprehensible to other English speakers. But such changes accumulate over time so that to modern speakers the language of their linguistic ancestors may seem like a different language. To illustrate this point, here is a passage, originally written in Greek, that has been translated into English at different times. It is taken from the Christian Bible, which, as a sacred text, has been translated particularly often. The first version given here is from *The New English Bible*, which was produced in England in 1961; it thus represents *Modern English*, that is, the English of the period since the end of the eighteenth century. The second is from *The King James Bible*, otherwise known as the *Authorized Version*, which was written at the command of King James I of England in 1611, whereas the third is from a translation made by William Tyndale in 1525, whose work strongly influenced the writers of *The King James Bible*. The two translations are therefore similar, but the spelling in the King James version has been modernized here, whereas in Tyndale's it has not. These two versions together represent the period known as *Early Modern English*, which is generally taken to extend from the early 16th to the end of the 18th century. The fourth text is taken from the *Wycliffite Bible*, so called because the man who inspired the translation was named John Wycliffe; the translation given here was a first draft written in about 1375, and so it represents a fairly literal rendering in what is known as *Middle English*, a period extending from the twelfth to the fifteenth centuries. The fifth, and earliest, version is taken from a translation of the Gospels made by a churchman and reformer named Ælfric in about 1000; this version, then, is a relatively late representative of *Old English*, which is the name given to the language from the earliest records up to the eleventh century. The texts are reprinted, in reverse order, from David Burnley's *The History of the English Language: A Source Book* (1992, pp. 356–360).

The Death of John the Baptist (Mark 6: 18–30)

Modern English: The New English Bible (1961)

18. John had told Herod, "You have no right to your brother's wife."

19. Thus Herodias nursed a grudge against him and would willingly have killed him, but she could not;

20. For Herod went in awe of John, knowing him to be a good and holy man; so he kept him in custody. He liked to listen to him, although the listening left him greatly perplexed.

21. Herodias found her opportunity when Herod on his birthday gave a banquet to his chief officials and commanders and the leading men of Galilee.

22. Her daughter came in and danced, and so delighted Herod and his guests that the king said to the girl, "Ask what you like and I will give it you."

23. And he swore an oath to her: "whatever you ask I will give you, up to half my kingdom."

24. She went out and said to her mother, "What shall I ask for?" She replied, "The head of John the Baptist."

25. The girl hastened back at once to the king with her request: "I want you to give me here and now, on a dish, the head of John the Baptist."

26. The king was greatly distressed, but out of regard for his oath and for his guests he could not bring himself to refuse her.

27. So the king sent a soldier of the guard with orders to bring John's head. The soldier went off and beheaded him in the prison,

28. Brought the head on a dish, and gave it to the girl; and she gave it to her mother.

29. When John's disciples heard the news, they came and took his body away and laid it in a tomb.

30. The apostles now rejoined Jesus and reported to him all that they had done and taught.

Early Modern English: The King James Bible (1611)

18. For John had said unto Herod, "It is not lawful for thee to have thy brother's wife."

19. Therefore Herodias had a quarrel against him, and would have killed him; but she could not.

20. For Herod feared John, knowing that he was a just man and an holy, and observed him; and when he heard him, he did many things, and heard him gladly.

21. And when a convenient day was come, that Herod on his birthday made a supper to his lords, high captains, and chief estates of Galilee;

22. And when the daughter of the said Herodias came in, and danced, and pleased Herod and them that sat with him, the king said unto the damsel, "Ask of me whatsoever thou wilt, and I will give it thee."

23. And he sware unto her, "Whatsoever thou shalt ask of me, I will give it thee, unto the half of my kingdom."

24. And she went forth, and said unto her mother, "What shall I ask?" And she said, "The head of John the Baptist."

25. And she came in straightway with haste unto the king, and asked, saying, "I will that thou give me by and by in a charger the head of John the Baptist."

26. And the king was exceeding sorry; yet for his oath's sake, and for their sakes which sat with him, he would not reject her.

27. And immediately the king sent an executioner, and commanded his head to be brought: and he went and beheaded him in the prison,

28. And brought his head in a charger, and gave it to the damsel: and the damsel gave it to her mother.

29. And when his disciples heard of it, they came and took up his corpse, and laid it in a tomb.

30. And the apostles gathered themselves together unto Jesus, and told him all things, both what they had done, and what they had taught.

Early Modern English: Tyndale's Bible (1525)

18. Jhon said vnto Herode, "It is not laufull for the, to have thy brothers wyfe."

19. Herodias layd waite for him, and wolde have killed him, butt she coulde not;

20. For Herode feared Jhon, knowynge that he was iuste and holy, and gave him reverence. And when he herde him, he did many thinges, and herde him gladly.

21. And when a convenyent daye was come, Herode on hys birth daye made a supper to the lordes, captayns, and chefe estates of Galile.

22. And the doughter of the same Herodias cam in, and daunsed, and pleased Herode and them that sate att bourde also. Then the kinge sayd unto the mayden: "Axe of me what thou wilt, and I will geve it the";

23. And he sware vnto her, "What soever thou shalt axe of me, I will geve it the, even vnto the one halfe of my kyngdom."

24. And she went forth, and sayde to her mother, "What shall I axe?" And she sayde: "Jhon Baptistes heed."

25. And she cam in streigth waye with haste vnto the kinge and axed, sayinge: "I wyll that thou geve me by and by in a charger the heed of Jhon Baptist."

26. And the kinge was sorye, yet for hys othes sake, and for their sakes which sate att supper also, he wolde not put her besyde her purpost;

27. And immediatly the kynge sent the hangman, and commaunded his heed to be brought in. And he went and beheeded him in the preson,

28. And brought his heedde in a charger, and gave it to the mayden, and the mayden gave it to her mother.

29. When his disciples herde of it, they cam and tooke vppe his body, and put it in a toumbe.

30. And the apostles gaddered them selves to geddre to Jesus, and tolde him all thynges, booth what they had done and what they had taught.

Middle English: the Wycliffite Bible (ca. 1375)

18. Sothly Johne seide to Eroude, "It is not leefful to thee, for to haue the wyf of thi brother."

19. Erodias forsothe leide aspies to him, and wolde sle him, and miȝte not.

20. Sothly Eroude drede John, witinge him a iust man and hooly, and kepte him. And him herd, he dide many thingis, and gladly herde hym.

21. And whanne a couenable day hadde fallun, Eroude in his birthe day made soupere to the princis and tribunys and to the firste of Galilee.

22. And whanne the douȝter of thilke Erodias hadde intride yn, and lepte, and pleside to Eroude, and also to men restynge, the kyng seide to the wenche, "Axe thou of me what thou wolt, and I shal ȝiue to thee";

23. And he swoor to hir: "For what euere thou schalt axe, I schal ȝive to thee, thouȝ the half of my kyngdom."

24. The whiche, whanne sche hadde gon out, seide to hir modir, "What schal I axe?" And sche seide, "The heed of John Baptist."

25. And whanne sche hadde entrid anon with haste to the kyng, she axide, seyinge, "I wole that anoon thou ȝyve to me in a dische the heed of John Baptist."

26. And the kyng was sory for the ooth, and for men sittinge to gidere at mete he wolde not hir be maad sory;

27. But a manquellere sent, he comaundide the heed of John Baptist for to be brouȝt. And he bihedide him in the prison,

28. And brouȝte his heed in a dische, and ȝaf it to the wenche, and the wench ȝaf to hir modir.

29. The which thing herd, his disciplis camen, and token his body, and puttiden it in a buriel.

30. And apostlis comynge to giderere to Jhesu, tolden to hym all thingis that thei hadden done and tauȝt

Ælfric's translation of the Gospels (ca. 1000)

18. Da sæde Iohannes Herode: "Nis þe alyfed to hæbenne þines broðer wif."

19. Da syrwde Herodias ymbe hine, and wolde hine ofslean, and heo ne mihte.

20. Soðlice Herodes ondræd Iohannem, and wiste þæt he wæs rihtwis and halig, and he heold hine on cwerterne. And he gehierde þæt he fela wundra worhte, and he lufelice him hierde.

21. þa se dæg com Herodes gebyrdtide, he gegearwode micele feorme his ealdor-mannum, and þæm fyrmestum on Galilea.

22. And þa ða þære Herodiadiscan dohtor inn-eode and tumbode; hit licode Herode and eallum þæm ðe him mid sæton. Se cyning cwæð þa to ðæm mægdene: "Bidde me swa hwæt swa þu wille, and ic þe selle";

23. And he swor hire, "Soðes ic þe selle swa hwæt swa þu me bitst, þeah þu wille healf min rice."

24. Da heo ut-eode, heo cwæð to hire meder, "Hwæs bidde ic?" þa cwæþ heo, "Iohannes heafod þæs fulluhteres."

25. Sona þa heo mid ofste inn to þæm cyninge eode; heo bæd and þus cwæð: "Ic wille þæt ðu me hrædlice on anum disce selle Iohannes heafod."

26. þa wearð se cyning geunret for þæm aðe, and forþæm ðe him mid sæton nolde þeah hie geunretan,

27. Ac sende anne cwellere, and bebead þæt man his heafod on anum disce brohte. And he hine þa on cwerterne beheafdode,

28. And his heafod on disce brohte, and hit sealde þæm mægdene, and þæt mægden hit sealde hire meder.

29. Da his cnihtas þæt gehierdon, hie comon, and his lichaman namon, and hine on byrgene legdon.

30. Soðlice þa ða apostolas togædere comon, hie cyddon þæm Hælende eall þæt hie didon and hie lærdon.

These translations are not exactly parallel to one another because they were pro-duced from different sources and with different intentions (Burnley 1992, p. 355). Tyndale and his successors consulted the original Greek text, whereas the Wycliffites and Ælfric worked from the Latin Vulgate translation. *The New English Bible* is by far the most liberal; the earlier translators tended to keep closer to the original that they were working from. Nevertheless, these five versions illustrate clearly how the standard written English of today has evolved through the past thousand years.

First, much of the vocabulary has changed. *The New English Bible* writes of Herod's daughter as a *girl* (verses 22, 25, and 28); the *King James* uses the word *damsel*, the Wycliffites' version, *wenche*, and Tyndale's and Ælfric's, different spellings of the word *maiden*. All four words exist in modern English, but *girl* is by far the most common; both *damsel* and *maiden* are distinctly old-fashioned, and *wench* is both old-fashioned and slightly insulting. Other words used in the older versions are still less familiar: The man who beheads John the Baptist is called a *manquellere* in the Wycliffite version and a *cwellere* in Ælfric's; they are not easily recognizable as variants of the modern word *killer*. Some words from Ælfric's text have disappeared entirely: *cweterne* (verses 20 and 27) has been displaced by *prison*, *fulluhteres* (verse 24) by *baptist*. Others survive but in a different meaning: *selle*, used in verses 22, 23, and 25 (and in the past tense form *sealde* in verse 28), is the modern verb *sell/sold*, but here it means "give"—there is no money involved; *ealdormannum* (verse 21) is now rendered by *lords*, but it survives as the narrower and less high status word *alderman*; *cnihtas* (verse 29) is used to mean "followers" (*disciples* in the later versions) but the modern form of the word is *knight*— quite a different kind of person.

Not only have the words of the language changed; so has the grammar. All the versions before 1961 use (in verses 18, 22, 23, and 25) singular forms of the second person pronoun: *thou/thee/thy* (1611), *thou/the/thy* (1525), *thou/thee/thi* (1375), and *þu* (or *ðu*)/*þe/þi[nes]* (1000); modern standard English has only one set of forms for both singular and plural, *you/your*. Another pronoun that has changed is the third person singular feminine: It is *she/her* in the 1961, 1611, and 1525 versions (see verses 19, 21, 22, 23, 24, 25, 26, and 28) and *sche/hir* in the 1375 one, but in 1000 it is *heo/hire*. The third person plural pronoun has also changed: What is *they* in the 1961, 1611, and 1525 versions and *thei* in the 1375 one was *hie* in 1000 (see verses 29 and 30). The rules concerning word order have changed too, as becomes clear if we make a word for word modern translation of Ælfric's version:

Verse 19: Da syrwde Herodias ymbe hine, and wolde hine ofslean and heo ne mihte.
   Then plotted Herodias against him, and would him slay and she not might.
Verse 23: Da heo ut-eode, heo cwæð to hire meder "Hwæs bidde ic?"
   Then she out-went, she said to her mother "What ask I?"
   þa cwæð heo, "Iohannes heafod þæs fulluhteres."
   Then said she, "John's head the Baptist's."

Another grammatical feature of Ælfric's language is that most words had a greater variety of grammatical endings or *inflections* than their modern equivalents. For example, the name *Herod* is presented as *Herodes* in verse 20 and as *Herode* in verse 18; the word *king* is *cyning* in verse 22 and *cyninge* in verse 25; *maiden* is *mægden* in the second mention in verse 28 and *mægdene* in the first mention. The choice of form is determined in each case by the function of the word in the sentence: *Herodes*, *cyning*, and *mægden* are all *subject* (or *nominative*) forms; they name the doer of the action described:

Verse 20: ... Herodes ondræd Iohannem.
   ... *Herod feared John.*
Verse 22: ... Se cyning cwæð þa to ðæm mægdene ...
   ... *The king said then to the maiden ...*
Verse 28: ... and þæt mægden hit sealde hire meder.
   ... *and that maiden it gave hir mother.*

The other forms in these examples are all *dative*; they name the *indirect object* or the direction of the action. The idea is usually expressed in modern English by using the preposition *to* before the noun in question. In Old English this preposition is also used, but the dative form is still needed after it, and often the dative can be used by itself.

Verse 18: Da sæde Iohannes Herode...
          Then said John [to] Herod...
Verse 25: Sona þa heo mid ofste inn to þæm cyninge eode ...
          Soon then she with haste in to the king went...
Verse 28: ...and hit sealde þæm mægdene...
          ...and it gave [to] the maiden

This analysis of the grammatical differences between the different versions of this text is by no means complete, but enough has been said to show that the grammar of English has changed significantly over the centuries, especially between the Old English and Middle English periods.

Another factor that makes the older texts, especially the Old English one, seem strange, is the spelling. The 1611 version has been modernized here, but its original spelling was as peculiar, to modern eyes, as Tyndale's is, illustrating the fact that spelling was not yet fixed; the spelling in Tyndale's rendering of this story is not even consistent within itself. The 1375 version is still more different from modern spelling, not only because the conventions for rendering particular sounds were different (*u*, for example, is used to represent the sound that we now spell with a *v*), but also because the pronunciation has changed: the spelling of *leefful* for *lawful* (verse 18) indicates that the word was then pronounced like *lay-full*; the use of *e* at the end of a word indicates a short unstressed vowel like the one at the end of *Anna*, so that the name *Eroude* would have been pronounced something like *eh-roo-duh*. The pronunciation of Old English was, naturally, still more different. The letter *y*, for example, represents a sound that disappeared in the Middle English period (Millward 1989, p. 74, 129): it was like the modern German *ü*, being made as if one was saying *ee*, but with the lips rounded (when the rounding disappeared, the *y* spelling was sometimes retained, as in *kyng*, verses 22 and 25 in the Wycliffite translation; but then it represented a sound like *i*, as in modern *king*). The letter *h* also represents a sound that no longer exists in English: it was like the *ch* in German *nicht* or in Scots *loch*. In addition, Old English used a few letters that have since been abandoned: æ is called *ash* and represents a sound between modern *a* and *e*; ð, called *eth*, and þ, called *thorn*, both represent the sounds expressed in modern English by *th*; ȝ, or *yogh* (which was used in Middle English too and is represented here only in the 1375 text), was used like modern *g* or *y*, as well as in other ways that need not concern us here. (For a description of Old English spelling, see Burnley 1992, pp. 1–3.)

So in these texts, we can see how changes at all the levels of the language have combined and accumulated so as to make the oldest records of English seem, to a modern reader, like texts in a foreign language. Yet, even in the Old English text, incomprehensible as it may seem, there are relatively few words that have no trace in modern English, and its relationship to the modern text is quite clear when we look at the intermediate versions. Change in language is striking, but we can only see it when we compare records that are widely separated in time. When we read only modern texts and listen only to modern speakers, we do not notice it; but change is continuing nonetheless, and much of the contemporary variation that we can perceive is a sign that it is going on.

These passages represent only one phase of the history of English: It will be called here the *European* phase, since it is the story of how the language developed in the minds, mouths, and hands of speakers who lived and continue to live in Europe. This phase is both the earliest and the longest because while there were people speaking the language in Europe long before they migrated anywhere else, there are people still speaking it there now.

NOTE

[1] This article is the first chapter of a work-in-progress, provisionally entitled *English Speakers: A Social and Linguistic History.*

REFERENCES

Aitchison, J. (1996). *The seeds of speech: Language origin and evolution.* Cambridge: Cambridge University Press.

Bruner, J. S. (1993). Learning the Mother Tongue. In L. M. Cleary & M. D. Linn. (Eds.), *Linguistics for teachers* (pp. 55–66), New York: McGraw-Hill.

Burnley, D. (1992). *The history of the English language: A source book.* London: Longman.

Carver, C. M. (1989). *American regional dialects: A word geography.* Ann Arbor: University of Michigan Press.

Coulmas, F. (1989). *Writing systems of the world.* Oxford: Blackwell.

Crosby, A. W. (1986). *Ecological Imperialism: The biological expansion of Europe, 900–1900.* Cambridge: Cambridge University Press.

Crystal, D. (1998). *English as a global language.* Cambridge: Cambridge University Press.

Eisenstein, E. (1979). *The printing press as an agent of change: Communications and cultural transformations in early-modern Europe* (Vols. 1–2). New York: Cambridge University Press.

Fennel, B. A. (2001). *A history of English: A sociolinguistic approach.* Oxford: Blackwell.

Goody, J. (1986). *The logic of writing and the organization of society.* Cambridge: Cambridge University Press.

Graff, H. J. (1979). *The literacy myth: Literacy and social structure in the 19th century city.* New York: Academic Press.

Graff, H. J. (1987). *The legacies of literacy: Continuities and contradictions in western culture and society.* Bloomington: Indiana University Press.

Heath, S. B. (1983). *Ways with words: Language, life, and work in communities and classrooms.* Cambridge: Cambridge University Press.

Leith, D. (1997). *A social history of english* (2nd ed.). London and New York: Routledge.

McArthur, T. (1998). *The English languages.* Cambridge: Cambridge University Press.

Millward, C. M. (1989). *A biography of the English language.* Fort Worth, TX: Holt, Rinehart and Winston.

Milroy, J. (1992). *Linguistic variation and change.* Oxford, England, and Cambridge: MA, Blackwell.

Milroy, L. (1987). *Language and social networks* (2nd ed). Oxford: Blackwell.

Nettle, D., & Suzanne R. (2000). *Vanishing voices: The extinction of the world's languages.* Oxford: Oxford University Press.

Ong, W. J. (1982). *Orality and literacy: The technologizing of the word.* London: Methuen.

Parry, K. (1986). *Readers in context: A study of northern Nigerian students and school certificate texts.* Unpublished doctoral dissertation. Teachers College, Columbia University.

Parry, K., & Xiaojun, S. (Eds.). (1998). *Culture, literacy, and learning english: Voices from the Chinese classroom.* Portsmouth, NH: Heinemann.

Pinker, S. (1995). *The language instinct: The new science of language and mind.* London: Penguin Books.

Price, G. (1984). *The languages of Britain.* London: Edward Arnold.

Prinsloo, M., & Mignonne B. (1996). *The social uses of literacy: Theory and practice in contemporary South Africa.* Philadelphia, PA: John Benjamins.

Pyles, T., & John A. (1982). *The Origins and development of the English language* (3rd ed.). San Diego, CA: Harcourt Brace Jovanovich.

Schmied, J. (1991). *English in Africa: An introduction.* London: Longman.

Scribner, S., & Michael C. (1981). *The psychology of literacy.* Cambridge, MA: Harvard University Press.

Street, B. V. (1984). *Literacy in theory and practice.* Cambridge: Cambridge University Press.

Thomason, S. G. (2001). *Language contact.* Washington, DC: Georgetown University Press.

Thomason, S. G., & Clarence K. (1988). *Language contact, creolization, and genetic linguistics.* Berkeley: University of California Press.

Weinreich, U. (1966). *Languages in contact: Findings and problems.* The Hague: Mouton.

QUESTIONS TO THINK ABOUT

1. The difference between *diglossia* and *bilingualism* is subtle, as you may have encountered in this reading. How would you draw this distinction, after having read the selection by Parry?
2. Parry refers to "the limitations of the writing system itself." What are some of these limitations? How do they cause writing and the printed word to be "an inadequate representation of speech," as Parry mentions in this context?
3. What are some of the features of Old English and Middle English texts presented by Parry that seem odd to speakers of Present Day English?
4. *Extending your understanding*: Consider some of the effects of literacy mentioned by Parry on language and its users. How do these effects impact the teaching of reading and writing both to first language students and to second language students?

TERMS TO DEFINE

Define the following words and phrases as they are presented within the context of the reading. Comment on your understanding of the significance of each one.

Lingua franca
Global language
Standard English
Language mixing
Language shift
Literacy

Queen's English

Homi K. Bhabha
University of Chicago

[Gary Dauphin]: So Black English is for secret stuff?
Reesie: It's not secret secret. But it's private.
— "Schoolyard Sages: New York City School Kids Weigh In on Ebonics,"
The Village Voice

Returning this winter to Chicago from Bombay with the sweet singsong of my native Bombay Bazaar English still sounding in my ears, I'm confronted with the latest American cultural brouhaha—the Ebonic plague. Like my friend and quasi-compatriot Mr. Rushdie, I am now quite convinced that writing about something can actually make it happen—to you. So there I am, Ms. Respected Reader, Dear Madam, as we are politely saying always in Bombay. So I'm trying too too hard to speak without mistake, sounding totally like polite, proper BBC English, not yankee crude, "ya" this, "gonna" that—always opening bigmouth and talking through nose. No, I'm trying for pure Westminster-Oxford-Waterloo English when I'm dispatched to write about Ebonics! Ebonic-bubonic plague, I thought. OOOOhhhh, my good god, why I should write and spoil more my English—nothing be cool or phat in dat. Out damn spot! If something wrotten (or written) in state of Oakland, why drag that damn disease here? So I picked up only one lovely, lovely bombay poetry, to forget all this hopeless culture wars and culture whores, and calmly read:

Friends, our dear sister is departing for foreign in two three days, and we are meeting today to wish her bon voyage.

You are all knowing, friends, what sweetness is in Miss Pushpa. I don't mean only external sweetness but internal sweetness. Miss Pushpa is smiling and smiling even for no reason but simply because she is feeling.

Reproduced with permission from *Artforum* (March 1997). © 1997 Artforum International Magazine, Inc.

Whenever I asked her to do anything, she was saying, "Just now only I will do it." That is showing good spirit. I am always appreciating the good spirit. Pushpa Miss is never saying no. Whatever I or anybody is asking she is always saying yes, and today she is going to improve her prospect, and we are wishing her bon voyage.

Reesie Otulana, nine, from Cambria Heights, Queens, New York, and Miss Pushpa T. S., nineteen, of Laburnum Buildings, Hanuman Vihar, Bombay, are hardly soul sisters. They come from vastly different cultural backgrounds: their social worlds are equally strange to one another. Reesie (as we have been repeatedly reminded by the ethnographers of Ebonics) is the descendant of West African slaves, suspended in the lower depths of urban American society. She is in danger of becoming just another percentage point in a deadening survey of the growing body of semi-literate and underemployed youth that come out of underfunded public schools located in areas of economic attrition. ("One half of all African-American youth are born into poverty": Jesse Jackson, *The New York Times*, Dec. 31, 1996; "71 percent of Oakland's 28,000 blacks are in special education classes . . . [the] average grade point on a 4.0 system is 1.8": Courtland Milloy, *Washington Post*, Dec. 22, 1996.) Reesie may well turn out to be "Baad!" in the nonstandard, "black English" sense of the word. Miss Pushpa, on the other hand, is undeniably good. As a clerical cog in the archaic wheel of Bombay's Byzantine bureaucracy, her "low" economic status has kept her from an improving, Westernized "convent" education. Her cute and creaky English has been picked up at a deeply disciplinary state school through the rote repetition of cliches, commonplace idioms, and readings out of Victorian-style "self-help" primers. Infantalized and exploited both at home and work, she is poised to escape this pervasive patriarchy, to better her prospects, by being "diasporized," going "to foreign" where, as a Non-Resident Indian in the United States or the Gulf States, she will, of course, be the good daughter and continue obediently to support her family back home. Miss Pushpa T. S. is "internal sweetness itself!" in Bombay Bazaar English—as the poet says, "Pushpa Miss is never saying no."

Reesie, the great-granddaughter of slaves; Pushpa T. S., the stepchild of the postcolonial state: What do they have in common? As their divergent "colonial" histories—of American slavery and British imperialism—circumnavigate the globe in opposite directions, they meet on the margins of nonstandard "vernaculars" or hybridized orders of speech. These are twisted versions of the language of the master, alienating the syntactical "eloquence" and intonational "elegance" through which "standard" English naturalizes itself as a national cultural norm. Whether or not these hybrid speech genres are a species of African-American Vernacular English (AAVE) or something like Bombay Bazaar Hindi-English (BBHE), whether the grammatical structure of "Ain't nobody sing like Chaka Khan" comes from the Niger-Congo Basin, or the rhetorical particularity of "Miss Pushpa is smiling and smiling/even for no reason" can be traced back to Hindi speech patterns common to Bombay's Bhindi Bazaar, the world of these utterances cannot be reduced to the description of speech as an "object" of linguistic study or a functionalist form of verbal communication without doing violence to the living tongue.

The sociolinguistic descriptions and definitions of vernacularization certainly have an important pedagogical contribution to make. Who could deny that a knowledge of the deep structure of black English would not assist teachers in their attempts to assess performance and to elicit the best results from those who are educationally disadvantaged? In *The Village Voice's* "Schoolyard Sages: New York City School Kids Weigh in on Ebonics," sixteen-year-old Keith Meyers, also from Cambria Heights, put it succinctly: "Teachers could make some room for different ways of speaking. Not teach it, but at least understand what we're saying," But rather than draw wide and increasingly general circles around the "academic" issue of what is black English, I want to deal with its more demotic address: What are Keith and Reesie and their friends doing when they act cool and "be all like., 'Yo, what's up?'"

These communal forms of utterance resemble what Roland Barthes describes as an "idiolect" in his influential early work *Elements of Semiology*. Ingeniously broadening the notion beyond its customary focus on an individual's given linguistic repertoire, Barthes defines the idiolect as the whole set of speech habits of a linguistic community that reflect "the need for a speech which is already institutionalized but not yet radically open to formalization, as the language is." The idiolect—as an intermediate practice between speech and language—resists "formalization," as Barthes put it, because its ability to confer a shared totemic identity on those who "miss-peak," those who are phat, is a process of cultural performance rooted in the passing, transitory moment of utterance itself. The idiolect is, quite literally, informal because it depends for its communal effect on rhythm, slang, gesture, dress—signs that express its particularity. Black talk certainly fits this description, but as the speech act of a minority, its particularity further connotes its sense of peripherality—of the eagerly guarded "privacy" that Reesie and her friends talk about. Listen, for instance, to Keith:

> We all have our individual way of speaking. It doesn't hurt anybody most of the time. You can do what you want on your personal time, but when you're getting paid to do something, you want to speak properly.... The slang comes in when you talk with your friends.

Keith's ventriloquism, the act of switching between "proper English" and "black English," redraws the public/private distinction through the medium of language, making both audible and visible the ways in which minorities are positioned as, at once, insiders and outsiders within the society of their belonging. "Privacy," in this context, is not the essential liberal virtue of having "a room of one's own," in Virginia Woolf's felicitous phrase, a sign of the sovereignty of self-hood, a place for meditation and reflection. This much more communal "privacy" lived out, ironically, in public—is a way of establishing a kind of cultural intimacy, even indegeneity, for a minority group that is too often in the public eye for its lack of commercial success, its educational failure, its high ratings in the crime statistics. Surveyed and punished, measured and mapped, the desire for privacy on the part of the kids of Cambria Heights is a way of claiming a linguistic territory that is playful, rude, riffy, ironic, and, above all, their very own. For Keith and his teenage friends, however, the division between the private and public spheres seems, at this stage, to be as fluid and pliable as the passage between the playground and the schoolroom. But as legal theorist Patricia J. Williams reminds us on the December 29, 1996 Op-Ed page of *The New York Times*, such ventriloquism, a verbal practice common to us all, exacts a special price in a racialized cultural context. The real argument, she writes, is not the genteel one about the structure and origin of a language. It is the ambivalent and antagonistic ways in which the vernacular comes to be socially valued within the ideological structure of mainstream culture that constitutes a major class—and race—contradiction. "Perhaps the real argument is not about whether Ebonics is a language or not. Rather, the tension is revealed in the contradiction of black speech simultaneously being understood yet not understood.... Colorfully comprehensible ... in sports and entertainment, yet deemed so utterly incapable of effective communication when it comes to finding a job."

Some elements of black "underclass" culture, from the worlds of sport and entertainment, are readily transformed into "style" via the yuppie collaboration with the culture industry (MTV, Rupert Murdoch's Fox Broadcasting Company, Time Warner, Inc.) and commodity fetishes (mile-high Nikes; low-slung Levis, "prison style" laceless boots). Then, suddenly, just as the melting pot or "tossed salad" models of cultural assimilation seem to be yielding to the apparently mixed (read integrated) metaphors of the pulled-pork "po' boy," the running buffet of bicultural (read multi-cultural) options and choices suddenly dries up. In an ambivalent reversal, those very icons of incorporation become the barriers to a creative cultural hybridization when the unlaced rapping classes come off the video screen or the vinyl track to claim their place within those market institutions that control the conditions of economic and cultural "choice," while shaping the menu of social mores. What you see or hear is not what you get.

Nobody could be more foreign to this world of diss and dat than the sweet child that is Miss Pushpa T. S. Except, of course, that she is about to leave for "foreign" where, as a migrant belonging to a minority culture, her own idiolect will, no doubt, be open to all kinds of symbolic readings and status responses. If one of the marks of "Ebonics" is the use of the "habitual be"—she be reading—then such a sense of the ongoing nature of actions or states is curiously close to Pushpa's present continuous: whatever I or anybody is asking/she is always saying yes. But her connection with Reesie is, I believe, best seen on home territory, in the vernacular world of Bombay's low-paid clerical workers and the hybrid languages that the public world of business and bureaucracy demands of them.

The poet's ironic mode of address frames Bombay Bazaar English (BBC, uh, E) and reveals its contradictory cultural connotations. Miss Pushpa hardly speaks in the poem, except in parentheses ("Just now only/I will do it"). Ever compliant, she lets both her employer and the poet speak for her. And it is because she is "spoken for" while in fact becoming the only realized persona in the poem that the language actually seems to circulate around her—as her speech—although she is not the speaker. Framed in this way, Miss Pushpa's idiolect is open to two forms of irony. First, in the very foregrounding of BBE, the well-versed "English" poet inscribes the bazaar vernacular as a figure of fun and irony—a little cruel, no doubt, but sufficiently part of the repertoire of Bombay "in" jokes to count as the irony of an insider, something like the equivalent of Jewish humor. But, beyond that, there is a more reflective, sadder irony involved in this portraiture of a group of speakers whose working lives demand that they speak a language in which they always come off like awkward "poreigners," as they would say, with the aspirated p sound of BBE, always already diasporic without even leaving home. Such an irony is compounded by a poignant reality: the vernacular that enables Pushpa and her class to survive economically is what severely limits her prospects for social advancement. She is going "to foreign" to "improve her prospect" and to improve her English, too. To the extent that Reesie's black talk is a sign of the informality of the "private" in the world of the minority, Pushpa's Bazaar English is the other side of the same coin: the official language of a public sphere that is, in part, "poreign." Her idiolect's vernacular culture—an awkwardly blended Hindi-English milieu—is part of a wider public ambivalence through which strategies of inclusion and exclusion, opportunity and discrimination, are set in motion. If there is a deeper, mocking laugh buried in the poem's lines, it is aimed at the arrogant and restricted vision that often accompanies social and linguistic propriety outside the schoolhouse. Are we to be blind to the sincerity and solidarity, the playfulness and privacy, through which people build their lives and words under conditions of duress, just because the poem got the grammar wrong?

QUESTIONS TO THINK ABOUT

1. What connections does Bhabha make among language dialects in India, England, and the United States? How does he bring us, the readers, into his attitude and point of view? For example, what kinds of language and discourse does he include in his writing from the first paragraph on? How does he merge this discourse style with his message about language and direct relationships across location and cultures? What do Reesle and Pushpa T.S. have in common?

2. When talking about nonstandard dialects, particularly African American Vernacular English, Bhabha says that the speech of the underclass is "readily transformed into 'style' [on videos] . . . and commodity fetishes, . . . [which] become the barriers to a creative cultural hybridization when the unlaced rapping classes come off the video screen or the vinyl track." Do you agree with Bhabha's assessment of how African American Vernacular English (AAVE) has both an insider and an outsider status? Generally, why is low prestige accorded to dialects of English other than standard English in the "public world of business and bureaucracy?"

3. In discussing Roland Barthes' notion of an "idiolect," Bhabha calls it an "intermediate practice between speech and language" that resists "formalization." What does an idiolect signify and what are its extended meanings? Where does it fit in Bhabha's examination of African American Vernacular English and Bombay Bazaar Hindi-English?

4. *Extending your understanding*: One suggestion that linguists have often made is that "a language is only equivalent to the sum of its various dialects." What is meant by this statement? Do a short writing, about one page long, on the implications of this idea. What implications does the statement have for (a) defining what "the English language" is, and (b) distinguishing English from other similar and related languages?

TERMS TO DEFINE

Define the following words and phrases as they are presented within the context of the reading. Comment on your understanding of the significance of each one.

Queen's English
Diasporized
Vernacularization
Idiolect
Ebonics
Bombay Bazaar English

The New Linguistic Order

Joshua A. Fishman
Yeshiva University

As you read this sentence, you are one of approximately 1.6 billion people—nearly one-third of the world's population—who will use English in some form today. Although English is the mother tongue of only 380 million people, it is the language of the lion's share of the world's books, academic papers, newspapers, and magazines. American radio, television, and blockbuster films export English-language pop culture worldwide. More than 80 percent of the content posted on the Internet is in English, even though an estimated 44 percent of online users speak another language in the home. Not surprisingly, both the global supply of and the demand for English instruction are exploding. Whether we consider English a "killer language" or not, whether we regard its spread as benign globalization or linguistic imperialism, its expansive reach is undeniable and, for the time being, unstoppable. Never before in human history has one language been spoken (let alone semi-spoken) so widely and by so many.

With unprecedented reach comes a form of unprecedented power. Although language is synonymous with neither ideology nor national interest, English's role as the medium for everything from high-stakes diplomacy to air traffic control confers certain advantages on those who speak it. Predominantly English-speaking countries account for approximately 40 percent of the world's total gross domestic product. More and more companies worldwide are making English competency a prerequisite for promotions or appointments. The success of politicians around the world also increasingly depends on their facility in English. When (newly elected) German chancellor Gerhard Schroeder and French president Jacques Chirac met in September to discuss future cooperation, they spoke neither French nor German, but English. And English is the official language of the European Central Bank, despite the fact that the United Kingdom has not joined the European Monetary Union, the bank is located in Frankfurt, and only 10 percent of the bank's staff are British. The predominance of English has become such a sore point within the European Union that its leadership now provides incentives for staff members to learn any other official languages.

Reproduced with permission from *Foreign Policy* (winter 1998): 26–38. © 1998 by J. A. *Fishman*.

Yet professional linguists hesitate to predict far into the future the further globalization of English. Historically, languages have risen and fallen with the military, economic, cultural, or religious powers that supported them. Beyond the ebb and flow of history, there are other reasons to believe that the English language will eventually wane in influence. For one, English actually reaches and is then utilized by only a small and atypically fortunate minority. Furthermore, the kinds of interactions identified with globalization, from trade to communications, have also encouraged regionalization and with it the spread of regional languages. Arabic, Chinese, Hindi, Spanish, and a handful of other regional tongues already command a significant reach and their major growth is still ahead. Finally, the spread of English and these regional languages collectively—not to mention the sweeping forces driving them—have created a squeeze effect on small communities, producing pockets of anxious localization and local-language revival resistant to global change.

LOVE THY NEIGHBOR'S LANGUAGE

English came to Massachusetts the same way it did to Mumbai: on a British ship. For all the talk of Microsoft and Disney, the vast reach of English owes its origins to centuries of successful colonization by England. Of the 100 colonies that achieved independence between 1940 and 1990, 56 were former British colonies and 1 was an American possession. Almost every colony that won its independence from England either kept English as an official language or at least recognized its utility.

The continued spread of English today is both a consequence of and a contributor to globalization. Some factors are obvious: the growth in international trade and multinational corporations; the ever widening reach of American mass media; the expanding electronic network created by the Internet; and the linguistic impact of American songs, dress, food, sports, and recreation. Other factors are perhaps less visible but no less powerful, such as the growth in the study of English overseas and the swelling number of students who go abroad to study in English-speaking countries. In 1992, almost half of the world's million-plus population of foreign students were enrolled at institutions in six English mother-tongue countries: Australia, Canada, Ireland, New Zealand, the United Kingdom, and the United States.

Yet globalization has done little to change the reality that, regardless of location, the spread of English is closely linked to social class, age, gender, and profession. Just because a wide array of young people around the world may be able to sing along to a new Madonna song does not mean that they can hold a rudimentary conversation in English, or even understand what Madonna is saying. The brief formal educational contact that most learners have with English is too scant to produce lasting literacy, fluency, or even comprehension. Indeed, for all the enthusiasm and vitriol generated by grand-scale globalization, it is the growth in regional interactions—trade, travel, the spread of religions, interethnic marriages—that touches the widest array of local populations. These interactions promote the spread of regional languages.

Consider the case of Africa, where some 2,000 of the modern world's approximately 6,000 languages are spoken and 13 percent of the world's population lives. English is neither the only nor even the best means to navigate this linguistic obstacle course. Throughout East Africa, Swahili is typically the first language that two strangers attempt upon meeting. The average East African encounters Swahili in a variety of contexts, from the market, elementary education, and government "how to" publications, to popular radio programming and films. New movies from India are often dubbed in Swahili and shown in towns and villages throughout Kenya, Tanzania, and Uganda. In West Africa, some 25 million people speak Hausa natively and perhaps double that number speak it as a second or third language, due in large part to burgeoning regional commerce at local markets throughout the region. Since most Hausa speakers are Muslim, many of them also attend Koranic schools where they learn Arabic, itself a major regional language in North Africa. Thus, many Africans are trilingual on a functional basis: local mother tongues when among "their own," Hausa for trade and secular literacy, and Arabic for prayer and Koranic study. Hausa speakers firmly believe that Hausa has great prospects as a unifying language for even more of West Africa than it already reaches. Its main competition will not likely come from English but rather from other regional languages such as Woloff—which is also spreading in markets in and around Senegal—and Pidgin English.

Increased regional communication, informal market interaction, and migration are driving regional language spread around the world just as they are in Africa. Mandarin Chinese is spreading throughout China and in some of its southern neighbors. Spanish is spreading in the Americas. Hundreds of varieties of Pidgin English have emerged informally among diverse groups in Australia, the Caribbean, Papua New Guinea, and West Africa. The use of French is still increasing in many former French colonies, albeit much more slowly than at its peak of colonial influence. Hindi is reaching new learners in multilingual, multiethnic India. And Arabic is spreading in North Africa and Southeast Asia both as the language of Islam and as an important language of regional trade.

Some regional languages are spreading in part due to the efforts of organizations and government committees. France spends billions of francs annually to support French-language conferences, schools, and media that promote French as a vehicle for a common French culture. Muslim organizations in the Middle East spread knowledge about Islam worldwide with an extensive array of English pamphlets and other literature, but they cultivate their ties with each other in Arabic. Moreover, in promoting Islam within their borders, many governments seek to Arabize local ethnic minorities (for example Berbers in Morocco and Christians in Sudan). The German government funds 78 Goethe Institutes, scattered from Beirut to Jakarta, that offer regular German language courses as well as German plays, art exhibits, lectures, and film festivals. Singapore, a tiny country with four official languages, is in the nineteenth year of its national "Speak Mandarin" campaign. Singapore designed the campaign to encourage dialect-speaking Chinese to adopt a common language and facilitate the use of Mandarin as a regional tongue.

The importance of regional languages should increase in the near future. Popular writers, itinerant merchants, bazaar marketers, literacy advocates, relief workers, filmmakers, and missionaries all tend to bank on regional lingua francas whenever there is an opportunity to reach larger, even if less affluent, populations. In many developing areas, regional languages facilitate agricultural, industrial, and commercial expansion across local cultural and governmental boundaries. They also foster literacy and formal adult or even elementary education in highly multilingual areas. Wherever the local vernaculars are just too many to handle, regional languages come to the fore.

HOME IS WHERE THE TONGUE IS

For all the pressures and rewards of regionalization and globalization, local identities remain the most ingrained. Even if the end result of globalization is to make the world smaller, its scope seems to foster the need for more intimate local connections among many individuals. As Bernard Poignant, mayor of the town of Quimper in Brittany, told the Washington Post, "Man is a fragile animal and he needs his close attachments. The more open the world becomes the more ties there will be to one's roots and one's land."

In most communities, local languages such as Poignant's Breton serve a strong symbolic function as a clear mark of "authenticity." The sum total of a community's shared historical experience, authenticity reflects a perceived line from a culturally idealized past to the present, carried by the language and traditions associated (sometimes dubiously) with the community's origins. A concern for authenticity leads most secular Israelis to champion Hebrew among themselves while also acquiring English and even Arabic. The same obsession with authenticity drives Hasidic Jews in Israel or the Diaspora to champion Yiddish while also learning Hebrew and English. In each case, authenticity amounts to a central core of cultural beliefs and interpretations that are not only resistant to globalization but are actually reinforced by the "threat" that globalization seems to present to these historical values. Scholars may argue that cultural identities change over time in response to specific reward systems. But locals often resist such explanations and defend authenticity and local mother tongues against the perceived threat of globalization with near religious ardor.

As a result, never before in history have there been as many standardized languages as there are today: roughly 1,200. Many smaller languages, even those with far fewer than one million speakers, have benefited from state-sponsored or voluntary preservation movements. On the most informal level, communities in Alaska and the American northwest have formed Internet discussion groups in an attempt to pass on Native American languages to younger generations. In the Basque, Catalan, and Galician regions of Spain, such movements are fiercely political and frequently involve staunch resistance to the Spanish government over political and linguistic rights. Projects have ranged from a campaign to print Spanish money in the four official languages of the state to the creation of language immersion nursery and primary schools. Zapatistas in Mexico are championing the revival of Mayan languages in an equally political campaign for local autonomy.

In addition to invoking the subjective importance of local roots, proponents of local languages defend their continued use on pragmatic grounds. Local tongues foster higher levels of school success, higher degrees of participation in local government, more informed citizenship, and better knowledge of one's own culture, history, and faith. Navajo children in Rough Rock, Arizona, who were schooled initially in Navajo were found to have higher reading competency in English than those who were first schooled in English. Governments and relief agencies can also use local languages to spread information about industrial and agricultural techniques as well as modern health care to diverse audiences. Development workers in West Africa, for example, have found that the best way to teach the vast number of farmers with little or no formal education how to sow and rotate crops for higher yields is in these local tongues. From Asturian to Zulu, the world's practical reliance on local languages today is every bit as great as the identity roles these languages fulfill. Nevertheless, both regionalization and globalization require that more and more speakers and readers of local languages be multiliterate.

LOOKING AHEAD

Since all larger language communities have opted to maintain their own languages in the face of globalization, it should come as no surprise that many smaller ones have pursued the same goal. If Germans can pursue globalization and yet remain German-speaking among themselves, why should Telegus in India not aspire to do the same?

Multilingualism allows a people this choice. Each language in a multilingual society has its own distinctive functions. The language characteristically used with intimate family and friends, the language generally used with coworkers or neighbors, and the language used with one's bosses or government need not be one and the same. Reading advanced technical or economic material may require literacy in a different language than reading a local gossip column. As long as no two or more languages are rivals for the same societal function, a linguistic division of labor can be both amicable and long-standing. Few English speakers in India, for example, have given up their local mother tongues or their regional languages. Similarly, in Puerto Rico and Mexico, English is typically "a sometime tongue," even among those who have learned it for occupational or educational rewards.

There will of course be conflict, not to mention winners and losers. Language conflict occurs when there is competition between two languages for exclusive use in the same power-related function—for example, government or schooling. Most frequently, this friction occurs when one regional or local language seeks to usurp roles traditionally associated with another local tongue. In the Soviet era, Moscow took an aggressive line on local languages, instituting Russian as the sole language of education and government in the Baltics and Central Asia. In the 1990s, however, many of these states have slowly de-emphasized Russian in schools, government, and even theaters and publishing houses, in favor of their national tongues. Estonia, Latvia, and Lithuania have passed the strictest laws, placing education, science, and culture within the exclusive purview of their national languages and (until just recently) leaving ethnic Russians out in the cold.

Even though local and regional regimes are most likely to use language for political ends, global languages (including English, the language of globalization) can also foster conflict. France's anxiety over the spread of English is well documented. The government in Paris forbids English in advertising and regulates the number of English-language films that may be shown in the country. A cabinet-level official, the minister of culture and communication, is responsible for monitoring the well-being of the national tongue. The Academie FRANCAISE, France's national arbiter of language and style, approves official neologisms for Anglo-American slang to guard the French language against "corruption." Yet French schools are introducing students to English earlier and earlier.

Those who speak and master the languages of globalization often suggest that "upstart" local tongues pose a risk to world peace and prosperity. Throughout most of recorded history, strong languages have refused to share power with smaller ones and have accused them of making trouble—disturbing the peace and promoting ethnic violence and separatism. Purging Ireland of Gaelic in the nineteenth century, however, did not convince many Irish of their bonds with England. Those who fear their own powerlessness and the demise of their beloved languages of authenticity have reasons to believe that most of the trouble comes from the opposite end of the language-and-power continuum. Small communities accuse these linguistic Big Brothers of imperialism, linguicide, genocide, and mind control.

Globalization, regionalization, and localization are all happening concurrently. They are, however, at different strengths in different parts of the world at any given time. Each can become enmeshed in social, cultural, economic, and even political change. English is frequently the language of choice for Tamils in India who want to communicate with Hindi-speaking northerners. Ironically, for many Tamils—who maintain frosty relations with the central authorities in Delhi—English seems less like a colonial language than does Hindi. In Indonesia, however, English may be associated with the military, the denial of civil rights, and the exploitation of workers, since the United States has long supported Jakarta's oligarchic regime. Although English is spreading among Indonesia's upper classes, the government stresses the use of Indonesia's official language, Bahasa Indonesia, in all contact with the general public. Local languages are denied any symbolic recognition at all. The traditional leadership and the common population in Java, heirs to a classical literary tradition in Javanese, resent the favoritism shown to English and Indonesian. Spreading languages often come to be hated because they can disadvantage many as they provide advantages for some.

English itself is becoming regionalized informally and orally, particularly among young people, because most speakers today use it as a second or third language. As students of English are increasingly taught by instructors who have had little or no contact with native speakers, spoken English acquires strong regional idiosyncrasies. At the same time, however, English is being globalized in the realms of business, government, entertainment, and education. However, Hindi and Urdu, Mandarin Chinese, Spanish, and vernacular varieties of Arabic can all expect a boom in these areas in the years to come—the result of both a population explosion in the communities that speak these tongues natively and the inevitable migrations that follow such growth.

The smallest languages on the world scene will be squeezed between their immediate regional neighbors on one side and English on the other. Most purely local languages (those with fewer than a million speakers) will be threatened with extinction during the next century. As a result, many smaller communities will not only seek to foster their own tongues but also to limit the encroachments of more powerful surrounding languages. Even in a democratic setting, "ethnolinguistic democracy" is rarely on the agenda. The U.S. government was designed to protect the rights of individuals; it is no accident that its founding fathers chose not to declare an official language. Yet given the vocal opposition to Spanish-language and bilingual education in many quarters of the United States, it seems not everyone holds the right to choose a language as fundamental.

What is to come of English? It may well gravitate increasingly toward the higher social classes, as those of more modest status turn to regional languages for more modest gains. It might even help the future of English in the long run if its proponents sought less local and regional supremacy and fewer exclusive functions in the United Nations and in the world at large. A bully is more likely to be feared than popular. Most non-native English speakers may come to love the language far less in the twenty-first century than most native English speakers seem to anticipate. Germans are alarmed that their scientists are publishing overwhelmingly in English. And France remains highly resistant to English in mass media, diplomacy, and technology. Even as English is widely learned, it may become even more widely disliked. Resentment of both the predominance of English and its tendency to spread along class lines could in the long term prove a check against its further globalization.

There is no reason to assume that English will always be necessary, as it is today, for technology, higher education, and social mobility, particularly after its regional rivals experience their own growth spurts. Civilization will not sink into the sea if and when that happens. The decline of French from its peak of influence has not irreparably harmed art, music, or diplomacy. The similar decline of German has not harmed the exact sciences. Ancient Greek, Aramaic, Latin, and Sanskrit—once world languages representing military might, sophistication, commerce, and spirituality—are mere relics in the modern world. The might of English will not long outlive the technical, commercial, and military ascendancy of its Anglo-American power base, particularly if a stronger power arises to challenge it. But just because the use of English around the world might decline does not mean the values associated today with its spread must also decline. Ultimately, democracy, international trade, and economic development can flourish in any tongue.

QUESTIONS TO THINK ABOUT

1. Fishman says that "Whether we consider English a 'killer language' or not, whether we regard its spread as benign globalization or linguistic imperialism, its expansive reach is undeniable and, for the time being, unstoppable." Given this assessment, why does he believe that there are "reasons . . . that the English language will eventually wane in influence"?

2. Fishman also says that "increased regional communication, informal market interaction, and migration are driving regional language spread around the world just as they are in Africa." What are the functions of these regional languages? How do these relate to the title of his article, "The New Linguistic Order"?

3. On a more personal level, if you had come (or did come) to English as a result of colonization or decolonization, which side would you be on: return to the use of local or regional languages or continue the spread of English? What do you think would influence your decision? Another way to think about this question is to consider the many variations of English within the United States. Which regional language or dialect in various regions is dominant?

4. *Extending your understanding*: What does Fishman mean by "authenticity" in his description of the experience of Israelis with Hebrew, English, and Arabic and the experience of some Jews with Yiddish, Hebrew, and English? How is globalization perceived as impacting on this stated authenticity? Why do you think people consider maintaining the use of these languages as resisting this perceived threat? Do you know of any other populations who have maintained a language for the purposes of authenticity? Who are they, and what are the languages?

TERMS TO DEFINE

Define the following words and phrases as they are presented within the context of the reading. Comment on your understanding of the significance of each one.

Globalization of English
Regionalization
Localization
Language conflict
Linguicide
Ethnolinguistic democracy

The African Writer and the English Language

Chinua Achebe
Bard College

In June 1952, there was a writers' gathering at Makerere, impressively styled: "A Conference of African Writers of English Expression." Despite this sonorous and rather solemn title, it turned out to be a very lively affair and a very exciting and useful experience for many of us. But there was something which we tried to do and failed—that was to define "African literature" satisfactorily.

Was it literature produced *in* Africa or *about* Africa? Could African literature be on any subject, or must it have an African theme? Should it embrace the whole continent or south of the Sahara, or just *Black* Africa? And then the question of language. Should it be in indigenous African languages or should it include Arabic, English, French, Portuguese, Afrikaans, et cetera?

In the end we gave up trying to find an answer, partly—I should admit—on my own instigation. Perhaps we should not have given up so easily. It seems to me from some of the things I have since heard and read that we may have given the impression of not knowing what we were doing; or worse, not daring to look too closely at it.

A Nigerian critic, Obi Wali, writing in *Transition* 10, said: "Perhaps the most important achievement of the conference . . . is that African literature as now defined and understood leads nowhere." I am sure that Obi Wali must have felt triumphantly vindicated when he saw the report of a different kind of conference held later at Fourah Bay to discuss African literature and the University curriculum. This conference produced a tentative definition of African literature as follows: "Creative writing in which an African setting is authentically handled or to which experiences originating in Africa are integral." We are told specifically that Conrad's *Heart of Darkness* qualifies as African literature while Graham Greene's *Heart of the Matter* fails because it could have been set anywhere outside Africa.

A number of interesting speculations issue from this definition which admittedly is only an interim formulation designed to produce an indisputably desirable end, namely to introduce African students to literature set in their environment. But I could not help being amused by the curious circumstance in which Conrad, a Pole, writing in English

Reprinted with permission from *Morning yet on creation day*. © 1975 by Anchor Press/Doubleday.

could produce African literature while Peter Abrahams would be ineligible should he write a novel based on his experiences in the West Indies.

What all this suggests to me is that you cannot cram African literature into a small, neat definition. I do not see African literature as one unit but as a group of associated units—in fact the sum total of all the *national* and *ethnic* literatures of Africa.

A national literature is one that takes the whole nation for its province and has a realized or potential audience throughout its territory. In other words a literature that is written in the *national* language. An ethnic literature is one which is available only to one ethnic group within the nation. If you take Nigeria as an example, the national literature, as I see it, is the literature written in English; and the ethnic literatures are in Hausa, Ibo, Yoruba, Efik, Edo, Ijaw, etc., etc.

Any attempt to define African literature in terms which overlook the complexities of the African scene at the material time is doomed to failure. After the elimination of white rule shall have been completed, the single most important fact in Africa in the second half of the twentieth century will appear to be the rise of individual nation-states. I believe that African literature will follow the same pattern.

What we tend to do today is to think of African literature as a newborn infant. But in fact what we have is a whole generation of newborn infants. Of course, if you only look cursorily, one infant is pretty much like another; but in reality each is already set on its own separate journey. Of course, you may group them together on the basis of anything you choose—the color of their hair, for instance. Or you may group them together on the basis of the language they will speak or the religion of their fathers. Those would all be valid distinctions; but they could not begin to account fully for each individual person carrying, as it were, his own little, unique lodestar of genes.

Those who in talking about African literature want to exclude North Africa because it belongs to a different tradition surely do not suggest that Black Africa is anything like homogeneous. What does Shabaan Robert have in common with Christopher Okigbo or Awoonor-Williams? Or Mongo Beti of Cameroun and Paris with Nzekwu of Nigeria? What does the champagne-drinking upper-class Creole society described by Easmon of Sierra Leone have in common with the rural folk and fishermen of J. P. Clark's plays? Of course, some of these differences could be accounted for on individual rather than national grounds, but a good deal of it is also environmental.

I have indicated somewhat offhandedly that the national literature of Nigeria and of many other countries of Africa is, or will be, written in English. This may sound like a controversial statement, but it isn't. All I have done has been to look at the reality of present-day Africa. This "reality" may change as a result of deliberate, e.g., political, action. If it does, an entirely new situation will arise, and there will be plenty of time to examine it. At present it may be more profitable to look at the scene as it is.

What are the factors which have conspired to place English in the position of national language in many parts of Africa? Quite simply the reason is that these nations were created in the first place by the intervention of the British, which I hasten to add, is not saying that the peoples comprising these nations were invented by the British.

The country which we know as Nigeria today began not so very long ago as the arbitrary creation of the British. It is true, as William Fagg says in his excellent new book *Nigerian Images,* that this arbitrary action has proved as lucky in terms of African art history as any enterprise of the fortunate Princess of Serendip. And I believe that in political and economic terms too this arbitrary creation called Nigeria holds out great prospects. Yet the fact remains that Nigeria was created by the British—for their own ends. Let us give the devil his due: colonialism in Africa disrupted many things, but it did create big political units where there were small, scattered ones before. Nigeria had hundreds of autonomous communities ranging in size from the vast Fulani Empire founded by Usman dan Fodio in the north to tiny village entities in the east. Today it is one country.

Of course, there are areas of Africa where colonialism divided up a single ethnic group among two or even three powers. But on the whole it did bring together many peoples that had hitherto gone their several ways. And it gave them a language with which to talk to one another. If it failed to give them a song, it at least gave them a tongue, for sighing. There are not many countries in Africa today where you could abolish the language of the erstwhile colonial powers and still retain the facility for mutual communication. Therefore those African writers who have chosen to write in English or French are not unpatriotic smart alecks with an eye on the main chance—outside their own countries. They are by-products of the same process that made the new nation-states of Africa.

You can take this argument a stage further to include other countries of Africa. The only reason why we can even talk about African unity is that when we get together, we can have a manageable number of languages to talk in—English, French, Arabic.

The other day, I had a visit from Joseph Kariuki of Kenya. Although I had read some of his poems and he had read my novels, we had not met before. But it didn't seem to matter. In fact I had met him through his poems, especially through his love poem 'Come away my love', in which he captures in so few words the trials and tensions of an African in love with a white girl in Britain:

Come away, my love, from streets
Where unkind eyes divide
And shop windows reflect our difference.

By contrast, when in 1960 I was traveling in East Africa and went to the home of the late Shabaan Robert, the Swahili poet of Tanganyika, things had been different. We spent some time talking about writing, but there was no real contact. I knew from all accounts that I was talking to an important writer, but of the nature of his work I had no idea. He gave me two books of his poems which I treasure but cannot read—until I have learned Swahili.

And there are scores of languages I would want to learn if it were possible. Where am I to find the time to learn the half dozen or so Nigerian languages, each of which can sustain a literature? I am afraid it cannot be done. These languages will just have to develop as tributaries to feed the one central language enjoying nationwide currency. Today, for good or ill, that language is English. Tomorrow it may be something else, although I very much doubt it.

Those of us who have inherited the English language may not be in a position to appreciate the value of the inheritance. Or we may go on resenting it because it came as part of a package deal which included many other items of doubtful value and the positive atrocity of racial arrogance and prejudice which may yet set the world on fire. But let us not in rejecting the evil throw out the good with it.

Some time last year, I was traveling in Brazil meeting Brazilian writers and artists. A number of the writers I spoke to were concerned about the restrictions imposed on them by their use of the Portuguese language. I remember a woman poet saying she had given serious thought to writing in French! And yet their problem is not half as difficult as ours. Portuguese may not have the universal currency of English or French but at least it is the national language of Brazil with her eighty million or so people, to say nothing of the people of Portugal, Angola, Mozambique, etc.

Of Brazilian authors, I have only read one novel, in translation, by Jorge Amado, who is not only Brazil's leading novelist but one of the most important writers in the world. From that one novel, *Gabriella*, I was able to glimpse something of the exciting Afro-Latin culture which is the pride of Brazil and is quite unlike any other culture. Jorge Amado is only one of the many writers Brazil has produced. At their national writers' festival there were literally hundreds of them. But the work of the vast majority will be closed to the rest of the world forever, including no doubt the work of some excellent writers. There is certainly a great advantage to writing in a world language.

I think I have said enough to give an indication of my thinking on the importance of the world language which history has forced down our throats. Now let us look at some of the most serious handicaps. And let me say straightaway that one of the most serious handicaps is not the one people talk about most often, namely, that it is impossible for anyone ever to use a second language as effectively as his first. This assertion is compounded of half truth and half bogus mystique. Of course, it is true that the vast majority of people are happier with their first language than with any other. But then the majority of people are not writers. We do have enough examples of writers who have performed the feat of writing effectively in a second language. And I am not thinking of the obvious names like Conrad. It would be more germane to our subject to choose African examples.

The first name that comes to my mind is Olauda Equiano, better known as Gustavus Vassa, the African. Equiano was an Ibo, I believe from the village of Iseke in the Orlu division of Eastern Nigeria. He was sold as a slave at a very early age and transported to America. Later he bought his freedom and lived in England. In 1789 he published his life story, a beautifully written document which, among other things, set down for the Europe of his time something of the life and habit of his people in Africa, in an attempt to counteract the lies and slander invented by some Europeans to justify the slave trade.

Coming nearer to our times, we may recall the attempts in the first quarter of this century by West African nationalists to come together and press for a greater say in the management of their own affairs. One of the most eloquent of that band was the Honorable Casely Hayford of the Gold Coast. His presidential address to the National Congress of British West Africa in 1925 was memorable not only for its sound common sense but as a fine example of elegant prose. The governor of Nigeria at the time was compelled to take notice and he did so in characteristic style: he called Hayford's Congress "a self-selected and self-appointed congregation of educated African gentlemen." We may derive some amusement from the fact that British colonial administrators learned very little in the following quarter of a century. But at least they did learn in the end—which is more than one can say for some others. It is when we come to what is commonly called creative literature that most doubt seems to arise. Obi Wali, whose article "Dead End of African Literature" I referred to, has this to say:

> Until these writers and their Western midwives accept the fact that any true African literature must be written in African languages, they would be merely pursuing a dead end, which can only lead to sterility, uncreativity and frustration.

But far from leading to sterility, the work of many new African writers is full of the most exciting possibilities. Take this from Christopher Okigbo's "Limits":

Suddenly becoming talkative
  like weaverbird
Summoned at offside of
  dream remembered
Between sleep and waking
I hand up my egg-shells
To you of palm grove,
Upon whose bamboo cowers hang
Dripping with yesterupwine
A tiger mask and nude spear. . . .

Queen of the damp half light,
  I have had my cleansing.
Emigrant with air-borne nose,
  The he-goat-on-heat.

Or take the poem, "Night Rain," in which J. P. Clark captures so well the fear and wonder felt by a child as rain clamors on the thatch roof at night and his mother, walking about in the dark, moves her simple belongings

Out of the run of water
That like ants filing out of the wood
Will scatter and gain possession
Of the floor. . . .

I think that the picture of water spreading on the floor "like ants filing out of the wood" is beautiful. Of course if you had never made fire with faggots, you may miss it. But, Clark's inspiration derives from the same source which gave birth to the saying that a man who brings home ant-ridden faggots must be ready for the visit of lizards.

I do not see any signs of sterility anywhere here. What I do see is a new voice coming out of Africa, speaking of African experience in a worldwide language. So my answer to the question *Can an African ever learn English well enough to be able to use it effectively in creative writing?* is certainly yes. If on the other hand you ask: *Can he ever learn to use it like a native speaker?* I should say, I hope not. It is neither necessary nor desirable for him to be able to do so. The price a world language must be prepared to pay is submission to many different kinds of use. The African writer should aim to use English in a way that brings out his message best without altering the language to the extent that its value as a medium of international exchange will be lost. He should aim at fashioning out an English which is at once universal and able to carry his peculiar experience. I have in mind here the writer who has something new, something different to say. The nondescript writer has little to tell us, anyway, so he might as well tell it in conventional language and get it over with. If I may use an extravagant simile, he is like a man offering a small, nondescript routine sacrifice for which a chick, or less, will do. A serious writer must look for an animal whose blood can match the power of his offering.

In this respect Amos Tutuola is a natural. A good instinct has turned his apparent limitation in language into a weapon of great strength—a half-strange dialect that serves him perfectly in the evocation of his bizarre world. His last book, and to my mind, his finest, is proof enough that one can make even an imperfectly learned second language do amazing things. In this book, *The Feather Woman of the Jungle,* Tutuola's superb storytelling is at last cast in the episodic form which he handles best instead of being painfully stretched on the rack of the novel.

From a natural to a conscious artist: myself, in fact. Allow me to quote a small example from *Arrow of God,* which may give some idea of how I approach the use of English. The Chief Priest in the story is telling one of his sons why it is necessary to send him to church:

I want one of my sons to join these people and be my eyes there. If there is nothing in it you will come back. But if there is something there you will bring home my share. The world is like a Mask, dancing. If you want to see it well you do not stand in one place. My spirit tells me that those who do not befriend the white man today will be saying *had we known* tomorrow.

Now supposing I had put it another way. Like this for instance:

I am sending you as my representative among these people—just to be on the safe side in case the new religion develops. One has to move with the times or else one is left behind. I have a hunch that those who fail to come to terms with the white man may well regret their lack of foresight.

The material is the same. But the form of the one is *in character* and the other is not. It is largely a matter of instinct, but judgment comes into it too.

You read quite often nowadays of the problems of the African writer having first to think in his mother tongue and then to translate what he has thought into English. If it were such a simple, mechanical process, I would agree that it was pointless—the kind of eccentric pursuit you might expect to see in a modern Academy of Lagado; and such a process could not possibly produce some of the exciting poetry and prose which is already appearing.

One final point remains for me to make. The real question is not whether Africans *could* write in English but whether they *ought* to. Is it right that a man should abandon his mother tongue for someone else's? It looks like a dreadful betrayal and produces a guilty feeling.

But for me there is no other choice. I have been given this language and I intend to use it. I hope, though, that there always will be men, like the late Chief Fagunwa, who will choose to write in their native tongue and insure that our ethnic literature will flourish side by side with the national ones. For those of us who opt for English, there is much work ahead and much excitement. Writing in the *London Observer* recently, James Baldwin said:

> My quarrel with the English language has been that the language reflected none of my experience. But now I began to see the matter another way. . . . Perhaps the language was not my own because I had never attempted to use it, had only learned to imitate it. If this were so, then it might be made to bear the burden of my experience if I could have the stamina to challenge it, and me, to such a test.

I recognize, of course, that Baldwin's problem is not exactly mine, but I feel that the English language will be able to carry the weight of my African experience. But it will have to be a new English, still in full communion with its ancestral home, but altered to suit its new African surroundings.

QUESTIONS TO THINK ABOUT

1. Achebe refers both directly and indirectly to historical circumstances and language processes that bring about language change and variation. Make two lists: one of the historical circumstances to which he is referring and another of the language processes that bring about language change and variation. Discuss the connection between them and the relative importance of each.

2. Achebe concludes that "the English language will be able to carry the weight of my African experience. But it will have to be a new English." What does he mean by these statements? Do you think his conclusion is correct and possible? Why or why not?

3. Achebe poses a critical question that applies to classroom situations around the world: "The real question is not whether Africans *could* write in English, but whether they *ought* to. Is it right that a man should abandon his mother tongue for someone else's? It looks like a dreadful betrayal and produces a guilty feeling." What are the implications of Achebe's questions for the teacher and for English language classrooms?

4. *Extending your understanding:* Achebe asks, "What are the factors which have conspired to place English in the position of national language in many parts of Africa?" Based on your reading and experience, what do you perceive as the critical factors that contribute to the world-wide use of English? You may want to consider knowledge you have from other fields, including history, economics, anthropology, sociology, literature, and ethnic studies.

TERMS TO DEFINE

Define the following words and phrases as they are presented within the context of the reading. Comment on your understanding of the significance of each one.

National language
National literature
Ethnic literature
Colonialism
World language
Mother tongue

Ebonic Need Not Be English

Ralph W. Fasold
Georgetown University

Since the 1996 Oakland School Board decision regarding the use of Ebonics as a tool of instruction, opinions have clashed over whether Ebonics is a separate language or merely a dialect of English. Called Black Vernacular English (BVE) in the 1960s and 70s and African American Vernacular English (AAVE) in the 1980s and 90s, Ebonics has traditionally been considered a dialect of English by educators and linguists (e.g., Fromkin & Rodman, 1998; Tshudi & Thomas, 1998). To understand why Ebonics might be considered a language other than English requires a closer look at what it takes to make a language, as well as what the differences are between a language and a dialect.

First, I would like to point out that the term *Ebonics* is not an appropriate name for a linguistic entity. However, the coinage is actually very close to a natural way of naming languages. There are languages that end in "ic," like Arabic and Amharic, as well as language family names of that form, like Slavic and Germanic. *Ebonic*, in such a naming system, is a clear way to specify *black language*. Thus, in this paper, I use the term *Ebonic*.

WHAT DOES IT TAKE TO MAKE A LANGUAGE?

Linguists generally agree that the notion of a language is largely, or entirely, social and political. What it takes to make a language is not a set of structural linguistic properties or lack of intelligibility with related linguistic systems, but rather the conviction that the linguistic system in question is a symbol of nationalist or ethnic identity. There are cases around the world of the two logical possibilities, cases in which mutually unintelligible linguistic varieties belong to the same language and others where mutually intelligible varieties are separate languages. For example, the dialects of Chinese are distinct from each other, at least as much so as the modern Romance languages. Yet they remain dialects of the Chinese language. The constellation of languages that includes Dutch, Flemish, and Afrikaans is a case of the other type. Each of these languages is easily understood by speakers of the others. Yet for most Afrikaners, Afrikaans is certainly neither Dutch nor

Flemish, but a new language that grew from the South African soil. Nor are many Belgian Flemings inclined to accept Flemish as a dialect of Dutch. These examples suggest that linguistically similar varieties can be languages if they are identified with different countries. The Nguni language family of South Africa shows that linguistically similar varieties can be separate languages even if they are spoken within the same country. There are four Nguni languages: Xhosa, Zulu, Swati, and Ndebele, each of which is generally reported to be readily understood by speakers of the others. Nevertheless, proposals to unify the languages of this group into a single standard language have been resisted, largely because of a general belief that the languages to be unified are each languages in their own right.

There is, therefore, no linguistic or geographical reason that Ebonic could not achieve status as a language distinct from English. Two objections that are likely to be raised are that 1) Ebonic is not a language, but rather English corrupted by bad grammar and excessive slang, and 2) Ebonic and English are too similar to each other to be different languages.

IS EBONIC BAD ENGLISH?

The idea that Ebonic is very bad English is obviously false to linguists who have studied it in detail (e.g., Mufwene, Rickford, Bailey, & Baugh, 1998; Wolfram & Schilling-Estes, 1998). Outside the realm of academic linguistics, however, the idea that Ebonic is bad English is generally held to be uncontroversially true. Hence, it is necessary to demonstrate that this notion is untenable. It is clear on examination that Ebonic, far from being bad English, is actually superior to English in one of its subsystems, the verbal tense-aspect system. In addition to the verb structure that English also has, Ebonic provides its speakers with rich resources for making distinctions among kinds and times of actions and states that can be made in English only awkwardly through use of a longer and more awkward expression. For example, Ebonic has several aspect markers; one is the habitual, exemplified below:

- She be eatin/She do be eatin.
  She is sometimes/usually/always eating.
- She don't be eatin.
  She is not sometimes/usually/always eating.

These forms are often used as illustrations that Ebonic is simply corrupt English. The habitual is invariably used ungrammatically in such illustrations, where it is taken as a corruption of "She is eating." Of course, the habitual progressive in Ebonic contrasts with the present progressive, which would be "She eatin" or, under emphasis, "She is eatin." It also contrasts with the simple present. It would be perfectly reasonable, for example, for an Ebonic speaker to say, "She not writin' right now but she be writin' mostly every day and she write good." This would mean that the person referred to is not in the process of writing at the moment, but that one would find her in the process of writing almost daily, and she characteristically writes well.

Such verb forms are frequently cited as evidence of slovenly English. Under analysis, however, they are shown to fit into an impressive verbal system that functions more efficiently than the English system does. Once this becomes clear, it is amazing to see Ebonic presented as inferior to English. The three-way distinction in Ebonic among the present, the present progressive, and the habitual progressive contrasts with a more limited two-way distinction between the present and present progressive in English.

IS EBONIC A LANGUAGE OR A DIALECT?

The second objection, that Ebonic and English are too similar to be different languages, is overtly or tacitly considered valid even by linguists. This argument is also faulty. To demonstrate, we can look at another speech system that is very similar to English, Scots. One of the three languages of Scotland, Scots is a Germanic language that was once the language of the court and that has largely been displaced by English. Because of its relatedness to English, Scots is now considered by many in Scotland to be a corrupted dialect of English, a similar attitude to the one directed toward Ebonic in the United States. The differences between Scots and English seem comparable to those between Ebonic and English, as the following example, from a World Wide Web site maintained by Clive P. L. Young (www.umist.ac.uk/UMIST_CAL/Scots/haunbuik.htm) illustrates:

> The wirdleet kivvers aboot 700 o the maist cowmon wirds in onie leid (A wisna luikin fur jist kenspeckle Scots wirds). The spellins come frae the School Scots Dictionary. A warnin thou, the file is muckle an maun tak a wee tae doonload.

> The word list covers about 700 of the most common words in any language (I wasn't just looking for well-known Scots words). The spellings are from the School Scots Dictionary. A warning, though; the file is large and may take a while to download.

To the naive eye, the Scots version for the most part looks like English badly spelled. There are a few vocabulary differences, like "kenspeckle," "leid," and "muckle," but most of the excerpt contains words that are close cognates of English words. Historically, and in the view of present day activists, however, Scots is not a degenerate form of English, but a language distinct from English. Merlin Press, a small publishing house that puts out instructional materials for teaching Scots, has posted the following questions and answers on its World Wide Web site (www.sol.co.uk/m/merlinpress/):

Q: In what form does Scots exist in the present day?

A: It exists in a multiplicity of dialect forms but without a Standard Scots to correspond to Standard English. There is nothing linguistically wrong with the forms of Scots we have, but for political and social reasons our children have been discouraged from using them for nearly three hundred years, on the grounds that they are incorrect, inferior or corrupt forms of English.

Q: Isn't Scots just a form of slang?

A: Absolutely not. When teaching Scots, one of your first tasks will be to show children the difference between Scots and slang.

Q: What is the best way to teach Scots in the classroom?

A: The best way is to start with what you have: The children themselves hear Scots every day, and many of them actually speak it without realising it. Start by recognising this and allowing its use in the classroom.

To those who followed the Ebonic debate, this discussion has an almost eerie familiarity. Scots has to be defended from charges that it is an incorrect form of English and just slang. Children grow up speaking Scots but are discouraged from using it. The suggestion in answer to the question, "What is the best way to teach Scots in the classroom?" is almost identical to the proposal by the Oakland School Board that provoked the furor in late 1996 and early 1997, except that the Oakland Board proposed the use of Ebonic in the classroom as a bridge to English.

We can see the case of Scots as an example of a linguistic variety viewed by some as a corrupted dialect of English but also having status as a language. As a language, Scots has important advantages over Ebonic. It has its own recognized grammar and dictionary. It is taught as a subject at several of Scotland's oldest universities. While not widely taught at the primary and secondary school levels, it is not considered outrageous to teach Scots in these schools, and there are published materials for use in teaching it.

On the other hand, Ebonic has one great advantage over Scots. It appears that without successful efforts to maintain and revive it, Scots is in danger of dying out completely in a few generations. Ebonic, in spite of almost universal opinion against it and a total lack of support in the educational system, is one of the most robustly maintained minority languages in existence. There is no hint that it is in any danger of dying out in the foreseeable future.

WHY CONSIDER EBONIC A SEPARATE LANGUAGE?

I have argued that Ebonic need not be English, but that instead there is every reason to suppose it is capable of being a language in its own right. There are several advantages to considering Ebonic a language separate from English rather than as an orderly and systematic dialect of English. The major advantage is that when one speaks of Ebonic as a language, rather than as a dialect, it reforms the discourse in a way that makes it easier to address the common misconceptions about Ebonic that have kept the debate at such an uninformed level. To begin with, when Ebonic is defended as a systematic and well-ordered dialect, it is inevitably contrasted with *standard* English. The concept *standard* has two meanings: minimum standards and arbitrary standards. Minimum standards are specifications that must be met for acceptability. Safety standards for automobiles are one example. If an automobile does not have the designated safety features, it fails the standards, and the manufacturer will not be able to sell it. In short, minimum standards must be met in order for an item to be good enough. Arbitrary standards are entirely different. For example, the United States uses Fahrenheit degrees to measure temperatures. Most of the rest of the world measures temperatures in degrees Celsius. One could argue that the Fahrenheit system is the inferior system. However that may be, Fahrenheit degrees serve an important function. They serve as an agreed upon arbitrary standard that everyone in the United States understands and uses. It is not so important that the best system of temperature measurement be used as it is that everyone agree on the same arbitrary standard.

When linguists use the term *standard language*, they invariably and implicitly mean an arbitrary standard. Just as in the case of the measurement standard for temperature, there are advantages to having agreement on certain arbitrary standards for some language uses. The standard language may not be the best possible constellation of linguistic features available. In fact, I have argued that in some ways, standard English is demonstrably inferior to Ebonic. But just as there is general agreement in favor of the Fahrenheit standard, the arbitrary standards we have agreed on for American English are unlikely to be abandoned any time soon. It is general social acceptance that creates a workable arbitrary standard, not the inherent superiority of the item it specifies.

However, the assumption made by the vast majority of people who have not studied the nature of language in depth is that the term *standard English* refers to minimum standards. Just like a house that fails to meet building code standards, nonstandard language is considered not fit to be used. The users of these dialects must, in this view, be brought up to the minimum standard for their own good as well as for the good of the society in general.

Another problem involves the term *dialect*. For linguists, dialects are speech varieties that make up a language, somewhat the way slices make up a pie. For the general public, though, a dialect is a perhaps quaint but surely faulty way of speaking a language. In that sense, it is on a par with slips of the tongue, slang-laced conversation, excessive use of profanity, and other perceived abuses of language. The linguist's view is quite different. For linguists, there are several levels of analysis of a language, each just a different view of the same phenomenon. The language is the largest level, but it can be viewed in greater detail as the dialects of which it is composed, and these, in turn, can be more closely examined as the various styles of each dialect.

When linguists refer to Ebonic as a dialect of English, they intend to make a simple to understand statement that the dialect Ebonic is one of a number of equally orderly dialects of English, including the standard one. It is not comparable to slurred speech or slips of the tongue, which lie at a much lower level of language analysis. The nonlinguist, though, hears the word dialect and interprets it in this way. Because dialects are presupposed to be corruptions of language, the claim that Ebonic is orderly and rule-governed can hardly make sense. The linguist's analysis will make no dent in the nonlinguist's conviction that anyone who is able to speak only a dialect has an immediate need to replace the dialect with the real language. This person will never hear that the linguist is actually saying that the dialect Ebonic is on a par with the standardized dialect and, given different historical developments, might even have been the standard.

For linguists to attempt to convey what we have learned about Ebonic using terms like *standard English* and *African American English dialect* starts us off immediately with a double handicap. Somehow, we have to dislodge the idea of minimum standard as applied to language and replace it with the concept of arbitrary standard. At the same time, we have to redefine dialect, moving away from the notion of dialect as a corruption of the real language to a notion of dialect as a legitimate component of all languages. On the other hand, if Ebonic were a language and not a dialect, it would not be assumed to be a corruption of anything. A language has its own standards. The standards of some other language are simply irrelevant. The way we discuss these matters would immediately change. Imagine the following hypothetical conversations:

Q: Isn't Ebonic just bad English?

A: Linguist: Certainly Ebonic is bad English, in the same sense that French is bad English. English is bad Ebonic, too.

Q: Why don't these so-called Ebonic speakers inflect the verb "to be." Why do they say "He be eatin" when they mean "He is eating?"

A: Linguist: Unlike English, which has only one form for "to be," Ebonic has two words for "to be." One of them is inflected and the other is not. The grammar of Ebonic makes a distinction not found in English. The difference is quite subtle and not easy for English speakers to master.

CONCLUSION

Simply speaking of Ebonic as a language rather than a dialect will not immediately cause linguists' discoveries about Ebonic to become universally accepted. There would be massive resistance to the idea that Ebonic is a language. Even if by dint of charisma and eloquence linguists manage to convince some nonlinguists that Ebonic could be a language, the struggle would not be over. However, I would find the new struggle easier to deal with. I know that, at least in teaching my own students, I have been able to get across the linguistic perception of the nature of Ebonic much more efficiently by framing its relation to English as one of language to language.

REFERENCES

Fromkin, V., & Rodman, R. (1998). *An introduction to language* (6th ed.). Fort Worth, TX: Harcourt College.

Mufwene, S. S., Rickford, J. R., Bailey, G., & Baugh, J. (Eds.). (1998). *African-American English: Structure, history and use.* London: Routledge.

Tshudi, S., & Thomas, L. (1998). *The English language: An owner's manual.* Boston: Allyn and Bacon.

Wolfram, W., & Schilling-Estes, N. (1998). *American English.* Oxford: Blackwell.

QUESTIONS TO THINK ABOUT

1. Fasold states that "linguists generally agree that the notion of language is largely, or entirely, social and political." Furthermore, he asserts that a language is "the conviction that the linguistic system in question is a symbol of nationalist or ethnic identity." What does he mean by these statements? Which pieces of evidence does he provide that you find provocative or convincing?

2. Whereas linguists analyze features of language and dialects according to the ways they are used and the functions they serve, most people consider low prestige dialects—for example, "Ebonics"—"bad English." How does Fasold refute this commonly held view of Ebonic, particularly through his description of the verb system?

3. Considering the continued use of Ebonic, Fasold says that "in spite of almost universal opinion against it and a total lack of support in the educational system, [Ebonic] is one of the most robustly maintained minority languages in existence. There is no hint that it is in any danger of dying out in the foreseeable future." From what you have learned about language processes, the relationship between language and culture, and language variation, comment on why you think Ebonic is so healthy in spite of its lack of recognition and esteem.

4. *Extending your understanding*: Consider the imaginary question/answer Fasold presents concerning Scots and English. Based on this, extrapolate and speculate about what Fasold believes is the way to deal with Ebonic speakers—or any speakers of a nonstandard dialect or another first language—in an English classroom.

TERMS TO DEFINE

Define the following words and phrases as they are presented within the context of the reading. Comment on your understanding of the significance of each one.

Ebonic
Dialect
Slang
Standard language
Arbitrary standard
African American English dialect

Languages and Language Learning in the Face of World English

John Edwards
St. Francis Xavier University

ENGLISH IN THE WORLD

These are difficult times for some languages—the small ones, the stateless ones, those of lesser-used or minority status, and so on. An exchange taken from a recent conference transcript is illustrative here:

> "What do you think of Gallic now—be honest!"
>
> "Well, it's a language that may still do you some good in the Highlands and Islands, maybe still in parts of Cape Breton, but outside those little areas, it isn't going to take you very far . . . "
>
> "Isn't it used in any other settings, then?"
>
> "No, it's simple, really—no one to speak it with. Who did you have in mind?"
>
> "Maybe Scots abroad . . . ?"
>
> "Listen, outside Scotland, Gallic speakers hardly use the language at all, even amongst themselves."
>
> "OK, but what d'you think of the language itself—is it a good sort of language, or what?"
>
> "Actually, I'm not too keen on it, as a language per se. It has become pretty bastardised, you know, bit of a mixture really—different dialects, English borrowings . . . "

This little discussion surely has a familiar ring to it: a "small" language struggling against larger forces, a variety increasingly confined geographically and socially, a medium whose intrinsic status is often seen as degraded and impure. And, if it proves difficult to maintain such a language in something like its native state, what attraction does it possess for language learners elsewhere? Why would anyone study it at school or university? The elementary catch-22 operates here: how can you induce the learning of a language when its

---

Reprinted with permission of the Modern Language Association, from *Profession* 2001: 109–120.

community of use is negligible, but how will that community ever grow unless more join it? The dreary downward spiral seems fated to continue, resulting in a native community that is small and a secondary community that may become the preserve of a tiny band of consciously committed enthusiasts.

I have been deceitful here. The exchange about Scots Gaelic never took place. It is modeled, however, on this earlier passage:

> "What think you of this English tongue, tell me, I pray you?"
>
> "It is a language that wyl do you good in England, but passe Douer, it is woorth nothing."
>
> "It is not used then in other countreyes?"
>
> "No sir, with whom wyl you that they speake?"
>
> "With English marchants."
>
> "English marchantes, when they are out of England, it liketh them not, and they doo not speake it."
>
> "But yet what think you of the speech, is it gallant and gentle, or els contrary?"
>
> "Certis if you wyl beleeue me, it doth not like me at al, because it is a language confused, bepeesed with many tongues: it taketh many words of the latine, & mo from the French, & mo from the Italian, and many mo from the Duitch [. . .]."
>
> (Yates 32)

This is taken from John Florin's *First Fruits*, published in 1578, it is a textbook and manual for the teaching of Italian to English gentlemen. The fruits "*yeelde familiar speech, merie Proverbes, wittie Sentences, and golden sayings. Also a perfect Induction to the Italian, and English tongues [. . .]. The like heretofore, never by any man published*" (as Florio modestly points out in his fuller title). John Florio was, of course, an exceedingly interesting character who played many different roles, language teacher and translator among them. He provided, for instance, an engaging—if sometimes rather loose—translation of Montaigne's *Essays*, a translation read and used by Shakespeare. In his time (ca. 1553–1625), French, Italian, and Spanish were the powerful international languages, widely studied in Tudor and Stuart England. Italian challenged the supremacy of French in both the cultural and the commercial worlds, and many prominent Elizabethans studied it. Indeed, the queen herself was a student, along with luminaries like Edmund Spenser and the earl of Southampton, Henry Wriothesly—a literary patron to Florio and, more famously, to Shakespeare (Yates; Acheson).

Very few people in the sixteenth century would have predicted global status for English, a language with four or five million speakers and well back in the linguistic sweepstakes. The point is a simple one: the fortunes of language rise and fall; the variety that today wields international influence on a scale never before seen was once of very secondary importance and restricted utility. It is easy to lose sight of this immediately demonstrable fact—particularly, of course, at a time when historical knowledge and the contextualization of current events to which its application must inevitably lead are commodities of little priority. It is sometimes imagined that the global power of English represents a new phenomenon. It is, however, only the most recent manifestation of a very old one, although its strength and its scope are arguably neater than those possessed by earlier "world" languages: the difference, then, is one of degree rather than of principle. I don't mean to argue that all this somehow lessens the impact of English on other varieties; I simply want to suggest that social and linguistic struggles to resist the encroachments of English are not battles against demons never seen before. I would also not wish to belittle the anxieties felt by those whose languages and cultures are under threat. I only wish to say that all these things have happened before and will no doubt happen again: it is an old play we are looking at here, a play whose plot endures while the cast changes.

Languages of "wider communication" have no special linguistic capabilities to recommend them; they are simply the varieties of those who have power and prestige. It seems necessary to repeat this truism quite frequently, and not merely for the benefit of those languishing in ignorance outside the academy. I find in the Fall 1999 *ADFL Bulletin*, for example, a piece that suggests that current linguistic dominance

> lies very simply in the fact that English is more responsive than any other language to the growing knowledge base that is the hallmark of these postmodern times. It is this ability to be eclectically open to new thoughts, new ideas, new concepts that has predisposed English to be the major medium of modern communication.
>
> (Eoyang 27)

It is undoubtedly the case that, more than (some) other languages, English has been an open and "loose" medium—ready to take what was needed from other varieties, to be flexible in the face of modern necessity, and so on. It is an egregious mistake, however, to think that such "openness" accounts for its dominance. The truth is rather more brutal. (I note in passing here that one occasionally reads a defense of some threatened "small" variety that is based on its elegance of phrasing, its regularities, its linguistic "purity," its marvelous literature: this language is just as good as the hulking neighbor next door. Unfortunately, as Mae West once said, apropos of diamonds, goodness has nothing to do with it.)

The reasons for the relative "openness" of English are not entirely transparent, but they certainly are entwined with many historical threads. There exist, today, a strength and practicality about English that make a relaxed stance easy; that is, a secure and powerful medium need not worry very much about borrowings and hybrids, about localizations and colloquialism, about purism and prescriptivism. But even if we go back to periods in which English was not dominant, back (say) to the sixteenth and seventeenth centuries, when "standard" national languages were beginning to emerge in Europe, we find English linguistic reflexes to be unlike those elsewhere. The most notable example is the lack of a language academy whose purpose is to help standardize, yes, but usually also to protect, to keep out foreign influence, to manage neologisms, and so on. Some years ago, Randolph Quirk pointed to an "Anglo Saxon" aversion to "linguistic engineering," a disdain for language academies and their purposes—goals that, he felt, were "fundamentally alien" to English speakers' conceptions of language (68). This is putting things too strongly, perhaps, but it is certainly noteworthy that the United Kingdom and the United States are virtually the only countries not to have (or to have had) formal bodies charged with maintaining linguistic standards. It is also interesting to consider that—given the obvious need for standardization, even in English—both countries essentially appointed one-man academies; the great lexicographers Samuel Johnson and Noah Webster produced dictionaries that became the arbiters of standards and of "correctness."

One aspect of English "openness," and another indication of its strength, can be found in the degree of its localization around the world, and—more important, perhaps—the attitudes attaching to this localization. Compare the recent history of English with French in this regard. The latter has seen its influence shrink dramatically, and it is unsurprising that the current stance is often one of protection and defense. Part of this involves a renewed vigor—for the basic tendency was always there—in what might be called linguistic centralism. French is certainly interested in expansion—in bringing Antoine Rivarol's language of clarity to more people—but this is to be accomplished in a guarded and centralist way. English, however, is much more decentralized, less guarded, and more expansive. Local varieties achieve considerable status (Indian English provides perhaps the single best example of a developing and accepted indigenized model) and, indeed, some predict an increasing divergence, reminiscent of the birth of the Romance languages; but it must be noted that there are strong countertendencies to this. In any event, a language once tainted by imperialism is rapidly becoming one of "our" languages in many parts of the world. It is suggestive that we see books devoted to the "new Englishes," that there are journals called *World Englishes* and *English World-Wide*, and that these have essentially no equivalents in French scholarly circles.[1]

It is obvious that even "big" languages now worry about English—examples can easily be found of English usages common in France, in Japan, in Germany. It is worth noting, though, that these usages do not simply fill new needs or avoid translations for words in common international exchange; they can also push aside already-existing equivalents. It is one thing, then, to refer to *das Web-Design* or *der Cursor*, and perhaps another to employ *der Trend* or *der Team* or *der Cash-Flow*. External pressures often lead to internal division. "E-mail" is commonly used in French, for example, even though the Academie Francaise has endorsed *message electronique* (or *mel*, an abbreviated version), and Quebec's Office de la Langue Francaise has plumped for *courriel*. It is not very surprising, either, that within the wider language community the more threatened sectors will tend to be the most linguistically watchful. Canada's sovereigntist Parti Quebecois recently accused France of not being French enough, of not sufficiently guarding the barriers, when it was announced that Air France pilots would now speak English to air-traffic controllers in Paris. This is in line with international practice, which makes English the norm in aviation, but French has been allowed in Quebec airspace for twenty years, and its place there has considerable symbolic importance. French pilots may inform ground control that they are about to commence *le fuel dumping*, but their Quebecois counterparts are more likely to refer to *delestage*. All this suggests that there now exists a division in the ranks of "big" languages: English is the sole occupant of one category, while French, German, Spanish, Russian, and other languages jostle among themselves in the second.[2]

LEARNING LANGUAGES IN NORTH AMERICA

It has always been more difficult to teach and to learn foreign languages in North America than in Europe. Within Europe, the difficulties have—in recent times, at least—been greater in Britain than on the Continent. Do we observe here some genetic anglophone linguistic deficiency? Are the British and the Americans right when they say, "I'm just no good at foreign languages"? Are they right to envy those clever Europeans (or, indeed, Americans and Asians) who slide effortlessly from one mode to another? The answers here obviously involve environmental conditions, not genetic ones, but I present these rather silly notions because—to the extent to which they are believed or half-believed or inarticulately felt—they constitute a type of self-fulfilling prophecy that adds to the difficulty of language learning. I use the word *adds* here because the real difficulties, the important contextual conditions, the soil in which such prophecies flourish have to do with power and dominance. Anglophone linguistic laments perhaps involve some crocodile tears or, at least, can seem rather hollow: the regrets of those who lack competence, but who need not, after all, really bother to acquire it.

Given what I've said earlier about the status of English in Florio's time, for instance, we could assume that English speakers, when not globally dominant, were actually assiduous language learners. This is a view endorsed by Norman Davies in his recent popular history: before the twentieth century, the idea that the British were somehow innately ill-equipped to speak foreign languages would have seemed ludicrous, and most educated people (not just the royals, not just Victoria and Albert chatting away in German) were, in fact, bilingual or better. There are counterindications, however, and, indeed, one of those takes us back exactly to Florio's day. In *The Merchant of Venice*, Portia complains of Falconbridge, one of her suitors, that "he understands not me, nor I him: he hath neither Latin, French, nor Italian" (1.2). All her admirers, including a Scot, are criticized, but only the English one is slated for linguistic incompetence. (Nick Oulton provides the Shakespearean example here—noting that perhaps the pre–twentieth-century competence attributed by Davies to the "British" might exclude the English!)

Well, we need not take Shakespeare as an infallible guide to language abilities here, but, in any event, there is no real paradox. Educated English speakers were, at once, more broadly capable in foreign languages than they are now and increasingly less capable—because of the growing clout of their maternal variety—than their Continental colleagues. A related and relevant point is that as we approach the modern era we find that linguistic competence becomes more and more associated with formal educational instruction and less driven by mundane necessity. Of course, this is a very general statement, and there are all sorts of exceptions to it. Nonetheless, the correlation between the social, political, and economic dominance of the English-speaking world and the decline in its foreign language competence—for those reasons already touched on—means that language learning becomes more a matter of the classroom than of the street. And this has clear implications for both students and teachers. These implications are, if anything, rather more pointed in North America than they are in Britain (or should I say England?), and they rest on an interesting point. It is commonly accepted that favorable attitudes and positive motivations are central to successful second-language learning. There is, indeed, a very large literature on this theme (see, e.g., Edwards, *Multilingualism*; Noels and Clément). The importance of favorable attitudes, however, *varies inversely with real linguistic necessity*. Historically, most changes in language-use patterns owe much more to socioeconomic and political pressures than they do to attitudes. Some have suggested that one sort of motivation may play a part here. A mid–nineteenth-century Irishman, for instance, could well have loathed English and what it represented, while still realizing the mundane necessity to change. This *instrumental* motivation is, of course, a grudging quantity and quite unlike what has been termed an *integrative* one—that is, one based on genuine interest in another group and its language, perhaps involving a desire to move toward that group in some sense. There might also be a useful distinction to be drawn here between *favorable* and *positive* attitudes (to cite the adjectives I used above). To stay with the Irish example, one could say that the language attitudes toward English were typically instrumental—and positive in the sense of commitment or emphasis—but not necessarily integrative or favorable. Of course, attempting to separate instrumentality from "integrativeness" may prove, in practice, to be difficult and, as well, the relation between the two no doubt alters over the course of language shift. But there is a distinction between, say, the English needed by Japanese engineers and that sought by Japanese professors of American literature; the difference is one of depth of fluency, to be sure, but it goes beyond that (Edwards, *Language*).

Similarly, the language teaching of most interest here is something that goes beyond language training, although it must build on that and although some students are primarily interested in acquiring what we could now call an instrumental fluency. It has been argued that since attitudes (favorable ones, at least) are often of little consequence in real-life situations of language contact and shift, they are trivial elsewhere, too. My point is simply that attitudes may assume *greater* importance in many teaching settings: if the context is *not* perceived to be very pertinent in any immediate or personal way; if the participant is *not* there out of real, mundane necessity, then attitudes may make a real difference. In this way—leaving ability out of the equation, of course—language classes may become just like all others.

In a society that rewards narrow and immediately applicable learning, in educational systems that are increasingly corporatized, in the thousand-channel universe that confuses information with knowledge (awash in the former and inimical to the latter), and in a world made more and more safe for anglophones, language learning and all its ramifications lose immediacy. Not only does instrumental appeal lessen, but the more intangible and more profound attractions—to which instrumentality leads and with which it is entwined—also inevitably decline. These are the social constraints within which language teaching and learning occur, and they tend to dwarf more specific settings. At a recent seminar, Janet Swaffar made some suggestions (which were reprinted in the *ADFL Bulletin*) "to help foreign language departments assume command of their destinies," and the usual suspects were pedantically rounded up: a redefinition of the discipline ("as a distinct and sequenced inquiry into the constituents and applications of meaningful communication"); more emphasis on communication and less on narrow grammatical accuracy; the establishmet of standards, models, and common curricula (for "consistent pedagogical rhetoric"), and so on (10–11). All very laudable, no doubt, but why do I think of Nero? It has always been difficult to sell languages in Kansas; wherever you go, for thousands of miles, English will take you to McDonald's, get you a burger, and bring you safely home again—and a thorough reworking of pedagogical rhetoric doesn't amount to sale prices.

Broadly speaking, there are two paths through the woods, although occasionally they share the same ground. The first is for foreign language teaching to satisfy itself with that shrinking pool of students intrinsically interested in languages and their cultures. These are, after all, the students nearest to one's own intellectual heart. The problem is that the natural constituency here might prove too small to support a discipline at desired levels, and it is hard to nurture it in any direct way. The other is to hope and work for a renewed instrumental interest, with whatever longer term fallout that might lead to. On the one hand, this is dependent on a context that extends well beyond national borders and on alterations in global linguistic circumstance that, while inevitable, are not always easy to predict. On the other hand, things might be done at home—a home that is, after all, culturally diverse, in which the loss of a hundred native languages to English is seen as uneconomic, in which the rights of immigrants (particularly those who are entitled to vote) attract social and political attention, and so on. In a word, we look at Spanish.

The importance of the study of Spanish in the United States is self-evident. It is a language that has a lengthy cultural and literary tradition with many interesting branches to the original trunk, and it remains a widely used variety around the world; with something like 30 million speakers, it runs fourth (behind Hindi, Chinese, and English) in the usage sweepstakes. Academically, then, it is the ideal second language. More immediately, recent reports show that there are over 30 million people of Hispanic background in America (about 12% of the population); that this group is the fastest-growing minority; and that in fifty years' time its proportions will double, so that one in four Americans will be of this ethnic origin. (These are informed speculations, of course, and there is room for variation: Carlos Fuentes recently said that by 2050 three out of every five Americans will speak Spanish.) The figures, impressive as they are on their own, take on more weight when we consider their traditionally concentrated nature: millions of people living more or less together are a different sociological phenomenon than if they are scattered among others. At the same time, not all Hispanic people live in the Southwest or the Southeast. In the last ten years, their numbers have more than doubled in Iowa (to take one example), and they are now more numerous than black Americans there (Bohrer; see also Fuentes). All in all, a powerful and growing population.

Considering both the global and the national presence of Spanish, it is little wonder that the language is the linchpin of modern language teaching in the United States. The whole discipline, however, remains weak: even though recent (1998) MLA statistics suggest an overall increase of about 5% in foreign language enrollments since 1995, only 1.2 million college students are represented here, fewer than 8% of the total. There have been, indeed, steep declines in some quarters; enrollments in German were reportedly down by 7.5% (90,000 students altogether), and those in French decreased by 3% (to about 200,000). But for Spanish, the figures are better: enrollments are up by about 8%, which translates to some 660,000 students. And to complete this part of the story one can see that students of Spanish thus constitute 55% of *all* language students. Is Spanish learning in a healthy situation, then, or does it only seem so in comparison with weaker sisters?[3]

This may be an impossible question to answer. How many students *ought* to be studying Spanish—or archaeology, or quantum mechanics, or sculpture? Still, one might expect that language study would be more immediately related to extraeducational factors, for example, jobs, mobility, and opportunity, and, if that is so, then one might wonder why the strength of the American Hispanic community does not bolster the educational effort more.

In fact, despite America's multiethnic status in general, and its powerful Hispanic components more specifically, the country remains resolutely anglophone in all important domains and, indeed, the chief supporter of English as a global language. Historically, the melting pot has been most effective at the level of language; that is, while aspects of cultural continuity can be discerned in various groups, languages other than English typically last no longer than the second or third generation, and the normal pattern has meant moving from one monolingualism to another. This is true, even for the two special cases, francophones in New England and hispanophones in the Southwest—special, inasmuch as they, unlike all other arrivals, remain close to their heartlands, the borders of which are easily and frequently crossed. The timing of language shift is naturally dependent on such variables, but the overall shape of the curve is remarkably similar across groups.

All this makes Carlos Fuentes's remarks rather naive, even though they are eminently understandable, reflective of the view of many, and, indeed, attractive in their impulse. He asks why most Americans know only English and sees their monolingualism as a "great paradox": the United States is at once the supreme and the most isolated world ever. Why, he continues, does America "want to be a monolingual country?" All twenty-first century Americans ought to know more than one language in order to better understand the world and deal with problems. And so on and so on. Obviously, monolingualism is not a paradox, and to say that Americans "want" to be monolingual would seem to miss the point—it is simply that English serves them across domains.

In more subtle ways, though, it could be argued that Americans do "want" to be monolingual—or, to put it more aptly, see no reason to expand their repertoires. They therefore resist the institutionalization of other languages. In a climate like this, especially a long-standing one, such an outlook—arguably based on perceived practicality—can expand on less immediate and more unpleasant levels. Not only do languages other than English appear unnecessary, their use can be seen as downright un-American, their speakers as unwilling to throw themselves wholeheartedly into that wonderful pot, their continuing linkage to other cultures as a suspect commodity. It is surely not surprising that, given the right context, these sorts of views would find formal expression, that organizations like U.S. English would flourish, that many states would enact English-only legislation, that bilingual education would be progressively de-emphasized and, in one or two notorious cases, scrapped entirely. Nor is it surprising that the central part of that "right context" would be an increasingly worried sense that the nonanglophone "others" are becoming too potent. English only, therefore, typically means not-Spanish. And so another circle is completed: the very language community that, by its power and number, ought logically to blaze the way in foreign language teaching and learning is under attack by powerful bodies that are either nostalgia-ridden yearners for some selective status quo or, worse, carriers of the most abhorrent social virus. And, even if these bodies were absent from the political landscape, one could only expect from the public at large a lukewarm and uninformed stance.

I have aimed here only at some slight elucidation of the social context relevant to languages and language learning. Large forces and weighty histories are at work, and their presence should be acknowledged and thought about, I didn't intend to write a jeremiad although I know that, for many, English is a lowering villain depriving other mediums of their rightful inheritance. I would simply reiterate that the factors at work here are neither unfamiliar nor unpredictable. We have seen transitional linguistic and social times before—and transition is, almost by definition, a painful and wrenching experience for those whose lives are directly affected.

It is a truism to say that the teaching and the learning of languages are influenced by the state of affairs outside the walls of the academy. It would be heartening—in a world in which, for all the power of English, bilingual or multilingual competences are still the norm—if the North American academy were dealing with a constituency that acknowledged and accepted such repertoires. The products on offer would not then require such advertising; the demand would arise naturally and would not itself have first to be suggested to the consumers. But this is a setting in which some linguistic analogy of Gresham's law seems to operate. As well, one recalls the (perhaps apocryphal) remark of that school superintendent in Arkansas, who steadfastly refused to have foreign languages taught at the secondary level: "If English was good enough for Jesus, it's good enough for you" (qtd. in Ricks and Michaels xvii).

We should recall, though, that there remains on this continent a rich linguistic and cultural diversity, and in many instances this continues to be a visible and powerful quantity. We have also engaged, over the last few years, in an unprecedented debate about multiculturalism and pluralism, about identity and citizenship. The field here remains terribly disputed and highly politicized, but the debate is far from over and the valuable middle ground has yet to be charted. Although the most active participants in the discussion have not been those whose primary concerns are linguistic, the latter have a role to play and a contribution to make.

NOTES

[1] On academics, dictionaries, Rivarol, and journals devoted to "Englishes," see Edwards, *Language* and *Multilingualism*.

[2] For recent French and German developments, see Séguin, "France," "Reverse Role"; Freeman; Gagnon; Ribbans. See also Edwards, "Language."

[3] See recent editorials in the *Times Higher Education Supplement*, 17 Dec. 1999, commenting on the meetings of the MLA: "German—Fewer than 100 Jobs" and "Literature Moves to a New Latin Rhythm."

Works Cited

Acheson, Arthur. *Shakespeare's Lost Years in London, 1586–1592*. London: Quaritch, 1920.

Bohrer, Becky. "U.S. Hispanic Population the Fastest-Growing Group." *Globe and Mail* [Toronto] 13 May 2000: 12.

Davies, Norman. *The Isles: A History*. London: Macmillan, 1999.

Edwards, John. "Language and the Future: Choices and Constraints." Conference on Language in the Twenty-First Century. Whitney Center, Yale U, June 1999.

Edwards, John. *Language, Society and Identity*. Oxford: Blackwell, 1985.

Edwards, John. *Multilingualism*. London: Penguin, 1995.

Eoyang, Eugene. "The Worldliness of the English Language: A Lingua Franca Past and Future." *ADFL Bulletin* 31.1 (1999): 26–32.

Freeman, Alan. "The English Patience of France." *Globe and Mail* 1 Apr. 2000: 22.

Fuentes, Carlos. "A Cure for Monolingualism." *Times Higher Education Supplement* 17 Dec. 1999: 4.

Gagnon, Lysiane. "Back in the Trenches of the Language War." *Globe and Mail* 3 Apr. 2000: 18.

"German—Fewer than 100 Jobs." *Times Higher Education Supplement* 17 Dec. 1999: 6.

"Literature Moves to a New Latin Rhythm." *Times Higher Education Supplement* 17 Dec. 1999: 4.

Noels, Kimberly, and Richard Clément. "Language Education." *Language in Canada*. Ed. John Edwards. Cambridge: Cambridge UP, 1998. 102–24.

Oulton, Nick. Letter. *Times Literary Supplement* 17 Mar. 2000: 21.

Quirk, Randolph. *Style and Communication in the English Language*. London: Arnold, 1982.

Ribbans, Elisabeth. "Germans Bemoan Popularity of English." *Globe and Mail* 27 Apr. 2000: 11.

Ricks, Christopher, and Leonard Michaels. *The State of the Language*. London: Faber, 1990.

Séguin, Rhéal. "France Not French Enough, PQ Says." *Globe and Mail* 29 Mar. 2000: 4.

Séguin, Rhéal. "Reverse Role Model Made in Canada." *Globe and Mail* 1 Apr. 2000: 22.

Shakespeare, William. *The Merchant of Venice. The Riverside Shakespeare*. Vol: 1. Boston: Houghton, 1974. 254–85.

Swaffar, Janet. "The Case for Foreign Languages as a Discipline." *ADFL Bulletin* 30.3 (1999): 6–12.

Yates, Frances. *John Florio*. Cambridge: Cambridge UP, 1934.

QUESTIONS TO THINK ABOUT

1. Why does Edwards say that "these are difficult times for some languages—the small ones." What are some of the difficulties these languages face in the 21st century, according to Edwards? What does Edwards mean by languages becoming "bastardised?"

2. What does Edwards intend when he says that it seems necessary to repeat the truism that languages of "wider communication" have no special capabilities to recommend them? Why does he find it necessary to repeat this idea? How does the quote from the Fall 1999 *ADFL Bulletin* help to demonstrate his point? How does this quote relate to Edwards' further discussion about English "openness?"

3. Edwards explains the difference between *instrumental* and *integrative* motivations to change spoken language. What is the difference? Provide an example that illustrates a change in spoken language for instrumental reasons rather than integrative reasons. Under what circumstances would you imagine that a person would learn a new language for integrative reasons?

4. *Extending your understanding*: One paradox shown by Edwards is that although English achieved its world status quite specifically because of its long history of speaker multilingualism and incorporation of words from other languages, most English speakers today are monolingual and actually resist the learning of other languages (unless actually forced by circumstances to do so). How do you think this phenomenon will affect the English language in the long run? Do you think English will lose its world status if the current trend of monolingualism continues? What other factors—in addition to linguistic factors—might affect the global status of English in the next centuries? Draw up a list of possible factors that might impact English and its status in the world over the next 200 years.

TERMS TO DEFINE

Define the following words and phrases as they are presented within the context of the reading. Comment on your understanding of the significance of each one.

"Small" language
Languages of "wider communication"
Linguistic "purity"
Linguistic engineering
Linguistic necessity
Monolingual

Gender Issues in Language Change

Deborah Cameron
University of London

There is a relatively long history of folk and scholarly interest in the differing roles played by women and men in processes of language change. In 1922, Otto Jespersen repeated (albeit with some caveats) the observation that "women do nothing more than keep to the traditional language which they have learnt from their parents and hand on to their children, while innovations are due to the initiative of men" (Jespersen, 1998, p. 230). Somewhat later, by contrast, the English dialectologist Harold Orton preferred male to female informants on the ground that the speech of older rural men was most likely to preserve traditional dialect forms (Orton, 1962). In the 1970s, variationist sociolinguists using quantitative methods to study language change in progress noted that women were typically more advanced than men in changes toward a prestige norm. This linguistic innovation was attributed, however, to a kind of social conservatism: women were motivated to adopt standard forms because of their greater "status consciousness" or "linguistic insecurity." Clearly, then, debates about men, women, and language change have been going on for some time: this review does not deal with a sudden flowering of interest in a previously neglected topic. Rather, it considers the influence on recent research of new ideas about gender and its relationship to linguistic phenomena.

Before proceeding, I should clarify what is encompassed by the term *language change*. In some discussions the term is used narrowly, to refer to changes within a single language system (albeit such changes may involve contact between subsystems, e.g., dialects spoken in adjacent areas). The prototypical phenomenon studied under this heading is sound change, a topic that continues to dominate research in variationist sociolinguistics. In addition to discussing recent work on sound change, however, I will consider several other types of change that are of interest to applied linguists. One is language shift, where one language in the repertoire of a bilingual speech community progressively encroaches on the functions of the other and eventually replaces it. Shift typically occurs intergenerationally, as younger community members become increasingly

Reprinted with permission of Cambridge University Press, from *Annual Review of Applied Linguistics* 23 (2003): 187–201.

limited in their bilingual competence, and eventually monolingual. Since women and girls in most societies are the primary carers for young children, researchers have paid attention to their role in promoting shift—and, conversely, in maintaining ancestral languages or revitalizing those which have become endangered. The formation of pidgins, the development of some pidgins into creoles, and the process of decreolization that creoles may subsequently undergo are also relevant topics, and I will comment briefly on recent work which addresses the relationship of gender to pidgin and creole development (see also McWhorter). Finally, I will consider the influence on language of recent and ongoing social changes relating to gender. An obvious case in point is the impact of overtly feminist linguistic reforms such as the promulgation of "nonsexist" or "inclusive" language policies. Also of interest are shifts in gendered language ideologies and verbal hygiene practices (i.e., representations of language and efforts to regulate its use in accordance with particular value judgments—for more detailed definitions and illustrations see Bergvall, Bing, & Freed, 1997; Cameron, 1995; Finegan; and Woolard, 1998). Though not, strictly speaking, examples of language change, these developments affect the value attached to different ways of speaking, and thus have the potential to influence the direction of language change in the future.

RETHINKING GENDER: THE RISE AND RISE
OF SOCIAL CONSTRUCTIONISM

In modern feminist theory, it is axiomatic that gender—socially constructed masculinity or femininity—is not reducible to biological maleness or femaleness. The sex/gender distinction was not, however, available to pre-feminist scholars like Jespersen, and many later researchers in practice made no use of it (Eckert, 1990). The explanations most commonly proposed for observed linguistic differences between women and men relied on large-scale generalizations about the roles or personality traits that were supposedly typical of each sex; even when the term "gender" was used, accounts of it were often shaped by an underlying assumption that it referred to an inherent natural attribute.

Feminists always regarded gender as a social rather than natural phenomenon, but in feminist theory during the 1990s there was a shift in the direction of a more radically social constructionist approach. In that approach gender is not seen as the stable outcome of early socialization, but as something constructed, continually in social interaction. It is recognized that the construction of gender takes different forms across cultures and through time—there is no universal essence of masculinity or femininity—and that gender may be produced differently by individuals in a single society or community. "Women" and "men" are no longer treated as discrete and internally homogeneous categories about which one can make universal statements ("women do X, men do Y"); there is variation within each group, and overlap between the two. In language and gender studies, researchers have turned away from the quest for universal generalizations about men's or women's speech, and focused instead on the particular conditions shaping the behavior of men and women in specific locales. More attention has been paid to the interaction of gender with other dimensions of social identity such as race, ethnicity, class, generation, and sexuality (see contributions to Hall & Bucholtz, 1995); gender is no longer conceived as a simple binary opposition (Bing & Bergvall, 1997), and explanations of gender differences have accordingly shifted away from generalities about sex roles or personality traits. Alternative frameworks adopted by researchers have included variants of post-structuralist postmodernist theory (cf. Livia & Hall, 1997) and the notion of the "community of practice" drawn from the work of Jean Lave and Etienne Wenger (e.g., Wenger, 1998; for the application of this model to language and gender studies, see Eckert & McConnell-Ginet 1992; 1999).

The impact of new theoretical approaches on the study of gender and language change has been mixed. Since the topic is of interest to scholars located in several fields and traditions, not all of them committed to feminist approaches or conversant with feminist theory, more conservative theoretical assumptions persist alongside accounts that challenge them. There has also been at least one recent theoretical development that goes strikingly against the social constructionist grain, namely a revival of interest in quasi-biological (neo-Darwinist) explanations for sex-differentiated linguistic behavior. The evolutionary scientist Robin Dunbar (1996), for instance, has proposed that the main survival advantage conferred on humans by language was the ability to maintain cohesion in larger social groupings. He argues that women (playing *ex hypothesi* the same pivotal role in early human social groups as females do in many nonhuman primate species) were the major force in the evolution of natural languages, and that this may have a bearing on the contemporary observation that women outperform men on various tests of verbal ability. The sociolinguist Jack Chambers (1992; 1995) has also cited women's evolved, neurobiologically-based verbal superiority as a potential factor explaining their tendency to display greater "stylistic flexibility" than men. This is relevant to the question of linguistic change because social and stylistic variation is the synchronic raw material from which change over time is produced. It should be noted, however, that the postulate of female verbal superiority is controversial (Hyde & Linn, 1988). At present, discussions framed in terms of Darwinian natural selection remain highly speculative, and I will concentrate here on the social constructionist approach.

GENDER AND LANGUAGE CHANGE IN RECENT VARIATIONIST SOCIOLINGUISTICS

Since its beginnings in the 1960s, variationist sociolinguistics has attended to differences between women and men, but the perceived importance of those differences has increased over time. Gender is no longer considered, as it was in the early years of the paradigm, secondary to class as a factor influencing language change. The ubiquity of gender differentiation within speech communities offers a particularly compelling illustration of the point that linguistic variation (and therefore, language change) is not simply the outcome of separation between groups in society, while conversely, sustained close contact does not necessarily produce homogeneity. In the words of William Labov: "No one can deny that husbands and wives, brothers and sisters, are involved in intimate communication in everyday life. Yet gender is a powerful differentiating factor in almost every case of stable social stratification and change in progress that has been studied" (Labov, 2001, p. 262).

As I noted above, variationist sociolinguists using quantitative methods to study language change (typically, sound change) in progress developed an early account of the relationship of gender to change, which laid emphasis on the "status consciousness" and "linguistic insecurity" of women. That account was later refined, however, in the light of accumulating evidence. After reviewing relevant research, Labov (1990) proposed the following generalizations (the formulation below is from Dubois and Horvath, 2000, p. 289, parenthetical explanations mine):

- Principle I: For stable sociolinguistic variables (i.e., those not involved in change), men use a higher frequency of nonstandard forms than women.
- Principle Ia: In change from above (i.e., where speakers are conscious of the existence and social meaning of competing variants), women favor the incoming prestige form more than men.
- Principle II: In change from below (i.e., where speakers are not conscious that change is occurring), women are most often the innovators.

Labov has drawn attention to the "gender paradox" his principles embody: women as a group "conform more closely than men to sociolinguistic norms that are overtly prescribed, but conform less than men when they are not" (Labov, 2001, p. 293). Though studies have documented the existence of individual women speakers whose behavior exemplifies the predicted pattern—simultaneously conservative with respect to stigma-tized changes and innovative with respect to nonstigmatized changes (e.g., Maclagan, Gordon, & Lewis, 1999)—it is also important to note that the leaders of change from above and change from below may be different individuals. In the communities stud-ied by Labov and his associates in Philadelphia, the leaders of both kinds of change are upper working class women, but they are distinguished by their degree of social conformity. Women's behavior is not uniform, then, and cannot be explained in terms of some essential characteristic common to all members of the group. The question does remain, however, of why the leaders of most changes are women rather than men.

Labov (2001) offers a multicausal account. In relation to change from above, he cites women's greater concern or responsibility for ensuring the social mobility of their children as a key motivation for adopting prestige norms, while his discussion of change from below refers to an assortment of proposals by other scholars—some of them problematic from the point of view of social constructionism, since they belong to the "biological" tendency mentioned above (e.g., Chambers, 1995; Gordon & Heath, 1998).[1] In line with the overall aims of this review, the discussion below will not look closely at arguments to which sex rather than gender is central, but will concentrate on accounts framed in social constructionist terms.

One such account is particularly associated with the sociolinguist Penelope Eckert, though it has also been taken up by others (an accessible recent summary appears in Eck-ert, 1998, see also Eckert & McConnell-Ginet, 1999; Wolfram & Schilling-Estes, 1998). This account suggests that women as social subordinates are more dependent than men on sym-bolic resources for asserting identity and group membership. Eckert carried out research in a suburban high school near Detroit, Michigan, where identity and social practice were organized around the contrast between "jocks" (who embraced the official definition of school success, e.g., participating actively in both academic and extracurricular pursuits and going on to college) and "burnouts" (who rejected the school's values and resisted active participation in its official culture). The contrast was also marked linguistically, with particular phonological variables that are involved in an ongoing change in the Detroit area (the Northern Cities Vowel Shift) being appropriated differentially to mark either jock or burnout identity. Eckert found that in both the jock and the burnout groups, young women were more advanced than young men in their use of the innovative variants marking group membership. This cannot be explained as status consciousness in the sense earlier sociolinguists used the concept, for the vowel shift is a case of change from below and the innovative variants are vernacular rather than standard. The kind of status sought by the young women is not the prestige associated with correct pronunciation; rather, they assert their status as "good jocks" or "good burnouts" by carrying their use of variants that function as group identity markers to a greater extreme than their male counterparts do. Eckert observes that nonlinguistic markers of status within the group—for instance, ath-letic prowess and fighting skills—are not available to women on the same terms as to men. Even if they possess the same skills, women are not rewarded for them in the same way. Their capital as jocks and burnouts is largely symbolic, and so they work harder to assert in-group status through symbolic details like the styling of their jeans and the pronunciation of their vowels.

Similar considerations may be invoked to account for women's role in changes from above. The labor market both exploits and reproduces female dependence on symbolic capital, channeling women into jobs that place emphasis on interpersonal communication (e.g., nursing, social work, customer service) and/or require a high level of standard language competence (e.g., school teaching, secretarial work). As Gordon (1997) has observed, too, an important form of symbolic capital for girls and women across classes and ethnic groups is sexual reputation. In a subjective reaction study carried out in New Zealand, Gordon found attributions of "looseness" to female speakers to be associated with nonstandard speech. She proposes this as a potentially powerful motivation for women's behavior in relation to Principles I and Ia above, i.e., women avoid stigmatized linguistic variants in an effort to avoid a kind of social stigma that is specific to their gender.

Labov's principles have provided a starting point for many more recent empirical variationist studies, and while some of these have offered further support for his generalizations, it has also been noted that specific local conditions may produce divergence from the expected patterns. Dubois and Horvath (2000), for instance, report on a study involving three generations of Cajun English speakers in Louisiana. The generations represent different phases of a historical process whereby originally monolingual French speakers became first bilingual and ultimately monolingual in English. The oldest speakers' English is strongly marked by the phonological influence of Ll French, whereas the middle generation, whose upbringing and education made them conscious of the stigma attached to French influenced pronunciation, uses a less markedly Cajun English. Among the youngest speakers, however, for whom English monolingualism is the norm, Cajun variants have made a dramatic comeback—particularly among young men. This "recycling" of French-influenced variants is a way of asserting Cajun identity via English (the only language available for the purpose since the younger speakers have no command of French itself); but since it is a case of change from below, the question arises why men rather than women are leading it. Dubois and Horvath explain this by noting that the revival of Cajun variants accompanies a resurgence of ethnic pride (the Cajun Renaissance) whose most important public symbols are traditionally masculine activities such as boating, hunting, fishing, and performing Cajun music. At the same time, language shift has eliminated the important role traditionally played by women in passing on the community's ancestral language to children. In the particular sociohistorical conditions of this community, then, it is young men who have the greater motivation to acquire and display symbolic capital as Cajuns.

GENDER AS AN INFLUENCE ON LANGUAGE SHIFT

Dubois and Horvath's study demonstrates that language shift may have consequences for the subsequent sociolinguistic positioning of women and men (in the Louisiana case, men have become torchbearers for Cajun language and culture). The reverse is also true: gender relations in bilingual communities may be consequential for the process of language shift. This emerges clearly from Susan Gal's classic study of the Austrian town of Oberwart (Gal, 1978; 1979). Here Hungarian-German bilingualism was in the process of yielding to German monolingualism, and young women were most advanced in their preference for German. Hungarian had come to be associated with a "peasant" identity, while speaking German only was associated with a "worker" identity; the linguistic choices of young women reflected their calculations regarding which category of man it would be preferable to marry. Many or most viewed the role of peasant's wife as less desirable than that of worker's wife, and planned to marry German-speaking workers from outside the community. This also implied that young bilingual men would have to seek marriage partners outside their own community, making German the de facto choice for the dominant language of their own future households.

In Oberwart, the symbolic association of Hungarian with peasant status and German with worker status caused the languages to be evaluated differently by women and men because of the greater unattractiveness of peasant life to women. But in some cases, gender may be part of what a language actually symbolizes, and this may affect the way it is evaluated by the whole community. One such instance is discussed by Don Kulick (1992; 1998), who studied language shift in a small and remote village, Gapun, in Papua New Guinea. Gapuners were until recently bilingual in the local vernacular Taiap and the creole language that serves as a lingua franca across the country, Tok Pisin. At the time of Kulick's original fieldwork in 1986–87, however, Tok Pisin was in the process of superseding Taiap, and when he returned a few years later he found that no villager younger than 14 had an active command of Taiap. Kulick analyzes the underlying reasons for shift in ideological and symbolic terms, noting that the contrast between Taiap and Tok Pisin has come to symbolize a series of other contrasts. For instance, Taiap is associated with the ancestral past whereas Tok Pisin is associated with modernization, development, and Christianization. The contrast between the languages has also come to symbolize an important local contrast between *hed* (willfulness, which may lead to unthinking or unguarded expression of one's thoughts and feelings) and *save* (knowledge, which implies the ability to control and manage the expression of potentially dangerous ideas and emotions). Gapuners associate the control that is central to *save* with men and the dangerous emotional excess that is part of *hed* with women. Oratories in the men's house, which are delivered in a highly indirect language and have the production of consensus and avoidance of conflict as primary goals, are predominantly in Tok Pisin. Taiap predominates, however, in the angry, obscene, and abusive monologues known as *kroses*, which are virtually always delivered by women. The association of Taiap with *hed* and Tok Pisin with *save* both underwrites and reinforces their symbolic gendering, i.e., Taiap is associated with women and Tok Pisin with men, even though both sexes use both languages. Kulick argues that the intertwined negative symbolic associations of Taiap—with women, *hed*, anger, and the past—are at the root of the actual language practices that propel the shift towards Tok Pisin.

Gal and Kulick studied language shift in communities which had not, or at least not recently, been displaced from their ancestral locations and ways of life. In contemporary global conditions, however, language shift is also often observed and studied in migrant and diasporic communities. In such communities the question is less about what motivates shift than it is about the course the process takes in particular circumstances: i.e., how quickly and extensively an additional language is adopted, and how far migrants and their descendants seek, or are able, to maintain heritage languages over time. A related question is whether patterns of shift and retention vary among different groups within the community. Research has shown that gender may be one source of variation, since opportunities for contact with the majority community (e.g., through participation in the labor market, or through intermarriage) may be markedly different for women and men. Once again, though, the effect is mediated by the particular form gender relations take in a given community; researchers pay attention to the local particularities of gender rather than treating it as a *global* category whose influence will be the same in every context.

In an analysis of Australian census data, Clyne and Kipp (1997) observe that different minority communities show different gendered patterns of shift to English. In the more established communities (e.g., Greek Australians), first generation migrant women have higher rates of L1 retention than men; but there are also cases (e.g., migrants from the Philippines speaking Tagalog, Ilokano, and Cebuano) where women are ahead of men in shifting to English. The most obvious explanation concerns exogamy rates. Women are a relatively large majority (65%) of Australians born in the Philippines, and a high proportion of them are married to Australian-born or European immigrant men. Clyne and Kipp report, however, that among the children of migrants in Australia (the second generation), gender differences are greatly reduced or eliminated for most groups.

Joanne Winter and Anne Pauwels (2000) note that the interpretation of patterns based on large-scale surveyor census data often relies on generalizations about gender that recent scholarship has called into question. The finding that, in many communities, first generation migrant women have higher L1 retention rates is typically explained as a consequence of *deficit* (women have restricted access to instruction in L2 and so experience a "linguistic lag" relative to men; see Ehrlich, 1997) and/or *difference* (women are cast within their communities as the primary guardians of ethnic and linguistic heritage). Investigating language maintenance among German, Greek, and Vietnamese speakers in Melbourne, Winter and Pauwels observed patterns similar to those reported by Clyne and Kipp, but they argue for a more nuanced approach to explanation, which takes account of the complexities of women's and men's experience within bilingual communities. They suggest that for second generation speakers particularly, the analysis of surveyor census data needs to be complemented by in-depth interviewing and ethnographic research in order to gain a better understanding of how women and men themselves perceive the connection between gender identity and the retention or loss of a minority language.

Along somewhat similar lines, Aneta Pavlenko (200la, b; 2002) has used language-learning memoirs to illuminate the experience of migrant and minority women in the United States, while Suzanne Sinke (1999) consulted literary and autobiographical works, immigrant letters, community newspapers, and the records of religious and philanthropic organizations for her account of gendered patterns of language shift among Dutch Americans at the turn of the (nineteenth to twentieth) century. The use of these sources enables Pavlenko and Sinke to probe the complex, often conflictual relationship between gender and ethnicity that is part of the hidden history of language shift in migrant communities. Sinke presents evidence that women in the communities she studied were at the extremes of both maintenance and shift, thus underlining the need for methods that can shed light on differences within gender groups as well as the differences between them.

GENDER INFLUENCES ON PIDGIN AND CREOLE DEVELOPMENT

Pidgins are auxiliary languages used in contexts where there is a need for a lingua franca to facilitate commerce or cooperative working between people with no other common language. The activities that have been most associated with the formation and use of pidgins historically include trade, plantation labor, and military or police service—all of which are predominantly associated with men (McWhorter, 1996). In some communities, it appears that men sought actively to prevent women from learning a pidgin, possibly because the use of pidgin among women was associated with prostitutes and so was not considered respectable (this should remind us that not all forms of commerce have been male monopolies).[2] As with language shift, though, the role played by women and girls in the language socialization of children in many societies may be a significant factor in the ongoing development of pidgins and creoles: creolization, like shift, is an intergenerational process (also see McWhorter). Thus when women do begin to use pidgin languages, this has potentially far-reaching consequences for subsequent linguistic change. In Gapun, for instance, Kulick (1992) notes that Tok Pisin was originally introduced to the village by men who had spent periods away working on plantations, and it remained for some time a male language, which boys picked up from older men. Only later did it come to be used regularly by women, but since this meant that younger children in the process of acquiring language were exposed to Tok Pisin as well as Taiap input, it was a crucial factor in the development of a fully bilingual speech community, which in turn paved the way for the now far-advanced shift to Tok Pisin.

GENDER IDEOLOGIES AS AN INFLUENCE ON LANGUAGE CHANGE

The last 30 years have seen major changes in the social position of women; while the impact has undoubtedly been greater in some places than in others, sociologists have noted that ideals of gender egalitarianism now have global currency (e.g., Giddens, 2000). Changing ideologies of gender have affected language and language-use just as they have affected many other social institutions and practices, and their linguistic reflexes have been studied by a number of researchers.

One focus of interest is linguistic reform, enacted by state and other institutions (e.g., educational, commercial, religious) in the context of policy initiatives promoting equal opportunities. For example, legislation prohibiting sex discrimination in the workplace creates a need for gender-inclusive or gender-neutral occupational terms (e.g., chairperson, firefighter) in job advertisements, job descriptions, employment contracts, and employment laws. Concern about the effects of sexism in educational and other materials which play a role in the socialization of children has led to the adoption of inclusive or nonsexist language by many producers and publishers (for a recent discussion of inclusiveness in EFL teaching materials, see Gray, 2002).

Whereas many early texts dealing with feminist linguistic reform were oriented to practice and activism (cf. Miller & Swift, 1980), some recent scholarship has taken a more theoretical and critical approach. Anne Pauwels's *Women Changing Language* (1998), for instance, not only provides comparative descriptive material on reform efforts across a range of languages and societies (including some non-Indo-European examples), it also advances the theoretical discussion by placing feminist linguistic reform in the conceptual framework of language planning. Pauwels notes that feminist reformers confront the same kinds of problems and choices as other language planners: she examines the issues they must deal with systematically, and in some cases criticizes their solutions as linguistically uninformed or overly narrow in focus. One limitation she identifies is the focus on replacing single items (words or morphemes), as if the goal were simply to substitute one form for another, and not to alter the repertoire of meanings. A number of researchers (e.g., Ehrlich & King, 1992; Kitzinger & Thomas, 1995) have examined the discursive "afterlife" of planned changes, noting that it is in discourse—language in use—that meanings are negotiated and contested. Consequently, substituted or newly coined terms may acquire meanings that were not intended by their instigators. Examples in English include the reinterpretation of *Ms.* so that it functions not as the intended parallel to *Mr.* but as a third term alongside *Miss* and *Mrs.*, applied to anomalous women such as lesbians and divorcees; and the use of -*person* suffixes with female referents only, while -*man* continues to be used for male referents.

Discourse patterns have been a long-standing concern of language and gender researchers, with interest typically centering on gender differences in preferred discourse strategies and styles, and the often negative consequences of those differences for women (Lakoff, 1975; Tannen, 1990). Recently, however, researchers have noted a new idealization of the cooperative, emotionally expressive discourse styles popularly (if not always accurately) associated with women. Cameron (2000) observes that feminine speech styles are being commodified in the new globalized service sector, where they are frequently prescribed to workers regardless of gender. Montgomery (1999) analyzes the reception of tributes to Princess Diana following her death in 1997, arguing that in contemporary mass-mediated public arenas, old-style (and symbolically masculine) oratory is now devalued by comparison with a (symbolically feminine) speech-style foregrounding sincerity and emotional openness. It appears then that language ideologies relating to gender may be shifting, prompting a certain feminization of public discourse, and a tendency to view masculine communication styles as problematic or dysfunctional (see Cameron, 2003, for examples). In the view of both Cameron and Montgomery, these developments have been prompted less by feminist critiques of patriarchal values than by new management practices and the demands of media performance in an age of global communication. But if, for whatever reason, feminine speech patterns are gaining prestige, that may have implications for the direction of future linguistic changes.

CONCLUSION: RECENT ADVANCES AND FUTURE TRENDS

Modern sociolinguistics is based on an understanding of language change as something other than random drift or functional adaptation: it is the product of choices made (not always consciously) by social actors using linguistic variation as a symbolic resource. In recent years, researchers working on various aspects of gender and language change have been challenged to engage with the argument that gender, too, is a form of social and symbolic practice. While responses to this challenge have varied, few researchers or research paradigms have remained untouched by it.

Yet this is not to say that a consensus has emerged on every subject. There is, for instance, ongoing discussion of appropriate research methods. While no one disputes the utility of quantification per se—the use of census data to map language shift/retention, or the statistical analysis which is central to variationist studies of sound change in progress—there have been calls for these techniques to be combined with ethnography and/or other qualitative methods to provide a more nuanced understanding of gender relations in specific communities and so illuminate the *why* as well as the *what* of gendered behavior.

Another issue that is likely to be the focus of continuing debate is the status of *generalization* in research carried out within a social constructionist framework. For some researchers, "looking locally" means that generalization is no longer an important goal, and may even be suspect. Others appear willing in principle to move from detailed observations of gender in particular communities of practice to more abstract and general statements, such as the proposal that women are in general more dependent than men on symbolic capital. This does not depend on presupposing some essential characteristic shared by all women in all times and places, but it does imply there may be some virtue in attending to larger structural factors shaping gender relations across communities. It is my own view that generalization remains a legitimate goal for social science, and is not necessarily incompatible with contemporary feminist views of gender as social construct and social practice. However, future attempts to generalize about gender and language change must be judged not only on their theoretical and political merits, but also on their ability to accommodate the complexity that recent empirical research has revealed.

NOTES

[1] Gordon and Heath (1998) believe that the tendency for women to favor certain kinds of vowel shifts (those that lead to an overall dispersion of vowels in phonetic space) while men tend to favor others (centralizing changes that concentrate vowels in a more restricted space), may be rooted in a "natural" sound symbolism which is ultimately linked to physiological sex differences. Labov (2001, p. 291) treats this proposal sceptically but seriously, noting empirical counterexamples but suggesting we should not be too quick to dismiss the general line of argument.

[2] I owe this point to Miriam Meyerhoff (personal communication, December, 2001), who observed the persistence of the association firsthand in field research among Bislama speakers in Vanuatu. I am also much indebted to her for more general guidance on the literature on pidgins and creoles. I should note however that this is very far from being a comprehensive survey of recent research on gender and language change in pidgin- and creole-speaking communities. Such research raises interesting and complex questions about, for instance, the applicability of Labov's 1990 principles to the kind of fluid multilingual situation in which pidgins and creoles typically arise (what, in such a situation, does one count as the prestige norm or as change from above?). Limitations of space prevent me from doing justice to these issues, however, and they will not be considered further here.

ANNOTATED BIBLIOGRAPHY

Eckert, P., & McConnell-Ginet, S. (1999). New generalizations and explanations in language and gender research. *Language in Society*, 28, 185–201.

This article is an important recent theoretical statement, summarizing and explicating the now influential approach to language and gender research that makes use of the concept of the "Community of Practice" (CoP). Focusing mainly though not exclusively on the application of this concept to variationist studies of language change, the article contains a usefully explicit discussion of the tension between recognizing local specificity/complexity and not losing sight of more general patterns. It also touches on arguments for using ethnography alongside quantification. It appeared in a special issue of *Language in Society* devoted to the CoP approach in language and gender studies, the other contributions to which are also informative.

Labov, W. (2001). *Principles of linguistic change, Vol II: Social factors.* Oxford: Blackwell. (See especially Chs. 8–11.)

> At the time of writing, this is Labov's most recent examination of the relationship of gender to sound change, continuing the discussion of his influential 1990 principles, and offering a useful (if densely written) summary of relevant variationist research evidence as well as some indication of the range of explanations scholars have proposed for empirically observed patterns of gender differentiation.

Pauwels, A. (1998). *Women changing language.* London: Longman.

> This full length book is the most comprehensive recent study of the phenomenon of feminist/anti-sexist linguistic reform, which is treated here as an instance of language planning. Pauwels provides valuable comparative information on feminist reform efforts across a range of languages and societies.

Pavlenko, A., Blackledge, A., Piller, I., & Teutsch-Dwyer, M. (Eds.). (2001). *Multilingualism, second language learning, and gender.* Berlin: Mouton de Gruyter.

> This is a wide-ranging collection whose primary focus is not gender and language change but gender and second language learning. However, several contributions focus on the meaning of bilingualism and language shift for women and men, particularly in contexts of migration; this is a theme that is increasingly emphasized in other research on gender and language change.

OTHER REFERENCES

Bergvall, V., Bing, J., & Freed, A. (Eds.). (1997). *Rethinking language and gender research.* London: Longman.

Bing, J., & Bergvall, V. (1997). The question of questions: Beyond binary thinking. In V. Bergvall, J. Bing, & A. Freed (Eds.), *Rethinking language and gender research: Theory and practice* (pp. 1–30). London: Longman.

Cameron, D. (1995). *Verbal hygiene.* London: Routledge.

Cameron, D. (2000). Styling the worker: Gender and the commodification of language in the globalized service economy. *Journal of Sociolinguistics, 4,* 323–347.

Cameron, D. (2003). Gender and language ideologies. In J. Holmes & M. Meyerhoff (Eds.), *The handbook of language and gender* (pp. 447–467). Oxford: Blackwell.

Chambers, J. K. (1992). Linguistic correlates of gender and sex. *English Worldwide, 13,* 173–218.

Chambers, J. K. (1995). *Sociolinguistic theory.* Oxford: Blackwell.

Clyne, M., & Kipp, S. (1997). Trends and changes in home language use and shift in Australia, 1986-1996. *Journal of Multilingual and Multicultural Development, 18,* 451–473.

Dubois, S., & Horvath, B. (2000). When the music changes, you change too: Gender and language change in Cajun English. *Language Variation and Change, 1,* 287–313.

Dunbar, R. (1996). *Grooming, gossip and the evolution of language.* London: Faber.

Eckert, P. (1990). The whole woman: Sex and gender differences in variation. *Language Variation and Change, 1,* 245–268.

Eckert, P. (1998). Gender and sociolinguistic variation. In J. Coates (Ed.), *Language and gender: A reader* (pp. 64–75). Oxford: Blackwell.

Eckert, P., & McConnell-Ginet, S. (1992). Think practically and look locally: Language and gender as community-based practice. *Annual Review of Anthropology, 12,* 461–490.

Ehrlich, S. (1997). Gender as social practice: Implications for second language acquisition. *Studies in Second Language Acquisition, 19,* 421–446.

Ehrlich, S., & King, R. (1992). Gender-based language reform and the social construction of meaning. *Discourse & Society, 3,* 516–566.

Finegan, E. (2003). Linguistic prescription: Familiar practices and new perspectives. *Annual Review of Applied Linguistics, 23*, pp. 213–224.

Gal, S. (1978). Peasant men can't get wives: Language and sex roles in a bilingual community. *Language in Society, 7*, 1–17.

Gal, S. (1979). *Language shift: Social determinants of linguistic change in bilingual Austria.* New York: Academic Press.

Giddens, A. (2000). *Runaway world: How globalization is reshaping our lives.* London: Routledge.

Gordon, E. (1997). Sex, speech and stereotypes: Why women use prestige speech forms more than men. *Language in Society, 26*, 1–14.

Gordon, M., & Heath, J. (1998). Sex, sound symbolism and sociolinguistics. *Current Anthropology, 39*, 421–449.

Gray, J. (2002). The global coursebook in ELT. In D. Block & D. Cameron (Eds.), *Globalization and language teaching* (pp. 151–167). London: Routledge.

Hall, K., & Bucholtz, M. (Eds.). (1995). *Gender articulated: Language and the socially constructed self.* London: Routledge.

Hyde, J. S., & Linn, M. (1988). Gender differences in verbal ability: A meta-analysis. *Psychological Bulletin, 104*, 53–69.

Jespersen, O. (1998 [1922]). The woman. In D. Cameron (Ed.), *The feminist critique of language* (2nd ed., pp. 225–241). London: Routledge.

Kitzinger, C., & Thomas, A. (1995). Sexual harassment: A discursive approach. In S. Wilkinson & C. Kitzinger (Eds.), *Feminism and discourse* (pp. 32–48). London: Sage.

Kulick, D. (1992). *Language shift and cultural reproduction: Self, syncretism and society in a Papua New Guinea Village.* Cambridge: Cambridge University Press.

Kulick, D. (1998). Anger, gender, language shift and the politics of revelation in a Papua New Guinean village. In B. Schieffelin, K. Woolard, & P. Kroskrity (Eds.), *Language ideologies: Practice and theory* (pp. 87–102). New York: Oxford University Press.

Labov, W. (1990). The intersection of sex and social class in the course of linguistic change. *Language Variation and Change, 2*, 205–254.

Lakoff, R. (1975). *Language and woman's place.* New York: Harper and Row.

Livia, A., & Hall, K. (Eds.). (1997). *Queerly phrased: Language, gender and sexuality.* New York: Oxford University Press.

Maclagan, M. A., Gordon, E., & Lewis, G. (1999). Women and sound change: Conservative and innovative behavior by the same speakers. *Language Variation and Change, 11*, 19–41.

McWhorter, J. (1996). Bringing gender into creole studies. In N. Warner, J. Ahlers, L. Bilmes, M. Oliver, S. Wertheim, & M. Chen (Eds.), *Gender and belief systems: Proceedings of the Fourth Berkeley Women and Language Conference* (pp. 501–508). Berkeley, CA: Berkeley Women and Language Group.

McWhorter, 1. (2003). Pidgins and creoles as models of language change: The state of the art. *Annual Review of Applied Linguistics, 23*, pp. 202–212.

Miller, C., & Swift, K. (1980). *The handbook of nonsexist language.* London: Women's Press.

Montgomery, M. (1999). Speaking sincerely: Public reactions to the death of Diana. *Language and Literature, 8*, 5–33.

Orton, H. (1962). *Introduction to the Survey of English Dialects.* Leeds: Arnold.

Pavlenko, A. (2001a). Language learning memoirs as a gendered genre. *Applied Linguistics, 9*, 3–19.

Pavlenko, A. (200lb). "How am I to become a woman in an American vein?": Transformations of gender performance in second language learning. In A. Pavlenko, A. Blackledge, I. Piller, & M. Teutsch-Dwyer (Eds.), *Multilingualism, second language learning and gender* (pp. 133–174). Berlin: Mouton de Gruyter.

Pavlenko, A. (2002). Narrative study: Whose story is it, anyway? *TESOL Quarterly, 36*(2), 213–218.

Sinke, S. (1999, Winter). Gender in language and life: A Dutch American example. *Gender Issues*, 26–51.

Tannen, D. (1990). *You just don't understand: Men and women in conversation.* New York: Morrow.

Wenger, E. (1998). *Communities of practice.* New York: Cambridge University Press.

Winter, J., & Pauwels, A. (2000). Gender and language contact research in the Australian context. *Journal of Multilingual and Multicultural Development, 21*, 508–522.

Wolfram, W., & Schilling-Estes, N. (1998). *American English.* Oxford: Blackwell.

Woolard, K. (1998). Language ideology as a field of inquiry. In B. Schieffelin, K. Woolard, & P. Kroskrity (Eds.), *Language ideologies: Practice and theory* (pp. 3–47). New York: Oxford University Press.

QUESTIONS TO THINK ABOUT

1. Cameron begins the reading with a quote from Otto Jespersen, one of the most respected and acclaimed linguists of our time. How does this quote immediately predispose you to a particular stance regarding language innovation and change? Why do you think Cameron chose this quote to begin her piece? How does it set up the quotes that follow in the introductory paragraph?

2. What does Cameron mean by language change? How is her definition broader than that of actual change within a linguistic system itself? How does she bring the influences of gender to bear on this particular definition of language change throughout the reading?

3. How does gender interact with other dimensions of social identity such as race/ethnicity, class, generation, and sexuality? Why is the notion of gender different than the notion of sexuality, according to Cameron? Why is it important that these two concepts be distinguished?

4. *Extending your understanding*: Cameron explains, in the context of the Eckert study she cites, that

   > [women's] capital as jocks and burnouts is largely symbolic, and so they work harder to assert in-group status through symbolic details like the styling of their jeans and the pronunciation of their vowels.

   What does Cameron mean by this assessment? Describe other situations in which a particular group uses linguistic attributes (technical language, slang, certain pronunciations, etc.) to show in-group status. Does the group seem to feel the need to exaggerate these linguistic attributes? Explain the implicit connection between marginalization by the in-group and in-group behavior inherent in such examples.

TERMS TO DEFINE

Define the following words and phrases as they are presented within the context of the reading. Comment on your understanding of the significance of each one.

Language change
Social constructionism
Variationist sociolinguistics
Gender paradox
Diasporic community
Creolization

Homophobic Slang as Coercive Discourse Among College Students

James D. Armstrong
State University of New York at Plattsburgh

An article in the 24 August 1988 issue of the *New York Times* reported that two men attacked by armed teenagers were also verbally degraded with "anti-homosexual epithets" (Wolinsky and Sherrill 1993: 53). Physical attacks on gay men (i.e., "gay bashing") are often accompanied by verbal assaults. On my campus and on others, "Take Back the Night" rallies sponsored by women's groups and activities organized by gay men and lesbian women sometimes evoke verbal assaults from male bystanders, who express their hostility with homophobic language. This is not so surprising given that language is an act that can be violent, exclusionary, and coercive. Furthermore, America's history of religious intolerance, stigmatization, and prejudice against homosexuals creates a context in which open derogation of homosexuality and homosexuals might be expected. In recent years, after some progress toward mainstream acceptance occurred during the 1970s, there has been an upturn in hostility toward gays and lesbians. This hostility has been accompanied by increased violence toward homosexuals and reinforced both by the fear generated by the AIDS pandemic and by the political power of the religious right (Blumenfeld and Raymond 1988; Perrow and Guillen 1990; Peters 1991). Against this background, gays and lesbians are likely to be "bashed" by both homophobic words and deeds.

Homophobia, however, is not limited to physical and verbal attacks on homosexuals and overt intolerance toward individuals suspected of being gay. Often in public interactions, people who might not think of openly attacking homosexuals use language that derogates homosexuality. Often those who employ this language in public are males, usually young, and presumably heterosexual. Use of such language creates an atmosphere of uncritical acceptance of intolerance toward homosexuality, while reinforcing stereotypical attitudes toward gays. At the same time, as this paper demonstrates, in some contexts this language asserts male (heterosexual) dominance by confirming presumed masculine values, while degrading presumed feminine gender attributes. Sociolinguists and feminist theorists have noted that the language used by men, including much of the slang, carries negative implications for the status of women in this society, and that male speech styles and language usage serve to reinforce male dominance (Lakoff 1975; Schultz 1975; Sutton, 1995). They have not considered, however, that the language men sometimes direct toward one another also serves to maintain their hegemonic power over women.

In this paper I explore the usage of some common slang terms that refer to homosexuals, especially when these terms are clearly used in derogatory or pejorative ways as a means of coercing others into behaving in a manner deemed appropriate by their users. The communicative acts that constitute the basis for my analysis are generally limited to situations where the target of the derogation is present. Usually in these situations the target is not suspected of being a homosexual. Rather, the usage is based on the linkage of some act or object to presumed attributes of homosexuals. Thus, this type of usage amounts to a connotative extension of the culturally based schema defining homosexuality to the referent. From an extensionist semantic view, focal types or prototypical schemata are defined in terms of attributes or features. In order to sensibly apply (or extend) a term to an object or person, the user evokes the relationship between the features that define an exemplar and the behavior, form, or function of the person or object to which the term is applied. In actual usage the similarities between exemplars and targets are not absolute but are influenced by contexts and by the cultural implications of one usage as opposed to another (Kronenfeld, Armstrong, and Wilmoth 1985).

Two more specific examples will clarify this process. Sweet (1997) reflects on the usage of *feygele*, a Yiddish word meaning "little bird." American Jews might use this term to refer to gay or effeminate males. Such usage illustrates the process of metaphoric extension. This class of extension is metaphoric because a gay or effeminate male is not a little bird, but the user presumes that somehow the target possesses or exemplifies an attribute of "little birdishness" such as delicacy. In contrast, application of the slang term *homo* to an individual is a connotative extension because a person may actually be a homosexual. The extension of the term in this case is based on the user's presumption that the target shares some connotative attribute(s) with the prototype of the category "homo."

In the discussion that follows I will treat all terms under consideration as semantic equivalents,[1] although there are differences in their connotations. All of them, however, do connote effeminacy and nonconformity to the prevailing cultural code regarding appropriate sexual choice and behavior. As will be shown, in most cases the extension of these terms to a person is based on the linkage between the person's behavior and effeminate or nonconformist attributions concerning homosexuality.

For the purposes of this paper, homophobic slang is any adaptation and extension of terms referring to homosexuals that can be interpreted as derogatory in the sense that the quality, action, attribute, or individual to which the term refers is being devalued (Pei and Gaynor 1975). For example, use of the slang term *homo* to refer to an individual is the result of the adaptation and extension of the term *homosexual.* Its usage is almost inevitably derogatory. As John Boswell, the noted historian of homosexuality, argues in his affidavit in the case of *Joseph C. Steffan v. Richard B. Cheney, Secretary of Defense:*[2]

> "[H]omo" became a widespread obloquy, especially among adolescents and those openly hostile to homosexuals. It is almost an exact lexical equivalent of the anti-Semitic "Hebe": both are abbreviations of terms applied by a suspicious majority to the minority in question ("homo" from "homosexual"; "Hebe" from "Hebrew"), as opposed to the terms used by the groups themselves ("gay" and "Jewish," respectively) and by those who are not hostile to them. Apocation of names is a common mode of intensification: ... for groups, especially suspect groups, the foreshortening usually betrays intensified hostility. (Boswell 1993: 51)

The hostility and the devaluation implicit in the usage of homophobic terms, as illustrated by Boswell's discussion of the term *homo,* occur by virtue of the assumed correctness of anything heterosexual. Thus, associating anything or anybody with the "other" category (i.e., homosexual) automatically makes it nonconformist at best.

METHODOLOGY

With the assistance of several students, I have been collecting instances in which terms that fit our definition of homophobic slang have been used in our presence.[3] In each instance we have attempted to describe the social context of the usage as completely as possible, paying special attention to the relationship of the user to others present, especially to the referent. The overwhelming majority of our examples were taken from conversations involving white male college students on this campus, although in some instances women and minority students were present. In addition, I conducted a number of interviews with students to explore the usage of this terminology more generally in the student culture of SUNY Plattsburgh. Since my student assistants had little access to the gay subculture in our area, I also interviewed several gay men and lesbian women about the usage of this terminology among gays and about their reaction to such usage by heterosexuals. The interviews were used to inform the other data and to fill in gaps in these data, not as a primary source of cases.

SOCIAL CONTEXT AND MEANING

Homophobic language is used in a variety of ways. For example, it is not unusual to hear someone use a term such as *fag* to refer to another individual who is not within earshot. One of my students heard a classmate refer to the members of a local fraternity as a "bunch of fags." In cases such as this it is not possible for the observer (or often even for the speaker) to know if this represents some kind of denotatively "accurate" attribution about the referent, nor is it always possible to ascertain the attribute of the individual(s) on which the extension is based. Even though the terms are usually intended to be derogatory in these cases, they are not very interesting from a semantic point of view since the referent is not present and there is usually no clear action that elicits these usages. Thus, although I have a number of instances of this type, they will not be considered in the analysis.

When the referent is present, it is relatively easy to identify both the intention of the user and the attribute on which extension is made. In this research the most frequently recorded homophobic usage was to employ the term *gay* to refer to any object, possession, attribute, or behavior of others, in their presence or not, deemed by the user to be nonnormative.[4] For example, I was present when a male friend of my daughter referred to another friend, who was also present, as "gay" because he spilled catsup on his shirt. I questioned those present about this usage and its relationship to conceptions we have about homosexuality. The young man who used the term in this case said, somewhat defensively, "I didn't mean anything by it. It's got nothing to do with homosexuals. I just kinda thought Jim acted sorta uncool." It seems from such examples that many young people will refer to almost anything or anybody as "gay" if they disapprove of it or find it "uncool" or odd. Thus, in this region, at least, young people have expropriated the preferred neutral sexual identity marker for males with a homoerotic orientation and, through connotative extension, given it a negative value.

Next to the usage of *gay* just described, the most frequently observed homophobic language occurs in multimale groupings, where one participant refers to another with a slang term synonymous for homosexual. This is pervasive behavior. Every student we interviewed has witnessed usages of this type on more than one occasion. Generally, the context is predominantly male, but it need not be limited to males. These usages usually occur in small groups of friends, with others within earshot. Usage of homophobic terminology in these contexts is often part of what is termed "busting" or "ranking." According to Moffatt, "In male lockerroom talk the term [to bust] was short for 'to bust their chops' or 'to bust their balls'" (1989: 67). These speech acts are a form of verbal aggression in which the user mocks the victim, usually to challenge the victim's authority or to undermine his pretensions. It is characteristically an all-male activity in which the participants know each other. Still, in current student culture, women are allowed to participate, although their participation is contingent on sticking to the male-defined rules of the game (Moffatt 1989). In the situations under consideration here, one participant will refer to another as a "fag," "homo," "queer," or other term intended to be even more derogatory from the point of view of the user. The reference is usually generated by some action of the target, such as refusing to join in a homosocial activity. In interviews, students claimed that such exchanges also occurred in cross-sex interactions, but we have only one example of a female employing a term in this way.

1. A group of four male students sitting in a dorm lounge is discussing plans for the evening, which include the usual drinking and carousing. One of them claims that he needs to study. The others "bust" on him. His closest friend in the group pleads, "Don't be a *fag*, you can study any time."

2. A student whom I know well is in my office after an afternoon class with another student we both know. We are chatting sociably. He invites me "downtown" for a beer. I decline his offer, explaining that I have to go home to cook dinner and watch my kids. In reaction to my refusal of his invitation, he says, "Come on, you big *homo*. You can have one beer."

3. A man in a relatively quiet residential neighborhood observes a car speeding down the street. He runs to the curb and yells at the driver to slow down. The driver slams on his brakes and backs up to within earshot of the man. The man, in a stern tone, tells the driver to be more careful because of the kids playing in the area. The driver responds, "Fuck you, you *faggot*."

These examples represent the range of speech acts that serve as the corpus of my data. They share two main features. In each case (and in all the collected cases) the action being labeled by the derogatory term has nothing to do with the denotative meaning of the term employed. In each case the usage takes its meaning from extension to the effeminate connotation of the term. From the speaker's point of view, the actions of studying, cooking, and being concerned about the welfare of neighborhood kids are unmasculine (conversely, the actions they are justifying are manly and virile).

These examples also indicate a means by which young men affirm their masculinity. By referring to others as "homos" or "fags" in these contexts, the speakers are referencing their own heterosexuality and masculinity, while coercing the referents to adopt the same values. Peggy Sanday, in her book *Fraternity Gang Rape*, discusses the process by which fraternity hazing rituals symbolically make boys into men. She claims, "These rituals stamp the pledge with two collective images: one image is of the cleansed and purified 'manly' self bonded to the brotherhood; the second image is of the despised and dirty feminine, 'nerdy,' and 'faggot' self bonded to the mother" (1990: 157). Most boys and young men in American society are likely to experience this kind of affirmation process as part of membership in all male groups. Insiders remake newcomers in their "manly" image by frequently and often ritualistically referencing the "loser" status of outsiders (Sanday 1990: 136). From our observations, for example, we discovered that in the hazing rituals of one of the fraternities on this campus, the "brothers" routinely refer to the pledges as "faggots" even when they weren't present. In doing so, the "brothers" aren't merely indexing the "otherness" of the pledges, they are announcing to themselves that they are heterosexual men.

Each of these examples, especially the first one, illustrates how young men affirm their maleness. The speakers in each case are saying to themselves and to the others present, "I am a man because my behavior is not contaminated by the feminine quality of 'homos' and 'faggots.'"

Neither of the first two examples is particularly derogatory. Students I interviewed felt that these kinds of usages mark the "take-it-for-granted" attitude that words are just words, similar to my daughter's friend's defense that his use of "gay" didn't really mean anything.

Furthermore, in both these cases and in most other examples of this kind, the speakers are indicating their affection for and equality to the referent in a joking manner that is especially common in locker-room discourse. In all three examples the usage stems from the association of stereotypically feminine behavior with homosexuality. Thus, the basis of the extension of the term is the connoted feminine quality of the refusal to join in the carousing, the need to look after one's children, and the warning about speeding. The extension in each of these cases represents the common confusion in American culture of gender-role behavior (studying, performing childcare, and being careful) with sexual orientation (homosexuality).

The first example is a classic "bust" in which it is acceptable to degrade a friend. Usage, in this almost ritualistic context, reinforces referent group values, broadcasts the manliness of the user, defines what the group expects of its members, and establishes boundaries for the group (Moffat 1989).

The second example, which, by the way, motivated my interest in this research, has "busting" qualities, but the power asymmetry between the student and me makes it interesting for other reasons. The student had to assume a sufficient degree of familiarity and equality with me in order for him to "bust" me. "Busting" is a form of one-upmanship, but it requires a certain level of equality among those who engage in it. The student also had to assume that I wouldn't take offense, that I was one of the guys, and that I wouldn't view his attribution as "fighting words." In the indirect style characteristic of male interactions, he was telling me that he liked me. This assumption indexes the heterosexist ethos of American culture. If I am a heterosexual and I am "cool," I won't misinterpret his "bust." I'll let it slide. In fact, he assumed that our male bond would be affirmed. He wouldn't have called me a "homo" if he assumed I was one.

The final example is clearly more derogatory. It shares some of the violent overtones possessed by verbal and physical attacks on gay men. The speaker intended to hurt the referent with his language. He presumably did not know the target, nor did he appreciate the warning, although it was well deserved, according to the observer. Still, the use of the term *faggot* is generated by the association between caring about the well-being of children and being effeminate, in contrast to the manliness of speeding down a residential street (i.e., risk-taking).

In student interviews it was unanimously agreed that terms like *homo, fag,* and *queer* were routinely used to refer to behaviors that didn't conform to what was considered "manly," such as playing sports, drinking, and general risk-taking behavior. In one of the cases collected, for example, preferring to go out with a girlfriend over playing touch football with male friends evoked a homophobic response. I find it particularly noteworthy and ironic that the speaker could "demean" his friend for preferring to go out with a woman (a fairly heterosexual thing to do) in an attempt to coerce the victim into engaging in a homosocial activity—going out with the guys is often valued above heterosocial activities like dating. What all these instances share in common is the implication that "manly" behavior (i.e., drinking, playing sports, driving fast) is valued, while stereotypically feminine behavior should be avoided.

CONCLUSIONS

To conclude, I would like to make several points about the material discussed in this chapter. First, most of the examples cited demonstrate how particular usages (homophobic slang) or styles ("busting") signal inclusion in reference groups. If individuals value inclusion in groups where homophobic language is commonly employed, they will be likely to employ it in order to signal their inclusion. Second, for the social contexts that are the focus of this research, this type of language functions to define for some and confirm for others appropriate gender attributes and behaviors.

Third, this language is coercive in a number of ways. The link between homosexuality and nonconformity, gender-inappropriate behavior, and femininity pressures members of reference groups to act in ways they might not wish to in order to avoid labeling, even if the underlying tone is friendly. This coercion is not limited to the referents but includes all potential participants in these exchanges.

Use of homophobic language is coercive in other, less obvious ways. First, degrading homosexuality in public contexts serves to maintain the invisibility of homosexuals. All the gay men and lesbian women I interviewed made this point in one way or another. Their main reaction to my examples of homophobic usage was to point out that this language makes them feel excluded, devalued, and invisible. Implicit in these usages is the assumption that all those present are heterosexual and share a negative evaluation of homosexuality. The pervasiveness of such language is another indication to gays and lesbians that "mainstream" American culture remains intolerant of homosexuality. For young men on college campuses, who are often unsure of their sexuality and who usually want to be included in reference groups, it is, at least, uncomfortable, if not dangerous, to oppose these assertions of the value of heterosexuality. Usage of this kind of language, therefore, by disregarding the hurt that it may cause to some, indicates how unimportant the feelings of these people are. That is, homophobic slang implicitly disregards the existence of homosexuals. Furthermore, since, in most everyday contexts, gays and lesbians are not particularly identifiable, their presence does not constrain the usage of derogatory terminology. In most contexts on college campuses, gay and lesbian identities remain hidden. The sexual orientation of some activists may be known by many, but the sexual identities of most gays and lesbians are known only to those relatively familiar to them. In contrast to gays and lesbians, Asian and African Americans and women, by virtue of their identifiability, constrain the use of racist and sexist language in many contexts (Smith 1993).

Finally, this language usage affirms male dominance and defines the terms, at least in certain contexts, for gender equality. This last point was driven home to me by one of the examples I collected. Two teenage sisters were preparing to walk over to a friend's house on a rainy day. One of the sisters was less than enthusiastic because of the rain. The other sister called her a "homo" for not wanting to go out in the rain. Thus, as this example indicates, and female participation on male terms in "busting sessions" confirms, the hegemonic language of males defines the terms for equality. Women may be permitted to participate in male groups if they talk like males, willingly "bashing" homosexuality and by extension the qualities traditionally associated with women. Of course, when women opt in, they are often degraded for being too "butch."

NOTES

[1] I limit my discussion to terms that denote a homosexual orientation. There are differences among such terms, mainly in their severity and, as a consequence, in the contexts in which they are used and the behaviors that evoke them.

[2] Joseph Steffan brought suit against the U.S. government because of his dismissal from the U.S. Naval Academy. Steffan admitted that he was gay. Defense Department regulations required that he be discharged, even though he was singled out as a model cadet and ranked at the very top of his class (Wolinsky and Sherrill 1993).

[3] I wish to acknowledge the help of Matt Zeitler, Doug Leonard, and Jennifer Mesiano, whose contribution to this project was invaluable.

[4] I do not put much stock in the frequency with which usage classes or terms occurred in the data set. I overheard or had reported to me more than one hundred instances of the "gay" usage and ceased collecting them because there was so little variety. Further, since neither my assistants nor I had easy access to the kinds of contexts where male-male "busting" takes place, this class of usage is probably underrepresented.

REFERENCES

Blumenfeld, Warren J., and Diane Raymond (1989). *Looking at Gay and Lesbian Life*. Boston: Beacon Press.

Boswell, John (1993). "Affidavit II of John Boswell: On the Use of the Term 'Homo' as a Derogatory Epithet." In Marc Wolinsky and Kenneth Sherrill (eds.), *Gays and the Military*. Princeton, NJ: Princeton University Press.

Kronenfeld, D., J. Armstrong, and S. Wilmoth (1985). "Exploring the Internal Structure of Linguistic Categories: An Extensionist Semantic View." In Jane W. D. Dougherty (ed.), *Directions in Cognitive Anthropology*. Urbana: University of Illinois Press.

Lakoff, Robin (1975). *Language and Woman's Place*. New York: Harper & Row.

Moffat, Michael (1989). *Coming of Age in New Jersey*. New Brunswick: Rutgers University Press.

Pei, Mario, and Frank Gaynor (1975). *Dictionary of Linguistics*. Totowa, NJ: Littlefield, Adams.

Perrow, Charles, and Mauro Guillen (1990). *The AIDS Disaster*. New Haven: Yale University Press.

Peters, Jeff (1991). "When Fear Turns to Hate and Hate to Violence" *Human Rights* 18: 1.

Sanday, Peggy R. (1990). *Fraternity Gang Rape*. New York: New York University Press.

Schultz, Muriel R. (1975). "The Semantic Derogation of Women." In Barrie Thorne and Nancie Henley (eds.), *Language and Sex: Difference and Dominance*. Roxbury, MA: Newbury House.

Smith, Barbara (1993). "Homophobia: Why Bring it Up?" In Henry Abelove, Michele Barale, and David Halperin (cds.), *The Lesbian and Gay Studies Reader*. New York: Routledge.

Sutton, Laurel A. (1995). "Bitches and Skankly Hobags: The Place of Women in Contemporary Slang." In Kira Hall and Mary Bucholtz (eds.), *Gender Articulated: Language and the Socially Constructed Self*. New York: Routledge.

Sweet, Michael J. (1997). "Taking About Feygelekh: A Queer Male Representation in Jewish American Speech." In Annalivica & Kira Hall (eds.), *Queerly Phrased: Language, Gender, and Sexuality*. New York: Oxford University Press.

Wolinsky, Marc, and Kenneth Sherrill, eds. (1993). *Gays and the Military*. Princeton, NJ: Princeton University Press.

QUESTIONS TO THINK ABOUT

1. Armstrong says that "language is an act that can be violent, exclusionary, and coercive." Discuss several examples he presents of the uses and functions of homophobic language showing how they document and substantiate his hypothesis.

2. A common development in the use of language—part of the dynamic change we see in language—is the process of semantic generalization in which word meaning is extended, strengthened, or weakened. Armstrong shows a shift in the meanings of the words "gay," "homo," and "queer," as used by young people today. What semantic generalizations are being applied to these words? Why do you think these newer connotations have gained popularity? How does social context affect word use in cases like these?

3. Another common lexical semantic process in language change is pejoration, or the degeneration of meaning over time. This is a shift from a positive or neutral meaning to a more negative, or pejorative, meaning for a word. Words like "gay" and "queer" have undergone this sort of pejoration over time, especially in past decades. Using a good, unabridged dictionary, see if you can trace the path of meaning shift for these words.

4. *Extending your understanding*: Imagine that derogatory language is being used in the classroom—words that connote sexual orientation, racial or ethnic groupings, social class background, religious differences, or something else. If you were a teacher or a teacher's assistant witnessing the use of disparaging and offensive terms, what would you do? Create several different scenarios and possibilities for responding to them.

TERMS TO DEFINE

Define the following words and phrases as they are presented within the context of the reading. Comment on your understanding of the significance of each one.

Homophobic language
Prototypical schemata
Metaphoric extension
Slang
Apocation
Busting

Unit II: Questions, Activities, and Resources

EXTENDING YOUR UNDERSTANDING AND MAKING CONNECTIONS

1. How would you integrate the information in the readings by Green and Trask to construct a tree of the Indo-European languages, with a fairly detailed Germanic branch?

2. Together with two partners, choose three dialects of English and have each member of your group investigate the historical origins of one of the dialects by doing library research, on-line research, and interviews of speakers. After each member reports back to the group, incorporate your findings in an essay comparing the histories and features of the three dialects. In the essay, you should consider whether or not the three dialects are closely related, and the evidence you have for your decision.

3. Translation studies is an area gaining popularity in academia today. Looking at the quote in the Barber selection from the *Chronicle of William of Gloucester*, analyze the comment William of Gloucester was making on the role and status of languages spoken by people of his time. Then do some library or on-line research about what translation scholars are saying about the status of differing languages in the world today. How do the opinions of this Middle English speaker compare to the opinions of those studying marginal languages today? Why, in your estimation, has so little changed in the politics of language over the course of time?

4. As a class, examine opinions on what the notion of an English standard dialect is:

Each member of the class: Ask five people (who are not in your class) to define what they think constitutes the standard variety of English—What are its features? Who speaks it? Who doesn't speak it? Why not?

Keep a log of the responses you receive. When your interviews are complete, summarize the opinions you recorded. Were you surprised at the responses you received? How did the ideas you recorded compare with your own ideas about standard English?

Compare your summary with those of others in your class. Can you reach a consensus on this topic? What are some of the differences of opinion? Why do you think people differ on this issue?

APPLICATIONS FOR TEACHING

1. Bhabha asks, "Are we to be blind to the sincerity and solidarity, the playfulness and privacy, through which people build their lives and words under conditions of duress, just because the poem got the grammar wrong?" This is an important question, especially considered in the social and cultural context of the classroom. What issues and questions must teachers confront in a linguistically varied environment? Discuss how these issues affect teaching, from grading and assessment to strategies for teaching grammar while still respecting the integrity of a student's written work.

2. Based on a "pragmatic" assessment, Fishman comments that

> Local tongues foster higher levels of school success.... Navajo children in Rough Rock, Arizona, who were schooled initially in Navajo were found to have higher reading competency in English than those who were first schooled in English.

What are the implications of these assertions for teaching students from diverse language backgrounds? If teaching isn't conducted in the students' first language, make a list of what else could be done within the classroom and school setting to maintain connections between first language (and culture) and the target language, English. Discuss your lists in groups. How could such suggestions be implemented?

3. If, as suggested by Cameron and others, differences in language use by females and males reflect social constructions, and not biological facts, should teachers privilege one type of discourse over another, teach several discourses, attempt to heighten consciousness, or ignore these distinctions? One way to think about your response is to consider which type of discourse was favored in your elementary, junior high, and high school experience, and how you were guided toward socially acceptable ways of using language. What kind of discourse is privileged in the academic/college environment? Write an essay on the role of the teacher, the classroom, and the student in this power relationship.

4. *Lesson Plan*: Create a lesson in which you summarize and briefly describe the history of English. Various readings in this unit of *Language and Linguistics in Context* should get you started on the research for this lesson. In addition, the Internet can prove a valuable tool for locating material about specific stages of English development, as well as samples of literature and writings (such as personal letters) from these stages. You might want to stimulate class discussion by introducing the idea that language is a dynamic, or ever-changing, human process, and that historical developments in English reflect how much languages can change over time. Indicate also some of the reasons why languages change as much as they do. As a homework assignment, you might ask your students to describe in writing, to the best of their ability, where, when, and how they think their own dialect of English came about.

PRINT AND WEB RESOURCES

Print Resources

Adams, J. N. (2002). *Bilingualism and the Latin language.* Cambridge: Cambridge University Press.

Fussell, S. R. (Ed.). (2002). *The verbal communication of emotions.* Mahwah, NJ: Lawrence Erlbaum Associates.

Joseph, B. D., & Janda, R. D. (Eds.). (2003). *The handbook of historical linguistics.* Blackwell Handbooks in Linguistics. Oxford: Blackwell.

Kiesling, S. F., & Paulston, C. B. (2004). *Intercultural discourse and communication: The essential readings.* Oxford: Blackwell.

Muthwii, M. J., & Kioko, A. N. (Eds.). (2004). *New language bearings in Africa: A fresh quest.* United Kingdom: Multilingual Matters.

Web Resources

http://www.iele.au.edu/resources/biblio/we.shtml
(English as a global language)

http://www.ling.nwu.edu/~ward/gaybib.html
(Gay and lesbian language)

http://www.linguistlist.org/ask~ling/
(Ask a linguist any question about language)

http://www.stanford.edu/~rickford/ebonics/
(Ebonics)

http://www.utexas.edu/cola/depts/lrc/
(Linguistics Research Center, University of Texas at Austin: Various topics)

WHAT IS LITERACY?

Introduction to Unit III:
Literacy and Education in a Globalized World

Harriet Luria
Hunter College, CUNY

SCOPE OF DIFFERENCES IN LITERACY

Using the commonly held though narrow definition of literacy as the ability to read and write, UNESCO, as of 2000, found that there are an estimated 862 million illiterate adults in the world, two-thirds of whom are women. Additionally, Mohamed Maamouri (2000) found that "the number of illiterate people in many developing countries still represents more than half their youth and adult populations...representing nearly 25 per cent of the world's youth and adults." In the United States, considered one of the developed countries, even though basic literacy rates are quite high (with some estimates at 98%), 23% of adult females and 17% of adult males have severely limited literacy skills.

Side by side with these staggering figures of world-wide illiteracy and functional illiteracy rates are figures presented by the United Nations Development Program (Warschauer, 2001), estimating that there are 700 million Internet users, who obviously are able to read, write, and understand printed text, constituting more than 10% of the world's population. These discrepancies between those who possess what we call "literacy"—more broadly defined not only as the ability to speak, read, and write, but also to do math, use the computer, and possess knowledge of one's place or situation within the local and larger society—and those who do not, represent a significant social and educational challenge in an increasingly globalized, interconnected world.

Do these figures represent a hopeless dichotomy that cannot be bridged, with those who possess "literacy" moving farther and farther ahead in the 21st century and leaving those who do not lagging inevitably behind? Or, is there an indication—implicit in the multiplicity of definitions of literacy, its varied history through the ages, the models of educational programs that lead to literacy acquisition, and its uses and functions across languages and cultures—that access to literacy can lead to a significant increase in its acquisition? For example, in those regions of the world that lead in illiteracy rates (e.g., South Asia, Arab States, Sub-Saharan Africa), basic education may not go beyond primary schooling, economies fluctuate and decline, allowing less money to be allocated to education, and on-going wars and conflicts combined with poverty lead to unstable educational structures. Although lack of literacy may not have created these transnational problems of poverty and inequality, access to literacy could play an important role in changing the conditions of individuals' lives. Thus, in the consideration of literacy, political and educational issues that influence literacy practice are also an important part of the discussion of what literacy is, how and by whom it is acquired, and how it is used.

BACKGROUND TO LITERACY THEORY

Linguists generally assert that all human beings are capable of language—are in effect hard-wired for language—but differentiate between this ability or competency and the performance of language. Perhaps, we can extend this assertion to say that all human beings are capable of being literate, placing language at the center of literacy inquiry. Put another way, we may all be competent (i.e., have the ability to become literate) but may perform differently based on many factors, including the social contexts we find ourselves in, the expectations of what it means to be literate, differences in language and language use, the tools (e.g., pens, books, computers) available for use in literacy performance and practice, and the way in which literacy is conceived and measured.

In the history of literacy, scholars differentiate between oral and written literacy, usually attributing primacy to writing as a form that moves beyond the immediacy of sound (phonology) and, thus, allows for a more permanent and widely disseminated record. From pictographs as a significant form of written communication to syllabaries and alphabets, wide-ranging claims are made for the effects of alphabets, not only on writing, but on the dissemination of ideas and culture. Thus, Jack Goody and Ian Watt, for example, claim that through use of the alphabet, the Greeks were able to develop democracy, invent categories (taxonomies), and evolve a unique logic. (For a full discussion see Cushman et al. [2001] and Newman in this unit.) Claims are made that access to the alphabet, as well as to pens, scrolls, and other materials connecting the word and the text, resulted not only in written text but in altering how the world is perceived and in improving cognitive ability.

Psychologists, anthropologists, and historians have spent considerable time thinking about and studying the supposed effects of writing on thought or cognition. (See Newman, Hull & Schultz, and Nieto in this unit.) Socrates pondered this relationship, concluding that writing in effect supplants thought. Psychologists such as Alexander Luria set up studies to prove the connection between literacy and the ability to reason and think. Although the findings were often inconclusive or showed some small differences in thinking between those who are literate (i.e., have some schooling) and those who are not, the assumption of a causal relationship between the ability to read and write and the ability to think became an accepted idea. Whereas Luria, Vygotsky, and others were, thus, concerned with the connections between literacy and a consequent ability of the individual to reason, cognitive psychologists today look at the actual processes involved in language, literacy, and thinking to see if there are connections among them and what the points of intersection and influence may be. (Again, see Cushman et al.)

Parallel to and emerging from these studies, psychologists and anthropologists considered the use of language in relation to literacy across cultures. Sylvia Scribner and Michael Cole, in their groundbreaking work (1981), examined the relationship between language use and cognition among the Vai people in West Africa. They show that literacy may affect cognition, but the way in which it does is dependent on particular social and cultural contexts, differentiating among kinds and uses of writing as well as different types of literacy. For example, expository writing, privileged in the West, particularly the English-speaking world, is often tied to cognition, schooling, and the subsequent advances it facilitates in science through reporting, arguing, theorizing, and so forth. Scribner and Cole found that the Vai, by comparison, had at least three literacy systems, only one of them tied to schooling. Their indigenous alphabetic script system was used for administrative and popular purposes; their use of Arabic and memorization and verbalization of the Qur'an lead to increased memory skills; English was learned through formal schooling. Scribner and Cole concluded that each of these distinct literacy systems lead to different skills and different cognitive effects.

Key findings from the Scribner and Cole studies have become the basis for a great deal of subsequent inquiry into the relationship between forms of language use and language practice. First, they provide a different way of thinking about what writing is, and by extension, of literacy. They broaden its definition from that of expository text that informs and persuades to text, the purpose of which is embedded in particular social practices and the use of which is derived from specific contexts. Second, they highlight the importance of practice and uses of literacy outside "schooled" contexts. Third, these studies and the alternative views they present question the assumption that writing and literacy are the main or only causes of the West's development; literacy is seen as *instrumental* rather than causal. Put another way, the West's particular type of literacy may not have caused the development of its systems of law, science, documents, bureaucracy, and government structures, but instead served as the instrument that moved these from oral "procedures" to their formalization and dissemination through written "procedures." These studies further urge us to question the supremacy of the Roman alphabet over nonalphabetic and other alphabetic systems. They also question the perception that individuals and groups from a predominantly oral tradition, a different alphabetic system, or a non-Western knowledge base, are illiterate and cognitively deficient.

THEORY AND ITS APPLICATION

What we subscribe to today as constituting literacy derives from these notions tied to concepts of progress, public education, increased access to books through the invention of printing and mass production, and the idea that knowledge is critical to progress. Speech and orality, although important, are seen as the first step in this road to progress, a road culminating in schooling, reading, writing, and the acquisition and dissemination of knowledge. Literacy, thus, continues to be seen as the *causal* factor of societal progress, with related consequences:

> Because literacy and schooling were seen as the causes or engines of social change, then the obvious means to producing psychological and social change was through imposing literacy and schooling on the ignorant and illiterate. The personal and social aspirations, interests, competencies and traditions of the learners could be ignored and overwritten by imposing literate standards and literate practices on them. (Olson & Torrance, 2001, p. 4)

The relationship between literacy and progress is articulated throughout the history of the United States. In the early part of U.S. history, literacy was used mainly for commerce and for religious reasons (i.e., to read the Bible). Evidence of signatures on deeds, marriage certificates, and wills, as well as ownership of books, attest to the increasing rates of basic literacy: from 70% of white men and 45% of white women in 1750 in the northeastern part of the United States to over 80% for these same groups by 1800. According to data from the National Center for Education Statistics (1993), in 1880 in the United States, approximately 92% of native-born Whites and 88% of foreign-born Whites were considered literate; by contrast, among Blacks and others, 30% were deemed literate. As the decades progress, literacy rates increased among native-born Whites to 98% in 1940. However, as the United States went through periods of increased immigration, illiteracy rates for foreign-born Whites decreased. For example, in 1920, when native-born White literacy stood at 98%, foreign-born White literacy was at 86%; among Blacks and others, literacy was at 77% in 1920. These literacy rates represent a basic ability to read and write.

What these literacy and illiteracy rates also signify, in a larger way, is the particular history of the United States, including settlement by Europeans, enslavement of Africans, enclosure of Native Americans, and immigration of millions of Europeans, Russians, Asians, Africans, and South Americans to the United States, global migrations that continue today. The implications of this history for literacy are varied: Euro-Americans used reading and writing for communication, commerce, and educational development; access to education among this group was differentiated by class and gender. African Americans were denied basic literacy and education both out of fear that it could contribute to resistance and rebellion and a denial of the basic humanness of the slave population. Coming to English from a variety of African languages meant that pidgins and creoles developed and solidified into what we now refer to as African American Vernacular English. Immigrants usually arrived in America with a first language other than English, often unable to read or write their first language, and because of economic and class reasons had limited access to the American educational system.

Throughout the 20th century, the United States moved to prepare its population to be a productive, industrialized work force. In a country based on a narrative of taming and settling the land, individualism, and opportunity, educational differences were seen as deficits that schools and teachers could fix as long as students worked hard and seemed educable. The school became a prime site for the integration and assimilation into mainstream American language, culture, and values. It seemed that a linear, skills-based pedagogy in which students first learned basic skills such as the alphabet, sounding out letters and groups of letters, and then sounding out words, would lead to skill in basic reading. Identifying topics, main ideas, and significant details would lead to an ability to make inferences and form conclusions, that is, to reading comprehension. Learning how to use a pencil and write letters would result in learning how to write words, sentences, paragraphs, and, finally, essays. Learning to write numbers, then to do basic mathematical operations, such as addition, subtraction, multiplication, and division, would lead to understanding numeracy. However, when it became apparent that massive numbers of students were not adequately learning to read, write, and speak English and understand and perform mathematical operations at a level necessary for a modernized, technologically developing country, student background, student ability, and educational pedagogy came under scrutiny, and remedial measures instituted.

Thus, during the 1960s, as part of the War on Poverty, Head Start Programs were initiated to introduce children from lower socioeconomic English and non-English backgrounds to the alphabet, to the sound system of standard English, to basic English vocabulary, and to the syntax of standard English. Parents were encouraged to read aloud to their children to engage them with text so that they could hear the syntax of English and learn a basic narrative structure of story, event, and logical development. Programs using television such as Sesame Street were funded by the government and national foundations to provide literacy instruction for children. Within the schools, debates over ways of teaching reading and writing ensued. Schools and teachers were torn between teaching with the "phonics" method versus the "whole word" method. Because of these challenges, direct instruction in writing, spelling, grammatical analysis, and basic numeracy were often replaced with what were labeled progressive methods. The latter were an attempt to replace rote learning and constant correction with allowing the language abilities of children to develop in a more "natural" manner, for example, by dictating stories using their own vocabularies and then learning to read that vocabulary through context rather than "sounding out words," or by writing words as they seemed to sound rather than by following standardized English spelling. What had been considered children's errors in reading (e.g., saying "She run" when the text indicated "She runs") was seen as indicative of comprehension on the part of the student. In fact, linguistically, what the student is said to have done is quite complicated: Translate the text from standard English into the student's own dialect of English, showing comprehension of both the standard written form and the dialect or nonstandard spoken form.

These pedagogical differences between direct phonics instruction versus recognition of whole words often represented an argument between those who subscribe to a behaviorist model versus those who adhere to a more meaning creation model. Starting in the early 2000s, the government is once again attempting to ensure basic literacy skills through programs such as No Child Left Behind. Based on educational studies of the past decades, most literacy teaching today merges direct teaching of skills with students' meaning-making based on their language and experience.

BROADENING LITERACY STUDIES

For the past 30 years, literacy theorists have been looking at the kind of multilinguistic and multiethnic situations prevalent both in the United States and in most other parts of the world, to try to make sense of the significance of these variables to literacy. They explore why whole groups of children (and adults) do not perform in expected ways, examine the discontinuities between the home and community versus the school environment, and study the individual as a representation of a larger cultural context connecting language and social environment. Ethnographic studies of researchers such as Shirley Brice Heath document and examine differences in language use among children across class, race, and ethnicity and their implications for the school environment. For example, if in a child's home questioning a parent's statement is seen as a sign of disrespect, how would this same child learn to question in the classroom and learn to interrogate the authority of the text? Or, if writing is used predominantly to make lists or record important numbers, then viewing writing as a way of learning may seem alien.

Other theorists such as James Paul Gee have attempted to redefine and broaden the concept of literacy. (See Chapter 24, in this unit.) Preferring the term "discourse" to "literacy," Gee asserts that the first language we learn to speak, our primary acquired discourse, is our "identity kit," marking us in terms of status and power. For those whose primary discourse is not the same as the dominant discourse, access to institutional and social power is limited. Although it is possible to learn the dominant discourse, achieving the fluency of primary acquisition will be problematic. The implications of Gee's assertions, relating dominant discourse to power, privilege, and economic and social status, have met with considerable controversy. Lisa Delpit, for example, is particularly concerned with what this means for those African Americans who may not be born into the dominant discourse. (See her Chapter 25 in this unit.) Based on her interviews with African Americans who successfully use the dominant discourse (i.e., standard English), Gee's assertions appear extreme and can result in a kind of social determinism.

When we broaden discussion to include literacy and literacy practices outside the school and academic environments, we include workplace literacy that provides additional theories and levels of analysis. (See Hull & Schultz in this unit.) In workplace literacy, the contexts for work vary, and the idea of a multiplicity of literacies becomes more viable. Perhaps because work is valued and the work environment is central to making a living, its literacy tasks and events are valued. Knowledge brought to the work environment as well as what is learned there may offer more opportunities for expanded social, cultural, and linguistic representations than the "monolingual" school setting with its more narrowly conceived expectations and assessments of reading, writing, and speaking. This is not to ignore the class and educational differences—symbolized in the dominant discourse—in who gets what job or position in modern-day society.

Another way of broadening how we think about literacy is to acknowledge the multilinguistic and multiethnic character of the general population, especially in the United States, and how it is reflected in defining literacy and discourse. (See Nieto in this unit.) Where the goal was once assimilation to the norm, now multilingualism is valued in our globalized world. Rather than deny or erase cultural differences and knowledge of more than one language and varied dialects, a more recent critical perspective validates and links reading, writing, and language acquisition to race, culture, and ethnicity. In validating multilingualism, we also validate literacy in languages other than English. Otherwise, when we use the term literacy, we may implicitly mean being able to read, write, and speak in English. In a world where there is an increasing transnational population that moves back and forth between countries of origin and countries of emigration, literacy is required across languages.

Thus, we move from a view of literacy as responding to an autonomous text to a critical perspective that situates literacy in history, community, and sociopolitical contexts. It gives us as individuals a way to connect our language narratives to the larger forces that determine our identities. If we both construct and are constructed by the discourses around us, then all the parts of our identity are reflected in these discourses. So it is not surprising that gender is an important variable in the discussion of what it means to be literate. As we see from global literacy statistics, women usually lag in their access to and attainment of basic literacy in the form of reading, writing, and numeracy. However, in terms of using their knowledge of their culture, their position, their language, and the roles they are expected to play, women can be seen as highly literate in their engagement with the conditions of their everyday lives and social practices. Additionally, nations are attempting to globally address the gender inequities in access to literacy learning through school and work programs. (See Ghose, Chapter 31, in this unit.)

Finally, another important area in the consideration of literacy and its practice focuses on the teachers of literacy, who they are, and how they view their mandate and their students. Curriculum and pedagogy, whether in school or out-of-school settings, have undergone considerable examination with a recognition that effective teaching is central to literacy learning. Teachers' backgrounds, language use, and knowledge levels are questioned, along with questions of who and what determines the curriculum, how and where teaching takes place, and what kinds of assessment of learning are used. We can learn a great deal about these issues from formal program assessments, including qualitative and quantitative school and workplace evaluations. We can also learn from self-conscious narratives of literacy practitioners (e.g., teachers) about how they view their own language and literacy background, about their beliefs concerning their students' competencies and ability to perform, about their students' language use, and about how they see their role and interaction in varied learning environments.

Although we looked initially at rather grim literacy statistics around the world, as we continue in the 21st century, what these theorists and theories about language use seem to tell us is that knowledge of reading, writing, speaking, numeracy, and screen-based technologies is not a monolithic skill based in one language. Instead, literacy is embedded across languages, technologies, cultures, and societies. And, as Paolo Freire has stated, to be able to read the text is in effect to be able to read the world. But, to understand what is in the text, we need to understand the world in which we live and the world, which the text represents. Then, literacy is as broad or as narrow as the situation demands, but implicit in any literacy practice or event is the acknowledgment of the varied understandings that constitute literacy. Although lack of literacy does not cause the social problems or create the social conditions that exist in the world, access to literacy can be a significant, instrumental force in broad-based social change.

REFERENCES

Cushman, E., Kintgen, E. R., Kroll, B. M., & Rose, M. (Eds.). (2001). *Literacy: A critical sourcebook.* Boston: Bedford/St. Martin's.

Freire, P. (1985). *Pedagogy of the oppressed.* New York: Continuum.

Heath, S. B. (1983). *Ways with words: Language, life, and work in communities and classrooms,* Cambridge, UK: Cambridge University Press.

Maamouri, M. (2000). World literacy: What went wrong? Retrieved September 30, 2004, from http://www.unesco.org/courier/2000_03/uk/dossier/txt21.htm.

National Center for Education Statistics (1993). Literacy from 1870–1979: Illiteracy. Retrieved October 1, 2004 from http://nces.ed.gov/naal/historicaldata/illiteracy.asp

Olson, D. R., & Torrance, N. (Eds.). (2001). *The making of literate societies.* Oxford: Blackwell.

Scribner, S., & Cole, M. (1981). *The psychology of literacy.* Cambridge: Harvard University Press.

UNESCO, UNESCO Institute for Statistics. (2004). *UNESCO Public Reports, 2004* [Data file]. Available from UNESCO Web site, http://stats.uis.unesco.org

Warschauer, M. (2001). Millenialism and media: Language, literacy, and technology in the 21st century. *AILA Review 14,* 49–59.

A BRIEF OVERVIEW OF UNIT III SELECTIONS

In Unit III, the authors define, redefine, and expand the concept of literacy, recognizing the complexity that is inherent in this "simple" word. Literacy refers to more than the ability to read and write, although these abilities are assumed to be part of the word's meaning. The authors in this section address numerous questions in their attempt to define and explore literacy: What is literacy? What is the context where literacy occurs?

What is its purpose? What is literacy's relationship to language, to culture, to gender, to power, to education, and to politics? What is the result of being judged illiterate? What is the result of becoming literate? In our globalized, mobile world, what happens when individuals literate in one language need to learn to communicate in a new language?

The questions are seemingly endless because literacy is related to so many aspects of living, understanding, and functioning in the world. Although these selections do not answer all of the above questions, they provide overviews, theoretical discussions, and varied educational program descriptions. In the first selection, Michael Newman's "Definitions of Literacy and Their Consequences," offers a history of literacy from earliest times, differentiates between oral versus written form, and summarizes differing theoretical schools that cross fields of psychology, anthropology, and sociolinguistics, outlining the principal premise of each. Newman contends that our understanding of literacy needs to be broadened to include not only the easily tested bottom-up skills perspective (i.e., that there are a series of micro skills that need to be mastered before one can be termed literate) but must also include the cultural and social contexts of literacy. In his broadening of the definition, Newman implies that everyone, in some sense, is literate.

Continuing to define literacy, James Gee tells us in his essay "What Is Literacy?" that every time we act or speak, we instantiate historically and socially defined discourses. Asserting that the discourse we engage in is our identity kit, which marks our status on many levels (i.e., social, economic, educational, cultural) Gee also argues that not all discourses are equal in nature and that some lead to success and power while others do not. Gee differentiates between primary and secondary discourses, asserting that "literacy is the control of secondary uses of language," as well as distinguishes between acquisition and learning. In response to Gee's arguments, Lisa Delpit, in "The Politics of Teaching Literate Discourse," questions the implications of Gee's assertions, believing instead that students can learn the dominant discourse even if it is not their primary language. Delpit says that teachers have a responsibility to teach the dominant discourse, or the discourse of power, to their students. She stresses the need to explicitly teach the grammar, punctuation, style, and mechanics of Standard English. She believes that students can learn a new discourse without being taught to reject their primary discourse. Delpit presents teaching techniques that can facilitate learning the dominant discourse and relates success stories of students who have mastered it, despite its not being their primary language.

Moving from discussions of literacy in school settings, Glynda Hull and Katherine Schultz broaden the scope of the literacy context through a comprehensive overview of theories and research concerning out-of-school literacy. Through their discussion and "vignettes" we see a multiplicity of literacies in aspects of everyday life, in the workplace, and in community organizations. The functions of literacy outside school and the literacy competency of large numbers of the population in out-of-school settings lead them to ask whether what has been learned in these extra-school settings about effective teaching and learning can be transferred to the school setting.

A. Suresh Canagarajah presents a theory of critical literacy in which he moves from the concept of the autonomous model of the text to one that sees the text (which could be in written form or a literacy event) as situated in history, community, and sociopolitical realities. In considering the multilingual writer, Canagarajah connects pedagogy to what he refers to as "text-internal and text-external factors, discursive and historical forces, [and] linguistics and social considerations." He suggests that though we should not "essentialize" students from other languages and cultures, we should acknowledge that literacy is related to different cultural beliefs and practices and that what goes on in the school is connected to the wider social and political world.

Again subscribing to a critical perspective, Sonia Nieto looks at literacy for bilingual and multilingual students, contending, like Canagarajah, that language and cultural differences may reflect differences of social and political power. She uses concepts such as identity/hybridity and context/situatedness/positionality to analyze what influences student performance and achievement in educational institutions. Nieto connects reading, writing, and language acquisition to racial, ethnic, and cultural positions. In "Educational Policy for the Transnational Dominican Community," Marianne D. Pita and Sharon Utakis are concerned with bi- and multilingual students who move back and forth between countries. They include in their discussion not just the globalization of language and literacy, with English often at the center of educational pedagogy, but the transnational nature of language and literacy. When students move back and forth on a regular basis, living in two countries with at least two languages, the situation has implications for educational institutions.

The next two chapters focus on language, literacy, and gender. Gloria Nardini, in her ethnographic study "Italian Patterns in the American Collandia Ladies' Club: How Do Women Make *Bella Figura*," demonstrates how gender and cultural knowledge interact with literacy activities. When the women in the Italian-American cultural club need to negotiate their budgets with their authority figure, they perform gendered discourse, using culturally approved language styles to achieve their aims. In Malini Ghose's "Women and Empowerment Through Literacy," we see how gendered access to educational programs is often complicated. Around the world, women may need the permission of their communities, particularly the male members, to participate in literacy programs. Ghose describes an educational attempt to establish less traditional school settings with teachers who had once been program participants, and with content that is mutually determined. The experiment meets with mixed results, but through its descriptions of internal struggle, it gives us a picture of a rich, contextualized literacy program that engages students with texts, as well as cultural beliefs, and confronts language and dialect differences. Perhaps, one of the most significant results is that many students and teachers want to continue their educational experience.

We move from theoretical and educational contexts to individual narratives of literacy acquisition and its consequences. Robert Ku, of Korean background, grew up in Hawaii and lives on the "mainland" of the United States. In his contribution, he questions the globalization of English and its relation to literacy through his own literacy narrative. Having experienced various languages and dialects of English, he explores the "sociodynamics of Standard English," acknowledging the contradictions that an educated speaker of English faces when he is multilingual and bidialectal. Ku shows how the individual narrative is representative of larger social issues.

Finally, Gary Tate, John McMillan, and Elizabeth Woodworth ponder and critique their own social-class narratives, thereby, discovering the importance of these narratives to their teaching. Their narratives explore why Americans in particular have difficulty acknowledging class differences and the implications of these differences for educational practice. Through their "stories" we see them grapple with issues of Standard English and dialect use, the relationship between how one feels about the class and group of one's primary affiliation, and how these self-concepts relate to who teaches, how they teach, and what they teach in the context of college composition classes. They conclude that "class markers are not brands that prevent success in the academy, but rather marks of distinction that need not—should not—be negative" if they are acknowledged and examined.

Thus, what began as an exploration of definitions of literacy and discussions of literacy theories, moved through literacy practice, among various contexts, cultures, and learners (including in-school and out-of-school contexts, bilingual and multilingual learners), and ends with teachers and composition classes in the university, the ultimate institutionalized, academic literacy context. All of these settings represent an exploration of the factors that go into the construction of literacy, or, as many of the authors contend, "multiliteracies," and the significance of literacy in a globalized, multicultural world.

Definitions of Literacy and Their Consequences

Michael Newman
Queens College, CUNY

Before World War II, the Soviet educational psychologist Lev Vygotsky and his disciple Alexander Luria developed the hypothesis that literacy alters a number of basic cognitive processes. One curious but testable consequence of their proposal was that uneducated people should not see certain types of what we usually think of as visual illusions. For instance, in the figure below illiterates should not see the circle on the left as larger than the one on the right. Instead, they should see them as they really are, that is, as the same size (Luria, 1976):

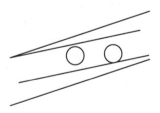

Luria tested this and other related hypotheses during a two-year investigation in Soviet Central Asia, particularly Uzbekistan and Kryzikistan, areas that had many unschooled adults. One story about this famous fieldwork has it that when Luria found that the first cohort of Uzbek illiterates actually did see the circles as the same size, he wished to inform Vygotsky without delay. So he telegraphed him the good news—"Uzbeks have few illusions"—before returning to Moscow. Upon his arrival, he was met by Stalin's secret police. They had intercepted the cable and, interpreting the "illusions" to be the political ones the regime was spinning, arrested the unfortunate psychologist for sounding out the skepticism of the Uzbeks.

Whether or not these events actually happened as told, this story could serve as a parable of the broad and sometimes unanticipated consequences, ideological repercussions, contradictions, and conflicts that continue to plague our attempts to understand literacy.

LITERACY AS TEXT DECODING

Take, for example, the definition assumed by Luria, that literacy is the ability to decode graphic representations of language. The first consequence of this view is that it centers literacy around what is known in cognitive science as *bottom-up* processing, the piecing together of wholes from their parts. If readers identify the phonological values of letters, they can discern the word the letters form. If they identify words, they can piece together phrases. If they understand phrases, they get the propositional meaning of the text. They can then use the propositional meaning together with knowledge and reasoning to determine inferences.

In some versions of this view, an alphabet is the gold standard of graphic systems because it is "the most abstract form of writing" (Ong, 1992, p. 312). The alphabet can also be seen as the culmination of the evolution of systems of writing. After all, the first writing began with the adaptation of pictures, or *pictographs*, to represent words, much as when we use a heart to represent "love" on a T-shirt or bumper sticker. These are referred to as *logographs*. Gradually, the pictures became more abstract and less iconic, much as the simplicity of a vertical line, |, whose singularity is evident and can develop various extensions, 1 or *1*. These variants are less iconically singular, but they maintain the meaning intact. At the same time, these symbols began to stand for homonyms of the words they originally represented, as when we use the number *2* to stand for the word *too*. In both cases the "symbol can represent something it does not really denote" (Daniels, 1992, p. 94), which is characteristic of true writing. In Sumerian, the language for which this process first happened, each morpheme constituted a syllable, and the system developed into a *syllabary* in which each symbol represents a syllable regardless of whether that syllable is a word or not.[1] The Phoenicians subsequently modified the syllabary to represent individual consonants. Their system was finally adapted by the Greeks, who added vowels. So for the Greeks, each grapheme represented a phoneme, and thus, inventing the alphabet. The Greek alphabet evolved into other shapes, as in the Roman and Cyrillic, and in some cases maintained less fidelity to the phonological basis, as in English. Still, the principle is unchanged today, almost 3,000 years later. It was precisely the ability to take apart language and put it back together, associated with the alphabet, that led to the more abstract way of thinking that allows literates to see illusions, according to advocates of this view.

A second consequence of this view of literacy is that it emphasizes the differences between written and oral language (Goody & Watt, 1968; Ong, 1982, 1992). Written text, unlike oral discourse, is meant to last, and this permanence has been assumed to make it more independent of context. Until the invention of the phonograph, oral language was always evanescent and, to this day, the vast majority of oral utterances disappear with the sound waves that carry them. Because situations change over time, it has been argued that written language cannot depend on a context of situation to elucidate its meaning, but must supply its own context. Street (1984, 1993) famously calls this view the "autonomous model of literacy" because a written text is seen as an autonomous entity.

The emphases on bottom-up skills in general and the alphabet in particular together with the notion of texts as autonomous have broad educational consequences. For one thing, if context is unimportant and if mastering the relations between sounds and graphemes is key to reading and writing, then intensive practice in this relation—known as *phonics*—should take up the lion's share of early literacy education.[2] If bottom-up *microskills* are crucial, then taking information from texts on the levels of words, phrases, and sentences should also be fomented.

Another educational consequence is that freedom from the complicating factor of context and looking at literacy as composed of microskills mean that literacy is relatively easy to measure. The amount of information—be it phonic, factual, or even inferential in nature—readers are able to extract and produce determines their level of literacy. Not surprisingly, then, this view is embodied in many reading tests, including virtually all those created before 1990. A look at these tests shows items designed to determine letter and word identification in early literacy and finding facts, main ideas, and inferences at more advanced levels (e.g, verbal SATs).

Even more extensive implications of this view extend beyond education, including wide-ranging claims regarding society and even civilizations. If abstract thought is improved by knowing and using alphabetic scripts, perhaps, this ability is responsible for the very nature of Western civilization, which after all is pervaded by alphabetic texts. In this view, it would not be a coincidence that the ancient Greeks were the first not only to use a fully alphabetic system but also to develop rationalistic philosophy (Havelock, 1976). In this way, alphabets now generalized among western European civilizations can explain their political and technological predominance. Conversely, if this position is true, alphabetization represents a specifically westernizing influence. So it is a potential threat to nonalphabetic, southern, and eastern cultures (Mühlhausler, 1990) if one starts from the presuppositions that all cultures are equally valid and that change from the outside damages them.

These implications, not the efficacy of bottom-up approaches, explain why graphic-centered views of literacy have proved attractive to movements on the right of the political spectrum in the United States. They support a number of values generally associated with conservative ideology:

1. *Tradition*: The viewpoint was dominant during most of the last century.
2. *Simplicity*: It defines literacy in basic terms of mastery of written language.
3. *Cultural affinity*: It supports Western civilization.
4. *Accountability*: It implies that literacy is relatively easy to measure.

In fact, there is nothing necessarily conservative about this view. Vygotsky and Luria were convinced Marxists, and plenty of politically conservative educators are convinced opponents of intensive phonics- and skills-based instruction if only because they doubt its efficacy.

Politics aside, this definition of literacy has received support from a number of cognitive tests, such as those of Luria, which showed that literates handle abstract cognitive tasks better than illiterates. However, it is problematic in a number of ways. One is that the equation of literacy with decoding creates a "great divide" (Street, 1984,1993) between literates and illiterates, oral and written (particularly alphabetic) language and the abstract and concrete. This divide is not only too simple, but it smacks of ethnocentricity. It assumes a superiority of alphabetic civilizations over technologically advanced nonalphabetic ones, such as the Chinese and Japanese civilizations. It also asserts that alphabets without vowels, such as Arabic and Hebrew, are not as highly developed as those with vowels. Yet, the selection and adequacy of specific writing systems may respond better to the grammatical structure of the languages being written (Daniels, 1992) than to the speakers' cultural levels of development. In other words, an alphabet works well for Indo-European languages, but an ideographic system works equally well for Chinese.

Another problem is that—even leaving out the specifically alphabetic claims—an exclusive concern with decoding ignores the fact that reading is used primarily as a tool and not as an end in itself. Many teachers, for instance, are familiar with children who can demonstrate the ability to decode by reading aloud but cannot make any use of the information contained in what they are reading. To call such children "literate" seems counterintuitive.

A related problem is that the bottom-up definition cannot capture the fact that readers and writers are inevitably better at some genres of text and some tasks using text than others. It is well known, for example, that many children suffer difficulties as they begin to read expository prose, usually starting in the 4th grade in the United States. These children, who seemed to be literate when reading stories in their earlier grades, have reading problems as their books begin to discuss science and history. Comprehension declines sharply, and even decoding can reappear as a problem. Similar effects are observable for writing in Language Arts and Second Language classes even as late as college.

Finally, there is evidence that the vaunted cognitive advantages offered by a strictly alphabetic literacy are not the result of an ability to decode. After all, reading and writing usually come combined with an intensive and systematic sort of cognitive training, namely, formal schooling. In a seminal ethnographic study of literacy, two anthropologists, Scribner and Cole (1981), examined a community in Liberia called the Vai, in which there existed a form of vernacular literacy that is learned without recourse to formal education. Of course, some Vai do receive formal education in addition to their vernacular literacy. When given cognitive tasks used in other studies, it turned out that the Vai with only vernacular literacy resembled the illiterates elsewhere, whereas those with formal education resembled other literates. Thus, schooling, not alphabetization, seems to be key to more abstract thought.

LITERACY AS USE OF WRITTEN LANGUAGE

Scribner and Cole's work demonstrated not only a major flaw in the "great divide" argument, but also the dangers of examining literacy outside its cultural and social contexts. In doing so, they inspired a large body of research on literacy that makes use of ethnographic methods and assumes a quite different definition of literacy. This research tradition is referred to as the New Literacy Studies (Street, 1993) and Socioliteracy (Johns, 1997).

According to most of these studies, literacy is not the ability to decode and encode written language per se but is instead the knowledge of a *practice*, that is, the ability to use it in specific contexts, a far more relativized definition. In this view, someone can be considered literate in one context (e.g., a child reading stories in third grade) but not in another (e.g., the same pupil reading history in 4th grade). An adult can similarly be literate at reading sports magazines for pleasure but not manuals to solve software problems.

This more nuanced viewpoint offers a number of practical advantages. Researchers can, for instance, pinpoint how the ways of oral language *use* at home interacts with learning literacy in schools. The reason is that different cultures use language following different norms and socialize their children into these norms. Schools, however, particularly when they are based on the culture of a different group, may not take these starting points into account.

One of the best examples is a classic study by Heath (1982, 1983) of three communities in the Piedmont area of South Carolina. One, consisting of African American and European American middle classes, used oral and written language with their preschoolers in ways that anticipated school genres and practices. They read to their children and asked them the types of questions that a teacher might ask. They also promoted complex interactions with the fictional worlds presented in children's books. Their children tended to succeed in school. By contrast, a community of working class European Americans of Appalachian origin read to their children and emphasized the importance of reading. However, they did not support complex interactions with texts and did not read much themselves beyond certain narrow genres. Their children tended to do well in early schooling but failed as more sophisticated interplay became required. Finally, a group of African American working-class families did support quite sophisticated oral interactions with narrative, but these varied from those used in school, particularly in the early grades. Also, their home use of written language was quite limited. Their children tended to do poorly right from the beginning. Significantly, by explicitly and systematically addressing the areas of mismatch between school and home, educators were able to improve the rates of success among the two disadvantaged groups.

Many other studies have confirmed and expanded this understanding of the importance of cultural values in literacy. Cazden (1988), for example, shows how differences in what counts as a good narrative between mainstream and minority cultures can lead to difficulties as children tell stories in class. Similarly, Fishman (1988) shows how the particular religious and secular values of the Amish are realized in their literacy practices. The schools they have created—and have stubbornly defended against state attacks—support precisely these practices. Their schools work because the values and practices they support are part and parcel of the larger community.

Other researchers have shown how communities use written language together with oral language in certain culturally relevant ways outside of school. One example is a fascinating study of writing and reading in a New Guinea village (Kulick & Stroud, 1993). The authors argue that the relatively recent arrival of written language had less social impact than might be expected. Far from changing the culture, as Mühlhausler (1990) believed would happen, writing was actually adopted as a tool to be used according to villagers' preexisting language and social norms. Even the fact that written language was associated with foreign cultural influences such as Christianity was not enough to make more than trivial changes in the villagers' worldview. The point of all these studies is that literacy practices, not the graphic representation of language per se, have value for and impact on users. Therefore, literacy, if it is to be socially and educationally meaningful, must be understood relative to social practices and cultures.

As these examples show, socioliteracy makes important contributions. However, just as happened with the graphic definition, it also gives rise to unexpected consequences. For instance, it is not clear what role decoding and other bottom-up skills actually play in constituting literacy, nor is it easy to determine that role using the ethnographic method this approach favors. As a result, a number of conflicts over the place of the explicit teaching of bottom-up skills have split socioliteracy into various factions. On one extreme is the denial of any importance to overt instruction of this kind, a position that is often associated with the *whole language* and *process writing* movements. In fact, many advocates of these philosophies do support teaching of some bottom-up skills (e.g., Cunningham, 1995), but it is fair to say that these movements are characterized by predominantly *top-down* instruction. Whereas bottom-up perspectives start with phonics, whole language instruction tends to work from context to text, from text to words, and words to phonemes or letters, if the instruction gets to letters at all. According to this view, reading is a "psycholinguistic guessing game" (Goodman, 1967) in which the words on the page serve only to confirm or disconfirm conclusions already arrived at through context. In writing instruction, it is possible to find a parallel approach (e.g., Calkins, 1995; Elbow, 1998).

Other authors assuming a socioliterate perspective have strongly defended explicit instruction of bottom-up skills as a necessary component of literacy instruction, though admittedly not the main goal. Delpit (1995), in particular, has argued that an exclusively top-down approach tends to help children who were already getting access to the alphabet and the ways of using language that she calls "codes of power" in the home.

As can be seen from Delpit's arguments, there are political ramifications that have arisen with the definition of literacy as the use of writing and reading practices. Generally, the emphasis on culture, the focus on issues of power, and goals of understanding disadvantaged groups have made socioliteracy congenial to many on the left of the political spectrum. This political dimension is particularly prominent in a third pedagogical tendency, Critical Literacy, inspired by the work of Paulo Freire (1970). In this view, the obstacles faced by literacy learners from marginalized groups are functions of social power in origin and in solution. The teaching and learning of literacy, within this movement, is tightly bound around understanding and resolving political issues that students face (e.g., Benesch, 1995, 1999).

As a result of this vagueness, a number of authors have searched for somewhat narrower definitions within socioliteracy based on critical issues in using written language. Barton (1994), for example, defines literacy "ecologically," that is, in terms of the function of written language in a society. Street (1984, 1993) defines it "ideologically." Someone is labeled literate or illiterate depending on the uses of written language privileged in a culture. Hill and Parry (1992, 1994) propose a definition whereby literacy consists of the mastery of the linguistic pragmatics associated with written language use. Thus, socioliteracy provides a wide spectrum of different viewpoints that pedagogically agree only in that bottom-up instruction is not enough. That is a useful enough point, but one that tells teachers what not to do rather than guides them toward effective practice.

LITERACY AS GENERIC COMPETENCE

The most highly developed narrowing of the socioliterate definition can be found among the *genre* school of literacy theorists. These authors (e.g., Walvoord & McCarthy, 1990; Swales, 1994; Berkenkotter & Huckin, 1995; Johns, 1997) define literacy in terms of control of written *genres*. In this perspective, a genre is not understood simply as a text type, such as epic poems, business letters, term papers, or country-western songs. Instead, and in tune with the emphasis on social context within socioliteracy in general, a genre is a type of text used within a specific context for a specific purpose by members of a community.

This position allows the genre view to elucidate otherwise surprising outcomes in school settings. Take, for example, a problem brought to me by an English teacher in Brooklyn. Why did his class of inner-city 10th graders have difficulty demonstrating knowledge of rhymes on tests when the students were universally familiar with rap music, in which rhyme has a central role? Many of these teens not only listen to recorded works of rap artists, in which rhymes appear in abundance, but create their own spontaneous rhymes. Even those who do not do this "free stylin'," as it is called, often judge other's efforts in contests called "battles" in which audience response decides the victor. The judgments made by the audience depend on a sophisticated understanding of rhythm and rhyme as well as the content presented by the combatants.

A genre view is helpful in explaining the students' paradoxical failure at learning rhymes in school because it focuses attention on the context of culture and situation, not just specific skills, such as identifying rhymes, in isolation. Free stylin' takes place within a peer culture of Hip-Hop, and the values associated with that culture are chosen and accepted by the communities of youths. The learning in which the teens have difficulty, by contrast, takes place within an entirely different social context, that of the formal structure of "school," imposed by adults. Moreover, the rhymes the students do not appear to see are often found in poetry of another age and culture, embodying what may appear to be an alien set of values that the students do not understand or may not wish to accept. Finally, instead of evaluating the rhymes holistically, that is, as intimately linked to a larger context, students are expected to respond analytically, naming patterns in isolation. Although the formal content is the same—a rhyme by definition is a specific type of phonological pattern—the differences in task, context, culture, and values obscure the similarity. The knowledge used in one setting does not necessarily transfer to another.

A genre approach depicts these students as highly literate in the world of Hip-Hop and its component genres, and so it acknowledges their competence at rhyming and their conscious awareness of rhymes, the bottom-up skills that are essential to this vernacular literacy. The point is that they are not yet literate in *academic* poetry analysis. Thus, unlike socioliteracy in general, the genre position can inform pedagogy in specific ways that are crucially respectful of learners' prior knowledge. For example, it tells the teacher not to teach the students what a rhyme is. It is apparent that they already know that. Instead, the teacher needs to make that knowledge explicit and to indicate the similarities that exist between the free stylin' they do or appreciate in their peers, and what Homer, Blake, Dickinson, and Lorca did in their day and in their way.

LITERACY AS COMPETENCE IN THE GENERAL USE OF LANGUAGE

Although the pedagogical consequences seem useful, this view is not exempt from conceptual contradictions. As this example shows, a definition of literacy based on genres tends to marginalize the role of written language. Although rap may be written, it may also be entirely oral. To decide that only written rhymes involve literacy, whereas oral free stylin' does not, appears artificial and counterproductive. Similarly, to say that rap is a form of literacy because some rhymes are sometimes written seems to include it on a technicality. On this point, note that genres such as those in film, video, sharing time in kindergarten, and even computer games, show that the notion of genre extends well beyond written texts or even language of any kind. So, given a genre definition, the use of writing as a necessary criterion for defining an act as literacy can come to seem superfluous. What then do we mean by literacy?

This broadening has provoked dismay in some (Snow & Dickenson, 1991), but it has been embraced by others, particularly in education. In English Language Arts classes, and increasingly on tests of language arts and ESL, oral language has increasingly taken on weight. Thus, Wells (1986) argues for a definition of literacy that includes *educated* oral genres of language. The New York State Regents in their regulations and the U.S. Congress in the National Literacy Act have similarly defined literacy as the use of oral and written language in educational settings.

Again, a look at the effects on assessment reveals the consequences of this approach as well as an indication of its influence on practice. Newer standardized English Language Arts exams tend to replace the microskills approach with sets of genres, both written and oral, and tasks deemed to be important for further schooling or professional life. Thus, these assessments tend to be full of business letters, academic note taking, and literary analysis. Similarly, on portfolio and performance assessments, context is usually exploited as a resource rather than looked at as a problem. Students are asked to write or speak as if they were in specific situations or faced certain life problems.

However, the seeming consensus that led to the adoption of this view in assessment only masks a continuing conflict in literacy education. It has been argued (Hill & Parry, 1994) that tests that are superficially more communicative and appear to use authentic genres can be misleading. Once a story is placed on a test, it ceases to be treated as a story because what students are asked to do with stories on tests is so different from what they do with them when they are not being evaluated. Similarly, Freedman, Adam, and Smart (1994) showed that students presenting a mock business presentation ended up displaying information in ways similar to those they would use on an essay test or paper rather than those they would use in the real business world.

Finally, this definition leaves out vernacular genres such as rap. To include such genres means reducing the definition to mean being competent at language, and that would seem to vacate the concept of any meaning at all. If literacy means mastery of language, then virtually everyone is literate because all but the severely mentally retarded can speak.

LITERACY AS INFORMATION MANAGEMENT

Actually, the addition of oral language may only be a way station to an even broader definition of literacy, one that paradoxically restores usefulness by adding coherence and encompasses meanings of *literacy* that have developed spontaneously in lay usage. The reason is that once writing is eliminated as a criterion, the door is open to asking why language itself need be present for an activity to be deemed literate. After all, de Castell and Luke (1983) and Jennings and Purves (1991) noted how information may be encoded also in different nonverbal semiotic systems. It is easy to see that numbers, computer code, maps and other graphics, videos, dances, paintings, and so on are used systematically for communication.

This insight has been solidified through the Multiliteracies Project, the brainchild of a collaboration of a number of prominent literacy researchers joined in what they call the "New London Group." One member of this group, Kress (2000a, p. 157), defines literacy as all "socially made forms of representing and communicating." The emphasis on the process of representation and communication necessarily shifts the focus away from the particularities of a modality such as written language or language itself. Instead, the concept comes to highlight the ways that encoded information is processed generally or the ways the different modalities act and interact. In other words, once we become less concerned with one supposedly crucial form of representation such as print and its supposed effects, we can see literacy as a certain way of understanding communication.

In this view, the encoding and decoding of information becomes the common denominator in literacy because information is the substance of communication—much as an electron is the substance of electricity. An important motivation for the resulting *information-based* view is the rise of a broad spectrum of information technologies in which print may be absent or combined with other modalities of encoding. This is currently most evident on the World Wide Web and in other forms of multimedia, where sound, graphics, and print are typically integrated in various combinations. This multimodality (Kress, 2000b) implies a decline of the role of print as the culturally-privileged vehicle for information management, and with it what might be called the cult of the written word.[3] It is not coincidence then that these changes are reflected in common usages of the term literacy, such as *geographic literacy, numeracy,* and *media literacy.* All these terms share a common sense of competence at information management within their respective domains. This commonality encompasses the traditional definition, what can now be called *print literacy,* which involves information in written text. The change in definition and theory thus reflects the changes in society.

Again, there are unexpected, though perhaps not unwelcome, consequences. First, this shift towards multimodality is supported by the development of what James Gee, another member of the New London Group, calls "fast capitalism" (Gee, 2000; Gee, Hull, & Lankshear, 1996). The use of information as a prime commodity creates a new kind of business model in which knowledge replaces physical plants as key capital. It is literacy in this new sense of information management and multimodality, rather than print literacy alone, that is needed in this new economy. Whatever one's opinions regarding fast capitalism and its correlates such as globalization, this view of literacy appears to be more in tune with emerging trends in contemporary society than a print-based one.

A second consequence of an information-based definition is that it includes what had previously been thought of as preliterate expressions, from pottery styles and dances to oral performances. All these forms of communication share with print the ability to express ideas, feelings, and identities as well as systematicity. Furthermore, all can be combined in multimodal genres, in which each form augments the other.

The New London Group (1996) has argued that all literacies have a Design. Design is both a structure that serves as a resource for meaning making and a process of creating that structure. As we speak, write, create computer programs, or dance, we follow certain rules that make our creation coherent and understandable. This structure has been most investigated in language, in which the most highly structured—and arguably the most important—element of Design is called grammar.

Grammar, like other Designs, crucially provides flexibility as well as organization. If English speakers did not expect, for example, a subject-verb-object order, except under specific circumstances such as questions, the language would cease to be comprehensible. Yet at the same time, the rules of language are not so rigid as to overly constrain our ability to adapt them (Wittgenstein, 1953). We use slightly different grammars of English when we speak to friends or talk in front of a class. These differences, called *registers*, mark the situation we are in. The rules ordering their use—for example, those that say that we use slang when talking to friends in a bar but not when writing a term paper—form another Design-element of language. The flexibility inherent in Design is seen in how languages and styles evolve both in the long term, as linguistic evolution takes place, or short term as registers shift during a conversation.

The notion of Design combined with the recognition that language should no longer be the only focus of literacy education leads the New London Group to propose a more ample form of instruction. In this pedagogy, practice using literacies of various Designs is combined with the explicit learning of Design elements, critical analysis, and transformation of Designs (New London Group, 1996; Cope & Kalantzis, 2000). The pedagogy provides control of the rulelike structure and the flexibility of that structure that characterizes the mastery of a literacy.

This is not the place to go into the Multiliteracies pedagogy in depth; it is enough to point out that the elements outlined above and even their combination is not new. The contribution of the New London Group has been to provide successful eclectic pedagogies with a coherent and theoretically based foundation. In this sense, the Multiliteracies Project has learned from the errors of previous educators who have tended to reinvent wheel after wheel, leading to the notorious swings of the pedagogical pendulum. Literacy education has been plagued with approaches that have not been as useful for teachers or helpful for students as they have been theoretically or ideologically attractive. Of course, the information-based definition of literacy and the Multiliteracies approach are quite new. It is perfectly possible that unanticipated consequences and ideological fallout may yet rear their ugly heads.

CONCLUSION

Another way to avoid some of the conflicts and incoherencies that have marked various attempts to capture the meaning of literacy is to acknowledge that there is no one sense of the word, and that there does not need to be. As Wittgenstein (1953) observed, it is often impossible to reduce the meaning of a concept to a single essence, although the various meanings will be related to each other. Ultimately, the actual meaning assigned to a word depends on the function of that word in a particular utterance. What is important is not to find a single overarching meaning but to use the word clearly and unambiguously.

It is certainly possible to find uses in which it makes sense to mean "literacy" as the ability to decode written text. To give just two examples, it is sometimes necessary to distinguish written text from oral discourse (e.g., Daniels, 1992) or to look at specific problems children may have in decoding it (e.g., Clay, 1993). Shifts in the meaning of literacy, therefore, do not need to be problematic as long as the context is made clear and the assumptions are sound.

Yet, as I hope readers have noticed, there are implications, including the difficult issue of ideology, that historically have determined our understanding of literacy. In the end it has often been the ideological and philosophical affinities of teachers, researchers, theorists, politicians, parents, and the general public that have determined which definition is adopted. Nevertheless, it is hard to defend definitions of literacy because they justify specific models of education or models of society that may be attractive for other reasons. To do so is to put the cart before the horse, unless one believes that the only way to help learners is to first change society.

Nor does it make sense to maintain models of literacy that developed for historical reasons (e.g., dominance of the printed word) when the historical realities that support them have changed. The definitions of literacy that teachers, researchers, theorists, and the public in general adopt may be multiple. Nevertheless, they must in all cases find their support in increasing our understanding of specific communication practices and in how individuals learn and use those practices.

NOTES

[1] In English, we have some morphemes that are syllables, including words such as *word* and derivational morphemes such as *-tion*. We also have morphemes that are less than a syllable, such as *-s* in *thinks* and those that are more than one syllable, such as *pizza* or *anti-*.

[2] To avoid common confusions, *phonics* should be understood as the association of graphemes and phonemes. It is not *phonetics*, which is the study of the physical aspects of human speech, nor *phonology*, which is the study of the mental representation of the sound systems of language. Only phonics, not phonetics or phonology, is the basis of a pedagogy. There is no such thing as a phonetic system of reading; nor is phonics a branch of linguistics.

[3] The term is not taken lightly. The religious connotations are seen literally in different ways in Islam, Judaism, and Christianity. A less confessional reverence can be seen in the notion of "freedom of the press," and contrariwise in the symbolism present in attacks on ideas, such as in the Nazi book burnings during the 1930s.

REFERENCES

Barton, D. (1994). *Literacy: An introduction to the ecology of written language.* London: Blackwell.

Benesch, S. (1995). Genres and processes in a sociocultural context. *Journal of Second Language Writing, 4*(2), 191–195.

Benesch, S. (1999). Rights analysis: Studying power relations in an academic setting. *English for Specific Purposes, 18*(4), 313–327.

Berkenkotter, C., & Huckin, T. N. (1995). *Genre knowledge in disciplinary communities.* Hillsdale, NJ: Lawrence Erlbaum Associates.

Calkins, L. M. (1994). *The art of teaching writing.* New York: Heinemann.

Cazden, C. B. (1988). *Classroom discourse.* Portsmouth, NH: Heinemann-Boynton Cook.

Clay, M. M. (1993). *Reading recovery: a guidebook for teachers in training.* Portsmouth, NH: Heinemann.

Cope, B., & Kalantzis, M. (2000). Designs for social futures. In B. Cope & M. Kalantzis (Eds.), *Multiliteracies: Literacy learning and the design of social futures* (pp. 203–234). London: Routledge.

Cunningham, P. M. (1995). *Phonics they use: Words for reading and writing.* New York: Addison Wesley.

Daniels, P. (1992). The syllabic origin of writing and the segmental origin of the alphabet. In P. Downing, S. Lima, & M. Noonan (Eds.), *The linguistics of literacy* (pp. 83–110). Philadelphia: Benjamins.

de Castell, S., & Luke, A. (1983). Defining 'literacy' in North American schools: Social and historical conditions and consequences. *Journal of Curriculum Studies, 15*(4), 373–389.

Delpit, L. (1995). *Other people's children: Cultural conflict in the classroom.* New York: New Press.

Elbow, P. (1998). *Writing with power: Techniques for mastering the writing process* (2nd ed.). New York: Oxford University Press.

Fishman, A. (1988). *Amish literacy: What and how it means.* Portsmouth, NH: Heinemann.

Freedman, A., Adam, C., & Smart, G. (1994). Wearing suits to class: Simulating genres and simulations as genre. *Written Communication, 11,* 193–226.

Freire, P. (1970). *Pedagogy of the oppressed.* New York: Continuum.

Gee, J. P. (2000). New people in new worlds: Networks, the new capitalism and schools. In B. Cope & M. Kalantzis (Eds.), *Multiliteracies: Literacy learning and the design of social futures* (pp. 43–68). London: Routledge.

Gee, J. P., Hull, G., & Lankshear, C. (1996). *The new work order: Behind the language of the new capitalism.* Boulder, CO: Westview.

Goodman, K. (1967). Reading: A psycholinguistic guessing game. *Journal of the Reading Specialist, 6*(1), pp. 126–35.

Goody, J., & Watt, I. (1968). The consequences of literacy. In J. Goody (Ed.), *Literacy in traditional societies* (pp. 27–68). Cambridge, UK/NY: Cambridge University Press.

Havelock, E. A. (1976). *Origins of Western literacy.* Toronto: OISE.

Heath, S. B. (1982). What no bedtime story means: Narrative skills at home and in school. *Language in Society, 11,* 49–76.

Heath, S. B. (1983). *Ways with words: Language life, and work in communities and classrooms.* Cambridge, UK: Cambridge University Press.

Hill, C., & Parry, K. (1992). The test at the gate: Models of literacy in reading assessment. *TESOL Quarterly, 26*(3), 433–461.

Hill, C., & Parry, K. (1994). *From testing to assessment: English as an international language.* New York: Longman.

Jennings, E. M., & Purves, A. C. (1991). Introduction. In E. M. Jennings & A. C. Purves (Eds.), *Literate systems and individual lives: Perspectives on literacy and schooling* (pp. 1–28). Albany: State University of New York Press.

Johns, A. M. (1997). *Text, role, and context.* Cambridge, UK: Cambridge University Press.

Kress, G. (2000a). Design and transformation: New theories of meaning. In B. Cope & M. Kalantzis (Eds.), *Multiliteracies: Literacy learning and the design of social futures* (pp. 153–161). London: Routledge.

Kress, G. (2000b). Multimodality. In B. Cope & M. Kalantzis (Eds.), *Multiliteracies: Literacy learning and the design of social futures* (pp. 182–202). London: Routledge.

Kulick, D., & Stroud, C. (1993). Conceptions and uses of literacy in a Papua New Guinean village. In B. Street (Ed.), *Crosscultural approaches to literacy* (pp. 30–61). Cambridge, UK: Cambridge University Press.

Luria, A. R. (1974/1976). *Cognitive development: Its cultural and social foundations* (M. L. Morillas & L. Solotaroff, Trans.). Cambridge, MA: Harvard University Press.

Muhlhäusler, P. (1990). Reducing Pacific languages to writing. In T. J. Taylor (Ed.), *Ideologies of language.* London: Croom Helm.

New London Group (1996). A pedagogy of multiliteracies: Designing social futures. *Harvard Educational Review, 66*(1), 60–92.

Ong, W. J. (1982). *Orality and literacy.* London: Methuen Press.

Ong, W. J. (1992). Writing is a technology that restructures thought. In P. Downing, S. Lima & M. Noonan (Eds.), *The linguistics of literacy* (pp. 293–320). Philadelphia: Benjamins.

Scribner, S., & Cole, M. (1981). *The psychology of literacy.* Cambridge, MA: Harvard University Press.

Snow, C. E., & Dickinson, D. K. (1991). Skills that aren't basic in a new conception of literacy. In E. M. Jennings & A. C. Purves (Eds.), *Literate systems and individual lives: Perspectives on literacy and schooling* (pp. 179–191). Albany: State University of New York Press.

Street, B. V. (1984). *Literacy in theory and practice.* Cambridge, UK: Cambridge University Press.

Street, B. V. (1993). The new literacy studies. In B. Street (Ed.), *Crosscultural approaches to literacy* (pp. 1–21). Cambridge, UK: Cambridge University Press.

Swales, J. M. (1990). *Genre analysis: English in academic research settings.* New York: Cambridge University Press.

Walvoord, B. E., & McCarthy, L. P. (1990). *Thinking and writing in College: A naturalistic study of students in four disciplines.* Urbana, IL: National Council of Teachers of English.

Wells, G. (1986). *The meaning makers: Children learning language and using language to learn.* Portsmouth, NH: Heinemann.

Wittgenstein, L. (1953). *Philosophical investigations.* New York: Macmillan.

QUESTIONS TO THINK ABOUT

1. Briefly summarize the various definitions and theories of literacy Newman presents, as well as the advantages, problems, and "expected and unexpected" consequences of each perspective. Then consider why Newman concludes that "The definitions of literacy that teachers, researchers, theorists, and the public in general adopt may be multiple."

2. Newman asserts that it does not "make sense to maintain models of literacy that developed for historical reasons (such as the dominance of the printed word) when the historical realities that support them have changed." In referring to the alphabetic system and text decoding, Newman says that "implications of this view extend beyond education, including wide-ranging claims regarding society and even civilizations." Views on phonics versus whole language instruction, as well as on assessment and accountability versus acceptance of multiple literacies also generate intense debate. Why do you think there has recently been so much political controversy raging around these assertions, educational theories and various pedagogies?

3. Consider your own literacy narrative. First, using the more traditional definition of literacy as decoding and then encoding the printed text, describe how you achieved literacy and enumerate and assess your literacy strengths. Next, consider your strengths based on an expanded definition of literacy as a multiple modality with many different types of literacy practices. Does your conception of your literacy strengths also expand? What do you learn from this exercise about the changing notions of literacy?

4. *Extending your understanding*: Newman outlines the possibility of pedagogical practices to complement particular literacy perspectives. Choose one of the definitions/theories and speculate about its possible teaching implications. For example, how might conceiving of literacy instruction as a bottom-up phonics approach be achieved in the classroom? What do the genre school, the New London Group, and the Multiliteracies approach offer that the earlier bottom-up and top-down approaches don't? How is the classroom reconceived once the definition of literacy moves from decoding printed text to multiple modalities?

TERMS TO DEFINE

Define the following words and phrases as they are presented within the context of the reading. Comment on your understanding of the significance of each one.

Autonomous model
Socioliteracy
Bottom-up approach
Top-down approach
New London Group
Multiliteracies/multimodality
Genre

What Is Literacy?

James Paul Gee
University of Wisconsin, Madison

It is a piece of folk wisdom that part of what linguists do is define words. In over a decade as a linguist, however, no one, until now, has asked me to define a word. So my first try: What does "literacy" mean? It won't surprise you that we have to define some other words first. So let me begin my giving a technical meaning to an old term which, unfortunately, already has a variety of other meanings. The term is "discourse." I will use the word as a count term ("a discourse," "discourses," "many discourses"), not as a mass term ("discourse," "much discourse"). By "a discourse" I will mean:

> a socially accepted association among ways of using language, of thinking, and of acting that can be used to identify oneself as a member of a socially meaningful group or "social network."

Think of discourse as an "identity kit" which comes complete with the appropriate costume and instructions on how to act and talk so as to take on a particular role that others will recognize. Let me give an example: Being "trained" as a linguist meant that I learned to speak, think and act like a linguist, and to recognize others when they do so. Now actually matters are not that simple: The larger discourse of linguistics contains many subdiscourses, different socially accepted ways of being a linguist. But the master discourse is not just the sum of its parts, it is something also over and above them. Every act of speaking, writing and behaving a linguist does as a linguist is meaningful only against the background of the whole social institution of linguistics, and that institution is made up of concrete things like people, books and buildings; abstract things like bodies of knowledge, values, norms and beliefs; mixtures of concrete and abstract things like universities, journals and publishers; as well as a shared history and shared stories. Some other examples of discourses: being an American or a Russian, being a man or a woman, being a member of a certain socio-economic class, being a factory worker or a boardroom executive, being a doctor or a hospital patient, being a teacher, an administrator, or a student, being a member of a sewing circle, a club, a street gang, a lunchtime social gathering, or a regular at a local watering hole.

Reprinted with permission from *Teaching and Learning: The Journal of Natural Inquiry*, pp. 3–11. © 1987 by J. P. Gee.

There are a number of important points that one can make about discourses, none of which, for some reason, are very popular to Americans, though they seem to be commonplace in European social theory (Belsey, 1980; Eagleton, 1983; Jameson, 1981; Macdonell, 1986; Thompson, 1984):

1. Discourses are inherently "ideological." They crucially involve a set of values and viewpoints in terms of which one must speak and act, at least while being in the discourse; otherwise one doesn't count as being in it.

2. Discourses are resistant to internal criticism and self-scrutiny since uttering viewpoints that seriously undermine them defines one as being outside them. The discourse itself defines what counts as acceptable criticism. Of course, one can criticize a particular discourse from the viewpoint of another one (e.g., psychology criticizing linguistics). But what one cannot do is stand outside all discourse and criticize anyone or all of them—that would be like trying to repair a jet in flight by stepping outside it.

3. Discourse-defined positions from which to speak and behave are not, however, just defined internal to a discourse, but also as standpoints taken up by the discourse in its relation to other, ultimately opposing, discourses. The discourse of managers in an industry is partly defined by their opposition to analogous points in the discourse of workers (Macdonell, 1986: 1–7). The discourse we identify with being a feminist is radically changed if all male discourses disappear.

4. Any discourse concerns itself with certain objects and puts forward certain concepts, viewpoints and values at the expense of others. In doing so it will marginalize viewpoints and values central to other discourses (Macdonell, 1986: 1–7). In fact, a discourse can call for one to accept values in conflict with other discourses one is a member of—for example, the discourse used in literature departments used to marginalize popular literature and women's writings. Further, women readers of Hemingway, for instance, when acting as "acceptable readers" by the standards of the discourse of literary criticism, might find themselves complicit with values which conflict with those of various other discourses they belong to as women (Culler, 1982: 43–64).

5. Finally, discourses are intimately related to the distribution of social power and hierarchical structure in society. Control over certain discourses can lead to the acquisition of social goods (money, power, status) in a society. These discourses empower those groups who have the least conflicts with their other discourses when they use them. For example, many academic, legalistic and bureaucratic discourses in our society contain a moral subdiscourse that sees "right" as what is derivable from general abstract principles. This can conflict to a degree with a discourse about morality that appears to be more often associated with women than men in terms of which "wrong" is seen as the disruption of social networks, and "right" as the repair of those networks (Gilligan, 1982). Or, to take another example, the discourse of literary criticism was a standard route to success as a professor of literature. Since it conflicted less with the other discourses of white, middle class men than it did with those of women, men were empowered by it. Women were not, as they were often at cross-purposes when engaging in it. Let us call discourses that lead to social goods in a society "dominant discourses" and let us refer to those groups that have the fewest conflicts when using them as "dominant groups." Obviously these are both matters of degree and change to a certain extent in different contexts.

It is sometimes helpful to say that it is not individuals who speak and act, but rather historically and socially defined discourses speak to each other through individuals. The individual instantiates, gives body to, a discourse every time he acts or speaks and thus carries it, and ultimately changes it, through time. Americans tend to be very focused on the individual, and thus often miss the fact that the individual is simply the meeting point of many, sometimes conflicting, socially and historically defined discourses.

The crucial question is: How does one come by the discourses that he controls? And here it is necessary, before answering the question, to make an important distinction, a distinction that does not exist in non-technical parlance, but one which is important to a linguist: a distinction between "acquisition" and "learning" (Krashen, 1982, 1985; Krashen & Terrell, 1983). I will distinguish these two as follows:

> Acquisition is a process of acquiring something subconsciously by exposure to models and a process of trial and error, without a process of formal teaching. It happens in natural settings which are meaningful and functional in the sense that the acquirer knows that he needs to acquire the thing he is exposed to in order to function and the acquirer in fact wants to so function. This is how most people come to control their first language.

> Learning is a process that involves conscious knowledge gained through teaching, though not necessarily from someone officially designated a teacher. This teaching involves explanation and analysis, that is, breaking down the thing to be learned into its analytic parts. It inherently involves attaining, along with the matter being taught, some degree of meta-knowledge about the matter.

Much of what we come by in life, after our initial enculturation, involves a mixture of acquisition and learning. However, the balance between the two can be quite different in different cases and different at different stages in the process. For instance, I initially learned to drive a car by instruction, but thereafter acquired, rather than learned, most of what I know. Some cultures highly value acquisition and so tend simply to expose children to adults modeling some activity and eventually the child picks it up, picks it up as a gestalt, rather than as a series of analytic bits (Heath, 1983; Scollon & Scollon, 1981). Other cultural groups highly value teaching and thus break down what is to be mastered into sequential steps and analytic parts and engage in explicit explanation. There is an up side and a down side to both that can be expressed as follows: "We are better at what we acquire, but we consciously know more about what we have learned." For most of us, playing a musical instrument, or dancing, or using a second language are skills we attained by some mixture of acquisition and learning. But it is a safe bet that, over the same amount of time, people are better at these activities if acquisition predominated during that time. The point can be made using second language as the example: Most people aren't very good at attaining a second language in any very functional way through formal instruction in a classroom. That's why teaching grammar is not a very good way of getting people to control a language. However, people who have acquired a second language in a natural setting don't thereby make good linguists, and some good linguists can't speak the languages they learned in a classroom. What is said here about second languages is true, I believe, of all of what I will later refer to as "secondary discourses": Acquisition is good for performance, learning is good for metalevel knowledge (cf. Scribner & Cole, 1981). Acquisition and learning are thus, too, differential sources of power: Acquirers usually beat learners at performance, learners usually beat acquirers at talking about it, that is, at explication, explanation, analysis and criticism.

Now what has this got to do with literacy? First, let me point out that it renders the common sense understanding of literacy very problematic. Take the notion of a "reading class." I don't know if they are still prevalent, but when I was in grammar school we had a special time set aside each day for "reading class" where we would learn to read. Reading is at the very least the ability to interpret print (surely not just the ability to call out the names of letters), but an interpretation of print is just a viewpoint on a set of symbols, and viewpoints are always embedded in a discourse. Thus, while many different discourses use reading, even in opposing ways, and while there could well be classes devoted to these discourses, reading outside such a discourse or class would be truly "in a vacuum," much like our repairman above trying to repair the jet in flight by jumping out the door. Learning to read is always learning some aspect of some discourse. One can trivialize this insight to a certain degree by trivializing the notion of interpretation (of printed words), until one gets to reading as calling out the names of letters. Analogously, one can deepen the insight by taking successively deeper views of what interpretation means. But, there is also the problem with "reading class," that it stresses learning and not acquisition. To the extent that reading as both decoding and interpretation is a performance, learning stresses the production of poor performers. If we wanted to stress acquisition we would have to expose children to reading and this would always be to expose them to a discourse whose name would never be "Reading" (at least until the student went to the university and earned a degree called "Reading"). To the extent that it is important to have meta-level skills in regard to language, reading class as a place of learning rather than of acquisition might facilitate this, but it is arguable that a reading class would hardly be the best place to do this. While reading classes like mine might not be around any more, it encapsulated the common sense notion of literacy as "the ability to read and write" (intransitively), a notion that is nowhere near as coherent as it at first sounds.

Now I will approach a more positive connection between a viable notion of literacy and the concepts we have dealt with above. All humans, barring serious disorder, get one form of discourse free, so to speak, and this through acquisition. This is our socio-culturally determined way of using our native language in face-to-face communication with intimates (intimates are people with whom we share a great deal of knowledge because of a great deal of contact and similar experiences). This is sometimes referred to as "the oral mode" (Gee, 1986b)—it is the birth right of every human and comes through the process of primary socialization within the family as this is defined within a given culture. Some small, so-called "primitive," cultures function almost like extended families (though never completely so) in that this type of discourse is usable in a very wide array of social contacts. This is due to the fact that these cultures are small enough to function as a "society of intimates" (Givon, 1979). In modern technological and urban societies which function as a "society of strangers," the oral mode is more narrowly useful. Let us refer then to this oral mode, developed in the primary process of enculturation, as the "primary discourse." It is important to realize that even among speakers of English there are socio-culturally different primary discourses. For example, lower socio-economic black children use English to make sense of their experience differently than do middle class children; they have a different primary discourse (Gee, 1985; 1986a; Michaels, 1981; 1985). And this is not due merely to the fact that they have a different dialect of English. So-called "Black Vernacular English" is, on structural grounds, only trivially different from standard English by the norms of linguists accustomed to dialect differences around the world (Labov, 1972). Rather, these children use language, behavior, values and beliefs to give a different shape to their experience.

Beyond the primary discourse, however, are other discourses which crucially involve social institutions beyond the family (or the primary socialization group as defined by the culture), no matter how much they also involve the family. These institutions all share the factor that they require one to communicate with non-intimates (or to treat intimates as if they were not intimates). Let us refer to these as "secondary institutions" (such as, schools, workplaces, stores, government offices, businesses, churches, etc.). Discourses beyond the primary discourse are developed in association with and by having access to and practice with these secondary institutions. Thus, we will refer to them as "secondary discourses." These secondary discourses all build on, and extend, the uses of language we acquired as part of our primary discourse, and they may be more or less compatible with the primary discourses of different social groups. It is, of course, a great advantage when the secondary discourse is compatible with your primary one. But all these secondary discourses involve uses of language, either written or oral, or both, that go beyond our primary discourse no matter what group we belong to. Let's call those uses of language in secondary discourses which go beyond the uses of language stemming from our primary discourse "secondary uses of language." Telling your mother you love her is a primary use of language, telling your teacher you don't have your homework is a secondary use. It can be noted, however, that sometimes people must fall back on their primary uses of language in inappropriate circumstances when they fail to control the requisite secondary use.

Now we can get to what I believe is a useful definition of literacy:

> Literacy is control of secondary uses of language (i.e., uses of language in secondary discourses).

Thus, there are as many applications of the word "literacy" as there are secondary discourses, which is many. We can define various types of literacy as follows:

> Dominant literacy is control of a secondary use of language used in what I called above a "dominant discourse".

> Powerful literacy is control of a secondary use of language used in a secondary discourse that can serve as a meta-discourse to critique the primary discourse or other secondary discourses, including dominant discourses.

What do I mean by "control" in the above definitions? I mean some degree of being able to "use," to "function" with, so "control" is a matter of degree. "Mastery" I define as "full and effortless control." In these terms I will state a principle having to do with acquisition which I believe is true:

> Any discourse (primary or secondary) is for most people most of the time only mastered through acquisition, not learning. Thus, literacy is mastered through acquisition, not learning, that is, it requires exposure to models in natural, meaningful, and functional settings, and teaching is not liable to be very successful—it may even initially get in the way. Time spent on learning and not acquisition is time not well spent if the goal is mastery in performance.

There is also a principle having to do with learning that I think true:

> One cannot critique one discourse with another one (which is the only way to seriously criticize and thus change a discourse) unless one has meta-level knowledge in both discourses. And this meta-knowledge is best developed through learning, though often learning applied to a discourse one has to a certain extent already acquired. Thus, powerful literacy, as defined above, almost always involves learning, and not just acquisition.

The point is that acquisition and learning are means to quite different goals, though in our culture we very often confuse these means and thus don't get what we thought and hoped we would.

Let me just briefly mention some practical connections of the above remarks. Mainstream middle class children often look like they are learning literacy (of various sorts) in school. But, in fact, I believe much research shows they are acquiring these literacies through experiences in the home both before and during school, as well as by the opportunities school gives them to practice what they are acquiring (Wells, 1985; 1986a, b). The learning they are doing, provided it is tied to good teaching, is giving them not the literacies, but meta-level cognitive and linguistic skills that they can use to critique various discourses throughout their lives. However, we all know that teaching is not by any means always that good—though it should be one of our goals to see to it that it is. Children from non-mainstream homes often do not get the opportunities to acquire dominant secondary discourses, for example those connected with the school, prior to school in their homes, due to the lack of access their parents have to these secondary discourses. Thus, when coming to school they cannot practice what they haven't yet got and they are exposed mostly to a process of learning and not acquisition. Since little acquisition thereby goes on, they often cannot use this learning-teaching to develop meta-level skills since this re-quires some degree of acquisition of secondary discourses to use in the critical process. Further, research pretty clearly shows that many school-based secondary discourses conflict with the values and viewpoints in some non-mainstream children's primary discourses and other community-based secondary discourses (e.g., stemming from religious institutions) (Gumperz, 1982; Heath, 1983; Cook-Gumperz, 1986).

While the above remarks may all seem rather theoretical, they do in fact lead to some obvious practical suggestions for directions future research and intervention efforts ought to take. As far as I can see some of these are as follows:

1. Settings which focus on acquisition, not learning, should be stressed if the goal is to help non-mainstream children attain mastery of literacies. This is certainly not liable to be a traditional classroom setting (let alone my "reading class"), but rather natural and functional environments, which may or may not happen to be inside a school.

2. We should realize that teaching and learning are connected with the development of meta-level cognitive and linguistic skills. They will work better if we explicitly realize this and build this realization into our curricula. Further, they must be ordered and integrated with acquisition in viable ways if they are to have any effect other than obstruction.

3. Mainstream children are actually using much of the teaching-learning they get not to learn but to acquire, by practicing developing skills. We should thus honor this practice effect directly and build on it, rather than leave it as a surreptitious and indirect by-product of teaching-learning.

4. Learning should lead to the ability for all children—mainstream and non-mainstream—to critique their primary discourses and secondary discourses, including dominant secondary discourses. This requires exposing children to a variety of alternative primary discourses and secondary ones (not necessarily so that they acquire them, but so that they learn about them). It also requires realizing explicitly that this is what good teaching and learning is good at. We rarely realize that this is where we fail mainstream children just as much as non-mainstream ones.

5. We must take seriously that no matter how good our schools become, both as envi-ronments where acquisition can go on (so involving meaningful and functional settings) and where learning can go on, the non-mainstream child will always have more conflicts in using and thus mastering dominant secondary discourses, since they conflict more se-riously with his primary discourse and community-based secondary ones. This is precisely what it means (by my definitions above) to be "non-mainstream." This does not mean we should give up. It also does not mean merely that research and intervention efforts must have sensitivity to these conflicts built into them, though it certainly does mean this. It also requires, I believe, that we must also stress research and intervention efforts that facilitate the development of wider and more humane concepts of mastery and its connections to gate-keeping. We must remember that conflicts, while they do very often detract from standard sorts of full mastery, can give rise to new sorts of mastery. This is commonplace in the realm of art. We must make it commonplace in society at large.

REFERENCES

Belsey, C. (1980). *Critical Practice.* London: Methuen.

Cook-Gumperz, J., Ed. (1986). *The Social Construction of Literacy.* Cambridge: Cambridge University Press.

Culler, J. (1982). *On Deconstruction: Theory and Criticism After Structuralism.* Ithaca, NY: Cornell University Press.

Eagleton, T. (1983). *Literary Theory: An Introduction.* Minneapolis: University of Minnesota Press.

Gee, J. P. (1985). The narrativization of experience in the oral mode, *Journal of Education, 167*, 9–35.

Gee, J. P. (1986a). Units in the production of discourse, *Discourse Processes, 9*, 391–422.

Gee, J. P. (1986b). Orality and literacy: From the *Savage Mind to Ways with Words, TESOL Quarterly, 20*, 719–746.

Gilligan, C. (1982). *In a Different Voice*. Cambridge: Harvard University Press.

Givon, T. (1979). *On Understanding Grammar*. New York: Academic Press.

Gumperz, J. J., Ed. (1982). *Language and Social Identity*. Cambridge: Cambridge University Press.

Heath, S. B. (1983). *Ways with Words: Language, Life, and Work in Communities and Classrooms*. Cambridge: Cambridge University Press.

Jameson, F. (1981). *The Political Unconscious: Narrative as a Socially Symbolic Act*. Ithaca, NY: Cornell University Press.

Krashen, S. (1982). *Principles and Practice in Second Language Acquisition*. Hayward, CA: Alemany Press.

Krashen, S. (1985). *Inquiries and Insights*. Hayward, CA: Alemany Press.

Krashen, S., & Terrell, T. (1983). *The Natural Approach: Language Acquisition in the Classroom*. Hayward, CA: Alemany Press.

Labov, W. (1972). *Language in the Inner City*. Philadelphia: University of Pennsylvania Press.

Macdonell, D. (1986). *Theories of Discourse: An Introduction*. Oxford: Basil Blackwell.

Michaels, S. (1981). "Sharing time": Children's narrative styles and differential access to literacy, *Language in Society, 10*, 423–442.

Michaels, S. (1985). Hearing the connections in children's oral and written discourse, *Journal of Education, 167*, 36–56.

Scollon, R. & Scollon, S. B. K. (1981). *Narrative, Literacy, and Face in Inter-Ethnic Communication*. Norwood, NJ: Ablex.

Scribner, S. & Cole, M. (1981). *The Psychology of Literacy*. Cambridge: Harvard University Press.

Thompson, J. B. (1984). *Studies in the Theory of Ideology*. Berkeley and Los Angeles: University of California Press.

Wells, G. (1985). "Preschool literacy-related activities and success in school," in D. R. Olson, N. Torrance, & A. Hildyard, eds. *Literacy, Language, and Learning*. Cambridge: Cambridge University Press.

Wells, G. (1986a). "The language experience of five-year-old children at home and at school" in J. Cook-Gumperz, ed. *The Social Construction of Literacy*. Cambridge: Cambridge University Press.

Wells, G. (1986b). *The Meaning Makers: Children Learning Language and Using Language to Learn*. New York: Heinemann.

QUESTIONS TO THINK ABOUT

1. Gee discusses several important concepts in this article including literacy, primary and secondary discourses, and identity. Summarize Gee's definitions of these terms as comprehensively as you can, then comment on his assertion that we should "think of discourse as an 'identity kit' which comes complete with the appropriate costume and instructions on how to act and talk." Do you think Gee has made a strong theoretical case connecting discourse, literacy, and identity?

2. Gee lists five important points about discourses, stating that "none of these are very popular to Americans, though they seem to be commonplace in European social theory." Gee also says "Americans tend to be very focused on the individual." Speculate about why Americans might have difficulty with these five points and whether and how they conflict with an emphasis on individuality.

3. Consider Gee's concepts of acquisition and learning and their significance for the classroom. What are the differences between them and how do they relate to literacy and language learning? Are the five "practical suggestions for . . . intervention" at the end of his article viable ways to bridge acquisition and learning? Choose one of these practical suggestions and demonstrate how you might translate it into a viable teaching methodology and plan.

4. *Extending your understanding*: According to Gee, "lower socio-economic black children use English to make sense of their experience differently than do middle class children; they have a different primary discourse." He further claims that "this is not due merely to the fact that they have a different dialect of English." What is your analysis of Gee's assertions? Does he provide any basis or evidence for them? Do you think they are controversial and if so, how? You may find it useful to consult an educational database for recent articles on African American Vernacular English (AAVE) for other viewpoints; see Delpit, Fasold, and Gilyard in this text.

TERMS TO DEFINE

Define the following words and phrases as they are presented within the context of the reading. Comment on your understanding of the significance of each one.

Literacy
Primary and secondary discourses
Dominant discourse
Acquisition
Learning
Oral mode
Enculturation

The Politics of Teaching Literate Discourse

Lisa D. Delpit
Georgia State University

I have encountered a certain sense of powerlessness and paralysis among many sensitive and well-meaning literacy educators who appear to be caught in the throes of a dilemma. Although their job is to teach literate discourse styles to all of their students, they question whether that is a task they can actually accomplish for poor students and students of color. Furthermore, they question whether they are acting as agents of oppression by insisting that students who are not already a part of the "mainstream" learn that discourse. Does it not smack of racism or classism to demand that these students put aside the language of their homes and communities and adopt a discourse that is not only alien, but that has often been instrumental in furthering their oppression? I hope here to speak to and help dispel that sense of paralysis and powerlessness and suggest a path of commitment and action that not only frees teachers to teach what they know, but to do so in a way that can transform and subsequently liberate their students.

DISCOURSE, LITERACY, AND GEE

This chapter got its start as I pondered the dilemmas expressed by educators. It continued to evolve when a colleague sent a set of papers to me for comment. The papers, authored by literacy specialist James Paul Gee ("Literacy, Discourse, and Linguistics: Introduction" and "What Is Literacy?"), are the lead articles of a special issue of the *Journal of Education*[1] devoted solely to Gee's work. The papers brought to mind many of the perspectives of the educators I describe. My colleague, an academic with an interest in literacy issues in communities of color, was disturbed by much of what she read in the articles and wanted a second opinion.

As I first read the far-reaching, politically sensitive articles, I found that I agreed with much that Gee wrote, as I have with much of his previous work. He argues that literacy is much more than reading and writing, but rather, that it is part of a larger political entity.

This larger entity he calls a Discourse, construed as something of an "identity kit," that is, ways of "saying-writing-doing-being-valuing-believing," examples of which might be the Discourse of lawyers, the Discourse of academics, or the Discourse of men. He adds that one never learns simply to read or write, but to read and write within some larger Discourse, and therefore within some larger set of values and beliefs.

Gee maintains that there are primary Discourses, those learned in the home, and secondary Discourses, which are attached to institutions or groups one might later encounter. He also argues that all Discourses are not equal in status, that some are socially dominant— carry with them social power and access to economic success—and some nondominant. The status of individuals born into a particular Discourse tends to be maintained because primary Discourses are related to secondary Discourses of similar status in our society (for example, the middle-class home Discourse to school Discourse, or the working class African American home Discourse to the black church Discourse). Status is also maintained because dominant groups in a society apply frequent "tests" of fluency in the dominant Discourses, often focused on its most superficial aspects—grammar, style, mechanics—so as to exclude from full participation those who are not born to positions of power.

These arguments resonate in many ways with what I also believe to be true. However, as I reread and pondered the articles, I began to get a sense of my colleague's discomfort. I also began to understand how that discomfort related to some concerns I have about the perspectives of educators who sincerely hope to help educate poor children and children of color to become successful and literate, but who find themselves paralyzed by their own conception of the task.

There are two aspects of Gee's arguments which I find problematic. First is Gee's notion that people who have not been born into dominant Discourses will find it exceedingly difficult, if not impossible, to acquire such a Discourse. He argues strongly that Discourses cannot be "overtly" taught, particularly in a classroom, but can only be acquired by encul-turation in the home or by "apprenticeship" into social practices. Those who wish to gain access to the goods and status connected to a dominant Discourse must have access to the social practices related to that Discourse. That is, to learn the "rules" required for admission into a particular dominant Discourse, individuals must already have access to the social institutions connected to that Discourse—if you're not already in, don't expect to get in.

This argument is one of the issues that concerned my colleague. As she put it, Gee's argument suggests a dangerous kind of determinism as flagrant as that espoused by the ge-neticists: Instead of being locked into "your place" by your genes, you are now locked hope-lessly into a lower-class status by your Discourse. Clearly, such a stance can leave a teacher feeling powerless to effect change, and a student feeling hopeless that change can occur.

The second aspect of Gee's work that I find troubling suggests that an individual who is born into one Discourse with one set of values may experience major conflicts when attempting to acquire another Discourse with another set of values. Gee defines this as especially pertinent to "women and minorities," who, when they seek to acquire status Discourses, may be faced with adopting values which deny their primary identities. When teachers believe that this acceptance of self-deprecatory values is *inevitable* in order for people of color to acquire status Discourses, then their sense of justice and fair play might hinder their teaching these Discourses.

If teachers were to adopt both of these premises suggested by Gee's work, not only would they view the acquisition of a new Discourse in a classroom impossible to achieve, but they might also view the goal of acquiring such a Discourse questionable at best. The sensitive teacher might well conclude that even to try to teach a dominant Discourse to students who are members of a nondominant oppressed group would be to oppress them further. And it is this potential conclusion which concerns me. While I do agree that Discourses may embody conflicting values, I also believe there are many individuals who have faced and overcome the problems that such a coflict might cause. I hope to provide another perspective on both of these premises.

OVERCOMING OBSTACLES TO ACQUISITION

One remedy to the paralysis suffered by many teachers is to bring to the fore stories of the real people whose histories directly challenge unproductive beliefs. Mike Rose[2] has done a poignantly convincing job detailing the role of committed teachers in his own journey toward accessing literate Discourse, and his own role as a teacher of disenfranchised veterans who desperately needed the kind of explicit and focused instruction Rose was able to provide in order to "make it" in an alien academic setting. But there are many stories not yet documented which exemplify similar journeys, supported by similar teaching.

A friend and colleague who teaches in a college of education at a major mid-Western university told me of one of her graduate students whom we'll call Marge. Marge received a special fellowship funded by a private foundation designed to increase the numbers of faculty holding doctorates at black colleges. She applied to the doctoral program at my friend's university and traveled to the institution to take a few classes while awaiting the decision. Apparently, the admissions committee did not quite know what to do with her, for here was someone who was already on campus with a fellowship, but who, based on GRE scores and writing samples, they determined was not capable of doing doctoral level work. Finally, the committee agreed to admit Marge into the master's program, even though she already held a master's degree. Marge accepted the offer. My friend—we'll call her Susan—got to know Marge when the department head asked her to "work with" the new student who was considered "at risk" of not successfully completing the degree.

Susan began a program to help Marge learn how to cope with the academic setting. Susan recognized early on that Marge was very talented, but that she did not understand how to maneuver her way through academic writing, reading, and talking. In their first encounters, Susan and Marge discussed the comments instructors had written on Marge's papers, and how the next paper might incorporate the professor's concerns. The next summer Susan had Marge write weekly synopses of articles related to educational issues. When they met, Marge talked through her ideas while Susan took notes. Together they translated the ideas into the "discourse of teacher education." Marge then rewrote the papers referring to their conversations and Susan's extensive written comments.

Susan continued to work with Marge, both in and out of the classroom, during the following year. By the end of that year, Marge's instructors began telling Susan that Marge was a real star, that she had written the best papers in their classes. When faculty got funding for various projects, she became one of the most sought after research assistants in the college. And when she applied for entry into the doctoral program the next fall, even though her GRE scores were still low, she was accepted with no hesitation. Her work now includes research and writing that challenge dominant attitudes about the potential of poor children to achieve.

The stories of two successful African American men also challenge the belief that literate Discourses cannot be acquired in classroom settings, and highlight the significance of teachers in transforming students' futures. Clarence Cunningham, now a Vice Chancellor at the largest historically black institution in the United States, grew up in a painfully poor comunity in rural Illinois. He attended an all-African-American elementary school in the 1930s in a community where the parents of most of the children never even considered attending high school. There is a school picture of a ragtag group of about 35 children hanging in his den. As he shows me that picture, he talks about the one boy who grew up to be a principal in Philadelphia, one who is now a vice president of a major computer company, one who was recently elected Attorney General of Chicago, another who is a vice president of Harris Bank in Chicago, another who was the first black pilot hired by a major airline. He points to a little girl who is now an administrator, another who is a union leader. Almost all of the children in the photo eventually left their home community, and almost all achieved impressive goals in life.

Another colleague and friend, Bill Trent, who is a professor and researcher at a major research university, has told me of growing up in inner-city Richmond, Virginia, "the capitol of the Confederacy" in the 1940s and 1950s (personal communication, April, 1991). His father, a cook, earned an eighth-grade education by going to night school. His mother, a domestic, had a third-grade education. Neither he nor his classmates had aspirations beyond their immediate environment. Yet, many of these students completed college, and almost all were successful, many notable. There are teachers, ministers, an electronics wizard, state officials, career Army officers, tennis ace Arthur Ashe, and the brothers Max and Randall Robinson, the national newscaster and the director of Trans-Africa, respectively.

How do these men explain the transformations that occurred in them and their classmates' lives? Both attribute their ability to transcend the circumstances into which they were born directly to their teachers. First, their teachers successfully taught what Gee calls the "superficial features" of middle-class Discourse—grammar, style, mechanics—features that Gee claims are particularly resistant to classroom instruction. And the students successfully learned them.

These teachers also successfully taught the more subtle aspects of dominant Discourse. According to both Trent and Cunningham, their teachers insisted that students be able to speak and write eloquently, maintain neatness, think carefully, exude character, and conduct themselves with decorum. They even found ways to mediate class differences by attending themselves to the hygiene of students who needed such attention—washing faces, cutting fingernails, and handing out deodorant.

Perhaps more significant than what they taught is what they believed. As Trent says, "They held visions of us that we could not imagine for ourselves. And they held those visions even when they themselves were denied entry into the larger white world. They were determined that, despite all odds, we would achieve." In an era of overt racism when much was denied African Americans, the message drilled into students was "The one thing people can't take away from you is what's between your ears." The teachers of both men insisted that they must achieve because "You must do twice as well as white people to be considered half as good."

As Cunningham says, "Those teachers pushed us, they wouldn't let us fail. They'd say, 'The world is tough out there, and you have to be tougher'" (personal communication, April, 1991). Trent recalls that growing up in the "inner-city," he had no conception of life beyond high school, but his high school teachers helped him to envision one. While he happily maintained a C average, putting all of his energy into playing football, he experienced a turning point one day when his coach called him inside in the middle of practice. There, while he was still suited up for football, all of his teachers gathered to explain to him that if he thought he could continue making C's and stay on the team he had another thought coming. They were there to tell him that if he did not get his act together and make the grades they knew he was capable of, then his football career would be over.

Like similar teachers chronicled elsewhere (for example, Ladson-Billings,[3] and Walker[4]), these teachers put in overtime to ensure that the students were able to live up to their expectations. They set high standards and then carefully and explicitly instructed students in how to meet them. "You can and will do well," they insisted, as they taught at break times, after school, and on weekends to ensure that their students met their expectations. All of these teachers were able to teach in classrooms the rules for dominant Discourses, allowing students to succeed in mainstream America who were not only born outside of the realms of power and status, but who had no access to status institutions. These teachers were not themselves a part of the power elite, not members of dominant Discourses. Yet they were able to provide the keys for their students' entry into the larger world, never knowing if the doors would ever swing open to allow them in.

The renowned African American sociologist E. Franklin Frazier also successfully acquired a Discourse into which he was not born. Born in poverty to unschooled parents,

Frazier learned to want to learn from his teachers and from his self-taught father. He learned his lessons so well that his achievements provided what must be the ultimate proof of the ability to acquire a secondary dominant Discourse, no matter what one's beginnings. After Frazier completed his master's degree at Clark University, he went on to challenge many aspects of the white-dominated oppressive system of segregation. Ironically, at the time Frazier graduated from Clark, he received a reference from its president, G. Stanley Hall, who gave Frazier what he must have thought was the highest praise possible in a predominantly white university in 1920. "Mr. Frazier ... seems to me to be quite gentlemanly and *mentally white*" (emphasis added, quoted in Platt,[5] p. 15). What better evidence of Frazier's having successfully acquired the dominant Discourse of academe?

These stories are of commitment and transformation. They show how people, given the proper support, can "make it" in culturally alien environments. They make clear that standardized test scores have little to say about one's actual ability. And they demonstrate that supporting students' transformation demands an extraordinary amount of time and commitment, but that teachers *can* make a difference if they are willing to make that commitment.

Despite the difficulty entailed in the process, almost any African American or other disenfranchised individual who has become "successful" has done so by acquiring a Discourse other than the one into which he or she was born. And almost all can attribute that acquisition to what happened as a result of the work of one or more committed teachers.

ACQUISITION AND TRANSFORMATION

But the issue is not only whether students can learn a dominant secondary Discourse in the classroom. Perhaps the more significant issue is, should they attempt to do so? Gee contends that for those who have been barred from the mainstream, "acquisition of many mainstream Discourses ... involves active complicity with the values that conflict with one's home and community-based Discourses." There can be no doubt that in classrooms students of color do reject literacy, for they feel that literate Discourses reject them. Keith Gilyard, in his jolting autobiographical study of language competence, graphically details his attempt to achieve in schools that denied the very existence of his community reality:

> I was torn between institutions, between value systems. At times the tug of school was greater, therefore the 90.2 average. On other occasions the streets were a more powerful lure, thus the heroin and the 40 in English and a brief visit to the Adolescent Remand Shelter. I ... saw no middle ground, or more accurately, no total ground on which anomalies like me could gather. I tried to be a hip schoolboy, but it was impossible to achieve that persona. In the group I most loved, to be fully hip meant to repudiate a school system in which African-American consciousness was undervalued or ignored; in which, in spite of the many nightmares around us, I was urged to keep my mind on the Dream, to play the fortunate token, to keep my head straight down and "make it." And I pumped more and more dope into my arms. It was a nearly fatal response, but an almost inevitable one.[6] (p. 60)

Herb Kohl[7] writes powerfully about individuals, young and old, who choose to "not-learn" what is expected of them rather than to learn that which denies them their sense of who they are:

> Not-learning tends to take place when someone has to deal with unavoidable challenges to her or his personal and family loyalties, integrity, and identity. In such situations there are forced choices and no apparent middle ground. To agree to learn from a stranger who does not respect your integrity causes a major loss of self. The only alternative is to not-learn and reject the stranger's world. (pp. 15–16)

I have met many radical or progressive teachers of literacy who attempt to resolve the problem of students who choose to "not learn" by essentially deciding to "not teach." They appear to believe that to remain true to their ideology, their role must be to empower and politicize their most disenfranchised students by refusing to teach what Gee calls the superficial features (grammar, form, style, and so forth) of dominant Discourses.[8] Believing themselves to be contributing to their students' liberation by deemphasizing dominant Discourses, they instead seek to develop literacy solely within the language and style of the students' home Discourse.

Feminist writer bell hooks writes of one of the consequences of this teaching methodology.[9] During much of her post-secondary school career she was the only black student in her writing courses. Whenever she would write a poem in black Southern dialect, the teachers and fellow students would praise her for using her "true authentic voice" and encourage her to write more in this voice (p. 11). Hooks writes of her frustration with these teachers who, like the teachers I describe, did not recognize the need for African American students to have access to many voices and who maintained their stance even when adult students or the parents of younger students demanded that they do otherwise.

I am reminded of one educator of adult African American veterans who insisted that her students needed to develop their "own voices" by developing "fluency" in their home language. Her students vociferously objected, demanding that they be taught grammar, punctuation, and "standard English." The teacher insisted that such a mode of study was "oppressive." The students continued venting their objections in loud and certain tones. When asked why she thought her students had not developed "voice" when they were using their voices to loudly express their displeasure, she responded that it was "Because of who they are," that is, apparently because they were working class, black, and disagreed with her. Another educator of adults told me that she based her teaching on liberating principles. She voiced her anger with her mostly poor, working-class students because they rejected her pedagogy and "refused to be liberated." There are many such stories to recount (see, also, Yorio[10]).

There are several reasons why students- and parents-of-color take a position that differs from the well-intentioned position of the teachers I have described. First, they know that members of society need access to dominant Discourses to (legally) have access to economic power. Second, they know that such Discourses can be and have been acquired in classrooms because they know individuals who have done so. And third, and most significant to the point I wish to make now, they know that individuals have the ability to transform dominant Discourses for liberatory purposes—to engage in what Henry Louis Gates calls, "changing the joke and slipping the yoke" (quoted in Martin[11] p. 204), that is, using European philosophical and critical standards to challenge the tenets of European belief systems.

bell hooks[12] speaks of her black women teachers in the segregated South as being the model from which she acquired both access to dominant Discourses and a sense of the validity of the primary Discourse of working-class African American people. From their instruction, she learned that black poets were capable of speaking in many voices, that the Dunbar who wrote in dialect was as valid as the Dunbar who wrote sonnets. She also learned from these women that she was capable of not only participating in the mainstream, but redirecting its currents: "Their work was truly education for critical consciousness....They were the teachers who conceptualized oppositional world views, who taught us young black women to exult and glory in the power and beauty of our intellect. They offered to us a legacy of liberatory pedagogy that demanded active resistance and rebellion against sexism and racism" (p. 50).

Carter G. Woodson called for similar pedagogy almost 70 years ago. He extolled teachers in his 1933 *Mis-Education of the Negro* to teach African-American students not only the language and canon of the European "mainstream," but to teach as well the life, history, language, philosophy, and literature of their own people. Only this kind of education, he argued, would prepare an educated class which would serve the needs of the African-American community.

Acquiring the ability to function in a dominant Discourse need not mean that one must reject one's home identity and values, for Discourses are not static, but are shaped, however reluctantly, by those who participate within them and by the form of their participation. Many who have played significant roles in fighting for the liberation of people of color have done so through the language of dominant Discourses, from Frederick Douglass to Ida B. Wells, to Mary McCloud Bethune, to Martin Luther King, to Malcolm X. As did bell hooks' teachers, today's teachers can help economically disenfranchised students and students of color both to master the dominant Discourses and to transform them. How is the teacher to accomplish this? I suggest several possibilities.

WHAT CAN TEACHERS DO?

First, teachers must acknowledge and validate students' home language without using it to limit students' potential. Students' home Discourses are vital to their perception of self and sense of community connectedness. One Native American college student I know says he cannot write in standard English when he writes about his village "because that's about me!" Then he must use his own "village English" or his voice rings hollow even to himself. June Jordan[13] has written a powerful essay about teaching a course in black English and the class's decision to write a letter of protest in that language when the brother of one of the students was killed by police. The point must not be to eliminate students' home languages, but rather to add other voices and Discourses to their repertoires. As bell hooks[14] and Henry Gates[15] have poignantly reminded us, racism and oppression must be fought on as many fronts and in as many voices as we can muster.

Second, teachers must recognize the conflict Gee details between students' home Discourses and the Discourse of school. They must understand that students who appear to be unable to learn are in many instances choosing to "not learn" as Kohl puts it, choosing to maintain their sense of identity in the face of what they perceive as a painful choice between allegiance to "them" or "us." The teacher, however, can reduce this sense of choice by transforming the new Discourse so that it contains within it a place for the students' selves. To do so, they must saturate the dominant Discourse with new meanings, must wrest from it a place for the glorification of their students and their forbears.

An interesting historical example is documented by James Anderson.[16] Anderson writes of Richard Wright, an African American educator in the post-Reconstruction era, who found a way through the study of the "classical" curriculum to claim a place of intellectual respect for himself and his people. When examined by the U.S. Senate Committee on Education and Labor, one senator questioned Wright about the comparative inferiority and superiority of the races. Wright replied:

> It is generally admitted that religion has been a great means of human development and progress, and I think that about all the great religions which have blest this world have come from the colored races—all ... I believe, too, that our methods of alphabetic writing all came from the colored race, and I think the majority of the sciences in their origin have come from the colored races. ... Now I take the testimony of those people who know, and who, I feel are capable of instructing me on this point, and I find them saying that the Egyptians were actually wooly-haired negroes. In Humboldt's Cosmos (Vol. 2, p. 531) you will find that testimony, and Humboldt, I presume, is pretty good authority. The same thing is stated in Herodotus, and in a number of other authors with whom you gentlemen are doubtless familiar. Now if that is true, the idea that the negro race is inherently inferior, seems to me to be at least a little limping. (p. 30)

Noted educator Jaime Escalante prepared poor Latino students to pass the tests for advanced calculus when everyone else thought they would do well to master fractions. To do so, he also transformed a new Discourse by placing his students and their ancestors firmly within its boundaries. In a line from the movie chronicling his success, *"Stand and Deliver,"* he entreated his students, "You *have* to learn math. The Mayans discovered zero. Math is in your blood!"

And this is also what those who create what has been called "Afrocentric" curricula do. They too seek to illuminate for students (and their teachers) a world in which people with brown and black skin have achieved greatness and have developed a large part of what is considered the great classical tradition. They also seek to teach students about those who have taken the language born in Europe and transformed it into an emancipatory tool for those facing oppression in the "new world." In the mouths and pens of Bill Trent, Clarence Cunningham, bell hooks, Henry Louis Gates, Paul Lawrence Dunbar, and countless others, the "language of the master" has been used for liberatory ends. Students can learn of that rich legacy, and they can also learn that they are its inheritors and rightful heirs.

A final role that teachers can take is to acknowledge the unfair "Discourse-stacking" that our society engages in. They can discuss openly the injustices of allowing certain people to succeed, based not upon merit, but upon which family they were born into, upon which Discourse they had access to as children. The students, of course, already know this, but the open acknowledgment of it in the very institution which facilitates the sorting process is liberating in itself. In short, teachers must allow discussions of oppression to become a part of language and literature instruction. Only after acknowledging the inequity of the system, can the teacher's stance then be "Let me show you how to cheat!" And of course, to cheat is to learn the Discourse which would otherwise be used to exclude them from participating in and transforming the mainstream. This is what many black teachers of the segregated South intended when they, like the teachers of Bill Trent and Clarence Cunningham, told their students that they had to "do better than those white kids." We can again let our students know that they can resist a system that seeks to limit them to the bottom rung of the social and economic ladder.

Gee may not agree with my analysis of his work, for, in truth, his writings are so multifaceted as not to be easily reduced to simplistic positions. But that is not the issue. The point is that some aspects of his work can be disturbing for the African American reader, and reinforcing for those who choose—wrongly, but for "right" reasons—not to educate black and poor children.

Individuals *can* learn the "superficial features" of dominant Discourses, as well as their more subtle aspects. Such acquisition can provide a way both to turn the sorting system on its head and to make available one more voice for resisting and reshaping an oppressive system. This is the alternative perspective I want to give to teachers of poor children and children of color, and this is the perspective I hope will end the paralysis and set teachers free to teach, and thereby to liberate. When teachers are committed to teaching all students, and when they understand that through their teaching change can occur, then the chance for transformation is great.

NOTES

[1] James P. Gee, *Journal of Education: Literacy, Discourse, and Linguistics, Essays by James Paul Gee,* Vol. 171, No. 1, 1989.

[2] Mike Rose. *Lives on the Boundary* (New York: The Free Press, 1989).

[3] Gloria Ladson-Billings and Annette Henry, "Blurring the Borders: Voices of African Liberatory Pedagogy in the United States and Canada," *Journal of Education,* Vol. 172, No. 2, pp. 72–88, 1990.

[4] Emilie V. Siddle Walker, "Caswell County Training School, 1933–1969: Relationships Between Community and School," *Harvard Educational Review,* in press.

[5] Anthony M. Platt, *E. Franklin Frazier Reconsidered* (New Brunswick, NJ: Rutgers University Press, 1991).

[6] Keith Gilyard, *Voices of the Self* (Detroit: Wayne State University Press, 1991).

[7] Herb Kohl, *I Won't Learn From You! The Role of Assent in Education* (Minneapolis, MN: Milkweed Editions, 1991).

[8] Gee's position here is somewhat different. He argues that grammar and form should be taught in classrooms, but that students will never acquire them with sufficient fluency as to gain entry into dominant Discourses. Rather, he states, such teaching is important because it allows students to gain "meta-knowledge" of how language works, which in turn, "leads to the ability to manipulalte, to analyze, to resist while advancing" (p. 13).

[9] bell hooks. *Talking Back* (Boston, MA: South End Press, 1989).

[10] Carlos Yorio, "The Other Side of the Looking Glass," *Journal of Basic Writing*, Vol. 8, No. 1, 1989.

[11] Reginald Martin, "Black Writer as Black Critic: Recent Afro-American Writing," *College English*, Vol. 52, No. 2, Feb. 1990.

[12] hooks, op. cit.

[13] June Jordan, "Nobody Mean More to Me Than You and the Future Life of Willie Jordan," *Harvard Educational Review*, Vol. 58, No. 3, 1988.

[14] hooks, op. cit.

[15] Henry L. Gates, *Race, Writing and Difference* (Chicago: University of Chicago Press, 1986).

[16] James D. Anderson, *The Education of Blacks in the South, 1860–1935* (Chapel Hill, NC: University of North Carolina Press, 1988).

QUESTIONS TO THINK ABOUT

1. Delpit appears to have written this article in response to James Paul Gee's assertions about primary and secondary discourses and their implications for language learning and successful participation in the educational mainstream. What is it she takes issue with and why is it important? Why does she say that Gee's assertions are social and linguistic "determinism" leading to helplessness and powerlessness?

2. To substantiate her belief that "individuals have the ability to transform dominant discourses for liberatory purposes," Delpit offers narratives of success with these dominant discourses by those who initially were outsiders to it. What are the significant variables in these narratives that help explain educational success and mastery of dominant discourses? Do you think Delpit adequately counters Gee's assertions?

3. List and discuss the three reasons Delpit offers why "students- and parents-of-color" believe it is a necessity to learn the dominant discourse. Why does Delpit even have to present these arguments and how is her defense related to the title "The Politics of Teaching Literate Discourse"? Why do some believe students should not learn the dominant discourse? What are the ways Delpit believes teachers can help students master and transform the dominant discourse?

4. *Extending your understanding*: Think about what type of discourse was privileged in the various classroom settings you have experienced, including the one you are in right now. Based on your analysis of these discourses, do you think the dominant, privileged discourse should or should not be required? You may want to consider how the dominant discourse could be required, whether it is possible and/or desirable to teach several discourses, or whether it is preferable to ignore distinctions in students' language use. Explain your response as fully as you can.

TERMS TO DEFINE

Define the following words and phrases as they are presented within the context of the reading. Comment on your understanding of the significance of each one.

Discourse
Literacy
Dominant discourses
Transformation

Literacy and Learning Out of School: A Review of Theory and Research

Glynda Hull
University of California, Berkeley

Katherine Schultz
University of Pennsylvania

During the last two decades, researchers from a range of disciplines have documented the considerable intellectual accomplishments of children, adolescents, and adults in out-of-school settings, accomplishments that often contrast with their poor school-based performances and suggest a different view of their potential as capable learners and doers in the world.[1] Much of this research has dealt with the practice of mathematics—for example, young candy-sellers in Brazil who, despite being unschooled, develop flexible methods for arriving at the correct answers to math problems important to their vending (Saxe, 1988; see also Cole, 1996). Worlds away, southern California suburbanites have shown a comparable competence in real-world arithmetic problem solving—figuring out the best bargain in supermarkets or calculating precise portions as part of weight-watching activities (Lave, 1988). Like the children in South America, these adults provide the illusion of incompetence in their performance on formal tests of the same mathematical operations.

In literacy research, too, there has been much interest in recent years in documenting and analyzing the writing and reading activities that take place outside school, activities diverse in function, form, and purpose. Some of these studies highlight the kinds of writing that adults do as part of everyday life (Barton & Hamilton, 1998; Barton & Ivanic, 1991). Others examine the literacy-related activities that many adolescents pursue on their own, including keeping diaries and writing plays (e.g., Camitta, 1993; Finders, 1997; Mahiri, 1998; Schultz , 2002). Some researchers, while also focusing on youth culture, include in their analyses of literature activity a notion of "text" more broadly conceived—the graffiti produced by youth in gangs (Cintron, 1991; Moje, 2000), for example, or Internet surfing and chat (e.g., Lankshear, 1997; Lankshear & Knobel, 1997b; cf. Kolko, Nakamura, & Rodman, 2000). In addition to personal literacy practices and those that flourish in friendship or peer networks, some researchers have noted the considerable literacy and language-based components that develop as part of a variety of community activities (e.g., Cushman, 1998; Heath & McLaughlin, 1993; Moss, 1994).

Reprinted with permission from *Review of Educational Research* 71:4 (winter 2001): 589–611.
© 2001 by The American Educational Research Association.

Others, notably Flower and Cole and colleagues (Cole, 1996; Flower, in press; Flower, Long, & Higgins, 2000) have directed their energies toward designing and organizing theory-driven after-school programs that link universities to surrounding communities. A similar structure has proved generative for researchers and teachers in the field of composition studies, who have developed "service-learning courses" in which college students volunteer their time in a variety of organizations in exchange for real-world practice in writing (e.g., Adler-Kassner, Crooks, & Watters, 1997). After-school programs have also been of interest to researchers in the field of reading, who have identified the value of children's participation in after-school book clubs (cf. Alvermann, Moon, & Hagood, 1999; Alvermann, Young, Green, & Wiseman, 1999).

Still another branch of out-of-school research on literacy has been attentive to the considerable pressures on recent immigrants to learn and put to use the literate practices of their adopted countries (e.g., Skilton-Sylvester, 2002; Weinstein-Shr, 1993; see also Norton Peirce, 1995). And finally, first spurred by worries about the economy and then inspired by features of our new capitalism, researchers and corporate leaders alike have become interested in the role of literacy in the context of work (e.g., Gee, Hull , & Lankshear, 1996; Hart-Landsberg & Reder, 1997).

In this article, we review research on literacy in out-of-school settings, research conducted from various theoretical perspectives with various populations in various contexts but with the commonality of a focus on nonschool practice. Our first purpose is to identify the conceptual advances in how researchers think about literacy that have arisen from non-school-based research, with a special focus on tracing the evolution of the research. As we shall see, accounts of literacy outside school have, in fact, played pivotal roles in the history and development of literacy research and literacy theory. The first half of this review is organized around the major theoretical traditions that have shaped various strands of work on out-of-school literacy. These are the ethnography of communication (e.g., Heath, 1983; Taylor & Dorsey-Gaines, 1988), Vygotskian perspectives and activity theory (e.g., Engeström, 1998; Scribner & Cole, 1981), and the New Literacy Studies (NLS) (e.g., Gee, 1996; Street, 1993a, 1993b). To be sure, such categories are not hard and fast; a current project, for example, might draw on methodological insights from the ethnography of communication and also on the interest in power relations made manifest by the NLS. And in some important ways, the more recent theoretical points of view are made possible by—even draw their life from—the earlier ones. However, our theoretical categories provide a useful historical lens for seeing more clearly the pivotal role played by studies of out-of-school literacy, and they serve also as a heuristic for mapping the ever-growing territory of research and practice in out-of-school settings.

A second purpose of this review is to feature recent research on literacy in out-of-school settings, research that we have selected to illustrate the range and dimensions of current work. Our primary intent here is not to critique these studies (although we do highlight certain strengths and shortcomings), nor to provide a comprehensive summary of the elements of each. Rather, we intend in the second half of our article to present studies of out-of-school literacy in such a way as to suggest, through example and vignette, the practical and conceptual incentives and rewards for conducting such work. Finally, we call for an examination of the relationships between school and nonschool contexts as a new direction for theory and research. We ask, How can research on literacy and out-of-school learning help us to think anew about literacy teaching and learning across a range of contexts, including school?

One caveat before we begin. In some ways the distinction between in-school and out-of-school sets up a false dichotomy. By emphasizing physical space (i.e., contexts outside the schoolhouse door) or time (i.e., after-school programs), we may ignore important conceptual dimensions that would more readily account for successful learning or its absence. We may, then, fail to see the presence of school-like practice at home (e.g., Street & Street, 1991), or non-school-like activities in the formal classroom. Such contexts are not sealed tight or boarded off; rather, one should expect to find, and should attempt to account for, movement from one context to the other. In a related way, Cole (1995) calls our attention to a possible danger in treating the notion of context as a container, as that which surrounds and therefore, of necessity, causes, influences, or shapes. Writing primarily about hierarchical levels, Cole (1995) worries about the tendency to see a larger context (i.e., the school) as determining the smaller (i.e., the classroom). But his comments can be extended to apply more simply to our case of the adjacent contexts of school and out-of-school. That is, in any analysis of out-of-school programs, we want to avoid the temptation to oversimplify the creative powers of context—for example, to assume that successful learning in an after-school program occurs merely or only because it takes place after school.

Nevertheless, school has come to be such a particular, specialized institution, with its own particular brand of learning (Miettinen, 1999), that to set it in contrast with other institutions and other contexts for learning seems useful. Doing so will allow us to reconsider what we have grown accustomed to taking as natural and normal and to recognize it as an artifact of a particular kind of learning that is associated primarily with schooling.

SELECTION OF STUDIES

Our review process began with the collection and systematic analysis of recent research on literacy in out-of-school settings. To identify this work we surveyed the past 10 years of publications in literacy and learning journals, including *Anthropology & Education Quarterly; College Composition and Communication; the Journal of Literacy Research; Mind, Culture, and Activity; Research in the Teaching of English; and Written Communication*. We also include works published in edited volumes and book-length studies during the same period. We looked at various aspects of this work, including the rationale that researchers gave for examining literacy out of school, types of questions and findings, whether researchers connected out-of-school literacy to in-school practice, and the theoretical traditions underpinning the work.

The next step in our process was to look at historical development, focusing especially on theoretical perspectives in order to better understand the traditions shaping current work. We reviewed the ethnography of communication, activity theory, and the NLS to understand the relationships between those traditions and empirical work in out-of-school settings.[2] It was here that we made our most important discovery: that empirical, field-based research on out-of-school literacy has led to some major theoretical advances in how we conceptualize literacy. We are not suggesting that studies of literacy in school were unimportant in this regard. But as we will illustrate below, when researchers examined literacy in out-of-school contexts, they often arrived at new constructs that proved generative for literacy studies. As part of our historical research, we identified central studies and researchers in each tradition.

The last stage of our review process was to return to current work on literacy in out-of-school settings and to inductively generate categories that captured the dimensions of this work. We noted, for example, the relationship of the studies to theoretical traditions, their conceptions of literacy, connections made or not made to schooling, communicative mode and primary medium, the age of participants and its significance for the research, types of out-of-school contexts, languages, and geographic locations. Such categories also helped us to see gaps in current research and to envision possible new directions for future work.

THE ETHNOGRAPHY OF COMMUNICATION

We turn first to a series of studies that take what is now known as a sociolinguistic perspective on literacy and schooling. These studies reflect the conceptual leap made by bringing anthropological and linguistic perspectives and research methods to the study of literacy.

In the 1960s and 1970s, scholars from traditions outside education—such as anthropology and linguistics—looked beyond schools to family and community settings to understand how urban schools might reach students from cultural, socioeconomic, and linguistic backgrounds that differed from the mainstream. Educators were concerned that students of color, and especially those from low-income families, were not doing well in school. Until that time, the prevalent explanations had been deficit theories that blamed the students and their families for poor performance in school. Anthropologists interested in the study of language and literacy in schools brought to the study of classrooms a view of culture as "patterns in a way of life characteristic of a bounded social group and passed down from one generation to the next" (Eisenhart, 2002, p. 210). This view of socialization and culture prompted them to look to settings outside schools to understand patterns of school success and school failure across groups of students.

In 1962, Dell Hymes and John Gumperz organized a panel for the American Anthropology Association that brought together researchers from the fields of linguistics and anthropology. In his introduction to the proceedings, Hymes (1964) urged linguists to study language in context and anthropologists to include the study of language in their description of cultures. Hymes proposed the concept of an "ethnography of communication," which would focus on the communicative patterns of a community and a comparison of those patterns across communities. Although Hymes intended the ethnography of communication to include writing and literacy, the early focus on speaking led many to believe that his emphasis was solely spoken language (Hornberger, 1995).

Just a few years later, in 1965, a group of scholars representing a range of disciplines— including linguistics, anthropology, psychology, and education—were brought together by the U.S. Office of Education to examine the relationship between children's language and school success. In the midst of President Lyndon B. Johnson's expansive Great Society programs, researchers were asked to consider why schools were failing "low-income and minority children" (Cazden, 1981). The conclusion reached by the group was that many school problems of minority students could be explained by discontinuities, and specifically by differences in how language was used, between a child's home and school communities (Cazden, John, & Hymes, 1972, p. vii). Thus the National Institute of Education funded a number of studies to examine these issues. A major finding from the initial work was that children who have been socialized in diverse contexts come to school differentially prepared and positioned to respond to the demands of school. Therefore, they experience school differently; the result is success for some and failure for others. Hymes's (e.g., 1974) notion of the communicative event, which included a range of components that characterize language use—setting, participants, norms, and genres—became a helpful framework for the documentation of language use in and out of school settings.

Following this initial work on language and speaking, Keith Basso (1974) suggested that an ethnography of writing should be the centerpiece of ethnographies of communication—in particular, writing as it is distributed across a community rather than just a classroom. He introduced the term *writing event*, describing it as an act of writing, and characterized writing, like speaking, as a social activity. Building in turn on Basso's work and prefiguring the theory behind the NLS (e.g., Gee, 1996; Street, 1993a), Szwed (1981), a folklorist by training, argued for an ethnography of literacy and proposed that, rather than a single continuum or level of literacy, we should imagine a variety of configurations or a plurality of literacies. Whereas Basso's description of writing events seemed to arise from an academic interest in bringing together sociolinguistics and anthropology, Szwed's focus on an ethnography of writing was a response to the "literacy crisis" of the 1980s. Szwed suggested that, despite the claims of a crisis of "illiteracy," we had yet to conceptualize literacy; moreover, we did not know how literacy or reading and writing are used in social life. He linked his research interest directly to schools and explained that the definitions of reading (and we can add writing) that schools use may not take into account the reading (and writing) that a student does out of school. He called for a study of the relationship between school and the outside world and specified that the focus should be an inventory of one community's needs and resources. Szwed's call for the cataloguing of how and where literacy occurred in the community was the basis for many studies that sought to document empirically this new concept of multiple literacies (cf. Hornberger, 1995; Shuman, 1986, 1993; Weinstein-Shr, 1993).

Around the same time, Shirley Brice Heath (1981) suggested the importance of documenting the social history of writing, which she termed the "ethnohistory" of writing. Like Szwed, Heath made explicit the links between writing in social or family settings and methods of writing instruction in school. Using preliminary data from what would become her groundbreaking ethnography (1983), Heath described ethnographic research begun in response to complaints made by junior and senior high school teachers that it was impossible to teach students to write. According to the teachers, their classrooms were filled with students who planned to work in the textile mills where reading and writing were unnecessary. Heath concluded that although there was a debate about how to teach writing in school, there was little systematic description of the functions of writing for specific groups of people. Her study revealed the potential for using ethnographic studies of writing to reorganize schooling with dramatic results. This early work, followed by her well-known study (1983) detailed below, supported the notion of teacher and student research and prompted both teachers and students to research the functions and uses of literacy in their communities in order to inform classroom practice.

Likewise, Hymes's ethnographic research (1981), funded by the National Institute of Education and including Heath as a team member, used conversations with teachers about their difficulties in teaching language arts as its starting point. Researchers worked with teachers to uncover the dimensions of their difficulties with students and to understand students' perspectives on their school experiences. The researchers were quickly convinced that any investigation of school phenomena would require the study of classroom and school structures as well as those in the children's homes and wider communities. This work became the core of Gilmore and Glatthorn's (1982) collection of educational ethnographies, *Children In and Out of School.* Throughout the studies reported in that volume, schools were portrayed as cultures organized around a set of values and beliefs that frequently were not shared by the students and the surrounding communities. This argument is now known as continuity-discontinuity theory (see Jacobs & Jordan, 1993). Heath explained in the Gilmore and Glatthorn volume (1982) that if education is seen as a process of cultural transmission, then formal schooling is only a part of the process. She thus made an early argument for the need to study schools and classrooms in relation to the broader community or culture and called for comprehensive, broad-based community studies.

Heath's (1983) long-term study of three contiguous communities over a decade in the 1960s and 1970s illustrated how each community—a Black working-class community, a White working-class community, and a racially mixed middle-class community—socialized their children into very different language practices. Heath documented each community's "ways with words" and found, for instance, that members of the White working-class community rarely used writing and generally viewed literacy as a tool to help them remember events and to buy and sell items. Although parents in this community collected reading and writing materials so that children were surrounded by print, the parents rarely read, themselves, and used reading and writing for mostly functional purposes. In contrast, although residents of the Black working-class community did not accumulate reading materials, reading was more seamlessly integrated into their daily activities and social interactions, and literacy was accomplished jointly in social settings. Heath concluded that "the place of language in the life of each social group [in these communities and throughout the world] is interdependent with the habits and values of behaving shared among members of that group" (p. 11). When children from these communities entered school, only the middle-class students whose language use was similar to that of the teachers were successful. Heath thus demonstrated how children from different communities were differentially prepared for schooling that promoted and privileged only middle-class ways of using language. This study engendered other research projects, which documented both the functions and uses of literacy practices in various communities and the differential preparation that children from various communities brought to school. These projects included Taylor and Dorsey-Gaines's (1988) study of the literacy practices in urban homes, Cochran-Smith's (1986) description of story reading in a private nursery school, Fishman's (1988) study of an Amish community, and Skilton-Sylvester's (2002) documentation of the literacy practices of Cambodian girls in the urban United States.

Begun as a turning away from schools and toward communities, Hymes's conception of the ethnography of communication gave researchers and educators a framework for noticing the resources that students bring to school and provided teachers with a way to imagine changing their pedagogy and curriculum instead of assuming that only students needed to change. Subsequently, many researchers began to catalogue and describe the ways that young people used language in competent and, indeed, exciting ways out of school, in a manner that teachers have not traditionally been primed to acknowledge or build on.

VYGOTSKIAN AND ACTIVITY THEORY PERSPECTIVES

If the ethnography of communication grew from the union of two fields—linguistics and anthropology—activity theory was born of the need to re-imagine a third discipline, that of psychology. As is richly documented in several accounts (e.g., Cole, 1996; Engeström, 1998; Wertsch, 1991), this effort has centered on theorizing and investigating not the mind in isolation or the mind as automaton, but the mind in society or culture in mind. Whereas ethnographies of communication took and continue to have as their main focus the role of language in learning, with a special emphasis on language differences in and out of school, activity theory chooses a different centerpiece: learning and human development. To be sure, activity theory had its origins in the work of the Soviet scholar Vygotsky (1978, 1986; see also Wertsch, 1985), who placed a premium on the role of language as the premier psychological tool; he gave pride of place as well to written language. But many researchers who adopt an activity theory perspective get along quite well without directing their research toward language or writing per se (cf. Engeström, Miettinen, & Punamäki, 1999). This is because they are interested instead in honoring "activity" as a unit of analysis, an enterprise that might or might not include sign-mediated communication per se as a principle concern.

Thus our discussion in this article of Vygotskian perspectives and activity theory represents but a small, if significant, slice of the pie: those pivotal activity theoretical studies that have examined literacy—literacy, that is, as part of integral units of human life, motivated by human goals and enacted in the course of everyday activities, especially beyond the school. We begin by briefly revisiting Vygotsky's ideas about the importance of writing, move next to attempts to test his claims empirically, and turn finally to a few projects that embody present-day formulations of activity theory. We ask, all the while, Why have these researchers been interested in examining literacy out of school, and what thereby have they learned?

Vygotsky (1978, 1986) believed that human sign systems, such as language, writing, and mathematics, have significant consequences for how we think and how we interact with the world. As products of human history that emerge over time and vary in their nature and their use from culture to culture, such sign systems, or psychological tools, as Vygotsky called them, structure mental activity, mediating between thought and action and interaction. Writing, Vygotsky reasoned, is a sign system that is especially noteworthy for its far-reaching effects on thinking. The effects of psychological tools such as writing will vary, he also wagered, depending on the nature of the symbol systems available at particular historical junctures and their uses in particular societies.

In the 1930s, with the help of Alexander Luria (cf. Luria, 1976), Vygotsky saw the opportunity to test this theory by investigating empirically how intellectual functioning might be affected by cultural change. Mounting a major field-based research project, Luria traveled to Central Asia, where vast and rapid reforms were at that time in progress— reforms requiring nonliterate farmers to take part in collective ownership, for example, to use new agricultural technologies, and to acquire literacy through schooling. Luria found that the participants in his research did indeed respond differently to a variety of experimental tasks related to perception, classification, and reasoning, depending on their exposure to literacy and schooling. This he took as confirmation of Vygotsky's theory that cultural change affects thinking. But, given the complexity of the setting, we might ask exactly which change affected thinking—was it literacy, or schooling, or collective farming, or other big shifts in the organization of everyday life? It is impossible to say. Furthermore, Luria seemed to put too much stock in certain culturally biased test materials, in particular the syllogisms that were for a long time a standard part of the cross-cultural researcher's experimental arsenal. He did not, that is, take into account that such materials might merely measure people's familiarity with school-based types of tasks rather than their ability to think abstractly or logically.

Thus a quick foray into the Soviet landscape of days gone by illustrates the preoccupation with literacy that was at the heart of Vygotsky's work, as well as aspects of his theorizing that still hold sway, especially his focus on writing as a mediational tool, or the power of written language as an instrument for thinking. But the excursion also allows us to introduce a first important rationale within this tradition of research for juxtaposing school and nonschool environments—that is, as a means (albeit often flawed) for ascertaining the effects of literacy and schooling on thought or cognitive development. If literacy is acquired in school, the reasoning went, and if adults and children differ in the amounts of schooling to which they have been exposed, then whatever differences appear on tests of mental activity can be attributed to literacy—or at least to literacy coupled with schooling. A great deal of cross-cultural research during the 1960s was driven by just such reasoning (cf. Cole & Means, 1981). Although the majority of this work was limited by methodologies with a Western cultural bias, not to mention what now appears to be a naïve faith in the efficacy of schooling, one within-culture comparison stands out for both its methodological savoir-faire and its contribution to current conceptions of literacy: the monumental analysis of literacy among the Vai conducted by Scribner and Cole (1981).

In the early 1970s, at the same time that linguists and ethnographers had begun to apply the approach called the ethnography of communication to problems of language differ-ence in and outside school in the United States, psychologists Sylvia Scribner and Michael Cole were organizing a research project in Liberia. Hoping to pick up where Vygotsky's theorizing had left off, they devised an ambitious plan to investigate the cognitive conse-quences of literacy but to avoid the methodological problems that marred Luria's work. In particular, Scribner and Cole drew on local cultural practices in designing the content of their experiments, and they also decoupled the effects of literacy from the effects of schooling. The latter they could accomplish handily, since the Vai boasted the unusual distinction of having invented an original writing system, the learning of which took place out of school. Government-sponsored schools were taught in English, and Qur'anic study was conducted in Arabic, but the Vai used their indigenous script for specialized purposes such as record keeping and letter writing. This unusual patterning of languages, scripts, and acquisition practices made it possible to find people who were literate but had be-come so outside school or who were literate through school and biliterate in two scripts acquired informally, and so on. Scribner and Cole's research team gathered ethnographic and survey-based descriptions of language and literacy use, and they also administered a complex battery of experimental tasks designed to tap the cognitive processes tradition-ally believed to be connected to literacy—abstraction, memorization, categorization, verbal explanation, and the like.

In a nutshell, Scribner and Cole did not find that literacy was responsible for great shifts in mental functioning of the sort that the Soviets had looked for and many policymakers and educators expect even today. But they did demonstrate that particular writing systems and particular reading and writing activities foster particular, specialized forms of thinking. For example, Qur'anic literacy improved people's performance on certain kinds of memory tasks, whereas Vai script literacy gave people an edge in certain varieties of phonological discrimination. In addition to sorting out the specialized effects of particular literacies, Scribner and Cole identified the equally specialized effects of schooling in and of itself apart from literacy—namely, the enhanced ability of schooled people to offer certain kinds of verbal explanations.

It should be noted that in scaling down the grand claims often made about the effects of literacy on cognition, Scribner and Cole took care to note that Vai literacy was a restricted literacy; it served relatively few, and a noticeably narrow range of functions. Scribner and Cole also made clear that in societies where economic, social, and technological conditions converge to warrant the increased use of literacy, the potential exists for literacy to serve many more functions and therefore to be more deeply implicated in thinking processes. The current moment, we would point out, is just such a time, as communication through the Internet for economic, social, and personal purposes becomes ubiquitous for many people. Yet if we have learned anything from Scribner and Cole, it should be that literacy is not literacy is not literacy. Specialized forms of reading and writing, both in school and out, have specialized and distinctive effects, even in an information age. Scribner and Cole were the very first to teach us this.

In fact, they were the first, to our knowledge, to introduce the now omnipresent term *practice* as a way to conceptualize literacy. Recently Cole (1995) wrote about the current popularity of terms such as practice in studies of cognitive development. He attributes this popularity, as well as that of related terms such as *activity*, *context*, and *situation*, to a widespread desire these days to move beyond a focus on the individual person as a unit for psychological analysis. Cole has also traced the theoretical origins of this new language (1995, 1996). Looking back to Marx, for example, he explains that the notion of practice was a way to get around the separation of the mental and the material. Consulting post-Marxist social theorists such as Giddens (1979), he reminds us that practice has also been offered as a construct that avoids the impasse of agency versus determinism.

In *The Psychology of Literacy*, Scribner and Cole (1981) did not reveal the theoretical etymology of their use of the term practice. But they did explain in some detail the framework that they had constructed to interpret their data, a framework centered on the notion of practice. They defined a practice "as a recurrent, goal-directed sequence of activities using a particular technology and particular systems of knowledge" (p. 236). Literacy, as a socially organized practice, "is not simply knowing how to read and write a particular script but applying this knowledge for specific purposes in specific contexts of use" (p. 236). It follows that, "in order to identify the consequences of literacy, we need to consider the specific characteristics of specific practices" (p. 237).

The notion of practice—with its emphasis on purpose within context and the patterned interplay of particular skills, knowledge, and technologies—is also central to a plurality of literacies. Within the Vygotskian tradition, research on out-of-school literacy sprang from the desire to contrast the schooled, and their presumed literacy-enhanced cognitive capabilities, with the nonschooled, who were suspected of thinking differently and less well. Aware of the pitfalls of the tradition of cross-cultural research, Scribner and Cole redirected such efforts through a complex and culturally sensitive—especially for that decade—research design, and thereby also changed our thinking in literacy studies. Like ethnographers of communication, they helped the field understand literacy as a multiple rather than a unitary construct, calling attention to the distinctive literacies that can exist beyond the schoolhouse door.

Scribner and Cole's project is an example of early research within a then-burgeoning activity theory perspective.[3] In subsequent years Scribner (cf. 1987) turned her attention to a major nonschool endeavor, that of work, while Cole became invested in establishing sustainable after-school activity systems for children that juxtapose learning and play (e.g., Cole, 1996). In both of their new research agendas, Scribner and Cole were interested in studying not the isolated mental tasks that were thought (erroneously) to be elicited by means of laboratory experiments, but thinking as part of activity. Activities, we learn from the theory by the same name, serve larger goals and life purposes rather than being ends in themselves.

Thus it makes sense from this theoretical perspective to study thinking as part of a dominant life activity—such as school—but more significantly, for our purposes in this essay, as part of play or work. As Scribner (1997) pointed out, we would be very remiss were our accounts of human development to ignore entire realms of activity. For example, she observed, "While we are certainly not wholly defined through our participation in society's labor, it is unlikely we can fully understand the life cycle of development without examining what adults do when they work" (p. 358). At its very core, then, activity theory reminds us to look not just in school and in research laboratories but outside them, always with the goal of capturing "human mental functioning and development in the full richness of its social and artifactual texture" (Cole, Engeström, & Vásquez, 1997, p. 13). For literacy, this perspective opens the door to studies of reading and writing within the context of a panoply of activities, activities themselves motivated by larger purposes and aims than literacy itself.

THE NEW LITERACY STUDIES

Located at the crossroads where sociolinguistic and anthropological theories of language and schooling meet ethnographic and discourse analytic methodologies is the recently conceptualized field of the NLS (Gee, 1996; Street, 1993a).[4] Like the perspectives on literacy that come out of the ethnography of communication and activity theory, the NLS is noteworthy for its emphasis on studying literacy in out-of-school contexts. However, while building on the ethnographic tradition of documenting literacy in local communities and the characterization of literacy as multiple and situated, the NLS also often makes central an analysis of the interplay between the meanings of local events and a structural analysis of broader cultural and political institutions and practices. It does so in large part through the construct of *discourses*. As compared with the focus on language and learning, writing, and development in the studies reviewed in the previous two sections, NLS research could be said to investigate literacy and discourse and to place a special emphasis on revealing, understanding, and addressing power relations.

According to James Gee, a linguist who has been a central figure in the NLS, "discourses are intimately related to the distribution of social power and hierarchical structure in society, which is why they are always and everywhere ideological" (1996, p. 132). Gee situates the NLS, as well as the ethnography of communication and studies based on activity theory, within a group of movements that have taken a "social turn," moving from a focus on the study of individuals to an emphasis on social and cultural interaction (Gee, 2000b). He points out that although all of these movements claim that meaning (or writing or literacy) is always situated, they often fail to articulate the mutually constitutive nature of their contexts (Gee, 2000b).

Although most of the studies in the field of the NLS use the term *literacy*, Gee popularized the broader term *Discourse*. He defines Discourses as "ways of behaving, interacting, valuing, thinking, believing, speaking, and often reading and writing that are accepted as instantiations of particular roles (or 'types of people') by specific *groups of people*. . . . [Discourses] are, thus, always and everywhere *social* and products of social histories" (1996, p. viii). When

Gee writes about Discourse, we hear echoes of Foucault's (cf. 1972) use of the term, as well as Bourdieu's (cf. 1977) related coinage, *habitus*. However, Gee's distinctive contribution has been to use the notion of Discourse to reframe understandings of literacy, especially in relation to identity. He explains that people use Discourses to affiliate and display their membership in particular social groups. Discourses are, in effect, an identity kit, or a group of behaviors, activities, and beliefs that are recognizable by others. Inherently ideological and embedded in social hierarchies, they reflect the distribution of power. By virtue of training our gaze on the larger construct of Discourse and insisting that literacy is always about more than literacy, Gee's framework draws our attention away from a solitary focus on learning and language use in school settings and positions us to understand learning, literacy, and identity construction in and out of schools and across the life span. His discussion of Discourses provides, then, a frame for understanding the connections between literacy, culture, identity, and power (cf. Maybin, 2000).

While Gee illustrates how the term literacy can be limiting, Brian Street (e.g., 1993a, 1995; Street & Street, 1991), often recognized jointly with Gee as the founder of the NLS, has argued that schooling and pedagogy constrain our conceptions of literacy practices. Street defines literacy as an ideological practice rather than a set of neutral or technical skills, as it has traditionally been conceived in schools, adult literacy programs, and mass literacy campaigns (Street, 1984, 1993a, 1993b, 1995). Rather than treating literacy as consisting of neutral bits of information, his conception highlights its embedded or social nature. Thus, according to Street, Western notions of schooling or academic literacy are just one form of literacy among many literacies.

Street's theoretical conceptualization of the NLS is derived from his fieldwork in Iran in the early 1970s (Street, 1984, 1995). Through a careful examination of and participation in village life, Street identified three different kinds of literacy practices used by youth and adults in the village where he resided. These included what he termed *maktab* literacy, or literacy associated with Islam and taught in the local Qur'anic schools; *commercial* literacy, or the reading and writing used for the management of fruit sales in the local village; and *school* literacy, associated with the state schools more recently built in the villages and located in the urban areas as well. Teaching and learning in the religious schools was based on memorizing portions of religious texts and involved traditional teaching methods. By contrast, in local reading groups connected to the maktab schools, participants gathered at each other's homes to read passages from the Qur'an and its commentary to generate discussions and interpretation. Street's close examination of literacy and learning in the context of village life and culture painted a portrait that differed from the conventional descriptions of religious training in Islamic schools as consisting exclusively of rote memorization.

Street described the ways in which the skills that students learned through this maktab literacy were hidden in relation to Western notions of literacy. Children and adults educated in this manner were considered "illiterate" as compared with those educated in the state schools designed to prepare youth for jobs in the modern sector. However, according to Street, the skills connected with maktab literacy were actually a preparation for the commercial literacy that turned out to be key to economic success during the early 1970s, when economic expansion resulted from oil production. During that period many students who went to the state-run schools in urban areas found themselves without work, while their peers educated in the "backward" villages and drawing from their maktab literacy practices prospered from their work selling fruit.

This study and others in the NLS tradition connect micro-analyses of language and literacy use with macro-analyses of discourse and power. They also point to the dangers of reifying schooled notions of literacy. As scholars in the field contend and as Street's ethnography exemplifies, literacy must be studied in its social, cultural, historical, economic, and political contexts, both in school and out (Gee, 1996, 2000b). In so doing Street could articulate a conception of literacy as tied to social practices and ideologies, such as economic, political, and social conditions, social structures, and local belief systems. He thereby was able to connect literacy practices with social positions in a manner that contrasted sharply with then-dominant characterizations of literacy as a neutral skill. Street used theoretical perspectives grounded in anthropological research to argue for research that makes visible the "complexity of local, everyday, community literacy practices, or literacy outside school settings" (Street, 2001, p. 22).

Over the years, Street (e.g., Street & Street, 1991) has repeatedly raised this question: When there are so many different types of literacy practices, why is it that school literacy has come to be seen as the defining form of reading and writing? In an article written with Joanna Street, he describes the "pedagogization" of literacy, or the phenomenon of defining literacy solely by means of reference to teaching and learning, while other forms of literacy are marginalized. Such a stance contrasts historical evidence suggesting that in the past literacy was associated with social institutions outside school (Street & Street, 1991; see also Cook-Gumperz, 1986). Educated middle-class women in 17th-century China, for example, wrote poems as a way to construct a community of women (Yin-yee Ko, 1989, in Street & Street, 1991). Historically, and across cultural contexts, women have used literacy in informal, nonreligious, and nonbureaucratic domains (Heller, 1997; Rockhill, 1993; Street & Street, 1991). Street and Street (1991) argue that such uses of writing have been marginalized and destroyed by modern, Western literacy "with its emphasis on formal, male, and schooled aspects of communication" (p. 146). One conclusion from this analysis is that rather than focusing on the continuities and discontinuities between home and school in ethnographic research, there is a need to focus on the ethnographies of literacies more broadly and to document, as do these authors, the ways that school can impose a version of literacy on the outside world (Street & Street, 1991).

Extending Street's framework, Barton and his colleagues (e.g., Barton, 1991) demonstrated the importance of carefully documenting literacy in everyday lives. Conducting their work primarily in Lancaster, England, they illustrate how everyday literacies involve various media and symbol systems, and they document how various literacies are associated with particular cultures and domains of life within those cultures. Rather than locating literacy solely within the lives of individuals, they emphasize the ways in which families and local communities regulate and are regulated by literacy practices (Barton, 1994; Barton & Hamilton, 1998; Clark & Ivanic, 1997). In a similar vein, Prinsloo and Breier (1996) draw from the theoretical perspectives lent by the NLS to look for the meanings of everyday literacy practices in a wide range of contexts in South Africa. Like Street's early study in Iran (1984), these studies point to the disjuncture between local practices and the new adult literacy programs begun in the post-Apartheid era. In addition, they describe the literate practices undertaken by people who might be considered illiterate by school or state standards. Consonant with the NLS, this work documented what people actually accomplished with literacy rather than beginning with an assumption of deficiency (Street, 1996). Prinsloo and Breier concluded that there needs to be a reconceptualization of literacy that takes it out of the context of school and into the context of local practices.

Most recently, Barton and colleagues have emphasized the interplay of structure and agency, focusing on insiders' perspectives on what constitutes local practices and the ways in which these practices reflect and shape social structures (Barton, Hamilton, & Ivanic, 2000). This focus on the term *literacy practices* draws from the anthropological tradition to describe ways of acting and behaving that reflect power positions and structures. Street (2001) makes a distinction between practices and events, explaining that one could photograph an event but not a practice. Literacy practices, according to Street, embody folk models and beliefs, whereas events might be repeated occurrences or instances where interaction surrounds the use of text (cf. Barton & Hamilton, 2000). Hornberger (2001) likewise offers a useful distinction between literacy practices and literacy events, explaining that bedtime story reading in U.S. middle-class homes is a literacy event (Heath, 1982), whereas these individual and repeated events are explained and undergirded by a set of literacy practices or conventions and beliefs about the value of reading to young children, assumptions about parent-child relationships, normative routines around bedtime, and the like.

It is important to note that although studies growing from an activity theory tradition and those taking the NLS as a starting point both use the term practice, their usage differs. In Scribner and Cole's early work (1981), for example, practice explicitly includes notions of skill, technology, and knowledge as well as patterned activity. In the NLS, on the other hand, the focus is clearly on the ways in which activity is infused by ideology, and there is little interest in specifying the cognitive dimensions of social practices. Thus, more recently, literacy theorists often employ the term practice in a narrower sense that is consonant with their focus on culture, ideology, and power, although their specialized use of the term usually is not made explicit.

Whereas literacy theorists have worked to conceptualize the NLS, there has been a parallel and, at times, overlapping focus by researchers and practitioners in a field captured by the term *critical literacy*.[5] Predating the work in NLS, much of this field is directly related to schools and pedagogy rather than to everyday practice out of school. The two fields share a commitment to defining literacy in relation to power and identity, but critical literacy has a stronger focus on praxis—action based on reflection—as well as schooling. Luke and Freebody (1997) recently defined the critical literacy movement "as a coalition of educational interests committed to engaging with the possibilities that the technologies of writing and other modes of inscription offer for social change, cultural diversity, economic equity, and political enfranchisement" (p. 1). This explicitly political agenda of course has strong ties to Paulo Freire (e.g., 1970; Freire & Macedo, 1987), whose teaching methods and politically and ethically alert conception of literacy have been pivotal for national literacy campaigns around the world. Freire's focus was on the ways in which education and literacy should support people in questioning and shaping their worlds. "Reading the world," he famously wrote, "always precedes reading the word, and reading the word implies continually reading the world ... [and] transforming it by means of conscious practical work" (Freire & Macedo, 1987, p. 35). Although many critical literacy projects have been school based, such work has clear implications for thinking about (and rethinking) writing out of school. Lankshear and Knobel (1997a), for example, propose a rereading and rewriting of our impoverished notions of citizenship to produce a new discourse of active citizenship that enables students to understand their social positionings in relation to their identity formation and subjectivities. Such an idea can surely inform learning broadly construed as well as learning within an English class. Thus, although most research that is part of the NLS is descriptive in nature, researchers and educators have also used the framework of multiple literacies to delineate possibilities for teaching and learning.

In 1996, a group of scholars from the United States, England, and Australia met and spent more than a year in dialogue to develop a way of talking about the social context of literacy learning, including the content and the form of literacy pedagogy. They built their dialogue in part on notions developed by researchers and practitioners identifying themselves with the critical literacy and NLS movements, as well as researchers from a range of disciplines. Calling themselves the "New London Group" (after the site of their first meeting in New London, New Hampshire), their findings can be summarized by a key term that they chose to use—*multiliteracies*—which signals multiple communication channels, hybrid text forms, new social relations, and the increasing salience of linguistic and cultural diversity (Cope & Kalantzis, 2000; New London Group, 1996). As they explain, "Multiliteracies also create a different kind of pedagogy, one in which language and other modes of meaning are dynamic representational resources, constantly being remade by their users as they work to achieve their various cultural purposes" (New London Group, 1996, p. 64). Furthermore, in their discussion of multiliteracies and the implications of what Gee and his colleagues have termed "fast capitalism" (Gee, Hull, & Lankshear, 1996),

Luke and Freebody (1997) raise the persistent questions about who will gain access to the new forms of writing and representations and how the traditional fractures of race, culture, class, gender, and sexuality will be reinscribed. In their words:

> The challenge then is not just one of equity of access (or lack of access) to such technologies and institutions, but also of the possibilities of using discourse and literacy to reinvent institutions, to critique and reform the rules for the conversion of cultural and textual capital in communities and workplaces, and to explore the possibilities of heteroglossic social contracts and hybrid cultural actions. The challenge is about what kinds of citizenship, public forums for discourse and difference are practicable and possible. (p. 9)

Gee, Hull, and Lankshear (1996) take up this challenge in their recent book, *The New Work Order*. They extend the notion of literacy as social practice to include their concept of sociotechnical practices, which they describe as "the design of technology and social relations within the workplace to facilitate productivity and commitment, sometimes in highly 'indoctrinating' ways" (p. 6). They go on to write that whereas old forms and organizational structures of work may have been alienating, new workplaces are asking workers to invest themselves in their work, merging public and private lives, in ways that might be considered coercive. They raise a number of questions that blur the lines separating literate practices in and out of school, including this one: "How should we construe learning and knowledge in general in a world where the new capitalism progressively seeks to define what counts as learning and knowledge in a 'knowledge economy' made up of 'knowledge workers' doing 'knowledge work'?" (p. 23).

The NLS thus focuses our attention on the shifting landscape of home, community, work, and schools and gives us a language and set of theoretical constructs for describing the close connections between literacy practices and identities. Perhaps more than any other theoretical tradition, NLS has embraced out-of-school contexts, almost to the exclusion of looking at schools, and has unabashedly valued out-of-school literacy practices as distinct from those associated with schools.

VIGNETTES FROM HOME, COMMUNITY, AND WORKPLACE

Thus far in this review we have traced the ways in which examinations of literacy in out-of-school settings have provided pivotal theoretical moments, pushing the field toward new understandings of "literacies" and into new lines of research. Indeed, we have argued that many theoretical advances in the field of literacy studies over the last 25 years have been made from discoveries about literacy and learning outside classrooms. To talk about literacy these days, both in school and out, is to speak of events, practices, activities, ideologies, discourses, and identities—and at times to do so unreflectively, so much a part of our customary thinking have these categories and terminologies become. Conceptual advances in literacy studies have of course also arisen from school-based research, and we do not mean to slight such contributions. But we do want to call attention to the fact that much of our current theoretical vocabulary has sprung from examinations of the uses and functions of literacy out of school.

Having traced the ways in which examinations of literacy in out-of-school settings have provided pivotal theoretical moments, we turn next to examples of current research. Drawing from multiple traditions and methodologies, set in a variety of contexts and representing various cultures and geographies, these studies suggest the range and dimensions of current work located in out-of-school contexts. As stated earlier, our primary intent here is not to critique the studies, although we will point to certain strengths and weaknesses. Nor do we provide a comprehensive summary of each; rather, we refer readers to the original texts for detail. Our purpose is to bring to the foreground the practical and conceptual incentives and rewards for conducting such work, and we want to raise the questions that yet remain for literacy education and research.

As centerpieces of this section, we offer four vignettes of children, youth, and adults engaged in literate activities outside of school, vignettes adapted from recent reports of research growing out of the three theoretical traditions reviewed above. We have chosen to construct vignettes—short descriptive sketches, moments, or scenes—in order to highlight representations of real people and their activities in what, thus far in this article, has been a very theoretical journey. One strength of the research conducted from all three traditions is bringing literacy activities to life through ethnographic and qualitative, fine-grained accounts of particular lives, contexts, and historical moments. Through such field-based research we come to know a panoply of individuals, families, networks, communities, organizations, and institutions. We also begin to understand some of the multifaceted ways in which literacy connects with learning, doing, and becoming outside school. By constructing vignettes we hope at least to hint at this richness. We begin with a page from down under, an account of a cool teenager, reluctant writer, and budding businessman in urban Australia.[6] And we ask, How might we draw on the out-of-school worlds that engage youth, even as we attempt to foster school-based expertise?

"I'm not a pencil man."

Jacques is thirteen years old and lives with his parents and siblings in a White, afflu-ent neighborhood of Brisbane. A disengaged student in the classroom, one who often "loses" his homework and would die a thousand deaths before volunteering an answer to a teacher's general query, he nonetheless provides a running sotto voce gloss on classroom activity, waxing in turn ironic, humorous, or dramatic. This self-designated joker has "great difficulty with literacy" according to his teacher. But he is quite good at derailing attempts to involve him in the classroom milieu. No "writing process" pedagogy for this young man. Rather than use the "Writer's Centre" to produce and publish a story, Jacques spends days stapling together a miniature book in which he writes, to his teacher's dismay and his peers' delight, a mere ten words. Made to repeat first grade, Jacques now patiently measures time until he can leave school for good. Neither professing nor demonstrating an interest in reading and writing, he explains, "'I'm like my dad. I'm not a pencil man'" (Knobel, 1999, p. 104).

Outside school, Jacques participates in two worlds valued in his family: work and religion. A member of the Jehovah's Witnesses, he takes part ably in a variety of literacy-related religious activities—scriptural exegesis, the distribution on Saturday rounds of church literature such as *The Watchtower*, and presentations at a weekly Theocratic School. But it is being a workingman, with certain specialized ways of interacting and valuing, that offers Jacques a current identity and a future vision of the person he expects and wants to become. His father owns a successful business as an excavator, and it is Jacques' potential role in this physically palpable occupation, revolving as it does around machines and action in and upon the world, that captures the young man's attention and energy. His involvement in and apprenticeship for the adult world of work also includes a few home-based literacy activities. On his home computer he designs and publishes an advertisement for a neighborhood mowing service. This professional-looking flyer promises "efficiency" and "reliability" and even offers "phone quotes"—turns of phrase we all can recognize as ubiquitous in the world of business advertising. Sadly, Jacques' out-of-school identity as an aspiring businessman and the social practices that support it, so obvious at home, are invisible in school, where he appears disengaged and less than competent. Yet one might speculate that he will nonetheless lead a successful adult life, finding a comfortable economic and social niche, given his cooperative immersion in valued and rewarded adult worlds.

This vignette of Jacques is adapted from Michele Knobel's recent book *Everyday Literacies: Students, Discourse, and Social Practices* (1999), an ethnographic case study of four adolescents coming of age in urban Australia. Framing her study with Gee's discourse theory (e.g., 1996) and methodological insights drawn from Green and the Santa Barbara Classroom Discourse Group (e.g., Green & Harker, 1988), Knobel poses the central question raised, but not yet answered, by years of research on out-of-school literacy. She asks, "What *is* the relationship between school learning and students' everyday lives, and what might an effective relationship between them be?" (p. 6).

Knobel's study reminds us, as does an important tradition of work in literacy theory and research, of the resources, both personal and community based, that children, adolescents, and adults bring to school. An important example is Moll's work with Latino communities in the Southwest and his generative term *funds of knowledge*, which he used to describe the networked expertise woven through community practices (Moll, 1992; Moll & Diaz, 1987; Moll & Greenberg, 1990; see also Vásquez, 1993). Moll's work provides a demonstration of how we can use funds of knowledge to bridge communities to classrooms when we acknowledge the expertise of parents and community members. Moll also offers examples of lessons in which teachers have brought community members into the schoolroom to share their knowledge and know-how, and he documents the positive effects of such activities on children's interest and investment in the curriculum.

Developing a culturally relevant pedagogy for teaching literary interpretation to African-American youth, Lee (1993) also illustrates cultural funds of knowledge, particularly language forms and discourse structures. In more recent work, Lee and her colleagues (Lee, 2000; Majors, 2000; Rivers, Hutchinson, & Dixon, 2000) examine language practices across contexts, identifying community participation structures in, for example, African-American hair salons, and using those structures to inform ways of conducting classroom discussions about texts. This research shows the potential for engaging students in high levels of reasoning about literary texts by drawing on their tacit knowledge of cultural forms found outside school.

Dyson's long-term studies of early writing development acknowledge especially well the resources that young children bring to their writing from their social worlds, including linguistic and symbolic tools appropriated from popular culture (Dyson, 1997, 1999, in press). Dyson has argued for the permeability of the curriculum, where teachers imagine their classrooms in such a way as to continually welcome the diverse resources that children of necessity bring to their writing. Dyson's research is situated physically within classroom walls, but her conceptual framework embraces children's out-of-school lives. Thus we see here two ways to bridge the home and school worlds. Moll and Lee literally go into homes, community centers, and other places outside school to learn about social and cultural resources; they then bring people and linguistic and cultural knowledge back into the classroom. Dyson, on the other hand, suggests the ways in which children themselves bring their outside worlds into the school through their writing and the oral performances that encircle literacy events.

Work in the vein of Moll, Lee, and Dyson provides persuasive examples of the necessity of attending to, building on, and incorporating the social, cultural, and linguistic resources that students bring to school, and it offers models of how to do so. Such studies thus helpfully extend the agenda first outlined through the ethnography of communication. We believe it is crucial that this kind of research continue, especially research that addresses those most alienated from school. Disaffected adults and youth such as Jacques are legion—individuals and groups for whom alienation from school-based learning seems sadly confirmed. For them, perhaps, community-based, out-of-school, or after-school opportunities are especially key. At the same time, we believe it equally important for school-based teachers to continue to ask, How might out-of-school identities, social practices, and the literacies that they recruit be leveraged in the classroom? How might teachers incorporate students' out-of-school interests and predilections but also extend the range of the literacies with which youth are conversant? And in what ways must our ways of thinking about what constitutes curriculum and pedagogy be modified to appeal to students who do not fit the common mold? How, to ask the hardest question, do we keep youth involved in school when their adult lives hold small promise of work or civic activity or personal fulfillment that draws strongly on school-based literacy?

"You gotta pay."

Marquis (aged 11 years), Delilah (10), and Samson (9) are at a community center when Ellen arrives, parking ticket in hand. A volunteer at the center and a friend of the children, she asks what to do with the ticket. Marquis asks where she found it, and Ellen answers, "On my windshield." "Oooo, you got a ticket for parking where you shouldn't have!" Delilah quickly chides, while Samson teases that she'll surely go to jail. Marquis states with the wisdom of his years, "She ain't going to jail for no ticket. She gonna pay somen." And then Marquis and Delilah set about problem solving, analyzing the ticket and sorting through strategies for dealing with it.

Delilah suggests that Ellen will need to go downtown to pay it, but on reexamining the ticket Samson concludes that it can be mailed and that the ticket itself, once folded over, will serve as an envelope. Marquis recommends simply putting it on someone else's car. "Yeah, on another Mazda," Deliah adds. But once the children deduce that Ellen's license number is recorded on the ticket, that plan seems less than ideal. "They got a copy of the ticket at the office, and if she don't pay she'll go to jail," a sober child concludes. Marquis and Delilah have the final say: "You gotta pay." And they commiserate over the steep fine of $25. "You got it?" Delilah asks. The problem-solving moment ends with a story. Marquis tells how his little brother once gave him a ticket for parking his big wheel in front of the house, a ticket for a hundred dollars. "Said I had to give it to him too, or I was going to jail!" Everyone joins in the laughter.

And so we see a group of African-American inner-city children turning a parking ticket this way and that, holding it up to the light, both literally and metaphorically. They draw on various literate and discursive strategies to find a way to obviate its influence—trying out scenarios, studying the artifact for information and directives, enumerating and questioning options. In other words, the children employ their developing language skills to solve a material problem in a resource-scarce community. Their negotiation of the traffic ticket thus lays bare a host of literate and problem-solving practices and also reveals the ways in which urban youth learn to hone their abilities to understand, function within, and circumvent the powers that be.

We are introduced to these children in Ellen Cushman's recent ethnography *The Struggle and the Tools* (1998), a book that celebrates inner-city residents' institutional language—those oral and literate skills crucial for daily negotiations with gatekeeping institutions. Taking issue with critical scholars who too quickly resort to notions of hegemony and false consciousness when they theorize the "underclass" or the "marginalized," Cushman takes as her project redefining critical consciousness. She demonstrates, and pays homage to, the ways in which the individuals she came to know as part of her research navigate the social structures that constrain them, both accommodating and resisting and even undermining such constraints through everyday language and literacy activities. In so doing, Cushman adopts what she calls an activist methodology, one that lays bare her role as a participant in the research and the community (notice her presence in the vignette above) and one that makes possible reciprocally beneficial relationships with the people who took part in her study.

Cushman's study vividly illustrates the communicative competence displayed by people in their everyday lives. She examines youths' conversations and finds, for example, not just chitchat but the deployment of a particular kind of strategic oral language in service of analyzing that most common of local literacy artifacts, the dreaded parking ticket. Indeed, much of the work on out-of-school literacy has had as its starting place a respect for and ac-knowledgement of people's abilities. As McDermott (1993) has noted, the stance that peo-ple are okay, that they are competent within their cultural milieu, is common within the field of anthropology—but expecting people to fail is often an artifact of schooling. Nowhere in the out-of-school research is an expectation for success more evident than in Shirley Heath's recent, long-term work in a multitude of out-of-school youth organizations around the United States (e.g., Heath, 1994, 1996, 1998a, 1998b; Heath & McLaughlin, 1993). Heath has documented young people's participation in arts-based organizations, among other community-based efforts, and offers this description of their important features:

> Within the organizations that host these arts programs, opportunities for young people to learn derive primarily from an ethos that actively considers them to be resources for themselves, their peers, families and communities. These programs thus engage the young in learning, both for themselves and for others, through highly participatory projects that encompass listening, writing and reading, as well as mathematical, scientific and social skills and strategies. (Heath, 1998a, p. 2)

To be sure, one of the most important lessons to be gleaned from research on literacy and out-of-school contexts is the benefits that can accrue from assuming competence. As Griffin and Cole (1987; see also Cole & Traupmann, 1981; McDermott, 1993) have discovered in their work with after-school programs, competence becomes most apparent when we allow many starting points for learning and many paths to progress.

In response to Cushman's study, we ask what we must do to cultivate such attitudes about children's and adults' competence in formal classrooms. The competence that often is assumed in after-school settings must too often, it seems to us, be proved in classrooms. How can we support educators in developing the habit of mind that students are variously able? And what have after-school settings to teach us in this regard? Furthermore, what special skills are required of teachers to nurture students whose critical consciousness as members of oppressed groups is finely honed and who may not be predisposed to display the competence they possess? Finally, how can teachers and researchers learn about and participate in communities apart from school in a respectful and reciprocal manner? The metaphor of journey is often invoked as part of much research on literacy out-of-school, as researchers voyage into less familiar communities and cultures to collect information and artifacts for their scholarship and the classroom. These studies have been valuable as ways of unveiling and emphasizing language and literacy practices that differ from those of the mainstream. Yet we would argue that it is time to find a different metaphor and another reason for traveling, one that facilitates the sharing of projects with participants and that directs research toward the amelioration of problems that community members, with researchers and teachers, find compelling. Work that Flower and colleagues have begun in Pittsburgh (Flower, 1997, in press; Flower, Long, & Higgins, 2000; Long, Peck, & Baskins, 2002; Peck, Flower, & Higgins, 1995) and work that Engeström (1987, 1993, 1998) and his colleagues are carrying out in Finland, are illustrative in this regard.

Of Mice and Managers

In a high-technology workplace in the Silicon Valley of northern California, frontline workers, most of them recent immigrants, participate in a sortie of literacy-rich activities, activities that accompany their participation in "self-directed" work teams, their documen-tation of their own productivity and quality scores, and the oral presentation of problem-solving data. Literacy is everywhere in this factory, serving some eighty-odd functions and ranging from simple copying and decoding to marshaling reading and writing to argue points of view. Managers and supervisors have quite definite ideas about the purposes that literacy activities should serve in this workplace. Yet the most carefully scripted plans of mice and managers often go astray. Here is Mr. San, one of several frontline workers at the

factory who is taking his turn in front of supervisors and co-workers to practice the computation and reporting of quality and productivity numbers. He begins innocently enough:

> Okay [puts transparency on the overhead projector]. Our team name is Turbo, Team number
> 31, and the area is First Mechanical and Handload. Shift—day, and my coach is Engineer
> Kartano.

But it soon becomes apparent that Mr. San is about to seize the moment, having chosen
not merely to participate in a practice exercise on oral reporting. Instead, he demonstrates
that it is actually impossible to calculate productivity scores correctly because workers have
been given incorrect standard times, or the times allotted for accomplishing the multitude
of assembly tasks required throughout the workday. In a dramatic "voila" moment, Mr. San
unveils on the overhead projector a virtually unreadable chart, so thickly packed it is with
numbers. Although its details are obscured, the import of the chart is as clear as can be:
Mr. San has managed to requisition a new set of standard times:

> This is, now I just got this, that's why we are delayed in entering our data [puts a new transparency
> up on the overhead projector], here is the Standard Time. Wow! [laughter].... They're trying
> to modify the Standard Time because I complained all the datas that we got on the actual time
> that we finish one board doesn't count in the Standard Time.

The issue of speed at work is of course a theme that runs throughout the history of labor
relations; how fast work gets done, or the "standard time," as it is called in Mr. San's factory,
has been contested over and over again. In this most recent example of that long history,
Mr. San appropriates a company meeting at which workers were expected just to practice,
merely to get their feet wet, with public presentations of data by reading off their responses
to prefabricated questions in rote fashion. Mr. San chose not to be part of the dog-and-pony
show, just as he had refused even before the meeting to complete elaborate graphs and
charts and provide a discursive rationale for his team's quality and productivity goals. "How
can we write goals," he had argued, "if our Standard Times are incorrect?" Pressing his
point with an engineer, he eventually succeeded in having the company's time-study experts
recalculate the Standard Times. Only after all of this did Mr. San consent to learn how to
perform—and to encourage his team members to do so as well—the considerable new
literate components of work. In this case, it seems that Mr. San's willingness to participate
in literacy-related activities was linked to the identity he was constructing for himself as a
worker, an identity most aptly described as advocate for his team—"my people," as he liked
to call them.

Hull (2000b) provides our Silicon Valley vignette from her ethnographic examination
of two companies in the circuit board assembly industry (see also Hull , Jury, Ziv, & Katz,
1996). She and her research team asked what kinds of workers the companies were seeking
to hire or to fashion and what kinds of literacies the new forms of work, such as self-
directed work teams, seemed to privilege. Frameworks drawn from the NLS (e.g., Gee,
1996; Street, 1993a) and sociocultural perspectives on writing (e.g., Freedman, Dyson,
Flower, & Chafe, 1987) primed Hull to link literacy and identity, calling attention to how
particular work identities can recruit or repel certain literacy practices. Like much of
the NLS, this research traced the connections between literacy and power, revealing how
opportunities to engage in particular literacy practices were distributed and constrained,
as well as how new structures for participation created unexpected spaces for the exercise
of new literacies and literate roles.

Other researchers who have recently examined the literacy demands of entry-level work
in ethnographic detail include Gowen (1992) in her account of hospital workers, Darrah
(1996) in his analysis of the electronics industry, and Hart-Landsberg and Reder (1997) in
their examination of auto accessory manufacturers. More studies, however, have focused

on the work and writing lives of college graduates who enter managerial or technical positions in which writing mediates work in quite visible and powerful ways. (For a review of the particular tradition of such work that draws on activity theory approaches, see Russell, 1997.) These studies help us to look critically at how college writing courses, writing across the curriculum programs, and training in technical communication do and do not prepare students for professional lives in which the mastery of written genres is central. They also give us detailed understandings of the literacy requirements and literacy-related social practices of a variety of workplaces, often making the case that writing at school and at work are "worlds apart" (Dias, Freedman, Medway, & Paré, 1999). This body of research has provided, finally, compelling portraits of the struggles of competent writers engaged in high-stakes, real-world activity through which they become professional wordsmiths (e.g., Beaufort, 1999).

In addition to research exploring the functions of literacy in workplaces, much recent research catalogues literacy in a range of contexts, often where we might least expect it—among taxi-drivers in South Africa (Breier, Taetsane, & Sait, 1996); at a cattle auction in Wales (Jones, 2000); in youth basketball leagues in the American Midwest (Mahiri, 1998); as part of household accounts and horse racing in Lancaster, England (Barton & Hamilton, 1998); and in a women's group in the San Francisco Tenderloin, a down-and-out part of the city associated with drugs and crime, not literacy (Heller, 1997). Collectively, this work illustrates Geertz's observation that "man's mental processes indeed take place at the scholar's desk or the football field, in the studio or lorry-driver's seat, on the platform, the chessboard, or the judge's bench" (quoted in Cole, Engeström, & Vásquez, 1997, p. 13). And it denotes as well the enlivened interest of current-day researchers from a range of fields in everyday practical activity (see the review and discussion in Cole, Engeström, & Vásquez).

This variety of literate forms in the workplace and elsewhere raises for us the broad question of what the relationship should be between the literacies taught at school and the literacies practiced in other contexts. How much, for example, should the workplace influence the curriculum? Research on literacy at work, such as that by Hull (1999, 2000b), argues for a broadening and rethinking of school-based literacy, especially the standard curricular fare for non-college-bound youth. Rather than the restricted literacies often associated with vocational tracks, schooling for such youth needs to more closely approximate the increased expectations of a working world where one must excel at literate activities and develop a working identity that involves a sense of oneself as a proficient user of multiple semiotic systems. This research also calls for, in the Freirean sense, an education for reading the world as well as reading the word—for example, the ways in which literacy practices can be implicated in the maintenance of the status quo, even in those workplaces striving to reinvent themselves around high performance models.

Evidence of the abundant, diverse forms of out-of-school literacy—crossing class, race, gender, culture, and nationality—enrich our definitions, making us think again of school-based, "academic" literacy and causing us to ask, What is or might be the value of essayist texts? The Tenderloin women writers group described by Heller (1997) wrote in many of the genres generally associated with school—essays, poems, short stories, other fiction, and imaginative writing. These longer texts contrast sharply with the lists, letters, notes, and advertisements that make up much everyday reading and writing in terms of form and purpose. They suggest, in fact, the permeability of the borders between in-school and out-of-school. We suggest that, in our efforts to document and validate the plethora of personal and local literacy practices, we should not abandon the opportunities that school historically has provided to develop particular forms of text-based expertise, forms that may provide a power absent in many everyday literacies. Although Damon (1990) notes that "children will adapt intelligently to their worlds" (p. 34), he also acknowledges the tension between youths' perceptions of what it is useful to know about the world and adults' understandings. Calling attention to the tendency to valorize out-of-school "skills" and to put

294 HULL AND SCHULTZ

them on equal footing with schooled knowledge (perhaps, he speculates, in reaction to the long-standing tendency among academics to denigrate the nonacademic), he asserts that

> it serves no useful purpose to imbue unschooled forms of knowledge with a sentimental gloss. Just as we should not lose sight of the remarkable adaptiveness of some unschooled abilities, we also must guard against expecting more from them than they can deliver. (p. 38)

We ask, then, what forms of schooled literacy are powerful intellectual tools, appropriate for these new times, and what forms are mere conventions or historical artifacts?

Kalantzis and Cope (2000) argue persuasively for pluralism as an organizing concept for education in new times, and similarly, they suggest that in imagining new work orders, we must work toward "productive diversity," wherein people are valued in their difference, and expertise at work centers on the ability to engage and negotiate difference. Gee (2000a) wonders whether the new capitalist rhetoric and practice—flexibility, teamwork, communities of practice—can be reclaimed for more radical social and educational ends. For our own part, we see promise in new coalitions of community organizations, schools, and universities that are attempting to sponsor job training for older youth and young adults, technology-rich after-school programs for children, and technology access for the wider community (Hill, 2001; Hull , 2000a), all in an effort to close the "digital divide," develop local expertise, and assist residents of low-income communities in laying claim to current economic opportunities. Documenting the development of such coalitions and assessing their influence on individuals and communities are important focuses for research.

We ignore at our students' peril the close connections that exist between economic change, the material conditions of people's lives, and literacy and literacy learning. Yet these connections have not often been acknowledged in school-based research on literacy. Brandt (1999) provides a cogent warning:

> Downsizing, migrations, welfare cutbacks, commercial development, transportation, consolidation, or technological innovations do not merely form the background buzz of contemporary life. These changes, where they occur, can wipe out as well as create access to supports for literacy learning. They also can inflate or deflate the value of existing forms of literacy in the lives of students. Any of these changes can have implications for the status of literacy practices in school and for the ways students might interact with literacy lessons. (p. 391)

In our theorizing, Brandt's concerns direct us to place at center stage a historical awareness of the relationship between literacy, the economy, and work and to determine "what enhances or impedes literacy learning under conditions of change" (Brandt, 1999, p. 391).

"Yo no sabia que era bilingue."
(I did not know that you were bilingual.)

A bilingual Latina in the third grade, Martha likes to tell jokes and show her wit when she interacts with people she knows and trusts, such as friends at Las Redes, their after-school program. During the program, children not only collaborate with each other and UCLA undergraduates as they play and master a variety of computer-related games and puzzles but also venture into cyberspace. A centerpiece of the children's activities is an e-mail exchange with a mysterious entity named "El Maga," whose identity and gender are objects of great speculation but ultimately remain unknown. Children recount to El Maga their progress in completing various computer games and related activities and report any difficulties they encounter. El Maga, for his or her part, is known to ask a lot of questions, as well as to initiate quite personal dialogues with individual children. The intent of these e-mail exchanges is fostering children's participation in and affiliation with Las Redes—socializing them, if you will, into the culture of an after-school activity system.

Martha begins her correspondence with El Maga by referencing the, at times, frustrating experiences she has had playing a computer game that has as its central character a frog. Martha writes in one early message:

dear El Maga, are are you? The pond was little bit harder. I couldn't understand the game and Christina [UCLA undergraduate] helped me figure it out. In the end, I passed the first level and I was surprised. thanks for writing to me.

And El Maga responds:

Dear Martha,

   I am doing pretty good, thank you for asking!!! How are you?? I hope you still have that big smile!!! The pond was difficult to figure out, huh? That frog causes many of us problems. It has a mind of its own and sometimes it does not want to do what we program it to do. Que ranita . . . [That mischievous little frog].
   I am glad that Christian helped you figure out the game. What kinds of things did you both do?? Did the frog do every thing you told it to do???

Write back,

El Maga

The next time Martha writes an e-mail message to El Maga, she composes in Spanish. She professes her surprise that El Maga is bilingual, presses El Maga for information on his/her gender, and reports her recent computer game activities. In so doing, Martha demonstrates certain Spanish literacy skills, such as knowledge about formal register, and she indicates as well, through her more familiar salutation and closing, that she is ready to establish a more intimate relationship with El Maga:

Querido/a

Yo no sabia que era bilingue. Usted es mujer or hombre? Haora juque boggle, y un rompe cabesas de batman, y Bertha nos ayudo armario.

Adios, Martha

(Dear

I did not know that you were bilingual. Are you a man or a woman? Today I played boggle, and a Batman puzzle. And Bertha helped us put it together.

Goodbye, Martha.)

Soon, Martha's correspondence with El Maga exhibits not just her proficiency in Spanish, but her "bilingual, bicultural, and biliterate knowledge and skills" (Gutiérrez, Baquedano-López, Alverez, & Chiu, 1999, p. 91), including an interest in cross-cultural language play. Consider the following message:

Dear La Maga

   Don't you like tortillas? Today I played *La Corrida de Toros*. The game was too easy for me, but in the hard level I was too confused because I didn't read the word list because I was too *floja* [lazy]. My brother gave me some candy. The candy was so delicious. Quiere probar some candy? [Would you want to try some candy?] You could . . . buy it in the store! Ha, ha, ha. . . . La Maga, I decided that you are a girl to me because I am a girl and Oscar de la Hoya told me El Maga is *mi admirador preferido* [my biggest fan]. . . . see you later alligator! Ha, ha, ha. I'm soooo happy . . . because I'm scooby-doooooooooooooooooooo! Where are you?∗∗∗ I'm right here∗∗ ha, ha, ha,

Martha

Over the next weeks, Martha continues to demonstrate through her e-mail exchanges with El Maga her fluency in both English and Spanish and a certain sophistication in her choices of language and register. Code-switching words and clauses, she also draws playfully on assumed shared cultural knowledge, alluding in the example above to the well-known Mexican-American boxer, Oscar de la Hoya, as well as to elements of children's popular culture, such as cartoons. A happy, outgoing, playful child at Las Redes, Martha soon begins, in collaboration with the undergraduates and El Maga, to use an array of written language skills to represent these facets of herself in print as well as in speech.

Martha's story comes from Gutiérrez, Baquedano-Löpez, Alverez, and Chiu (1999), who bring activity theory to bear on the study of children's language and literacy development. The Las Redes after-school club operates out of an urban elementary school located near the Los Angeles International Airport and represents one instantiation of Cole's Fifth Dimension project (e.g., Cole, 1996). Combining play and learning, Las Redes provides a context where collaboration is the order of the day and where the children and their undergraduate amigos/as from UCLA can mix languages, registers, and genres, or in Gutiérrez's terms, engage in hybrid language and literacy practices. Gutiérrez and colleagues argue the importance of creating such contexts for learning where hybridity can flourish, "particularly in a time when English-only, anti-immigrant, and anti-affirmative action sentiments influence, if not dominate, educational policy and practice" (p. 92).

The work of Gutiérrez and her colleagues (see also Gutiérrez, Baquedano-Löpez, & Tejeda, 1999; Gutiérrez, Baquedano-Löpez, & Turner, 1997) calls attention to after-school programs that support children's and youths' intellectual and social development by providing supplementary instruction and, as in this and other instantiations of Cole's Fifth Dimension project, constructing new, theoretically motivated learning environments or "activity systems." Such programs can serve a range of important functions, including helping us to re-imagine classrooms and students. As Gutiérrez and others have shown, children often interact and learn in very competent ways after school, despite poor records and reputations within traditional classrooms (Gutiérrez, Baquedano-Löpez, & Turner, 1997). And as Cole points out, after-school programs can reorganize learning so that typical student-teacher relationships and participant structures are turned on their heads. He writes, "This unusually heterogeneous distribution of knowledge and skill is a great resource for reordering everyday power relations, thereby creating interesting changes in the typical division of labor" (Cole, 1996, p. 298). He emphasizes, as well, the importance of choice–children participate voluntarily—but choice balanced by discipline and learning infused with play and imagination.

One of the complexities of such programs is the need, often voiced by funders, for formal evaluations to determine whether and how such programs promote in-school academic achievement. There is little research in that area, nor do investigators frequently address the various purposes and various kinds of achievement characteristic of in- and out-of-school programs. Another important issue is sustainability. Cole (1996) and Underwood, Welsh, Gauvain, and Duffy (2000) caution that after-school programs must confront issues of sustainability at an early stage. If such programs are to last, to become viable community institutions that outlast their founders' interest, then they must be accompanied by structural changes within both community institutions, such as YMCAs and Boys' and Girls' Clubs and churches, and university partners. Documenting the development and evolution of such community institutions as well as their impact on individual and community development is an important task for research.

There is a further tension that after-school programs must continually address: To what extent should they become school-like organizations—serving essentially as arms of classrooms that extend the school day, providing assistance with homework and safe spaces for youth after school—and to what extent might they define themselves apart from schools as alternative sites for alternative learning? The push will be for the former, given the current availability of federal and local funding for after-school programs and given the tendency of textbook publishers and other vendors to provide standardized and pre-packaged materials. The danger is that we will lose a currently available creative space for doing academics differently as well as for broadening learning opportunities (Eidman-Aadahl, 2002).

When researchers such as Dyson (1987) first began to document unofficial literacy practices in school, such as passing notes, there was worry that bringing those forms of writing into the official curriculum would take away the interest and delight that students found in them. In a similar vein, there is sometimes concern about attempts to import to school new literacy practices that flourish in after-school programs and other after-school settings. This concern often arises in connection with new technologies, such as multimedia composition, Web-based writing, and chat rooms and other sites for identity construction and playful writing, such as those documented by Lankshear and Knobel (1997b). The concern is that, if school appropriates these subversive forms, they may become domesticated and lose their vigor and appeal. On the other hand, an important opportunity to address the "digital divide" comes with preparing teachers to think differently about what counts as literacy in new times and to provide schools with technology, making these opportunities available to more students. We urge researchers and educators to ask, How can schools and classrooms, after-school programs, and other informal educational settings incorporate, without co-opting, children and youth's sub rosa literacy practices?

CONCLUSION

At the heart of the theoretical positions that we have rehearsed above, and at least implicitly the raison d'être for much of the research on out-of-school literacy and learning that we have reviewed, is the democratic impulse of inclusiveness. With the realization that so many children, youth, and adults have fared poorly at schooling came the desire to understand why, and that analysis moved forward by moving away from a sole focus on classrooms and toward a broader examination of life and learning in families, communities, and organizations. In this article we aimed to identify and salute the conceptual advances in theories of literacy that have arisen from non-school-based research, giving special attention to the historical roots of current theories. A second aim was to highlight recent research on literacy in out-of-school settings that exemplifies the range and dimensions of current work to suggest future directions for literacy theory and practice.

As we have illustrated, when researchers have looked at literacy out of school, their goals have been several:

1. Decouple the effects of literacy from the effects of schooling, asking,
   a. What are the cognitive consequences of literacy separate from the always-mediating impact of formal schooling?
   b. How are our conceptions of literacy constrained by one version of literacy—schooled literacy?
2. Develop the notion of literacy as multiple, asking,
   a. How do language and literacy practices in homes and communities differ from those valued in school?
   b. What new forms of and technologies for literacy exist out of school?
3. Account for school failure and out-of-school success, asking,
   a. What resources do children and youth from diverse backgrounds and cultures and socioeconomic groups bring to the classroom?
   b. What are the differences between contexts, conceptions of knowledge, and performance for successful learners outside school and unsuccessful learners in school?

4. Identify additional support mechanisms for children, youth, and adults, asking,
   a. What institutions can support learning in addition to our beleaguered schools?
   b. How can out-of-school learning environments serve as stimuli for rethinking schools and classrooms?

5. Push our notions of learning and development, asking,
   a. What understandings of mature versions of social practices can be found in out-of-school settings that we can connect to child or adult learning?
   b. How might we document the intersection of literacy with social identity or study the connection of ways of reading and writing to ways of talking, acting, interacting, valuing, and being in the world?
   c. How might we cultivate a long and broad view of learning, one that focuses on "human lives seen as trajectories through multiple social practices in various social institutions"? (This quotation is from Gee, Hull, & Lankshear, 1996, p. 4.)

As a future direction for theory and research, we call for an examination of the relationships between school and nonschool contexts. Surveying the recent research on out-of-school literacies, we see four categories of questions that are useful for shaping a new research agenda. First are questions about how to bridge students' worlds with classroom practice, including the following: How might out-of-school identities, social practices, and the literacies that they recruit be leveraged in the classroom? How might teachers incorporate students' out-of-school interests and predilections but also extend the range of the literacies with which they are conversant?

Second are questions about (re)conceptualizing students and communities: How can we support educators in developing the habit of mind that students are able, and what can after-school settings teach us in this regard? What special skills are required of teachers to nurture students whose critical consciousness as members of oppressed groups is finely honed and who may not be predisposed to display the competence they possess? How can teachers and researchers learn about and participate in communities apart from school in a respectful and reciprocal manner?

Third are questions that bridge theory and practice in their interrogation of the relative value and place of diverse literacy practices: What should the relationship be between the literacies taught at school and the literacies practiced in other contexts? How much, for example, should the workplace influence the curriculum, and what is the value of essayist texts? What forms of schooled literacy are powerful intellectual tools, appropriate for these new times, and what forms are mere conventions or historical artifacts?

Finally, there are numerous questions about the nature, development, and practices of after-school programs: How might we document the development of coalitions among community-based organizations, schools, and universities and assess their influence on individuals and communities? How can after-school programs be sustained? What purposes do such programs serve and what kinds of achievement do they foster, in contrast to and in complementarity with schools? How can schools and classrooms, after-school programs, and other informal educational settings incorporate, without co-opting, children and youths' sub rosa literacy practices?

Research on literacy and out-of-school learning, we have argued, can help us think anew about literacy teaching and learning across a range of contexts, including school. Given the vast gulfs that separate and continue to widen between children and youth who flourish in school and those who do not, between the privileged and the disenfranchised, there is no better time for literacy theorists and researchers, long practiced in detailing the successful literate practices that occur outside school, to direct their energies toward investigating potential relationships, collaborations, and helpful divisions of labor between schools and formal classrooms and the informal learning that flourishes in a range of out-of-school settings.

NOTES

[1] The authors gratefully acknowledge the detailed and insightful commentary provided by three anonymous RER reviewers. An expanded version of this article appears in Hull & Schultz (2002).

[2] A fourth theoretical tradition that we included in our early analysis was sociocultural perspectives on writing. We have not included that tradition in this article because it was primarily school based and because it drew heavily on other traditions, especially the ethnography of communication in combination with cognitively oriented studies of writing. See Freedman, Dyson, Flower, & Chafe (1987).

[3] Later, Scribner provided an account of her literacy research with Cole in terms of contemporary activity theory (1997).

[4] Because the New Literacy Studies is new as a tradition of research in comparison with the other traditions that we review, our account of its historical development is relatively truncated.

[5] We do not review here but want to acknowledge the important scholarship associated with "critical discourse analysis," a field that, like the critical literacy area, is politically alert but uses the tools of discourse analysis to critique and challenge dominant institutional practices. See, for example, Fairclough (1995).

[6] Most of our vignettes are written in the ethnographic present. We are aware of the dangers of representing people as static and their situations as perpetual, but have chosen to write in present tense in an effort to make our vignettes more engaging.

REFERENCES

Adler-Kassner, L., Crooks, R., & Watters, A. (Eds.). (1997). *Writing in the community: Concepts and models for service-learning in composition.* Washington, DC: American Association for Higher Education.

Alvermann, D. E., Moon, J. S., & Hagood, M. C. (1999). *Popular culture in the classroom: Teaching and researching critical media literacy.* Newark, DE: International Reading Association.

Alvermann, D. E., Young, J. P., Green, C., & Wiseman, J. M. (1999). Adolescents' perceptions and negotiations of literacy practices in afterschool read and talk clubs. *American Educational Research Journal, 36,* 221–264.

Barton, D. (1991). The social nature of writing. In D. Barton & R. Ivanic (Eds.), *Writing in the community* (pp. 1–13). Newbury Park, CA: Sage.

Barton, D. (1994). *Literacy: An introduction to the ecology of written language.* Oxford, UK: Blackwell.

Barton, D., & Hamilton, M. (1998). *Local literacies: Reading and writing in one community.* London: Routledge.

Barton, D., & Hamilton, M. (2000). Literacy practices. In D. Barton, M. Hamilton, & R. Ivanic (Eds.), *Situated literacies: Reading and writing in context* (pp. 180–196). London: Routledge.

Barton, D., Hamilton, M., & Ivanic, R. (Eds.). (2000). *Situated literacies: Reading and writing in context.* London: Routledge.

Barton, D., & Ivanic, R. (Eds.). (1991). *Writing in the community.* Newbury Park, CA: Sage Publications.

Basso, K. (1974). The ethnography of writing. In R. Bauman & J. Sherzer (Eds.), *Explorations in the ethnography of speaking* (pp. 425–432). Cambridge, UK: Cambridge University Press.

Beaufort, A. (1999). *Writing in the real world: Making the transition from school to work.* New York: Teachers College Press.

Bourdieu, P. (1977). *Outline of a theory of practice* (R. Nice, Trans.). Cambridge, UK: Cambridge University Press.

Brandt, D. (1999). Literacy learning and economic change. *Harvard Educational Review, 69*(4), 373–394.

Breier, M., Taetsane, M., & Sait, L. (1996). Taking literacy for a ride—reading and writing in the taxi industry. In M. Prinsloo & M. Breier (Eds.), *The social uses of literacy: Theory and practice in contemporary South Africa* (pp. 213–233). Cape Town, South Africa: Sached Books.

Camitta, M. (1993). Vernacular writing: Varieties of literacy among Philadelphia high school students. In B. V. Street (Ed.), *Cross-cultural approaches to literacy* (pp. 228–246). Cambridge, UK: Cambridge University Press.

Cazden, C. B. (1981). Four comments. In D. H. Hymes (Ed.), *Ethnographic monitoring of children's acquisition of reading/language arts skills in and out of the classroom.* Final report for the National Institute of Education, Philadelphia.

Cazden, C. B., John, V. P., & Hymes, D. (Eds.). (1972). *Functions of language in the classroom.* New York: Teachers College Press.

Cintron, R. (1991). Reading and writing graffiti: A reading. *Quarterly Newsletter of the Laboratory of Comparative Human Cognition, 13,* 21–24.

Clark, R., & Ivanic, R. (1997). *The politics of writing.* London: Routledge.

Cochran-Smith, M. (1986). Reading to children: A model for understanding texts. In B. B. Schieffelin & P. Gilmore (Eds.), *The acquisition of literacy: Ethnographic perspectives* (pp. 35–54). Norwood, NJ: Ablex.

Cole, M. (1995). The supra-individual envelope of development: Activity and practice, situation and context. In J. J. Goodnow, P. J. Miller, & F. Kessel (Eds.), *Cultural practices as contexts for development* (pp. 105–118). San Francisco: Jossey-Bass.

Cole, M. (1996). *Cultural psychology: A once and future discipline.* Cambridge, MA: Harvard University Press.

Cole, M., Engeström, Y., & Vásquez, O. (1997). Introduction. In M. Cole, Y. Engeström, & O. Vásquez (Eds.), *Mind, culture, and activity: Seminal papers from the Laboratory of Comparative Human Cognition* (pp. 1–21). Cambridge, UK: Cambridge University Press.

Cole, M., & Means, B. (1981). *Comparative studies of how people think: An introduction.* Cambridge, MA: Harvard University Press.

Cole, M., & Traupmann, I. (1981). Comparative cognitive research: Learning from a learning disabled child. In W. A. Collins (Ed.), *Minnesota symposia on child psychology: Vol. 14. Aspects of the development of competence* (pp. 125–154). Hillsdale, NJ: Lawrence Erlbaum.

Cook-Gumperz, J. (1986). Literacy and schooling: An unchanging equation? In J. Cook-Gumperz (Ed.), *The social construction of literacy* (pp. 16–44). Cambridge, UK: Cambridge University Press.

Cope, B., & Kalantzis, M. (Eds.). (2000). *Multiliteracies: Literacy learning and the design of social futures.* London: Routledge.

Cushman, E. (1998). *The struggle and the tools: Oral and literate strategies in an inner city community.* Albany, NY: SUNY Press.

Damon, W. (1990). Reconciling the literacies of generations. *Daedalus, 119*(2), 33–53.

Darrah, C. (1996). *Learning and work: An exploration in industrial ethnography.* New York: Garland.

Dias, P., Freedman, A., Medway, P., & Paré, A. (1999). *Worlds apart: Acting and writing in academic and workplace contexts.* Mahwah, NJ: Lawrence Erlbaum.

Dyson, A. H. (1987). The value of time-off task: Young children's spontaneous talk and deliberate text. *Harvard Educational Review, 57,* 396–420.

Dyson, A. H. (1997). *Writing superheroes: Contemporary childhood, popular culture, and classroom literacy.* New York: Teachers College Press.

Dyson, A. H. (1999). Coach Bombay's kids learn to write: Children's appropriation of media material for school literacy. *Research in the Teaching of English, 33*(4), 367–402.

Dyson, A. H. (in press). The stolen lipstick of overheard song: Composing voices in child song, verse, and written text. In M. Nystrand & J. Duffy (Eds.), *Towards a rhetoric of everyday life.* Madison: University of Wisconsin Press.

Eidman-Aadahl, E. (2002). Got some time, got a place, got the word: Collaborating for literacy learning and youth development. In G. Hull & K. Schultz (Eds.), *School's out! Bridging out-of-school literacies with classroom practice* (pp. 241–260). New York: Teachers College Press.

Eisenhart, M. (2002). Changing conceptions of culture and ethnographic methodology: Recent thematic shifts and their implications for research on teaching. In V. Richardson (Ed.), *The handbook of research on teaching* (4th edition) (pp. 209–225). New York: Macmillan.

Engeström, Y. (1987). *Learning by expanding: An activity-theoretical approach to developmental research.* Helsinki: Orienta-Konsulit.

Engeström, Y. (1993). The working health center project: Materializing zones of proximal development in a network of organizational learning. Paper presented at the 10th annual Work Now and in the Future Conference, Portland, OR.

Engeström, Y. (1998). Distinguishing individual action and collective activity in the study of organizational literacy. Paper presented at the annual meeting of the American Educational Research Association, San Diego, CA.

Engeström, Y., Miettinen, R., & Punamäki, R-L. (Eds.). (1999). *Perspectives on activity theory.* Cambridge, UK: Cambridge University Press.

Fairclough, N. (1995). *Critical discourse analysis: The critical study of language.* New York: Longman.

Finders, M. J. (1997). *Just girls: Hidden literacies and life in junior high.* New York: Teachers College Press.

Fishman, A. (1988). *Amish literacy: What and how it means.* Portsmouth, NH: Heinemann.

Flower, L. (1997). Partners in inquiry: A logic for community outreach. In L. Adler-Kassner, R. Crooks, & A. Watters (Eds.), *Writing the community: Concepts and models for service-learning in composition* (pp. 95–117). Washington, DC: American Association of Higher Education.

Flower, L. (in press). Talking across difference: An activity analysis of situated knowledge, conflict, and construction. In C. Bazerman & D. R. Russell (Eds.), *Activity and interactivity: A collection of research and theory.*

Flower, L., Long, E., & Higgins, L. (2000). *Learning to rival: The practice of intercultural inquiry.* Hillsdale, NJ: Lawrence Erlbaum.

Foucault, M. (1972). *The archaeology of knowledge and the discourse on language* (A. M. Sheridan Smith, Trans.). New York: Pantheon Books.

Freedman, S. W., Dyson, A. H., Flower, L., & Chafe, W. (1987). *Research in writing: Past, present, and future* (Tech. Rep. No. 1). Berkeley and Pittsburgh: University of California, Berkeley, and Carnegie Mellon University, Center for the Study of Writing.

Freire, P. (1970). *Pedagogy of the oppressed.* New York: Seabury Press.

Freire, P., & Macedo, D. (1987). *Literacy: Reading the word and the world.* South Hadley, MA: Bergin and Garvey.

Gee, J. P. (1996). *Social linguistics and literacies: Ideology in Discourses* (2nd ed.). London: Falmer Press.

Gee, J. P. (2000a). New people in new worlds: Networks, the new capitalism and schools. In B. Cope & M. Kalantzis (Eds.), *Multiliteracies: Literacy learning and the design of social futures* (pp. 43–68). London: Routledge.

Gee, J. P. (2000b). The New Literacy Studies: From socially situated to the work of the social. In D. Barton, M. Hamilton, & R. Ivanic (Eds.), *Situated literacies: Reading and writing in context* (pp. 180–196). London: Routledge.

Gee, J. P., Hull, G., & Lankshear, C. (1996). *The new work order: Behind the language of the new capitalism.* Boulder, CO: Westview.

Giddens, A. (1979). *Central problems in social theory: Action, structure, and contradiction in social analysis.* Berkeley: University of California Press.

Gilmore, P., & Glatthorn, A. A. (Eds.). (1982). *Children in and out of school: Ethnography and education.* Washington, DC: Center for Applied Linguistics.

Gowen, S. (1992). *The politics of workplace literacy: A case study.* New York: Teachers College Press.

Green, J., & Harker, C. (Eds.). (1988). *Multiple perspective analyses of classroom discourse.* Norwood, NJ: Ablex.

Griffin, P., & Cole, M. (1987). New technologies, basic skills, and the underside of education. In J. A. Langer (Ed.), *Language, literacy and culture: Issues of society and schooling* (pp. 199–231). Norwood, NJ: Ablex.

Gutiérrez, K., Baquedano-López, P., Alverez, H. H., & Chiu, M. M. (1999). Building the culture of collaboration through hybrid language practices. *Theory into Practice, 38*(2), 87–93.

Gutiérrez, K., Baquedano-López, P., & Tejeda, C. (1999). Rethinking diversity: Hybridity and hybrid language practices in the third space. *Mind, Culture, and Activity, 6*(4), 286–303.

Gutiérrez, K., Baquedano-López, P., & Turner, M. G. (1997). Putting language back into language arts: When the radical middle meets the third space. *Language Arts, 74*(5), 368–378.

Hart-Landsberg, S., & Reder, S. (1997). Teamwork and literacy: Teaching and learning at Hardy Industries. In G. Hull (Ed.), *Changing work, changing workers: Critical perspectives on language, literacy, and skills* (pp. 359–382). Albany: State University of New York Press.

Heath, S. B. (1981). Ethnography in education. In D. Hymes (Ed)., *Ethnographic monitoring of children's acquisition of reading/language arts skills in and out of the classroom* (pp. 33–55). Final report for the National Institute of Education, Philadelphia.

Heath, S. B. (1982). Protean shapes in literacy events: Ever-shifting oral and literate traditions. In D. Tannen (Ed.), *Spoken and written language: Exploring orality and literacy* (pp. 91–118). Norwood, NJ: Ablex.

Heath, S. B. (1983). *Ways with words.* New York: Cambridge University Press.

Heath, S. B. (1994). The project of learning from the inner-city youth perspective. In F. A. Villarruel & R. M. Lerner (Eds.), *Promoting community-based programs for socialization and learning* (New Directions for Child Development, No. 63) (pp. 25–34). San Francisco: Jossey-Bass.

Heath, S. B. (1996). Ruling places: Adaptation in development by inner-city youth. In R. Jessor, A. Colby, & R. A. Shweder (Eds.), *Ethnography and human development: Context and meaning in social inquiry* (pp. 225–251). Chicago: University of Chicago Press.

Heath, S. B. (1998a). Living the arts through language plus learning: A report on community-based youth organizations. *Americans for the Arts Monographs, 2*(7), 1–19.

Heath, S. B. (1998b). Working through language. In S. M. Hoyle & C. T. Adger (Eds.), *Kids talk: Strategic language use in later childhood* (pp. 217–240). New York: Oxford University Press.

Heath, S. B., & McLaughlin, M. W. (1993). *Identity and inner-city youth: Beyond ethnicity and gender.* New York: Teachers College Press.

Heller, C. E. (1997). *Until we are strong together: Women writers in the Tenderloin.* New York: Teachers College Press.

Hill, L. (2001). Beyond access: Race, technology, community. In A. Nelson, T. L. N. Tu, & A. H. Hines (Eds.), *Technicolor: Race, technology, and everyday life* (pp. 13–33). New York: New York University Press.

Hornberger, N. H. (1995). Ethnography in linguistic perspective: Understanding school processes. *Language and Education, 9*(4), 233–248.

Hornberger, N. H. (2001). Afterword: Multilingual literacies, literacy practices and the continua of biliteracy. In K. Jones & M. Martin-Jones (Eds.), *Multilingual literacies: Reading and writing different worlds.* Amsterdam: John Benjamins.

Hull, G. (1999). What's in a label? Complicating notions of the skills poor worker. *Written Communication, 16*(4), 379–411.

Hull, G. (2000a). *Bridging the divides: An action research project linking after-school and job-training programs.* Proposal submitted to the University of California Office of the President, Presidential Grants in Education.

Hull, G. (2000b). Critical literacy at work. *Journal of Adolescent and Adult Literacy, 43*(1), 648–652.

Hull, G., Jury, M., Ziv, O., & Katz, M. (1996). *Changing work, changing literacy: A study of skill requirements and development in a traditional and a reorganized workplace.* Final Report to the National Center for Research in Vocational Education and the Center for the Study of Writing and Literacy, Berkeley, CA.

Hull, G., & Schultz, K. (Eds.) (2002). *School's out! Bridging out-of-school literacies with classroom practice.* New York: Teachers College Press.

Hymes, D. (1964). Introduction: Towards ethnographies of communication. In J. J. Gumperz & D. Hymes (Eds.), *The ethnography of communication* (pp. 1–34). Washington, DC: American Anthropology Association.

Hymes, D. (1974). *Foundations of sociolinguistics.* Philadelphia: University of Pennsylvania Press.

Hymes, D. (Ed.). (1981). *Ethnographic monitoring of children's acquisition of reading/language arts skills in and out of the classroom.* Final report for the National Institute of Education, Philadelphia.

Jacobs, E., & Jordan, C. (Eds.). (1993). *Minority education: Anthropological perspectives.* Norwood, NJ: Ablex.

Jones, K. (2000). Becoming just another alphanumeric code: Farmers' encounters with the literacy and discourse practices of agricultural bureaucracy at the livestock auction. In D. Barton, M. Hamilton, & R. Ivanic (Eds.), *Situated literacies: Reading and writing in context* (pp. 70–90). London: Routledge.

Kalantzis, M., & Cope, B. (2000). Changing the role of schools. In B. Cope & M. Kalantzis (Eds.), *Multiliteracies: Literacy learning and the design of social futures* (pp. 121–148). London: Routledge.

Knobel, M. (1999). *Everyday literacies: Students, discourse, and social practice.* New York: Peter Lang.

Kolko, B. E., Nakamura, L., & Rodman, G. B. (Eds.). (2000). *Race in cyberspace.* London: Routledge.

Lankshear, C. (1997). *Changing literacies.* Buckingham, UK: Open University Press.

Lankshear, C., & Knobel, M. (1997a). Critical literacy and active citizenship. In S. Muspratt, A. Luke, & P. Freebody (Eds.), *Constructing critical literacies: Teaching and learning textual practice.* Cresskill, NJ: Hampton Press.

Lankshear, C., & Knobel, M. (1997b). Different worlds? Technology-mediated classroom learning and students' social practices with new technologies in home and community settings. In C. Lankshear, *Changing literacies* (pp. 164–187). Buckingham, UK: Open University Press.

Lave, J. (1988). *Cognition in practice: Mind, mathematics, and culture in everyday life.* Cambridge, UK: Cambridge University Press.

Lee, C. D. (1993). *Signifying as a scaffold for literary interpretation: The pedagogical implications of an African American discourse genre.* Urbana, IL: National Council of Teachers of English.

Lee, C. D. (2000). The cultural modeling project's multimedia records of practice: Analyzing guided participation across time. Paper presented at the annual meeting of the American Educational Research Association, New Orleans.

Long, E., Peck, W. C., & Baskins, J. A. (2002). STRUGGLE: A literate practice supporting life-project planning. In G. Hull & K. Schultz (Eds.), *School's out! Bridging out-of-school literacies with classroom practice.* New York: Teachers College Press.

Luke, A., & Freebody, P. (1997). Critical literacy and the question of normativity: An introduction. In S. Muspratt, A. Luke, & P. Freebody (Eds.), *Constructing critical literacies: Teaching and learning textual practice.* Cresskill, NJ: Hampton Press.

Luria, A. R. (1976). *Cognitive development: Its cultural and social foundations* (M. Cole, Ed.; M. Lopez-Morillas & L. Solotarofs, Trans.). Cambridge, MA: Harvard University Press.

Mahiri, J. (1998). *Shooting for excellence: African American and youth culture in new century schools.* Urbana, IL: National Council of Teachers of English.

Majors, Y. (2000). Talk that talk: Discourse norms transversing school and community. Paper presented at the annual meeting of the American Educational Research Association, New Orleans.

Maybin, J. (2000). The New Literacy Studies: Context, intertextuality and discourse. In D. Barton, M. Hamilton, & R. Ivanic (Eds.), *Situated literacies: Reading and writing in context* (pp. 197–209). London: Routledge.

McDermott, R. (1993). The acquisition of a child by a learning disability. In S. Chaiklin & J. Lave (Eds.), *Understanding practice: Perspectives on activity and context* (pp. 269–305). New York: Cambridge University Press.

Miettinen, R. (1999). Transcending traditional school learning: Teachers' work and networks of learning. In Y. Engeström, R. Miettinen, & R-L. Punamäki (Eds.), *Perspectives on activity theory* (pp. 325–344). Cambridge, UK: Cambridge University Press.

Moje, E. B. (2000). To be part of the story: The literacy practices of gangsta adolescents. *Teachers College Record, 102*(3), 651–690.

Moll, L. C. (1992). Bilingual classroom studies and community analysis: Some recent trends. *Educational Researcher, 21*(3), 20–24.

Moll, L. C., & Diaz, S. (1987). Change as the goal of educational research. *Anthropology & Education Quarterly, 18,* 300–311.

Moll, L. C., & Greenberg, J. B. (1990). Creating zones of possibilities: Combining social context for instruction. In L. C. Moll (Ed.), *Vygotsky and education: Instructional implications and applications of sociohistorical psychology.* (pp. 319–348) Cambridge, UK: Cambridge University Press.

Moss, B. (Ed.). (1994). *Literacy across communities.* Cresskill, NJ: Hampton Press.

New London Group. (1996). A pedagogy of multiliteracies: Designing social futures. *Harvard Educational Review, 66*(1), 60–92.

Norton Peirce, B. (1995). Social identity, investment, and language learning. *TESOL Quarterly, 29*(1), 9–31.

Peck, W. C., Flower, L., & Higgins, L. (1995). Community literacy. *College Composition and Communication, 46,* 199–222.

Prinsloo, M., & Breier, M. (1996). *The social uses of literacy: Theory and practice in contemporary South Africa.* Bertsham, South Africa: Sached Books.

Rivers, A., Hutchinson, K., & Dixon, K. (2000). Participatory appropriation in a cultural modeling classroom. Paper presented at the annual meeting of the American Educational Research Association, New Orleans.

Rockhill, K. (1993). Gender, language and the politics of literacy. In B. V. Street (Ed.), *Cross-cultural approaches to literacy* (pp. 156–175). Cambridge, UK: Cambridge University Press.

Russell, D. R. (1997). Writing and genre in higher education and workplaces: A review of studies that use cultural-historical activity theory. *Mind, Culture, and Activity: An International Journal, 4*(4), 224–237.

Saxe, G. B. (1988). Candy selling and math learning. *Educational Researcher,* August-September, 14–21.

Schultz, K. (2002). Looking across space and time: Reconceptualizing literacy learning in and out of school. *Research in the Teaching of English, 36*(3), 356–390.

Scribner, S. (1997). Mind in action: A functional approach to thinking. In M. Cole, Y. Engeström, & O. Vösquez (Eds.), *Mind, culture, and activity: Seminal papers from the Laboratory of Comparative Human Cognition* (pp. 354–68). Cambridge, UK: Cambridge University Press.

Scribner, S., & Cole, M. (1981). *The psychology of literacy.* Cambridge, MA: Harvard University Press.

Shuman, A. (1986). *Storytelling rights: The uses of oral and written texts among urban adolescents.* Cambridge, UK: Cambridge University Press.

Shuman, A. (1993). Collaborative writing: Appropriating power or reproducing authority? In B. V. Street (Ed.), *Cross-cultural approaches to literacy* (pp. 247–271). Cambridge, UK: Cambridge University Press.

Skilton-Sylvester, E. (2002). Literate at home but not at school: A Cambodian girl's journey from playwright to struggling writer. In G. Hull & K. Schultz (Eds.), *School's out! Bridging out-of-school literacies with classroom practice.* (pp. 61–90) New York: Teachers College Press.

Street, B. V. (Ed.). (1993a). *Cross-cultural approaches to literacy.* Cambridge, UK: Cambridge University Press.

Street, B. V. (1993b). The New Literacy Studies: Guest editorial. *Journal of Research in Reading, 16*(2), 81–97.

Street, B. V. (1995). *Social literacies: Critical approaches to literacy in development, ethnography and education.* London: Longman.

Street, B. V. (1996). Preface. In M. Prinsloo & M. Breier (Eds.), *The social uses of literacy: Theory and practice in contemporary South Africa* (pp. 1–9). Bertsham, South Africa: Sached Books.

Street, B. V. (2001). Literacy events and literacy practices: Theory and practice in the New Literacy Studies. In K. Jones & M. Martin-Jones (Eds.), *Multilingual literacies: Comparative perspectives on research and practice* (pp. 17–29). Amsterdam: John Benjamins.

Street, J. C., & Street, B. V. (1991). The schooling of literacy. In D. Barton & R. Ivanic (Eds.), *Writing in the community* (pp. 106–131). Newbury Park, CA: Sage.

Szwed, J. F. (1981). The ethnography of literacy. In M. F. Whiteman (Ed.), *Writing: The nature, development, and teaching of written communication. Part 1* (pp. 13–23). Hillsdale, NJ: Lawrence Erlbaum.

Taylor, D., & Dorsey-Gaines, C. (1988). *Growing up literate: Learning from inner-city families.* Portsmouth, NH: Heinemann.

Underwood, C., Welsh, M., Gauvain, M., & Duffy, S. (2000). Learning at the edges: Challenges to the sustainability of service-learning in higher education. *Language and Learning Across the Disciplines, 4*(3), 7–26.

Vásquez, O. A. (1993). A look at language as resource: Lessons from La Clase Mögica. In B. Arias & U. Casanova (Eds.), *Bilingual education: Politics, research, and practice* (pp. 119–224). Chicago: National Society for the Study of Education.

Vygotsky, L. (1978). *Mind and society: The development of higher psychological processes.* (M. Cole, V. John-Steiner, S. Scribner, & E. Souberman, Eds.). Cambridge, MA: Harvard University Press.

Vygotsky, L. (1986). *Thought and language.* (A. Kozulin, Ed.). Cambridge, MA: MIT Press.

Weinstein-Shr, G. (1993). Literacy and social process: A community in transition. In B. V. Street (Ed.), *Cross-cultural approaches to literacy* (pp. 272–293). Cambridge, UK: Cambridge University Press.

Wertsch, J. (1985). *Vygotsky and the social formation of mind.* Cambridge, MA: Harvard University Press.

Wertsch, J. (1991). *Voices of the mind: A sociocultural approach to mediated action.* Cambridge, MA: Harvard University Press.

Yin-yee Ko, D. (1989). Toward a social history of women in 17th-century China. Unpublished doctoral dissertation, Stanford University.

QUESTIONS TO THINK ABOUT

1. Hull and Schultz trace the history of out-of-school literacy and document its theoretical basis. Make a chart listing the researchers, the significant points of their theories, and their relationship to out-of-school learning. Why, generally, are these theories important and what do you learn from this exercise about the changing ideas of what literacy is and its role across contexts and cultures?

2. To show how literacy occurs in various out-of-school settings, Hull and Schultz present four "vignettes" or case studies. Describe each one briefly, including the participants, the literacy activities they engage in, and the "literate and discursive strategies they use." How do these activities and practices draw on "tacit knowledge of cultural forms found outside school"? How are they related to activities of everyday living and the workplace?

3. The authors quote the Brazilian educator Paulo Freire, who said, "Reading the world always precedes reading the word, and reading the word implies continually reading the world . . . [and] transforming it by means of conscious practical work." Try to explain what you think Freire means. How are his ideas related to the general perspective Hull and Schultz present that literacy is connected to culture, identity, power, and language?

4. *Extending your understanding*: Hull and Schultz ask three related questions: "How might out-of-school identities, social practices, and the literacies that they recruit be leveraged in the classroom? How might teachers incorporate students' out-of-school interests and predilections but also extend the range of the literacies with which youth are conversant? And in what ways must our ways of thinking about what constitutes curriculum and pedagogy be modified to appeal to students who do not fit the common mold?" Based on what you have read as well as your own knowledge and experience, try to answer these three questions. Be as specific as you can in listing and explaining what could and probably should be transferred to the school environment.

TERMS TO DEFINE

Define the following words and phrases as they are presented within the context of the reading. Comment on your understanding of the significance of each one.

Dell Hymes
Shirley Brice Heath
New Literacy Studies
Literacy practices
Literacy events
Ethnography of communication
Continuity-discontinuity theory

Understanding Critical Writing

A. Suresh Canagarajah
Baruch College, CUNY

So what happens to writing when you attach the word *critical* to it? Does anything happen at all? Is this another newfangled label that promotes a novel pedagogy or method for purely commercial reasons or other ulterior motivations without substantially affecting the writing activity? Or, on the other hand, is too much happening—far too much for our liking—shifting our attention to things unrelated to writing? Is this label bringing into composition something extraneous to the writing activity, such as political causes and social concerns that are the whims of one scholarly circle or the other? We in the teaching profession are rightly suspicious of anything that claims to be new, fashionable, or revolutionary nowadays.

For me, the label *critical* brings into sharper focus matters that are always there in writing. It develops an attitude and a perspective that enable us to see some of the hidden components of text construction and the subtler ramifications of writing. We gain these insights by situating the text in a rich context comprising diverse social institutions and experiential domains. In doing so, the label also alerts us to the power—and dangers—of literacy. Texts can open up new possibilities for writers and their communities—just as illiteracy or ineffective writing can deny avenues for advancement. Writing can bring into being new orientations to the self and the world—just as passive, complacent, or mechanical writing parrots the established view of things (which may serve the unfair, partisan interests of dominant institutions and social groups). Indeed, the text is shaped by such processes of conflict, struggle, and change that characterize society. By connecting the text to context (or the word to the world), the critical perspective enables us to appreciate the complexity of writing and address issues of literacy that have far-reaching social implications.

DEFINING THE CRITICAL

Before I spell out how *critical* redefines writing, we should consider briefly the currency of the label itself. We have by now come across critical theory, critical thinking, critical pedagogy, critical ethnography, critical linguistics, critical discourse analysis, and even critical classroom discourse analysis—just to mention a few.[1] We can of course go on attaching this label to any field we want because there is something predictable and distinctive that happens when we do so. It is natural for us to think of *uncritical* as the opposite of this label. But it is unfair to say that those who don't practice a critical approach are choosing to be apathetic or naive. There are good reasons why someone may choose to adopt an alternative approach. Indicative of these more serious motivations are terms like *objective, detached, disinterested, pragmatic, formalistic,* and *abstract.* These adjectives are less pejorative antonyms for the term *critical.*

To understand the ways these terms relate to each other, we need to take a brief detour through history. The Enlightenment movement of seventeenth-century Europe has much to do with the values attached to these terms. Taking pride in adopting a more rational, systematic, and scientific approach to things, the movement initiated radical changes in many domains of inquiry. Its effects are still there in certain traditions of the study of writing. In order to understand writing, the movement would have said, we need first to identify and demarcate the object of our analysis—the text. We should separate the "text-in-itself" from other related activities and domains so that it can speak for itself. For example, the writer's intentions, feelings, values, and interests should be separated from the text. Neither is the text the reader's processing of it in terms of his or her intentions, feelings, values, and interests. Also, the scholar must see to it that he or she doesn't bring any biases or predisposition to the analysis. This disinterested attitude was considered favorable to letting the object speak for itself. At its best, the study of the text could be undertaken without any involvement of the scholar by employing predesigned procedures and methods. As a culmination of the Enlightenment tendency, Structuralism took the scholar further inside the isolated text. It claimed that if one entered the core of the text, cutting through the superficial clutter of content, meaning, and surface structural variations, one would discover the basic underlying rules that account for the text's universal laws of production and reception. This attitude encouraged an abstract and formalistic approach. Schools as diverse as New Criticism in literature, text linguistics in discourse analysis, and the "current traditional" paradigm in rhetoric display such an approach today. Literacy instruction, influenced by this tendency, has been formalistic, skill driven, and product oriented.

The cultivation of such an empirical perspective on texts was certainly productive in many ways. It brought a clarity, discipline, and rigor to the descriptive activity. Getting the predisposition of human subjects muddled in the analysis, or getting distracted by superficial variations, can be misleading. The approach certainly generated important insights into certain general properties of textuality and literacy. But there is also something lost in this type of approach. For the sake of analytical convenience we are deliberately simplifying the disposition and implications of texts. The text becomes more and more isolated, detached, abstract, and generic. The values that inform its structure and form are ignored. It becomes empty of content, losing its complexity and depth. With the decontextualized approach, the influences of social conditions and cultural diversity on text construction are lost. The ways in which texts are shaped by, and in turn shape, sociopolitical realities are obscured. Much of this happens because the text has become static, passive, and one-dimensional. Writers and readers themselves become automatons who employ predesigned formal procedures with detachment to generate texts. All this amounts to adopting an innocence and complacency toward the literate activity. As a corrective, the critical approach grounds the text in the material world to orientate to its troubling social functions, the value-ridden nature of its constitution, and the conflicting motivations behind its production and reception.

Now let's return to our original question: how does the critical orientation redefine writing? We may summarize the shifts in perspective in the following manner.

- *From writing as autonomous to writing as situated.* The production of texts is not an end in itself. We don't write simply to produce a text—and leave it at that. We produce texts to achieve certain interests and purposes. Furthermore, after a text is produced, it gets used in unanticipated ways. Launched into the public world, it takes a life of its own and effects results and processes totally unanticipated by the writer. Therefore, texts not only *mean* but *do.* Their functionality goes to the extent of reconstructing reality, rather than simply reflecting reality. We need to inquire what the word does to/in the world.

- *From writing as individualistic to writing as social.* For many of us, the stock image of writing is that of the lonely writer locked away in his small apartment (in crowded New York City) or a cabin (in the quiet woods of New England) pouring his thoughts on paper under mysteriously received inspiration. But writing is not a monologue; it is dialogical. One has to take account of the audience (implicitly or explicitly) while writing. This may involve a set of intended audiences, but it also involves an ever-expanding unintended audience (stretching limitlessly across time and space). In constructing a text, a writer is conducting a conversation with all this diversity of readers. This process is different from the definition of it we get from communication theory—which is often diagrammed as follows: writer → text → reader (or speaker → words → listener). Writing is not a one-way transmission of ideas, nor are constructs like writer and text autonomous. The writer's "intentions" and "thoughts" are considerably influenced by the expectations, norms, and values of the audience (or community). The text itself then becomes a *mediated* construct—one that is shaped by the struggle/collaboration/interplay between the writer, reader, and the community for thought. We have to become sensitive to how the text embodies the influences of this social interaction.

- *From writing as cognitive to writing as material.* For many, writing is a purely mental activity of putting down on paper the relevant ideas, words, and information that one has the capacity to generate. They view writing as a play between the mind and the text for meaning, order, and coherence. But there are many material resources required to do writing. At the simplest level, one needs a pencil, pen, typewriter, or computer to compose one's thoughts. Which of these one uses is often decided by one's economic status. Each of these instruments presents different levels of advantage to the writer. Furthermore, one needs to be privileged to devote the time required for writing. Writers also need the means to tap necessary resources from publishers, libraries, media industries, and the market. The text is shaped out of a negotiation of these constraints and resources. How these material factors impinge upon the text requires examination.

- *From writing as formal to writing as ideological.* Another commonsense assumption is that one only needs grammar, structure, and rules to construct a text. These are treated as abstract, value-free features of textual form. But writing is more than language or structure. It is also a representation of reality, an embodiment of values, and a presentation of self. Form itself is informed by diverse conventions of textuality, values of appropriacy, and attitudes to style. If writing is not just rules but how to use those rules—that is, for what purpose and with what attitude—then this is a contentious area of cultural difference and ideological preference. One has to consider what values are implied by the form and whether textual norms can be modified to represent alternate values.

- *From writing as spatial to writing as historical.* For many, the text (once produced) is an inert object that occupies a space. It is how words populate five pages, structured in a seamless manner, that is treated as the concern of writers and readers. But the text has evolved through time. While the writing was being done the writer took care of many other responsibilities in his or her everyday life. There were many false starts and failed attempts. There were many visions and revisions of what the writer wanted to say. There were collaborations and conflicts around the evolving text. The changing social conditions of the community and the personal fortunes of the writer also shape the text. After being produced, the text continues to live in history, being decoded differently according to differing social conditions. The text then is not a seamless whole that stands static through reading and writing. How it is shaped by the disjunctions, fissures, struggles, and conflicts during its construction and reception needs attention.

If we can summarize all these differences in one simple slogan, the shift is from writing as an *object* to writing as an *activity*. In integrating the text into the flow of sociohistoric currents and understanding it as one more purposive activity we do in everyday life, writing becomes not a product but a practice. It is in perceiving writing as a situated, mediated, dynamic social activity that the work of critical practice begins. We cannot stop with charting the internal linguistic structures and rhetorical patterns of the text. We have to also interrogate the values and ideologies that inform the text; the ways in which the external contexts of production and reception shape the text; the prospects for human possibilities to be limited or expanded by the text; and the ways in which the unequal status and differing identities of writers (and readers) affect the constitution of the text. In short, we begin to see how writing is implicated in social conflict, material inequality, cultural difference, and power relationships. In critical writing, students would become sensitive to these factors. They would wrestle with textual constraints, tap the available material resources, and negotiate the conflicting discourses in their favor to communicate effectively. In teaching critical writing, instructors have to make students aware of these diverse constraints and possibilities as they strive for a representation of knowledge that is emancipatory and empowering.

The orientations listed earlier differ from the perspectives of some other current schools of thinking that may employ similar constructs in their definitions. For example, that writing should be contextualized is widely held by many schools these days. But for some, contextualizing the text means seeing the specific details/words/images in terms of the total framework of the text. Or it can mean seeing the details in terms of rhetorical/genre conventions. But this sense of context is still "internal" to the text. I have articulated an ever-widening context that expands beyond the writer/reader and the community to historical and social conditions. On the other hand, even when social context is acknowledged by some schools, it is treated as lying outside the text; it doesn't affect the text's very constitution. Furthermore, theorizing the politics of writing has become fashionable in many circles today—especially among those influenced by poststructuralist and postmodernist perspectives. However, here again, politics is defined in terms of discursive and linguistic issues only, leaving more recalcitrant material factors out of consideration. This orientation explains the trend in Western academic circles toward celebrating the rhetorical activity of interpreting the tensions within the text to show how ideological struggle is manifested there. The poststructuralist schools perceive language as one of the tools that sustain inequality and domination at the microsocial level; therefore, deconstructing the written text to expose the tensions therein is treated as equal to bringing the whole unfair social edifice crumbling down. Though I acknowledge the importance of language and discourse in reflecting/sustaining/enforcing inequality, I still feel that the historical and material dimensions of power have to be addressed in their own terms. Therefore my perspective on writing brings together text-internal and text-external factors, discursive and historical forces, linguistic and social considerations.

ORIENTATING TO THE MULTILINGUAL WRITER

I have been talking of the writer in very generalized terms up to this point. It is time now to give flesh and blood to the type of writers this essay is concerned with. The pedagogical context assumed is the teaching of English for speakers of other languages (ESOL). The

ESOL student community includes those who are learning English as a second language—in other words, those living in former British colonies such as India, Nigeria, and Jamaica and those linguistic minorities living in the traditionally English-speaking countries of Canada, the United States, and Britain, all of whom actively use English as an additional language in social and educational life. These are largely bilinguals. Included in this group are speech communities for whom English has become considerably "nativized." Through a long history of interaction, English has now become locally rooted, accommodating lexical, grammatical, and discoursal features from native languages. While some of these speakers would consider English their native language (i.e., speaking English as their first or sole language), they will still face challenges in using the "standard" English dialects (of the Anglo-American variety) treated as the norm for academic writing. Therefore they should also be considered bidialectals who have to shift from one variant of English to another in their writing.

These groups (largely ESL) differ from those who learn English as a foreign language (EFL). In many parts of the contemporary world, English is an indispensable auxiliary language for a variety of specialized purposes. In addition to being proficient in the vernacular, and perhaps in some regional or colonial languages (French in Vietnam, Dutch in Indonesia, Portuguese in Brazil), students from these communities will still have some competence in English. This circle is largely multilingual, speaking English as a third or fourth language. However, the traditional distinction between EFL and ESL contexts is becoming fluid these days as English attains the position of a global language.[2] It is becoming indispensable for almost everyone in the postmodern world to hold some proficiency in English and use it for a variety of purposes in their everyday life. Despite the varying levels of linguistic competence possessed by the different ESOL subgroups identified earlier, in practicing academic writing in English they have to all acquire new discourses and conventions and represent their identities in novel ways.[3]

Do these students require a different teaching approach from those used for L1 students? To address this question clearly we have to first ask how ESOL and L1 student communities are different. (By "L1 students" I am referring here to those who are "traditionally native" in English, largely monolinguals, coming from the former colonizing communities that still claim ownership over the language.) It has become pedagogical common sense to distinguish these groups in terms of linguistic difference. ESOL teachers have treated multilingual students as strangers to English and thus aimed to develop their grammatical competence in order to facilitate their academic writing. But this approach is misdirected. We must note that many of these students have some competence in one or more dialects of English—sometimes speaking their local variants of English "natively." There is also widespread proficiency in specialized registers in English—such as the language of computers, technology, academia, and the professions (e.g., legalese, journalese). Moreover, writing involves not just grammatical competence. Therefore, different pedagogies are not warranted based purely on differences in grammatical proficiency.

Teachers have also focused on the cultural difference between both student groups. Apart from the larger differences in beliefs and practices, there can be more specific differences related to literacy. The genres and styles of communication, the practices and uses of literacy, and the attitudes and processes in composing can be different. The popularity of approaches like contrastive rhetoric explains the importance given by teachers to cultural differences in text construction. But even this mustn't be exaggerated too much. After the colonial experience, European culture has left an indelible mark on many local communities (see Canagarajah 1999b; Pennycook 1994). The general trend of globalization in the contemporary world has also resulted in the spreading of Anglo-American values and institutions worldwide. More relevant to our discussion, literacy has spread to such levels that we don't have any "pure" oral communities to speak of today. Even the communities that didn't have a written script have developed one through the help of missionary enterprises (though some of this resulted from the motivation of teaching the Bible).

In general, it is becoming more and more difficult to "essentialize" students in ESOL—that is, to generalize their identity and character according to a rigidly definable set of linguistic or cultural traits. We are unable to define them in ways that are diametrically opposed to the language and culture of L1 students. ESOL students are not aliens to the English language or Anglo-American culture anymore. The hybridity that characterizes communities and individuals in the postcolonial world complicates some of the easy distinctions teachers are used to making about ESOL students. In fact, it is difficult now to speak of uncontaminated "native" cultures or "vernaculars," as many communities have accommodated foreign traditions and practices through a history of cultural interaction and adaptation (see Appadurai 1996). Students in ESOL bring with them a mixture of local and Western linguistic/cultural characteristics, and we shouldn't assume that they all require an "introduction" to the English language and Anglo-American culture.

These qualifications don't mean that ESOL students are not different from L1 students but that "difference" has to be redefined in more complex terms. We have to move away from easy stereotypes about them. The fact that ESOL students display hybrid multicultural, multilingual tendencies doesn't make them the same as L1 students. Hybridity doesn't preclude questions of sociocultural uniqueness. These students may display conflicting attitudes toward the various cultures that make up their subjectivity. They may in fact suspect—and resist—their "Anglo-American" legacy, which has the potential to dominate or suppress their more "indigenous" side. They may also display a different subject position in terms of cultural identity. Their preferred choices of community solidarity and cultural identities have to be respected. While most ESOL students occupy a largely unequal status, as colored individuals from periphery communities, L1 students occupy a privileged position. The latter's cultural identity enjoys the power of dominant communities from the geopolitical center, providing a head start on the linguistic and cultural capital necessary for success in the contemporary world. Hybridity shouldn't be taken to mean, therefore, that issues of power and difference are irrelevant in today's world. Some postmodernist scholars have mistakenly assumed that the reality of cultural and linguistic mixing has defeated the designs of imperialistic forces. Nor should we assume that trends toward hybridity and globalization lead to a homogeneous world where difference doesn't matter anymore. In fact, these trends have inspired minority communities to celebrate their differences and develop their local knowledge and identities. Therefore, despite certain obvious signs toward homogeneity through forces of technology, multinational companies, market forces, and the media, we cannot say that difference has been eradicated altogether. Issues of power and difference have simply become more subtle and dispersed.

NOTES

[1] While the first few terms here are well known, the final three—especially those that concern our profession relatively more closely—may sound strange. For publications that employ these labels, see Fowler and Kress 1979 for *critical linguistics*; Fairclough 1995 for *critical discourse analysis*; and Kumaravadivelu 1999 for *critical classroom discourse analysis*.

[2] For a perspective on the need to reconsider these traditional dstinctions, see Nayar 1997.

[3] The new realizations about linguistic identity create a need for new terminology. In referring to students and teachers in second-language programs, I will use the term ESOL except when I make a specific point about the ESL/EFL situation or the L1/L2 distinction. Though this label is awkward, especially when it is used as an adjective to qualify teachers and students, it has been used in these contexts in the professional literature for a long time (see Canagarajah 1993; Harklau 2000). The term ESOL enables me to sidestep the question of whether the subjects are balanced bilinguals or not and of whether they are using English as a second language, a foreign language, or a nativized language.

[4] For a debate on this issue in the pages of the *ELT Journal*, see Rajagopalan 1999 and Canagarajah 1999b.

REFERENCES

Appadurai, A. (1996). *Modernity at large: Cultural dimensions of globalization*. Minneapolis, MN: University of Minnesota Press.

Canagarajah, A. S. (1993). Critical ethnography of a Sri Lankan classroom: Ambiguities in opposition to reproduction through ESOL. *TESOL Quarterly 27*(4), 601–626.

Canagarajah, A. S. (1999a). On EFL teachers, awareness, and agency. *ELT Journal 53*(3), 207–214.

Canagarajah, A. S. (1999b). *Resisting linguistic imperialism in English teaching*. Oxford: Oxford University Press.

Fairclough, N. (1995). *Critical discourse analysis: The critical study of language*. London: Longman.

Fowler, R., & Kress, G. (1979). Critical linguistics. In R. Fowler, B. Hodge, G. Kress, & A. Trew (Eds.), *Language and control* (pp. 185–213). London: Routledge.

Harklau, L. (2000). "From the 'good kids' to the 'worst' ": Representations of English language learners across educational settings. *TESOL Quarterly 34*(1), 35–68.

Kumaravadivelu, B. (1999). Critical classroom discourse analysis. *TESOL Quarterly 33*(3), 453–484.

Nayar, P. B. (1997). ESL/EFL dichotomy today: Language politics or pragmatics? *TESOL Quarterly 31*(1), 9–37.

Pennycook. A. (1994). *The cultural politics of English as an international language*. London: Longman.

Rajagopalan, K. (1999). Of EFL teachers, conscience, and cowardice. *ELT Journal 53*(3), 200–206.

QUESTIONS TO THINK ABOUT

1. Canagarajah says that a "critical perspective enables us to appreciate the complexity of writing and address issues of literacy that have far-reaching social implications." In arriving at his critical perspective toward writing, Canagarajah presents five shifts in perspective, moving "from writing as an *object* to writing as an *activity.*" What are these five shifts and what is the significance of each as well as its relationship to literacy in general. What does he mean by a "critical perspective," what is its connection to literacy, and what are the social implications he refers to?

2. Why does Canagarajah question whether multilingual speakers of English "require a different teaching approach from that used for L1 students"? To answer this question, you may want to consider who the multilingual writers he refers to are. What are the various kinds of English they use? What are the distinctions he makes among various English speakers (e.g., bidialectals, monolinguals, ESOLs)?

3. Why does Canagarajah say that "it is becoming more and more difficult to 'essentialize' students in ESOL—that is, to generalize their identity and character according to a rigidly definable set of linguistic or cultural traits"? What, if any, are the significant cultural differences among various English-speaking groups? In what ways does he suggest that literacy is related to beliefs, practices, genres, and styles of communication?

4. *Extending your understanding*: In his discussion of the multilingual writer, Canagarajah asserts that "It is becoming indispensable for almost everyone in the postmodern world to hold some proficiency in English and use it for a variety of purposes in their everyday life." Building on the examples Canagarajah gives, provide your own examples of English used in various parts of the world, of the different "specialized registers in English" you know of, and of the importance and necessity of English in the global context. See Pratt, Fishman, Ku, and others in this text who also provide an expanded sociopolitical perspective on the globalization of English

TERMS TO DEFINE

Define the following words and phrases as they are presented within the context of the reading. Comment on your understanding of the significance of each one.

Critical writing
Contextualized/decontextualized
Bidialectals
ESL/EFL/ESOL
Multilingual
Essentialize
Hybridity

Language, Literacy, and Culture: Intersections and Implications

Sonia Nieto
University of Massachusetts, Amherst

It has only been in the past several years that scholars have begun to connect the issues of language, literacy, and culture in any substantive way. Prior to this time, they were considered to exist largely separate from one another. As a result, educators usually thought about culture, for example, as distinct from language and from reading and writing except in the most superficial of ways; or as English as a Second Language (ESL) divorced from the influence of native culture on learning; or as the contentious debate about phonics and whole language as somehow separate from students' identities. These dichotomies have largely disappeared in the past 20 years. It is now evident that language, literacy, and culture are linked in numerous ways and that all teachers—whether they teach preschool art or high school math—need to become knowledgeable in how they affect students' schooling.

Even more crucial to our purposes in this textbook, until recently, critical perspectives were almost entirely missing from treatments of reading, writing, language acquisition and use, and an in-depth understanding of race, culture, and ethnicity. If broached at all, differences were "celebrated," typically in shallow ways such as diversity dinners and the commemoration of a select few African American and other heroes and through "ethnic" holiday fairs. But discussions of stratification and inequality were largely absent until recently in most teacher education courses. Despite their invisibility, questions about equity and social justice are at the core of education. As such, education is always a political undertaking.

The fact that education is not a neutral endeavor scares many people because it challenges cherished notions that education is based solely on equality and fair play. Power and privilege, and how they are implicated in language, culture, and learning, also typically have been invisible in school discourse. This situation is changing as the connections among language, literacy, and culture are becoming more firmly established, and as inequality and the lack of access to an equal education faced by many students is becoming more evident.

In this chapter, I describe the links among language, literacy, and culture beginning with my own story and concluding with some central tenets of sociocultural theory: agency, experience, identity/hybridity, context, and community. As you read this chapter, think about how your own understanding of language, literacy, and culture has shifted over the years, and how you have changed your ideas about teaching as a result.

INTRODUCTION: LANGUAGE, LITERACY, AND CULTURE: INTERSECTIONS AND IMPLICATIONS*

Given my background and early life experiences, I should not be here today talking with you about literacy and learning. According to the traditional educational literature, my home and family situation could not prepare me adequately for academic success. My mother did not graduate from high school, and my father never made it past fourth grade. They came to the United States as immigrants from Puerto Rico and they quietly took their place in the lower paid and lower status of society. In my family, we never had bedtime stories, much less books. At home, we didn't have a permanent place to study, nor did we have a desk with sufficient light and adequate ventilation, as teachers suggested. We didn't have many toys and I never got the piano lessons I wanted desperately from the age of five. As a family, we didn't go to museums or other places that would give us the cultural capital (Bourdieu, 1986) it was thought we needed to succeed in school. We spoke Spanish at home, even though teachers pleaded with my parents to stop doing so. And when we learned English, my sister and I spoke a nonstandard, urban Black and Puerto Rican version of English: we said *ain't* instead of *isn't* and *mines* instead of *mine*, and no matter how often our teachers corrected us, we persisted in saying these things. In a word, because of our social class, ethnicity, native language, and discourse practices, we were the epitome of what are now described as "children at risk," young people who were described when we were coming up as "disadvantaged," "culturally deprived," and even "problem" students.

I was fortunate that I had a family that, although unable to help me with homework, would make sure that it got done; a family who used "Education, Sonia, education!" as a mantra. But they kept right on speaking Spanish (even when my sister and I switched to English), they still didn't buy books for our home, and they never read us bedtime stories. My parents, just like all parents, were brimming with skills and talents: They were becoming bilingual, they told us many stories, riddles, tongue-twisters, and jokes; when my father, 20 years after coming to this country, bought a *bodega*, a small Caribbean grocery store, I was awed by the sight of him adding up a column of figures in seconds, without a calculator or even a pencil. My mother embroidered beautiful and intricate patterns on handkerchiefs, blouses, and tablecloths, a trade practiced by many poor women in Puerto Rico to stock the shelves of Lord and Taylor's and Saks' Fifth Avenue in New York. These skills, however, were never called on by my teachers; my parents were thought of as culturally deprived and disadvantaged, another segment of the urban poor with no discernible competencies.

Sometime in my early adolescence, we bought a small house in a lower middle-class neighborhood and I was able to attend a good junior high and an excellent high school. I didn't particularly like that high school—it was too competitive and impersonal and I felt invisible there—but in retrospect I realize that my sister and I got the education we needed to prepare us for college, a dream beyond the wildest imagination of my parents, most of my cousins, and the friends from our previous neighborhood. My new address made a profound difference in the education that I was able to get. I eventually dropped the *ain't* and the *mines*, and I hid the fact that I spoke Spanish.

I begin with my own story, not because I believe that autobiography is sacrosanct, or that it holds the answer to all educational problems. My story is not unique and I don't want to single myself out as an exception, in the way that Richard Rodriguez (1982) ended up doing, intentionally or not, in his painful autobiography *Hunger of Memory*. I use my story because it underscores the fact that young people of all backgrounds can learn and that they need not be compelled, as Rodriguez was, to abandon their family and home language in the process for the benefits of an education and a higher status in society. In many ways, I am like any of the millions of young people in our classrooms and schools who come to school eager (although perhaps not, in the current jargon, "ready") to learn, but who end up as the waste products of an educational system that does not understand the gifts they bring to their education. They are the reason that I speak with you today about language, literacy, and culture, and the implications that new ways of thinking about them have for these children.

Language, literacy, and culture have not always been linked, either conceptually or programmatically. But this is changing, as numerous schools and colleges of education around the country are beginning to reflect a growing awareness of their intersections, and of the promise they hold for rethinking teaching and learning. My own reconcep-tualized program at the University of Massachusetts, now called Language, Literacy, and Culture, mirrors this trend.[1] I believe the tendency to link these issues is giving us a richer picture of learning, especially for students whose identities—particularly those related to language, race, ethnicity, and immigrant status—have traditionally had a low status in our society. One result of this reconceptualization is that more education programs are reflecting and promoting a sociocultural perspective in language and literacy, that is, a perspective firmly rooted in an anthropological understanding of culture; a view of learn-ing as socially constructed and mutually negotiated; an understanding of how students from diverse segments of society—due to differential access, and cultural and linguistic differences—experience schooling; and a commitment to social justice. I know that multi-ple and conflicting ideas exist about these theoretical perspectives, but I believe some basic tenets of sociocultural theory can serve as a platform for discussion. I explore a number of these tenets, illustrating them with examples from my research and using the stories and experiences of young people in U.S. schools.

The language of sociocultural theory includes terms such as *discourse, hegemony, power, social practice, identity, hybridity,* and even the very word *literacy*. Today, these terms have become commonplace, but if we were to do a review of the literature of some 20 years ago or less, we would probably be hard pressed to find them, at least as currently used. What does this mean? How has our awareness and internalization of these terms and everything they imply changed how we look at teaching and learning? Let's look at literacy itself. It is generally accepted that certain family and home conditions promote literacy, including an abundant supply of books and other reading material, consistent conversations between adults and children about the books they read, and other such conditions (Snow, Barnes, Chandler, Goodman, & Hemphill, 1991). I have no doubt that this is true in many cases, and I made certain that my husband and I did these things with our own children. I am sure we made their lives easier as a result. But what of the children for whom these conditions are not present, but who nevertheless grow up literate (Taylor & Dorsey-Gaines, 1988)? Should children be doomed to educational failure because their parents did not live in the right neighborhood, were not privileged enough to be formally educated, or did not take their children to museums or plays? Should they be disqualified from learning because they did not have books at home?

TENETS OF SOCIOCULTURAL THEORY

I began with my story to situate myself not just personally, but socially and politically, a primary premise of sociocultural theory. Given traditional theories, the only way to understand my educational success was to use traditional metaphors: I had "pulled myself up by my bootstraps"; I had "melted"; I had joined the "mainstream." But I want to suggest that these traditional metaphors are as unsatisfactory as they are incomplete because they place individuals at the center, isolated from the social, cultural, historical, and political context in which they live. Traditional theories explain my experience, and those of others who do not fit the conventional pattern, as springing primarily if not solely from our personal psychological processes. Sociocultural theory, on the other hand, gives us different lenses with which to view learning, and different metaphors for describing it. This is significant because how one views learning leads to dramatically different curricular decisions, pedagogical approaches, expectations of learning, relationships among students, teachers and families, and indeed, educational outcomes.

Sociocultural and sociopolitical perspectives are first and foremost based on the assumption that social relationships and political realities are at the heart of teaching and learning. That is, learning emerges from the social, cultural, and political spaces in which it takes place, and through the interactions and relationships that occur between learners and teachers. In what follows, I propose five interrelated concepts that undergird sociocultural and sociopolitical perspectives. These concepts are the basis of my own work, and they help me make sense of my experience and the experiences of countless youngsters that challenge traditional deficit views of learning. The concepts are also highly consistent with a critical multi-cultural perspective, that is, one that is broader than superficial additions to content or "holidays and heroes" approaches.

I focus on five concepts: *agency/co-constructed learning; experience; identity/hybridity; context/situatedness/positionality;* and *community*. Needless to say, each of these words holds many meanings, but I use them here to locate some fundamental principles of sociocultural and sociopolitical theory. In addition, the terms are both deeply connected and overlapping. I separate them here for matters of convenience, not because I see them as fundamentally independent concepts.

Agency

In many classrooms and schools, learning continues to be thought of as transmission rather than as *agency*, or mutual discovery by students and teachers. At the crudest level, learning is thought to be the reproduction of socially sanctioned knowledge, or what Michael Apple (1991) has called "official knowledge." These are the dominant attitudes and behaviors that society deems basic to functioning. The most extreme manifestation of this theory of learning is what Paulo Freire (1970) called "banking education," that is, the simple depositing of knowledge into students who are thought to be empty receptacles. In an elegant rejection of the banking concept of education, Freire instead defined the act of study as constructed by active agents. According to Freire (1985), "To study is not to consume ideas, but to create and re-create them" (p. 4).

Although learning as the reproduction of socially sanctioned knowledge is repudiated by teachers and theorists alike, it continues to exist in many schools and classrooms. It is the very foundation of such ideas as "teacher-proof curriculum," the need to "cover the material" in a given subject, and the endless lists of skills and competencies "that every student should know" (Hirsch, 1987). This contradiction was evident even near the beginning of the 20th century when John Dewey (1916) asked:

> Why is it, in spite of the fact that teaching by pouring in, learning by a passive absorption, are universally condemned, that they are still so entrenched in practice? That education is not an affair of "telling" and being told but an active and constructive process, is a principle almost as generally violated in practice as conceded in theory, (p. 38)

Why does this continue to happen? One reason is probably the doubt among the public that teachers and students have the ability to construct meaningful and important knowledge. Likewise, in low-income schools with students from diverse cultural and linguistic backgrounds, very little agency exists on the part of either students or teachers. In such schools, teachers learn that their primary responsibility is to "teach the basics" because students are thought to have neither the innate ability nor the experiential background of more privileged students. In the case of students for whom English is a second language, the assumption that they must master English before they can think and reason may prevail.

Let me share some examples of agency, or lack of it, from the words of students of diverse backgrounds who a number of colleagues[2] and I interviewed for my first book (Nieto, 1992, 2000). We found that students' views largely echoed those of educational researchers who have found that teaching methods in most classrooms, especially those in secondary schools and even more so in secondary schools attended by poor students of all backgrounds, vary little from traditional "chalk and talk" methods; that textbooks are the dominant teaching materials used; that routine and rote learning are generally favored over creativity and critical thinking; and that teacher-centered transmission models still prevail (Cummins, 1994; Goodlad, 1984). Students in my study (Nieto, 2000) had more to say about pedagogy than about anything else, and they were especially critical of teachers who provided only passive learning environments for students. Linda Howard, who was just graduating as the valedictorian of her class in an Urban high school, is a case in point. Although now at the top of her class, Linda had failed seventh and eighth grade twice, for a variety of reasons, both academic and medical. She had this to say about pedagogy:

> Because I know there were plenty of classes where I lost complete interest. But those were all because the teachers just said, "Open the books to this page." They never made up problems out of their head. Everything came out of the book. You didn't ask questions. If you asked them questions, then the answer was "in the book." And if you asked the question and the answer *wasn't* in the book, then you shouldn't have asked that question! (pp. 55–56)

Rich Miller, a young man who planned to attend pharmacy school after graduation, described a "normal teacher" as one who "gets up, gives you a lecture, or there's teachers that just pass out the work, you do the work, pass it in, get a grade, good-bye!" (p. 66).

The students were especially critical of teachers who relied on textbooks and blackboards. Avi Abramson, a young man who had attended Jewish day schools and was now in a public high school, had some difficulty adjusting to the differences in pedagogy. He believed that some teachers did better because they taught from the point of view of the students: "They don't just come out and say, 'All right, do this, blah, blah, blah.' . . . They're not so *one-tone voice*" (p. 116). Yolanda Piedra, a Mexican student, said that her English teacher "just does the things and sits down" (p. 221). Another student mentioned that some teachers "just teach the stuff. 'Here,' write a couple of things on the board, 'see, that's how you do it. Go ahead, page 25'" (p. 166).

These students didn't just criticize, however; they also gave examples of teachers who promoted their active learning. Hoang Vinh, in his junior year of high school, spoke with feeling about teachers who allowed him to speak Vietnamese with other students in class. He also loved working in groups, contrary to conventional wisdom about Asian students' preference for individual work (demonstrating the dangers of generalizing about fixed cultural traits). Vinh particularly appreciated the teacher who asked students to discuss important issues, rather than focus only on learning what he called "the word's *meaning*" (p. 143) by writing and memorizing lists of words. Students also offered thoughtful suggestions to teachers to make their classrooms more engaging places. One student recommended that teachers involve more students actively: "More like making the whole class be involved, not making only the two smartest people up here do the whole work for the whole class" (p. 125).

Teaching becomes much more complex when learning is based on the idea that all students have the ability to think and reason. Sociocultural and sociopolitical theories emphasize that learning is not simply a question of transmitting knowledge, but rather of working with students so that they can reflect, theorize, and create knowledge. Given this theory of agency, "banking education" (Freire 1970) makes little sense. Instead, the focus on reflective questions invites students to consider different options, to question taken-for-granted truths, and to delve more deeply into problems.

Experience

That learning needs to build on experience is a taken-for-granted maxim, based on the idea that it is an innately human endeavor accessible to all people. But somehow this principle is often ignored when it comes to young people who have not had the *kinds* of experiences that are thought to prepare them for academic success, particularly those students who have not been raised within "the culture of power" (Delpit, 1988), or who have not explicitly learned the rules of the game for academic success. The experiences of these students— usually young people of culturally and linguistically diverse backgrounds and those raised in poverty—tend to be quite different from the experiences of more economically and socially advantaged students, and these differences become evident when they go to school.

Pierre Bourdieu (1986) described how different forms of cultural capital help maintain economic privilege, even if these forms of capital are not themselves strictly related to economy. Cultural capital is evident in such intangibles as values, tastes, and behaviors and through cultural identities such as language, dialect, and ethnicity. Some signs of cultural capital have more social worth, although not necessarily more intrinsic worth, than others. If this is true, then youngsters from some communities are placed at a disadvantage relative to their peers simply because of their experiences and identities. Understanding this reality means that power relations are a fundamental, although largely unspoken, aspect of school life.

We also need to consider the impact of teachers' attitudes concerning the cultural capital that their students *do* bring to school, and teachers' subsequent behaviors relative to this cultural capital. Sociocultural theories help to foreground these concerns. For example, a 1971 article by Annie Stein cited a New York City study in which kindergarten teachers were asked to list in order of their importance the things a child should learn in order to prepare for first grade. In schools with large Puerto Rican and Black student populations, socialization goals were predominant, but in mostly White schools, educational goals were invariably first. "In fact," according to Stein, "in a list of six or seven goals, several teachers in the minority-group kindergartners forgot to mention any educational goals at all" (p. 167). This is an insidious kind of tracking, where educational ends for some students were sacrificed for social aims. The effects of this early tracking were already evident in kindergarten.

All children come to school as thinkers and learners, aptitudes usually recognized as important building blocks for further learning. But there seems to be a curious refusal on the part of many educators to accept as valid the *kinds* of knowledge and experiences with which some students come to school. For instance, speaking languages other than English, especially those languages with low status, is often thought of by teachers as a potential detriment rather than a benefit to learning. Likewise, although traveling to Europe to ski is generally considered culturally enriching, the same is not true of traveling to North Carolina, Haiti, or the Dominican Republic to visit relatives. The reason that these kinds of experiences are evaluated differently by teachers, and in fact in the general society, has more to do with their cultural capital than with their educational potential or intrinsic worth.

The reluctance or inability to accept and build on students' experiences is poignantly described by Mary Ginley, a teacher in Massachusetts who taught in a small city with a large

Puerto Rican student population. A gifted teacher, Mary also knew that "being nice is not enough," an idea she elaborated on in a journal she kept for a class she took with me:

> Every child needs to feel welcome, to feel comfortable. School is a foreign land to most kids (where else in the world would you spend time circling answers and filling in the blanks?), but the more distant a child's culture and language are from the culture and language of school, the more at risk that child is. A warm, friendly, helpful teacher is nice but it isn't enough. We have plenty of warm friendly teachers who tell the kids nicely to forget their Spanish and ask mommy and daddy to speak to them in English at home; who give them easier tasks so they won't feel badly when the work becomes difficult; who never learn about what life is like at home or what they eat or what music they like or what stories they have been told or what their history is. Instead, we smile and give them a hug and tell them to eat our food and listen to our stories and dance to our music. We teach them to read with our words and wonder why it's so hard for them. We ask them to sit quietly and we'll tell them what's important and what they must know to "get ready for the next grade." And we never ask them who they are and where they want to go. (Nieto, 1999, pp. 85–86)

A case in point is Hoang Vinh, the Vietnamese student I mentioned previously. Vinh was literate in Vietnamese and he made certain that his younger siblings spoke it exclusively at home and they all wrote to their parents in Vietnam weekly. He was a good student, but he was also struggling to learn English, something that his teachers didn't always understand. He described how some teachers described his native language as "funny," and even laughed at it. But as he explained, "[To keep reading and writing Vietnamese] is very important. . . . So, I like to learn English, but I like to learn my language too" (Nieto, 2000, p. 178). Even more fundamental for Vinh was that teachers try to understand their students' experiences and culture. He explained: "[My teachers] understand some things, just not all Vietnamese culture. Like they just understand some things *outside*. . . . But they cannot understand something inside our hearts" (p. 178). Vinh's words are a good reminder that when students' skills and knowledge are dismissed as inappropriate for the school setting, schools lose a golden opportunity to build on their students' lives in the service of their learning.

Identity/Hybridity

How students benefit from schooling or not is influenced by many things including the particular individual personalities of students and the values of the cultural context in which they have been raised. Traditional theories, however, privilege individual differences above all other circumstances. As a result, it is primarily through tests and other measures of students' individual abilities that their intelligence is determined. Sociocultural theory goes beyond this limited perspective to include other issues such as students' cultural identities. But culture should not be thought of in this context as unproblematic. Mary Kalantzis, Bill Cope, and Diana Slade (1989) remind us that

> we are not simply bearers of cultures, languages, and histories, with a duty to reproduce them. We are the products of linguistic-cultural circumstances, actors with a capacity to resynthesize what we have been socialized into and to solve new and emerging problems of existence. We are not duty-bound to conserve ancestral characteristics which are not structurally useful. We are both socially determined and creators of human futures. (p. 18)

Culture is complex and intricate; it cannot be reduced to holidays, foods, or dances, although these are of course elements of culture. Everyone has a culture because all people participate in the world through social and political relationships informed by history as well as by race, ethnicity, language, social class, sexual orientation, gender, and other circumstances related to identity and experience.

If culture is thought of in a sentimental way then it becomes little more than a yearning for a past that never existed, or an idealized, sanitized version of what exists in reality. The result may be an unadulterated, essentialized "culture on a pedestal" that bears little resemblance to the messy and contradictory culture of real life. The problem of viewing some aspects of culture as indispensable attributes that must be shared by all people within a particular group springs from a romanticized and uncritical understanding of culture.

Let me share an example of this with you: Last year, I received an e-mail message with the subject heading "You Know You're Puerto Rican When. . . ." The message was meant to be humorous, and it included a long list of experiences and characteristics that presumably describe what it means to be Puerto Rican in the United States (e.g., being chased by your mother with a *chancleta*, or slipper in hand; always having a dinner that consists of rice and beans and some kind of meat; having a grandmother who thinks Vick's Vapor Rub is the miracle cure for everything). I laughed at many of these things (and I shared a good number of these experiences when I was growing up in New York City), but it was also sobering to read the list because it felt like a litmus test for *puertorriqueñidad* (Puerto Ricanness). If you could prove that you had these particular experiences, you could claim to be authentic; otherwise, you could not. By putting them to paper, the author was making it clear that these experiences defined the very essence of being Puerto Rican.

Reading the list made me reflect on my own daughters, born and raised in the United States by highly educated middle-class parents. My daughters would likely not pass the Puerto Rican litmus test: Their dinner was just as likely to consist of take-out Chinese or pizza as of rice and beans; they barely knew what Vick's Vapor Rub was; and I don't remember ever chasing them with *chancleta* in hand. But both of them identify as Puerto Rican, and they speak Spanish to varying degrees and enjoy rice and beans as much as the next Puerto Rican. But they also eat salmon and frog's legs and pizza and Thai food. The e-mail message I received made it seem as if there was only one way to be Puerto Rican. The result of this kind of thinking is that we are left with just two alternatives: either complete adherence to one definition of identity, or total and unequivocal assimilation. We are, in the words of Anthony Appiah (1994), replacing "one kind of tyranny with another" (p. 163).

My daughters' identities are complicated. They live in a highly diverse society in terms of race, ethnicity, social class, and other differences, and they enjoy the privileges they have received as a result of their parents' social-class position in society. The point of this story is to emphasize that culture does not exist in a vacuum but rather is situated in particular historical, social, political, and economic conditions, another major tenet of sociocultural theory. That is, culture needs to be understood as dynamic; multifaceted; embedded in context; influenced by social, economic, and political factors; created and socially constructed; learned; and dialectical (Nieto, 1999). Steven Arvizu's (1994) wonderful description of culture as a *verb* rather than a *noun* captures the essence of culture beautifully. That is, culture is dynamic, active, changing, always on the move. Even within their native contexts, cultures are always changing as a result of political, social, and other modifications in the immediate environment. When people with different backgrounds come in contact with one another, such change is to be expected even more.

Let me once again use the example of Linda Howard, one of the young women we interviewed for *Affirming Diversity* (2000). As I mentioned, Linda was a talented young woman who was graduating as valedictorian of her class. But the issue of identity was a complicated one for her. Being biracial, she identified as "Black American and White American," and she said:

> I don't always fit in—unless I'm in a mixed group . . . because if I'm in a group of people who are all one race, then they seem to look at me as being the *other* race . . . whereas if I'm in a group full of [racially mixed] people, my race doesn't seem to matter to everybody else. . . . Then I don't feel like I'm standing out . . . It's hard. I look at history and I feel really bad for what some of my ancestors did to some of my other ancestors. Unless you're mixed, you don't know what it's like to be mixed (pp. 51–52).

The tension of Linda's identity was not simply a personal problem, however. It was evident throughout her schooling, and especially when she reached secondary school. She found that teachers jumped to conclusions about her identity, assuming she was Latina or even Chinese, and identifying her as such on forms without even asking her. Linda won a scholarship to a highly regarded university. When discussing her future, she exclaimed proudly, "I've got it all laid out. I've got a 4-year scholarship to one of the best schools in New England. All I've gotta do is go there and make the grade."

Linda's future seemed hopeful, overflowing with possibilities, but she didn't quite "make the grade." When Paula Elliott, who interviewed Linda the first time, spoke with her again 10 years later, she found out that Linda dropped out of college after just a few months, and she never returned. Over dinner, Linda described her experience at the university in this way: "I felt like a pea on a big pile of rice." Using a sociocultural lens, we can see that identity is not simply a personal issue, but that it is deeply embedded in institutional life. Had there been a way to validate her hybridity, perhaps Linda might have graduated. She certainly had the intellectual training and resources; what she didn't have was the support for her identity to ease the way.

In some ways, we can think of culture as having both surface and deep structure, to borrow a concept from linguistics (Chomsky, 1965). For instance, in the interviews of students of diverse backgrounds that I mentioned previously (Nieto, 2000), we were initially surprised by the seeming homogeneity of the youth culture they manifested. Regardless of racial, ethnic, linguistic background, or time in the United States—but usually intimately connected to a shared urban culture and social class—the youths often expressed strikingly similar tastes in music, food, clothes, television viewing habits, and so on. When I probed more deeply, however, I also found evidence of deeply held values from their ethnic heritage. For instance, Marisol, a Puerto Rican high school student, loved hip hop and rap music, pizza, and lasagna. She never mentioned Puerto Rican food, and Puerto Rican music to her was just the "old-fashioned" and boring music her parents listened to. But in her everyday interactions with parents and siblings, and in the answers she gave to my interview questions, she reflected deep aspects of Puerto Rican culture such as respect for elders, a profound kinship with and devotion to family, and a desire to up-hold important traditions such as staying with family rather than going out with friends on important holidays. Just as there is no such thing as a "pure race," there is likewise no "pure culture." That is, cultures influence one another, and even minority cultures and those with less status have an impact, on majority cultures, sometimes in dramatic ways.

Power is deeply implicated in notions of culture and language (Fairclough, 1989). Indeed, what are often presented as cultural and linguistic differences are above all differences in power. Put another way, cultural conflict is sometimes little more than political conflict. Let me give you another example concerning the link between culture and context based on an experience I had that took me by surprise even as a young adult. As you probably know, rice is a primary Puerto Rican staple. There is a saying in Spanish that demonstrates how common it is: "*Puertorriqueños somos como el arroz blanco: estamos por todas partes*" (Puerto Ricans are like white rice: we are everywhere), an adage that says as much about rice as it does about the diaspora of the Puerto Rican people, almost half of whom live outside the island. As a rule, Puerto Ricans eat short-grained rice, but I have always preferred long-grained rice. Some Puerto Ricans have made me feel practically like a cultural traitor when I admitted it. I remember my surprise when a fellow academic, a renowned Puerto Rican historian, explained the real reason behind the preference for short-grained rice. This preference did not grow out of the blue, nor does any particular quality of the rice make it innately better. On the contrary, the predilection for short-grained rice was influenced by the historical context of Puerto Ricans as a colonized people.

It seems that, near the beginning of the 20th century when Puerto Rico was first taken over by the United States as spoils of the Spanish-American War, there was a surplus of short-grained rice in the United States. Colonies have frequently been the destination for unwanted or surplus goods from the metropolis, so Puerto Rico became the dumping ground for short-grained rice, which had lower status than long-grained rice in the United States. After this, of course, the preference for short-grained rice became part of the culture. As is true of all cultural values, however, this particular taste was influenced by history, economics, and power. This example was a good lesson to me that culture is not something inherent, but often arbitrary and negotiated.

Hybridity complicates the idea of cultural identity. It means that culture is always heterogeneous and complex; it also implies that assimilation or cultural preservation are not the only alternatives. Ariel Dorfman's (1998) autobiography *Heading South, Looking North: A Bilingual Journey* eloquently describes the turmoil he experienced as a child in developing his identity, first in New York City and later in Chile: "I instinctively chose to refuse the multiple, complex, in-between person I would someday become, this man who is shared by two equal languages and who has come to believe that to tolerate differences and indeed embody them personally and collectively might be our only salvation as a species" (p. 42). As an adult, he reflected on the demand to be "culturally pure" that he experienced in the United States as a graduate student:

> Sitting at my typewriter in Berkeley, California, that day, precariously balanced between Spanish and English, for the first time perhaps fully aware of how extraordinarily bicultural I was, I did not have the maturity—or the emotional or ideological space, probably not even the vocabulary—to answer that I was a hybrid, part Yankee, part Chilean, a pinch of Jew, a mestizo in search of a center, I was unable to look directly in the face the divergent mystery of who I was, the abyss of being bilingual and binational, at a time when everything demanded that we be unequivocal and immaculate, (p. 22)

The idea of hybridity, and of culture as implicated with power and privilege, complicate culturally responsive pedagogy. Rather than simply an incorporation of the cultural practices of students' families in the curriculum, or a replication of stereotypical ideas about "learning styles," culturally responsive pedagogy in the broadest sense is a political project that is, according to Gloria Ladson-Billings (1994) about "questioning (and preparing students to question) the structural inequality, the racism, and the injustice that exist in society" (p. 128). Culturally responsive pedagogy is not simply about instilling pride in one's identity or boosting self-esteem. It is also about context and positionality, to which I now turn.

Context/Situatedness/Positionality

When culture is thought of as if it were context-free, we fragment people's lives, in the words of Frederick Erickson (1990), "as we freeze them outside time, outside a world of struggle in concrete history" (p. 34). Context is also about *situatedness* and *positionality*, reminding us that culture is not simply the rituals, foods, and holidays of specific groups of people, but also the social markers that differentiate that group from others. It is once again the recognition that questions of power are at the very heart of learning. This view of culture also implies that differences in ethnicity, language, social class, and gender need not, in and of themselves, be barriers to learning. Instead, it is how these differences are viewed in society that can make the difference in whether and to what extent young people learn.

Judith Solsken's (1993) definition of *literacy* as the "negotiation of one's orientation toward written language and thus one's position within multiple relations of power and status" (p. 6) brings up a number of questions that have traditionally been neglected in discussions of reading and writing, questions such as: How do students learn to use language in a way that both acknowledges the context in which they find themselves, and challenges the rules of that context? How do young people learn to negotiate the chasm that exists between their home languages and cultures and those of school? Let me share with you another example from Linda Howard. What helped Linda go from a struggling student in junior high to valedictorian of her class several years later? There are probably many answers to this question, but one ingredient that made a tremendous difference was Mr. Benson, her favorite teacher in high school. He too was biracial, and Linda talked about some of the things she had learned from Mr. Benson about positionality and context:

> I've enjoyed all my English teachers at Jefferson. But Mr. Benson, my English Honors teacher, he just threw me for a whirl! 'Cause Mr. Benson, he says, I can go into Harvard and converse with those people, and I can go out in the street and rap with y'all. It's that type of thing, I love it. I try and be like that myself. I have my street talk. I get out in the street and I say "ain't" this and "ain't" that and "your momma" or "wha's up?" But I get somewhere where I know the people aren't familiar with that language or aren't accepting that language, and I will talk properly.... I walk into a place and I listen to how people are talking, and it just automatically comes to me. (Nieto, 2000, p. 56)

Linda's statement is an example of the tremendous intelligence needed by young people whose Discourses (Gee, 1990) are not endorsed by schools, and who need to negotiate these differences on their own. Linda's words are also a graphic illustration of James Baldwin's (1997) characterization of language as "a political instrument, means, and proof of power" (p. 16). In the case of African American discourse, Baldwin suggested—as Linda learned through her own experience—"It is not the Black child's language that is in question, it is not his language that is despised: It is his experience" (p. 16). As David Corson (1993) reminds us, "...education can routinely repress, dominate, and disempower language users whose practices differ from the norms that it establishes" (p. 7).

What does this mean for teachers? Situations such as Linda Howard's suggest that, in the words of Sharon Nelson-Barber and Elise Trumbull Estrin (1995), "We are faced with essential epistemological questions such as, what counts as important knowledge or knowing?" (p. 178). These questions are at the core of sociocultural theory, and they are neither neutral nor innocent. They are rarely addressed openly in school, although they should be. As Ira Shor (1992) said, "A curriculum that avoids questioning school and society is not, as is commonly supposed, politically neutral. It cuts off the students' development as critical thinkers about their world" (p. 12).

Sociocultural and sociopolitical perspectives have been especially consequential because they have shattered the perception that teaching and learning are neutral processes uncontaminated by the idiosyncrasies of particular contexts. Whether and to what extent teachers realize the influence social and political context have on learning can alter how they perceive their students and, consequently, what and how they teach them. A good example of positionality is the status of bilingual education. Bilingualism is only viewed as a problem and a deficit in a context where speakers of a particular language are held in low esteem or seen as a threat to national unity. This is the case of bilingual education in the United States, and especially for children who speak Spanish. That is, there is nothing inherently negative about the project of becoming bilingual (many wealthy parents pay dearly for the privilege), but rather it is the identities of the students, and the status of the language variety they speak, that make bilingual education problematic. This was clearly explained by Lizette Román, a bilingual teacher whose journal entry for one of my classes reads as follows:

> Unfortunately, most bilingual programs exist because they are mandated by law, not because they are perceived as a necessity by many school systems. The main problem that we bilingual teachers face every day is the misconception that mainstream teachers, principals, and even entire school systems have about bilingual education.... As a consequence, in many school districts bilingual education is doubly disadvantaged, first because it is seen as remedial and, second, because little attention is paid to it. Many mainstream teachers and administrators see bilingual education as a remediation program and do not validate what bilingual teachers do

in their classrooms even when what they are teaching is part of the same curriculum. . . . The majority think that there must be something wrong with these children who cannot perform well in English. As soon as the children transfer out of the bilingual program, these teachers believe that *this* is the moment when the learning of these children starts. The perception of the majority distorts the importance and the purpose of bilingual education. It extends to bilingual children and their parents. Bilingual children and their parents sense that their language places them in a program where they are perceived to be inferior to the rest of the children. What isolates children in the bilingual program is not the way the program is conducted, but the perceptions the majority has about people who speak a language different from the mainstream. (Nieto, 1999, pp. 87–88)

Lizette's reflections suggest that if teachers believe that intelligence and learning are somehow divorced from context, then they will conclude that the political and economic realities of their students' lives—including their school environments—have nothing to do with learning. In short, teachers can delude themselves by believing that they and the schools in which they work inhabit an "ideology-free zone" in which dominant attitudes and values play no role in learning. When students are asked to give up their identities for an elusive goal that they may never reach because of the negative context in which they learn, students may be quite correct in rejecting the trade.

Community

How we define and describe *community* is of central significance in sociocultural theory. Lev Vygotsky's (1978) research in the first decades of the 20th century was a catalyst for the viewpoint that learning is above all a social practice. Vygotsky suggested that development and learning are firmly rooted in—and influenced by—society and culture. Accepting this idea means that it is no longer possible to separate learning from the context in which it takes place, nor from an understanding of how culture and society influence and are influenced by learning.

Vygotsky and others who have advanced the sociocultural foundation of cognition (Cole & Griffin, 1983; Scribner & Cole, 1981) have provided us with a framework for understanding how schools can either encourage or discourage the development of learning communities. Because schools organize themselves in specific ways, they are more or less comfortable and inviting for students of particular backgrounds. Most schools closely reflect the traditional image of the intelligent, academically prepared young person, and consequently, these are the young people who tend to feel most comfortable in school settings. But institutional environments are never neutral; they are always based on particular views of human development, of what is worth knowing, and of what it means to be educated. When young people enter schools, they are entering institutions that have already made some fundamental decisions about such matters, and in the process, some of these children may be left out through no fault of their own. The ability to create community, so important in sociocultural theory, is lost.

Maria Botelho, a doctoral student of mine and a former early childhood teacher and librarian, remembers very clearly what it was like to begin school as a young immigrant student in Cambridge, Massachusetts. After viewing a short video on bilingual education in one of my classes, she felt almost as if she had stepped back in time. The video highlights a number of students, one of them Carla, a young Portuguese student in a bilingual class in Cambridge. Maria reflected on her reactions to the video in the journal she kept for my class:

I viewed the video "Quality Bilingual Education" twice. I wept both times. The Portuguese-speaking girl, Carla, attended kindergarten in a school that is less than a block from where my parents live in Cambridge; it was too close to home, so to speak. Like Carla, I entered the Cambridge Public Schools speaking only Portuguese. Unlike Carla, I was placed in a mainstream first-grade class. I still remember my teacher bringing over a piece of paper with some writing on it (a worksheet) and crayons. I fell asleep. There I learned quietly about her world, and my world was left with my coat, outside the classroom door. (Nieto, 1999, p. 110)

Sociocultural theories are a radical departure from conventional viewpoints that posit learning as largely unaffected by context. Traditional viewpoints often consider that children such as Maria who do not speak English have low intelligence. As a result, such children are automatically barred from entering a community of learners. A Vygotskian perspective provides a more hopeful framework for thinking about learning because if learning can be influenced by social mediation, then conditions can be created in schools that can help most students learn. These conditions can result in what Carmen Mercado (1998) described as the "fashioning of new texts—texts of our collective voices" (p. 92) that emerge as a result of organizing a learning environment in which literacy is for sharing and reflecting. Particularly significant in this regard is the idea of the *zone of proximal development* or ZPD (Vygotsky, 1978). But the ZPD is not simply an *individual* space, but a *social* one. Thus, according to Henry Trueba (1989), if we accept Vygotsky's theory of ZPD, then failure to learn cannot be defined as *individual* failure but rather as *systemic* failure, that is, as the failure of the social system to provide the learner with an opportunity for successful social interactions.

In order to change academic failure to success, appropriate social and instructional interventions need to occur. For teachers, this means that they need to first acknowledge students' differences and then act as a bridge between their students' differences and the culture of the dominant society. The metaphor of a bridge is an appropriate one for teachers who want to be effective with students of diverse backgrounds. This is a lesson I learned from Diane Sweet, a former student who had been an engineer until she fell in love with teaching ESL at the plant where she worked and decided to become a teacher. Diane was well aware of the benefits of bridges, and she applied the metaphor to teaching: A bridge provides access to a different shore without closing off the possibility of returning home; a bridge is built on solid ground but soars toward the heavens; a bridge connects two places that might otherwise never be able to meet. The best thing about bridges is that they do not need to be burned once they are used; on the contrary, they become more valuable with use because they help visitors from both sides become adjusted to different contexts. This is, however, a far cry from how diverse languages and cultures tend to be viewed in schools: the conventional wisdom is that, if native languages and cultures are used at all, it should be only until one learns the *important* language and culture, and then they should be discarded or burned. It is definitely a one-way street with no turning back.

The metaphor of the bridge suggests a different stance: You can have two homes, and the bridge can help you cross the difficult and conflict-laden spaces between them. Teachers who take seriously their responsibility for working with students of diverse backgrounds become bridges, or what Estéban Díaz and his colleagues (1992) called *sociocultural mediators*. That is, they accept and validate the cultural symbols used by all their students, not just by those from majority backgrounds. In sociocultural theory, learning and achievement are not merely cognitive processes, but complex issues that need to be understood in the development of community.

Three of my colleagues provide a hopeful example of using students' experiences and identities as a basis for creating community. Jo-Anne Wilson Keenan, a teacher researcher, working with Judith Solsken and Jerri Willett, professors at the University of Massachusetts, developed a collaborative action research project in a school in Springfield, Massachusetts, with a very diverse student body. The project—based on the premise that parents and other family members of children from widely diverse back-grounds have a lot to offer schools to enhance their children's learning—was distinct from others in which parents are simply invited to speak about their culture and to share food. Instead, their research focused on demonstrating how parents, through visits that highlight their daily lives, talents, and skills, can promote student learning by transforming the curriculum. But engaging in this kind of project is not always easy. The researchers pointed out that collaborating with families "requires that we confront our own fears of difference and open our classrooms to discussions of topics that may raise tensions among the values of different individuals, groups, and institutions" (p. 64). Through inspiring stories based on indepth analysis of the families' visits, Wilson Keenan, Solsken, and Willett (1999) described how they attempted to build reciprocal relationships with parents. They concluded:

> Both the extent and the quality of participation by the parents belies the common perception that low-income and minority parents are unable or unwilling to collaborate with the school. Even more important, our study documents the wide range of knowledge, skills, and teaching capabilities that parents are already sharing with their children at home and that are available to enrich the education of their own and other children in school. (p. 64)

The important work of Luis Moll, Norma Gónzalez, and their colleagues (1997) is another well-known example of research that builds on family knowledge.

CONCLUSION

No theory can provide all the answers to the persistent problems of education because these problems are not just about teaching and learning, but about a society's ideology. But sociocultural theories give us different insights into these problems. Although we need to accept the inconclusiveness of what we know, we also need to find new and more empowering ways of addressing these concerns. Maxine Greene (1994), in a discussion of postmodernism, poststructuralism, feminism, literary criticism, and other sociocultural theories, discussed both the possibilities and the limits they have. She wrote: "The point is to open a number of fresh perspectives on epistemology in its connection with educational research" (p. 426). But she added, "no universalized or totalized viewing, even of a revised sort ... " (p. 426) is possible.

Nevertheless, despite this inconclusiveness, we know enough to know that teachers need to respect students' identities and they need to learn about their students if they are to be effective with them. This means understanding the students we teach, and building relationships with them. Ron Morris, a young man attending an alternative school in Boston, described the disappointing relationships he had with teachers before attending the alternative school where he now found himself, a school that finally allowed him to have the relationships he craved. He said:

> When a teacher becomes a teacher, she acts like a teacher instead of a person. She takes her title as now she's mechanical, somebody just running it. Teachers shouldn't deal with students like we're machines. You're a person. I'm a person. We come to school and we all act like people. (Nieto, 2000, p. 265)

Ron reminds us that we do not have all the answers, and indeed, that some of the answers we have are clearly wrong. Ray McDermott (1977), in an early ethnography, described this fact beautifully: "We are all embedded in our own procedures, which make us both very smart in one situation and blind and stupid in the next" (p. 202). More recently, Herbert Kohl (1995) suggested that students' failure to learn is not always caused by a lack of intelligence, motivation, or self-esteem. On the contrary, he maintained that "to agree to learn from a stranger who does not respect your integrity causes a major loss of self" (p. 6), or what Carol Locust (1988) called "wounding the spirit" (p. 315).

Much has been written in the past few years about teachers' reluctance to broach issues of difference, both among themselves and with their students (Fine, 1992; Jervis, 1996; McIntyre, 1997; Sleeter, 1994; Solomon, 1995; Tatum, 1997). This is especially true of racism, which is most often addressed in schools as if it were a personality problem. But prejudice and discrimination are not just personality traits or psychological phenomena; they are also manifestations of economic, political, and social power. The institutional definition of racism is not always easy for teachers to accept because it goes against deeply held theories of equality and justice in our nation. Bias as an institutional system implies that some people and groups benefit and others lose. Whites, whether they want to or not, benefit in a racist society; males benefit in a sexist society. Discrimination always helps somebody—those with the most power—which explains why racism, sexism, and other forms of discrimination continue to exist. Having a different language to speak about differences in privilege and power is the first step in acquiring the courage to make changes.

Finally, sociocultural and sociopolitical concepts give us a way to confront what Henry Giroux (1992) called our nation's "retreat from democracy" (p. 4). Paulo Freire (1998), writing a series of letters to teachers, focused on this problem:

> When inexperienced middle-class teachers take teaching positions in peripheral areas of the city, class-specific tastes, values, language, discourse, syntax, semantics, everything about the students may seem contradictory to the point of being shocking and frightening. It is necessary, however, that teachers understand that the students' syntax; their manners, tastes, and ways of addressing teachers and colleagues; and the rules governing their fighting and playing among themselves are all part of their *cultural identity*, which never lacks an element of class. All that has to be accepted. Only as learners recognize themselves democratically and see that their right to say "I be" is respected will they become able to learn the dominant grammatical reasons why they should say "I am." (p. 49)

All students are individuals as well as members of particular groups whose identities are either disdained or respected in society. When we understand this, then my own story and those of countless others, can be understood not simply as someone "pulling herself up by her bootstraps," or "melting," or joining "the mainstream," but as a story that the concepts I've spoken about today—*agency/co-constructed learning; experience; identity/hybridity; context/situatedness/positionality;* and *community*—can begin to explain. When language, literacy, and culture are approached in these ways, we have a more hopeful way of addressing teaching and learning for all students.

NOTES

* This material is based on a keynote address given at the National Reading Conference in December, 2000.

[1] I wish to acknowledge my colleagues in the Language, Literacy, and Culture Doctoral Research Area, School of Education at the University of Massachusetts, Amherst: Jerri Willett, Judith Solsken, Masha Rudman, Catherine Luna, and Theresa Austin. Working with them to conceptualize and develop our program over the past 3 years has had a profound influence on my thinking about these issues.

[2] I am very grateful to those who assisted me with the interviews and gave me suggestions for crafting the case studies: Paula Elliott, Haydée Font, Maya Gillingham, Beatriz McConnie.

REFERENCES

Appiah, A. (1994). Identity, authenticity, survival: Multicultural societies and social reproduction. In A. Gutmann (Ed.), *Multiculturalism* (pp. 149–163). Princeton, NJ: Princeton University.

Apple, M. W. (1993). The politics of official knowledge: Does a national curriculum make sense? *Teachers College Record, 95*(2), 222–241.

Arvizu, S. F. (1994). Building bridges for the future: Anthropological contributions to diversity and classroom practice. In R. A. DeVillar, C. J. Faltis, & J. P. Cummins (Eds.), *Cultural diversity in schools: From rhetoric to reality* (pp. 75–97). Albany: State University of New York Press.

Baldwin, J. (1997). If Black English isn't a language, then tell me, what is? *Rethinking Schools, 12*(1), p. 16.

Bourdieu, P. (1986). The forms of capital. In Richardson, J. G. (Ed.), *Handbook of theory and research for the sociology of education* (pp. 241–248). Westport, CT: Greenwood Press.

Chomsky, N. (1965). *Aspects of the theory of syntax.* Cambridge, MA: MIT.

Cole, M., & Griffin, P. (1983). A socio-historical approach to re-mediation. *The Quarterly Newsletter of the Laboratory of Comparative Human Cognition, 5*(4), 69–74.

Corson, D. (1993). *Language, minority education and gender: Linking social justice and power.* Clevedon, UK: Multilingual Matters.

Cummins, J. (1994). Knowledge, power, and identity in teaching English as a second language. In F. Genesee (Ed.), *Educating second language children: The whole child, the whole curriculum, the whole community* (pp. 33–58). Cambridge, UK: Cambridge University.

Delpit, L. D. (1988). The silenced dialogue: Power and pedagogy in educating other people's children. *Harvard Educational Review, 58,* 280–298.

Dewey, J. (1916). *Democracy and education.* New York: The Free Press.

Díaz, E., Flores, B., Cousin, P. T., & Soo Hoo, S. (1992, April). *Teacher as sociocultural mediator.* Paper presented at the annual meeting of the American Educational Research Association, San Francisco, CA.

Dorfman, A. (1998). *Heading south, looking north: A bilingual journey.* New York: Penguin.

Erickson, F. (1990). Culture, politics, and educational practice. *Educational Foundations, 4*(2), 21–45.

Fairclough, N. (1989). *Language and power.* New York: Longman.

Fine, M. (1991). *Framing dropouts: Notes on the politics of an urban high school.* Albany, NY: SUNY.

Freire, P. (1970). *Pedagogy of the oppressed.* New York: Seabury.

Freire, P. (1985). *The politics of education: Culture, power, and liberation.* New York: Bergin & Garvey.

Freire, P. (1998). *Teachers as cultural workers: Letters to those who dare teach.* Boulder, CO: Westview.

Gee, J. P. (1990). *Social linguistics and literacies: Ideologies in discourse.* Bristol, PA: Falmer.

Giroux, H. (1992). Educational leadership and the crisis of democratic government. *Educational Researcher, 21*(4), 4–11.

Goodlad, J. I. (1984). *A place called school.* New York: McGraw-Hill.

Greene, M. (1994). Epistemology and educational research: The influence of recent approaches to knowledge. In L. Darling-Hammond (Ed.), *Review of research in education* (Vol. 20; pp. 423–464). Washington, DC: American Educational Research Association.

Hirsch, E. D. (1987). *Cultural literacy: What every American needs to know.* Boston: Houghton Mifflin.

Jervis, K. (1996). "How come there are no brothers on that list?": Hearing the hard questions all children ask. *Harvard Educational Review, 66,* 546–576.

Kalantzis, M., Cope, B., & Slade, D. (1989). *Minority languages.* London: The Falmer Press.

Kohl, H. (1994). *"I won't learn from you" and other thoughts on creative maladjustment.* New York: The New Press.

Ladson-Billings, G. (1994). *The dreamkeepers: Successful teachers of African American children.* San Francisco: Jossey-Bass.

Locust, C. (1988). Wounding the spirit: Discrimination and traditional American Indian belief systems. *Harvard Educational Review, 3,* 315–330.

Mercado, C. I. (1998). When young people from marginalized communities enter the world of ethnographic research: Scribing, planning, reflecting, and sharing. In A. Egan-Robertson & D. Bloome (Eds.), *Students as researchers of culture and language in their own communities* (pp. 69–92). Cresskill, NJ: Hampton.

McDermott, R. P. (1977). Social relations as contexts for learning in school. *Harvard Educational Review, 47,* 198–213.

McIntyre, A. (1997). Constructing an image of a white teacher. *Teachers College Press, 98*(4), 653–681.

Moll, L., & Gonzalez, N. (1997). Teachers as social scientists: Learning about culture from household research. In P. M. Hall (Ed.), *Race, ethnicity, and multiculturalism* (Vol. 1; pp. 89–114). New York: Garland.

Nelson-Barber, S., & Estrin, E. T. (1995). Bringing Native American perspectives to mathematics and science teaching. *Theory into Practice, 34*(3), 174–185.

Nieto, S. (1999). *The light in their eyes: Creating multicultural learning communities.* New York: Teachers College Press.

Nieto, S. (2000). *Affirming diversity: The sociopolitical context of multicultural education* (3rd ed.). New York: Longman.

Perry, T., & Delpit, L. (Eds.). (1998). *The real ebonics debate: Power, language, and the education of African-American children.* Boston: Beacon Press & Rethinking Schools.

Rodriguez, R. (1982). *Hunger of memory: The education of Richard Rodriguez.* Boston: David R. Godine.

Scribner, S., & Cole, M. (1981). *The psychology of literacy.* Cambridge, MA: Harvard University.

Shor, I. (1992). *Empowering education: Critical teaching for social change.* Chicago: University of Chicago.

Sleeter, C. E. (1994). White racism. *Multicultural Education, 1*(4), 5–8, 39.

Snow, C. E., Barnes, W. S., Chandler, J., Goodman, I. F., & Hemphill, L. (1991). *Unfulfilled expectations: Home and school influences on literacy.* Cambridge, MA: Harvard University.

Solomon, R. P. (1995). Beyond prescriptive pedagogy: Teacher inservice education for cultural diversity. *Journal of Teacher Education, 46*(4), 251–258.

Solsken, J. W. (1993). *Literacy, gender, and work in families and in school.* Norwood, NJ: Ablex.

Stein, A. (1971). Strategies for failure. *Harvard Educational Review, 41,* 133–179.

Taylor, D., & Dorsey-Gaines, C. (1988). *Growing up literate: Learning from inner-city families.* Portsmouth, NH: Heinemann.

Tatum, B. D. (1997). *"Why are all the Black kids sitting together in the cafeteria?" and other conversations about race.* New York: Harper Collins.

Trueba, H. T. (1989). *Raising silent voices: Educating the linguistic minorities for the 21st century.* Cambridge, MA: Newbury House.

Vygotsky, L. S. (1978). *Thought and language,* Cambridge, MA: MIT Press.

Wilson Keenan, J., Solsken, J., & Willett, J. (1999). "Only boys can jump high": Reconstructing gender relations in a first/second grade classroom. In B. Kamler (Ed.), *Constructing Gender and Difference: Critical Research Perspectives on Early Childhood* (pp. 33–70) Cresskill, NJ: Hampton Press.

QUESTIONS TO THINK ABOUT

1. Nieto says that "Given my background and early life experiences, I should not be here today talking with you about literacy and learning." What does she mean by this? Why does she use her own language and cultural background in talking about language and literacy in general? What do you consider the key variables in her language and cultural background and how do you think they have influenced her view of learning as "socially constructed and mutually negotiated."

2. Nieto presents five concepts she believes "challenge traditional deficit views of learning": agency, experience, identity/hybridity, context/situatedness/positionality, and community. Define as best you can each concept and its key characteristics, give at least one example, and summarize its importance to literacy and learning. Consider why Nieto says that "teaching becomes much more complex when learning is based on the idea that all students have the ability to think and reason." How do these concepts challenge traditional beliefs?

3. In discussing identity/hybridity, Nieto asserts that "Power is deeply implicated in notions of culture and language (Fairclough, 1989). Indeed, what are often presented as cultural and linguistic differences are above all differences in power." What does she mean by this and how does it relate to her discussion of Pierre Bourdieu's concept of "cultural capital"? What is the importance of power and position in relation to literacy and learning?

4. *Extending your understanding*: Through autobiography, Nieto defines her vision of literacy and its educational implications. Based on the theories and concepts Nieto presents, explain the critical events in your literacy achievements. What are your learning strengths and weaknesses, what particular individual, social, political, and economic conditions influenced your learning situation, and what social practices can you identify as significant in your literacy narrative? What conditions in your school environment might have been changed so that your learning would have been more effective?

TERMS TO DEFINE

Define the following words and phrases as they are presented within the context of the reading. Comment on your understanding of the significance of each one.

Agency
Identity/hybridity
Banking education
Cultural capital
Context

Educational Policy for the Transnational Dominican Community

Marianne D. Pita and Sharon Utakis
Bronx Community College

The increasingly transnational character of many immigrant communities necessitates changes in educational policy. We use the Dominican neighborhoods in New York City as our local case, examining the economic, political, social, cultural, and linguistic evidence of the transnationalism of this community. Many Dominicans maintain close ties to their native country through global networks that facilitate language and cultural maintenance. In spite of discrimination, Dominicans in the United States need to maintain their Spanish and want their children to develop fluent Spanish. Neglecting the language needs of transnational children leads to serious academic and social problems. Enriched bilingual bicultural programs would promote parallel development in both languages, providing cultural as well as linguistic instruction so that students can succeed in either country.

Global economic changes have led to a new paradigm of migration and the creation of communities that transcend national boundaries (Glick Schiller, 1999; Glick Schiller, Basch, & Blaric-Szanton, 1992). Some immigrants travel back and forth between native and host countries, weaving an economic, political, social, cultural, and linguistic web between two places. In the interstices of the global economy, these transnational communities have found ways to exploit global transportation and communication networks to maintain their native language and culture.

Bilingual education and English as a second language (ESL) programs in the United States have been designed to serve immigrants who settle here and wish to assimilate (Crawford, 1992). However, changes in migration patterns should lead to changes in language programs to meet the needs of transnational communities. Educational policy cannot be formulated exclusively from above, for immigrants in general. It must be responsive to local context, to a particular population, to their lives, their histories, and their goals (Skutnabb-Kangas, 1988). Local knowledge must inform educational policy to effectively serve the needs of a community. In the case of a transnational community, local knowledge

Reprinted with permission from the *Journal of Language, Identity and Education* 1:4 (2002). © 2002 by Lawrence Erlbaum Associates, Inc.

must include an understanding of both native and host contexts and how the transnational community experiences the connection between the two places.

As English teachers at Bronx Community College, we have noticed a disconnect between educational policy in New York City (NYC) and the needs of our transnational students and their children. Most of our ESL students at Bronx Community College are Dominican, and many go back and forth between the Dominican Republic and New York. Using the Dominican[1] neighborhoods in New York City as our local case, we argue that the increasingly transnational character of this immigrant community necessitates changes in educational policy. Since the community is transnational, students need to learn two languages and be able to live in two cultures. Schools should help students develop and maintain fluency and literacy in both languages and should help students understand both cultures. In this article, we provide an overview of the Dominican community in New York City and advocate changes in educational policy for this transnational community.

THE TRANSNATIONAL NATURE OF THE DOMINICAN COMMUNITY IN NEW YORK CITY

The Dominicans are the largest immigrant group in New York City (Sontag & Dugger, 1998). Jennifer Chait of the New York Department of City Planning estimates that there are 600,000 people of Dominican origin in the city (Kugel, 2001). However, although Cuban, Mexican, and Puerto Rican immigrant communities in the United States have been the subject of extensive linguistic and sociological studies (e.g., García & Otheguy, 1987; Peñalosa, 1980; Zentella, 1997a), Dominican immigrants, who have come to the United States more recently, have been the subject of significantly less research (Bailey, 2000b; Hernández & Torres-Saillant, 1996).

According to an article in the *New York Times*, "Dominicans, regardless of class, are probably the most transnational of all New York's immigrants ... they have transformed their nation while laying claim to whole New York neighborhoods" (Sontag & Dugger, 1998, p. A28). Dominicans maintain close ties to their native country through global networks that facilitate language and cultural maintenance. These migrants can go back for vacations or extended visits because of inexpensive plane fares, and they stay in regular contact with family, friends, and institutions through phone calls, faxes, and the Internet. A 1997 poll published in the Dominican Republic reports that half of all Dominicans have family in the United States, and more than 65% would move here if they had the opportunity (Rohter, 1997). In a monograph on the Dominican community in Washington Heights, Jorge Duany (1994) describes transnational communities as, "characterized by a constant flow of people in both directions, a dual sense of identity, ambivalent attachment to two nations and a far-flung network of kinship and friendship ties across state frontiers" (p. 2). The transnationalism of the Dominican community can be seen in its economic, political, social, cultural, and linguistic characteristics.

Evidence of the economic ties between New York City and the Dominican Republic can be seen in the businesses that proliferate in the Dominican neighborhoods of New York: *agentes de dinero extranjero* (foreign money brokers), *mudanzas* (movers), *envios* (shipping), and *agencias de turismo* (travel agencies). Dominican entrepreneurs have created an economic infrastructure that forms the basis of transnational exchange. As noticeable as the economic impact of this transnational community is on New York City, the impact on the Dominican economy is even more substantial. Dominicans living in the United States send more than 1 billion dollars a year back to the island (Kugel, 2001).

Transnational political ties attest to the importance of transmigrants on the island. In recognition of the dual identity of many Dominican migrants, the Dominican Republic changed its constitution to allow citizens living abroad to hold dual citizenship and vote in national elections (Smith, 1997). However, there is no mechanism for Dominicans living abroad to cast their ballots, so thousands fly back for national elections. In May 2001, hundreds of Dominicans marched in Manhattan to demand the right to vote from abroad in the 2004 Dominican presidential election (Kugel, 2001). In the 1996 election, Leonel Fernández, a transmigrant, was elected President of the Dominican Republic. Fernández, who holds a green card, moved to New York City in the 1960s, attended public school in Washington Heights, then returned to the Dominican Republic to attend law school (Guarnizo, 1997a; Smith, 1997).

Dominicans place a strong value on *familismo*, commitment to extended family (Castillo, 1996; Pita, 2000). In this transnational community, many families have relatives in both countries, and strong kinship ties are maintained by regular travel. Lacking adequate daycare facilities in New York, parents often send their young children back to be cared for by grandparents. With family in both countries, parents can send teenagers to the Dominican Republic to shelter them from gangs, drugs, and early sex. Our students at Bronx Community College sometimes leave in the middle of the semester to go back to care for sick relatives or attend funerals. Many Dominicans save up so they can buy a house and/or a business in their native country and retire there, rejoining family left behind. In 1996 more than 50% of the Dominicans who died in New York City were returned to the Dominican Republic for burial (Sontag & Dugger, 1998).

Second generation Dominican Americans are still strongly tied to the Dominican Republic. A qualitative study of a small group of Dominican girls born and raised in New York City revealed that these children often went back to their country for summer vacation (Pita, 2000). They identified themselves as Dominican and maintained many Dominican customs. For example, these preadolescent girls were expected to maintain complete innocence in appearance, thought, word, and deed, a state of innocence called *pudor* in the Dominican Republic. Their Dominican parents were trying to raise children with traditional Dominican values.

Dominican migrants maintain their ties to their native land on a daily basis. *El Nacional*, a leading newspaper in the Dominican Republic, has a New York edition with a circulation of 25,000 copies every day. In addition, five more dailies from the Dominican Republic are sold in northern Manhattan and the Bronx, among other places in New York (Smith, 1997).

Sue Dicker and Hafiz Mahmoud (2001) of Hostos Community College have made an extensive survey of language use in the Dominican community in Washington Heights. The results indicate that these migrants are moving toward acquisition of English and greater participation in the larger society, while simultaneously maintaining their native language and their involvement and interest in Spanish cultural activities. Whether this transnational community can maintain their native language over the long term is a question for further research. The final item in Dicker and Mahmoud's language survey asked participants whether they plan to stay in the United States or return to the Dominican Republic. Among those planning to stay in this country, a significant number also indicated plans to return to the Dominican Republic. Staying in this country and returning to their native country were not seen as mutually exclusive.

Dominican migrants are forging a transnational identity that spans the two countries. Many of these migrants view their own identity positively. In a survey of Dominican high school students in New York City, Castillo (1996) found that 95% considered themselves "Dominicans and proud of it, regardless of where they were born" (p. 51). Fernando Mateo, a businessman who shuttles between New York and Santo Domingo, is quoted in the *New York Times* as saying, "I believe people like us have the best of two worlds. We have two countries, two homes. It doesn't make any sense to be either this or that. We're both" (Sontag & Dugger, 1998).

However, many Dominican migrants face conflicts in trying to create a transnational identity. In the Dominican Republic, transmigrants are called *Dominicanyorks* by the elite, a pejorative term for transnationals stereotyped as drug traffickers (Castillo, 1996; Duany, 1994; Smith, 1997) and discriminated against in business associations, private social clubs, schools, and housing (Guarnizo, 1997b). Nevertheless, lower nonmigrant classes look up to the migrants as role models and "a sort of revenge against the traditional elites" (Guarnizo, 1997a, p. 305).

In the United States, many Dominicans feel they have to choose between being Dominican or being "American."[2] This forced choice pushes some to cling tightly to their own language and culture, making it difficult for them to learn English. In New York City, Dominicans tend to live in segregated neighborhoods in northern Manhattan and the west Bronx where they have little need to speak English (Duany, 1994; Smith, 1997). Dominicans are disparaged for not becoming "American" quickly or completely enough. Other migrants, particularly adolescents and children, feel that in order to be accepted in this country, they need to abandon their native language and culture.

The process of forging a transnational identity is made more difficult by the discrimination against Dominican migrants based on race, language, and social class. Although 90% of the population of the Dominican Republic is of African descent, Dominicans in the United States resist categorization as Black, preferring to identify as "Spanish" because they speak Spanish (Bailey, 2000a). Nevertheless, "Negative stereotypes promoted by the mass media, especially since the 1992 riots in Washington Heights, have stigmatized the entire Dominican community as violent drug-trafficking gangsters" (Duany, 1994, pp. 43–44). Our Dominican students report discrimination in the workplace, schools, housing, hospitals, and streets. Although we focus on language-based discrimination, this form of discrimination is inextricably bound with racism and class discrimination.

Discrimination based on language, or linguicism, leads to a hierarchy of language varieties, in which some varieties have lower prestige than others (Phillipson, 1992). In this country, Spanish, especially the Spanish of poor and working class immigrants, has low prestige relative to English (Dicker, 2000–2001). Furthermore, different varieties of Spanish have different levels of prestige within the Spanish-speaking community. Among Spanish speakers in New York, both Dominican and Puerto Rican Spanish have low prestige, according to Ana Celia Zentella (1997b). Why do Spanish speakers look down on Dominican Spanish? Zentella argues that, "The negative impact of U.S. language policies on Puerto Rico and of decades of dictatorial repression in the Dominican Republic, as well as the lower incomes and darker skins of Dominicans and Puerto Ricans in NYC, place them at the bottom of the language status ladder" (1997b, p. 175). Even among Dominicans themselves, Zentella found that 35% of Dominicans expressed negative opinions about Dominican Spanish, and 80% said that Dominican Spanish should not be taught in schools (1990). The question of which language or which language variety should be used in schools is of vital importance for the success of Dominican transnational students.

CURRENT EDUCATIONAL POLICY IN THE DOMINICAN COMMUNITY

Children from the Dominican community move between two school systems and, as a result, may suffer academically in both countries. Neglecting the needs of these transnational children can lead to devastating academic and social outcomes. According to a study by Luis Guarnizo (1997b), many Dominican Americans, concerned about the influence of New York culture on their school-age children, send the children back to the Dominican Republic to continue their schooling, often against the children's wishes. Some of these children were born in the United States or migrated here at a very young age. Guarnizo notes that "many return children had undergone their primary socialization in the United States and did not even speak Spanish—or if they did, theirs was a limited, domestic Spanish inadequate for schoolwork or 'proper' social communication" (p. 42). At best, these children suffered from a difficult adjustment period with poor academic performance. At worst, they resisted their new environment in socially unacceptable ways. Guarnizo notes that the challenges posed by these children went beyond the domestic sphere to create "a widespread and neglected social problem" (p. 42) in the Dominican Republic.

Peggy Levitt (2001) gives further evidence of the academic challenges transnational children face: "Because these students lack full linguistic or cultural fluency in either setting, they often fall irrevocably behind. Just as they begin to catch up ... their parents move them again" (p. 84). Because the children may well return to this country, the schools in Dominican neighborhoods in New York City have an interest in preparing students for an educational future in both the Dominican Republic and New York.

One of the most important assumptions underlying educational policy for immigrants in the United States is that people come to settle permanently, and to be successful they need to master English and assimilate as quickly as possible (Crawford, 1992). Historically, ESL teachers have been responsible for helping students to assimilate by teaching them English and those aspects of middle-class Anglo culture that are supposed to help them survive in the United States. Implicit in this view is the idea that immigrants do not need to develop or even retain their native language or learn about their own culture. The arguments in favor of bilingual education tend to be about affective aspects of language learning, how important it is for students' self-esteem and family connection to maintain some level of proficiency in the native language (e.g., Skutnabb-Kangas, 1988; Zentella, 1997a). Researchers have also argued that academic proficiency in the native language leads to more rapid acquisition of English (Cummins, 1989; Krashen, 1991). In fact, students who have mastered their native language have an advantage in learning a second language because of the transfer of academic skills (Cummins, 1986; Krashen, 1996; Zentella, 1997b). Although we agree with these arguments in favor of bilingual education in general, for transnational Dominican students the need to develop high levels of proficiency in Spanish is not merely affective, nor simply a matter of the most effective way to learn English. Their academic and economic survival depends on knowing both languages well.

Dominicans in the United States want to maintain their Spanish and want their children to develop fluent Spanish (Castillo, 1996) in spite of some negative feelings about their language variety. Zentella (1990) found that 94% of Dominicans surveyed wanted their children to be bilingual.

How well do the language programs available in New York City public schools serve the needs of transnational Dominican students? According to the Chancellor's *Report on the Education of English Language Learners* (New York City Board of Education, 2000) in New York City, four programs are recommended: freestanding ESL, accelerated academic English language, transitional bilingual, and dual language.

Freestanding ESL programs immerse students in content area instruction in English for most of the day. ESL instruction may occur in the classroom or in pull-out settings. Currently in an experimental phase, accelerated academic English-language programs, also called "High Intensity English," employ content area teachers trained in ESL methodology. All instruction is in English. Both programs focus solely on the acquisition of English; students are typically given no support for their native language and, in fact, are encouraged to discard it. Although there is evidence that students acquire the language variety of their peers in English-speaking classrooms, academic competence in their native language (and in all academic subjects other than English) is sacrificed to expedient and cost-effective English learning. While they may maintain fluency in Spanish because of their home environment, they rarely develop further competence in their native language, and reading and writing skills are likely to deteriorate. Students who return to their native country suffer academically from having been deprived of continued instruction in their mother tongue.

Transitional (short-term) bilingual programs are the most common form of bilingual education in New York City. In District 6, which has the highest concentration of Dominican students, 79% of English-language learners are in transitional bilingual programs.[3] Such programs are an improvement over English immersion, but their goal is still monolingualism in English, "to transition students to regular English only classes as quickly as possible" (New York City Board of Education, 2000, p. 17). The native language is used to keep students from falling behind in other subjects while they learn English, but these programs shortchange students because after they are mainstreamed, language maintenance is ignored and academic competence in the native language atrophies (Skutnabb-Kangas & Garcia, 1995). Students in transitional bilingual programs are penalized for learning English quickly: As soon as they have reached minimal competence in English, their studies in Spanish are terminated (Cummins, 1980; Krashen, 1996). In New York City, students are expected to exit from bilingual and ESL programs after 3 years (New York City Board of Education, 2000).

Next we come to dual language programs, in which the focus is on the development of proficiency in English within three years, with the additional goal of mastery of both English and a second language (New York City Board of Education, 2000). Evelyn Linares is the principal of the 21st Century Academy (*Academia del Siglo 21*), a dual-language public school in District 6. She believes that of the programs currently available in New York City, dual-language programs best serve the needs of Dominican children because "They recognize from the beginning that the [Spanish] language is important . . . they put stress on learning the language in a deeper way" (personal communication, November 30, 2001).

Although dual language programs are currently the best alternative available for transnational Dominican students in New York City, they are small, limited in number, and often serve only elementary school students. According to Linares, her school suffers from high attrition as transnational students return to the Dominican Republic, and it is difficult to integrate new students beyond the second grade and maintain a balance between English and Spanish dominant students.

The educational establishments in both New York and the Dominican Republic are beginning to recognize the challenges that these school systems face in trying to meet the needs of transnational Dominican students. The State Education Department of New York and the Dominican Department of Education called an Education Summit in April 2001. A Memorandum of Understanding between the two education departments was signed and included the following statement:

> Each year, large numbers of elementary and secondary school students of Dominican Republic heritage and their families migrate between the Dominican Republic and the State of New York, sometimes more than once in a school year; . . . such two-way migration impacts on the continuity and effectiveness of the education of such students . . . increased communication, collaboration and sharing between DR [Dominican Republic] and SED [State Education Department] . . . is in the best interests of such students of Dominican Republic heritage and of such educational systems. (New York State Education Department, 2001, p. 1)

Both the New York State Education Department and the Dominican Department of Education recognize the educational impact of this two-way migration on students. Although there are suggestions in the Memorandum for information sharing, instructional material exchange, and school staff exchange programs, bilingual education is not even mentioned, perhaps because bilingual education is so controversial in the United States.[4]

TOWARD A COHERENT EDUCATIONAL POLICY

The Education Summit is a starting point, but New York City needs a more coherent language policy for Dominican students. Public school students, who may go back to the Dominican Republic at any time, need to continue to develop competence in both languages for as long as they are in school. The educational system should help students develop and maintain fluency and literacy in both languages.

We are proposing an *enriched bilingual bicultural program*, so that students can succeed in school systems in either New York or the Dominican Republic. Students in a transnational community need a bicultural as well as a bilingual program. Josh DeWind (1997) describes the goals of such programs as follows: "Bilingual/bicultural programs are intended not only to help students develop dual language skills but also to help them become comfortable in both their native and American cultural contexts" (p. 141). As it stands, students in this country study U.S. history, and students in the Dominican Republic study Dominican history. A survey of Dominican high school students in New York City showed that they have very little knowledge of Dominican literature, art, folk culture, and history (Castillo, 1996). In a bicultural program in New York, students would study both histories and the relationship between the two countries. The history of U.S. political and economic intervention in the Dominican Republic and the resulting immigration patterns are an integral part of students' own histories. The curriculum should integrate materials that are relevant to students' lives, from their home country as well as the United States. Thus, this model is different from dual language programs that focus only on language instruction without giving equal consideration for culture.

Furthermore, students in 12th grade in New York City should have a 12th-grade Spanish reading and writing level, even if they came to this country in 4th or 5th grade. Basic education with native language instruction would also help students who may well return to the Dominican Republic to develop further their literacy in Spanish. In the long run, education in the native language may help the transnational Dominican community to maintain Spanish in future generations. Zentella argues that "All groups . . . are unlikely to pass Spanish on to the next generations, despite their fervent desire to do so, if they do not make special efforts to raise their children bilingually. These include insisting on Spanish at home and demanding developmental—not transitional—bilingual education in the public schools, and Spanish for Native Speakers courses at the university level" (Zentella, 1997b, p. 195). In this sense, the model we propose differs from the other available programs— such as freestanding ESL, accelerated academic English language, and transitional bilingual models—which favor the dominant host language (English) and lead to monolingualism among immigrant students.

This does not mean that the acquisition of English should be de-emphasized. In spite of the need for and interest in Spanish in the Dominican community in the United States, English is the language of power, and students want to learn that language because of the material advantages and increased security accruing from mastery of English. Even some of our students planning to return to the Dominican Republic report that they want to learn English because they will be better situated to get a good job in the Dominican Republic and to choose where they settle.

However, teaching Standard English uncritically reinforces notions of the superiority of English and inferiority of Dominican Spanish. Since Dominicans in New York City speak a low prestige variety of a low prestige language, it is particularly important for teachers to help students value their own language. One way to do this is by helping students become aware of the historic, social, and economic reasons why some language varieties are more valued than others. Critical language awareness gives students the tools to understand the relationship between language and power. Teachers can create a space where explicitly sociopolitical and linguistic discussions can occur. For example, readings on bilingual education, the English Only movement, and assimilation have provoked intense discussions in our classrooms. This transnational perspective can lead to a critique of conditions in the United States and in the Dominican Republic.

Ideally, educators from the same background (in this case Dominican teachers) can serve as role models of how students can become bilingual and bicultural (Auerbach, 1996). Furthermore, with Dominican teachers, students can learn to value their own language variety.

The linguistic and cultural needs of Dominican transmigrants are increasingly complex, and educational policy should be responsive to students' changing needs. School systems and educators need to work with the transnational community to develop programs that bridge continents, cultures, and languages.

ACKNOWLEDGMENTS

Thanks to Angus Grieve-Smith, Sue Dicker, Len Fox, Frederick De Naples, and Michael Denbo for their comments and suggestions; to the Dominican Studies Institute and John Acompore of the New York City Board of Education for help in finding information; and to Evelyn Linares for sharing her experience and insight. We especially thank Suresh Canagarajah for his thoughtful comments. All errors are our own.

NOTES

[1] We have generally used the term Dominican, rather than Dominican American. Because of the transnational nature of this community, many migrants prefer the unhyphenated term. The question of identity is an important topic for future research.

[2] Clearly, "American" could refer to anyone from North, Central, or South America. However, we use the term in quotation marks in reference to people associated with the United States.

[3] John Acompore, Deputy Director of the NYC Board of Education Office of English Language Learners, reported in spring of 2001 that out of 9,937 general education English Language Learners in District 6 entitled to bilingual or ESL services, 7,850 were in bilingual education, 1,874 were in ESL, and 214 were in neither.

[4] The controversy surrounding bilingual education, in particular the 1998 California Referendum rejecting bilingual education, led to the "re-examination of current practices in educating ELLs [English language learners]" in New York City according to the Chancellor's Report (New York City Board of Education, 2000, p. i).

REFERENCES

Auerbach, E. R. (1996). *From the community to the community: A guidebook for participatory literacy training.* Mahwah, NJ: Lawrence Erlbaum Associates, Inc.

Bailey, B. (2000a). Language and negotiation of ethnic/racial identity among Dominican Americans. *Language in Society, 29,* 555–582.

Bailey, B. (2000b). Social/interactional functions of code switching among Dominican Americans. *Pragmatics, 10,* 165–193.

Castillo, J. (1996). *Young Dominicans in New York City.* Unpublished master's thesis, Teachers College, Columbia University, New York.

Crawford, J. (1992). *Hold your tongue: Bilingualism and the politics of "English only."* Reading, MA: Addison-Wesley.

Cummins, J. (1980). The exit and entry fallacy in bilingual education. *NABE Journal, 4,* 25–60.

Cummins, J. (1986). Bilingual education and anti-racist education. *Interracial Books for Children Bulletin, 17*(3 & 4), 9–12.

Cummins, J. (1989). *Empowering minority students.* Sacramento, CA: California Association for Bilingual Education.

DeWind, J. (1997). Educating the children of immigrants in New York's restructured economy. In M. E. Crahan & A. Vourvoulias-Bush (Eds.), *The city and the world: New York's global future* (pp. 133–146). New York: Council on Foreign Relations.

Dicker, S. J. (Winter 2000–2001). Hispanics and the Spanish language: Is their status rising? *NYS TESOL Idiom, 30*(4), 18–19.

Dicker, S. J., & Mahmoud, H. (2001, February). *Survey of a bilingual community: Dominicans in Washington Heights.* Paper presented at the 23rd Annual NYS-TESOL Applied Linguistics Conference, New York.

Duany, J. (1994). *Quisqueya on the Hudson: The transnational identity of Dominicans in Washington Heights.* New York: The CUNY Dominican Studies Institute.

García, O., & Otheguy, R. (1987). The bilingual education of Cuban-American children in Dade County's ethnic schools. *Language and Education, 1*(2), 83–95.

Glick Schiller, N. (1999). Who are these guys?: A transnational reading of the U.S. immigrant experience. In L. R. Goldin (Ed.), *Identities on the move: Transnational processes in North America and the Caribbean Basin* (pp. 15–43). Austin: The University of Texas Press.

Glick Schiller, N., Basch, L., & Blanc-Szanton, C. (1992). Transnationalism: A new analytic framework for understanding migration. In N. Glick Schiller, L. Basch, & C. Blanc-Szanton (Eds.), *Towards a transnational perspective on migration: Race, class, ethnicity, and nationalism reconsidered: Vol. 645. Annals of the New York Academy of Sciences* (pp. 1–24). New York: New York Academy of Sciences.

Guarnizo, L. E. (1997a). The emergence of a transnational social formation and the mirage of return migration among Dominican transmigrants. *Identities, 4*, 281–322.

Guarnizo, L. E. (1997b). "Going home": Class, gender and household transformation among Dominican return migrants. In P. R. Pessar (Ed.), *Caribbean circuits: New directions in the study of Caribbean migration.* (pp. 13–60). New York: Center for Migration Studies.

Hernández, R., & Torres-Saillant, S. (1996). Dominicans in New York: Men, women, and prospects. In G. Haslip-Viera & S. Bauer (Eds.), *Latinos in New York: Communities in transition.* Notre Dame, IN: University of Notre Dame Press.

Krashen, S. (1991). Bilingual education: A focus on current research. *NCBE Focus: Occasional Papers in Bilingual Education, 3.*

Krashen, S. D. (1996). *Under attack: The case against bilingual education.* Culver City, CA: Language Education Associates.

Kugel, S. (2001, May 20). Dominicans march for voting rights (on the island). *The New York Times*, p. B4.

Levitt, P. (2001). *The transnational villagers.* Berkeley: The University of California Press.

New York City Board of Education. (2000, December 19). *Chancellor's report on the education of English language learners.* New York City:

New York State Education Department. (2001). *Memorandum of understanding between the Department of Education of the Dominican Republic and the New York State Education Department.*

Peñalosa, F. (1980). *Chicano sociolinguistics: A brief introduction.* Rowley, MA: Newbury House.

Phillipson, R. (1992). *Linguistic imperialism.* Oxford, England: Oxford University Press.

Pita, M. (2000). *Reading Dominican girls: The experiences of four participants in Herstory, a literature discussion group.* Unpublished doctoral dissertation, New York University, New York.

Rohter, L. (1997, February 19). Flood of Dominicans lets some enter U.S. by fraud. *The New York Times*, p. A4.

Skutnabb-Kangas, T. (1988). Multilingualism and the education of minority children. In T. Skutnabb-Kangas & J. Cummins (Eds.), *Minority education: From shame to struggle* (pp. 9–44). Clevedon, England: Multilingual Matters.

Skutnabb-Kangas, T., & Garcia, O. (1995). Multilingualism for all—General principles? In T. Skutnabb-Kangas (Ed.), *Multilingualism for all* (pp. 221–256). Lisse, The Netherlands: Swets & Zeitlinger B.V.

Smith, R. C. (1997). Transnational migration, assimilation, and political community. In M. E. Crahan & A. Vourvoulias-Bush (Eds.), *The city and the world: New York's global future* (pp. 110–132). New York: Council on Foreign Relations.

Sontag, D., & Dugger, C. W. (1998, July 19). The new immigrant tide: A shuttle between worlds. *The New York Times*, p. A1, A28–A30.

Zentella, A. C. (1990). Lexical leveling in four New York City Spanish dialects: Linguistic and social factors. *Hispania, 73*, 1094–1105.

Zentella, A. C. (1997a). *Growing up bilingual: Puerto Rican children in New York City.* Cambridge, MA: Basil Blackwell.

Zentella, A. C. (1997b). Spanish in New York. In O. García & J. A. Fishman (Eds.), *The multilingual apple: Languages in New York City* (pp. 167–201). New York: Mouton de Gruyter.

QUESTIONS TO THINK ABOUT

1. Pita and Utakis provide various definitions and characteristics of a transnational community. List as many of these as you can (e.g., two-way migration, economic, political, and family ties, dual identities and language, etc.), and comment on how the Dominican community in New York City serves as a model of a transnational community. How is the concept of a transnational community related to language and literacy?

2. In their discussion of the Dominican transnational community, Pita and Utakis contend that "Schools should help students develop and maintain fluency and literacy in both languages and should help students understand both cultures." What are the language, literacy, and educational implication of their assertions in the United States, within the Dominican community, and in the Dominican Republic? What are the advantages and disadvantages of attempting to develop literacy in both languages and cultures through the school and its curriculum?

3. The New York City public schools, according to Pita and Utakis, presently have four types of "language programs . . . [to] serve the needs of transnational Dominican students." Describe each of these programs, give its strengths and weaknesses, and assess its pertinence to transnational students. Which pedagogy and methodology do you think the authors subscribe to and what is the basis for your conclusion?

4. *Extending your understanding*: Pita and Utakis suggest that "bilingual education is . . . controversial in the United States," but nonetheless recommend an "*enriched bilingual bicultural program*, so that students can succeed in school systems in either New York or the Dominican Republic." What do you know about bilingual programs in the United States, their history, and the controversies swirling around them? You might read other authors in this text or consult journals and books for information. Based on your reading of Pita and Utakis, what do you see as possible difficulties in implementing bilingual programs in general and bicultural ones in particular? Do you think the United States educational system has an obligation to implement such programs? How might the transnational concept be connected to and facilitate the globalization of English?

TERMS TO DEFINE

Define the following words and phrases as they are presented within the context of the reading. Comment on your understanding of the significance of each one.

Transnational communities
Bilingual education
Assimilation
Freestanding ESL
Accelerated academic English language
Transitional bilingual
Dual language

Italian Patterns in the American Collandia Ladies' Club: How Do Women Make *Bella Figura?*

Gloria Nardini
University of Illinois at Chicago

Italians have immigrated to Chicago since about 1850. The greatest numbers came between 1880 and 1914, with additional peaks in the 1920s and in the period from 1946 to the 1980s, when Italian immigration ended.

According to Rudolph Vecoli, early immigrant colonies consisted of the Assumption Church neighborhood, early Chinatown, the Taylor Street area, the Northwest Side Santa Maria Addolorata parish, the North Side 22nd ward known as "Little Sicily," the Tuscan settlement on 24th and Oakley, and assorted South Side communities. Suburbs included Blue Island, Chicago Heights, Melrose Park, and Highwood (Candeloro, 1995, pp. 229–234).[1]

World War II saw the end of a geographic base for the Italian community as people moved out of their Little Italies. What survived was "a community of interest based almost entirely on voluntary associations and self-conscious identification with Italian-ness" (Candeloro, 1995, p. 245).

The Collandia Ladies' Club[2] was founded in Chicago in the 1950s as an auxiliary to the Collandia Men's Club, started in the 1930s by immigrants from Lucca.[3] It consists of American-born Italian women and Italian-born post–World War II immigrant women.[4] Entitled to membership because they have husbands in the Men's Club, these women have as their purpose "to help the men."[5]

The Collandia Club is recreational, its heart simple. Lifetime friendships are formed and fostered here where members come to play cards, to place *bocce*, and to speak Italian. Everyone knows about everyone else's troubles and pleasures. People get married, raise children, and grow old together. In some ways the Collandia represents the *caffe* and the *piazza* of the *paese* left behind.

At the Collandia, I engaged in 2 $\frac{1}{2}$ years of long-term participant observation (Hymes, 1974) to reach an emic interpretation of the culture. I came to realize the importance of being not just bilingual, but also bicultural.[6] That is, I came to understand the extent to which language and culture are inextricably bound at the Collandia Club. Despite 30 to

Reprinted with permission from *Ethnolinguistic Chicago: Language and literacy in the city's neighborhoods,* edited by Marcia Farr. © 2004 by Lawrence Erlbaum Associates, Inc.

40 years of living in Chicago, a familiarity with English, and incorporation of American holidays, the underlying mores of this club are Italian.

Of these underlying mores, the most important phenomenon is the Italian cultural construction known as *fare bella figura*, literally "to make a beautiful figure." Figuratively, the phrase means "to engage in appropriate visual display, to look good, to show off, to put on the dog"—in short, "to perform." Its opposite is *fare brutta figura*, literally, "to make an ugly figure," which means to engage in behavior lacking in appropriate style, flair, or *sprezzatura*. This last term, coined in 1528 by Baldassarre Castiglione in *The Book of the Courtier*, purports to be the key to explain correct "gentlemanly" behavior. Castiglione (1528) urged his courtier to

> steer away from affectation at all costs, as if it were a rough and dangerous reef, and (to use perhaps a novel word for it) to practise in all things a certain *sprezzatura* which conceals all artistry and makes whatever one says or does seem uncontrived and effortless.... So we can truthfully say that true art is what does not seem to be art; and the most important thing is to conceal it, because if it is revealed this discredits a man completely and ruins his reputation. (p. 67)

At the Collandia Club, a *bella figura* performance is always expected, encouraged, and constituted.[7]

Analysis of a partial transcript of a Collandia Ladies' Club financial meeting shows that within this bilingual, bicultural community, the concept of *bella figura* is transferred into speech in English, too. That is, whether speaking Italian or English, one must *fare bella figura*.

This analysis answers the following questions:

> What is the social context of this interaction? That is, how do these women "present" themselves? How are they members of the same speech community?

> What are the communicative strategies at work here? How do the women create "conversational involvement"?

> Where does "performance" occur? How is this an example of a communally constituted performance?

> What role does indirection and the view of women as "powerless" users of language play in this discourse?

The overarching question of this analysis remains: How are language and culture inextricably bound? I maintain that in this transcript[8] the Collandia Ladies claim social power for themselves through their linguistic use of *bella figura*. Thus, interpretation of their ways of speaking, both gendered and culture rich, is dependent on the social context of the Collandia Club for its full meaning.

To use Hymesean terms, in this communicative situation, otherwise known as the end-of-the-year Collandia Ladies' Club officers' financial meeting, a communicative event takes place: The women ask the Men's Club president for a reduction in Ladies' Club debt as they attend to finalizing their books. Within this event occur discrete communicative acts, specifically, a series of performances, one defined as a "starring moment." This dazzling act is a definitive performance of *bella figura* by the Ladies' Club treasurer.

Analyzing a communicative event requires that attention be paid to its salient components. Adapting Hymes' (1974) framework, Saville-Troike (1982) treated scene as composed of genre, topic, purpose/function, and setting (pp. 137–150).

In this case, the genre is persuasive discourse. Rina, the treasurer, wants the ladies to help her convince Ciro, the Men's Club president, that less money is owed to the men than is actually shown in their books. First, the Ladies' Club paid for expenses that, by rights, do not belong to them, and for which the Men's Club should reimburse them. Second, they were not reimbursed even for bills, such as for the stamps used on New Year's Eve mailings, for which the Men's Club does accept responsibility. Therefore, instead of paying the total, which they owe to the Collandia Men's Club for the Ladies' Christmas Party, Rina wants Ciro to acknowledge the Men's Club's expenses so she can deduct them. Thus, her topic and function are straightening out who is responsible for what so that efficient payment can be made.

The setting for this meeting is the banquet room of the clubhouse. At this point, having clarified their finances for themselves, the women are waiting for the Men's Club president. When Ciro enters, he participates from a standing position next to the seated ladies.

The participants are nine women,[9] only two of whom do not speak and understand Italian. Six women are members of 15 or 20 years' standing.[10] They have held myriad offices, chaired important events, played *bocce*, decorated, cleaned, and performed the thousands of functions that the Collandia Ladies' Club yearly takes upon itself. They present themselves, therefore, as a formidable force of actors whose current routine is to verify that money has been appropriately allocated so that the yearly books can be closed to everyone's satisfaction. This routine is not new, for there is a tradition that the Ladies' Club meets with the Men's Club president at the beginning of each fiscal year to finalize expenses. Not new, either, is the tension located in gender, which always arises about what, specifically, the women owe the men.

The message form is colloquial English, with occasional code switching to Italian. Much of the nitty-gritty of the exchange, the message content about who owes what, occurs between Rina and Ciro so that they fall into an act sequence of rhythmic exchange that moves to a quicker, louder pace, ultimately leading to a temporary "rupture" of sudden silence. Much overlapping, some unintelligible, goes on throughout except during these "ruptures." Sometimes side conversations can also be heard.

The components called "rules for interaction" are defined by Saville-Troike (1982) as "prescriptive statements of behavior, of how people 'should' act, which are tied to the shared values of the speech community" (p. 147). In this instance, they define what topics the women are allowed to discuss publicly. Namely, there are to be no complaints about whether it is correct to follow the bylaws, which prescribe that only $1,000 may be kept in the Ladies' Club treasury. What should be discussed is how the bylaws are being followed. The burden of explaining is put upon treasurer Rina, who should do most of the talking to Ciro. Any public entreaty she makes to lessen the financial responsibility of the Ladies' Club can be accepted or denied by him, because he is in full agreement that the Ladies' Club exists to "help the men." In the midst of refurbishing the banquet room and the kitchen, he is eager for money.[11] As president of the dominant male club, Ciro can say pretty much anything he wants.

The norms of interpretation concern following the "real rules" of the Collandia Club. These involve working hard to make money, being frugal, accepting what one is entitled to and nothing more, and following tradition.[12] Because these "real rules" rely upon oral tradition, their reconstruction depends on the memories of long-time members. Therefore, much of the conversation between the women specifies who has always done or paid for what. Much discussion also seeks to enculturate newcomers into these long-standing traditions.

According to Stubbs (1983), "transcribing conversation into the visual medium is a useful estrangement device, which can show up complex aspects of conversational coherence which pass us by as real-time conversationalists or observers" (p. 20). I use the "estrangement device" of discourse analysis to look at gendered notions of power and powerlessness as encoded in language. Here I use a feminist frame of reference that takes as (historically) important the things men do. In it, men operate as the default category and women operate as "other." I show how in their discourse these Collandia women recreate the man-as-powerful and woman-as-powerless themes with which they are societally familiar. "Power" in this case has to do with who controls the purse strings of their auxiliary. I also show how the women's language is imbedded in a microcosm of strategies, mostly of indirection, which historically have been used by the powerless against the powerful. Actually, this is my point, that the participants in this discourse are not fully aware of the deeper implications of gender roles and *bella figura*, the cultural code, which constrain them to act in the ways that they do. This transcript shows them seamlessly bringing the two together. For, as Goffman (1959) said, "We all act better than we know how" (p. 74). This meeting is ostensibly about money, but money is really a moot point because profits beyond $1,000 go to the men anyway.

What then is the meeting really about? I think it concerns the tensions involved in maintaining *bella figura* in the handling of this money. That is, the Collandia Ladies' Club accepts that the dominant club is the Collandia Men's Club, but they want acknowledgment for themselves, not just for their part in making this club work, but for their organized, rule-bound, tradition-following part in making this club work. Scott (1990) called this kind of discourse a hidden transcript of resistance, a "creation of autonomous social space for assertion of dignity" (p. 198). In other words, the Collandia Ladies' Club wants acknowledgement of their *bella figura*, as is evident in the following transcript.

TRANSCRIPT OF FINANCIAL MEETING

Lines represent breath groups; CAPS imply that the tone is louder and the pitch higher; bold-faced italicized comments (to right and left of dialogue) are explained later in the text of the chapter; and English translations are in brackets after the Italian.

The Prologue (no man present)
1 Rina: Pretty soon Ciro's going to come—*#2 powerless*
2   you're all here. You're all officers.
3   Ask him to deduct this $826.95
4   It's all their expenses.
5   Easter, Mother's day, Xmas decortions . . .
               {overlapping comments}
6 Jeanne: But wait, you owe them for the dinner yet.
#1 direct
7   Deduct that 800 . . .
8 Rina: You, you deduct.
#2 powerless
9 Frida: That's right.
Echo #1 direct with no man present
10 Rina: You deduct.
#2 powerless
11   See if they're willing to do it.
12   If they're willing to deduct, you do it.
13 Jeanne: That's right.
#1 direct
14 Sofia: Why not?
Echo #1 direct with no man present
15 Jeanne: It comes down to a matter of
#1 direct
16   you guys are letting them do it to you.
17 Sofia: That's right.
Echo #1 direct with no man present
18 Jeanne: They're going to get it anyway,

#1 direct

19	but to me it's the principle.
20	If they want to put these women down,
21	I mean let's . . .

Act One: The Show

{"Hi, Ciro" from many as Men's President walks in.}

22 Rina:	Whenever you have a moment, eh . . .
23 Sofia:	Sit down, Cirino.
24	*Metteti al tavolo, Ciro.* (in baby voice)
	[Sit at the table, little Ciro.]
25 Rina:	Whenever you have a moment, we're ready.
26	We want to show you our books.
27	We want to pay the bills.

{Some comments unintelligible. Ciro briefly goes elsewhere.}

Prologue (continued)

28 Nora:	*Questa roba che l'hai scritta te,*

Language of power with no man present

29	*l'hai fatti te i soldi di quelle li?*
30	*Allora perché devi paga'?*
	[This stuff that you wrote down,
	did you make the money from it?
	Then why do you have to pay?!]
31 Rina:	Well, we gotta.

#2 powerless

32	That's why we're here.
33 Sofia:	That's because they find the women so soft.

Echo language of power with no man present

Act One (continued)

{Ciro returns.}

34 Sofia:	Sit down, Ciro.	
35 Dora:	Did you hear how nice Sofia's saying,	
36	"Sit down, Honey?"	
	{overlapping comments—much back channel "uhhm"	
	as approval throughout following section}	
37 Rina:	Of all the money that was passed to us from last year,	
	song	
38	all the . . . everything that we collected . . .	
39	all the profits that we made . . .	*enreaty*
40 Ciro:	(Yeah) . . .	
41 Rina:	The money that we have outstanding . . .	*and*
42	it	
43	or how it all was spent . . .	
44 Ciro:	(Yeah), where's my money?	
45 Rina:	Wait.	
	{general laughter}	
46 Rina:	*Ora questi qui, questi qui,*	*dance*
	[now these here, these here]	
47	they were spent like at Easter,	
48	Easter eggs . . .	*incantation*
49 Ciro:	(Yeah) . . .	

50 Rina: <u>Easter bunny</u>
51   and then for <u>Mother's Day</u>
52   and <u>the presidential banquet</u> . . . so the ladies feel that this . . .
               {many unintelligible comments}
53 Rina: They want to take it off the money
#1 direct (first time)
54   that we owe you for the Xmas party.
55 Ciro: *Porca Miseria!* (walks off)   *temporary rupture*
               [For crying out loud!]
               {confusion}
56 Sofia: Come over here, Ciro, Ciro . . .   ***rupture commented on***
57 Rina: See, I mean—why do we want to get aggravated?
               {many comments}
58 Gloria: No, he's coming back.
59   He's going to go to the bathroom.
60 Rina: No, he's going to go . . .

Act Two
{Ciro returns.}

61 Jeanne: No, the men—it comes down to a matter of
#1 direct
62   principle . . .
63 Ciro: Okay.
64 Jeanne: We have to give it up anyway,
#1 direct
65   but we want to be reimbursed by you
66   so that our books reflect what we've really done.
67   Do you know what I'm saying?
68   When we send out your cenettas,
69   you should be paying for those stamps.
70   Normally they do.
               {Nora chimes in approval.}
71 Ciro: We do. We pay for those cenettas.
72 Rina: But like—I sent out New Year's Eve.   *song*
73   I sent out New Year's Eve.   *and*
74   Nobody reimbursed us for that.   *dance*
75 Ciro: If you sent out New Year's Eve,
76   you got the bill,
77   we pay you for New Year's Eve.
78 Jeanne: There—see?
#1 direct
79 Rina: Oh, well,   *final performance*
80   I don'T HAAAVE the BILLLL.   *re-starts argument*
               (Louder tone, higher pitch)
81 Ciro: (continuing) because everybody come with the bill
82   They say here
83   so many stamps for that
               {overlapping unintelligible comments}
84 Rina: Okay here, you know how many members we have;
85   one to every member—
86   We have a hundred and sixty seven.
87 Ciro: (overlapping) But you gotta . . .
88 Nora: But they have to have a voucher

89		to put in their books.	
90	Jeanne:	Eighty-seven dollars is …	
91	Rina:	Well, who <u>bought the stamps?</u>	*entrapment/indirect*
92	Frida:	Excuse me … I know that Norma … (unintelligible)	
93	Rina:	(overlap) Whoever <u>bought the stamps</u> …	*song*
94	Ciro:	Well, who <u>bought the stamps?</u>	*and*
95		Maybe we <u>bought the stamps!</u>	*dance*
96	Rina:	No, no, no!	
97	Ciro:	How do you know?	
98		If we don't know who <u>bought the stamps</u> …	*song*
99	Rina:	Because I have them all in here	*and*
100		from the—	*dance*
101		<u>They were bought</u>—	*(cont.)*
102		<u>they were bought</u> from the E. Postmaster—	
103		E.P. postmaster.	
104		I have the check!	*invoking authority*
105	Ciro:	(continuing and overlapping) because …	
106	Gloria:	(overlapping and correcting) E.P. she's saying	
107	Rina:	E.P. …	
108	Dora:	Oh, Matilda!	
		{several voices: Matilda B!}	
109	Ciro:	Matilda—	
110		Maybe we give her the money; *song and*	
111		we are giving the money …	*dance*
112	Rina:	(overlapping) III gave her the CHECK—	
113		how could you—	*powerful starring moment*
114		WHAT YOU SAYING—	
115		THAT SHE GETS THE MONEY TWICE?	
116	Ciro:	I don't know. (very softly)	*temporary rupture*

Different women see this issue differently. Jeanne, not Italian at all—only married to a second-generation Italian American—adopts the most direct method of negotiating with Ciro, the Men's Club president. (On the transcript I have marked her comments "#1 direct.") For her, the issue is clear-cut: "They're going to get it, anyway" (line 18), but it has to do with the "principle" in "our books" (lines 19, 62, 66). Jeanne expects that saying what she means will accomplish what she wants—that Ciro will reimburse her for expenses that are rightly his, that monies used by the women will be shown by the women as their expenses, and that the logic and "justice" of her method will be recognized by all. As an American-born feminist, for her the most important issue has to do with equality of representation. She is involved in establishing her role in the discourse of power, but she fails to understand *bella figura*. So when she says "There—see?" (line 78) to the others to indicate Ciro's compliance and fairness, she is the only one to view the matter as closed.

Rina, an Italian who migrated to Chicago at age 12, engages in almost total indirection. (I mark her comments "#2 powerless." They form part of the prologue.) She looks for solidarity: "Pretty soon he's going to come—you're all here. You're all officers. Ask him to deduct … ." (lines 1–3). In lines 28–30 when Nora code switches to Italian to ask why the Ladies' Club has to pay for events wherein they did not take in the profits, she answers, "Well, we gotta. That's why we're here" (lines 31–32). Rina speaks the quintessential language of the powerless: We are here to fulfill an agenda that we do not really control. While establishing this conflict, she seems to be reciting lines to a script. (I mark this "entreaty.") Note especially the rhythmically balanced way she sets up her initial exchange of appositives with Ciro. Twice she speaks in breath groups of threes, repeating "all" four times. I have underlined the lines:

```
37  Rina:   Of all the money that was passed to us
                from last year,
38              all the ... everything that we collected....
39              all the profits that we made .....
40  Ciro:   Yeah ...
41  Rina:   The money that we have outstanding....
42              it
43              or how it all was spent....
```

The language and prosody here are similar to classical dramatic exposition, in which the conflict is briefly encapsulated for the audience at the beginning of Act One. It seems fair to say that there is more (unconsciously?) going on in Rina's discourse than meets the eye.

In fact, The Prologue can be regarded as a contest between the language of the powerless and the "direct" language of power,[13] all spoken with no man present. None of this is performative language, for it is private and not meant to impress —the women are simply discussing what they should do before their dialogue with the Men's Club president.

When Ciro, an Italian who immigrated at 17 years of age, appears, the action becomes almost like a play, with the women as the chorus and Ciro as the main actor. (This section is marked "Act One, the Show.") Here is the Don with his handmaidens metaphorically kissing his hand. In the opening lines, Rina has set the stage for her entreaty. Her words are graceful, almost poetic:

```
25  Rina:   Whenever you have a moment, we're ready.
26              We want to show you our books.
27              We want to pay the bills.
```

She now takes the main role opposite Ciro, and the rest of the women, unconsciously perhaps, drift back and forth between being performers and audience, but all—except Jeanne—are privy to the fact that this is a "show."

Sofia too has entered into the play by code switching into diminuitives. "Cirino" she calls him in line 23, perhaps to mimic a sort of tongue-in-cheek playfulness appropriate to the unfolding drama in which he must be cajoled. This mood contrasts with her "why not?/that's right" refrain in lines 14 and 17, dead serious throughout the earlier transcript, where in line 33 she also called the women "so soft." However, that was the discourse of power, appropriate, she seems to think, when only the ladies are present. That this language is a public departure for Sofia is evidenced by the fact that President Dora remarks on her sweetness in lines 35–36, "Did you hear how nice Sofia's saying, 'Sit down, Honey?'"

Throughout "The Show, Act One," a rhythm is established as if for the performance of a metaphorical song and dance. For example, Ciro reiterates "yeah" three times as Rina dances around him with a recitation of the financial items to be discussed.

```
40  Ciro:   Yeah....
41  Rina:   The money that we have outstanding....
42              it
43              or how it all was spent....
44  Ciro:   Yeah, where's my money?
45  Rina:   Wait.
                {general laughter}
46  Rina:   Ora questi qui, questi qui,
                [now these here, these here]
47              they were spent like at Easter,
48              Easter eggs.... *incantation*
49  Ciro:   Yeah...
```

My circling of "yeah" in lines 40, 44, and 49 indicates that Ciro, too, is circling, waiting for the request he knows is about to come, for in lines 37–43 Rina had used seven synonyms as a sort of introductory refrain: "money," "everything," "collected," "profits," "money," "outstanding," "spent." In line 44 the first comment Ciro makes before walking off— "where's my money?"—reiterates the "money" of Rina's refrain.

"Wait," she says in line 45, postponing an answer to his question. It is as if he has disturbed her rhythmic, repetitive incantation of what he owes her. These are her "lines," so to speak:

46 Rina: *Ora questi qui, questi qui,*
                 [now these here, these here]
47   they were <u>spent like at Easter,</u>
48   <u>Easter eggs</u>. . .
49 Ciro: Yeah . . .
50 Rina: <u>Easter bunny</u>
51   and then for <u>Mother's Day</u>
52   and <u>the presidential banquet</u>. . . so the ladies
                 feel that this . . .

My underlining shows how she repeats herself with every breath, five times in all, always in breath groups of three, as if chanting a mantra designed to change Ciro's mind.

Finally, she gets to the point in lines 52–54, which is that "the ladies feel" that they have been shortchanged.[14] "They want to take it off the money that we owe you for the Xmas party," she states bluntly. It is her first direct statement. Hearing her request, Ciro becomes angry. In line 55 he cries, "*Porca Miseria*"—glossed to "for crying out loud"—an expression of annoyance, and intentionally walks off. So this act comes to an abrupt and dramatic close, marked "temporary rupture."

52   and the presidential banquet . . . so the ladies
                 feel that this . . .
                 {many unintelligible comments}
53 Rina: They want to take it off the money
    #1 direct (first time)
54   that we owe you for the Xmas party.
55 Ciro: *Porca Miseria!* (walks off) ***temporary rupture***
                 [For crying out loud!]
                 {confusion}
                 The attention is clearly on Ciro now. In fact, his performance
                 is so terribly important that we all comment on it.
56 Sofia: Come over here, Ciro, Ciro . . . ***rupture commented on***
57 Rina: See, I mean—why do we want to get aggravated?
                 {many comments}
58 Gloria: No, he's coming back.
59   He's going to go to the bathroom.
60 Rina: No, he's going to go . . .

In this interlude, the women become audience to Ciro, for his departure has brought the song and dance to a close. Rina, who had briefly tried a somewhat direct approach to set up her plea, drops this rhetorical strategy in line 57: "See, I mean, why do we want to get aggravated?" Thus she replicates the age-old powerlessness of women theme, the role of accepting subservience. Italian-born Sofia drops her former playfulness to speak directly in line 56, "Come over here, Ciro." I attempt a Jeanne-like logic, which does not fail to take into account the drama Ciro has invoked. "He's coming back," I say in line 58, implying that we get another chance at the dialogue. Is this an aside? Do I sense that we have not yet finished the play? Only Jeanne remains silent. Has she not perceived Ciro's leaving as an "exit" in the play?

When Ciro returns, Act Two begins. Jeanne again approaches him (lines 61–70) with the direct, logical discourse of the American feminist. She acknowledges that "we have to give it [the money] up anyway," but she is still concerned with the "principle" she mentioned earlier. "Normally," she says, the men pay for the stamps used on their mailings.

She implies that his response will not be anything other than "normal," almost as if she has not seen him yell, "*Porca Miseria*" (line 55) and run off. Notice how Jeanne's dialogue in lines 61–70, which I have marked "#1 direct," sounds more like written prose than oral discourse.

It could be written like this:

> We have to give it up anyway, but we want to be reimbursed by you so that our books reflect what we've really done. Do you know what I'm saying? When we send out your cenettas, you should be paying for those stamps. Normally they do.

Only "Do you know what I'm saying?" sounds like real talk. In the rest of her lines, there are no repetitions, no incomplete phrases, none of the emotional sense of the previous responses to Ciro's leave-taking. When Ciro says in line 71, "We do. We pay for those cenettas," Jeanne seems content that they have reached consensus about the New Year's Eve mailing. So she says in line 78, "There—see?," meaning that everything is now settled.

Rina, however, is unwilling to "settle," so she begins another song and dance.

```
72  Rina:   But like—I sent out New Year's Eve. song
73           I sent out New Year's Eve. and
74           Nobody reimbursed us for that. dance
75  Ciro:   If you sent out New Year's Eve,
76           you got the bill
77           we pay you for New Year's Eve.
```

The phrase "New Year's Eve," which I have underlined along with its pronoun subjects, is rhythmically invoked twice by both Rina and Ciro, but for different purposes. She means it as an example of how the Men's Club has overlooked her; he means it as an example of their willingness to be equitable. These lines repeat the song and dance of lines 37–51 in Act One, which Ciro had brought to an abrupt close with *Porca Miseria*!)

Now when Jeanne says, "There-see?" (line 78), Rina launches her final—and most important—performance. She says, "Oh, well, I don't HAAAVE the BILLLL," (lines 79–80) with great emphasis on both "HAAAVE" and "BILLLL," thereby contesting Jeanne's direct "settling" of the account. Ciro, too, has been involved by agreeing to the "bill" as proof of sale. We can look at this indignant comment of Rina's two ways. Either she is implying that "having the bill" is not necessary for someone of her moral fiber, the treasurer who would never attempt to get reimbursed for any illegitimate expense. Or, because she knows that she has the canceled check from the E.P. post office, which is better than having the "bill," she is setting Ciro up for a fall. Whatever she means—and I suggest that she is (subconsciously) out to ensnare Ciro—she effectively re-starts the argument.

Next, in line 91 she asks a (seemingly) innocent question, "Who bought the stamps?" to which she already has the answer. (I have marked it "entrapment/indirect.") Ciro speaks from a position of power. "Maybe we bought the stamps," he says in line 95. Again, they engage in a song and dance in which each takes a turn repeating the significant words of the other. (I have underlined their seven repetitions of "bought the stamps.") It is a prelude leading up to Rina's invoking of authority in lines 102–104. When she mentions the "E.P. postmaster" and the "check," she has won, at least directly, the battle for financial credibility.

91	Rina:	Well, who <u>bought the stamps</u>? *entrapment/indirect*
92	Frida:	Excuse me . . . I know that Norma . . . (unintelligible)
93	Rina:	(overlap) Whoever <u>bought the stamps</u> . . . *song*
94	Ciro:	Well, <u>who bought the stamps</u>? *and*
95		Maybe we <u>bought the stamps</u>! *dance*
96	Rina:	No, no, no!
97	Ciro:	How do you know?
98		If we don't know who <u>bought the stamps</u> . . . *song*
99	Rina:	Because I have them all in here and
100		from the—*dance*
101		<u>They were bought</u>—*(cont.)*
102		<u>they were bought</u> from the E. Postmaster—
103		E.P. postmaster.
104		I have the check! *invoking authority*

But Ciro is not quite ready to give up, despite everyone's realization that "Matilda" in line 108 "bought the stamps" from the "E.P. postmaster." So another song and dance scene occurs in which he and Rina repeat "money" and "check." It is almost a reprise. Notice how the lines are parallel in structure: first the subject pronoun—he says "we" twice, but she corrects him with "III"—then the verb "give" and then "money." Her line 112 is said at the same time as his line 111, thus leading to the finale.

110	Ciro:	Maybe we give her the money;	*song and*
111		we are giving the money . . .	*dance*
112	Rina:	III gave her the CHECK—(overlapping)	

It is interesting that ostensible powerlessness (indirection) seems to be the position with which Rina is most comfortable, because she reacts against Ciro in a wonderfully dramatic scene.

112	Rina:	(overlapping) III gave her the CHECK—	
113		how could you—	*powerful starring moment*
114		WHAT YOU SAYING—	
115		THAT SHE GETS THE MONEY TWICE?	
116	Ciro:	I don't know. (very softly) *temporary rupture*	

She shouts in indignation. It is her starring moment. In it she upstages Ciro.

Another temporary rupture occurs. Ciro's ending comment of "I don't know" is spoken softly, no longer a part of the tempo previously established. Unlike his parallelism in lines 110–111 "Maybe we give her the money/we are giving the money," it is now clear that Rina has outperformed him. He knows it, she knows it, and so do all the women who have been part of the chorus. Only Jeanne, perhaps, oblivious to the subtleties of the discourse, does not.

According to Tannen (1989), "Cultural patterns . . . . provide a range from which individuals choose strategies that they habitually use in expressing their individual styles" (*Talking Voices*, p. 80). My explanation of Rina's style is that she has created the strategy of *sprezzatura* or "studied carelessness," as recommended by Castiglione (1528) in *The Courtier*. Her repetitions of "You—you deduct" (line 8) and "I sent out New Year's Eve" (lines 72–73) and "who bought the stamps?" (line 91) imply a lack of entitlement for the Ladies' Club, even though she knows better. Despite the fact that she is legitimately in the right, she chooses not to make her claims outright to Ciro. After all, she could have said, "I don't have the bill. I have the canceled check for the stamps." But she deliberately withholds this information until later. When she finally does tell him, she invokes the authority of "postmaster" and "check" two times (lines 102–104, 112)—Ciro never mentions these words.

Perhaps she senses that she needs a moment of highly emotional display, a *figura* of sorts, in order to have him realize the legitimacy of what she has to say, for whenever the argument appears to be settled, she brings it up again. The first temporary rupture—his yelling out of "*Porca Miseria*" in line 55—occurs because Ciro is in control; the second temporary rupture—when he almost whispers "I don't know"—occurs because he is not. At the end, if Ciro answers "no" to "What you saying . . . that she gets the money twice?" he admits Rina was right; if he says "yes," he makes himself look stupid. So he has no viable answer. Therefore, Rina's performance, embedded in the context of (seemingly) powerless female discourse, has invoked the all important cultural construct of *bella figura* by putting Ciro in the position of making a *brutta figura* no matter what answer he gives. By saying "I don't know," he admits that she has won the challenge. The power of the performance is hers—there are no words left for him.

All of us, except possibly Jeanne, are, in some sense, engaged in performing a role in this play. Nora, in describing the unresolved gender tensions at the Collandia, is initiating me into the discourse. Sofia is pretending to believe in male dominance with Ciro, yet acting directly powerful with the women. Ciro himself is acting like the Men's Club president. The other women provide the choral backdrop. Rina's role is the most directly performed of all because in her attempt to impose her views upon Ciro, she is most in need of the performative persuasion drama affords (Goffman, 1959). Thus, she chooses to perform *bella figura*, a juxtapositioning of cultural forms, which she is able to invoke because she is both bilingual and bicultural.

But Ciro is bilingual and bicultural, too. He knows exactly what she is doing, and—perhaps—even admires and approves of it. So he acquiesces in applauding her performance, and they are able to move on to the business at hand. Ciro's quiet "I don't know" of line 116, his second "temporary rupture" which might seem almost a defeat, in actuality simply marks a shift in his behavior. The play is finished. "Come on, Ciro," Rina says when it's all over, "we've gotta take care of this." She sits down. He sits down. The bills get paid with very little drama. Rina has "won," so to speak, her right to deduct.

By the end of my analysis of this transcript, we can understand the culturally-specific drama captured within it. So we return to the questions posed at the beginning.

What is the social context of this interaction? That is, how do these women "present" themselves? How are they members of the same speech community?

The social context is that all the women are members of the Collandia Ladies' Club who know the "real rules" and are familiar with the issue of entitlement—namely, who has the right to do what?—the topic of almost all their overt discussions. This entitlement obtains both among the women themselves and between the women and the men. Moreover, their familiarity with the code of *bella figura* gives them a shared knowledge of rules both for their own conduct—for how they "present" themselves—and for interpreting each other's speech.

The women show this knowledge by attempting to get Ciro to return after the first "rupture," after he has shown the necessary pizzazz to win the first round. They need to engage with him again to make their entreaty work. At the second "rupture," however, they realize that the *tour de force* has been Rina's, and they say nothing, knowing that there is nothing to say. She has won.

What are the communicative strategies at work here? How do they create "conversational involvement"?

The overlapping, the frequently poetic-like repetition, the pace of what could be called a "high-involvement" style are what Tannen (1991) considered "ethnic style," as are Rina's (and Sofia's) strategies of indirection. "Conversational involvement" in the drama comes from all the participants' realization that a *bella figura* performance has occurred. Thus, except for Jeanne, they are speaking in English but "performing" in Italian. As "insiders," they are able to weave for themselves an emotional and philosophical involvement that operates throughout their conversation with Ciro.

Where does "performance" occur? How is it communally constituted and recognized?

"Performance" occurs twice, both times co-constructed by Rina and Ciro as they battle for control of the finances. Both performances end in a temporary "rupture." In the first case, we know that Rina is starting a performance (line 37) because she begins a list of synonyms, items for which the Men's Club bears responsibility. She speaks in breath groups of threes four different times (lines 37–39, 41–43, 46–48, and 50–52), frequently repeating herself, using repetition as "the central linguistic meaning-making strategy" (Tannen [1989], *Talking Voices,* p. 97) of poetics. Except for the one time she directly asks Ciro for what she wants, Rina engages in indirect language, also a poetic strategy. But her performance does not work because Ciro abruptly walks off without giving her an answer.

The second time, Rina signals her performance with a change in stress, pitch, and duration. Again, she speaks in breath groups of three lines (lines 72–74); again she uses repetition to create a poetic parallelism that becomes more and more authoritative as it escalates. The words she chooses invoke an official financial authority: "stamps," "postmaster," "check." At the end, her voice becomes the loudest it ever has been on the tape. She also uses a pause right before the *coup de grace* in line 115, "THAT SHE GETS THE MONEY TWICE?" as a signal to pay attention. This time her performance works because she has cowed Ciro. All he can do is mumble softly, "I don't know."

We know when the performances have ended because, in both cases, the normal give and take of conversation ends. The first time (line 55) entails a confusion of overlapping comments in which all the women become an audience to Ciro's dramatic exit; the second time (line 116), the silence signals Ciro's and the audience's acknowledgment of his defeat. According to Bauman (1977), "A not insignificant part of the capacity of performance to transform social structure ... resides in the power that the performer derives from the control over his audience afforded him by the formal appeal of his performance" (p. 16). In this case, "control" means the power to stop what had been proceeding conversationally. In other words, Rina achieves power because her audience is stopped in its tracks by her cleverness.

The ladies have helped constitute this "performance" by their willingness to let Rina speak for them; their willingness to be the audience is heard in back-channel hums of approval throughout. Rina, too, is clearly considering and speaking for them as she states in her entreaty: "You're all here, you're all officers, ask him to deduct." During her second performance, their mention of "Matilda" as the woman "who bought the stamps" lends credibility to her outrage at Ciro for implying that he gave her the money.

What role does indirection and the view of women as "powerless" users of language play in this discourse?

Stubbs (1983) maintained that much of language use is indirect, and that "a central problem for analysis is therefore the depth of indirection involved" (p. 147). This insight allows us to view much of this discourse as meaning other than what it literally says. For example, Rina's lines 26–27 "We want to show you our books. We want to pay the bills," probably really means "We want you to acknowledge that some of what we have paid was not really our responsibility." But because her meaning is expressed indirectly, if she happens to be wrong, she can save face later by claiming that she really wanted simply to "show our books." This is the power of indirection: Paradoxically, it can claim powerlessness for itself and so not be left without any way to repair a *brutta figura.*

How are language and culture inextricably bound?

Discourse analysis serves as an important tool in describing this bond, because it shows us how one creates and, at the same time, is created by the other. That is, to examine the language of this transcript without acknowledging the primacy of the cultural construct of *bella figura* as a frame is virtually impossible. Otherwise, much of what goes on becomes unclear, or worse—nonsensical. But we also cannot understand *bella figura* as a cultural construct unless it is played out as a specific linguistic performance. Otherwise, there is no meaning in what occurs. They are two sides of the same coin. That is, if we do not understand the intense importance of display and spectacle in this speech community, we also fail to realize how Rina's artful performance operates in the claiming of power. And if we do not understand how Rina's artful performance operates in the claiming of power, we also fail to realize the intense importance of display and spectacle in this speech community.

In conclusion, these women's ways of speaking, both gendered and cultured, are dependent on the context of the Collandia Ladies' Club for their full meaning. This transcript, a wonderfully rich and woven tapestry, allows us to understand that *bella figura* operates in language as well as in nonverbal behavior. Rina's performance, a dazzling display of verbal art, validates yet again the cultural code in which it is embedded.

NOTES

[1] Generally speaking, these neighborhoods were formed by chain migration patterns, with immigrants coming to live alongside others from their same town or region.

[2] The name is a pseudonym, as are all the women's names except mine.

[3] Lucca is a province located in Tuscany in north central Italy, where the dialect spoken is very close to standard Italian. By contrast, most Italian immigration to Chicago was from southern Italy.

[4] The conditions they encountered, although challenging, were not the *miseria* attributed to the illiterate waves of the early 1900s. Generally, these *lucchesi* arrived equipped with literacy, job skills, and contacts already in place.

[5] These words were told to me over and over again by different members.

[6] I, too, am bicultural and bilingual, for my father was born in Lucca; I was born in Chicago, as was my mother, whose parents came from Liguria and Tuscany.

[7] It goes without saying that to encourage *bella figura* means to avoid *brutta figura*. The latter may be even more important.

[8] It is a transcribed audiotape.

[9] Five of the Italian speakers were born in Italy, four in Lucca. The other two, American-born, come from Lucchesi parents. The non-Italian speakers are married to bilingual *Lucchese* men and identify strongly with the Italian community.

[10] Newcomers are monolingual president Dora, monolingual Jeanne, and bilingual Gloria (me).

[11] The Collandia Club has owned its own clubhouse since the early 1970s. Expenses for the building are constant.

[12] See Nardini (1999) *Che Bella Figura! The Power of Performance in an Italian Ladies' Club in Chicago*, State University of New York Press for a full explanation of the "real rules" of the club.

[13] Farr's (2000) Mexican ranchero franqueza seems to be a similar phenomenon.

[14] Note Rina's use of "feel," which implies a sort of weblike intuition. Jeanne had said, "Do you know what I'm saying?," which is more of an intellectualization

REFERENCES

Bauman, R. (1977). *Verbal art as performance*. Prospect Heights, IL: Waveland Press.

Candeloro, D. (1995). Chicago's Italians: A survey of the ethnic factor 1850–1985. In M. G. Holli & P. d'A. Jones (Eds.), *Ethnic Chicago: A multicultural portrait* (pp. 229–259). Grand Rapids, MI: Eerdmans.

Castiglione, B. (1528). *The book of the courtier*. (Trans. Sir Thomas Hoby, 1994). London: J.M. Dent and Sons.

Farr, M. (2000). *A Mi No Me Manda Nadie!* Individualism and identity in mexican ranchero speech. *Pragmatics, 10*, 61–85.

Goffman, E. (1959). *The presentation of self in everyday life*. New York: Anchor Books.

Hymes, D. (1974). *Foundations in sociolinguistics: An ethnographic approach.* Philadelphia: University of Pennsylvania Press.

Nardini, G. (1999). *Che bella figura! The power of performance in an Italian ladies' club in chicago.* Albany: State University of New York Press.

Saville-Troike M. (1982). *The ethnography of communication.* Oxford: Basil Blackwell.

Scott, J. (1990). *Domination and the arts of resistance: Hidden transcripts.* New York, London: Yale University Press.

Stubbs, M. (1983). *Discourse analysis: The sociolinguistic analysis of natural language.* Chicago: The University of Chicago Press.

Tannen, D. (1989). *Talking voices: Repetition, dialogue, and imagery in conversational discourse.* Cambridge, UK: Cambridge University Press.

Tannen, D. (1991). Indirectness in discourse: Ethnicity as conversational style. *Discourse Processes, 4,* 221–238.

QUESTIONS TO THINK ABOUT

1. Nardini uses a particular speech community and its "Italian cultural construction known as *fare bella figura*" to explore relationships among language, literacy, power, and gender. How does she conduct her study? What is the social context, who is involved, and in what ways are they members of the same speech community? How do they incorporate literate practice into their communal/organizational lives?

2. Nardini says that she "uses ... discourse analysis to look at gendered notions of power and powerlessness as encoded in language." What does she mean by this? What instances of this can you find in various parts of the script she presents? As Nardini asks, "What then is the meeting really about?" How does she answer the question? What would you add to her analysis? Do you think the people in the study understand the meanings of their verbal and nonverbal speech strategies in their performance? Why do they participate in this gendered "performance" on a regular basis?

3. Nardini asks "What are the communicative strategies at work here? How do the women create 'conversational involvement'?" Refer to both verbal and nonverbal strategies in the script as well as Nardini's discussion of the interactions to answer these questions. You may want to act out as many parts of the transcript as you can either as a class or in small groups in order to experience the strategies in a more immediate manner.

4. *Extending your understanding:* In this selection, Nardini illustrates communication within a bilingual and bicultural community. The participants, for the most part, know their gendered roles, and perform them in English, although the norms and boundaries may come from a different time, place, and language. Because we live in a diverse, multiracial, multiethnic, multilingual society, these instances probably occur more often than we realize. Refer to your own "ethnic community" or to instances in literature or movies, or to your observations, to provide an example when "meaning is expressed indirectly," and at the same time confirms how "language and culture [are] inextricably bound."

TERMS TO DEFINE

Define the following words and phrases as they are presented within the context of the reading. Comment on your understanding of the significance of each one.

Discourse analysis
Code switching
Ethnography
Gendered
Performative

Women and Empowerment Through Literacy

Malini Ghose
Centre for Women and Education, New Delhi, India

Learning to read and write may involve considerably more than the direct acquisition of a skill. For the women in rural India it is a matter of recognizing and in some cases taking power over some aspects of language, literacy, and life. This paper discusses a literacy program[1] based on the collaborative work of Nirantar, a women's collective working in the area of education, and Mahila Samakhya, a women's empowerment program in Banda, a "backward" district in the north Indian state of Uttar Pradesh. The analysis of power structures and dynamics at play in literacy work is based on reports of three teaching/learning environments, a residential literacy camp, a participatory primer development workshop, and a six-month residential educational course for rural women.

GOALS

As feminist literacy practitioners, we believe that education is not neutral, nor are we in the business of merely delivering certain skills—such as literacy—to women. Our concern has been explicitly with changing power relations at a social and individual level. We are also bound to a pedagogy which sees process and consequence as part of the same continuum, and to a belief that for women to feel empowered as a result of an engagement with education, they must be empowered within the educational practice. How power dynamics play themselves out in literacy programs, which consciously attempt an empowering and participarory pedagogy such as ours, forms the focus of this paper.

Having said this, we should add that the working understanding of power used in empowerment programs such as ours, draws on dichotomous categories like "powerful and powerless," and images of "grabbing power," "redistributing power," and the like, all of which suggest an understanding of power as a finite commodity. We appreciate the limitations of this approach, but we also find it a valid entry point to discussions when we are interacting with women who relate to the concept of power as something lacking in their own lives, and an asset of their oppressors.

On the other hand, our practice is also informed by a view of power at another level of definition: we see power as a phenomenon of structured but mutable social relationships, in patriarchy for example (see Street, 1995). This vision of power is elegantly stated by Isaac:

> the exercise of power is always contingent, it is chronically negotiated in the course of everyday life.... Thus power relations approximate less a model of stimulus and response, and more a model of endemic reciprocity, negotiation, and struggle, with both dominant and subordinate groups mobilizing their specific powers and resources (and for the subordinate solidarity is always the greatest resource). (Isaac, 1986)

This chapter is about just such struggles and negotiation; it is about the reproduction and transformation of power relations in certain literacy learning situations.

Such an analysis of power has of course been at the core of feminism, as have issues of knowledge and representation, control and resistance, authority and subordination, construction of subjectivities, and, above all, a concern for the everyday realities of women's lives. The concept of empowerment too—though now a buzzword—has been crucial in problematizing the issue of power and bringing a theoretical construct within the realm of practice. Our own work, and certainly the Mahila Samakhya program, has its antecedents in this process.

PROGRAMS

Mahila Samakhya

As women's issues came to the center stage of the "development" arena in the 1980s in India, a number of empowerment programs for women were formulated. Some were programs mooted by the government. The women's movement in India, through protest, lobbying, and critiquing patriarchal structures and institutions, had created an "alternative space" in the previously forbidden terrain of government programs. Partnerships between women's groups and government agencies, previously unthinkable, began to be forged.

As women's groups attempted to translate feminist constructs into concrete programs of action, there was a shift from looking at power as simply a negative or coercive force to regarding it as a generative, transformative, and productive force as well (Batliwala, 1993). These programs became spaces to introduce a different culture of power. Mahila Samakhya (hereafter MS),[2] originally outlined in the policy document of the Ministry of Human Resource Development (1988), was a product of this period.

The MS program works on issues of women's education and empowerment. Banda, the MS district that is the focus of this paper, is one of the poorest districts in India; it is *dacoit* (bandit) ridden, extremely poor, with a significant tribal and low-caste population, low literacy levels, and a high degree of violence towards women. Over the past six years MS in Banda has addressed a number of issues: struggles against landlords and forest contractors, education, health, and water. A particularly innovative effort has been training illiterate rural women as hand-pump mechanics. It was born out of a need to redress the water scarcity in the region and a nonfunctioning government water department. This intervention has had a number of spin-offs—a growing demand for literacy, the acquisition of new skills like masonry, and a demand for information. All these efforts have been built on a bedrock of women's understanding of their life situation—their subordination, as well as strengths.

Although it is a central government program, MS's broad mandate did encourage the development of a flexible, responsive organizational structure. Autonomous MS societies were set up, a structure that involved the state but also allowed nongovernmental organizations (NGOs), particularly women's groups, to play a role in operationalizing the project. At the core of the organizational structure were village-level women's groups called *mahila sanghas.* Village-level activists or *sakhis* were instrumental in activating the *sangha* of their village, taking up issues, discussing problems, and holding village meetings. They usually were nonliterate, poor, lower-caste women. *Sahayoginis* coordinated the work of 10 villages. They provided leadership and played a catalytic role in building and sustaining the *sangha*, and provided a link with the District Office. They had some formal education. The District Office in turn coordinated, helped plan and oversee the work of the entire district, and was staffed by a district coordinator and resource person.

The education team in Banda initially consisted of a few *sahayoginis* and teachers, called *sahelis.* The formal schooling levels of the *sahelis*, compared to the educational qualifications of teachers in general, were low, though most had completed their primary education. But this is an area where literacy levels for women are abysmally low, somewhere between 8 and 16 percent, and it was often difficult to find even a single literate woman in some villages.

The decision to work with teachers with such low levels of formal education was in part born out of necessity, but also out of programmatic principle. The program decided that it was preferable to train and work with local women, who were culturally rooted, and to create local resources rather than settle for the easier option of getting more qualified women from elsewhere. In fact the education team in Banda today includes some *sahelis* who became literate through the literacy camps organized by MS—an uncommon occurrence as far as education programs go.

Nirantar

Several of the Nirantar[3] members, of which the author is one, have been actively involved in the work in Banda since 1989, with concrete work on literacy beginning in 1991. Our involvement with the gender training and other aspects of the program provided the base for building a common understanding of education and women's empowerment between Nirantar and the Banda team.

THE APPROACH TO LITERACY WORK IN BANDA

It is important to understand the context of the women's demand for literacy. It grew out of their involvement with MS, an experience which affirmed their own knowledge and skills, and encouraged them to question, critique, and reflect on their life situation. Literacy was gradually seen as a skill that would enable women to deal with their environment from a position of strength. For the *sakhis*, their new roles as village activists demanded that they interact with the bureaucracy, schools, and other mainstream institutions on a regular basis. The women hand-pump mechanics needed literacy for specific reasons: to maintain records of spare parts, other repairs, depths of bores, etc. They expressed a sense of humiliation at having to get their log books updated by the male mechanics of the government department; *"Baar baar un ko poochna padta, achcha nahin lagta"* (We constantly have to ask the male mechanics to write our records for us. We do not like it). The demand for literacy was linked to women redefining their lived realities—which now included learning new skills, interacting with mainstream structures of power, greater mobility and self-confidence, and the desire for information on a range of issues.

Initially, the articulation of this demand compelled the program functionaries to quickly get into the act of "delivering literacy." However, each new intervention has led to an evolution of the team's (and our) perspective on education. The group now considers literacy to be instrumental to the development of a critical understanding of their lifeworld, their experiences of struggle, of joy, as well as their folklore, language, and indigenous ways of knowing. On the other hand, education for many continues to be equated with knowledge, power, jobs, and the path to a better life.

The complexities and contradictions in the approach to literacy closely resemble our understanding of power outlined above. Thus, just as on the one hand we accept power as a concrete asset or a lack, we also find ourselves treating (or being forced to treat) literacy and education as a concrete asset which we must deliver to those lacking it. Then again, we also treat power as a more abstract, contingent, and open-ended phenomenon, and we try quite hard to bring the same openness to our literacy work.

The tension between these two broad perspectives of power and education is probably the most striking feature that emerges in the experiences narrated below. There is, however, another basic thread running through these episodes—the power dynamic between "us" and "them," "teachers" and "participants." This again was an area fraught with contradictions, a situation we both accepted and tried to get past. In truth, we were generally at pains to overcome this divide, but often we reinforced it, as we certainly could not escape it.

An Experience From a Literacy Camp

Literacy camps are residential programs that initiate women into the world of letters. Through the use of locally relevant key words, discussion, and creation of learner-generated texts, these literacy camps provide a supportive learning atmosphere which dispels women's initial lack of confidence about being able to read and write. Since 1990 a number of such camps have been held in Banda. A literacy course consists of a series of three residential camps. Each camp lasts 10 days with a month-long break between each. Nirantar members were involved in evolving an appropriate teaching/learning methodology and training the local team.

What follows is an experience from one such literacy camp. By this time, the Banda education team was familiar with the methodology. This camp was being coordinated by two *sahayoginis*, a group of *sahelis*, and a facilitator from Nirantar.

> Durga (a *sahayogini*) began writing the names of the months on chart paper. As she wrote "*Chait*" (approximately corresponding to the month of April) the women in her group read out "*Chaiyat*"; she wrote "*Baisaakh*" they read "*Bayeesaakh*." This continued for a while. I wondered if this was a problem of differences in pronunciation. Or could it be that they were just reading incorrectly.
>
> It soon struck me that the *sahelis* had written the names of the month in standard Hindi and what the women (even some *sahelis*) were reading aloud was in Bundeli—the local language—the language of all oral communication in the area. I posed a question to the *sahelis*—would it not be simpler to write "*Chaiyat*" instead?
>
> There were a flood of protests—"*Chaiyat*" was not "proper" or "correct." "But you speak it?" I inquired. One *saheli* said, "We are teachers, how can we teach them incorrectly? When the women return to their villages their books will be scrutinized by family members and others in the community, like the *pradhan* (village headman). It will reflect badly on us and the program." Said another, "Besides they were learning to read and write to be able to access information. All calendars were written in standard Hindi." I was in a quandary.
>
> If "*Chaiyat*" is how they say it, how they identify with it, they should write it as such. But in the face of such strong protest, could I push my views, it will not be what they want. But then I thought, "*Chait*" for that matter was "incorrect," the "proper" (sanskritized) Hindi word is "*Chaitra*." In fact that is how it is written in most calendars. When I pointed this out to the sahelis, they said that while they were familiar with "*Chaitra*" it would be too difficult for the women to learn and pronounce.
>
> On that occasion the women learned to write "*Chait*."
>
> (From the diary of a Nirantar member, Nov. 1993)

The "*Chaiyat*," "*Chait*," "*Chaitra*" incident might appear trivial to some, especially as the words are so close—*chait* and *chaiyat* do not sound very different—but it threw up a number of issues. Questions of power were central to this. Who decides what is "correct" and what is not? As we had seen, the boundaries between the regional language and standard Hindi were not as clear as we had initially assumed. As "trainers" we could have pulled rank on the *sahelis* and insisted on *Chaitra* being taught. Or we could have ignored their need to access the mainstream and insisted on their learning the months in the local language—the language they identify with.

Decisions on language policies in the formal education system we know are made by governments on behalf of the people, but the issue of language in the nonformal system is not given serious consideration. Decisions are either not taken, implying that the dominant language is used *de facto*, or at the most a "transitional approach" is adopted where the regional or local language is used as a bridge to ultimately take the learner towards learning the mainstream language.

The *sahelis*, despite the local inflections in their own Hindi, saw themselves as "teachers" representing positions of authority and as providers of information. They were worried that this position would be open to question by other mainstream institutions. They had low levels of education, and would not have been accepted as "teachers" in a formal context. But having become teachers in MS, they had acquired a certain social standing, and they quickly stepped into their roles.

The contradiction lies in the fact that they are aware that in other areas of the MS program primacy is given to women's ways of knowing and forms of expression. Yet when it came to literacy, the *sahelis* became sticklers for formality and purity. They also felt that they needed validation from the community for something as small as writing the names of the months, despite their involvement in processes which question this "authority" in much more direct and visible ways.

This episode forced us to deal with the issue of language in literacy teaching. Then, as now, while the verbal teaching/learning transaction was done in Bundeli, the actual words being taught and the texts being created were in Hindi. Was this instrumental approach to the local language limiting the women's creativity, inhibiting expression and communication of their thoughts and experiences? Was this approach, thereby, making invisible the women's culture and ways of defining and categorizing their lifeworld? If this was so, then it was our limitation in not knowing the local language. We were Hindi-speaking people.

However, the situation was not really all that simple. Hindi symbolized the language of power; the *sakhis* themselves perceived their language as inferior. It was, they said, a *dehati* (rustic), *lath maar bhasha* (rough-and-ready language)—a poor alternative to Hindi. Bundeli had no credibility—a reflection of the inferiority they experienced *vis-a-vis* their caste, class, and gender identities.

Three broad categories of power structures came into play in this incident. At a macro level, we see the process through which dominant values, specifically dominant national languages, enforce their hegemony. It is interesting of course that literacy lends itself to this process. That is, the norms of correctness are applied to spelling but not to pronunciation. Second, there is an appeal to the power structures of the educational system. Although this incident occurred in an apparently alternative educational system, expectations of what teachers should teach and learners learn were clearly derived from the mainstream system. Finally, the incident expresses some of the power dynamics between the trainers and the *sahelis*. In this case, the trainers intervened to question the teacher's literacy practice. While we did not enforce any change, the intervention itself opened the issue for negotiation later.

Creating a Primer

We decided to develop a new primer for the program. Having a primer that the women identify with, one that reflects the beliefs of the program, was felt to be important, as it is very often the only teaching material that the *sahelis* have. A group of 10-12 *sahelis* and *sahayoginis* and members from Nirantar got together to develop a primer through a series of participatory workshops in 1993. Developing the primer threw up some important power-related issues of a participatory process of materials production. The incidents described below will highlight the issues around language hierarchies and knowledge creation, between oral and written language, literacy pedagogy and participatory processes.

Tackling Language Hierarchies

At the outset the following exchange occurred:

Facilitator (F): In what language should your primer be?

> The responses of the participants (P) varied but were unanimously in favor of Hindi:
>
> P: It should not be in the local language.
>
> P: We speak our language, there is nothing new in it, so why teach in Bundeli?
>
> P: If we teach them in their language they will remain where they are.
>
> P: How will they read other books if they are taught only in Bundeli?
>
> P: We should teach only the pure and correct form—both in the written and oral mode.

We felt differently. Language in literacy work was not merely a conduit to pass messages from a group of information providers to passive recipients. While we could not disregard the participants' strong notions of and aspirations for mainstream education, we felt that education work in the local language should at least be experimented with. Still, their strong articulation in favor of Hindi put us in a dilemma. Could we push our agenda? After all, we were committed to a "participatory" approach. Finally, drawing on the same methodology, we reasoned that it would be unfair if we were not able to find the space to express our views. We thought it necessary to make explicit the issues of power within the question of language.

We decided that a dialogue on the issue was in order. We told the group we wanted to challenge their notions of purity and correctness in the context of language. This proved to be a difficult exercise. We raised with the group issues about the politics of language and the asymmetry of power that exists in the Indian context between the use of standardized (official) languages (like Hindi) and regional languages and local dialects. We tried, through numerous illustrations, to bring home the point that language was a means to exercise control and domination, as well as self-determination, and a strong cultural expression. While they relate to the concept of "power" or "paua" (as they refer to it) and experience it—viz. the landlords (class), by upper-castes, and as women, it was difficult for them to do so within the context of language.

Not having made any headway we decided to explore the issue differently rather than drop it completely. To not make explicit the various dimensions of subordination of Bundeli would have been to perpetuate unequal power relations. We undertook an exercise where we developed word lists in Bundeli in certain categories—items found in the house including architectural terms; kinship patterns; different idioms and qualities related to men, women, and children; adjectives used for different types of personalities; jewelry items, etc. The corresponding words in Hindi and English were written alongside. This exercise generated excitement. Every word brought with it an outpouring of stories—intensely personal, but also humorous and satirical: "they used to tell me not to laugh like that . . . my mother got these kinds of earrings made when I got married . . . they used to shout and call him a 'belli' [nut] . . . the milk used to be hidden in this kind of cupboard . . ."

Though each story, even around the same word, was different, they all shared a common cultural experience. Experiences, from which we were excluded, but became a part of, in the narration. Our interest somehow seemed to affirm their experiences and the stories kept flowing. (Excerpts from the workshop report)

The process revealed a wealth of indigenous cultural experiences and the richness of the local language while simultaneously inverting the power dynamics between Nirantar members and the *sahelis*. For instance, the group found that there were words in Bundeli that had no equivalent in Hindi. English was able to capture even fewer nuances. In English you have only uncle and aunt, in Hindi there are special terms for every kind of uncle or aunt; your father's sister is *bua*, and mother's sister is *maasi*; and Bundeli is even more nuanced. Each term carries connotations of a unique relationship. In other categories too there were Bundeli words that found no place in Hindi. If these words were not within the mainstream language should they be deleted from our vocabulary as well? Were these words "incorrect"? As the discussion flowed the group decided that they would settle for a mix of Hindi and Bundeli.

This exercise brought into focus the main issues or assumptions. First, that writing, unlike speech, calls for the authorized version. Second, new learners and their teachers are faced with this issue of power and who has the right to say how something will be written.

Participatory Writing Process: The Complexities Involved

So far so good. But the next day when we attempted to build on this fruitful exercise we were in for a surprise.

On the basis of the previous day's exercise we asked them to select key words and create reading texts. They wrote: "Minu fetch water," "Ramu go to the fields," "Rita cook the food." Everything was an instruction. The readers were passive receivers. We took their work and read it back to them. They looked unmoved. We asked them, where was the laughter and animation of the previous day? If we had enjoyed the stories so much could that not then form part of their primer? They said, "But then we were 'telling' the story. Those kinds of stories are never in books. We never thought they were worth anything much." "But then you never wrote books before," we replied. "Now you will, so you can put what you want into them."

It is evident from this incident that there was a sharp distinction in the women's minds between what is appropriate for oral and for written communication. While indigenous language and images find reflection in the oral mode, literacy and the written mode is concerned with instructions, development, and information, and always reflects the images and perceptions of the mainstream language. We felt we had to intervene again to make the group realize that they had the power to shape the primer as they chose, to include their images and content. The conflicting images of that content held by teachers and learners had to be reconciled. It was a realization of the power they would wield, as well as the potential power to change and redefine what counts as knowledge. To make the alternative possible we had to first validate their language and cultural experiences and establish that language was central to knowledge creation. And it was not insignificant that the validation was coming from us—people who to them represented the mainstream.

How Did We Select What to Include in the Primer?

In the previous day's exercise they had listed Bundeli words for architectural features within their houses. One such feature was a special cupboard called a *kimaria*, where all the precious "goodies"—like extra milk or ghee or some sweets—would be stored. Numerous stories had been narrated about the *kimaria*. Most of them had to do with women or young girls being denied access to the *kimaria*. One story was slightly different. One of the *sahayoginis* as a young girl was caught stealing milk from the *kimaria*. It was humorous, used the local idiom, and had caused much merriment in its narration. This type of story was finally selected for the primer.

When it came to making a selection a majority of the group suggested one of the denial stories. But we felt very strongly that selecting that story would only reinforce the stereotypical relationship between a mother-in-law and young bride which is usually portrayed as being tense, strained, and one of restriction and denial. Was it not possible to present a more humorous side to women's and young girls' lives? Although many of the books available portray young girls as being burdened with work and discriminated against, we emphasized that every time we present a story (written or oral) we are implicated in a particular way of understanding the world and our place in it (Simon, 1987). Do we then always want to produce narratives that represent women as "victims"—denied, burdened, and discriminated against?

Maniya's Story: When Real Events Become Material for Texts

As we were working on the primer that evening some women from the Mahila Samakhya office rushed into the room saying, "A young woman, Maniya, has been burnt to death by her husband. A group of us are going to Manikpur [a nearby town] to try and catch him."

We all dropped our work and prepared to leave with them. No one needed any prompting.

A group of about 15 women from Mahila Samakhya reached Manikpur. We gathered the women of Maniya's neighborhood and began having a meeting. All of a sudden the dead women's husband appeared—dressed in white, feigning a deep sense of loss at his wife's death. He thought we had come to pay a condolence visit. But the women were in no mood to be taken in by his deceit. We accused him of the crime. He denied having committed it. The women did not relent. He finally admitted that he was guilty, but with no hint of remorse or shame. We were enraged and started beating him. We painted his face black, made him wear a garland of slippers, and paraded him through the town.

On returning to the workshop everyone started writing out the story as a lesson in the primer. There had been no consultation. The key word selected for the lesson was "*chadchatta*" (a deceitful fraudulent person), a word in Bundeli that had emerged in the previous day's exercise. They were convinced that no other word could describe the man. (From Nirantar's workshop report)

The primer workshop experience reveals an unusual sequence of events. Here the Nirantar members were obviously quite forceful in pushing the women to affirm their local tongue. But after the apparent success in generating a lively discussion on the joys of Bundeli, this momentum floundered the next day on the deeply ingrained association of literacy with the national language. Yet it was finally the intervention of "everyday life" or at least a common tragedy that shook the women into a realization of the virtues of their own language. This episode also reveals to us the virtues and limitations of "classroom exercises." The classroom discussion while creative and important did not seem to have any concrete significance for the women. But after the cathartic experience of punishing Maniya's husband, the women spontaneously drew on their vernacular for the unusual but plainly empowering act of labeling the murderous husband. It is, however, unlikely that this would have happened had the discussions not moved outside the language exercise.

Issues of Power Emerging From a Structured, Long-Term Educational Program

The women and adolescent girls who had acquired basic literacy skills at the literacy camps and centers articulated a strong demand for further education. A six-month residential course at the Mahila Shikshan Kendra (Women's Learning Center) began in January 1995 to meet this demand.

The examples below are drawn from the first course at the Mahila Shikshan Kendra (MSK). It was during this period that the curriculum was developed collaboratively by Nirantar, MS Banda, and the 28 participants.

MSK as a "School"

MSK was a long-term, structured educational activity. And it generated a set of power dynamics and negotiations unlike anything in the literacy camps and the primer development workshop. The participants came to the MSK with a fixed set of expectations. For them MSK symbolized a "school"—a school with a difference, but a school nonetheless. This carried with it the entire baggage of notions associated with School as a social institution which define a set of expectations about school and its outcomes. First, a school has a prescribed set of (power-laden) relationships between teacher and learner; teachers have authority over pace and content; they control discipline; the teacher is the "expert"; "knowledge" is what the teacher provides. These notions impacted directly upon the MSK structure and activity in a myriad of interesting ways.

The Power of the Participants

We know about our forest and trees. We know how integral forests are to our lives. We know what sources of water we have in our village and the problems around it. All you do is listen to us and give back what we have told you. What do you have to give us? Tell us what we do not know. You have not told us anything new in a week! (Participant's reactions a week after the MSK started, Jan. 1995)

We were stunned. We didn't know how to respond. We were all set to explore the possibilities of working on an alternative "learner-centered" curriculum where the learner and her lifeworld would be at the center of the educational experience. Were we free to do this?

We were forced to shift gear, teaching became more information oriented. Learners had an insatiable demand for information. We were doing a session on the movements of the earth—rotation, revolution, and the seasons, and before the session even ended we were questioned: "We want to know about rain and how the monsoons reach us. Why are you keeping this 'hidden' from us?"

They were here at the "school" to learn—learn not what they already knew but what we knew. (Nirantar members' field notes)

As practitioners committed to a learner-centered approach we had planned a curriculum that was not predetermined but loosely centered on issues of land, water, forest, and village and society. The starting-point would be to explore these aspects from the perspective of the participants' own environment, lived experiences, and needs. Around these we would structure new information areas, discussion, critical awareness, gender issues, etc. Texts written and created in the classroom and other informally produced material would be the learning material. This way participants and the local education team, we felt, would have some degree of control over the curriculum. But, as the quote above indicates, the participants clearly wanted otherwise.

The participants certainly had insights and information which we did not, but these were not always precise or comprehensive. It is a mistake, as is the case in many programs, to assume that all local people will be repositories of local knowledge. There certainly existed experts in particular areas of local knowledge, but these specialists were not at the MSK classroom. We continue to struggle with the issue of how to add substantively to learners' knowledge about the local environment, history, and culture.

This is not to say that we were denying them all mainstream information. The need for MSK to achieve equivalency with the primary school level had been articulated at an early stage of its planning. What we were unprepared for was the intensity and single-mindedness of the demand from the learners.

The demand for equivalency made sense for the girls, some of whom wanted to enter mainstream schools after the MSK. But did the women want mainstream content as well? We knew that rural women reject formal schooling (and have done so for years) precisely because they see it as irrelevant. They don't believe it can change their lives. At the same time many of them were closely scrutinizing the textbooks of their school-going children, probably to make sure that the MSK was not cheating them of mainstream content. This might appear contradictory; it is in fact a reflection of the complex relationships poor rural women have with mainstream education structures. On the one hand, by rejecting the mainstream, they acknowledge that mainstream curriculum content does not address their needs, and that the teaching methodology of the formal system does not help them learn. On the other hand, the kind of education they desire continues to be influenced by that which is taught in school. This education would give them the knowledge they have been denied; knowledge and information that allowed the "educated" to remain powerful.

Thus, in a sense, while we saw the MSK educational intervention as "providing them with an opportunity," they saw it as "redressing denial."

We gradually found the MSK taking on the trappings of formal education. A Nirantar member wrote in her field-notes: "They are getting too schoolish in their style—sit in straight lines, walk in straight lines, say prayers in the morning, ring bells in between sessions..."

These routines were not initiated by us, but were things the participants wanted at the MSK, even as they admitted that their children learned nothing at school. These seemingly contradictory responses had to be negotiated constantly at the MSK. It was both interesting and ironical that the power exercised by the learners in this process of negotiation was a power given to them by our commitment to a feminist, participatory pedagogy. Certainly a traditional "school" would not have allowed learners to determine the content. Yet this very power was subverting our pedagogy!

It was not as if dialogue, discussion, and critical awareness were abandoned altogether, but it had to be woven in with their demands. Thus began a process of negotiation; a negotiation which forced all of us to change. We altered our approach to include some aspects of more mainstream curricula, not completely at the expense of other subject areas. Consequently the learners, having compared the MSK curriculum with school textbooks, felt satisfied that their education was at par with formal school education. They grew to see that dialogue, discussion, and role-playing of local issues, even if they did not deliver "mainstream information," were not a waste of time, but critical to the learning process. They responded enthusiastically to alternative content and methods. They were excited by debates—on whether large dams are more beneficial than small ones, or whether the Taj Mahal should be protected from industrial pollution by shutting down local factories; and animated discussions took place on the healthcare system, on women, and on violence. Just as we negotiated content we established the validity of dialogues, discussions, and role-playing as important educational tools.

The learners were able to determine the pace and the content of learning because their responses were our only source of affirmation of the entire MSK process. The process was validated when the learners responded, when they asked questions, when interaction took place. And if they chose to be silent, then we were rendered entirely powerless. They could exercise power by simply refusing to learn. Unlike in the formal educational system, where failure rests on the students, in our system it rested on the teachers and us. Because MSK was an "alternative" educational activity it could ultimately only be validated by the learners themselves.

The Empowerment of the MSK Sahelis

"Everything was new. We have taught in numerous literacy camps but here the process of teaching was very different. We had to teach them things we ourselves did not know and also discuss it with them. We didn't feel competent."

"During a session on eclipses somebody asked how many days does it take for the moon to revolve around the earth? I didn't know, so I diverted the participants' attention and desperately searched for the information."

Why was the diversion necessary?, we asked.

"Otherwise our credibility would be lost. Anyway they are always trying to think of ways to catch us out." (Minakshi, the MSK coordinator, during the review meeting)

Among the defined sets of relationships in a traditional school is that of teacher-learner. The teacher is the expert, the empowered one, the knowledge-giver. But in the MSK, the teachers were initially the most disempowered group. The *sahelis* who taught at the MSK not only had low levels of formal education, but the quality of education they had received was poor—typical of government schools in rural areas. As the quotation above reflects, they had a limited information base, were not confident of their teaching abilities or their own information levels, nor were they familiar with teaching methodology beyond literacy teaching. To make matters worse they were young, and from the same caste and class as the learners. A traditional, educated, upper-caste teacher would have fitted the bill better. All these factors worked against the teachers being accorded any kind of respect by the learners. In the participants' perception, these teachers simply did not command authority.

The teachers were desperate to establish their credibility. And their position was a constant source of anxiety for us.

> I have been feeling deep anxiety about how the *sahelis* are going to manage . . . their informa-
> tion levels are so low . . . they have forgotten completely what they learnt in school . . . quite a
> reflection on how ineffective the formal system is . . . but on the 17th they sat down to do their
> own reading . . . what was good was that they at least were able to grasp what information was
> being given without us holding their hand—so I guess we have something to be grateful about.
> (Nirantar, member's diary)

In a traditional school setting we would have been concerned with challenging the all-powerful role of the teacher as the "repository of knowledge." Here, our task was just the opposite. The teaching/learning process had to empower not only the participants, but the teachers as well. Therefore, instead of questioning, we bolstered the teachers' role as "information-givers," allowing them and the participants to feel that the *sahelis* were in control of the information they were giving. On several occasions when some learners were intent on picking out the teachers' mistakes we had to actively intervene and put a stop to it.

It was paradoxical to our pedagogy, that we had to "empower" the teacher by invoking a traditional teacher-student relationship, even as we tried to alter and redefine it. It was a contradiction because it was our participatory approach and MS's philosophy of empowerment which were the source of the power and confidence that led the learners to disrespect the teacher in the first place.

Nirantar's Power

During the first few months, as everyone was trying to cope there was little time ro reflect. We were all consumed with issues such as: how to teach a particular topic, how to collect the necessary information on such-and-such, and how to prepare the *sahelis* to take the session. In this process a division of roles emerged. As the *sahelis*' own levels of information were so low, it became Nirantar's task to do the research for the sessions, take decisions on what to teach, and plan the lessons as well. The actual teaching, however, was done by the *sahelis*. This role reinforced the notion of the outsider being the "providers of information," a notion we were simultaneously trying to break.

This role also gave us tremendous power over the *sahelis*; for them, we were the "experts"—a role which they began to accept unquestioningly, to the point of total dependence. Breaking free from that role meant disempowering the *sahelis vis-a-vis* the learners. We were caught in a double bind.

Social Context of an Alternative Educational Activity

The nature of Nirantar's involvement with the program, the *sahelis*, and the learners left us with no choice but to accept certain problematic power dynamics with the MSK. Among these was Nirantar reinforcing the powerful role of the "outside expert." We were accountable for seeing that the effort was a "success." This must be seen within the context of rural reality.

Those working in literacy are well aware of what it means for rural women to leave their homes for a period of six months to attend an educational program. Behind each woman's presence at the MSK was a story of long struggle and months of negotiations with the family and community. This was an unprecedented occurrence for the area; an effort which, if rejected by the community or learners, would have serious implications for doing education work in the area. That the women should remain, learn, and enjoy their educational experience was uppermost on our minds.

The women's presence at the MSK was not entirely within our control. They were there so long as their community, their families, or rather the men in the families, saw fit for them to be there. Literacy efforts and what happens within them cannot be seen as isolated little conclaves, they must be placed within the realities of the sociocultural context in which they are situated.

The Relations Between Knowledge and Power

How do different belief systems and ways of seeing the world impact upon an educational process? This issue came up starkly in certain sessions but was an underlying concern throughout.

Are Rivers and the Earth Living or Nonliving?

During one of the sessions in the MSK devoted to looking at different ways of categorizing, the participants were categorizing the world around them into "living" and "nonliving." The lesson progressed smoothly till they came to classifying soil and river. The participants classified both as living. The *sahelis* too believed this. There was a moment of confusion as the MS resource person present had a niggling feeling of doubt. A science textbook she had read had classified soil as nonliving. But the *sahelis* were not persuaded. Not being absolutely certain, and fearing that the *sahelis'* confidence would be undermined, the MS resource person let it pass and the lesson proceeded without further hiccups.

That afternoon two members from Nirantar reached the MSK. On hearing about the morning's sessions they expressed alarm; it was factually incorrect to classify river and soil as living. A hasty meeting was convened. The *sahelis* defended their position. They eventually referred to the background material that had been given to them by Nirantar, which said, "*Jaise hamare shareer ko hava, pani, aur khana takat badane ke liye zaroori hota hain, vaise hi mitti ko bhi zinda rehne ke liye in sab ki zaroorat hoti hai*" (Just as human beings require air, water, and food to keep alive, soil too requires the above). The lifelike quality attributed to soil was a turn of phrase, and not to be taken literally. For the *sahelis* it only served to reinforce what they already believed. We defended our position by checking both soil and river against the listed characteristics of living things. They did not fit. Science textbooks were referred to. The *sahelis* fell silent. They were uncomfortable about announcing to the class that they had made a mistake. We decided to reopen the discussion and try and rectify things.

Some excerpts from the discussion:

Intervenors (I): Which of you think that soil and rivers are living? [All the learners (except one) raised their hands.] Why do you think they are living?

Participants (P): River is our devi (goddess) and "dharti" (earth) is our mother.

        I: Your real mother is living. Earth and rivers are mother images, not your real mother.

       P: They both give life—our grain, plants, forests grow in soil. Rivers give us life-giving water. Our mothers give life.

       I: It is true that they are life supporting but that does not mean they are living themselves. We eat food and grains to live but the grain itself is not living. They do not grow. They do not procreate.

P: But if soil did not have life it would not produce life. Rivers grow. They grow in the monsoons and shrink in the summers. They do give birth to other rivers.

Chamela, a learner, challenged her colleagues: A river is nonliving because rivers dry up in the summer. Something living cannot periodically live and die.

P: River is a mother and mothers can have many children. If one child dies do we say all others are dead or that the mother is dead? Earth is our mother and earth drinks water.

I: But a piece of cloth also soaks water, it is not living.

I: What is a river made of?

P: Water.

I: Is water living?

P: Water in a glass is not living but a river is living. A river is living because it flows, it moves, it cuts its own course.

I: You are saying that soil is living, but is this (holding up a lump of soil) living?

P: No, in this form it is not living but the earth is living. Gods and goddesses give birth to river. Earth is a goddess. We pray to them.

I: That is a matter of your belief. Your religion. Others religions or belief systems may not accept this. For instance, scientists believe that they are nonliving. Everyone is free to have their own beliefs and that is nice. The logic you put forward holds for the way you look at the world and similarly the logic within the other system is consistent.

This interaction, very early on in the semester, compelled us to reflect on our practice. There was a distinct polarization between the way we categorized the world and their ways of looking or knowing. The interaction described above pitted one belief system against the other. However, the manner in which the interaction unfolded, with us trying to counter every point they made with a different logic, was not fruitful. The two systems really had no basis for comparison. And though we gave value to their ways of seeing, we did try and uphold a scientific, positivist conception of knowledge. Categories such as living and nonliving had been emphasized as "scientific" and "logical," and the task of teaching and learning had to do with the acquisition of "universal," neutral content.

Yet the situation was not simply about imposing our worldview and disregarding theirs. And the episode in many ways was a dialogue among equals. Learners, till the end, were far from convinced that the categorization we were trying to suggest had any value or validity. Their beliefs that earth and river are "goddesses," "life-giving," and "mother" could not be separated or broken down into components such as "river is made of water and water is nonliving." The power and meaning that River and Earth hold in their lifeworld is too great and too integral to their existence. "Humanizing" or giving things human attributes was also integral to the participants' language use—branches are children, sap is blood, when you cut a tree it bleeds, and the rustling of the leaves when a tree or branch is being cut are cries of pain.

Such an intellectual stance by Western standards exhibits what is called "animism" and is frequently labeled a "misconception" to be overcome. However, Western researchers report the common failure of even systematic instruction to overturn such views (diSessa, 1996; Mintzes, Wandersee, & Novak, 1997). Divorcing this language use when trying to categorize is also not possible. Cultural roots are far more resistant and educational interventions cannot wipe these out so quickly or simply. Furthermore, the dangers of negating the learners' lifeworld are immense. Most education programs pay little attention, as we did on that occasion, to the connections that exist between knowledge and its practical, cultural, and linguistic realities in the learners' lives. Teaching and learning is not simply the acquisition of universal, neutral content; rather, knowledge is an instrument of reflection and insight.

This stalemate was not the last word on the issue of living and nonliving; the dialogue resurfaced on another occasion. The same group of women, when discussing how rivers are formed, unhesitatingly declared that they are formed from melting snow of the mountains. This also brought home the fact that people are products of a complex reality, have different "voices" (Wertsch, 1991), and do not necessarily believe in "one truth." The voice that argues strongly for the river being a mother, living, a goddess, and created by gods, also believes that rivers are born from melting mountain snows. Both voices are equally real.

The interaction also brought out power dynamics in relation to the *sahelis*. The *sahelis* had not really been convinced of our argument but possibly did not feel on strong enough ground to counter our views. In a polarized situation they felt they must team up with us rather than the learners.

Some final questions arise: What made us include this in the curriculum? Why try and teach adult women categories like living and nonliving? They already had well-defined ways of seeing and categorizing. We realized that this decision was unconsciously determined by our own primary-level schooling, and not by any carefully thought-out criteria. And indeed the distinction between living and nonliving is one of the first lessons in most school textbooks. But then, if we did not bring in such topics would we be excluding them from a way of seeing shared with a large section of society? Such questions remain unanswered.

Is There a Difference Between "Forced" and "Genuine" Sati?

We decided to discuss the issue of *sati* by analyzing the Roop Kanwar Case—a controversial case which brought together women's groups from across the country to protest and lobby for legislative changes. *Sati* is the practice of burning a widow on her husband's funeral pyre. It was widely prevalent in the early nineteenth century in parts of India. Despite legislation against it, some cases of *sati* have been reported in India in the past 40 years. Roop Kanwar, a young widow, was burned alive on a husband's funeral pyre on September 4, 1987, in Deorala village, Rajasthan. When we decided to take up the issue of *sati*, we were aware that many in the group probably believed that women who immolate themselves on their husband's pyre are goddesses and should be revered. They do, however, make a distinction between "forced" and "genuine" *sati*: the latter occurs when women "possessed" by *sat* or truth, after their husband's death throw themselves "willingly" into the fire. It is believed that in this state the widow becomes so powerful that she does not feel pain and can perform miracles. Though *sati* is certainly not a common occurrence, it is integral to their belief system.

> As the *sahelis* were unfamiliar with the case I discussed it with them in great detail—the gender, caste, and political dimensions and the strategies adopted by the women's groups. This was easy as I had been so involved with the case myself. I told them about the family members, how the politicians and police had reacted, and how we had countered all that. The sahelis were meant to facilitate the session, and I was to support them.
>
> The discussion had hardly begun when the women made the (expected) distinction between "forced" and "genuine" *sati*. While they upheld genuine *sati* they sympathized with forced *satis*. From this point on *sahelis* were unable to take the discussion forward. They didn't know whether to take on the women and counter genuine *sati* or to elaborate upon the details of the case. The former they were not equipped to do. Some still believed in it themselves.
>
> I had to take over because there was a danger that the discussion would only reaffirm *sati*. I deconstructed the Roop Kanwar Case and discussed the issue of why women should feel the need to commit *sati* in the first place. I linked this to women's status as widows. Many in the group were widows. They shared their experiences of discrimination and hardship. However, they continued to put forward arguments to defend genuine *sati*... after becoming *sati* women

become goddesses and are revered...That is the only time women are powerful...if Roop Kanwar had been coerced then we oppose it...

It was at this point that I stated in no uncertain terms that "I believe that *sati* is murder," and by upholding *sati*, genuine or otherwise, they were participating in creating conditions to make women believe that. My declaration was met with silence. (Nirantar member's diary)

Here again we had two positions pitted against each other. But the dynamics were different. The learners were a group of women who were in the process of developing a feminist perspective and would instinctively pick up cudgels to fight cases of rape and domestic violence. Why was there a resistance to questioning this form of violence against women? As in the previous example, here too we have a case of women speaking in different voices—hence the distinction between "forced" and "genuine" *sati*. Their feminist voice allowed them to acknowledge that there was "forced" *sati*, which was wrong and should be condemned; and their other voice, which was rooted in religious and cultural beliefs, made them say "genuine" *satis* were possible and were divine acts. By making this distinction, they gave themselves the space to hold on to their religious and cultural beliefs, while simultaneously allowing their feminist voice to speak.

In an education space like the MSK, such plurality was constantly expressed. However, upholding plurality could not become an end in itself. Thus it was important for us to state our position unequivocally and from a position of power. There is no genuine *sati*. While in the living/nonliving example, we stated our position, we did it with trepidation, wanting to acknowledge the other belief system. In this case, we were clear about wanting to state our position and even replacing theirs with it.

CONCLUDING COMMENTS

The three teaching/learning activities raise important questions for people who are working in the area of education and literacy. Often by defining education and literacy as empowering and describing our practice as "participatory," we do away with the uncomfortable question of power. Participation embodies the notion of equality—since everyone participated in the activity, they all had an equal say. We also do away with questions of power by invoking the fact that we do not work on or for people but we work with people. In this case study an attempt has been made to unpack the concept of participation and to demonstrate that we are constantly working in situations that are ridden with inequalities. An analysis of power in our daily practice becomes critical, as the teaching/learning situation is not a neutral one. It is a real material site of social relations.

The other element that runs through all these experiences is the constant tension that exists between the mainstream and the creation of an alternative. The experiences demonstrate that neither can we in our practice do away entirely with the mainstream, nor can we simply construct the "other" in opposition to the mainstream. Negotiating between the two becomes crucial to the construction of a sustainable literacy intervention, where there is an integrated "participation" of the two rather than mere substitution. This brings us back to our understanding of power, where the two notions of power—one as a commodity and the other as generated through structured relationships that are mutable—become part of this negotiation with marginalized groups who experience power only as a lack.

NOTES

[1] A version of this chapter was presented by Nirantar at the International Seminar on Literacy and Power held in Harare, Zimbabwe in Aug. 1995. The field experiences recounted in this paper date from the period between 1991 and 1995.

[2] Mahila Samakhya or Education for Women's Equality is an Indian central-government program of the Department of Education, Ministry of Human Resources Development. It was launched in 1989 in the states of Karnataka, Gujarat, and Uttar Pradesh, and has since expanded to cover several other states. Banda is one of the districts in Uttar Pradesh, where the program was first launched. The program was launched in pursuance of the National Policy on Education in 1986, which was the first policy-level expression of the belief that education can bring about changes in the status of women.

[3] Nirantar, a Gender and Education resource center, was set up in 1993. Our mandate, very briefly, is to make education an enabling and sustainable process for women. We work in close collaboration with field-based nongovernmental organizations to plan and implement education strategies, produce alternative curricula and reading material for newly literate adults, and conduct gender sensitization trainings. The dissemination of these experiences is an important part of our work. We are involved in action research and various campaigns on women's issues, especially violence against women.

REFERENCES

Batliwala, S. (1993). *Empowerment of Women in South Asia: Concepts and practices*. New Delhi: Food and Agriculture Organization of the United Nations.

diSessa, A. (1996). What do "just plain folk" know about physics? In D. R. Olson and N. Torrance (eds.), *The Handbook of Education and Human Development: New models of learning, teaching and schooling*. Cambridge, Mass. and Oxford: Blackwell Publishers.

Isaac, J. (1987). Beyond the Three Faces of Power: A realist critique. *Polity, 20*(1), 4–31.

Ministry of Human Resource Development. (1988). *Mahila Samakhya*. New Delhi: Government of India.

Mintzes, J., Wandersee, J., and Novak, J. (1997). Meaning learning in science: The human constructivist perspective. In G. D. Phye (ed.), *Handbook of Academic Learning: Construction of knowledge*. San Diego: Academic Press.

Simon, R. (1987). Empowerment as a pedagogy of possibililty. *Language Arts, 64*(4), 370–382.

Street, B. (1995). Literacy and power? Paper presented at the International Seminar on Literacy and Power, Harare.

Wertsch, J. (1991). *Voices of the Mind: A sociocultural approach to mediated action*. Cambridge, Mass.: Harvard University Press.

QUESTIONS TO THINK ABOUT

1. In the beginning, Ghose says that "learning to read and write may involve considerably more than the direct acquisition of a skill." She also says, "it is a matter of recognizing and in some cases taking power over some aspects of language, literacy, and life." What does she mean by this? What are the various definitions of literacy she offers throughout this piece? How does she expand the concept of literacy and relate it to language, gender, social practices, and life in general?

2. Ghose presents literacy programs that include teachers with varied educational levels and backgrounds. How did this happen and what is the rationale she offers for this configuration? What are the advantages, disadvantages, and problems that are encountered by this diverse group of teachers? How do varied teacher preparation and experience affect questions of power, of who decides the language of instruction, of what is and isn't correct pedagogy and English usage, and of what content should be included?

3. One of the results of these programs is that "The women and adolescent girls who had acquired basic literacy skills at the literacy camps and center articulated a strong demand for further education." What do you think were the factors that lead to this result? What allowed women to participate in the programs and what would be critical in determining their continued engagement with education? Do you believe that this should be one of the critical consequences of literacy? Finally, based on your reading of Ghose, what do you consider the transformative power of literacy?

4. *Extending your understanding:* Following her discussion of "rivers and earth [as] living or nonliving," Ghose says in regard to conflicting belief systems: "Cultural roots are far more resistant and educational interventions cannot wipe these out so quickly or simply. Furthermore, the dangers of negating the learners' lifeworld are immense." Think about the meaning and implications of these statements. Then consider an educational intervention that has the potential to meet with resistance and that could negate a learner's "lifeworld," or one that has actually happened. There are many instances in American, as well as international, history you can refer to: removing native American children from their homes and sending them to special boarding schools that would "teach" them mainstream culture and eradicate their Indian roots; or instances of not allowing Spanish-speaking children to use Spanish in the United States classroom, etc. So what are the dangers of "negating the learners' lifeworld," educationally as well as socially and psychologically? Do you think it is ever worth it?

TERMS TO DEFINE

Define the following words and phrases as they are presented within the context of the reading. Comment on your understanding of the significance of each one.

Feminist literacy practitioners
Sahelis
Participatory writing
Empowerment
Sati

Confessions of an English Professor: Globalization and the Anxiety of the (Standard) English Practice

Robert Ji-Song Ku
California Polytechnic State University

I am an English professor. The principal business of the English professor is to study and teach English. Like most people in my line of work, I have acquired my position by earning an advanced degree—the highest one that exists, in fact—*in* English. This indicates that I have consciously, systematically, and, yes, even monastically, studied English for a long time. In short, I have *practiced* English for a very long time.

Practice. By evoking *practice* over other related terms in this exploratory essay, I am hoping to benefit from this particular word's specific valences of possible meanings:

- First, by practice, I mean to imply the idea of profession, vocation, occupation, or career. Thus, I wish to consider the practice of English as one might consider the practices of law or medicine. Is it possible to somehow make good use of the odd sounding combination of the two words, *English* and *practice?*

- Second, by practice, I speak of the habitual and systematized behavior for the purposes of attaining proficiency in a particular activity. This is the meaning of the word that makes possible the old adage: "practice makes perfect." Question: If one is to become "perfect" in English, say, because of years and years of monastic devotion and practice, what does one really achieve? What does it mean to be "good" (let alone "perfect") in English? Unless you are Madonna, the American pop icon, who has recently decided to take on an English accent, why practice English? Is perfection in it really attainable, let alone desirable?

- Third, by practice, I mean to excavate a meaning of the word that is, according to the *Oxford English Dictionary* (perhaps the only true Sacred Text of the English practice), "the earliest recorded sense" but is "now archaic": "the action of scheming or planning, especially in an underhanded way and for an evil purpose; treachery; trickery, artifice." Evil purpose? So, what *really* lies in the heart of the English practice? What rough beast lurks in the shadows of its grammar, phonology, and syntax, slouching towards every corner of the globe to be born?

- Fourth and finally, by practice, I wish to contemplate the meaning of the word as it typically stands in opposition to the word *theory*. In thinking seriously about the English language, must theory and practice forever remain apart, like doomed lovers in a 19th-century English novel or 21st-century Korean soap opera?

GLOBAL LANGUAGE, KILLER LANGUAGE

English is global. Of course, you do not need an English professor to tell you this. In *English as a Global Language* (1997), David Crystal, relying on a variety of statistical information on language, conservatively estimates some 2.1 billion people in the world who are, in theory, routinely exposed to English in their daily lives. Among them, about 337 to 450 million learned English as a first—or native—language. It is virtually impossible to attach a meaningful number indicating how many people around the world use English as a nonnative language, because of the difficulty of defining exactly what level of proficiency qualifies as "sufficiently proficient." Crystal offers as the lowest estimate "a grand total of 670 million people with a native or native-like command of English" (p. 61). If "reasonable competence" is the criterion, then 1.8 billion might be a conservatively reliable figure. Again, you do not need an English professor to tell you that this is nearly *half* of the world's population. What impresses Crystal more so than the *degree* to which English has spread globally is the *accelerated pace* of this expansion. He writes: "In 1950, the case of English as a world language would have been no more than plausible. Fifty years on, and the case is virtually unassailable. What happened in this fifty years—a mere eye-blink in the history of a language—to cause such a massive change of stature?" (p. 63).

Indeed, what has happened in the past fifty years? Braj B. Kachru's essay "The Second Diaspora of English" (1992) is quite helpful in considering both the historical and contemporary phenomenon of English as a global language. Kachru divides the geopolitical diffusion of the English language into two major diasporic periods:

1st Diaspora, Phase 1: The British Isles. In 1535, the English language expands to Wales, as Wales unites with England. It then extends to Scotland in 1603 as the Scottish and English monarchies merge. With the integration of parts of Ireland into its fold, the state of Great Britain, along with the primacy of English within it, is established in 1707.

1st Diaspora, Phase 2: United States, Canada, Australia, and New Zealand. English settles two different continents with the creation of new Anglo-dominant nations. At the turn of the 19th century, English becomes one of the "major" languages of the world, on par with Arabic, Spanish, French, Hindi, German, and Russian. (Although Kachru does not, I would add Chinese—the written form, as well as the Mandarin vernacular—to this mix.)

2nd Diaspora: Asia, Africa, and Latin America. Kachru writes: "Slowly, with the power of the expanding Empire behind it, English became a link language for elite populations in multilingual Asia and Africa. English contributed to the creation of a cross-linguistic and cross-cultural network of people who began to use it in the domains of science, technology, military, pan-regional business, and creative writing. It is primarily for these reasons that English eventually acquired its present status as a global language" (p. 234).

Tom McArthur, in *The English Languages* (1998), considers the global roles and status of English during this 2nd Diaspora in terms of its de facto and de jure uses: The United Kingdom and United States are two prime examples of places where English exists as a de facto official language. The list of places where English exists (or often coexists) as a de jure official language is quite expansive and includes: Jamaica, Barbados, Belize, Guyana, Trinidad and Tobago, Saint Lucia, Nigeria, Ghana, Sierra Leone, Canada, Cameroon, Botswana, Singapore, South Africa, Kenya, India, Bangladesh, Malaysia, among many others. In places like Denmark, Norway, Sweden, the Netherlands, and Israel, English holds an unofficial but significant status, and is used for personal and professional purposes by many. Also, English serves as an official language for international purposes in both the United Nations (as one of six official working languages) and the European Union (as one of eleven official languages).

The spread of English during the 1st Diaspora and the first part of the 2nd Diaspora was primarily due to the empire-building efforts of Great Britain. During the latter part of the 2nd Diaspora, however, and in particular, the 50 years before it, the United States replaced Great Britain as the major global diffuser of the English language, signaling to the world its linguistic dominance, along with its economic, military, and technological power.

All this in the past 50 years. But wait, there is more to this: According to Tove Skutnabb-Kangas, a scholar of linguistic human rights, there are currently "at least around 7000 (maybe up to 10,000) *oral* languages and thousands of *sign* languages" (p. 187) in the world. She tells us in her essay "Linguistic Diversity, Human Rights and the 'Free' Market" (1999) that demographically, "fewer than 300 languages account for a total of over 5 billion speakers, or close to 95% of the world's oral population" (p. 187). Moreover, "over half of the world's (oral) languages, and most of the sign languages, are used by communities of 10,000 speakers or less." In ecological terms, these are all *threatened* languages. "But, half of these . . . meaning around a quarter of the world's oral languages, are spoken by communities of 1,000 speakers or less," meaning that over "25% of the world's languages account for only 0.2% of speakers" (pp. 187–188). Again, in ecological terms, these are *endangered* languages. Skutnabb-Kangas cites the work of Michael Krauss, who claims that between "20 and 50% of the world's oral languages are no longer being learned by children, meaning they are 'beyond endangerment'" (p. 188). Rather, they are *living dead* languages that will be extinct in the next century. Skutnabb-Kangas writes: "Languages today are being killed and linguistic diversity is disappearing at a much faster pace than ever before in human history." She continues: "When linguistic diversity disappears through linguistic genocide (meaning languages are killed; they do NOT disappear through any kind of natural death, but are murdered), the speakers are assimilated into the realms of other languages. The top ten languages in terms of numbers are the real killer languages, and English is foremost among them" (p. 191).

I began this essay by admitting that I am an English professor. Let me be more precise in case there is some ambiguity: I am a professor of English, not a professor who happens to be an Englishman. In light of all the facts, figures, and frenzy surrounding the globalization of English, perhaps it takes a "real" Englishman, someone who is more perfect in (or at) English than I am, to declare the following:

From century to century the great river of English has flowed on, fed by all these streams [the languages of "copper-hued Native Americans, blacks kidnapped into bondage, liquid-eyed Indian rajahs and craftsmen, narrow-eyed Malay pirates and merchants of Cathay'], . . . As it enriched the lives of past generations, so it will continue to enrich the lives of our children and their children's children—provided we take care that they learn how to understand and appreciate it. (Pennycook, 1998, p. 138, quoting Clairborne, 1983)

What is worth noting here, aside from the unabashedly triumphalist tone, is the conditional warning embedded in the last sentence: "provided we take care they learn how to understand and appreciate it." No doubt the "they" refer, not only to "our children," but more so to the "Native Americans," "Blacks," "Indians," "Malays," and other former colonized peoples who increasingly find it necessary to adopt the use and demands of the English language for their economic survival. The message is clear: Yes, it's wonderful that English is so global, but let's not celebrate too soon because the integrity and purity of the English language is at stake. After all, although not everyone has the good fortune to have been *born* English, there is, fortunately, the various English standards that everyone can live up to. And, the first and foremost of these is Standard English.

STANDARD ENGLISH

What is Standard English? If we were to take Peter Trudgill's word for it, it is neither language nor accent, neither style nor register. It is—and Trudgill insists in his essay "Standard English: What It Isn't" (1999) that most British sociolinguists are agreed on this—a *dialect*, "simply one variety of English among many. *It is a sub-variety of English.* Sub-varieties of languages are usually referred to as *dialects*, and languages are often described as *consisting of* dialects" (p. 123). Moreover, Standard English is *purely a social dialect.* British Standard English might have once started out as a geographical dialect like most others, having its origins in specific areas of Southern England at the turn of the 16th, 17th or 18th century, depending on whom you ask, but it now resides entirely in the realm of socioeconomics across the entire geographic length of Britain, if not the globe. According to Trudgill, in Britain today, Standard English is spoken as a *native* dialect by less than 15% of the population, but this small percentage does not constitute a random cross-section of the population. They are concentrated at the very top of the social scale. "The further down the social scale one goes," he writes, "the more non-standard forms one finds" (p. 124). Simply put, Standard English is the dialect of English that belongs to the "social group with the highest degree of power, wealth, and prestige" (p. 124). By all indications, this appears true for all primary English speaking nations, most notably the United States, Australia, New Zealand, and Canada. Of course, each of these countries has fashioned a customized variety of Standard English so that what is Standard English in Australia or the United States is not considered Standard English in Britain. But, for clear, unabashedly *Anglocentric* reasons, British Standard English is the standard to which all other Standard Englishes are measured.

According to James Milroy's "The Consequences of Standardisation in Descriptive Linguistics" (1999), there are three main characteristics of standard languages: First, *the chief consequence of standardization is a high degree of uniformity of structures.* This is achieved by the suppression of linguistically legitimate but socially stigmatized variations. "Thus, standard languages are high level idealizations, in which uniformity or invariance is valued among all things" (p. 27). Second, *standardization is implemented and promoted through written forms of language.* "It is in this channel that uniformity of structure is most obviously functional" (p. 27). And third, *standardization inhibits linguistic change and variability.* There should "be no illusion as to what the aim of language standardization actually is: it is to fix and 'embalm' (Samuel Johnson's term) the structural properties of the language in a uniform state and *prevent* all structural change" (p. 28).

Given these observations, many sociolinguists have begun to venture outside narrow academic concerns to promote public tolerance of language variations and, according to Milroy, "to point out that it is wrong to discriminate against individuals on linguistic grounds, just as it is wrong to discriminate on grounds of race or colour of skin" (p. 19). Make no mistake, Standard English ideology is inseparable from the self-promotional desire of the nation-state to create a homogeneous citizenry. There is little or no tolerance for change and variability in the nation-state.

One more point about the sociodynamics of Standard English: Although Standard English is most often the acquired, *native* dialect of the most privileged class in the English speaking world, Standard English is not used exclusively by the members of this class. It is also the *learned* or *assimilated* dialect of those who, for whatever reasons, wish to be in the company of the most privileged class.

BLOODLETTING

It is really worth recognizing the fact that English has *not* obtained, and is *not continuing* to obtain, its prominent global status because of any *intrinsic linguistic* qualities. Rather, the spread of English has been achieved through much shedding of blood—Scottish, Irish, Chinese, Filipino, Indian, Arab, various aboriginal—you name it. In the words of Chris Searle, who is much more eloquent and pithy about it than I ever can be:

> Let us be clear that the English language has been a monumental force and institution of oppression and rabid exploitation throughout 400 years of imperialist history. It attacked the black person with its racist images and imperialist message, it battered the worker who toiled as its words expressed the parameters of his misery and the subjection of entire peoples in all the continents of the world. It was made to scorn the languages it sought to replace, and told the colonized peoples that mimicry of its primacy among languages was a necessary badge of their social mobility as well as their continued humiliation and subjection. Thus, when we talk of 'mastery' of the Standard language, we must be conscious of the terrible irony of the word, that the English language itself was the language of the master, the carrier of his arrogance and brutality. (Chris Searle, 1983, p. 6)

As Britain worked to establish its vast global dominance, the English language was an indispensable instrument of power and legislation, no less important to its empire-building mission than its military, clergy, or financiers. And so, it is quite surprising—and disappointing—to realize exactly how little study has actually been conducted in examining the role of the English practice in the conquering, occupying, and settling of the lands, bodies, and tongues of those who stood in the path of Britain's empire building. Perhaps even more shocking is the virtual absence of studies that interrogate the U.S. nation-state's use of the English practice in continuing to further its own empire-building mission.

CONCLUSION: WHY ME?

When you stop and think about it, the English practice is a rather strange occupation for someone like me. For one, as I established earlier, I am not an Englishman. For another, English was not my first language—Korean was. In fact, it was not even my second, according to most English professionals. I was born in Korea and immigrated to Hawaii when I was nine years old. For the next 6 or 7 years, I was placed in one ESL class after another, until I entered high school, when I finally graduated out of ESL into a "regular" classroom. But if you know anything about Hawaii, you know that Standard English is a foreign language to most—if not all—the locals there. So, while struggling to learn the Board of Education's officially mandated Standard English, I became more adept at assimilating the "outlawed" native tongue, pidgin or Hawaiian Creole English. After high school, I went off to college in the mainland, to California, then eventually to New York City, where I completed a Ph.D. in English. I now find myself earning a living in the English practice at a large, public, urban university, teaching English to students with whom I share an uncanny resemblance: nonwhite, immigrant, nonnative speakers of Standard English. Just from this brief overview of my life, you can see how large a territory English has settled in—or occupied, if you will—in my life. And, as you can see, I have steadfastly practiced English for almost the entire duration of my existence, and still do so—often until it bleeds.

REFERENCES

Crystal, D. (1997). *English as a global language.* Cambridge: Cambridge University Press.
Kachru, B. B. (1992). The Second Diaspora of English. In T. W. MacHan & C. T. Scott (Eds.), *English in its Social Context* (pp. 230–252). Oxford: Oxford University Press.
McArthur, T. (1998). *The English languages.* Cambridge: Cambridge University Press.
Milroy, J. (1999). The Consequences of Standardisation in descriptive linguistics. In T. Bex & R. J. Watts (Eds.), *Standard English: The widening debate* (pp. 16–39) London: Routledge.
Pennycook, A. (1998). *English and the discourse of colonialism.* New York: Routledge.
Skutnabb-Kangas, T. (1999). Linguistic diversity, human rights and the "free market." In M. Kontra, R. Phillipson, T. Skutnabb-Kangas, & T., Varady (Eds.) *Language: A right and a resource: Approaching linguistic human rights* (pp. 187–222). Budapest: Central European University Press.
Trudgill, P. (1999). Standard English: What it isn't. In T. Bex & R. J. Watts (Eds.), *Standard English: The widening debate.* (pp. 117–128). London: Routledge.

BIBLIOGRAPHY

Anzaldúa, G. (1987). *Borderlands/la frontera: The new mestiza.* San Francisco: Aunt Lute Book Company.
Arteaga, A. (Ed.). (1994). *An other tongue: Nation and ethnicity in the linguistic borderlands.* Durham: Duke University Press.
Bex, T., & Watts, R. J. (Eds.). *Standard English: The widening debate.* London: Routledge.
Clairborne, R. (1983). *The life and times of the English language: The history of our marvelous tongue.* London: Bloomsbury.
Fisher, J. H. (1996). *The emergence of standard English.* Lexington: The University Press of Kentucky.
Gee, J. P. (1996). *Social linguistics and literacies: Ideology in discourse.* (2nd ed.). Philadelphia: Palmer Press.
Kachru, B. B. (Ed.). (1992). *The other tongue: English across cultures* (2nd ed.). Urbana: University of Illinois Press.
Kontra, M., Phillipson, R., Skutnabb-Kangas, T., & Varady, T. (Eds.). (1999). *Language: A right and a Resource: Approaching linguistic human rights.* Budapest: Central European University Press.
Ku, R. J-S. (2000). The terrible tyranny of standard English: The lingua franca of Asian American literature. *Dialogue, 3*(1), 30–33.
Lippi-Green, R. (1997). *English with an accent: Language, ideology, and discrimination in the United States.* New York: Routledge.
Lyall, S. (1994, November 29). In furor over prize, novelist speaks up for his language. *The New York Times.* p. Axxx.
Nettle, D., & Romaine, S. (2000). *Vanishing voices: The extinction of the world's languages.* New York: Oxford University Press.
Pennycook, A. (1994). *The cultural politics of English as an international language.* London: Longman.

Phillipson, R. (1992). *Linguistic imperialism.* Oxford: Oxford University Press.

Sassan, S. (2000). *Globalization and its discontents.* New York: The New Press.

Searle, C. (1983). A common language. *Race and Class, 34*(3), 45–54.

Sebba, M. (1997). *Contact languages: Pidgins and creoles.* New York: St. Martin's Press.

Valdes, G. (2000, Winter). Nonnative English speakers: Language bigotry in English mainstream classrooms. *ADE Bulletin, 124,* 12–17.

QUESTIONS TO THINK ABOUT

1. In the beginning of the selection, Ku says that he has *"practiced* English for a very long time." What does he mean by this and what are the various definitions he offers for the term "practice"? What facts and context does he give you about his life throughout the text that explains and expands the significance of the idea of "practice"?

2. How does Ku account for the globalization of English? Include the significant historical events, facts and figures, reasons, and consequences he cites for this spread and globalization. What is the main point that Ku makes about the oral and sign languages that exist today? Why does he cite Skutnabb-Kangas's work as part of his argument? How is "bloodletting" connected to the globalization of English?

3. Ku asks, "What is Standard English?" Discuss the various definitions he offers to answer the question and then connect these to the three main characteristics of standard languages Ku cites from Milroy. What do you find insightful and what do you find problematic in his presentation of the "sociodynamics of Standard English"?

4. *Extending your understanding*: In discussing the globalization of English, Ku refers to places where English exists as a de facto official language (e.g., United States) and where it exists as a de jure official language (e.g., India). Find out as much as you can about the de facto and de jure distinction and then comment on its importance for teaching, literacy, and the international use of English. Do you think these distinctions as Ku presents them are static or are they subject to change? What are the factors that might contribute to change? In today's world, does being literate mean knowing English? Explain your responses as fully as you can.

TERMS TO DEFINE

Define the following words and phrases as they are presented within the context of the reading. Comment on your understanding of the significance of each one.

Practice
Diaspora
De facto/de jure
Endangered language
Living dead language
Standard English
Dialect

Class Talk

Gary Tate, John McMillan, and Elizabeth Woodworth
Texas Christian University

THINKING ABOUT OUR CLASS

Gary Tate

When I walked into the meeting room at the Hyatt in Phoenix where the basic writing workshop was to be held, I saw a room filled with round tables and chairs for participants and a microphone and lecture stand for the speakers. Because it seemed to me inappropriate to "lecture from above" on the topic of social class, I suggested that John, Elizabeth, and I just sit at one of the tables near the middle of the room so that our voices could be heard and so that we would be a part of the workshop. This worked well. And the presence of several workshop participants at our table as we talked gave me the feeling that a conversation was taking place. I began by pointing out that I would talk for a very few minutes about social class generally and about our feeling that teachers must attend to their own social class before bringing class into their classrooms, that John would talk, again briefly, about the power of storytelling in discussions of class, and that Elizabeth would then act as our teacher and give us all a writing assignment, the responses to which would be discussed later as the core of this portion of the workshop. Here is what I said:

Elizabeth and John and I are here today to propose four theses for your consideration:

1. that social class—the perennial third item in the familiar trio gender, race, and class—has been largely ignored in composition studies and in the academy generally,
2. that there are signs that this neglect is ending,
3. that the neglect of class must end if we are to understand our students as fully as we must if we are to teach them well,
4. and, finally, that before we can bring class into our classrooms in a meaningful, productive way, we must try to understand and come to terms with our own individual class histories, complex as these may often be.

Let me say just a few words about each of these points. Our neglect of class is not difficult to demonstrate, although it is difficult to understand. It has grown, I suspect, out of that peculiarly American feeling—a feeling praised by those who profit from it—that we are a classless society and that matters of class are, thus, insignificant, even embarrassing. Many of us have an easier time talking about sex than we do about social class. Whatever the cause, we have not attended to social class in the way we have attended in recent years to matters of gender and race. One searches in vain through composition journals for anything more than an occasional reference to the subject. And the books in the field do only slightly better. The names of Mike Rose, Jim Berlin, Ira Shor come to mind, but beyond that, very little.

Fortunately, and I move to our second thesis, the situation is changing. Let me mention some signs. At the meeting of this organization in Milwaukee last year, there were, if I count correctly, three sessions devoted to issues of class: two roundtable discussions and one special interest group. All three of these sessions were packed—people sitting on the floor, standing in doorways, and so on. A good sign, we thought. And we were right. This year, there are twenty-one panels and roundtables, two special interest groups, and this workshop. (Let me add, parenthetically, that the number of sessions on race has increased even more dramatically. Last year there were five; this year there are forty-five: this workshop, three special interest groups, and forty-one panels, roundtables, forums, etc.) More evidence of this new interest. Last October's issue of *College English* (1996) featured an article by Lynn Bloom on "Freshman English as a Middle-Class Enterprise" and my review of two books about working-class academics. A few issues before that Lynn Bloom had also reviewed a book about working-class women in the academy.

Not much, but certainly better than in years past. A Center for Working-Class Studies has been established at Youngstown State University in Ohio, and, in 1995, Youngstown State hosted a conference entitled Working-Class Lives/Working-Class Studies. They will host another such conference this coming June. To many of us, the '95 conference was a revelation. As I have said many times, it was the most exciting meeting I have ever attended, reminding me, as it did, of early 4C's meetings, where small groups of enthusiasts, not much honored back home, gathered together for support, education, good talk, and, indeed, inspiration. If you are free the next time this conference is held, find your way to Youngstown, Ohio. You will never regret it. Or go to Omaha, Nebraska, the next time the University of Nebraska at Omaha holds its Pedagogy of the Oppressed Conference. Both of these conferences are good signs that the landscape of class studies is changing.

Another positive sign is that at least three collections of original essays on issues of social class and teaching are being prepared for publication: one by E. J. Hinds of the University of Northern Colorado, one by Sherry Linkon at Youngstown State, and the one that Alan Shepard, John McMillan, and I are editing at TCU. Finally, a sure sign that the neglect of class is ending: Benjamin DeMott has just edited a reader for first-year composition courses, entitled *Created Equal: Reading and Writing About Class in America* (HarperCollins, 1996). When publishers of textbooks for first-year composition classes take an interest in a topic, I think we can say with some certainty that that topic has arrived, late though it may be.

Our third thesis, that we must attend to social class if we are to understand our students as fully as possible, makes sense to us and we hope that it will to you. Just as our lives and the lives of our students are profoundly affected by gender, race, sexual orientation, and so on, so they are profoundly affected by social class, be that working class, middle class, upper class, or whatever categories you choose to think in. Although the primary focus of the work I've mentioned—and of much of the important work being done today—is the working class, certainly the attitudes, linguistic habits, behavior patterns of all our students are influenced, in part at least, by their class histories. If we believe Lynn Bloom when she says that Freshman English is a middle-class enterprise, then we must assume that students and teachers from middle-class backgrounds will feel more at home in the course than will others. Be that as it may, there is a rapidly growing body of testimony about the difficulty that working-class students—and teachers—have adjusting to the demands of the academy. And there is some evidence that students from the upper classes have similar difficulties. One of the contributors to our book writes eloquently of her difficult transformation from her life of wealth to her life as a graduate student in English. Here are her words: "[I]n preparation for graduate school, I sold my Mercedes, put my Rolex watch in the vault, and boarded a private Lear jet [her father's] with one suitcase and my cat, headed for a different life." Now I suppose that most of us would have trouble seeing her difficulties as equivalent to the difficulties of a working-class student struggling to survive, but my point is that we should not—as some of my colleagues seem to suggest—ignore all class difficulties not associated with the working class. The tricky thing about class is not just its fluidity, its complexity, but that it is so easily hidden. Just as the woman I quoted tried to hide her upper-class upbringing—not successfully, I can testify—so working-class students can hide their identities—or try to. The right clothes, the right hairdo, will hide much. What can often not be hidden, however, are the bad teeth, bad skin, the too-loud voice or brash manner (or silence), the struggle with "standard" English, and a host of other signs that will not escape the observant, caring teacher.

And so we would urge you today not to ignore the class positions of your students, because we are beginning to understand more and more about how these positions influence their lives in school, their learning styles, their behavior, their choices. Some of you here today, especially those of you from working-class backgrounds, could, I am certain, join me in remembering the pain and estrangement we have felt, as students and teachers, as we have attempted to "fit into" this strange and often hostile world of higher education, a world that has caused many of us to deny our past and to resort to coping devices of a sometimes dangerous kind. Drugs became my favorite coping device for many years, the dirty secret behind a career that has looked, on the outside, to be moderately successful.

This brings me to our last thesis: that before we can make productive use of our knowledge of students' class positions, we must seek to understand and to come to terms with our own. And that is not easy to do, especially for those of us who have been hiding our past—from others, and, more important, from ourselves. Or we have been fooling ourselves into thinking that we have left all that behind. As my ten-year-old granddaughter is fond of saying airily, when I ask her if she still likes a certain kind of music or a certain kind of jelly, "Oh, I've moved on." The question is, can we move on? The answer, I think, is only a little. I very much like the way Janet Zandy puts it when writing about the working class in her anthology *Calling Home* (Rutgers UP, 1990): "If you are born into the working class and are willing to change your speech, your gestures, your appearance—in essence, to deny the culture of your home and the working-class self of your childhood—then you might 'pass' as a member of the dominant culture. But you will never *belong* there" (2).

So the question is: Where *do* we belong now? Where *have* we belonged? Who *have* we been? Who *are* we now? How we answer these questions depends, as Carolyn Steedman points out in her brilliant book *Landscape for a Good Woman* (Rutgers UP, 1987), not so much on what has actually happened to us in our lives as on the stories we tell ourselves about what has happened. As I have begun to try to come to terms with my working-class past and to see how it has influenced my life, I realize that I have suffered not so much from the actual circumstances of my life, but from the stories I have been telling myself about those circumstances, stories that, in my case, left out entirely anything about social class, stories that had me struggling alone, the victim of my own personal weaknesses, my own ignorance, my own loneliness. Slowly, I have begun to tell myself different stories and it has made an enormous difference—in how I think, how I teach, how I live.

And so, this morning, it is to narrative that we must turn, to storytelling. Back to our very beginnings.

SILO IN THE SUBURBS

John McMillan

When I think about my own social class, the best I can do is approximate. It is this about social class-talk that I particularly like, that it is overtly what perhaps every other kind of talk is covertly—a best guess, a shot in a dimly lit dark, a story. Of course, according to some definition of "common sense" you could quite easily say that I am middle-class. Certain stories of mine fit well with this common sense vision: I grew up in the suburbs, my dad has an MBA, I graduated from a private university.

But class is a sticky thing, and as there are problems in saying "men are like this, women are like that," etc., it seems to me that there are also some problems in resorting entirely to a kind of class-talk that says "middle-class people are like this, working-class people, that." Class talk can as quickly degenerate into overgeneralizations and proclamations as any other talk, I imagine. That is, it can morph into those kinds of declarations that are attempts to end conversations and to explain existing power relationships according to first principles. Nevertheless, class is sticky, and perhaps, above all, what I mean by this is that class-talk resists depersonalization; and personalization is about approximation, which is the best I can do. And so I am arguing that, more than a place for proclamations, social class is an occasion for stories. And so it is in the spirit of Jesus's reply to the young lawyer's "and who is my neighbor?" that I offer the following collage of tales, or you might say the stories, that are the beginning of my theory about my own social class.

Where it all began

Once, early in my undergraduate days, I was in a sort of church meeting where the preacher asked, "Did anyone here grow up on a farm?" Of course he didn't really ask it. He was trying to make a point about "real" work. He was talking about the loss of certain values. I raised my hand. I was the only one. There were two hundred people in that crowd.

I don't know why I did it. I'd done it without reflection. The preacher cocked his head and focused in on me. His look screamed that nobody was supposed to have answered that question affirmatively. It messed up his point. "You grew up on a farm?" he queried. "No," I stuttered, "I didn't." My voice was quivering. If I'd been standing I'm sure I would have fallen over. His face screwed up somewhere between a scowl and a snicker. He turned his head back and went on with his sermon.

Years later, older and tired of being embarrassed, I allowed myself to reflect a bit on that event. It was from that reflection that my theory grew. It is sufficient to say that, as random as my answer to the preacher was, I'm not so sure it was entirely wrong.

A Theory

There are silos in the suburbs. There are church pews from tiny Pennsylvania Baptist churches in the office buildings of the city. Pre-dawn milkings and prayer meetings give shape to our days. The best I can do is approximate. So I'll say it again, There are silos in the suburbs; and, of course, they're in my classroom too.

Allow me to explain myself. Let me tell you a story . . . or 3 or 6

My father was raised on a farm in Ohio; my mother was the oldest daughter of a Baptist minister who, over the course of her growing up, pastored congregations in rural parts of New York, Pennsylvania, and Ohio—places called Black Creek, Wellsville, Pavillion.

From what I can make of it, it went like this: when my father graduated from high school, he wanted to go to college. No one else in the family had ever considered such a thing. A few of them were even opposed to it. He enrolled at Ohio State University in

Columbus, paid his way working as an R.A. during semesters and by raking asphalt in the summers. Got a job at Kodak upon graduation. They funded his MBA. I know less about my mother. The oldest daughter in a family of seven children, after a year of business school in Olean, New York, she went to work as a secretary at Kodak. They met and married; I was born three years later.

I grew up in a suburb in upstate New York. I lived in the same house until I left for college. When my brother was born, rather than moving to a bigger house, my parents decided to add on. With the help of relatives (my mother's father built a fieldstone fireplace in the new addition, peppering it with "stones from the holy land," I was told, gathered from a recent trip to Israel.) They built the addition off the back and cut out of the attic a room for my sister. My brother moved into her old room, downstairs, next to mine.

I started delivering penny papers door to door when I was eleven. You could work that young if you had a permit, signed by your parents. I graduated to the city paper a couple of years later and remember something of the excitement I had at the prospects of a real job where I collected money and got Christmas tips, where someone actually read what I was delivering. Eventually I passed the route off to my little brother. Later, in high school I could be found working at the local pizza joint six days a week.

My dad retired at age 49. He and my mother bought an old farm house out in the country. They have a barn across the street. My mom works as a secretary at a real estate office in the city. My dad reads a lot and keeps up the yard, works on the house. They both tend to the garden.

I tell these stories because somehow they help explain me (me explain?) when I am confronted with questions about my own social class. In a world marked by commercials and Cliff's Notes, stories are terribly inefficient. They are long, slow, and, at their core, are in opposition to the illusion of exactitude we've all become addicted to. Jim Corder, in an unpublished manuscript, has said that his best guess is that even the most orthodox academic paper is really only the very end of a long, personal narrative ("On Argument, What Some Call 'Self Writing,' and Trying to See the Back Side of One's Own Eyeballs"). And Wayne Booth has suggested recently that "authoritative" discourse, whatever that might be, derives its power from its ability to conflate a reader's "narrative" and "authorial" audiences ("Where Is the Authorial Audience in Biblical Narrative—and in Other 'Authoritative' Texts?" *Narrative 4* [1996]: 235–253)—that is, if I understand Booth right, it could be said that a text's power comes from its ability to un-story itself, comes from its success in erasing and effacing the storyteller. I want to say that class-talk resists this erasing—which might explain why social class has been talked about so little in the academy. The personal narratives of class are written in permanent ink. To un-story class is to cease to talk about class.

From my own class stories I see characteristics I name "self-reliance," "discipline," "simplicity," "confidence," and "tempered defiance," the last term being a kind of encapsulation of the previous four. I'm not sure if I like it yet, but I see myself trying to engender these characteristics in my students in invitations to negotiate grades and assignments, in requiring self-assessments, and in my recent grappling with contract grading. These are the cells around which my stories of myself as a teacher grow. So that, finally, any account of the effects of my own social-class upon my teaching is double-deep in narrative: It is making sense of how the stories I tell myself about my class affect the way I story my teaching. Which is why I say that there are silos in the suburbs, and that they're in my classroom too.

CHAT AND WRITE: WRITE AND CHAT

Elizabeth D. Woodworth

During this "teaching" portion of the workshop, I offered participants this plan: "I'll talk briefly and generally about social class and me, and then I'll ask you to write a bit about your reflections on social class and you. Then we'll have a brilliant, lively, and illuminating discussion."

Chat: Preamble

Any time we want to talk about social class as an issue in a writing classroom, we have to first explore our own perceptions of our class. There are so many questions we can ask ourselves when we approach the issue of class it seems a monumental, even insurmountable, task. What is social class? Is a definition of class dependent upon our economic situation? Our race? Where we live? What we do for a living? What sex we are? Should all these factors be considered in our exploration of social class?

In fact, right when we start asking questions about what class might be and what that means, the topic of social class wriggles out from under the lens of our microscope and defies demarcations and categorizations. It's just two short words, "social class." It ought to be a simple thing to discuss, to explore, to contemplate, but no, the connotations intrinsic to these two short words depend so much upon the individual (despite and because of cultural, racial, sexual, tribal affiliations). This difficulty, this reflection inward to the one and outward to the many, at the same time, necessitates a circular, an open and enfolding, connective approach.

A linear approach—suggesting one definition of social class or another, one narrative for all—must be impossible—because how can we be precise when we talk about class? How can we talk about class without talking about everything else we believe ourselves to be? How do we sort this out then? If this is a topic that concerns us, and it does or we wouldn't be here now, we have to start somewhere. And to begin, you begin with yourself.

I have, like both Gary and John, looked to the stories I tell myself, have told myself about where I come from. I've looked to the stories others have told me about where I come from: my grandmother, my mother, my father, other family members, my friends, my neighbors. I've looked to the stories I tell others about me—and how that might differ from what I tell myself. Then I've looked at how these stories determine the person I am in the classroom. How have I presented myself to my students? Has my behavior somehow subtly or boldly declared what I believe about my social class?

When I began to dissect the narratives which fill my life—the stories about who I am, my gender, my race, my class—I began to see how all my perceptions about me affect who I am as a teacher. I wasn't surprised, really, or unhappy to find that as a teacher in a writing class I'm deeply influenced by my, and my family's, past and profoundly influenced by who I think I am at present, and the stories I tell myself and others about who I'll be in the future. By just knowing that I can somehow begin to grapple with myself and the slippery issues of social class, this knowledge of my confused state regarding social class helps me to begin finding new ways of attempting to reach students, no matter who they are, or where they come from, or where they're going, no matter what they believe, or what they look like. When I can begin to untangle my many narratives about me, then I can begin to unravel who I am as a teacher—keep the parts I like, discard what doesn't work, and even experiment a little. But most importantly, I can begin to ask my students to consider what "social class" means to them; I can ask them to write about such reflections; I can give my writing students the opportunity to talk about what has so rarely been discussed openly—but, I believe, so clearly needs open discussion.

Write: The Initial Assignment

At this point I concluded my chatting and asked participants to take twenty minutes or so to write about themselves and class. The prompt below was announced and the "write" portion of our presentation began:

> How do the stories you tell yourself and others—about yourself and your social class—influence your teaching and your life in the academy, especially in the basic writing classroom?

At the end of twenty minutes, I asked participants to share what they felt comfortable sharing, as little or as much as they had written.

Following this are two sections, responses and reflections: a response from one participant to the prompt, and my reflections on this and other's responses.

Chat Again: Response

One of the participants kindly offered us his text to include with this written version of our presentation. It is largely a reconstruction of what was written during the twenty minutes allocated (with some extra commentary where needed). The difficulty Gary wrote of earlier—that it's hard to talk about class, is evident here in my writing and in that of our volunteer participant/writer. But we did it anyway, difficult or not; we had a conversation about class and teaching and who we are and can be—contributing, in our own way, to the emergence of class studies as an important field of its own and an important part of composition studies.

Earlier John explained his notion that we "story" our teaching by using our own narratives to tell ourselves about ourselves as selves and as teachers. John says, "I tell these stories because somehow they help to explain me (me explain?) when I am confronted with questions about my own social class." The sample response works this way too: it is an explanation of self, self trying to understand social class, self-confronting social class histories. These are the stories that must be told so that we can, as Gary puts it, "bring class into our classrooms in a meaningful and productive way."

> Before I came to graduate studies, I was a bus driver in New York City for twenty-one years. After about thirteen or fourteen years, in the midst of a personal crisis, I decided I was living someone else's life, that I needed to make a drastic change of some kind.
>
> I am now a grad student and a teacher. Because I am a non-traditional working-class entrant in academe, I view my students differently than my colleagues who have traveled the traditional academic path. I used to think of the teacher/student exchange in terms of "otherness": I am their Other, and they are mine. I am now what they aspire to be, and they represent for me my past. But, increasingly, I think of this exchange less in terms of difference and more in terms of likeness. I am more like them, and less like other graduate students, than I was formerly aware. I can no longer ignore the elite and snobbish attitudes which constitute too much of the discourse of grad students about their own students. They can't wait to be rid of them and get back to their "real" work, their literary research. However, I try not to throw the baby out with the bath water; I condemn their attitudes and not their love of literature. Why? This is my love, as well. But I have learned that I am never more comfortable than when I am among other "nontraditional" students (grad students or composition students) because it is at these moments that I feel that I have come home.
>
> Leo Parascondola, The Graduate School, CUNY

Leo's response is an important one as it raises the issue of class within the academy, within English studies: the literature major vs. the composition major. Literature vs. rhetoric and composition—a rivalry that has long been a source of tension and also, as Leo suggests, split allegiances. A hierarchy exists in English studies which allocates rhet/comp studies to a second-class position. Talking about this class struggle is as vital for teachers of composition and literature as talking about their own social class histories, for by entering the profession of teaching English, they embark upon another journey in which class distinction is critical to self-perception, self-fulfillment. This is an issue that must always be part of our "class talk."

The Last Chat and Write: Some Reflections

I can only give impressions now of other responses, but the impressions have stayed with me long after the experience, long after the actual words shared by the participants.

Part of this lasting sense of what happened has to do with me personally—a personal class history thing that needs explanation, perhaps.

Every time I talk with someone about class issues and we exchange stories, I feel like I'm at one of those 12-step meetings: "Hi. My name is Elizabeth, and I'm confused about class—mine, yours, the definition of class." But the more I talk about class and writing, the more I listen to other's stories, the better I feel. I come from a strange place of mixed race, mixed class, mixed gender-role messages. I was raised in a German-Irish family but am of Hispanic descent (as I recently learned just before my adopted mother died). My mother's family were impoverished upper class from Chicago. Dad's family were dirt farmers and railroad workers from North Dakota with so many kids they shared shoes, and each kid only had one good set of clothes, one set of everyday clothes. My parents insisted that I get a good education, prepare for a career, be the ideal wife when I got married, be an ideal mother, the perfect super woman. Of everything I felt like I had to be, "educated" was the most important. My mother never finished college, despite several attempts over a twenty-year period, because she would not commit to school, but she insisted I totally commit to my education. Yet I also needed to know how to organize the perfect dinner party, how to garden, build shelves and such handy stuff, change a tire or an air filter, throw a baseball, cook tasty and nutritious meals, look great, be witty, be at home with a plumber or a CEO as my dinner partner, and throw a spiral pass (and when I wanted to grow up to be an NFL player, I was told ladies don't play football—huh?). My scattered sense of self, no doubt, contributed to the length of my undergraduate career—nine years, seven universities, six declared majors. I couldn't decide who I was—how could I possibly decide what I was going to do? And all along I feared that I would never graduate, or impossible of all dreams, get to graduate school and succeed.

Fortunately, John McMillan and I met the first day of graduate school and bonded over our shared fears that we somehow didn't quite belong. We confessed to each other that we felt uncomfortable in grad classes—just waiting for the elitist goon squad to come and knock on the door of the classroom: "Excuse us, we've come for Elizabeth and/ or John. There's been a mistake. You don't belong here. You must come with us." What happened after that neither of us was sure—but we were convinced about that much. In some ways, even before we started to think seriously about class studies, we were talking about our class backgrounds, sharing our stories, sharing our fears about who we were according to who our families had been, what they had done, who they knew, how we valued work.

Last year at 4Cs, I listened to Gary Tate confess similar feelings about his class and fears of belonging—or rather, not belonging—and how such fears, when repressed, could profoundly affect a life. I felt, with some variations, he was telling the same story John and I had told to each other several years before. For me, he crystallized what it was I had struggled for years to understand—my self-doubt came from my inability to talk about my class, from my unknown race, my mixed view of gender roles, my sense that somehow I might not belong to the academic set.

Listening to the workshop participants, many of whom confessed fears of inadequacy in academe, was like listening to myself. And their stories have stayed with me—melting into my own stories—the ones I tell myself, the ones I tell others, helping me to further explore the way my social class history has molded my present and is molding my future self.

A young woman spoke about her life, her class, her family, with tears in her eyes, trembling hands shuffling papers in front of her. She came from a working class family who had become increasingly distant from her as she became more formally educated. Both she and her family were proud of her achievement—a move to a higher class through education—but both wondered if she could really belong anymore. As she spoke, her words shook me—her worries were my worries—her experiences were mine. My dad's family of high-rise construction workers were pretty well split between pride in all my education and derision for my "useless" knowledge. Did I really belong among them anymore? Clearly we were both (she and I, dad's family and I) concerned about "class," status. Even my use of "dad's family" marks the distance I feel—somehow they don't feel like my own family, only a family of mine via Dad.

I became distressed, eyes making tears, as I saw her struggle to tell her story. Her courage made me want to jump up and run to her and tell her it was okay—she was telling the story of all of our struggles with class issues, she was telling the story of our shame, our discomfort with the very topic of class. The details didn't matter in a way. Not one other noise could be heard while she spoke. It was as if she had articulated the emotional and intellectual needs that had motivated the organization of the session, as if she had articulated the emotional and intellectual reasons we were there.

A shy young man shared his writing. He struggled to speak, too, as this young woman had, but was determined to do it. He was clearly shy about sharing, keeping his eyes on the text he'd just written, rarely looking up, pages shaking slightly as he read. His story was another one of fear and inadequacy in academe, exacerbated by his emphasis on composition studies. He had felt like the Other in the academy as a student, now he felt like the Other within his own academic department. Few teachers of composition could not relate. Class markers are everywhere—even in English departments—and it's a deeply moving experience to talk about what class means to each of us. And while it might have been difficult, it was necessary to the participants to share what they had discovered about themselves through writing.

An older man, brown of skin and with an accent I did not recognize, spoke about class as an issue for the new citizen, or the "alien." He spoke of the hope of the United States, the apparent "classlessness" of our society as it was perceived in his home country. But he realized after living here that there is a class system, even if not clearly articulated by our culture. He seemed less disconcerted by the class differential than the lack of articulation. And he admitted that this could be (and probably was) a result of other cultural influences. Living in a supposed "melting pot," concerned with class issues, it seems crucial that we ask how the mix and contact of many cultural ideas of class are brought to bear on our discussion.

A young black woman spoke of the shock on her students' faces in a heartland college when they realized she would be their teacher. Black, a woman, and teaching college. Wow. For her, she was also shocked by her entrance into university teaching because of the lower socio-economic background she came from—something the students could not see, but a reality which added to her anxiety about being an authority figure. Her case, her response, her students' reactions are argument for striving to look at class, gender, and race as related issues. Could she possibly separate these in her own life? Can we separate these issues in our own lives? Can we start with class and move to race and gender as issues under discussion in our writing classes? Can we discuss one without the others? I think not.

Many more shared their responses—many ages, many races, many classes, women and men—all concerned with the ways we define ourselves, our class, our race, our gender roles. What was most important for me, many spoke about the ways they connected their "class-talk" with their teaching, particularly about how it encouraged them to reach out to students who are worried about not belonging or not making it. There was a general eagerness to share, despite the difficulty of doing so for some.

Like the first time you taste, do, or see something—there's joy and freedom and the desire to describe, and the fear that others won't understand your special experience. What this part of the day's workshop did (for me and for others) was alleviate the fear that "no one can understand me," that "no one is like me." And this conversation about class is exactly where we can start and what we can share with basic writing students who so desperately need to know they are not alone, who need to know that someone can and will understand them. That class markers are not brands that prevent success in the academy, but rather marks of distinction that need not—should not—be negative.

Throughout the remainder of the conference, participants stopped me regularly to say what an impact the workshop had on their thinking, how they enjoyed what had happened throughout the day, but mostly what I heard was that being able to write and talk about social class in a safe place was liberating. Isn't this what we hope to give our students in writing classes—the chance to write in a safe place? Isn't our agenda to give our students a chance to grow as writers? Don't we hope we can help them to places where they can think beyond where they've been before? Don't we hope they will find new ways of seeing themselves and others through their writing?

For Gary, John, and I, the workshop proved to be a fertile ground for further thinking and talking about class and writing, basic writing especially, as we made new friends, shared stories and ideas, learned new strategies for helping the basic writer, and came to understand a bit more about ourselves as selves and teachers.

QUESTIONS TO THINK ABOUT

1. Explore the various direct and indirect meanings Tate, McMillan, and Woodworth attribute to the term "class" as you find it used in their article. How do these compare with ideas you brought to the selection from experience, reading, and what you have learned in other courses (particularly those in the social sciences) about what class and its significance mean? Based on these definitions, do you believe that their conclusion that knowing and thinking about their class background can help teachers "to reach out to students who are worried about not belonging or not making it" is justified?

2. Tate, McMillan, and Woodworth use narratives to talk about language, emphasizing the relationship between social class and language use. List as many of their literacy narratives as you can, the significant class characteristics of the speakers, and how their class affected their language use. Did any of these authors undergo transformations as they moved from their initial primary discourse to control or mastery of the dominant, standard discourse? In what ways are their narratives concerned with fitting in and "passing" in the academic world? Which of the "Class Talk" narratives do you find most compelling and why? How do you think about and deal with the continuities and discontinuities of your own "class" experiences?

3. The authors contend that Americans are uncomfortable acknowledging and talking about "class" and that "we have not attended to social class in the way we have attended in recent years to matters of gender and race." Do you agree with this assessment? What do you think is the basis for Americans' unwillingness to discuss class and class differences? Further, do you think that class background can be separated from other factors such as race, ethnicity, gender, economic status, age, politics, religion, occupation, etc.? How are literacy practices and language use influenced by these issues?

4. *Extending your understanding*: Social class is viewed as an important component of language variation. Linguists are able to identify social stratification and hierarchy across nations and cultures through language study and analysis. In a well-known study, linguist William Labov demonstrated how use of the /r/ in speech correlated with social class background in New York City. In a variety of department stores, he posed a question to numerous people that required the answer "fourth floor." Based on the responses, his data showed that speech variation can be connected to class background. With a small group of students in your class, consider a language usage in your area that serves as a "marker" of class background and gather data. You might look at differences in casual speech, the presence or absence of particular sounds in certain words (e.g., /t/), differences in pronouncing minimal pair word lists, (e.g., law/lore, boot/boat), use of nonstandard verb agreement (e.g., she know, we has). Although your measurements may be approximate and overlapping, what have you learned about the relationship between language use and class background from designing and carrying out this project?

TERMS TO DEFINE

Define the following words and phrases as they are presented within the context of the reading. Comment on your understanding of the significance of each one.

Class
Working class
Middle class
Gender
Race

Unit III: Questions, Activities, and Resources

EXTENDING YOUR UNDERSTANDING AND MAKING CONNECTIONS

1. Each author in this Unit grapples with defining the term or concept "literacy." First, think about your definition of the term, especially the one you held before reading these articles. Then list and summarize the definitions each author offers. Next, consider what these multiple definitions and ways of interpreting literacy are based on. And finally, explore how your ideas of literacy have changed through your engagement with these authors and ideas. What has been challenged and what has expanded in your initial beliefs?

2. Many of the authors in this Unit address literacy in a globalized world. Based on your reading of these selections, what do you think are the significant literacy issues confronting a world filled with the movement of peoples? What brings about the mobility? What facilitates it? What are the educational implications for literacy? What are the language implications in a multilingual world? What are the literacy issues for work environments that require communication skills? In addition to examining the evidence in these articles, think about the community in which you live and how global forces affect the social and political contexts of literacy demands locally as well as nationally and internationally.

3. The issue of the relationship of literacy to power is addressed by many (probably all) of the authors in this section. What do they mean by power and what are the questions they raise about power? What are the various ways they conceive of contexts of learning, including who decides what is to be learned, what is correct and incorrect, how learning will take place, what the role of the teacher is, what the different types of discourse are, what the relationship of discourse to identity is, how the language of instruction is important, what the importance of the learning environment is, and who will have access to learning?

4. Malina Ghose, in "Women and Empowerment Through Literacy," discusses the social implications of women's literacy programs, how women are affected by literacy practices and in turn alter these practices, and how literacy transforms women's lives. On the one hand, she says that women may "feel empowered as a result of an engagement with education." However, Ghose also notes that when viewed through the lens of different cultural perspectives and practices, "cultural roots are far more resistant [to] educational interventions. . . . Furthermore, the dangers of negating the learners' lifeworld are immense." Considering each of the readings in this unit, discuss what you learn about how literacy transforms lives and provides access to a wider world. Then consider the possible negative consequences of literacy suggested by authors in this section.

APPLICATIONS FOR TEACHING

1. Look at the various definitions of literacy that are presented in this Unit and that you listed in Question 1 above. What are the implications and applications to teaching for each of these definitions?

2. After reading the selections in this Unit, think about and list the ongoing political and educational issues that influence literacy practices. (See your thoughts to Question 2 above.) Then, connect these political and educational issues to the educational/ literacy practices that result from these influences. For example, if students are in a classroom as a result of political and social problems in the countries they come from, what are the educational implications of this? What is the role of dominant discourse in the classroom—that is, should it be taught and, if so, how? What are teaching practices that directly address the existence of multilingual, bilingual, bidialectal, and transnational students both in in-school and out-of-school settings?

3. Many of the authors in this Unit address issues around teachers and pedagogy. Ordinarily, we see teachers as objective, neutral information givers. However, teachers' belief systems, worldviews, and backgrounds (social class, ethnicity, race, gender, and language) influence the teaching environment. With a group of students, explore your "backgrounds" and how, for each of you, your personal biography might influence your educational practice. Look at both your strengths and the areas that may need change in making you an effective teacher.

4. *Lesson Plan*: Create a lesson plan based on what you consider the most effective literacy practices you read about in this Unit. First, imagine a setting (e.g., in-school classroom, out-of-school program or workplace), determine the students' age and level (e.g., from basic literacy to specialized learnings or from pre-K through college), describe the student characteristics of your imagined population (including social class, language, gender, racial/ethnic, and geographical backgrounds), and decide whether you are addressing a homogenous or heterogenous group of learners. Once you have done this, list the various literacy practices you believe can effectively help this group to increase its literacy. Describe the basic structure, issues, curriculum, and kinds of teachers and pedagogy that would be important to institute in this imagined teaching and learning environment. Be as specific as you can in all of your descriptions.

PRINT AND WEB RESOURCES

Print Resources

Cummins, J., Garner, B., & Smith, C. (Eds.). (2004). *Review of adult learning and literacy.* Mahwah, NJ: Lawrence Erlbaum Associates.

Cushman, E., Kintgen, E. R., Kroll, B. M., & Rose, M. (Eds.). (2001). *Literacy: A critical sourcebook.* Boston: Bedford/St. Martin's.

Delpit, L., & Dowdy, J. K. (Eds.). (2002). *The skin that we speak: Thoughts on language and culture in the classroom.* New York: The New Press.

Gee, J. P. (2004). *Situated language and learning: A critique of traditional schooling.* London: Routledge.

Hull, B., & Schultz, K. (2001). *School's out: Bridging out-of-school literacies with classroom practice.* New York: Teachers College Press.

Kucer, S. B. (Ed.). (2004). *The dimensions of literacy: A conceptual base for teaching reading and writing in school settings (4th ed.).* Mahwah, NJ: Lawrence Erlbaum Associates.

Olson, D. R., & Torrance, N. (Eds.). (2001). *The making of literate societies.* Oxford: Blackwell.

Zamel, V., & Spack, R. (Eds.). (2003). *Crossing the curriculum: Multilingual learners in college classrooms.* Mahwah, NJ: Lawrence Erlbaum Associates.

Web Resources

http://www.ed.gov
(U.S. Department of Education)

http://www.gse.harvard.edu/~ncsall
(National Center for the Study of Adult Learning and Literacy)

http://www.literacyonline.org/ncal
(National Center on Adult Literacy)

http://www.nifl.gov
(National Institute for Literacy)

http://www-personal.umich.edu/~jlawler/gender.html
(The Council on the Status of Women in Linguistics of Linguist List)

http://www.unesco.org
(United Nations Educational Scientific and Cultural Organization)

Credits

Author Index

Numbers in parenthesis indicate reference number, although author's name might not appear on page. Italic numbers indicate the pages where the complete reference is given.

Subject Index